Encyclopedia of the Black Death

Encyclopedia of the Black Death

Joseph P. Byrne

ABC-CLIO

Santa Barbara, California • Denver, Colorado • Oxford, England

Copyright 2012 by ABC-CLIO, LLC

Library of Congress Cataloging-in-Publication Data

Byrne, Joseph Patrick.
  Encyclopedia of the Black Death / Joseph P. Byrne.
    p. cm.
  Includes bibliographical references and index.
  ISBN 978–1–59884–253–1 (hardcopy : alk. paper) — ISBN 978–1–59884–254–8 (ebook)
1. Black Death—History—Encyclopedias. 2. Black Death—Encyclopedias. I. Title.
RC172.B98   2012
614.5′73203—dc23   2011031689

ISBN: 978–1–59884–253–1
EISBN: 978–1–59884–254–8

16 15 14 13 12   1 2 3 4 5

This book is also available on the World Wide Web as an eBook.
Visit www.abc-clio.com for details.

ABC-CLIO, LLC
130 Cremona Drive, P.O. Box 1911
Santa Barbara, California 93116-1911

This book is printed on acid-free paper ∞

Manufactured in the United States of America

Contents

List of Entries by Broad Topic

Art and Literature

Almanacs

Arrows

Art, Effects of Plague on

Ars moriendi (*The Art of Dying*)

Boccaccio, Giovanni

Books of Hours

Broadsheets, Broadsides, and Pamphlets

Bullein, William

Chaucer, Geoffrey

Chronicles and Annals

Churches, Plague

Danse Macabre

Death, Depictions of

Defoe, Daniel

Dekker, Thomas

Donne, John

Ex voto

I promessi sposi

Jonson, Ben

Langland, William

Lydgate, John

Metaphors for Plague

Morality Literature, Christian

Nashe, Thomas

Petrarch, Francesco

Poetry, European

Poetry, Islamic

Printing

Shakespeare, William

Tears against the Plague

"Three Living Meet Three Dead"

Transi Tombs

Triumph of Death

Wither, George

Biomedical Causes and Issues

Animals

Black Death: Debate over the Medical Nature of

Bubonic Plague

Bubonic Plague in North America

Diseases, Opportunistic and Subsidiary

DNA and the Second Plague Pandemic

End of Second Plague Pandemic: Theories

Epidemic and Pandemic

Fleas

Germ Theory

Little Ice Age

Morbidity, Mortality, and Virulence

Pneumonic Plague

Rats and Other Plague Carriers

Septicemic Plague

Virgin Soil Disease

Yersinia pestis

Coping Methods

Abandonment

Amulets, Talismans, and Magic

Bells

Bills of Health

Bills of Mortality

Cordons Sanitaires

Corpse Carriers

Corpses

Disinfection and Fumigation

Doors

Expulsion of Victims

Flight

Funerals, Catholic

Funerals, Muslim

Funerals, Protestant

Governments, Civil

Health Boards, Magistracies, and Commissions

Hospitals

Islamic Civil Responses

Islamic Religious Responses

Lazarettos and Pest Houses

Leprosy and Leprosarium

London's East Smithfield Plague Cemetery

Mass Graves and Plague Cemeteries

Moral Legislation

Parish

Plague Memorials

Plague Orders and National Authorities

Plague Stone

Prophylaxes

Public Health

Public Sanitation

Quarantine

Searchers

Shutting In

Social Construction of Disease

Sumptuary Laws

Tumbrels

Wands

Wills and Testaments

Epidemics and Pandemics

Athens, Plague of

Biblical Plagues

Black Death (1347–1352)

Black Death: Origins and Early Spread

Black Death, *Plague*, and *Pestilence* (Terms)

Dancing Mania

Justinian, Plague of (First Plague Pandemic)

London, Great Plague of

Plague in Europe, 1360–1500

Plague in Europe, 1500–1725

"Plagues" in the West, 900–1345

Second Plague Pandemic

Third Plague Pandemic

Groups

Apothecaries

Armies

Bishops and Popes

Children

Confraternities

Friars (Mendicants)

Gravediggers

Venice, Italy

Vienna, Austria

Religion

Allah

Apocalypse and Apocalypticism

Bible

Borromeo, Federigo

Borromeo, St. Charles (San Carlo)

Cellites and Alexians

Christ

Clement VI, Pope

Demons, Satan, and the Devil

Flagellants

God the Father

Gregory the Great, Pope

Grindal, Edmund

Heaven and Hell

Islamic Religious Responses

Islip, Simon

Job

Lazarus

Li Muisis, Gilles

Lollards

Luther, Martin

Muhammad the Prophet

Pilgrims and Pilgrimage

Plague Saints

Prayer and Fasting

Processions

Purgatory

Reformation and Protestantism

St. Januarius

St. Michael the Archangel

St. Nicholas of Tolentino

St. Roche

St. Rosalia

St. Sebastian

Sin

Virgin Mary

Societal Factors and Effects

AIDS and Plague

Anticlericalism

Anti–Semitism and Anti–Jewish Violence before the Black Death

Ciompi Revolt

Clothing

Crime and Punishment

Demographic and Economic Effects of Plague: The Islamic World

Demographic Effects of Plague: Europe 1347–1400

Demographic Effects of Plague: Europe 1400–1500

Demographic Effects of Plague: Europe 1500–1722

Demography

Economic Effects of Plague in Europe

Famine

Feudalism and Manorialism

Hundred Years War

Individualism and Individual Liberties

Jacquerie

Jewish Treasure Hoards

Labourers, Ordinance and Statute of

Languages: Vernacular and Latin

Malthusianism

Peasants' Revolt, English

Poisoning and Plague Spreading

Poverty and Plague

Repopulation

Taxes and Public Finance

Thirty Years' War

Introduction

When a student, I was exposed to the Black Plague or Black Death as an abstract, even soulless, historical phenomenon. It was a part of history, and I liked history, but, like the Holocaust or nuclear devastation, it was simply unimaginable even as an abstraction. And, unlike the Holocaust or nuclear war, it was a distant artifact. In the later 1960s and 1970s, there were few accessible books on the plague in English and no History Channel to recreate it for us. As a graduate student in European history, my eyes were opened when I discovered an entire course dedicated to the Black Death and even had its instructor as my mentor. But it was a lower-level course and I a doctoral student, so I passed it by.

Plague and I formally met near Florence, in the State Archives in Prato, Italy, in the papers of the 14th-century merchant Francesco Datini. He left a huge cache of letters and accounts when he died in 1410, and fortunately, no one saw fit to dispose of them. I chose as my dissertation topic his life, piety, and patronage. As I worked my way through some 10,000 original letters, I noted and set aside all references to plague, which first appeared and orphaned him when he was about 13 and affected him at least six times. Through the letters to and from the wealthy merchant—warning of plague's recurrence, requesting aid, inviting relocation, informing of friends' illness and death—the Black Death evolved from an abstraction to being a very real part of the lives I was encountering and a special part of the life I was reconstructing. I worked in the house he fled in 1390 and 1400 when plague threatened, and I daily wandered the streets down which the cry to "Bring forth your dead!" once echoed off the ancient stones.

Years later, I was given the opportunity to write a monograph on the medieval Black Death (1347–1500) in 2004, and then a second on daily life during the Black Death in 2006, which I extended to the end of the Second Plague Pandemic in Europe in the 1770s. By this time, new studies of plague in English were appearing about once a month, and my language skills allowed me to study works produced in French, Italian, Spanish, and German, and sources in Latin. The scholarly landscape had changed greatly since the 1960s. I set myself the task of combing and synthesizing what I could of the research and speculation being produced by the small army of medical and historical experts and students. This encyclopedia is a fruit of that synthesis, and, I hope, a tool in the ongoing campaign to bring further light to the subject.

The Second Plague Pandemic

Plague, as used throughout this work, refers to one or more of the three main manifestations of the human disease caused by the bacterium *Yersinia pestis*. Normally found in fleas and rodents, when transferred to humans, its effects may manifest as bubonic, pneumonic, or septicemic plague, depending on whether the pathogens concentrate in the lymphatic system, lungs, or bloodstream. Medieval and medical historians agree that the first widespread outbreak—or pandemic—of plague dates to the sixth century CE. It continued sporadically for more than two centuries in the Mediterranean and parts of Western Europe. Named after the Byzantine Emperor Justinian, under whom it first appeared, the recurring epidemics are collectively called the First Plague Pandemic. The disease seems to have gone underground—literally— in Eurasia until the mid-14th century. Its appearance in the Black Sea region around 1345 marks the beginning of the Second Plague Pandemic. Popularly known as the Black Death, this series of recurring epidemics in the parts of the world dominated by Christianity and Islam, and centered again on the Mediterranean, lasted in Europe until the 18th century and in Ottoman-controlled territories until about 1840. Some evidence suggests that China may have also suffered plague epidemics, though the Sahara protected Central and Southern Africa, and India seems to have been spared until the 17th century. No contemporary culture's science correctly explained the biological mechanisms of the disease or the environmental reasons for its recurrence and spread. It was as much an act of God as of nature.

The Third Plague Pandemic began in and spread from China in the 1880s and, in its early stage, met its match in the discoveries of plague researchers Alexandre Yersin and Shibasaburo Kitasato. Only in the 1890s and early 1900s did the chain of bacteria– flea–rodent–flea–human become clear, and could scientists and public health officials devise effective countermeasures. Even so, the Third Plague Pandemic only ended in the 1970s.

The Larger Picture

Over the past couple of decades, our society's interest in matters of disease, both contemporary and historical, has greatly increased. We feel hopeful about eradicating polio and TB, we fear emerging diseases both new and variant, and we shudder to think about biological warfare or terrorism. The gold standard for biological devastation remains the Black Death of Boccaccio, Defoe, and the creaking tumbrels piled high with corpses "whose arms hung akimbo." Study of the historical phenomenon may help students appreciate the potential for disaster; reflection on the futility of *that* society's responses may help contextualize our own bravado in claiming powers over nature we most certainly do not possess; and, finally, careful, balanced, and accepted scholarship may drive out the false images, facile generalizations, and falsehoods that are so often the "historical" stuff of pop culture.

About *Encyclopedia of the Black Death*

The late medieval and early modern Second Plague Pandemic is the subject of this encyclopedia. The *Second Plague Pandemic* is the term for a series of epidemics from around 1345 to around the 1770s in Europe and around 1840 in what is now Turkey. This long pandemic (an epidemic covering a large area and population) includes the Black Death of 1347–1352 and is sometimes more popularly known as the Black Death or simply the Plague.

Encyclopedia of the Black Death is a collection of 300 interdisciplinary entries covering plague and its effects on Western society across four centuries. People (Hippocrates, Avicenna, Pasteur, Yersin) and events (Biblical plagues, Plague of Justinian, Third Plague Pandemic, AIDS, and Plague) outside of the 1340 to 1840 time frame appear for the light they shed on the Second Plague Pandemic (often simply the Second Pandemic). I have striven to provide a balanced approach that represents the current state of research, debate, and consensus. The dominating coverage is of Western Europe, reflecting the state of primary sources, secondary scholarship, and the region's evident dynamism in dealing with the plague, but I have also been able to cover the Islamic world in these pages thanks to the interests and contributions of such scholars as Lawrence Conrad, Michael Dols, and Emilie Savage, as well as such relative newcomers as Nüklet Varlik, Miri Shefer-Mossensohn, and Michael Borsch.

At a glance, as the List of Entries by Broad Topic discloses, I have attempted to provide a wide range of interdisciplinary and multidisciplinary material. I have chosen subjects that are clearly pre-1340s because of their impact on how the people of that generation understood or reacted to the Black Death. These include medical scholars, epidemics, and saints. Several articles provide the modern, scientific understanding of plague and the pioneers in that realization, as well as recent scientific debates over the nature of the medieval disease and its relationship to modern HIV-AIDS.

In covering the Second Plague Pandemic itself, I break down the era into meaningful subperiods for general overviews that serve as introductions to the stages' characteristics and that interrelate the appropriate narrower entries. Some entries deal with the factors in plague's spread and recurrence, while others sketch the social, economic, political, and cultural effects of the epidemics. Another set lays out the various—usually European—ways of dealing with the plague, from prayer to useless remedies to flight to quarantine and isolation. Individual entries appear on doctors, scientists, religious leaders, and writers, and some who were all four. Though women have their own entry, none appears individually, a fault of the historical record. Many other major groups—for example, peasants, physicians, friars, Jews, armies, and notaries—are covered from three angles: how they suffered through the plague, whether they contributed to the plague's recurrence, and how the phenomenon affected the group (usually in Europe). Other cultural articles try to capture details of the epidemics, from amulets to tumbrels, doors, wands, corpse carriers, and toads. Entries on the medical practices and practitioners of the day lay out the range of medical responses available, from humoral theory to medical education to bedside procedures.

To help readers understand this period and scholarship better, I have created a brief timeline at the beginning of *Encyclopedia of the Black Death*, and nearly each entry includes valuable, up-to-date resources for further reading as well as an extensive bibliography at the end of the work. I have included almost exclusively English-language books and articles in the reference sections and in the bibliography, which reflect our intended audience. A comprehensive index adds to the encyclopedia's accessibility, as do cross-references throughout the work.

Timeline

Following is a brief list of the three plague pandemics and major events associated with them to help the reader's historical orientation to the Second Plague Pandemic and Black Death, the subject of this encyclopedia.

541–c. 750 CE   **The Plague of Justinian or First Plague Pandemic**
Emerging first from Egypt under Byzantine Emperor Justinian, this series of plague epidemics struck the early medieval Mediterranean Basin and Northwestern Europe for nearly two centuries. It appears to have disappeared until the Black Death of the 1340s.

c. 1345–c. 1840   **The Second Plague Pandemic**
From animal reservoirs in **Central Asia**, plague spread rapidly during the 1340s to Western Asia, Europe, and North Africa, and may have struck **China**. It recurred in epidemic form regionally in waves about every decade until c. 1500, then more sporadically in major cities. Between about 1650 and 1722, one by one, western European cities suffered their final epidemics (**Moscow** in 1770s). Plague continued in Ottoman Mediterranean ports until the early 1840s.

1347–1352   **The Black Death**, the initial and widespread outbreak of the Second Plague Pandemic, ravaged the Christian and western Islamic worlds, killing perhaps 40 percent of the population. Following trade and travel routes, the disease spread from the Black Sea region to Egypt and Italy, eventually engulfing lands from Persia to Ireland, and finally Russia.

1627–1634   The **Thirty Years War** (1618–1648) unleashed military campaigns and refugees that spread plague across central and southern Europe in a series of locally devastating urban epidemics.

1665–1666   **London's Great Plague**, England's last major plague epidemic, immortalized in Samuel Pepys's diary and Daniel Defoe's *Journal*. Killed perhaps 80,000 people.

1720–1722   **Marseille's final plague epidemic** was limited by swift action to the Marseille region but still killed some 50,000.

1866–1960s	**Third Plague Pandemic** Slowly spreading outbreaks originated in China. Thanks to steam shipping, outbreaks became worldwide, including Hawaii and San Francisco, and killed millions in dense, less-developed areas such as India.
1894–1914	Scientists **Alexandre Yersin** and **Shibasaburo Kitasato**, working in Hong Kong, isolated the plague bacillus in 1894, and subsequent research by **Paul-Louis Simond** and others uncovered the full bacteria–flea–rodent–flea–human plague chain.

A

Abandonment

Among the most heartrending passages in the Introduction to Giovanni Boccaccio's *Decameron* is his description of family members abandoning plague-struck parents, children, or siblings. Dying alone was not only a psychic horror, it also meant that one would not receive sacramental Last Rites, the highly desired Catholic spiritual aid for one's final journey. Abandonment had figured in descriptions from early medieval epidemics (e.g., Paul the Deacon), and it became a standard topic in later medieval and early modern plague literature (e.g., among early Italian chroniclers Agnolo di Tura, Marchionne di Stefano, Matteo Villani). Some emphasized the terrible nature of the disease, using abandonment as a measure of its effect even on kin. Others stressed the healthy person's fear of the sick and dead. The era's vague notions of contagion reasonably suggested that one could "catch" the disease from victims, living or dead. Though the theory was incorrect, carrier fleas did abandon dying victims for fresh flesh, spreading disease to new victims.

During early stages of epidemics, inns and households hid away plague victims, sometimes abandoning them to die in the process (easier with a servant or apprentice than a child, presumably). This reduced the risk of having the otherwise healthy business or family "shut in"—imprisoned in its own residence—by authorities. This form of isolation, itself a type of abandonment by the wider society, was employed increasingly frequently from the early 16th century. An even more brutal form of societal abandonment occurred when communities expelled the sick, literally parading them out the city gate to fend for themselves.

Fear of being abandoned led many to join organizations, for example, urban brotherhoods or confraternities, that ensured that last rites and burial would be provided, even in plague time. Some of these pious organizations, typically Catholic, were themselves dedicated to comforting the dying and burying the dead. During normal times, families generally saw that their deceased received proper burial, but when plague struck, these norms either broke down or were officially suspended. The need for efficient mass burial meant that families had to surrender their beloved dead to grotesque corpse carriers, who carted them off to the plague pits and anonymous graves. This severed familial traditions and connections in cities as well as villages.

Plague historians also recognize other applications of the concept of abandonment. When such professionals as doctors, pastors, notaries, and city officials followed medical advice and fled plague-struck areas, they were often criticized or even punished for unethically abandoning their obligations. In addition, economic and demographic historians note that plague losses created stocks of abandoned urban housing and made many rural communities unviably small, leading survivors to abandon them altogether.

See also: Causes of Plague: Historical Theories; Children; Confraternities; Contagion Theory; Corpses; Expulsion of Victims; Flight; Shutting In.

References

Beresford, Maurice, and John Hulst. *Deserted Medieval Villages*. Cambridge: Lutterworth Press, 1971.

Byrne, Joseph. *Daily Life during the Black Death*. Westport, CT: Greenwood, 2006.

Wear, Andrew. "Fear and Anxiety and the Plague in Early Modern England," in *Religion, Health and Suffering*, edited by J. R. Hinnells and Roy Porter (Oxford, UK: Taylor and Francis, 1999), 339–362.

AIDS and Plague

The Human Immunodeficiency Virus and Acquired Immune Deficiency Syndrome (HIV/AIDS) first appeared in the medical literature in 1981. Early cases were reported in south central Africa, Haiti, and with a very active homosexual flight attendant. Relation of the disease with two—from a typical American's point of view—very marginal regions and a nonmainstream man who spread the disease through homosexual activity made this disease of but passing interest. Gay activists and those who realized how devastating the disease was becoming for Africans countered this lack of concern by pointing to contaminations of blood supplies and to the argument that anyone might contract the disease. As cases multiplied, activists compared the disease to the Black Death.

Those supporting the comparison point to the utter novelty of the two in their day and of the inability of the day's medical profession to cure the disease (at least in the short run). Typically, the huge death tolls are mentioned, as is the (dubious) idea that anyone might contract the disease. Similar, too, were religious and moralistic responses to the diseases. God caused the Black Death to punish the sinful world, and throughout the Second Pandemic, moralists and Church leaders stressed penitence and amendment of life. Since AIDS in America has been located largely among active homosexuals, prostitutes, and illegal drug users, moralists and Church leaders have branded these "sinners" to be the objects of God's wrath for their immoral lifestyles. Related has been the issue of social class. From the later 16th century in Europe, social critics came to view plague as a matter of squalor, overcrowding, filth, poverty, laziness, immorality, and other attributes of the lowest urban class. The high incidence of AIDS among prostitutes, needle-sharing addicts, and other street people has created a similar sense of stigma. One might also compare some responses to public health responses: those who could regularly escaped quarantine and isolation, and crowds sometimes rioted against harsh public measures against plague. Gay activists fought against the closing of homosexual bathhouses in New York and San Francisco in the public's attempt to lessen AIDS incidence.

Major differences are important, however. Unlike the case with plague up to 1900, despite initial ignorance, modern medical science has come to understand and make huge leaps in treating HIV/AIDS. This is true in both medical science and public health. For a quarter century, apart from a relative few randomly stricken by tainted blood (transfusion recipients) or contact with tainted blood or other contaminated bodily fluids (physicians, EMTs), the groups whose behaviors put them at risk have known who they were and how to reduce their risk. With plague, everyone was a potential victim and for no reason they could fully understand. Authorities believed their actions could affect or stop outbreaks, but not understanding the rat–flea–bacterium chain, they were shooting in the dark.

An interesting sidebar is the 1997 announcement of a causal link between one's ancestors' exposure to plague and subsequent generations' reduced susceptibility to contracting AIDS. Briefly, a mutation in the white blood cells' CCR5-delta 32 gene can make it much harder for the HI virus to enter cells and reproduce. This appears first to have happened about 700 years ago, and repeated plagues may have privileged this mutation. Today, perhaps 10 to 15 percent of Europeans—especially from the far north—enjoy this resistance. Others have related this to smallpox rather than plague, but the jury is still out.

See also: Moral Legislation; Morality Literature, Christian; Poverty and Plague; Sin.

References

Duncan, S. R. "Reappraisal of Historical Selective Pressures for the CCR5-Delta Mutation." *Journal of Medical Genetics* 42 (2005): 205–208.

Editorial. "No Need for Panic about AIDS. Acquired Immune Deficiency Disease, Now Frequent Among Male Homosexuals in the United States, Is Not This Century's Black Death. The Most Urgent Need Is to Understand What Is Going On." *Nature* 302 (April 28, 1983): 749.

Galvani, Alison P., and Montgomery Slatkin. "Evaluating Plague and Smallpox as Historical Selective Pressures for the CCR5-Delta 32 HIV-Resistance Allele." *Proceedings of the National Academy of Science USA* Dec. 9: 100 (25, 2003): 15276–15279.

Jeffries, D. "AIDS—The New Black Death?" *Medical Legal Journal* 54 (1986): 158–175.

Scott, Susan, and Christopher Duncan. *The Return of the Black Death: The World's Greatest Serial Killer.* Hoboken, NJ: Wiley, 2004.

al-Asqalani, Ibn Hajar (1372–1449)

Ahmad ibn Ali ibn Muhamad ibn Muhamad ibn Ali ibn Ahmad Shihab al-Din Abu al-Fadl al-Kinani al Asqalani was born in Cairo in February 1372. Known as Ibn Hajar for some now obscure reason, he was raised to be a scholar, as was his father. His education spanned two dozen years and his expertise was in every major field of Muslim studies, including Hadith, jurisprudence (*fiqh*), and history. Ibn Hajar taught in numerous venues and authored more than 150 known books. He traveled to Alexandria, Yemen, Syria, and Mecca but settled in Cairo, where he served as Grand qadi (judge) of the Shafi'ite branch of Sharia law. Two of his six daughters died of plague in 1417, and he died at the beginning of the epidemic of 1449, having survived five major epidemics.

Ibn Hajar composed his plague treatise *Badl al-Ma'un fi fawaid al-Ta'un* during the plague year of 1431. His concern was for the community's moral failings and God's striking down of the infidel. His analysis is synthetic rather than original, with little in the way of description or narrative. Doctors could neither define nor combat the disease, and without knowing, they could not remedy it. True answers are religious: the Koran and Hadith provide the proper answers and responses. Plague is mercy to Muslims (martyrs) but a chastisement to infidels. The infidels indirectly caused the plague, so martyrs die at their hands as in jihad. As a member of the Shafi'ite school of religious jurisprudence, he rejected the severe resignation of such Hanbalites as Muhammad al-Manbiji. These, he said, uniquely equated plague and death, while Shafi'ites saw plague as one disease among many. They could in good conscience pray to have Allah lift it. Later Hanbalites refuted his interpretation of their beliefs and also accepted the licitness of prayer. Should such prayer be by individuals or in groups? Ibn Hajar pointed out that collective prayer had not succeeded.

See also: Islam and Medicine; Islamic Religious Responses; Muhammad the Prophet.

References

Kawash, Sabri K. "Ibn Hajar al-Asqalani (1372–1449 AD): A Study of the Background, Education, and Career of a 'Alim in Egypt." Ph.D. dissertation, Princeton University, 1969.

Sublet, Jacqueline. "La Peste prise aux rêts de la jurisprudence: le traité d'Ibn Hağar al-'Asqalana sur le peste." *Studia Islamica* 33 (1971): 141–149.

Alchemy

Alchemy was a body of theory and practice that sought to harness for human use certain hidden or "occult" powers in natural objects. It depended on the interconnectedness of all of nature and of nature with the celestial realm, with its planets and stars (the heart of astrology). Much of the alchemical

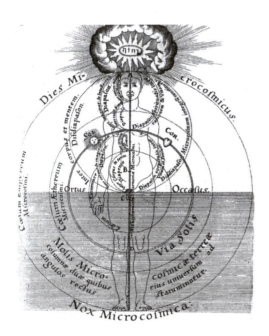

Alchemical chart showing the human body as the "world soul." This appears in a 17th-century publication by Robert Fludd. (Courtesy of the National Library of Medicine)

pursuit was purification of base, low-order substances and their transmutation into higher-order materials—turning base lead, sulphur, or mercury into valuable gold. This began among the ancient Greeks but was systematized by Jabir ibn Hayyan (Geber the Wise; c. 721–c. 815), court astrologer to Harun al-Rashid at Baghdad. He blended astrology with age-old magic and *khaffiyah* (science of the occult powers) into a pseudo-science called al-Kimiya that he hoped would extend the limits of natural philosophy. Jabir wrote 22 treatises on various techniques used by alchemists, including distillation, extraction, crystallization, and concoction (cooking together); the great physician Rhazes wrote three treatises linking the products of alchemical processes with the humoral system and the medicine based upon it.

Alchemia medica, the application of alchemy to medicine, entered the Latin-reading West at the same time as other Islamic medical, scientific, and philosophical works. By 1144, Latin works on alchemy began appearing. Though transmuting lead into gold may not sound like a medicinal procedure, it was seen as no different from blending herbs or minerals into medicines. Indeed, ingested gold was long used as a plague prophylactic: gold's perfection was meant to counteract the supposed poison's corruption. Alchemy and the pharmacist's tasks were similar, and the occupations of alchemist and apothecary developed simultaneously. Both sought to master and harness the hidden powers of natural objects, often for healing purposes, though the apothecary tended to work with organic substances and the alchemist with inorganic. Socially, apothecaries were often organized into societies or guilds, openly practiced their craft, and were considered vital to a community's health. Alchemists were often loners who operated on society's fringes, protecting their secrets and developing little or nothing of commercial value. Some worked in laboratories furnished by noble patrons, including Emperor Rudolf II. Unless protected, alchemists attracted suspicion since their search for occult powers paralleled that expected of witches and sorcerers. Indeed, the obscure alchemical vocabulary utilized such terms as *angels* and *spirits* that could have meant diabolical entities or something else (e.g., alcoholic spirits).

Since plague was considered a product of both celestial and natural forces and seemingly worked through hidden (occult) mechanisms, it was considered a natural subject for alchemical investigation. Neoplatonist and physician Marsilio Ficino helped link Renaissance astrology with alchemy, identifying the cosmic "vital spirit" with alchemy's fifth element or quintessence. A generation later, German Protestant physician Paracelsus made a career out of his attempts to harness mineral "powers" to human healing. The "philosopher's stone" was a universal cure-all that alchemists expended enormous efforts to produce in their laboratories through the processes and with the tools first outlined by Jabbir. Ben Jonson's plague-time comedy *The Alchemist* relies on popular perception of the fortune and the philanthropic coup to be had from its creation (and the charlatanism that took advantage of it).

The record of failure did little to dissuade physicians and others from pursuing the alchemist's dream. The Paracelsian emphasis on mineral rather than organic medical therapies seemed fruitful and utilized many alchemical principles and methods. Seventeenth-century scientists Robert Boyle and Isaac Newton were dedicated alchemists. Their efforts helped mutate the pseudoscience of alchemy into the modern science of chemistry, as they developed early instruments, procedures, and protocols. Slowly but surely, "occult" forces like magnetism and gravity gave up their secrets, and scientific societies blessed laboratory research.

See also: Amulets, Talismans, and Magic; Apothecaries; Arabic-Persian Medicine and Practitioners; Astrology; Ficino, Marsiglio; Gold; Jonson, Ben; Paracelsus and Paracelsianism.

References

Crisciani, Chiara. "Black Death and Golden Remedies: Some Remarks on Alchemy and the Plague," in *The Regulation of Evil*, edited by Agostino Paravicini Bagliani and Francesco Santi (Sismel: Galluzzo, 1998), 7–39.

Maxwell-Stuart, P. G. *The Chemical Choir: A History of Alchemy*. New York: Continuum, 2008.

Pereira, Michela. "Mater Medicinarum: English Physicians and the Alchemical Elixir in the Fifteenth Century," in *Medicine from the Black Death to the French Disease*, edited by Roger French et al. (Burlington, VT: Ashgate, 1998), 26–52.

Allah

According to Islam, Allah is the sole and all-powerful divinity or God. Traditionally spoken of in the masculine, he is creator and sustainer of all things, both transcending all of his creation and present to all of it. There are no human or spirit mediators nor intercessors in Allah's relationship with humanity. Islam's central tenet is submission to the will of Allah through faith in and obedience to him. His word is the Koran, which was recited to the Prophet Muhammad by the angel Gabriel during the early seventh century. Islam teaches, however, that Allah had revealed himself to the world through the monotheistic religions of Judaism and Christianity before Muhammad. Arabia, Muhammad's homeland, had been polytheistic before his time, and *Allah* was the name of an important provider deity. The Koran revealed this to be the name by which the true and singular God was to be known.

All that happens is according to Allah's will, so of course a plague has its ultimate source in God's will. The sickness's more immediate causes were debatable: was it nature as understood by Galenic medicine or the spirits known as *jinn*? Islam taught that those faithful Muslims who died of plague found immediate peace with God in Paradise; the faithless were damned. Muslim scholars differed on whether each person's fate was predetermined or whether one could escape plague by flight or counteract it by prayer, preventative measures, or remedies. Closely related was the issue of contagion: unless God will it, could one randomly catch the disease from another person or thing? Many physicians were also learned in religious law and had to be very careful: their observations indicated contagion while their religion taught against it. Legal scholars denied contagion quite readily, placing each person's fate directly in Allah's control. Because Allah is regularly recognized and praised in the Koran as merciful and compassionate, from time to time we read of Muslim prayer services and even processions during which believers prayed directly to Allah for relief. The Islamic healing tradition that privileges religious over classical Greek medicine is called prophetic medicine.

See also: Arabic-Persian Medicine and Practitioners; Contagion Theory; Islamic Religious Responses; Jinn; Muhammad the Prophet; Prayer and Fasting; *Ta'un.*

References

Ibn Qayyim al-Jawziyya. *Medicine of the Prophet.* Translated by Penelope Johnstone. Cambridge: Islamic Texts Society, 1998.

Pormann, Peter E., and Emilie Savage-Smith. *Medieval Islamic Medicine.* Washington, DC: Georgetown University Press, 2007.

Almanacs

Almanacs were inexpensive annual printed guides to the year's astronomical and meteorological events that came to include popular medical advice and advertisements. Directly related to both ecclesiastical and astrological calendars, almanacs may have originated in the Islamic world and entered the Christian West through Spain. Fourteenth-century English friars John Somer and Nicholas of Lynn combined astrological material with medical advice for popular consumption. But Johann Gutenberg's press in Mainz produced the first mass-media publication in 1448. As the printing press spread, so did the almanac, so profitable did it prove to be to publishers across the continent. In general the pamphlet or broadsheet was divided into the astrological and meteorological calendar and the more miscellaneous "prognostications." The latter varied by country, region, publisher/author, and time but generally contained some combination of Galenic medical advice, a zodiac man, local weights and measures, animal husbandry, legal advice, and predictions of disasters for the year.

In England, almanacs circulated from 1498 but for 40 years were translations of those by continental authors. In 1537, Carthusian priest and royal physician Andrew Boorde produced the first original English almanac. Many more followed, ranging in size from a single sheet to 16 pages. In 1603,

King James I granted a monopoly on the popular booklets to English Stock, a joint-stock company. The company's control ended with the early stages of the English Civil War in the 1640s, and the genre flourished until curbed by Charles II in 1662. Still, around 1700, English printers produced between 350,000 and 400,000 annual copies.

Circulating throughout much of the Second Pandemic, almanacs were important means of mediating elite, Galenic medicine—both prophylaxis and remedies—to the general population. They may also help explain the tenacity of the Galenic tradition and astrological medicine. Many also incorporated what historians consider folk traditions for maintaining and restoring health: certain herbs were most powerful when picked under a full moon, for example. Almanac authors tended to be physicians, astrologers, or astrological physicians. Astrology was at the heart of the almanac: marking the best times for bleeding and other purgations; noting times of potentially pestilential south winds; and predicting planetary conjunctions that presaged and caused plague. The zodiac man diagram was a common feature that linked body parts and organs to the zodiac signs, indicating the periods of potential danger or most effective medical intervention. Health could also be maintained, supposedly, by maintaining a balance of bodily humors through diet, and almanacs regularly provided dietary advice and recipes. Dietary regimen was also at the center of remedial medicine, restoring humoral balance when the body fell ill. Medications, too, were employed and touted in almanacs. From advice on individual herbs to advertisements for proprietary pills or potions, almanacs provided self-help for the suffering. In her study of English examples, Louise Curth noted that in 1640, only 7 percent of almanacs had advertisements, but the figure rose to more than 75 percent by 1700. Many of these were for plague remedies, for example, the "Excellent Lozenges" of Mr. Edmund Buckworth: "a great antidote against the plague" (1657). In the face of competition, his claim rose two years later: "a sovereign antidote against the plague." When plague hit London in 1665, the claims stopped.

Some almanacs blended religious elements—calls to repentance, prayers, predictions of the apocalypse—but more often, clerics challenged the authors' predictions and medical claims. In 1609, Thomas Dekker published the parody *The Raven's Almanac, Foretelling of a Plague, Famine, and Civil War*, making the point that all was ultimately in God's hands. But almanacs had a powerful hold across the continent as people tried to control their own lives through prediction and self-medication.

See also: Astrology; Bleeding/Phlebotomy; Broadsheets, Broadsides, and Pamphlets; Galen and Galenism; Humoral Theory; Zodiac Man.

References

Capp, Bernard. *Astrology and the Popular Press: English Almanacs, 1500–1800*. London: Faber and Faber, 1979.

Curth, Louise Hill. "The Medical Content of English Almanacs, 1640–1700." *Journal of the History of Medicine and Allied Sciences* 60 (2005): 255–282.

Slack, Paul. "Mirrors of Health and Treasures of Poor Men: The Uses of the Vernacular Medical Literature of Tudor England," in *Health, Medicine and Mortality in the Sixteenth Century*, edited by Charles Webster (New York: Cambridge University Press, 1979), 237–271.

al-Manbiji, Muhammad (d. 1383)

Muhammad al-Manbiji was born in Manbij in northern Syria. He grew to become an

Islamic legal and religious scholar of the conservative Hanibalite school of Sharia jurisprudence. Living in Aleppo, or perhaps Manbij, al-Manbiji was an eyewitness to the plagues of 1348 and its successors in 1362 to 1364 and 1373 to 1374. In the wake of the second, he composed a plague treatise *Fi Akhbar at-ta'un* (*Report on the Plague*), and after the third, he penned *Tasliyat ahl al-Masaib* (*Consolation for Those in Distress*), a work of spiritual comfort for those touched by the disease. The single surviving *Report* of 1363 to 1364 in Cairo has 22 chapters over 157 folio pages and is the earliest extant Muslim plague treatise that contains a list of regional epidemics from the First Pandemic to his own time. Al-Manbiji credits the pestilence to Allah, who used the jinn (not miasmas) to spread the disease. His explanations are standard: plague is a martyrdom and a mercy; virtuous Muslim victims are taken to Paradise, infidels are damned; one should pray to Allah, but not to end the outbreak; neither doctors' remedies nor magic can thwart Allah's will; neither enter nor leave a plague-stricken area; cultivate patience during plague; and so on. Descriptive or narrative passages are few, and he provides little in the way of prophylactics or remedies; it is clearly the work of an orthodox jurist and not a physician.

See also: Allah; Consilia and Plague Tracts; Islamic Religious Responses; Jinn; Muhammad the Prophet.

Reference

Dols, Michael W. "Al-Manbiji's *Report of the Plague*: A Treatise on the Plague of 764–5/1362–4 in the Middle East," in *The Black Death: The Impact of the Fourteenth-century Plague*, edited by Daniel Williman (Binghamton, NY: Medieval and Renaissance Texts and Studies, 1982), 65–76.

al-Maqrizi, Muhammad (al-Makrizi; 1363/4–1442)

Taki al-Din Abu l-Abbas Ahmad ibn Abd al-Kadir al-Maqrizi was born in Mamluk Cairo to a father who was a scholar in many disciplines, and Al-Maqrizi himself became a noted scholar, especially in history. He knew the great philosopher and historian Ibn Khaldun, who may have been responsible for his turning to history as a full-time occupation. In Cairo, Al-Maqrizi was a teacher, preacher, and administrator, and he was an inspector of the markets (*muhtasib*) for several six-month stints from 1399 to 1408. In 1409, he appears in Damascus and subsequently in Mecca and Cairo. He penned an unfinished world history, as well as histories of the Muslim rulers of Egypt, the Fatimids Ayyubids, and Mamluks of his day.

Plague plays an important role in his works, though he wrote no book specifically on the phenomenon. The further back he goes, the less reliable is his information. He borrowed a good deal from earlier accounts, in the process preserving these, but not always dealing with them critically. Some have accused him of plagiarism, but that would be to impose a modern standard on the medieval writer. His descriptions and interpretations of his own time are the most valuable of his work to historians. Though he was not an eyewitness to everything he recorded, he treats these sources far more critically. Especially important is his detailed discussion of rural depopulation due to plague deaths and flight to cities and the resulting decline and collapse in the irrigation infrastructure along the Nile River in 1403 to 1404. As a muhtasib, he was acutely aware of the economic impact of this blow.

His student and successor as chronicler of Mamluk Egypt was Yusuf ibn Taghri Birdi

(Taghribirdi; c. 1409–1470). Taghri Birdi's father was a mamluk who rose to lead Egypt's armies and serve as viceroy of Damascus, but he died when the boy was younger than five. He was raised under his sister's care to become a scholar in Persian, Turkish, and Mamluk traditions, especially military history. He wrote biographies of key individuals as well as a history of Egypt from the 640s to 1476. His most valuable contribution to plague studies is his eyewitness description of the terrible plague of 1429 to 1430 in Cairo and Fustat.

See also: Cairo, Egypt; Chronicles and Annals.

References

Borsch, Stuart. *The Black Death in Egypt and England.* Austin: University of Texas Press, 2005.

Dols, Michael W. *The Black Death in the Middle East.* Princeton, NJ: Princeton University Press, 1977.

Amulets, Talismans, and Magic

Magic was the exercise of power or control over the forces in the cosmos that were hidden from most people. When this involved invoking demons or angels for aid, both Islam and Christianity objected. When this meant using earthly objects as natural "lenses" for occult (hidden) powers, whether celestial or terrestrial, then neither pope nor Prophet took issue. Like alchemy and astrology, magic sought to bridge the gap between what humans normally sensed in the world and valuable potentials locked in or exercised by common objects. So, just as lead could be changed into healing gold (alchemy) and the stars had an impact on a human body, even at a great distance (astrology), so could stones, metal, and even scripts on parchment serve to prevent or heal illnesses. Magic was

empirical, relying on trial and error rather than theory, and was not part of the medical curriculum or most pharmaceutical training. Nonetheless, many of its forms were widely accepted within medical communities during the Second Pandemic.

Amulets or talismans were objects of various materials worn or carried on the body to ward off bad fortune, evil spirits, or plague. They were visible symbols of an invisible power and used as prophylactics by Christians, Muslims, and Jews. Despite belief in Allah's omnipotence, Muslims accepted the use of objects made of jewels or precious metals (often in the form of rings) or inscribed with Koranic passages, prayers, or mystical words or symbols. Though learned opinions varied, most Muslim plague tracts recommended incantations or prayers linked with amulets as valid defenses against plague-spreading jinn.

Arabic magical texts accompanied medical texts into the Christian world during the 1100s and 1200s. Christians linked the power of amulets to saint veneration, their relation with astrological powers, and, later, the Paracelsian homeopathic theory. Despite official Church disapproval, popular Catholicism embraced the use of charms, medallions, written prayers worn around the neck, and relics as effective plague prophylaxes. During the 1656 plague in Naples, disposable prints of St. Francis Xavier were worn on the chest: they were believed to absorb plague poison from the body. Since even the pope believed in the influence of celestial bodies on epidemics, astrological talismans, especially of gold and jewels thought to keep celestial powers at bay, were grudgingly accepted. Geoffrey Chaucer's pilgrim-physician was adept at astrology, natural magic, and the making of healing "ymages."

Largely Protestant Paracelsians created amulets as external remedies, partly magical, partly chemical in their actions. The most serious scientists experimented with toads, whose own poisons were believed to ward off or draw out plague poison. Gold contained the sun's cleansing power, and sapphires absorbed plague bubo pus. Small bags with ground herbs and minerals were also popular. A Milanese recipe (1631) contained sulphur, arsenic, incense, carnations, nutmeg, myrrh, radish leaves, ginger root, orange peel, peony leaves, mastic, and rue seeds. Anti–Paracelsians criticized chemical-based remedies; other physicians mocked their ineffectiveness or associated their use with witchcraft.

See also: Alchemy; Apothecaries; Arabic-Persian Medicine and Practitioners; Astrology; Bezoar Stones; Charlatans and Quacks; Contagion Theory; Empirics; Gold; Paracelsus and Paracelsianism; Prophylaxes; Remedies, External.

References

Baldwin, Martha. "Toads and Plague: Amulet Therapy in Seventeenth-century Medicine." *Bulletin of the History of Medicine* 67 (1993): 227–247.

Bühler, C. F. "Prayers and Charms in Certain Middle English Scrolls." *Speculum* 39 (1964): 270–278.

Pingree, David. "The Diffusion of Arabic Magical Texts in Western Europe," in *La diffusione delle scienze islamiche nel Medio Evo europeo* (Rome: Accademia Nazionale dei Lincei, 1987), 57–102.

Pormann, Peter E. and Emilie Savage-Smith. *Medieval Islamic Medicine.* Washington, DC: Georgetown University Press, 2007.

Skemer, Don C. *Binding Words: Textual Amulets in the Middle Ages.* University Park, PA: Pennsylvania State University Press, 2006.

Anatomy and Dissection

Anatomy was essentially knowledge of the structure of the human body as described verbally in books, depicted in drawings, or taught in medical school lectures or courses. *Dissection* refers to the investigative probing of the body beneath the skin by peeling back layers of skin and muscle. This might be done for self-education or publicly for teaching purposes. An autopsy is the same procedure, though with the purpose of determining the cause of the body's death. Vivisection is the same, though carried out on living animals or people, with the goal of understanding the functioning of a living body. Though the ancient Egyptians carefully treated the corpses of their aristocracy, especially pharaohs, most Western cultures shunned corpses as ritually defiling, disease-generating, or in need of immediate interment. Medical investigative dissection, as opposed to mummification, began in Alexandria, Egypt, under Ptolemy I Soter in the third century BCE. The descriptions of executed criminals' corpses by Herophilus and Erasistratus were studied by Galen and other Roman physicians, who themselves refrained. The practice was not unknown, however, and the Byzantine historian Procopius noted that plague corpses were dissected in Constantinople during the First Pandemic's early stage. Dissection never presented problems for Byzantines.

Despite their advances in surgery and internal medicine, Islamic physicians relied little on dissection, trusting heavily in Galen and in rather crude pictorial representations of anatomical features. Medieval Christians also avoided defiling corpses, though autopsies were carried out. The first court-ordered public autopsy on record was in Bologna in 1302 when Bartolomeo da Varignana opened Azzolino degli Onesti. Bologna's famed law school and professional, academic attitude toward surgery made it the early center for academic anatomy. Mondino dei Luzzi was the first to teach anatomy via dissection and wrote the famous manual *Anathomia*

(1316), which stood beside Galen's *Tegni*, a key portion of the *Articella*. Galen's hold on Western medicine was such that despite what Mondino actually observed, he repeated many of the false statements in Galen's work.

By 1347, only a few Italian medical schools required anatomical education and exposure to dissections, and Montpellier's required biannual public dissections from 1340 and annual events from 1376, with corpses provided by the Duke of Anjou. At Perugia in 1348, doctors autopsying a plague corpse believed they had located the sac of poison caused by the miasma, and in Florence, physicians and surgeons were not only allowed to do autopsies, they were hired to do so. In 1348, Pope Clement VI in Avignon required autopsies of plague corpses as a means of better understanding the disease, and this spurred required anatomical education and educational dissection in medical schools new and established. A few years later, papal surgeon Guy de Chauliac published his *Chirurgia*, which replaced Mondino in many schools.

But even with frequent dissections, medical students remained largely ignorant of even basic anatomy. In a typical public event, a surgeon cut the body open, a physician read from an anatomy manual in Latin, and a third used a pointer to indicate the feature being discussed. New, more or less Galenic manuals appeared in 1522 and 1536 by Berengario da Carpi and Guinter von Andernacht respectively, but Andreas Vesalius in Padua made the biggest leap with his hands-on instructional dissections and publication of *De Fabbrica* and its digests in 1543. During the same century, anatomical education became slightly more sophisticated, and permanent anatomical theaters replaced makeshift venues. Obtaining corpses remained a legal and ethical

Lesson in anatomy, from a 14th-century Italian manuscript. A physician reads from an anatomy text while a surgeon demonstrates on the corpse. (Courtesy of the National Library of Medicine)

issue, however. Executed criminals were convenient and presented few ethical qualms, though authorities did their best to ensure that they were not locals whose families might object. German student Felix Platter recalled disinterring corpses from a monastic cemetery until the monks armed themselves with crossbows to prevent the sacrilege.

With its Galenic preconceptions and ignorance of physiology and bacterial action, in the short run, Western epidemic medicine gained little from expanded anatomical education. Theories of plague still sent dissectors looking for abdominal sacs of poison, with no progress in understanding the plague-wracked body. Yet such gallant researchers as Samuel Pepys's physician contracted the disease while autopsying fresh corpses whose hungry fleas flocked to their new host. Contemporary physician George Thomson protected himself during autopsies by hanging a dried toad amulet around his neck. Though contracting the disease, he recovered and wrote a plague text, *Loimotomia* (1666).

See also: Arabic-Persian Medicine and Practitioners; *Articella*; Chauliac, Guy de (Guido de Cauliaco); Corpses; Galen and Galenism; Islam and Medicine; Medical Education (1300–1500, Medieval Europe); Medical Education (1500–1700, Early Modern Europe); Prisoners; Surgeons/Barbers; Vesalius, Andreas.

References

French, Roger. *Dissection and Vivisection in the European Renaissance*. Burlington, VT: Ashgate, 1999.

Savage-Smith, Emily. "Attitudes toward Dissection in Medieval Islam." *Journal of the History of Medicine and Allied Sciences* 50 (1995): 67–110.

Animals

Animals of many species played various roles throughout the Second Pandemic.

Animals and Bubonic Plague

Bubonic plague is a disease of animals (zoonosis) that, under certain circumstances, is transferred to humans. The pathogenic bacterium *Yersinia pestis* is carried by various types of fleas between infected and healthy rodents, including rats, squirrels, tarbagans, marmots, susliks, meriones, desert gerbils, and wild guinea pigs. Domesticated cats and dogs have also been infected, but they tend to survive. The commensal black rat *rattus rattus* is generally considered to be responsible for historical outbreaks, and the rat flea *Xenopsylla cheopis* is best adapted to transmit the disease. Though less efficient, the human flea *pulex irritans* may have also played an important role in spreading plague among people. None of this was known during the Second Pandemic, though some people believed that vapors from dead animal carcasses putrefied the air, causing pestilence. Muhammad al-Maqrizi stated that human plague pandemic originated with the stench of rotting animal carcasses in Uzbekistan.

Animals as Portents

Early in the Second Pandemic, observers claimed that unusual animal manifestations were plague harbingers. Gabriele de' Mussis reported that in China, serpents and toads fell from the sky, entered homes, and poisoned inhabitants before eating them. Louis Heyligen, a musician in Avignon, also related portents from "eastern India," including a rain of scorpions, frogs, lizards, snakes "and other poisonous animals." A similar, deadly rain of serpents and pestilential worms fell in the land where "ginger grows," said a monk of Neuberg in Austria. Closer to home, physician Heinrich of Bratislava claimed one epidemic portent listed by Avicenna, that mice and dormice (and, he added, toads and moles) would flee their subterranean homes as corrupting vapors gathered underground. Such later physicians as Ficino, Michele Savonarola, and Giovanni de Albertis added bugs, snails, scorpions, and snakes to Heinrich's list. Another cleric, at Salona on the Adriatic Sea, recounted the deaths by mange of sheep, goats, oxen, and horses—supposedly a global phenomenon—that immediately preceded the great pandemic.

Animals as Victims

Many observers claimed that animals died of plague, though rodents were never specified. Maqrizi declared that the whole animal world was eventually cut down by the pandemic. He specified species of birds and fishes, wild boars, lions, hares, onagers, and camels; somewhat later Muslim chronicler Ibn Taghri Birdi added wolves, gazelles, and Nile crocodiles. Significantly, these animals displayed swellings similar to buboes on humans. In his *Decameron*, Boccaccio claimed that two pigs rooting through infected clothing immediately seized and died. According to Henry of Hervordia, dogs, oxen, wolves, and birds were early plague victims, and Marchionne Stefani listed dogs, cats, oxen, sheep, chickens, and donkeys as early plague victims. Friar Michele da Piazza noted that whole families died, including their livestock and even cats; the Paduan chroniclers listed household dogs as victims, and Gilles li Muisit mentioned household cats and dogs. The Neuberg monk wrote of men and animals being struck motionless, as if turned to stone. In England, Thomas Walsingham of St. Albans monastery noted that murrain, a highly infectious disease that killed many animals, followed the plague, and Augustinian canon Henry Knighton of Leicester specified the death of many sheep by murrain.

Heyligen reported the belief that the corrupted air also affected sea life, and people avoided eating saltwater fish for fear of poison. Boccaccio mentioned that in rural areas, peasants abandoned their flocks ("oxen, asses, sheep, goats, pigs, chickens, and even dogs") to wander at will, feeding on unharvested crops, a phenomenon noted in Egypt as well. Knighton also reported cows and sheep wandering among ripened crops, most of them dying eventually from lack of proper attention.

Dog Massacres

Dogs, like other scavengers, fed on corpses when not normally cared for. They also had a tendency to unearth and chew on corpses when these were not buried deeply enough. From the later 15th century, such observers as Marsiglio Ficino began blaming animals—dogs that molested corpses made the most sense—for spreading plague, probably through miasma in their fur. Records show that individual households might have killed cats, dogs, and even rats lest they infect the family, and public action was close behind. Requiring dogs be chained was a first step, but many cities during the 16th and 17th centuries eventually required their extermination when plague struck. In 1499, Edinburgh required that stray cats, pigs, and dogs be killed, a law reiterated in 1505 and 1585. In April 1581, plague smothered Seville, Spain, but the Count of Villar reported that things had not gotten so bad that they had to start killing cats and dogs. London began killing cats and dogs in 1563, and such desperate cities as Rome and Amsterdam also carried out the grim practice. In July 1665, London's Lord Mayor ordered the "rakers" of every ward to remove carcasses of cats, dogs, "and other vermin" along with trash, and by spring 1666, the city's dogcatcher had been paid for killing 4,380 dogs. In 1720, authorities in plague-stricken Marseille had animal corpses tossed into the sea, only to have them wash ashore and rot on the causeways and strand. This left much public waste to contaminate the streets and eliminated one of the rats' prominent predators.

See also: Avicenna (Ibn Sina); Boccaccio, Giovanni; Bubonic Plague; Bubonic Plague in North America; Ficino, Marsiglio; Fleas; Public Sanitation; Rats and Other Plague Carriers; Toads; Tumbrels.

References

Cohn, Samuel. *The Black Death Transformed.* New York: Oxford University Press, 2002.

Horrox, Rosemary. *The Black Death.* New York: Manchester University Press, 1994.

Naphy, William and Andrew Spicer. *The Black Death.* Stroud, Gloucs., UK: Tempus, 2001.

Anticlericalism

Expressions of popular dissatisfaction with the Catholic priesthood (clergy) predate the Black Death by 250 years. Bishops and other priests complained, poets mocked, and laypeople from aristocrats to peasants condemned these men whose special spiritual and legal statuses seemed to set them above common humanity. During epidemics, they died by the scores serving their flocks, but many fled their responsibilities out of fear or greed for greener pastures. God was universally considered the ultimate cause of the plague, and clearly the clergy were not doing their job of pleasing him. Clerical sin and abuse were considered especially aggravating. After the initial outbreak, priests ran to lucrative positions as chaplains and chantry priests, abandoning shell-shocked flocks. Such English poets as Gower and Chaucer decried this in particular, while bishops sought to reduce the attractiveness by limiting what patrons could pay. When plague returned to Europe in the late 1350s and early 1360s and yet again in the 1370s, criticism increased and urban survivors often sought out mendicant friars in place of parish pastors when needed.

But not all criticism was anticlerical. Bishops railed that their clergy ignored their duties, scandalized their flocks, were poor role models, and "drown themselves in an abyss of vice," but bishops were hardly "anticlerical." Conversely, followers of English priest and heretic John Wycliffe, the Lollards, and Jan Hus's similar Hussites in Bohemia were openly hostile to the very notion of a Christian clergy, let alone a corrupted one. In between were most anticlericalists. They were plain folk who were disgusted by what they had witnessed, read, or heard, sought a scapegoat for their suffering, or simply resented the position and power of the clergy. Historians note dozens of outbreaks of open violence against bishops and priests in the wake of 14th-century plagues, though specific motivations are generally unclear.

By eliminating the ordained priesthood and redefining the clergy, Protestant Reformers eradicated anticlericalism from their territories. This success chastened Catholic leaders, who reformed the Church and its clergy in the mid-1500s and limited criticism via the Inquisition and Index of Forbidden Books.

See also: Bishops and Popes; Boccaccio, Giovanni; Chaucer, Geoffrey; Friars (Mendicants); Langland, William; Pastors, Preachers, and Ministers; Priests; Reformation and Protestantism.

References

Aberth, John. *From the Brink of the Apocalypse.* New York: Routledge, 2001.

Dohar, William. *The Black Death and Pastoral Leadership: The Diocese of Hereford in the Fourteenth Century.* Philadelphia: University of Pennsylvania Press, 1995.

Anti–Semitism and Anti–Jewish Violence before the Black Death

The roots of hatred by some Christians for people of the Jewish religion are deep and ancient. In the New Testament, Jewish leaders are depicted as opposing the teaching of Jesus and achieving his execution by bribing Judas. When Jews are given the option of freeing Jesus, one gospel of the New Testament, St. Matthew, has them shout, "Let his blood be on our hands and those of our children!" By the late Middle Ages, these scenes were recalled or reenacted each Easter season. For many Christians, Jews were guilty of deicide—killing God—even though Roman soldiers actually did the deed. Those who remained Jews despite Jesus's teaching were seen as blind, hard-hearted, or even evil.

During the medieval centuries, there was an underlying contempt for Jews in Christian Europe that emerged from time to time polemically and physically. In most places, Jews were forbidden to hold or own land, to attend universities, and often to hire Christians or join occupational guilds. Some became doctors and money lenders, drawing suspicion from the first and resentment from the second. They were the classic "other" in Christian communities: those whose customs and values were thought to be opposed to the community and whose ultimate desire was supposedly to destroy the Christians and their community. Their attention to personal hygiene and diet, their forms of worship, and cycles of holidays were off-puttingly different. Terrible myths grew up around these differences, especially in Germany: Jewish men menstruated as women do; ceremonial *matzo* bread was made with human blood; Christian children were captured, cooked, and eaten. These vile notions circulated orally and in writing and were preached by mendicant friars, who whipped up audiences against the Jews in their midst.

The years of the Black Death saw Jewish communities libeled, attacked, scattered, and even massacred. But patterns of anti–Jewish atrocities predated the mid-14th century. Libels hurled at Jews included the myths mentioned above, as well as specific accusations of cases of arson (Deggendorf, Bavaria, 1337); ritual murder and cannibalism (earliest 1144; and in Fulda, Germany in 1235; and Lincoln, England in1255); desecration of the Eucharistic bread or Host, believed to be the Body of Christ (in 1298 in 417 locales in Germany); working with Muslims, lepers, and even devils to poison wells (1161 in Bohemia, 1267 in Vienna, and 1321 in France); and practice of the Black Arts of sorcery (especially connected with doctors and druggists). Armed assaults on Jewish communities (usually special quarters of towns or cities) famously occurred during the First Crusade (1196), as Christian mobs worked their way through German territory south toward the Balkans. The feeling was, "why should we travel so far to fight the enemies of God when these live among us?" Much of the Rhine Valley that was scorched or soaked with Jewish blood in 1349 was first violated in 1096 by rogue crusaders who assaulted and murdered Jews in Speyer, Worms, Mainz, Cologne, and Metz. Others suffered in Prague and Regensburg, despite condemnations by bishops and the pope. Later violence included pogroms in Alsace in 1287, 1298, and 1336 to 1338. Blood libels also resulted in Jewish deaths: officials burned 34 Jews in Fulda in 1235, and 19 were executed in Lincoln in 1255. Some northern European Jews in the 12th and 13th centuries even accepted the persecution as martyrdom, a sanctification of God's name through blood sacrifice.

Officially, the Catholic Church sought to protect European Jews, taking them in some sense under their care, and urging Catholic rulers to do the same. Monarchs, nobles, and city patricians generally opposed and even blocked anti–Jewish mob violence, but often this was more a matter of maintaining order rather than aiding a beset minority. Though perhaps influenced by Church authorities, upper classes used the Jews as sources of credit and as communities that might be taxed for extraordinary income when necessary. Damage to these communities thus meant damage to the ruling class as well. Nonetheless, England's King Edward I banished all Jews from his kingdom in 1290 and the French followed in 1306.

See also: Black Death (1347–1352); Clement VI, Pope; Jewish Treasure Hoards; Jews; Physicians; Poisoning and Plague Spreading.

References

Almog, Shmuel, editor. *Antisemitism through the Ages*. Oxford: Pergamon Press, 1988.

Bauchau, Bénédicte. "Science et racisme: les Juifs, la lèpre et la peste." *Stanford French Review* 13 (1989): 21–35.

Nirenberg, David. *Communities of Violence: Persecution of Minorities in the Middle Ages*. Princeton, NJ: Princeton University Press, 1996.

Apocalypse and Apocalypticism

Around 1348, Agnolo di Tura of Siena wrote in his Italian *Cronica*, "So many have died that everyone believes it is the end of the world;" on Crete, Arab chronicler as-Suluk noted that Christians there "feared that it was the end of the world." The notion that the world as we experience it will end in one or a series of cataclysms is deeply embedded in Christian belief. Though never saying when it would occur, Jesus spoke of certain signs for which one could watch. The final book of the Christian Bible, known as the Apocalypse (Catholic) or the Revelation of St. John (Protestant), is a vivid and frightening description of the end of time, or *eschaton*. Much of the human race alive at the time is to be destroyed, not least by war, famine, and death, while seven angels pour vials of poison into the earth's atmosphere. Coincidently, the chief explanation for plague from the 13th through the 19th centuries was "corrupted" or poisoned air.

Seemingly every generation of Christians has had adherents who believe they live during the "end times." In the 14th century, however, the belief was especially widespread. During the previous century, southern Italian prophet Joachim of Fiore claimed the world was in its last phase, awaiting the arrival of Anti–Christ, the chief enemy of God and harbinger of the war that would end the world and bring Christ's return. War was endemic in many parts of Europe, and the Hundred Years War began in the 1330s; widespread famines struck repeatedly in the 1310s, 1320s, and 1340s. While some modern historians have seen societal reactions as having been caused by the tensions of an increasingly overcrowded landscape (Malthusianism), many at the time related disasters to God's will and his opening of humanity's last chapter. Well before the Black Death, people generated and read reports of unnatural (supernatural?) events including hailstorms and "rains" of fire, poisonous amphibians and reptiles, and deadly earthquakes and floods that leveled entire cities. Reports of—and then the appearance of—plague in 1347 seemed to fill out the picture (see Apoc/Rev 16: 8–11, 18: 8; Matt 24:7; and Lk: 21–11).

Some, like the clerics Englishman William Dene and German Heinrich of Hervordia, put the pieces together in their plague-time chronicles. Others excused the destruction of Jewish communities by Rhineland mobs as part of the inexorable unfolding of the eschaton. Some modern historians, and perhaps the participants themselves, linked the flagellant movement sparked by the Black Death to Millenarianism—the thousand-year reign of Christ.

When the first epidemic ended without the Second Coming of Christ, some dismissed the earlier apocalyptic fears, while others, for example recovered plague victim Franciscan friar John of Rupescissa, interpreted it as just stage one. When plague returned in the 1360s and 1370s, such new prophets arose as Tomassino da Foligno and Daniele the Minorite (Franciscan), who also renewed the Joachite predictions. Repeated epidemics dulled the effect the first ones had, however, and Apocalypticism faded from view.

The 16th century saw its revival in the wake of the religious schisms and identification of the popes with Antichrist. This accompanied a more general tendency to associate plague with God's wrath, sparked now by Protestant heresy or Catholic refusal to reform. In late-Tudor and Stuart England, moralistic plague literature reduced Apocalypticism to the plague itself: repent or the end of *your* world will occur. George Wither's *Britain's Remembrancer* (1628) captures the dual levels of the threat: both England and the individual will undergo devastation and be forgotten. Political Millenarianism that fueled the English Civil War (1641–1649) used recurring plague as part of its picture of the contemporaneity of End Times. The arts had long reflected the prophecies of Revelation, as in the ubiquitous medieval portrayals of the Last Judgment. Renaissance-era Catholic art intensified traditional motifs, as in Michelangelo's *Final Judgment* in the Sistine Chapel in Rome (1541), and turned what had been illustrative or even folk art into masterpieces. Albrecht Dürer transformed the Apocalypse's

normally tame Four Horsemen into a chilling squad of vengeful cavalry thundering from the sky (1498), and Pieter Breughel abandoned humanity to a skeletal army in a blasted landscape in his version of the *Triumph of Death* (c. 1562).

See also: Dietary Regimens; Earthquakes; Flagellants; Jews; Malthusianism; Triumph of Death.

References

Aberth, John. *From the Brink of the Apocalypse: Crisis and Recovery in Late Medieval England*. New York: Routledge, 2000.

Cunningham, Andrew and Ole Peter Grell. *The Four Horsemen of the Apocalypse: Religion, War, Famine and Death in Reformation Europe*. New York: Cambridge University Press, 2000.

Getz, Faye Marie. "Black Death and the Silver Lining: Meaning, Continuity, and Revolutionary Change in Histories of Medieval Plague." *Journal of the History of Biology* 24 (1991): 265–289.

Lerner, Robert E. "The Black Death and Western Eschatological Mentalities." *American Historical Review* 86 (1981): 533–552; also in *The Black Death: The Impact of the Fourteenth-century Plague*, edited by Daniel Williman, (Binghamton, New York: Medieval and Renaissance Texts and Studies, 1982), 77–106.

Smoller, Laura. "Of Earthquakes, Hail, Frogs, and Geography: Plague and the Investigation of the Apocalypse in the Later Middle Ages," in *Last Things: Death and the Apocalypse in the Middle Ages*, edited by Caroline Walker Bynum and Paul Freedman (Philadelphia: University of Pennsylvania Press, 2000), 156–187.

Apothecaries

Apothecaries were the druggists or pharmacists of the later medieval and early modern world. The name is derived from Greek *apotheke*, a storehouse. Greeks pioneered the literature on medical botany and the development of such drugs as theriac, but the profession of apothecary emerged first in the Islamic world during the early ninth century. Two centuries later, the scholar Abu al-Rayhan al-Biruni described the apothecary as one who possesses the finest drugs and who prepares them according to the physician's order. These might be individual materials (simples) or compounds containing a variety of organic and inorganic ingredients. In the Islamic world, apothecaries operated shops or worked in hospitals and palaces. Given their wide trading networks, Muslim merchants greatly expanded the *materia medica* of the Greeks. As apothecaries developed, so did the apparatus of state oversight. *Muhtasibs* held the office of *hisba*, which had local control over food shops, bazaars, apothecaries, and medical practitioners in general. They inspected weights, measures, and quality of merchandise sold.

The Latin West borrowed the apothecary and much of his pharmacopoeia, or catalogue of simples and compounds. By the Black Death, these specialists had shops across Europe. When organized, they were originally in guilds with such similar tradesmen as spice merchants, chandlers, painters, or grocers. They followed physicians and surgeons in gaining organizations of their own over time, but they were generally licensed and inspected by boards of local physicians. Valencia's formed a guild in 1441, and Venetian apothecaries formed the Collegio degli speziali in 1565 with 71 members, growing to 85 members in 1569—including five women—and more than 100 by 1600. London's apothecaries belonged to the Grocers' Company until 1617, when they formed the Worshipful Company of Apothecaries; they remained unable to prescribe medicines until early in the 18th century. In France, apothecary colleges or guilds emerged in the 1570s, along with requirements for Latin literacy, previously reserved for university-educated physicians. In the 1590s, Seville's druggists underwent apprenticeship, were tested and licensed by the *protomedico*, had to know Latin, had at least 500 ducats capital to open a shop, and accepted regular inspections by two city councilors, a physician, and a nonlocal apothecary. Some cities specified which medical manuals had to be present, and most required the keeping of detailed records.

When plague struck, apothecaries worked with physicians and empirics to provide clients with what they believed to be effective prophylactics, or remedies. While the physician might view the patient through a window rather than at bedside, the apothecary would minister the prescribed treatment. Given the spike in demand for medical service, apothecaries often visited sufferers and delivered appropriate medicines on their own. High demand also meant that supplies ran low, forcing apothecaries to suggest substitutions. Given the era's Galenic medical orthodoxy, the most common bodily response sought by physicians and apothecaries alike was purgation of tainted humors through one or more orifice. Inventories of 17th-century Norwich apothecary shops confirm that the majority of drugs were purgatives.

In Europe, apothecaries were entrepreneurs who supplied institutions as well as individuals. During epidemics, plague hospitals and pest houses required drugs, as did houses of those shut in by authorities. Officials usually assigned apothecaries to keep such places supplied, a task that also brought them into direct contact with the sick and dying. Before London's Great Plague (1665–1666), the city had about 475 apothecaries who oversaw some 875 apprentices; 275 remained after the Great Plague to serve Londoners, of whom 50 died leaving wills.

Street scene with interior view of an apothecary's shop; also miniatures depicting heliotherapy and balneology, a cupping procedure, bloodletting, and surgery on a patient's chest. (Courtesy of the National Library of Medicine)

See also: Armenian Bole; Bezoar Stones; Bimaristans; Charlatans and Quacks; Humoral Theory; Narwhal/Unicorn Horn Powder; Poisoning and Plague Spreading; Prophylaxes; Purgatives; Remedies, External; Remedies, Internal; Syrups and Electuaries; Theriac and Mithridatum; Tobacco.

References

Brévart, Francis B. "Between Medicine, Magic, and Religion: Wonder Drugs in German Medico-Pharmaceutical Treatises for the Thirteenth to the Sixteenth Centuries." *Speculum* 83 (2008): 1–57.

Curth, Louise Hill. *From Physick to Pharmacology: Five Hundred Years of British Drug Retailing.* Aldershot, UK: Ashgate, 2006.

Pormann, Peter E. and Emilie Savage-Smith. *Medieval Islamic Medicine.* Washington, DC: Georgetown University Press, 2007.

Stengaard, M. Kruse. "Drug Therapy in the Official Danish Plague Instructions, 1619–1709." *Pharmacy in History* 44 (2002): 95–104.

Arabic-Persian Medicine and Practitioners

When plague struck Islamic regions from the 14th century, the cultures unified by Islam had several approaches to the disease and to healing in general. These included pre–Islamic folkloric traditions and magic, Islamic prophetic medicine based upon the Hadith and traditions about Muhammad, strains of learned traditions of Persian and Indian Ayurvedic medicine, and the Greek medicine attributed to Hippocrates, Galen, and late antique successors.

Like most premodern peoples, the Arabs and others of the Near East and North Africa had ancient, oral lore regarding health and healing. This was rooted in various sources, including astrology, herbalism, myth, superstition, and experience. Explanations, remedies, and expectations differed among the widely scattered ethnic groups and tribes and never constituted a coherent system. Healers were charismatic or hereditary, deriving their authority from their command of the traditions. Supposed ability to control malicious jinn (spirits), to read the macrocosmic signage of the stars, to know which formulae to write into amulets for protection or remedy, or to choose the most appropriate medicinal plants or earths was of paramount importance.

The Koran says nothing about medicine or doctors, but the traditions and sayings attributed to the Prophet Muhammad form a loose body of medical teachings. Each collection of Hadith contains a specific medical chapter or book called the *Kitab at-Tibb*. Compilers drew from the Hadith themselves, as well as earlier folk traditions discussed above. The result was a "medicine" that was more a moral and ethical guide for believers than a textbook for surgical procedures or internal medicine. Those who relied upon and taught the Prophet's medicine were Muslim religious teachers and judges rather than medical practitioners, and the two groups often disagreed or even clashed. For example, prophetic medicine, like folkloric, accepted the role of spirits, or jinn, in causing disease. While pre–Islamic traditions allowed that jinn could act arbitrarily and maliciously in attacking whom they wished, prophetic medicine accepted a kind of predestination or fatalism according to the will of Allah. Jinn might act, but only as ordered by God, or so went one reading. In another clash, pre–Islamic healers apparently accepted the notion of contagion, while one Hadith appears to have Muhammad deny contagion, again on grounds of divine intentionality.

When Islam spread eastward during the seventh century, it conquered a severely weakened Persian Empire that had been battling Byzantine armies as well as pestilence. The Persians had a sophisticated scholarly tradition of medicine influenced by the Indians and the Greeks. Indian folk medicine, with its own malevolent and healing spirits, astrological influences, and *materia medica*, blended with native Persian and neighboring traditions. So did elements of India's Ayurvedic medicine, which had its experiential and theoretical equivalent in the Greek Hippocratic corpus and Galen's writings. Some Indian scholars and medical texts found their way to Baghdad under the Abbasid rulers, and Muslim medical men borrowed terminology, techniques, and *materia medica* from the ancient civilization.

The final and most powerful influence on Islamic medical practitioners before the later 16th century was Greek. Mediated through Byzantine manuscripts and Syriac translations, works of the Hippocratic Corpus, Galen, and such lesser lights as Rufus of Ephesus were quickly absorbed. Abbasid Caliph al-Ma'mun (813–833) had the House of Wisdom (Bayt al-Hikma) built in Baghdad as a center for text translation, collection, and study. An enormous program of absorption was carried out under Hunayn ibn-Ishaq (d. c. 873), firmly establishing Greek medical principles. Arabic commentaries accompanied translations, along with syncretistic elements of Arabic, Persian, and Indian traditions, including astrology, magic, and *materia medica* (also found in the Greeks—respectively—Ptolemy, Alexander of Tralles, and Dioscorides). Henceforth, learned medical practice in Muslim lands would be modified Galenism. Such encyclopedic works as the *Canon* of Avicenna provided systematic coverage of huge swaths of medical theory and technique that educated the neophytes and reminded the practicing physicians. It is clear that, as in the Christian West, authority trumped experience at the core of Islamic medicine.

A young man seeking to practice as a physician could teach himself a range of fundamentals through books; or could be apprenticed to a practicing physician; or could work and study in a bimaristan, usually under the direction of an expert. The earliest formal school (*madrasa*) for medical study appeared in Damascus in the early 13th century. All students were encouraged to work with patients in a bimaristan. Young practitioners were examined by local authorities—including the local chief physician—upon seeking the right to practice, a process that differed among regions of the Islamic world. Having dedicated so much time and effort to acquire skill and knowledge, not surprisingly, the well-trained physician sought social recognition and lucrative positions with clients among the well off, who were generally living in cities. The poor had recourse to informal practitioners of magic and other folk healing traditions and to bimaristans and those who worked within their walls.

See also: Amulets, Talismans, and Magic; Astrology; Avicenna (Ibn Sina); Bimaristans; Galen and Galenism; Hippocrates and the Hippocratic Corpus; Islam and Medicine; Jinn; Muhammad the Prophet; *Ta'un*.

References

Conrad, Laurence I. "*Ta'un* and *waba*: Conceptions of Plague and Pestilence in Early Islam." *Journal of the Economic and Social History of the Orient* 25 (1982): 268–307.

Dols, Michael W. *Medieval Islamic Medicine: Ibn Ridwan's Treatise "On the Prevention of Bodily Ills in Egypt*." Berkeley: University of California Press, 1984.

Ibn Qayyim al-Jawziyya. *Medicine of the Prophet*. Translated by Penelope Johnstone. Cambridge: Islamic Texts Society, 1998.

Kharmi, Ghada. "State Control of the Physician in the Middle Ages: An Islamic Model," in *Town and State Physicians in Europe from the Middle Ages to the Enlightenment*, edited by Andrew Russell (Wolfenbüttel Forschungen 17: Herzog August Bibliothek, 1981), 63–84.

Pormann, Peter E. and Emilie Savage-Smith. *Medieval Islamic Medicine*. Washington, DC: Georgetown University Press, 2007.

Stearns, Justin. *Infectious Ideas: Contagion in Premodern Islamic and Christian Thought in the Western Mediterranean*. Baltimore, MD: Johns Hopkins University Press, 2011.

Ullmann, Manfred. *Islamic Medicine*. Edinburgh: Edinburgh University Press, 1978.

Wujastyk, Dominik. *The Roots of Ayurveda*. New York: Penguin Books, 2003.

Armenian Bole

Also known as *bolus armenus*, bol armeniac, and bole armoniac, the iron oxide-rich clay was an often prescribed element in both internal and external plague remedies and prophylaxes. A special variety was *terra sigillata*—earth "sealed" with approval. In some cases, both ingredients were required. Purportedly recommended by Galen, the fine powder was mixed in a drink or dampened and placed on the body. Al-Maqrizi noted that during plague outbreaks, some Muslims covered their bodies, but most prescriptions called for smearing a mixture over the buboes. Some recipes for amulets called for the clay, which would have made modeling specific shapes much easier. Bole was believed to absorb the poison that entered or developed within the plague-struck body, either through the skin or through digestion and evacuation. Used throughout the Second Pandemic, bole taken internally may have been a mild emetic, and that slathered on buboes may have absorbed bacteria from the skin as it dried, though the effect would have been minimal.

See also: Amulets, Talismans, and Magic; Apothecaries; Prophylaxes; Remedies, External; Remedies, Internal.

Reference

Dols, Michael W. *The Black Death in the Middle East*. Princeton, NJ: Princeton University Press, 1977.

Armies

War brought more people together faster, from farther away, keeping them together and moving them around the countryside longer than any other human activity. Those who gathered and maneuvered premodern armies had little regard for disease. Camp life tended to be harsh and dirty, and rats, fleas, and illness were constant companions.

Though soldiers on campaign knew—or quickly learned—to avoid plague, hunger, fatigue, and callousness could drive them to ignore its signs as they fearlessly rummaged about for food, clothing, or sex across a devastated countryside. Such camp followers as mistresses, prostitutes, merchants, and servants came and went as armies marched, bringing diseases with them and taking them away if they were fortunate enough to survive. Infected soldiers would drop out of ranks or desert along the route, bringing disease and suffering to uninfected areas as they imposed themselves on civilians. When an army became plague stricken, it disintegrated as men sought to avoid the disease and return home. War brought disruption to daily life as food stocks were plundered or hoarded, houses were destroyed, and refugees with various diseases unleashed across the landscape or gathered into overcrowded and undersupplied cities. Plague ran rampant when such cities were besieged, sparing neither civilian nor soldier, defender nor attacker.

The Black Death itself brought an end to the siege of Caffa and destroyed Djanibeg's Tatar army; forced a seven-year truce during the Hundred Years War; killed Alfonso XI of Castile while besieging Gibraltar; reduced the effective size of the warring Venetian and Genoese fleets; opened the northern boundaries of the Byzantine Empire to a Serbian invasion; lured the Scots near Selkirk to attack the stricken English army and quickly acquire the disease; ended the sieges of Tabriz and Baghdad by Malik Ashraf; and scattered the army of Abu l-Hasan of Fez, who had invaded Tunisia, after the Battle of al-Qayrawan in June 1348. The Mamluks forwent offensives for a decade, and the Reconquista halted for more than a century.

Russian plagues in 1567 and 1570 undermined resistance to Tatar invasions, and pestilence in Ireland interfered with Tudor military recruitment. Plague killed off Danish mint and brewery workers in 1564 to 1565, keeping Frederick II from paying his troops. Armies spread plague domestically during the French Wars of Religion and England's Civil War, and troops returning from France in 1563 brought the disease with them. Disasters like the latter led to segregation of returning soldiers, adding to the hardships they faced.

See also: Caffa (Kaffa, Feodosiya), Ukraine; Hundred Years War; Moscow, Russia; Thirty Years' War.

References

Concannon, R. J. G. "The Third Enemy: The Role of Epidemics in the Thirty Years War." *Journal of World History* 10 (1967): 500–511.

Cunningham, Andrew and Ole Peter Grell. *The Four Horsemen of the Apocalypse: Religion, War, Famine and Death in Reformation Europe.* New York: Cambridge University Press, 2000.

Outram, Quentin. "The Socio-economic Relations of Warfare and the Military Mortality Crises of the Thirty Years' War." *Medical History* 45 (2001): 151–184.

Prinzing, Friedrich. *Epidemics Resulting from Wars.* Oxford: Oxford University Press, 1916.

Arrows

The most consistent metaphor for plague was the arrow. In *Iliad* (c. 800 BCE), Homer envisioned a plague in Agamemnon's camp as enraged Apollo stalking about shooting his victims randomly. Wrathful Yahweh in Deuteronomy (32:23–4) declares, "I will exhaust all my arrows against them: emaciating hunger and consuming fever and bitter pestilence," smiting those who oppose him. Sore-stricken Job, whose plague-like ailments made him a plague saint, lamented, "the arrows of the Almighty are within me." The Book of Revelation's four apocalyptic horsemen included an archer, and the founder of the Dominicans, St. Dominic, had a vision of Christ holding three arrows of just punishment, as described in Iacobus de Voragine's *Golden Legend* (c. 1280). In 590 CE, Honorius of Autun described the Justinianic Plague as "arrows falling from heaven."

In battle, arrows fell from heaven—purported source of plague—striking victims randomly. Skilled archers could transfix targets with great accuracy at long distances, silently and without warning. Just as arrow wounds did not always kill, neither did plague. Whether God's plague struck randomly or he targeted whom he would, the arrow metaphor worked brilliantly. It was not by accident that Italian notary Gabriele de' Mussis described plague as "sharp arrows of sudden death"; or that Flemish Abbot Gilles li Muisis celebrated the heaven-sent "arrows" that decimated the Mongol Tatars before striking Europe. Some Muslim poets also pictured plague as jinn-fired arrows.

Though Christian writers could be vague about heavenly archers, artists needed specificity. In some paintings and woodcuts, Christ—even Baby Jesus in Mary's lap—hurls them like small spears or drops them from an open palm. In scenes with interceding saints, the archers are often angels around Christ enthroned. More rarely, Death is the shooter and sometimes demons, perhaps reducing God's responsibility. Victims, often representing a range of social types, litter the ground. With time, the placement of arrows in victims became more precise: groin, neck, and armpit, the sites of plague victims' lymphatic buboes. Catholicism taught that saints serve as intercessors who pray to God for the living. Some artworks depict saints, usually

Mary, shielding devotees from divine arrows with her cloak, effectively thwarting God's will. The Council of Trent (1545–1563) banned these images as sacrilegious. Catholics invoked St. Sebastian as plague saint because third-century pagans initially martyred him with arrows. In early modern Catholic countries, Sebastian's ubiquitous arrow-pierced but living portrait kept the metaphor alive, while biblical arrow imagery inspired such Protestant tracts as William Gouge's *God's Three Arrowes, Plague, Famine, Sword* (London, 1631). Crossed arrows also appeared as talismans to ward off plague and, in Luxembourg, were painted on houses until the 1900s.

See also: Art, Effects of Plague on; Bible; Books of Hours; Broadsheets, Broadsides, and Pamphlets; Christ; Death, Depictions of; Ex voto; Heaven and Hell; Metaphors for Plague; Plague Saints; St. Sebastian; Triumph of Death; Virgin Mary.

References

Horrox, Rosemary. *The Black Death*. New York: Manchester University Press, 1994.

Marshall, Louise. "Manipulating the Sacred: Image and Plague in Renaissance Italy." *Renaissance Quarterly* 47 (1994): 485–532.

Mormando, Franco and Thomas Worcester, eds. *Piety and Plague from Byzantium to the Baroque*. Kirksville, MO: Truman State University Press, 2007.

Ars moriendi (The Art of Dying)

One of the most popular genres in literature from 1480 to 1650 was the "Art of Dying Well," in Latin called *Ars moriendi*, a guidebook for the dying and for those attending. It originated in the traditional Catholic deathbed sacrament of Last Rites, which included communion, confession, anointing, and prayers. This required a priest, but after waves of 14th-century plague, people realized that a clergyman's deathbed presence was unlikely during epidemics. Combined with growing literacy rates and increased comfort with expressions of popular lay piety by the later 15th century, this ritual need was filled by a handbook that led one to a "good death" without (or with) a clerical presence. Commentators have attributed the genre's formal origins to a Latin text (c. 1415) by the French theologian Jean Gerson and an anonymous early 15th-century tract, both of which contained the essential elements.

For Catholics, the time immediately before one's death is literally one's last opportunity to grasp at salvation: to repent of one's sins and to cry out for God's mercy. The bedside was a battleground between God's angels and Satan's demons, both of which claimed the sinner's soul. The priest's final ministrations were thought to tip the balance, but in his absence, the dying person (*moriens*) was on his or her own. The *Ars* provided three major tools meant to focus his attention. The first was discussion of the five temptations of the dying: against faith, and to despair, impatience, vainglory, and avarice. These were matched with five countering inspirations: to faith and against the others. In illustrated versions of the genre, these 10 struggles appear, complete with threatening devils, supportive angels, and saints surrounding the deathbed. One such image shows the soul as a baby rising into the waiting hands of Jesus. The second tool was a series of questions probing *moriens*'s spiritual state, leading him to contrition and repentance, as would a good sacramental confession. The third tool was a series of prayers on behalf of *moriens*'s soul, to be prayed with, for, and by the dying person. Most were printed as cheap booklets in Europe's vernaculars or as illustrated single sheets with text reduced to rhymed couplets.

Protestant versions vary in content, structure, and titles. Early Lutheran texts emphasize that *moriens* has no fear since he has certitude of salvation through faith alone: the good death is the witness of one's faith to those around. Prayers were only for the living: that they might remain steadfast and godly. For some, Christ's obedient death was to be the model to which one aspired. Anglicans rejected Lutheran certainty of salvation and emphasized the need for God's mercy. Calvinist authors, influenced by predestination, taught that the good death reflected the life well lived and inspired those around to emulate his good life.

See also: Bible; Books of Hours; Death, Depictions of; Prayer and Fasting; Purgatory; *Tears against the Plague*.

References

Beaty, Nancy Lee. *The Craft of Dying: A Study in the Literary Tradition of the 'Ars Moriendi' in England*. New Haven, CT: Yale University Press, 1970.

O'Connor, Mary C. *The Art of Dying Well: The Development of the* Ars Moriendi. New York: AMS, 1966.

Reinis, Austra. *Reforming the Art of Dying: The Ars Moriendi in the German Reformation (1519–1528)*. Burlington, VT: Ashgate, 2007.

Art, Effects of Plague on

The deaths of artists, craftsmen, apprentices, and sophisticated patrons had to have an effect on art after the Black Death. Some major projects, for example, Siena's planned cathedral, were stopped and never revived. Contemporary Agnolo Tura blamed this on the reduction in population and, specifically, the deaths of the skilled workers and the project oversight committee (*opera*). Some English architectural historians attribute the simpler lines and masses of the new perpendicular style to the lack of skilled masons and sculptors, others to the reduced expenditures on church buildings. Churches begun in the decorated style were finished in the bulkier perpendicular; then in the 1440s, English church building paused, probably for economic reasons. In Scandinavia, construction of the wooden stave churches ended around 1350.

Italianist Millard Meiss believed that northern Italy underwent a spiritual change post-1348 in which patrons demanded less sophisticated, more "spiritual," and stylistically more old fashioned religious painting. Developments toward greater naturalism were abandoned, he wrote. Later research undermined the so-called Meiss Thesis, usually accepting his observations but attributing the changes to economics, workshop deaths, and changing practice or patronage, and not spirituality. An attitudinal change on the part of patrons, however, may have played a major part in memorial art. The fear of anonymity in mass graves and being forgotten as plague wiped out whole families led upper-class heads of families to create family chapels, decorate altars, create realistic burial effigies, and mark their gifts and memorials clearly with coats of arms or other identifying symbols. Cohn uncovered clear patterns of patrons' intent in wills across northern Italy. Monumental transi tombs also marked the dead unambiguously. Like other memento mori art of the period, these were also meant to warn viewers: time is short and life fleeting.

Three popular artistic themes preceded the Black Death in their origins but gained great popularity after 1348. Each had a poetic component that usually accompanied the illustration, and each featured Death. The Danse macabre or Dance of Death was popular into the mid-1500s and depicted skeletal Death dancing away a representative variety of social types, from pauper to pope. Related was the Three Living meet the Three Dead, in which three wealthy, young horsemen come upon three corpses. The latter admonish the well off, "what we are now you will be." The third type is the Triumph of Death, which has cadaverous or skeletal figures representing Death arrayed in military formation and clearly victorious against terrified people. Iconography of Death and Plague is virtually interchangeable from the later Middle Ages and into the Renaissance, as artists shied from tackling the plague realistically.

Artists during the later Middle Ages developed pictorial themes that emphasized the physical suffering of Christ during the passion. Partly, this expressed a cult of guilt that reminded each believer that his or her sin bore responsibility, but it also embodied the shared suffering of man and God. Jesus knew human suffering and has compassion. Terribly realistic crucifixion scenes appeared, culminating in Grünewald's tortured tableaus of the early 1500s. The half-figure man of sorrows, called the pietà in Italy, depicted the dead savior with crown of thorns propped up behind an altar/slab. This was later softened to Mary supporting and meditating on the dead Christ, the most famous example of which is Michelangelo's in St. Peter's. Similar images focused on Jesus's five wounds (feet, hands, side) or the instruments of the passion, including the cross itself, the nails, crown of thorns, even the dice and rooster.

Art served to interpret the theological understandings of plague, its source in the divine, and spiritual remedies. A panel in the Carmelite church in Göttingen depicts Jesus himself hurling arrows, 16 transfixed victims lying around Him despite the presence of prayerful saints, including Mary, who catches some of the arrows in her upraised gown.

Because of the well-developed Catholic cult of saints—reliance on the prayers of those in heaven to help those left on earth— depictions of such plague saints as Sebastian and Roche and of the Virgin Mary protecting devotees with her cloak were a major product from about 1400 to the Pandemic's end. Sebastian gained his visual attribute of the arrow at least a century before the Black Death and went from being modestly clothed to being stripped to a loincloth like his savior. Roche was a newcomer: he had helped the plague-stricken, contracted the plague, with his dog's help recovered, and died falsely imprisoned. Along with the protective Mary, off of whose mantel plague arrows bounced harmlessly, Sebastian and Roche appeared as household icons, accompanying prayers on printed broadsheets, as stand-alone altarpieces, or as ensembles with other saints or shown pleading with Jesus on humanity's behalf.

During the period after the Council of Trent (1545–1563), dominated as it was by Baroque sensibilities, Catholic authorities and patrons commemorated heroic clergy and other Catholic leaders. Chief among these was Charles Borromeo, Archbishop of Milan during the epidemic of the mid-1570s. He was the model leader and Catholic: aiding the needy, self-sacrificing, providing the Eucharist, embracing humility, following Jesus. Another was Cardinal Barbarini, who, during Rome's final plague, selflessly distributed badly needed bread among the hungry. An anonymous treatment from c. 1657 depicts Rome's Sts. Peter and Paul hovering approvingly overhead. Divine approval also shows itself in the Archangel Michael sheathing his sword of death, a motif that originated with a sixth-century Roman epidemic. Catholic artists tended to embrace the death that plague meant but turned it to the positive, emphasizing heroes rather than victims and glory that can come from suffering and the performance of good works (Boeckl).

See also: Arrows; Biblical Plagues; Borromeo, St. Charles (San Carlo); Broadsheets, Broadsides, and Pamphlets; Christ; Churches, Plague; Corpses; Danse Macabre; Death, Depictions of; Ex voto; Flagellants; Gregory the Great, Pope; Individualism and Individual Liberties; Plague Memorials; Plague Saints; Printing; Processions; "Three Living Meet Three Dead;" Transi Tombs; Triumph of Death.

References

Bailey, Gauvin Alexander, et al., eds. *Hope and Healing: Painting in Italy in a Time of Plague, 1500–1800.* Chicago: University of Chicago Press, 2005.

Boeckl, Christine. *Images of Plague and Pestilence: Iconography and Iconology.* Kirksville, MO: Truman State University Press, 2000.

Cohn, Samuel K. *The Cult of Remembrance and the Black Death.* Baltimore, MD: The Johns Hopkins University Press, 1992.

Llewellyn, Nigel. *The Art of Death: Visual Culture in the English Death Ritual, c. 1500–c. 1800.* London: Reaktion and the Victoria and Albert Museum, 1991.

Marshall, Louise. "Manipulating the Sacred: Image and Plague in Renaissance Italy." *Renaissance Quarterly* 47 (1994): 485–532.

Meiss, Millard. *Painting in Florence and Siena after the Black Death: The Arts, Religion, and Society in the Mid-fourteenth Century.* Princeton, NJ: Princeton University Press, 1951.

Mormando, Franco and Thomas Worcester, eds. *Piety and Plague from Byzantium to the Baroque.* Kirksville, MO: Truman State University Press, 2007.

Norman, Diana. "Change and Continuity: Art and Religion after the Black Death," in her *Siena,*

Florence and Padua, I: Art, Society and Religion 1280–1400. Interpretative Essays (New Haven, CT: Yale University Press, 1995): 177–196.

Steinhoff, Judith B. *Sienese Painting after the Black Death: Artistic Pluralism, Politics, and the New Art Market.* New York: Cambridge University Press, 2006.

Van Os, Henk. "The Black Death and Sienese Painting: A Problem of Interpretation." *Art History* 4 (1981): 237–249.

Articella

Literally "Little Art," also known as *Art of Medicine*, *Articella* was the principal medical textbook of Western Christian medical faculties from the early 12th to mid-16th centuries. Originally a compendium of five short Greek texts translated into Latin, the work grew as more texts became available. The original text, introduced to the medical school at Salerno, Italy, by Johannes Afflacius, included Hippocrates's *Aphorisms* and *Prognostics*, probably translated by Constantine the African (Johannes's teacher), the Byzantine *Pulses* (by Philaretus) and *Urines* (Theophilus Protospatharius), and the digest of Galenic principles of health and disease, *Isagoge* (Introduction), composed by Hunayn ibn Ishaq, called "Johannitius." Added around 1150 was a Latin translation of Galen's *Tegni* (*Techne*), his own summary. Additional Arab works were added around the 1180s, and, in the mid-13th century, several Galenic commentaries on Hippocrates. Medical scholars composed their own commentaries on *Articella*'s components; these became as important as the text itself, and many were absorbed into it. As medical education became formalized into curricula at major medical schools, *Articella* provided the matrix well into the 16th century.

See also: Galen and Galenism; Hippocrates and the Hippocratic Corpus; Medical Education (1300–1500, Medieval Europe).

Reference

Siraisi, Nancy. *Medieval and Early Renaissance Medicine.* Chicago: University of Chicago Press, 1990.

Astrology

Astrology posits that celestial bodies—stars and planets—have a direct influence on the earth and its inhabitants and that these influences can be determined. While this has led some to try to "read" the heavens to predict the future, a task condemned by Christianity and Islam, others have read the skies as a scientist might read genes or meteorological reports. Rooted in the ancient Near East, astrology was rationalized by second-century Greco-Roman astronomer Ptolemy in his *Tetrabiblos* and *Almagest*.

Largely ignored by the rudimentary Western Christian medical tradition, such Islamic physicians as Abu Bakr al Razi (d. 925) adopted astrology as a vital tool in determining patients' constitutions, developing case histories, diagnosing ailments, and prescribing treatment. Despite opposition from Avicenna, Islamic medical astrology flourished. Abu Ma'shar (Albumasar; d. 887) related each zodiac sign to a human body part and humor in his *Introduction to Astronomy*, a work available in Latin from the 12th century. The Spanish Jew Abraham ibn Ezra (1086–1164) translated more than 50 astrological works from Arabic into Latin and other European languages at the same time that Arab medical works—and *Tetrabiblos*—were being translated. In the 13th century, Michael Scot introduced astrology to Emperor Frederick II in Palermo, Sicily. Meanwhile,

Oxford's Chancellor Robert Grosseteste rejected and Thomas Aquinas's teacher, Albertus Magnus, embraced and wrote much about astrology.

Abu Ma'shar had noted a recurrence of a Great Conjunction of Saturn, Jupiter, and Mars every 960 years, relating it to major natural and political disasters. Albertus Magnus did as well, and its appearance at 1:00 PM on March 23, 1345, was widely believed to have caused the Black Death. The influential *Compendium* composed by the medical faculty of the University of Paris adopted the Conjunction as a principle cause, and Liége cleric Simon de Couvin allegorized it in verse in his *Judgment of the Sun*. The effect was considered natural, though at a distance: the conjunction affected earthly water sources and gasses, which caused miasmas of corrupted air that poisoned plague victims. This narrative dominated plague causation theories for centuries.

Astrology also played an increasingly important role in plague medicine. In 1371, King Charles V joined a program in astrology to the Paris medical school. From 1405, the University of Bologna required four years of astrological study; similarly at the Universities of Montpellier, Erfurt, Krakow, Leipzig, and Vienna. Ironically, Paris was the first to back away, renouncing astrology in the late 1530s. About this time, Europe saw the rise of almanacs: cheap, popular books that featured a calendar with astronomical events, predictions for natural occurrences, medical suggestions, and advertisements. Popular culture held to what medical schools had rejected: the answers were in the stars.

See also: Almanacs; Arabic-Persian Medicine and Practitioners; Avicenna (Ibn Sina); Causes of Plague: Historical Theories; Medical Education (1300–1500, Medieval Europe); Miasma Theory; Zodiac Man.

References

Curth, Louise Hill. *English Almanacs, Astrology and Popular Medicine, 1500–1700*. New York: Manchester University Press, 2007.

MacDonald, Michael. "The Career of Astrological Medicine in England," in *Religio Medici*, edited by Peter Grell and Andrew Cunningham (Brookfield, VT: Ashgate, 1996), 62–90.

North, J. D. "Medieval Concepts of Celestial Influence," in *Astrology, Science and Society: Historical Essays*, edited by Patrick Curry (Wolfboro, NH: Boydell Press, 1987), 5–18.

Rawcliffe, Carole. *Medicine and Society in Later Medieval England*. Stroud, Gloucs, UK: Sutton, 1997.

Athens, Plague of

At the end of the first year of the Peloponnesian War, an epidemic (perhaps typhoid fever) broke out in Athens. Athenian historian Thucydides, both witness and victim, chronicled the plague (430–426 BCE) in Book Two of his *Peloponnesian War*. He described the plague's origins and symptoms and recounted the victims' suffering and frequent abandonment. Corpses littered the city, burial rites were suspended, and people seeking pleasure broke the laws of gods and men. This account remained well known to educated Greek speakers and shaped subsequent descriptions of epidemics and their effects (e.g., Lucretius, *De rerum* 1138–1286; Diodoros Siculus, *World History* 14:70–72). Descriptions of the sixth-century Plague of Justinian by Procopios and other Byzantine chroniclers echo Thucydides and re-emerged in the 14th century to be drawn upon by Emperor John VI and others. Western Europeans discovered Thucydides around 1450, prompting such writers on plague as Thomas Lodge to borrow freely

(*Treatise on the Plague*, 1603). When a writer uses an earlier literary model, historians must carefully distinguish writers' own observations from the model's influence.

See also: Abandonment; Chronicles and Annals; Constantinople/Istanbul; Hippocrates and the Hippocratic Corpus; Justinian, Plague of (First Plague Pandemic).

Reference

Miller, Timothy S. "The Plague in John VI Cantacuzenus and Thucydides." *Greek, Roman and Byzantine Studies* 17 (1976): 385–395.

Avicenna (Abu Ali al-Husayn ibn Abd Allah ibn Sina; 980–1037)

Avicenna—the Latinized form of his Arabic name—was born to a governmental administrator near Bukhara in present-day Uzbekistan. Though formally educated in Bukhara, he later attributed his enormous scholarship to his own reading. Eventually he produced between 300 and 450 books. The longest was *Kitab al-Shifa* (*Book of Healing*), an encyclopedic work organized around logic, physics, mathematics, and metaphysics. In this, he sought to reconcile Aristotelian scholarship with Islamic teaching. He served as scholar and physician in residence at Bukhara's court, moving when the dynasty changed. He went on to serve local rulers in Qayy, Qazvin, Hamadan, and finally Isfahan.

Though Avicenna did not witness plague, his major writing on medicine, *Qanun-fi-t-Tibb* (*Canon* [model] *of Medicine*) had an enormous impact on both Islamic and Christian medical theory and practice. Its attraction was due in part to its organization, clarity, and sense of completeness, in which Avicenna blended classical Galenism with his own observations and experience. He organized *Canon* into five books: the first covered medical theory, including anatomy and physiology, diseases causes, symptoms, diet, principles of treatment, and prevention of disease, or prophylaxis; the second dealt with simple pharmacological remedies; the third specific diseases and their remedies; the fourth contagious diseases; and the fifth composite or complex remedies. In Book IV, Avicenna discussed epidemics, outlining miasma theory of fumes corrupting or putrefying the atmosphere, which goes on to poison the human heart, causing it to rot. He blends this with the idea that people can transmit the poison to others by breath, a basic form of contagion theory. He also noted contagion with tuberculosis and transmission of "poison" through water and dirt. These mechanical explanations seemed to exclude Allah's all-powerful will, which spawned Muslim critics and opponents in Spain and Egypt.

In Toledo, Spain, 12th-century scholar Gerard of Cremona translated *Canon* into Latin, which served as the basic Western medical authority on classical medicine until medical humanists produced new editions of Hippocrates and Galen in the 16th century. Even so, Renaissance-era medical scholars continued to write commentaries on *Canon*, and both Gerard's and fresh translations appeared in more than 60 printed editions after 1500.

See also: Arabic-Persian Medicine and Practitioners; Contagion Theory; Galen and Galenism; Medical Humanism; Miasma Theory; Remedies, Internal.

References
Pormann, Peter E. and Emilie Savage-Smith. *Medieval Islamic Medicine*. Washington, DC: Georgetown University Press, 2007.

Siraisi, Nancy. *Avicenna in Renaissance Italy: The Canon and Medical Teaching in Italian University after 1500*. Princeton, NJ: Princeton University Press, 1987.

B

Barcelona, Spain

Barcelona was the Kingdom of Aragon's major city and chief seaport in the 14th century. Its Catalan language and culture set it apart from Spain and France, but commerce linked it to the Western Mediterranean via coastal roads and its great harbor. Plague's first appearance occurred in April of 1348, probably arriving by ship from Roussillon or Mallorca. Religious leaders immediately arranged processions and liturgies to placate an angry God, and the wealthy fled. Following the trade routes along the coast and inland, the plague moved with cargo and refugees. Barcelona's Jewish ghetto was ransacked amid claims of poisonings. Pedro IV ordered the perpetrators captured and punished, but none was. Civil order broke down as nearly all of the members of the Council of 100 died. Diocesan records suggest death rates of around 60 percent for clergy, and wills and other sources between 35 and 40 percent of the population, about 15,000. Pre-1348 population was between 40,000 and 45,000, a figure that held steady over 300 years.

Dates for post-1348 epidemics differ among historians, but the fullest accounting includes heavy death tolls in 1362 to 1363, 1371, 1422, 1457, and 1465 to 1466; with lighter attacks in 1371, 1375, 1394 to 1397, 1408 to 1410, 1416, 1429, 1441, 1448, 1452, 1456 to 1458, 1475 to 1478, 1483, 1486, 1489 to 1490, 1493 to 1494, and 1497. In 1408, the city first formed a temporary 12-man plague commission drawn from the four estates: aristocrats, merchants, and higher and lower guildsmen. The 16th century also saw a high rate of recurrence: 1501, 1515, 1521, 1530, 1558, 1560, 1564, and 1589 to 1590. This last year's total deaths were recorded in bills of mortality and reached 11,723 from July 1 to January 7, about 30 percent of the population.

Plague returned in 1607 and the devastating—and final—epidemic of 1651 to 1653. This last was indeed Barcelona's deadliest bout, killing 50 percent of 40,000. It produced the fullest European narrative by a commoner, the *Plague Diary* of the tanner Miquel Parets, who wrote with horrifying detail. In 1650, Barcelona's authorities hemmed in the stricken city of Gerona with a military cordon sanitaire, but in January 1651, the capital itself was suffering. The province responded in kind, which made food and other goods scarce and expensive. Barcelona itself contributed 700 men to guarding its borders. In March, processions invoked God and his saints. Quarantine was set up in the two waterfront bastions, and two monasteries provided pest houses. Most victims with houses were shut up in them. Those who broke in were supposed to be executed, but many were condemned to work in the pest houses, which held 3,000 to 4,000 victims at a time. The plague subsided in early 1652 but was sparked anew by returning troops in 1653.

See also: Black Death (1347–1352); Cordons Sanitaires; Lazarettos and Pest Houses; Merchants; Processions.

References

Betrán, José Luis. *La peste en la Barcelona de los Austrias.* Lleida: Milenio, 1996.

Gyug, Richard. "The Effects and Extent of the Black Death of 1348: New Evidence for Clerical

Mortality in Barcelona." *Mediaeval Studies* 45 (1983): 385–398.

Parets, Miquel. *A Journal of the Plague Year: The Diary of the Barcelona Tanner Miquel Parets, 1651*. Translated by James S. Amelang. New York: Oxford University Press, 1995.

Smith, Robert S. "Barcelona 'Bills of Mortality' and Population, 1457–1590." *Journal of Political Economy* 44 (1936): 84–93.

Bells

As in normal times, bells played highly important symbolic roles when plague struck. For centuries, large bells or groups of bells, each with its own distinctive sound, rang from high towers that were next to or part of Christian churches. These were rung to call worshipers to services in cities, in villages, and at monasteries. An old yet tenacious belief held that ringing bells chased or kept demons away. Perhaps this is why monks rang their bells at the point when one of their brothers passed on. Tolling bells at death and during funeral rituals had become customary across Europe by the 14th century. From the later 13th century, communal governments acquired their own bell and tower, used to gather citizens together or warn of emergencies.

During the early stages of plague outbreaks of the Second Pandemic, bells seemed endlessly to toll deaths and funerals. In Ben Jonson's play *Volpone*, a character remarks "The bells, in times of pestilence, ne'er made like noise, or were in that perpetual motion" (III.5). But bell ringing was also believed to break up miasmic air that caused the disease, and keeping demons away had its advantages. The city of Tournai (Belgium) claimed victory over pestilence after merely one day of miasma-clearing noise. During communal religious processions, tolling bells often marked the group's progress through the city. As time went on, though, the effect was numbing, and many felt that the ringing actually made people susceptible to plague by depressing them. Since funerals were held even at night, tolling interrupted sleep. One after another, cities began first limiting the use of bells and then banning them altogether. At Tournai, despite their success, bells were only to be rung for Sunday mass. Orvieto, Pistoia, and Venice in Italy each curbed or banned bell ringing, as did certain Aragonese towns in Spain, which did so "to avoid frightening the people." Protestant Londoners forbade bell tolling in 1547 and 1559 because of its association with Catholic ritual and belief. Nonetheless, the practice was curbed, not stopped, because of how deeply seeded the custom was. And so John Donne could make his famous admonition: "Ask not for whom the bell tolls . . ." Where bells had been silenced, their resounding marked the relief of thanksgiving celebration.

Smaller hand bells also played their part in plague time. Since lepers had long carried small bells to warn of their coming, in some cities, plague victims who might be out of doors were sometimes required to carry a small bell for the same reason. Once the tumbrels of the corpse carriers started to roll, the sharp clang of a hand bell often announced their approach. Along the northern Florentine border during the plague of 1630, residents were required to ring bells to warn border guards if unknown people crossed illicitly into Florentine territory.

See also: Civil Governments; Corpse Carriers; Funerals, Catholic; Funerals, Protestant; Wands.

Reference

Byrne, Joseph P. *Daily Life during the Black Death*. Westport, CT: Greenwood, 2006.

Bertrand, Jean-Baptiste (1670–1752)

Bertrand was born and raised in Martiques, Provence. He was educated at Marseille at the Jesuit College and in medicine in Avignon and Montpellier. His early experience came in Lyon hospitals, but he moved to Marseille in 1707 and joined the 12-man College of Physicians in 1708. In 1709, Bertrand was called upon to serve, along with three others, at the Hôtel Dieu hospital during an especially deep frost. He contracted fever but was the only College physician to remain at the hospital.

In May 1720, plague struck Marseille, as Bertrand explains, via a ship from the Levant. In July, he was assigned a quarter of the city and required to visit the sick and confirm the cause of death of corpses. He contracted fevers three times and watched his wife and two daughters die in January 1721. Subsequently, he was quarantined for 40 days. When the carnage ended in 1722, more than half of the city's population of 85,000 were dead, as were 37 percent of the province of Provence.

As the plague entered its final phase in 1721, Bertrand published his 500-page *Relation historique de la peste de Marseille*. Reviewing earlier plagues, he found this to have been the most deadly. He believed it a "severe chastisement exercised by an angry God" rather than natural and, thus, immune to medical science. Good order and severe measures within the city and the strict cordon thrown around it "diminished its ravages." In 1722, as the epidemic ended and other physicians and officials published their reports, Bertrand produced a second and shorter *Observations on the Plague that Currently Reigns at Marseille*. This continued a debate with Dr. François de Chicoyneau of Montpellier. Chicoyneau had argued that the disease was not contagious and that the source of plague was the fear of the plague. This was both in line with humoral medicine that claimed passions weakened bodily defenses and with Enlightenment belief that psychosomatic conditions could be cured by human intervention. Bertrand responded by reiterating God's wrath as ultimate cause but also by positing tiny organisms that can pass between people. Thus, contagion was very real, and the life cycle of such organisms explains why symptoms are not immediate.

See also: Cordons Sanitaires; Fracastoro, Girolamo; Kircher, Athanasius; Marseille, France; Physicians.

References

Bertrand, Jean Baptiste. *A Historical Relation of the Plague at Marseilles in the Year 1720*. Translated by Anne Plumtre (1805). New York: McGraw-Hill, 1973.

Gordon, Daniel. "Confrontations with the Plague in Eighteenth-century France," in *Dreadful Visitations*, edited by Alessa Johns (New York: Routledge, 1999), 3–30.

Bezoar Stones

Like gallstones and kidney stones, bezoar stones are formed when foreign material is lodged in an animal's digestive organ, collects other material around it, and, over time, hardens into a ball or lozenge. Spanish Muslim physician Avenzoar is thought to have made the oldest reference to these as medicinal items around 1000 CE. Shortly after, Al-Biruni explained in his *Book of Stones* that goats ate poisonous snakes and grass, and the snake balled up in the intestine and petrified, creating the stone. The poison in the snake remains gave the stone the power to counteract other poisons, including that involved in plague. Stones were worn as amulets, and in some places dipped into wines to create prophylaxes. Stones were laid on buboes (the swellings on the diseased person) to draw out the poison, and stone powder was mixed with various materials to create drinks, pills, and plasters. Critics included Nathaniel Hodges (1672), who debunked powdered stone but not whole stone's efficacy. Of course, the unscrupulous sold fake bezoar and underwent punishment, as in London in 1603 and 1630.

See also: Apothecaries; Charlatans and Quacks; Prophylaxes; Remedies, External; Remedies, Internal.

Reference

Pormann, Peter E. and Emilie Savage-Smith. *Medieval Islamic Medicine*. Washington, DC: Georgetown University Press, 2007.

Bible

In the Christian New Testament and the Hebrew Scriptures that together constitute the Christian Bible, one finds numerous references to plague and pestilence and several examples of plagues that were taken to be historically true (or certain to come) throughout the First and Second Pandemics. Jews, Christians, and Muslims shared belief in Scripture and tended to treat it literally, despite a long history of allegorical interpretation. The Bible provided supposed insight into divine causation of epidemic disease, including the reasons and means, and proper human responses. In the centuries before the Enlightenment and modern microbiology, these models shaped the Western plague experience.

Causation. The Bible makes clear that God is the source of plagues and pestilence.

Through prophets and in his own voice, God makes it clear that he controls these frightful events. In Exodus 12, 1 Chronicles 21, 2 Samuel 5 and 6, and Revelation, an angel or angels follow God's direction, mowing down the victims, or, in Revelation, pouring out the poison of plague onto the earth. Though Christian plague iconography often depicts angelic archers raining down plague arrows, and the divine voice in Scripture threatens with his arrows, angel archers are not biblical and God is never described as an archer.

Plague or divine threats of plague always proceed from God's wrath or vengeance. Naturally, God threatens his enemies, and Israel's, with pestilence, or rains it down upon them. Habakkuk at 3:5 describes prophetically God striding against his foes: "Before him goes pestilence, and plague follows in his steps." Ezekiel is to warn the city of Sidon, "I will send pestilence." God sent the famous 10 plagues of Egypt to soften the obstinate Egyptians' hearts that they might release the Israelites (Exodus 5:1–12:36). When the Philistines captured the Israelites' Ark of the Covenant, God rained plague upon their camp at Ashdod until the Philistines returned it (I Samuel 5, 6).

God also used plague to threaten or chastise his own people. Their disobedience and abandonment of him provoked his wrath. After the Golden Calf incident in the Sinai, God threatened "bitter pestilence" upon those who deserted him (Deuteronomy 32:34). Regarding the disgruntled who had lost faith in Moses: "I will strike them with pestilence and wipe them out" (Numbers 14:12). Disobedience of divine law would trigger "malignant and lasting maladies," an exterminating "pestilence" (Deut. 28:21, 59). "I will send in a pestilence among you," God warned the disobedient through Moses (Leviticus 26:25). When the Babylonian (Chaldean) king Nebuchadnezzar threatened Jerusalem, the prophetic priest Jeremiah warned the remaining inhabitants to surrender to the conqueror: God would hear no prayers and accept no sacrifices from the wicked. To those who proposed flight, God ensured death by sword, famine, and pestilence (Jeremiah 14:12, 24:10). The prophet Ezekiel added, "a third of your people shall die of pestilence," a number often used for medieval plague deaths. Failure of individual leadership also resulted in plague: when King David ordered a census, 70,000 Israelites died in a single day (1 Chronicles 21/2 Samuel 5, 6).

On a more individual level, the story of Job and Jesus's parable of Lazarus and Dives reminded believers that they could never know for certain why any given person suffered. God allowed Satan to inflict faithful Job, and we have no backstory on Lazarus. Muslims, who accepted the Bible (though believing it corrupted and inferior to the Koran), made no pretenses to know God's purposes in creating plagues. Noting that both the righteous and the infidel died side by side, Islamic theologians taught that the infidel's death was punishment, but the good Muslim's was martyrdom and assured his place with Allah.

Human responses. Lazarus's humility gained him eternal life, and Job's faithfulness despite suffering was rewarded with twice the wealth. By definition, God's actions are righteous, though he can be bargained with. When God threatened the Israelites, Moses talked him down to merely delaying entry into the Promised Land and denying it to certain people (Num. 14:20–25). David's repentance and sacrifice convinced God to lift the plague. The best prophylaxis against plague was obedience to the divine will; the best remedies were prayer, repentance of sin, and return to obedience. Sin was at the root of God's anger, and people had to repudiate the sin in their lives. When Solomon dedicated the Temple in Jerusalem, he prayed that God would listen to the prayers of those who revered God's House "when there is pestilence ... whenever there is a plague or sickness of any kind" (2 Chronicles 6:28/1 Kings 8:37). God responded, "If I send pestilence" and people "humble themselves and pray ... and turn from their evil ways," I will "pardon their sins and revive their land" (2 Chron. 7: 13–14). David's building of an altar for sacrifice and the rewards promised those who venerated the Jerusalem Temple convinced many later Catholic plague pandemic survivors to build, refurbish, or decorate churches where the Sacrifice of the Mass took place.

The End Times? Often serious students of Scripture, Protestant authors tended to concentrate on Christ's warning at Luke 21:11 of pestilence as a harbinger of the end of time and on the role of plague in John's Revelation (especially Revelation 6–16). Clearly echoing the Egyptian plagues and divine warnings of "famine, sword, and pestilence," Revelation convinced many Christians that plague was indeed introducing the last days. Though there was a strain of eschatological response among Catholics, especially the early flagellants, the Church had never sanctioned such speculation. Protestants were much freer to interpret the signs of the times. In plague tracts, their apprehensions became prophetic warnings to their countrymen.

See also: Apocalypse and Apocalypticism; Biblical Plagues; Causes of Plague: Historical Theories; Christ; Flagellants; Job; Lazarus;Moral Legislation; Morality Literature, Christian; Plague Memorials; Prayer and Fasting; Sin.

References

Gilman, Ernest B. *Plague Writing in Early Modern England.* Chicago: University of Chicago Press, 2009.

Lerner, Robert E. "The Black Death and Western Eschatological Mentalities." *American Historical Review* 86 (1981): 533–552.

Mormando, Franco and Thomas Worcester, editors. *Piety and Plague from Byzantium to the Baroque*. Kirksville, MO: Truman State University Press, 2007.

Biblical Plagues

These heaven-sent punishments of the wicked and chastisements of God's people became cultural models for Jews, Christians, and Muslims. They embedded notions of inevitability, divine causation brought on by sin, and the need for moral regeneration, especially among Christian populations.

The earliest case is the famous 10 plagues that afflicted the Egyptian Pharaoh and his people. Refusal to free the Israelites from servitude brought blood, frogs, gnats, animal deaths, pestilence, boils, hail, locusts, darkness, and finally angelic killing of every first-born. From Exodus 5:1 to 12:36, Moses and Aaron orchestrate and interpret the horrors, and Pharaoh repents, relents, and releases the Israelites.

In I Samuel 5 and 6, Philistines attack the Israelites and steal the sacred Ark of the Covenant. God punishes them with mice and plague of uncertain nature (dysentery?), causing the Philistines to relent and return the Ark. But even Israel's King David could bring down God's wrath. In 2 Samuel 24 (and 1 Chronicles 21), David decides to have a

The Philistines run through the street in fear of the plague; some cover their noses and mouths, some are dead, rats roam the street. (Courtesy of the National Library of Medicine)

census taken, which provokes God's anger. The prophet Gad informs David he had a choice of punishments: three-year famine; three months of his enemy's success; or a three-day plague. David chose plague. Seeing its destruction and the angel who carried it out, he relented, building an altar for sacrifices to appease God and end the suffering.

Finally, Christian author John foresees the destruction of the world by angel agents and four horsemen, one of which is "Pestilence" (Revelation 6–16). Now it is too late for penitence.

See also: Apocalypse and Apocalypticism; Bible; Causes of Plague: Historical Theories; Christ; Sin.

References

Ehrenkranz, N. Joel and Deborah Sampson. "Origins of the Old Testament Plagues." *Yale Journal of Biology and Medicine* 81 (2008): 31–42.

Köhler, W. and M. Köhler. "Plague as Rats, the Plague of the Philistines." *International Journal of Medical Microbiology* 293 (2003): 333–340.

Bills of Health

When a doctor presents one with a "clean bill of health," she is using a designation of health or fitness that originated during the Second Pandemic. Although the medical science of the day did not grasp the mechanisms by which plague spread from one place to another, both physicians and authorities recognized that the disease's dissemination was related directly to human and commercial traffic. When plague was in the neighborhood, the stranger at the city gate was a potential angel of death; even in seemingly normal times, a ship arriving in port could be carrying a most deadly cargo. The crux of the matter was where the traveler or ship had been and whether the plague had

been present there. Perhaps because of the famed initial importation of plague by ship to Messina, Pisa, Genoa, and Marseille in 1347, from about 1374, Mediterranean port cities began requiring arriving ships to obtain certification from previous ports of call that local conditions had been safe. No certificate, no entry. If the certificate read *brute*, then cargo and crew were quarantined before entry; if *nette*, and no news indicated otherwise, they were free to disembark.

In northern Italy, with its dense network of roads and walled urban centers, the practice of certifying individuals began. The cities' initial reaction was to deny entry to anyone from a known plague center, places often announced on posted broadsheets, and later banning anyone whose point of origin was unknown. Regional cooperation was strongest in Visconti-controlled Lombardy, and such inland cities as Mantua began relying upon *bolletini di sanità* around 1400. The success of any interregional use of such documentation required cooperation and trust among the participants. French and English commentators ridiculed Italian efforts along exactly these lines, but Italian states understood that their very survival depended on such measures.

The earliest known English example is York, which required certification from people arriving from plague-stricken Maldon in 1536; York was a century ahead of most of England. In 1575, Milanese authorities made their *bollette* more elaborate because the responsible parish authorities had been giving them out too freely. These now required residence by parish and gate, name, age, physical description, destination, and reason for trip. About the same time in Palermo, *protomedico* G. F. Ingrassia designed what amounted to passports, requiring name, workplace, and dates of departure and return to Palermo. In most places, the seal of a notary or priest made the document official. Seventeenth-century Europe began printing forms and tightened acceptance policies to prevent fraud. Tuscany used rural border guards to screen travelers, and many European cities established checkpoints well outside of their gates.

See also: Contagion Theory; Cordons Sanitaires; Health Boards, Magistracies, and Commissions; Ingrassia, Giovanni Filippo; Quarantine; Searchers; Shutting In.

References

Christensen, Daniel. *Politics and the Plague in Early Modern Germany: Political Efforts to Combat Epidemics in the Duchy of Braunschweig-Wolffenbüttel during the Seventeenth Century.* Saarbrücken: Verlag Müller, 2008.

Cipolla, Carlo. *Public Health and the Medical Profession in Renaissance Florence.* New York: Cambridge University Press, 1976.

Cook, Alexandra Parma and Noble David Cook. *The Plague Files: Crisis Management in Sixteenth-Century Seville.* Baton Rouge: University of Louisiana Press, 2009.

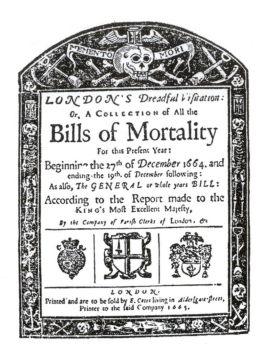

Title page of *Bills of Mortality*, the printed report of deaths in London from December 1664 to December 1665 during London's Great Plague. (Dover Pictorial Archives)

Bills of Mortality

A mark of the modern state is the generation and use of population statistics. The number of mouths to feed, hearths to tax, and young men to enlist in the military became increasingly important during the early modern period. The raw number of plague deaths, as well as trends up or down, also gained importance as civic authorities were required to judge whether the summer would bring a handful of cases or an epidemic that would empty the city and crash its economy. Systematically recording plague deaths was a daunting task, but English authorities took it up in the early 1500s. Concentrating on London, England's economic hub and capital, they produced and published "bills of mortality" that grew in complexity and coverage. But the English did not invent the bills, the Renaissance Italian city-states did.

The registering of baptisms and burials by parish authorities was sporadic during the later Middle Ages, and few of these records survive. Systematic registration of the dead followed three cycles of plague in Italy and is first noted in Arezzo, near Florence, in 1373. Other Tuscan towns followed: Borgo San Sepolcro, 1377; Siena, 1379; and Florence in 1385. Florence's "Books of the Dead," or *Libri della Grascia morti*, were kept by the Grain Office until the later 18th century and were based upon parish burial records. From 1424, cause of death was required for each entry. The accuracy of these determinations should not be assumed, and such categories as "old age" or "long illness" hardly meet modern standards of diagnosis. Milan began its civic record in 1452, specifically as a tool for identifying new outbreaks of plague. It required a physician or surgeon to certify every death: recording the date, name, age, address, cause of death, and duration of terminal illness. A continuous series exists from 1503. Mantua instituted a similar requirement in 1496 and Modena in 1554. Venice began a systematic record only in 1504, and from 1575, daily numbers were published during epidemics. By 1630, death record-keeping had become quite sophisticated. During the plague, each entry in the *Necrologi* included name, age, surname, occupation, cause of death, days sick, and residence. The state expected that all people resident in Venice would be counted, including infants, foreigners, and Jews. Requiring a doctor to visit every dying person during plague times helped regularize diagnoses and avoided the bias of relying upon Catholic parish authorities or burial accounts. In Barcelona, municipal authorities kept records of plague deaths from 1457, relying on the observations of letter carriers as they made their rounds.

In England, plague-time record-keeping began in the mid-1400s. Lists of dead were gathered at the parish level, and plague deaths were noted in Roman numerals. From 1519, collection of information for the City became regularized in form, but until 1563, collections were only intermittent; from 1563, they were generated weekly. The process evolved from then: in 1578, "searchers" were employed; in 1581, these were required to be "discrete matrons," sworn in at St. Mary-le-Bow Church, who carried white wands and could determine and report the cause of death; in 1582, London Stationers began

printing reports as a means of proving (or disproving) rumors of plague and making money; in 1603, they added remedy recipes and advertisements to bills. Early records only covered the City of London, but by 1603, they had expanded to include the "liberties and suburbes." By three royal charters from 1611, James I organized the Company of Parish Clerks, who were charged with overseeing searchers, organizing data, and circulating bills. Searchers were paired up in 1617 to improve accuracy. In 1629, officials segregated deaths by sex and added specific causes of death in addition to plague; unfortunately, these included "disappointed in love," "blasted and planet-struck," "suddenly," and "lunacy." During the 1665 London epidemic, surgeons had to confirm searchers' findings. Critics then and now dismiss the bills' accuracy, in part because searchers were usually untrained old women on poor relief; as a report from Yarmouth put it, "they are drunken persons and very poor, and may make false returns..." Other problems included poor addition, transcription errors, exclusion of Jews, Catholics, and Dissenters, under-reporting of infants, and people's hiding of dead relatives to avoid being shut in. Despite their problems, they proved invaluable to John Graunt, their earliest student and pioneer statistician and actuary.

See also: Barcelona, Spain; Florence, Italy; Graunt, John; Health Boards, Magistracies, and Commissions; London, England; London, Great Plague of; Public Health; Venice, Italy.

References

Cipolla, Carlo M. "The 'Bills of Mortality' of Florence." *Population Studies* 32 (1978): 541–548.

Munkhoff, Richelle. "Searchers of the Dead: Authority, Marginality, and the Interpretation of Plague in England, 1574–1665." *Gender and History* 11 (2002): 1–29.

Robertson, J. C. "Reckoning with London: Interpreting the Bills of Mortality before John Graunt." *Urban History* 23 (1996): 325–350.

Rusnock, Andrea A. *Vital Accounts: Quantifying Health and Population in Eighteenth-Century England and France*. New York: Cambridge University Press, 2002.

Smith, Robert S. "Barcelona 'Bills of Mortality' and Population, 1457–1590." *Journal of Political Economy* 44 (1936): 84–93.

Bimaristans (also Maristans)

The term for the Islamic equivalent of a hospital is from the Persian "place of the sick." The origins of these facilities is lost to history, with both Christian Byzantium and Sassanian Persia given credit. They certainly borrow a note of Christian philanthropy and classical public-spiritedness. Caliph Harun al-Rashid (r. 786–809) is said to be the founder of the first Baghdad bimaristan (though an older one is credited to Muslim Damascus). Like other Muslim institutions, it took on several functions: caring for the sick and wounded, sponsoring experiments in medical treatment, housing medical teaching by master physicians, and housing a medical library in which translations from Greek, Persian, Indian, Hebrew and other traditions took place. At least five additional bimaristans were built under aristocratic patronage in Baghdad during the 10th century and more in Mecca and Medina. The income from donated aristocratic estates and urban real estate (*waqf*) was provided as endowments to support the building and upkeep of the bimaristans and was considered a public as well as spiritual benefit. Aiding weakened or suffering pilgrims on the hajj to Mecca was especially valuable. Baghdad's largest 10th-century bimaristan was founded by Adud al-Dawla and is known as the bimaristan Adudi. Its early staff included 24 salaried physicians with various specialties.

In the 12th century, Nur al-Din ibn Zangi founded bimaristans in Damascus, Aleppo, and Mecca that continued to flourish into the 1500s. A ninth-century bimaristan served Alexandria, Egypt, and Cairo is said to have hosted Islam's finest institution. The Mansuri bimaristan was built in 1284 in a palace of the former Fatimid rulers and housed 8,000. Al-Andalus acquired its bimaristans rather late, with Granada's sultan Muhammad V constructing perhaps the first in 1367, following two bouts of plague. During the 150 years after Istanbul's conquest in 1453 by Ottoman Sultan Mehmet II, six major bimaristans rose alongside its mosques and other institutions. They were not always well provided for, however, and records show some foundations in decline, providing little more than food, a blanket, and a charcoal brazier for heat.

Like the Haruni in Baghdad, bimaristans always served multiple purposes, though the founders often set restrictions, for example, no soldiers or slaves were to be aided, or no gynecological procedures performed. The old and infirm joined the sick and injured, though in some bimaristans, they may have been segregated. The larger were complexes with multiple wards segregated by sex, including facilities for the insane, courtyards, lecturing areas, a dispensary, storehouses, a kitchen, private rooms for consultations and treatments, and plenty of latrines for the sake of hygiene. A mosque and sometimes the founder's tomb were also attached. Muslim physicians were taught and trained in bimaristans, a practice in Western medical education only from the 16th century. Galenic medicine was at the heart of treatment, from the orientation of windows and ventilation to the diets and remedies provided.

In the Christian West, hospitals were works of mercy and charity for the poor and physically damaged, whether acutely or for the long term. Bimaristans served a full range of social groups, though the wealthy could presumably afford to be treated at home. There was no stigma attached to hospitalization. We have indications that when an epidemic broke out, the sick were taken to bimaristans for treatment or to die, flooding the generous facilities. Personnel would have had to be added, including corpse carriers and probably gravediggers to handle the additional and rapidly growing duties. Records studied to date provide little insight into the operations of bimaristans during plague time, but one would hope that the wealthy in large cities would augment their donations to offset expenses incurred by increases in demand for services. The problem would be that the value of existing and new endowments would fall with the deaths or flight of those who generated the income stream through their payments to landlords: peasant laborers, renters, or shopkeepers.

See also: Arabic-Persian Medicine and Practitioners; Cairo, Egypt; Constantinople/Istanbul; Hospitals; Islam and Medicine; Leprosy (Hansen's Disease) and Leprosarium; Mecca; Pilgrims and Pilgrimage.

References

Horden, Peregrine. "The Earliest Hospitals in Byzantium, Western Europe and Islam." *Journal of Interdisciplinary History* 35 (2005): 361–389.

Pormann, Peter E. and Emilie Savage-Smith. *Medieval Islamic Medicine*. Washington, DC: Georgetown University Press, 2007.

Bishops and Popes

By 1347, the Christian churches were guided and administered by bishops (*episkopoi*). Each oversaw a territory—diocese—from a cathedral city or see. He was aided by other priests known as canons and other, increasingly lay, bureaucrats. In the Roman Catholic West, the Bishop of Rome administered Rome and its diocese but also served as pope, whose understood succession from biblical St. Peter gave him authority over the universal Church. Countries had hierarchies of bishops, with archbishops nominally above bishops and a primate, for example, England's Archbishop of Canterbury, over all. During the 16th-century Reformation, Calvinist and Radical churches disavowed the clerical model and drove out their bishops, while Anglicans and most Lutherans retained them as civil pastors and administrators. Orthodox bishops tended to serve the civil Church (Byzantium and Russia) or minority religious communities in Islamic lands. They looked for leadership to the Patriarch of Constantinople until 1453 and thereafter to the Patriarch of Moscow (called the "Third Rome").

Like all leaders, Pope Clement VI, living in Avignon, could only react to the Black Death, but he did so along a broad front. He fought chaos and terror in Avignon, blessing the river into which corpses were dumped, establishing cemeteries and a hospital, and leading penitential processions. Universally, he granted an indulgence to all who died of plague, allowed even women to hear confessions, formulated a new plague liturgy, and sped young men into the depleted priesthood. His was a model of the active Church leader. Later popes at Avignon and then Rome did not face the scope or the novelty of the Black Death and directed their attention to local needs, often relying from a distance on bureaucrats. No pope died of plague.

Bishops always bore the burden of spiritual leaders, comforters, and managers of the clergy. In England, there was no effective civil response until the Tudors, so bishops played a broader role, as displayed in their excellent records. At the top, three Archbishops of Canterbury ruled and died during 1348 to 1349, until Simon Islip finally stabilized the position. All told, England lost six of its 23 bishops; Norway lost four of five; Saxony buried 12 of theirs; but Sweden's bishops all survived. Besides replacing their own, bishops spent much time and effort replacing the parish clergy, who disappeared at three and four times normal rates. As Barcelona's records reveal, dioceses suspended much ordinary business, including detailed recordkeeping, in favor of the extraordinary demands. In England, this often meant frequent relocation to avoid pestilence and perhaps inspect conditions: Hereford's John Trillek moved four times before returning to his cathedral, and Lincoln's John Gynewell seemed in constant motion as he filled vacant positions and spread word of the pope's changes in important practices. Some of these were anticipated by the bishops themselves.

Bishops often clashed with secular authorities who sought, for example, to limit contagion-inducing crowds, while the churchmen insisted on the value of public religious processions and masses. Charisma as much as common sense determined who prevailed.

See also: Anticlericalism; Anti–Semitism and Anti–Jewish Violence before the Black Death; Borromeo, St. Charles (San Carlo); Borromeo, Federigo; Flagellants; Clement VI, Pope; Gregory the Great, Pope; Islip, Simon; Moral Legislation; Prayer and Fasting; Priests; Processions; Rome, Italy.

References

Aberth, John. "The Black Death in the Diocese of Ely: The Evidence of the Bishop's Register." *Journal of Medieval History* 21 (1995): 275–287.

Collinson, Patrick. *Archbishop Grindal, 1519–1583. The Struggle for a Reformed Church.* Berkeley: University of California Press, 1979.

Davies, R. H. "The Effect of the Black Death on the Parish Priests of the Medieval Diocese of Coventry and Lichfield." *Bulletin of the Institute of Historical Research* 62 (1989): 85–90.

Dohar, William J. *The Black Death and Pastoral Leadership: the Diocese of Hereford in the Fourteenth Century.* Philadelphia: University of Pennsylvania Press, 1995.

Moran, JoAnn Hoeppner. "Clerical Recruitment in the Diocese of York, 1340–1530: Data and Commentary." *Journal of Ecclesiastical History* 34 (1983): 19–54.

Utterback, Kristine T. "The Date and Composition of Bishops' Registers from the Plague Years in the Diocese of Barcelona." *Journal of Ecclesiastical History* 39 (1988): 412–432.

Wood, Diana. *Pope Clement VI: The Pontificate and Ideas of an Avignon Pope.* New York: Cambridge University Press, 1989.

Black Death (1347–1352)

The story began somewhere between China and the Crimean Peninsula. Lonely gravestones at Issyk Kul appear to testify to plague's passage in the 1330s. Modern theories point to Mongol horsemen disrupting reservoirs of plague-carrying rodents, who entered the stream of commerce and conquest. An incident during the Mongols' siege of Italians at Caffa on the Black Sea gave rise to the tale that plague-stricken warriors hurled plague victims' bodies into the town, panicked the Europeans, and caused them to take ship for the West with plague aboard. Evidence of political and social disruption in the Khanate of the Golden Horde suggests plague's depredations, which may have facilitated the rise of the Ottomans.

THE BLACK DEATH: GREAT PANDEMIC OF THE 14TH CENTURY

EUROPE 1347

Cologne
Paris
Jan.
1348
Genoa
Avignon
Nov.
Rome
Tunis
Messina
Oct.
Mediterranean Sea
Venice
Constantinople
Nov. - Dec.
Sarai
Astrakhan
Tana
Nov.
Kaffa
Trebizond
Damascus
Nov. - Dec.
Alexandria
Gaza

1346 Sarai
Astrakhan
Baghdad
Samakand
Kashgar
1338-1339
Peking
PERSIA
Mecca
1349
ARABIA
TURKESTAN
Sian
CHINA
1320's
Hangchow
TIBET
Chittagong
INDIA
1340's
Calcutta
CEYLON

■ Area's of Plague
1340 Date of outbreak
— Part of Silk Road
..... Land trade routes
- - - Sea trade routes

0   1000 mi
0   1000 km

Islamic records testify to epidemics cascading southward from the region between the Black and Caspian Seas. Spread by armies and caravans, the divine event that hurled the faithless into Hell and rewarded believers with a martyr's death wrought havoc in city after city from Afghanistan to Syria. However, the plague took ship and arrived in Constantinople; the Byzantine capital began to suffer and sent cargoes of death south to Alexandria and westward to Sicily. Today, we know that plague is a disease caused by bacteria carried by fleas that live on rodents. When rats lacking any immunity die, the fleas jump to other animals and people, sparking epizootics among

the animals and spreading quickly to humans. Frequently docking ships provided the perfect vessels for spreading the rats and their disease, as did the heavily laden caravans with their vulnerable food supplies. Ships and caravans circulated the plague down the Nile and the Red Sea to Mecca, as well as across North Africa and up the coast from the Sinai. Islamic cities suffered terribly, losing from a third to a half or more of their populations. Rural villages contracted the disease from merchants, pilgrims, soldiers, overseers, or villagers returning from stricken cities. No less than townsfolk, villagers died in horrific numbers; they depopulated and sometimes abandoned settlements, reduced food shipments to cities, and left necessary such infrastructure as canals and dikes to fall to nature. Muslims had a sophisticated version of ancient Greek medicine, but this availed little as it blamed the presence of contaminated air (miasma, caused by God) for the disease. Though Muslims tended and treated the sick and buried the dead, and some prayed that the scourge be lifted while others fled, Islamic leaders counseled resignation and acceptance rather than concerted action.

Plague arrived in Messina, Sicily, in late 1347 and proceeded up both lateral coasts of Italy. Michele da Piazza recorded the "terrible and unnatural event" in Messina, the eviction of the Genoese believed to have brought it, the faith people put in religious ritual, and the flight of Messinesi that helped the disease spread. It appeared along the coast of Dalmatia on its way north to Venice and Trieste and, to the west, moved upriver to Florence and rich Tuscany. Poet and humanist Giovanni Boccaccio later captured the terror and torpor, the lack of charity and even humanity the Tuscans displayed as they were ravaged. Coasting vessels took the plague across southern France and to Spanish ports in Aragon and Catalonia; river vessels and land cartage, along with refugees, served as capillaries that penetrated the countryside, targeting some settlements and ignoring others. Barcelona and Marseille suffered terribly while Milan's powerful rulers shut the gates and drove away contaminating visitors, reducing its death rate to a few in scores of thousands.

The Rhône River brought plague to the pope's door, and Clement VI proved unable to mitigate its effects. Prayers and masses gave way to new cemeteries and a blessing of the river that whisked away so many corpses. Faced with increasing levels of anti–Semitic violence against Jews "convicted" of spreading poison out of hatred for Christians or merely libeled and slaughtered, Clement condemned the lies (Jews died as readily as Christians) and the violence they sparked in an arc from Aragon to Savoy. Meanwhile, European physicians, both Christian and Muslim, sought to explain the disaster and to render relief. From the Italian Gentile da Foligno to the Muslim Ibn Khatimah to the Medical Faculty of the University of Paris, practitioners steeped in Galenic (Greek) medicine repeated the formula: God caused the planets to align malignantly, which caused poisoned air (miasmas) to develop on earth, killing those exposed who were susceptible to it. The Christian God unleashed fury and wrath, prompting ritual and personal attempts to placate His righteous anger. Here, Christ or the Trinity differed from the dispassionate Allah. Wicked Christendom began turning to saintly intercessors with prayers and offerings of art and charity. Physicians counseled flight to avoid the plague and humor-balancing diets and exercise to strengthen resistance. Though Muhammad denied the operation of contagion and miasma theory had no place for it, most medical men believed the disease could be caught and passed on, recommending that people minimize contacts. City governments, too, curtailed even religious gatherings and funerals while mandating the elimination of miasma-inducing sources of stench.

And still the Black Death proceeded northward. It was introduced to England with continental cargo and across the Alps into Germany and Austria from Italy. Monks, mendicants, and clerics dropped as they anointed the sick and blessed the dead, and bishops and orders were overwhelmed with demands for replacements. In Germany and the Low Countries, certain folks abandoned the clergy and followed self-whipping flagellants who processed through the countryside, stopping in town squares to perform penitential acts including hymns and prayers. Others turned on the enemies of God in their midst, the Jewish communities, whose purported culpability for Christian suffering was as much their refusal to convert as their supposed spread of plague. Gathered in their neighborhoods, Jews were easy targets for bloodthirsty mobs—both lower and upper class—that sought to (and did) destroy them. Innocent Jews died by the hundreds, sometimes killing themselves and their children. England, having driven out its Jews in 1290, witnessed no pogroms, and few instances of flagellant frenzy made history. At the same time, neither King nor civil governments did much of anything to alleviate the suffering or prevent its spread. Instead, Edward tried to maintain social control by forbidding the natural rise in wages and prices in the plague's immediate wake. His Ordinance of Laborers (June, 1349) was an unprecedented extension of royal writ into the economy and would be soon followed by further extensions. Several truces during the Hundred Years War recognized the Mortality's impact, but only temporarily.

The Scots felt the plague's putrid breath: finding the English army opposing them decimated by disease, they attacked and themselves fell prey. They naturally fled, disseminating plague as they returned to their homes. Eastern Europe, too, succumbed as the disease moved north from the Balkans and Hungary and eastward from the Rhine. Hansa towns along the Baltic fell early, and their ships introduced the plague to other Scandinavian ports. It appears to have been no less virulent here than in the sunny Mediterranean, with upward of half the population of any given city lost. Rural areas suffered no less, leaving crops and animals untended as peasants or farmers died or

fled. Where they could, wages and other perks rose as the labor pool shrank. In Catalonia and underurbanized Eastern Europe—that presented few alternatives to agricultural labor—the landlords maintained a steady and oppressive hand on those who survived. Despite their relative isolation, Scandinavian farms disappeared by the thousands.

The last regions savaged by the Black Death were the cities of Russia. Pskov, Novgorod, and Moscow recorded terrible onslaughts in 1352. Plague moved eastward and south from Europe rather than up the great rivers from its reservoir in the southern steppes, though for no clear reason. All ranks in society died, and the aristocracy's losses were so severe that Moscow's dynasty almost disappeared, and elsewhere, their balance against autocracy withered away.

The estimates of percentages and numbers who died between 1347 and 1352 have been rising over the past decades. Historical demography is an imprecise science, but with each new study and every overthrown theory, the trend seems clear. In 1969, Philip Ziegler accepted an average toll in Europe of about 33 percent, with an upward limit of 45 percent. Thirty-five years later, Benedictow, a historical demographer, presented a gross European population of around 80,000,000, and a death toll of about 60 percent overall in Europe, which is a total of about 48,000,000 dead. To this would be added the toll in the Muslim world: should it be any smaller in proportion? Even if the total figure were the well-worn 25,000,000 dead, the impact is absolutely staggering.

See also: Black Death: Origins and Early Spread; Boccaccio, Giovanni; Bubonic Plague; Caffa (Kaffa, Feodosiya), Ukraine; Causes of Plague: Historical Theories; Clement VI, Pope; *Compendium of Paris*; Contagion Theory; Demographic and Economic Effects of Plague: The Islamic

World; Demographic Effects of Plague: Europe 1347–1400; Economic Effects of Plague in Europe; Flagellants; Galen and Galenism; Gentile da Foligno; Hundred Years War; Ibn Khatimah, Abu Jafar Ahmed; Islam and Medicine; Islamic Civil Responses; Issyk Kul, Kyrgystan; Jews; Labourers, Ordinance and Statute of; Li Muisis, Gilles; Mongols; Plague Saints; individual cities.

References

Aberth, John. *The Black Death: The Great Mortality of 1348–1350*. New York: Bedford, 2005.

Benedictow, Ole. *The Black Death 1346–1353: The Complete History*. Rochester, NY: Boydell & Brewer, 2004.

Biraben, Jean-Noel. *Les hommes et la peste en France et dans les pays européens et méditeranéens*. 2 vols. Paris: Mouton, 1975, 1976.

Bisgaard, Lars and Leif Søndergaard, editors. *Living with the Black Death*. Odense: University of Southern Denmark Press, 2009.

Borsch, Stuart. *The Black Death in Egypt and England*. Austin: University of Texas Press, 2005.

Byrne, Joseph P. *The Black Death*. Westport, CT.: Greenwood Press, 2004.

Carmichael, Ann G. *Plague and the Poor in Renaissance Florence*. New York: Cambridge University Press, 1986.

Cohn, Samuel K. *The Black Death Transformed: Disease and Culture in Early Renaissance Europe*. New York: Oxford University Press, 2002.

Dohar, William J. *The Black Death and Pastoral Leadership: The Diocese of Hereford in the Fourteenth Century*. Philadelphia: University of Pennsylvania Press, 1995.

Dols, Michael W. *The Black Death in the Middle East*. Princeton, NJ: Princeton University Press, 1977.

Horrox, Rosemary. *The Black Death*. New York: Manchester University Press, 1994.

Jillings, Karen. *Scotland's Black Death: The Foul Death of the English*. London: Tempus Publishing, 2003.

Kelly, John. *The Great Mortality: An Intimate History of the Black Death*. New York: HarperCollins, 2005.

Kelly, Maria. *A History of the Black Death in Ireland*. Stroud, Gloucs, UK: Tempus, 2001.

Naphy, William G. and Andrew Spicer. *Plague: Black Death and Pestilence in Europe*. Stroud, Gloucs, UK: Tempus, 2004.

Nutton, Vivian, ed. *Pestilential Complexities: Understanding the Medieval Plague*. Supplement #27 to *Medical History*. London: Wellcome Trust for the History of Medicine, 2008.

Ormrod, W. M. and P. G. Lindley, eds. *The Black Death in England*. Stamford: Paul Watkins, 1996.

Platt, Colin. *King Death: The Black Death and its Aftermath in Late-medieval England*. Toronto: University of Toronto Press, 1996.

Smail, Daniel Lord. "Accommodating Plague in Medieval Marseille." *Continuity and Change* 11 (1996): 11–41.

Wray, Shona Kelly. *Communities and Crisis: Bologna during the Black Death*. Boston: Brill, 2009.

Ziegler, Philip. *The Black Death*. New York: Harper and Row, 1969.

Black Death: Debate over the Medical Nature of

In 1894, Alexandre Yersin discovered the bacillus that he identified correctly as the pathogen (*Yersinia pestis*) that caused the plague that raged around him in Hong Kong. He immediately wrote of it to his mother, adding pregnantly that he believed he had also found the cause of the medieval plagues. Published in the Pasteur Institute's *Annales*, Yersin's claim established a century-long paradigm that has only recently undergone systematic challenge. Subsequent discoveries of the flea that most easily spread the bacteria and the rat off of which it fed fleshed out the model. Certainly, if Chinese, Indian, and other modern peoples could suffer from commensal rats and their parasites, medieval

Europeans wallowing in imagined squalor could have been just as susceptible. Famous historical descriptions of buboes on medieval victims strengthened the case for bubonic plague, and within a decade, the identification of the Black Death and subsequent epidemics of "pestilence" as bubonic plague was settled. Though historians and epidemiologists noted important discrepancies between medieval and modern plague, for example, death rates and speed of dissemination, they tended to dismiss them as products of mutations in the bacterium or flea.

In 1970, historian J. F. Shrewsbury launched the first assault on the plague paradigm. He noted that modern, preantibiotic plague mortality rates ran around 5 percent and nowhere near the 30 percent or higher rates claimed by medieval documents and historians. Either the demographic impacts were much lower than reported or medieval pestilence was not modern plague. He kept the plague, dismissing reported death rates as medieval exaggerations. Biologist Graham Twigg has argued since 1985 that medieval epidemics in no way resembled modern plague: medieval plague spread too far too quickly and took too many lives. Since about 2000, a growing number of historians, biologists, and epidemiologists have elaborated on Shrewsbury and Twigg. Most develop one or more of the following arguments. Medieval symptoms as described by contemporaries fit other diagnoses as well or better; medieval pestilence was far more infectious than modern plague, even pneumonic plague; it spread far more quickly than modern plague; given the known ecologies of R. rattus and X. cheopis, medieval outbreaks do not mesh with expected patterns of humidity and temperature; there is no evidence of medieval epizootics and scant mention in records of dead rats; the density of black rat populations was not sufficient to support a

plague epizootic that would spill over into the human population; while modern outbreaks last several years in a given locale, medieval records claim durations of a single year or less; and the medieval disease recurred with a diminishing effect on populations, concentrating on urban areas, abandoning the countryside, and eventually disappearing from Europe altogether. Some critics suggest alternatives: Twigg likes anthrax as an alternative; Scott and Duncan make an argument for a hemorrhagic viral disease similar to Ebola, while historian Samuel Cohn claimed it "was any disease other than the rat-based bubonic plague …" (1) Modern proponents of bubonic plague sometimes attribute the discrepancies to epidemics of pneumonic and/or—to a lesser extent—septicemic plague, which are also caused by the Y. pestis bacterium. Pneumonic or pulmonary plague occurs when the bacillus concentrates in and disrupts the lungs. Septicemic plague occurs when the flea-induced bacillus concentrates in and disrupts the bloodstream from infection, causing septic shock.

Some blame the Pulex irritans, a human-targeting flea, for spreading Y. pestis, which would remove the rat as a vector. The presence of other, perhaps opportunistic, diseases might account for variations in symptoms and high death rates. Proponents often point to bacterial evolution and mutation as reasons for falling virulence (surviving hosts mean surviving bacteria) and credit such public health measures as quarantine and cordons sanitaires for the disease's disappearance. The absence of testimonials to rat die-offs may simply be a matter of the animal's ubiquity, and in any case, rat bones are quite fragile. Microbiologists have been studying 14th-century mass burial victims' tooth pulp for evidence of Y. pestis DNA, the presence of which might end the debate, but early positive conclusions have been challenged. Shortly before going to press (early 2011), a report was released by a European team that studied multiple cases from multiple sites and claimed proof of *Y. pestis*. As yet, their claim has not been critically assessed.

It is safe to say that, at present, most writers on the Black Death accept bubonic plague as paradigmatic, though critics across disciplines have asked important questions and raised important objections.

See also: AIDS and Plague; Black Death (1347–1352); Black Death: Origins and Early Spread; Bubonic Plague; Demographic Effects of Plague: Europe 1347–1400; Demographic Effects of Plague: Europe 1400–1500; Diagnosing Plague; Diseases, Opportunistic and Subsidiary; DNA; Fleas; Plague in Europe, 1360–1500; Pneumonic Plague; Rats and Other Plague Carriers; Septicemic Plague; Yersin, Alexandre; *Yersinia pestis*.

References

Benedictow, Ole. *The Black Death 1346–1353: The Complete History.* Rochester, NY: Boydell & Brewer, 2004.

Benedictow, Ole J. *What Disease Was Plague? On the Controversy over the Microbiological Identity of Plague Epidemics of the Past.* Boston: Brill, 2010.

Birkelbach, Karl. "Plague Debate: An Historiographical Analysis of the Retrospective Diagnosis of the Black Death." Ph.D. dissertation, University of Western Australia, 2010.

Cohn, Samuel K. *The Black Death Transformed: Disease and Culture in Early Renaissance Europe.* Oxford: Oxford University Press, 2002.

Lerner, Robert E. "Fleas: Some Scratchy Issues Concerning the Black Death." *The Historian* 8 (2008): 205–229.

Martin, A. Lynn. *Plague? Jesuit Accounts of Epidemic Disease in the Sixteenth Century.* Kirksville, MO: Sixteenth Century Journal Publishers, 1996.

Moseng, Ole Georg. "Climate, Ecology and Plague: The Second and the Third Pandemic Reconsidered," in *Living with the Black Death*, edited by Lars Bisgaard and Leif Sondergaard (Odense: University of Southern Denmark Press, 2009), 23–45.

Nutton, Vivian, ed. *Pestilential Complexities: Understanding the Medieval Plague.* Supplement #27 to *Medical History.* London: Wellcome Trust for the History of Medicine, 2008.

Scott, Susan and Christopher Duncan. *Biology of Plagues: Evidence from Historical Populations.* New York: Cambridge University Press, 2001.

Shrewsbury, J. F. *History of Bubonic Plague in the British Isles.* New York: Cambridge University Press, 1970.

Twigg, Graham. *The Black Death: A Biological Reappraisal.* New York: Schocken Books, 1985.

Black Death: Origins and Early Spread

Origins

There is no consensus among historians regarding the geographic origin of the Black Death. The candidates are China (McNeill), the shoulders of the Himalayas (McNeill), Kyrgystan, northern Iraq (Norris), and southern Russia (Benedictow). No contemporary records from Mongol-controlled China or Central Asia clearly indicate local epidemics, let alone pandemic plague. Apart from archeological evidence at Issyk Kul, no physical remains in Asia indicate large death tolls. Western Muslim and Christian chroniclers attribute the origins to China or points further west, but the accuracy of these usually conflicting statements has always been doubted.

The traditional and popular picture is that merchants and other travelers along the Silk

Road westward from China carried with them rats and their plague-infested fleas. Like embers shooting from a campfire, these animals infected virgin colonies of rodents that maintained the plague enzootically. The famed *Pax Mongolica* allowed for safe and relatively swift travel and, thus, migration of plague. A variation of this picture has the increased traffic disrupting local plague foci and putting the disturbed rodents and fleas in contact with the traveling people and animals. Of course, both could have been true serially. The problem is that as the western Mongol Empire Islamized and disintegrated, the political conditions in Central Asia were much less conducive to long-distance trade—especially with Christians—than once thought.

Recently, historians have been prone to move the point of origin closer to the Black Sea and Southern Russia, significantly reducing the distance the carriers would have had to travel. In 1977, John Norris critiqued the contemporary theories and, basing his own theory in part on biovariations of the bacteria, located the origin in northern Iraq or Kurdistan. From here, the plague would have migrated northward to the Black and Caspian Sea regions and, over a longer period, eastward in an arc from northern India to Manchuria. Most recently, Norwegian historian Ole Benedictow believes that the pandemic began in the Volga and Don basins, spreading south and westward to the Crimea and Southern Russia in the midst of the Golden Horde, closer still in time and place to the purported incidents at Caffa. He relies heavily on a medieval Russian chronicle that specifically mentions a 1346 epidemic striking the towns "Ornach . . . Khastorokan . . . Sarai . . . Bezdezh" and, more generically, the "Bessermens," Tatars, Armenians, Circassians, and "European foreigners."

If Norris is correct, then the plague spread north to the Kipchak Khanate, north and west into Syria and Anatolia, and south toward Baghdad. If the plague arrived from the east, then it moved in generally the opposite direction, flowing south between the Caspian and Black Seas and west into Southern Russia and the Crimea. The famous story is that from their plague-stricken Crimean colony, Italian sailors and merchants carried the pestilence to Constantinople, then south and west in 12 galleys directly to Messina, Sicily, site of the first recorded Western European epidemic.

Means of Spread

The picture above—Caffa to Messina—is simple, logical, dramatic, and unlikely. Plague may indeed have traveled by ship, however, since rats are notorious stowaways. Extensions of plague from Sicily to the mainland, from the Continent to Britain to Ireland, and to Scandinavia are all explainable only by ship-borne carriers. Spread along coastlines was also apparently by ship. Plague is also likely to have traveled up and down rivers, being deposited at ports along the way. Flea-bearing rats may also have hitched rides in carts traversing Europe's roads, especially those transporting such foodstuffs as grain. Once in a new locale, the rats would distribute their fleas among established and virgin rodent populations living commensally with people. As rat hosts died off, the fleas adopted human hosts, and the local epidemic began. If some specialists are correct and the human flea *Pulex irritans* also served as a carrier of the plague bacillus, then rats were not as needed and human movements alone explain the spread. When plague neared or struck a city, many fled, and many of these carried the disease with them. There is also the possibility of fleas residing in furs and textiles, bedding, or old clothes for a time, and if these materials were shipped any distance, they might serve to unleash a local outbreak, as at Eyam, England, in 1666.

The picture in Islamic countries is very similar. Trade and travel between Muslim cities, by ship and caravan, seem to be the means of disbursing the plague. As Norris points out, camels are actually good carriers of fleas. Coastal maritime traffic explains the plague's spread across much of North Africa to Morocco, and the Nile is the likely conduit for its penetration of Egypt. The hajj also provided a means for spread, since pilgrims usually traveled the deserts in caravans. Finally, armies—with their dense concentrations of people and supplies, poor sanitation, slow movements, and often disruptive demeanor—were ideal means of transporting plague, as was likely in the Kipchak Khanate. Plague-stricken armies often disbanded, sending thousands of men, some percentage of whom were carriers, across the landscape.

Geographic Patterns of Spread

The European historical records of first appearance of plague in a given place vary in quality, reliability, and levels of detail. Benedictow (2004) and Christakos and colleagues provide the fullest and most recent studies of the geographic dissemination of plague, which necessarily rely on these records. Little in their work contradicts such earlier studies as Biraben's magisterial work in French, since they used most of the same sources. In general, mapped incidences of plague by date of first appearance show a clear pattern of more or less consistent movement outward, north and west, from Sicily, and from coastlines inward. Typical maps show boundaries marking the advance every

six months or year, suggesting a wave-like motion across a broad front. Locally, of course, the picture is less neat, as interactive cities and towns became centers from which villages contracted the disease by chance encounters. Sometimes whole rural communities suffered sickness and death, while their near neighbors never experienced the epidemic; some regions including the Pyrenees and parts of Bohemia were seemingly spared the Black Death altogether. Benedictow (xviii–xxiv) presents a more accurate and interesting colored map that makes clearer and sharper spatio-temporal distinctions than wave maps.

However plague entered Messina, it did so around mid-August 1347. As it raged, it sent out infected refugees on foot and by ship to other Sicilian towns and nearby islands and onto the mainland. Marseille in southern France was suffering by early November and Tuscan Pisa by later the same month. Venetian ships, which may have dallied among and doomed the Republic's Aegean possessions, infected the Adriatic coastline before reaching their home lagoons in late autumn. Given the nature of the disease, it would have needed five to eight weeks to establish itself epidemically in a given city. Reports of first appearance—in Venice it was January 25, 1348—need to be adjusted backward when attempting to ascertain the date of the disease's arrival.

The year 1348 saw the explosion of the pandemic across the southern tier of Europe. Up the Arno to Florence and across central Italy, the plague raced along the dense old Roman road system. From the Genoese hub, the plague moved to Piedmont and Lombardy, sparing the cautious Milanese and crossing the Alps northward. Likewise, from the hub of Venice, plague moved into the Veneto and then north through Innsbruck and east into the Balkans. Another line of advance followed the Rhône River valley north from Marseille through papal Avignon and into the upper Rhine in early 1349. Christian Iberia was invaded overland from Marseille and by plague ships departing Majorca, which had suffered since the previous year. A westward wave also skirted the Pyrenees, striking Bordeaux, from which it coasted north to Normandy, down the Seine to Paris, and across the Channel to southern Britain and Dublin. From Bordeaux, the plague also moved south along Iberia's Atlantic seaboard.

Further expansion occurred in 1349. Gaelic Ireland, Wales, and England north of London hosted the disease, as did western Scandinavia—Bergen and Oslo serving as entry points. The Danube, Central Rhine, and upper Loire valleys suffered, as did the remainder of Muslim Iberia, or Andalusia. Scotland, most of Germany, the Netherlands, Denmark, and Sweden were stricken in 1350, as was a great swath that arced from German Frankfurt to Pskov in Russia. In 1351 and 1352, the plague spread along transportation routes and Russia's great rivers from Pskov south and east to Kiev, Novgorod, and Moscow. In 1353, Act I of the Second Pandemic in Europe came to an end.

Accepting the traditional Dols/Benedictow model, the plague spread from Constantinople into the western Muslim lands. Refugees probably carried it into Anatolia (Turkey), where it reached the Turk-dominated Central Plateau by 1349. In the fall of 1347, it leapt from the Byzantine capital to Alexandria, Egypt, by ship, a single merchant/slave ship, according to a contemporary source. From here, it spread slowly down the Nile, reaching Upper Egypt in February 1349. It also moved west and east, paralleling the Mediterranean shoreline. By April 1348, Gaza had been struck, and in July, Damascus, Syria, was suffering. Continuing north, plague devastated Aleppo in October. Fifteenth-century chronicler Al-Maqrizi relates that in 1346, Malik Ashraf's Muslim army fighting at Tabriz in Persia turned on Baghdad, Iraq, where both army and city contracted the disease. To the far south, pilgrims on hajj carried the plague to Mecca in 1348, and the ruler of Yemen, newly released from captivity in Egypt in 1351, carried the Black Death home with his entourage. In North Africa, plague traveled westward from Alexandria and south into Tunis from Sicily in April 1348. In Tunisia, it spread east and west, infecting yet another army, this one fighting to conquer Tunisia for Morocco. Its refugees and remnants disseminated the germs back to their homes, handing Morocco over to plague in late 1348. Northwest Africa may also have been infected from Muslim-controlled Almeria in southern Spain.

See also: Armies; Black Death (1347–1352); Caffa (Kaffa, Feodosiya), Ukraine; China; Flight; Issyk Kul, Kyrgystan; Merchants.

References

Benedictow, Ole. *The Black Death, 1346–1353: The Complete History.* Rochester, NY: Boydell and Brewer, 2004.

Biraben, Jean-Noel. *Les hommes et la peste en France et dans les pays européens et méditeranéens.* 2 vols. Paris: Mouton, 1975, 1976.

Christakos, George, et al. *Interdisciplinary Public Health Reasoning and Epistemic Modeling: The Case of the Black Death.* New York: Springer, 2005.

Christensen, Peter. "Appearance and Disappearance of the Plague: Still a Puzzle?" in *Living with the Black Death*, edited by Lars Bisgaard and Leif Søndergaard (Odense: University of Southern Denmark Press, 2009), 11–22.

Dols, Michael W. *The Black Death in the Middle East.* Princeton, NJ: Princeton University Press, 1977.

McNeill, William. *Plagues and Peoples.* Garden City, NY: Anchor Press, 1975.

Norris, John. "East or West? The Geographic Origin of the Black Death." *Bulletin of the History of Medicine* 51 (1977): 1–24; and his discussion with Dols in 52 (1978): 112–120.

Wheelis, Mark. "Biological Warfare at the 1346 Siege of Caffa." *Emerging Infectious Diseases* 8 (2002): 971–975.

Black Death, Plague, and Pestilence (Terms)

Terminology associated with the Second Pandemic (1347–1840s) can be confusing. It should be used consistently and as precisely as possible, though this is often not the case either historically or today. *Plague* is derived from Latin *plaga*, meaning a blow or sudden strike. In English, we use the term broadly, as in a "plague of locusts" or the plagues of biblical Egypt. *The plague* appears in early English-language accounts of epidemics associated today with *Yersinia pestis*, known for the past century as bubonic plague, which includes the Black Death and the Second Pandemic. Terms typically used for bubonic plague elsewhere in Europe were variations of the word *pest*, from the Latin *pestis* for a widespread disease. *Pestilence* also appears with variations—*pestilentis, pestilencia, pestilenzia*—generally with direct reference to bubonic plague, sometimes modified by *great*, as in the Latin *pestilentia magna*. Other terms varied by region and time: in late medieval Aragon, it was *pestilentis, epidemia, egritudo*, and *maladie*, often coupled with *great*; to Swedes, it was *sudden death* (*brådöda*); to Normans, *mortality* or *grande mortalité* and rarely *peste*; and in Germanic countries, *the great dying* (*grosse Sterben*).

Black in *Black Death* meant "terrible" and did not refer to plague's physical symptoms. *Black death* occurs in Latin texts from as early as 1350, though the label was not used systematically until the 1800s. Belgian astrologer Simon Couvin first used *mors nigra* in his allegorical poem on the epidemic of 1347 to 1352 and Venetian poet Giacomo Ruffini *atra lues* in his plague description of 1556. Both terms mean black death, and Ruffini underlines his usage by appending *monstra nigrantis*, or "monster of blackness." Sixteenth- and 17th-century Scandinavian texts use variations of *black death* more readily, but English use appears only after the "Great Plague" of 1665 to 1666, referring to the initial 14th-century outbreak, and first appears popularly in the 1823 historical writings of a Mrs. Penrose.

See also: Metaphors for Plague.

Bleeding/Phlebotomy

Also known as blood-letting, exsanguination, and venesection, phlebotomy is the medical procedure of removing blood from the body. In the Galenic system accepted by both Muslims and Christians, good health required the balance of the four humors, one of which was blood. Adding to humoral levels was a matter of good diet, but removal was trickier. Easiest to remove was blood. This could be done simply by opening a vein and draining out the requisite amount. In normal times, medieval and early modern people might undergo bleeding once or several times per year as a way of maintaining health. A good barber-surgeon would schedule these for appropriate days on the astrological calendar or according to one's horoscope. When sick, a person might be bled several times, both to achieve humoral balance and to drain off supposed toxins.

Since Galen was said to have saved himself by phlebotomy after contracting plague, medieval practitioners generally accepted the practice. For plague victims in 1348, both the Paris *Compendium on the Epidemic* and Italian physician Gentile da Foligno recommended draining blood until the person passed out, which would keep venomous fluids from reaching the heart. Others were less drastic: Dr. Dionysius Colle bled the mature but, based on experience, refrained from bleeding "the young." During the 1565 epidemic, French physician Ambroise Paré asked many doctors about bleeding, and most told him it weakened and killed patients. Yet it remained popular, and even William Harvey bled patients.

Bleeding was normally done by barbers or surgeons or, in Islamic, lands specialist phlebotomists, who had special knives and bowls to catch the blood. Artless "Vein Man" charts and phlebotomy manuals indicated where incisions should be made, and many plague *consilia* or such tracts as Gentile's directed: if the bubo is on the neck open the cephalic vein in the two thumbs . . .

See also: Arabic-Persian Medicine and Practitioners; Astrology; Galen and Galenism; Humoral Theory; Surgeons/Barbers.

References

Arikha, Noga. *Passions and Tempers. A History of the Humours*. New York: Ecco, 2007.

Niebyl, Peter H. "Galen, Van Helmont and Blood Letting," in *Science, Medicine and Society in the Renaissance*, vol. 2, edited by Allen G. Debus (New York: Neale Watkins, 1972), 13–22.

Pormann, Peter E. and Emilie Savage-Smith. *Medieval Islamic Medicine*. Washington, DC: Georgetown University Press, 2007.

Voigts, Linda E. and Michael McVaugh. *A Latin Technical Phlebotomy and Its Middle English Translation*. Philadelphia: American Philosophical Society, 1984.

Boccaccio, Giovanni (1313–1375)

Born to a merchant in Certaldo, near Florence, Giovanni was raised to follow his father. He spent a dozen years in Naples, learning to appreciate and write good literature and studying Canon Law. He gained a reputation for classicizing poetry but had trouble gaining patronage. He was probably in Florence when the Black Death struck, to which he lost his stepmother and possibly his father.

The plague clearly inspired his *Decameron*, which is neither classicizing nor poetic. It is a collection of one hundred vernacular short tales fitted into a frame-tale set in plague-wrecked Florence. His description of plague-wrecked Florence, perhaps the most

Illustration from an early-20th-century edition of Giovanni Boccaccio's masterpiece, the *Decameron*. Completed shortly after the Black Death struck Florence in 1348, the *Decameron* is considered one of the best contemporary accounts of the plague. (Library of Congress)

famous in any language, is horrifically realistic, from aching buboes to unleashed hedonism and criminality. At least some language and scenarios were borrowed from other sources, but his poet's eye and ear allowed him to create an unforgettable portrait of individual and social calamity. In its midst, seven young women and three young men meet in Santa Maria Novella Church during a service and decide that since they have no duties in Florence, they should relocate to a villa far from the city. Over 10 days, each tells 10—often ribald—stories in the placid setting. Most famous for its gritty introduction, *Decameron* stands as a masterpiece of early Renaissance literary realism, perhaps made possible by the shared experience of the plague.

See also: Abandonment; Chaucer, Geoffrey; Flight; Florence, Italy; Humoral Theory.

References

Levenstein, Jessica. "Out of Bounds: Passion and the Plague in Boccaccio's *Decameron*." *Italica* 73 (1996): 313–335.

Watkins, Renee Neu. "Boccaccio as Therapist: Plague Literature and the Soul of the City." *Psychohistory Review* 16 (1988): 173–200.

Books of Hours

The "hours" in a Book of Hours is the daily cycle of roughly 30-minute prayer sessions dictated by the Benedictine *Rule* for Christian monks. Beginning before dawn, eight times each day, the community would gather to chant biblical psalms, sing hymns, and hear Scriptural passages. These hours were named matins, lauds, prime, terce, sext, none, vespers, and compline. Collections of psalms were called psalters and were among the most common of early medieval books. Later, priests were required to pray a similar, if shorter, version of daily prayers; these were laid out in the breviary. By the 1100s, wealthy and literate laity began ordering similar prayer books based on the daily cycle of monastic hours for their use. A great many of these survive; scholars have said that Books of Hours constitute the largest category of medieval books to survive.

Before printing, each was hand produced and unique, though there are patterns of contents. The core was the Hours of the Virgin Mary, a variation of the monastic cycle dedicated to Jesus's mother. Second came an often beautifully and symbolically decorated calendar that included Church holidays, saints' feast days, and sometimes anniversaries meaningful to the patron. These were followed by some or all: prayers to Mary; Gospel selections; the Office of Mary; the Seven Penitential Psalms; a Litany of Saints ("St. Sebastian, pray for us"); a shorter version known as the Hours of the Cross; the Hours of the Holy Spirit; the Office (liturgy) of the Dead, with set prayers for those who had died, that they might be released from purgatory; and prayers to such specific saints as Sebastian, Roche, and Christopher, who were thought to provide aid during plague. Prayers for the dead also served as mementos mori, reminders of one's own mortality.

After 1350, prayers and imagery related to plague became very popular, especially in the final two categories of content. While these were also traditional, their presence became increasingly common down to the genre's end in the later 16th century. Prayers to plague saints were often illustrated with iconic images, for example, Sebastian being shot with arrows. The Office of the Dead could feature any combination of a number of images associated with plague: Pope St. Gregory during the First Pandemic; the Angel of Death with Arrow and Sword; King David prays to avert a plague; allegorical images of death; the Last Judgment; the Danse macabre; The Three Living Meet the Three Dead; the Triumph of Death; a funeral, procession, or burial; a contemporary burial in a used grave; Lazarus and Dives. The most famous example is the French *Tres Riches Heures of the Duc du Berry* by the Limbourg Brothers, begun 1410.

See also: Arrows; Art, Effects of Plague on; Danse Macabre; Death, Depictions of; Monks, Nuns, and Monasteries; Plague Saints; Prayer and Fasting; Purgatory; "Three Living Meet the Three Dead;" Triumph of Death; Virgin Mary.

References

Harthan, John P. *Books of Hours*. New York: Random House, 1988.

Stocks, Bronwyn. "Intersections of Time and Place in Books of Hours," in *Crossing Cultures: Conflict, Migration, and Convergence*, edited by Jaynie Anderson (Carlton, Australia: Miegunyah Press, 2009), 442–447.

Borromeo, Federigo (1564–1631)

Federigo was born to nobility in Milan and was the young cousin of Catholic Reformation Archbishop Charles Borromeo, who oversaw his education in Bologna in 1579 to 1580. While there, Charles decided Federigo had a religious vocation and Federigo announced for the Jesuit order. This displeased his cousin, who destined him to a diocesan career and sent him to the University of Pavia (1580–1585). Charles died in 1584, so Federigo traveled to Rome in search of patronage in 1585. He was a natural scholar, devoting his energy to the early Church, and was made a cardinal deacon in 1587.

Federigo was raised to Milan's throne in June 1595 and proved a spiritual rather than pragmatic leader. He oversaw Charles's canonization in 1610 and led the diocese through stressful periods of the Thirty Years' War. Famine struck in 1628 and plague in 1629 to 1630. He used his cousin's activity as a template and clashed with the secular authorities. The plague was not so much a medical disaster as an extension of the ages-old battle between God's love and light and demonic hatred and darkness. The Church's ministrations thus far outweighed civic precautions. He hurled his clergy into the corpse-choked streets, at the loss of two-thirds of them; he bullied the local mendicant orders and the Jesuits to fill the fallen ranks; and he urged nuns to serve in the city's huge lazaretto. On June 11, 1630, Federigo tried to catch some of Charles' charisma by leading a large procession through Milan's central streets. Those who died in the lazaretto and left their goods to the Church obtained an indulgence releasing them from spiritual penalties for their unconfessed sins.

In August 1630, shortly before his death, he penned *De pestilentia*, a collection of his observations of and ideas about plague. The government delayed declaring plague and closing access because of greed for gate taxes and customs duties. He blamed much of the carnage on "greasers," evil people who spread death through poisoned ointments; the authorities should have done more to stop them. Demons also provided poison formulas, wiped poisoners' memories clean, and deceived authorities into providing worthless remedies. To prepare for the postplague world, Borromeo advocated next time immediately sending out 300 of the expert craftspeople and the "strongest and best priests," without pastoral responsibilities, to preserve them from plague at city expense.

See also: Bishops and Popes; Borromeo, St. Charles (San Carlo); Milan, Italy; Poisoning and Plague Spreading; Thirty Years' War.

References

Borromeo, Federico. *La peste di Milano*. Milan: Rusconi, 1987.

Cohn, Samuel K. *Cultures of Plague: Medical Thinking at the End of the Renaissance*. New York: Oxford University Press, 2010.

Naphy, William G. *Plagues, Poisons and Potions: Plague Spreading Conspiracies in the Western Alps c. 1530–1640*. New York: Manchester University Press, 2002.

Borromeo, St. Charles (San Carlo; 1538–1484)

Born to a Milanese nobleman and his Medici wife, Charles was a second son who was early on dedicated to an ecclesiastical career. He graduated from the University of Pavia in Canon and Civil Law in 1559, the same year his uncle became Pope Pius IV. Charles was quickly named cardinal-deacon and made an administrator of the diocese of Milan, was ordained priest in 1563, and was elected Archbishop of Milan in 1564. He became a model administrator of the Tridentine Catholic Reform movement, working tirelessly to address ecclesiastical abuses and deficiencies in Milan's diocese.

When plague struck Milan in late July 1576, Borromeo was beloved and respected. Attributing the epidemic to God's wrath kindled by sins of the Milanesi, he immediately demanded prayer, repentance, and ritual. In October, with disease spreading and despite the civil authorities' objections, he personally led three processions through Milan's streets, barefoot and carrying a large wooden cross. Though urged to flee, he insisted on remaining and personally serving victims, encouraging his clergy to do the same. As depicted in later paintings, Borromeo preached, said Mass regularly, and dispensed alms, the Eucharist, and Last Rites to victims in their homes and the huge lazaretto. He actively sought to replace fallen clergy and stood in the midst of mass burial trenches to consecrate the ground. After distributing his own considerable wealth to sufferers, coining his own gold and silver plate, and transforming his personal and church textiles into winter clothing, he begged for charity on his people's behalf. When the epidemic subsided, Borromeo led more processions blessing the city and thanking God for deliverance.

Noted for his reformer's zeal and selfless modeling of Christian charity and leadership, Charles Borromeo was beatified in 1602 and named saint by Pope Pius V in 1610. His popular cult as plague saint was boosted by his nephew Federigo Borromeo, who served as Milan's Archbishop during the terrible plague of 1630.

See also: Bishops and Popes; Borromeo, Federigo; Milan, Italy; Plague Saints; Priests; Processions.

References

Giussano, Giovani Pietro. *The Life of St. Charles Borromeo, Cardinal Archbishop of Milan*. 2 vols. New York: Burns and Oates, 1884; facsimile edition of Vol. 1 by Bibliolife, 2010.

Jones, Pamela. "San Carlo Borromeo and Plague Imagery in Milan and Rome," in *Hope and Healing: Painting in Italy in a Time of Plague, 1500–1800*, edited by Gauvin Alexander Bailey et al. (Chicago: University of Chicago Press, 2005), 65–96.

Boyle, Robert (1627–1691)

Born at Lismore Castle in Ireland, 14th of 15 children of a self-promoting courtier and royal administrator, Robert received four years of formal education at Eton before undertaking the Grand Tour of Europe. Rebellion at home in 1642 cut this short, orphaned him, and forced his return to London. Robert inherited an estate at Stalbridge in Dorset, at which, for a dozen years, he engaged his interests in natural philosophy and experimentation in alchemy. A learned amateur, Boyle moved from alchemy to chemical medicine (iatrochemistry), influenced by Joan Van Helmont and the English Paracelsian movement. In 1656, Boyle joined other early scientists at Oxford, where he received an honorary M.D. degree in 1665. In 1660, he helped found London's Royal Society. He rode out the plague year of 1665 to 1666 in an Oxfordshire village and relocated to London's Pall Mall in 1668. A stroke in 1670 slowed but did not stop his work.

Though best known for his *Sceptical Chymist* and never a physician, Boyle scattered his ideas about epidemic disease across numerous works as they developed. These include *Tracts about the Cosmical Qualities of Things* (1671); *Essays of the strange Subtility, great Efficacy, determinate nature of Effluviums* (1673); *Suspicions about some Hidden Qualities of the Air* (1674); *Essay of the Great Effects of Languid and Unheeded Local Motion* (1685); the leechbook *Receipts* (Recipes) *sent to a Friend in America* (1688; expanded 1692); and *Experimenta et Observationes Physicae* (1691). His ideas borrowed widely from ancient atomism and Baconian science, Rene Descartes, and Pierre Gassendi. Boyle believed all natural things and phenomena were made of or caused by material corpuscles (molecules) made of atoms. The human body was a chemical machine that contracted plague when it absorbed through pores tiny "morbifick corpuscles" sloughed off by certain subterranean natural objects

and carried in the air. These particular corpuscles (effluvia) interfered with the body's systems and fluids, causing the symptoms and results of pestilence. Amulets worked similarly, infinitesimal layers of sloughed corpuscles entering pores and blocking "morbifick" ones from penetrating. A Christian, Boyle wrote a moralistic pamphlet in 1665, "The Plague of London from the Hand of God."

See also: Amulets, Talismans, and Magic; Causes of Plague: Historical Theories; Leechbooks; Paracelsus and Paracelsianism; Scientific Revolution; Sydenham, Thomas; Van Helmont, Joan Baptista.

Reference

Kaplan, Barbara Beigun. *"Divulging of Useful Truths in Physick": The Medical Agenda of Robert Boyle*. Baltimore, MD: Johns Hopkins University Press, 1993.

Broadsheets, Broadsides, and Pamphlets

With the advent of printing on cheap paper in the mid-15th century came inexpensive one- or two-sheet publications of popular interest. Often combining words with an appealing image or images, these publications could be religious or secular, official or dissident, newsworthy or the hoax of a charlatan. Text-dominant broadsides could contain new legal provisions, advice for just about anything, advertisements or recipes for medicines, prayers, and poems; broadsheets held images of strange events, recent civic events, saints, biblical figures, rulers, and pilgrim routes. Many were one-sided and meant to be posted on church doors, columns, and other public venues; others were sold for a few pennies to be hung in even the poorest homes. Vendors, booksellers, printers' shops, inns, and taverns hawked the latter.

During epidemics, ephemeral publications became important conduits of information between rulers and ruled. Since plague edicts and policies were sporadic and directly affected people's daily lives, their immediate posting where people expected to find them ensured familiarity, if not compliance. People sought the latest information since infractions often resulted in execution. In many cities, for example, Rome in 1656, a "crier" loudly announced new ordinances from street corners, at which the broadsheet would then be posted. Some ordinances required that the civic trumpeter precede the crier to draw the greatest possible attention. In Italy, official postings were variously known as *gride* (GREE-deh), *bandi*, *proclami*, or *provvisioni* and were most commonly found in Bologna, Milan, and Venice. Bologna's government released only two sets of sanitation orders prior to 1575, but up to 1600, five or more appeared every year. Most of these were prophylactic in nature.

Printers also produced medical material, from quack cures to the latest anatomical findings of such experts as Andreas Vesalius (1543). Such standard subjects as zodiac man and bloodletting charts, originally aimed at medical students and practitioners but increasingly of interest to the general public, were sold beside more sophisticated treatments of both Galenic and Paracelsian medicine. About 1540, Johann Vogt of Ulm produced a single-sheet "Cure for Pestilence," advertising his own gold-based medicine and recommending consumption of lamb and mutton. In 1555, Regensburg printer Hans Kohl produced a bloodletting chart with a descriptive paragraph for each of the seven recommended sites on the body.

"In time of pestilence," he noted, people had to care for themselves.

This applied to spirit as well as body. Early prayer broadsides were simple and featured one or more prayers unadorned by images, especially in areas affected by Calvinism. Catholic prayer sheets often featured Mary or St. Sebastian protecting devotees, or Christ's crucifixion. The suffering Redeemer or saint drew a parallel between salvific pain as depicted and anguish the viewer may have been undergoing. Many Catholic prayers were directed to plague saints, hence their images, as advocates before Christ the judge and plague's source. Protestant prayer sheets avoided Catholic imagery in favor of such symbols as skulls or corpses, as reminders of inevitable death, or kneeling figures or families with their prayers for divine mercy directed to God. Like quack medicines, fake rituals were broadcast to the gullible: during the epidemic of 1575 to 1577, printer Pietro de Faris peddled a set of prayers that, when thrice recited and accompanied by the sign of the cross, would provide immunity from plague. The Inquisition found this very interesting.

Some sheets featured images of suffering and the horrors of corpse collection or mass burial, for example, the famous plague etchings of Rome in 1656 to 1657 by Louis Rouhier, published by Giovanni de Rossi. Similar pictures accompanied English moralistic poetry and social criticism from around 1600. Ballads of lament and political criticism also appeared as single sheets, to be sung in taverns and at other gatherings.

See also: Almanacs; Apothecaries; Art, Effects of Plague on; Astrology; Charlatans and Quacks; Death, Depictions of; Dekker, Thomas; Governments, Civil; Morality Literature, Christian; Plague Saints; Poetry, European; Prayer and Fasting; Public Sanitation; Remedies, External; Remedies, Internal; Zodiac Man.

References

Achinstein, Sharon. "Plagues and Publication: Ballads and the Representation of Disease in the English Renaissance." *Criticism* 34 (1992): 27–49.

Cust, R. P. "News and Politics in Seventeenth-Century England." *Past and Present* 112 (1986): 60–90.

Jarcho, Saul. *Italian Broadsides Concerning Public Health*. Mount Kisko: Futura, 1986.

San Juan, Rose Marie. *Rome: A City Out of Print*. Minneapolis: University of Minnesota Press, 2001.

Watt, Teresa. *Cheap Print and Popular Piety*. New York: Cambridge University Press, 1993.

Buboes. *See* Bubonic Plague

Bubonic Plague

Bubonic plague is naturally a disease of animals. Like many diseases—bird flu, chicken pox, AIDS—it jumps to humans, becoming a zoonosis. Unlike others, however, plague requires the presence of animals to sustain itself over time. It is not caught directly from a carrier in normal contact, and in this sense it is not contagious. Even when the pathogens lodge in the lungs and the human victim coughs them into the air, it is usually to little effect. The key is a high level of proximity.

The Zoonosis

The disease known as plague is produced in the human body by the pathogen known as *Yersinia pestis*. This is a nonmotile, pleomorphic, and gram-negative bacterium of the bacillus type. It protects itself well after encountering an animal's immune system but does not last long in the open environment. The normal life cycle of the *Y. pestis* is spent in the bloodstreams of various types of rodents and other small mammals. More than 200 types of mammal carriers today are known to harbor *Y. pestis*, including prairie dogs, squirrels, and domestic cats. These animals, other than cats, tend to create communities that are stable and settled, and the bacteria live literally within that community enzootically, doing little damage to individual animals and none to the integrity of the community. Such a community is a focus of plague, and a large geographic area in which many of these lie is a plague reservoir. Within a reservoir, many types of mammal species may host the bacterium. Unless the natural balance within the community is disturbed, the focus will last indefinitely.

While *Y. pestis* may pass from rodent to rodent through a random mixing of blood, the *Y. pestis* has a much more reliable means of passing from a dying to a new and healthy host: fleas. Fleas regularly live within the fur of mammals and feed off of the animals' blood. They may also feed on grain dust and other detritus, but blood meals are needed for survival in the long run. There are many different types of fleas—between 80 and 100 can carry *Y. pestis*—but the *siphonaptera* are especially good at inserting their tiny tubes through the skin of the host and drawing the meal out. When that blood is contaminated with *Y. pestis*, then the flea ingests it. As long as the flea remains on the contaminated host, the cycle continues until the death of one or the other. When a new, healthy flea arrives and draws its first meal, it, too, is infected. When the body temperature of the host rodent begins to fall with death, from whatever cause, the fleas abandon it for a new host. This may or may not be a carrier but is likely to be infected by the infected fleas if not. And the cycle continues.

Among rodents, the black rat *Rattus rattus* is especially tasty to a particular flea, the siphonaptera known as *Xenopsylla cheopis*. *X. cheopis* is an especially efficient transmitter of *Y. pestis*. When *X. cheopis* draws a blood meal from a contaminated host, the bacteria are not immediately digested. Rather, thanks to an important mutation, they are collected in a sac known as the mid-gut, between the siphoning proboscis and the gut. The mid-gut fills and blocks the flea from successfully siphoning off its next meal. The blocked flea may repeatedly and unsuccessfully insert its proboscis, or it may regurgitate some or all of what is in its mid-gut. This is likely to be into the bloodstream of the host. Such a large injection may well overwhelm the host's immune system and eventually kill it. This is especially true if the host has never experienced the pathogen before and has limited natural defenses. *Rattus rattus* is a natural homebody that rarely strays more than a few meters from its home base unless disturbed. It also lives well in primitive housing material, for example, rooting thatch, and off of the unprotected or cast-off food from human tables, especially grains. In medieval and early modern Europe, *R. rattus* lived within human communities with little known cause for alarm.

Transmission

When an infected focus is disrupted, whether by a camper's nosy cat or a traveling Mongol with a tasty sack of flour, there may be trouble. The cat may kill and "play with" an infected rat, leading the fleas to jump into the cat's fur. A lone rat may take up residence in the flour sack and pass its fleas along to the lone rider. Alternately, the lone rat may abandon the sack at the next rest site and interject itself into a healthy colony of rats. Lacking attained immunity, the rats rather quickly die off in a epizootic (animal epidemic). If humans are in proximity, the fleas will take up residence among them, on their skin, to drink their blood.

And so the animal disease becomes a human disease.

Premodern humans suffered from many irritants, including such human fleas as *Pulex irritans*, and would have thought nothing of a few fleas or flea bites. Ironically, bathing was believed to be unhealthy and was rarely done. Though the fleas' first choice would have been the rat, the second choice of people or domestic animals would provide the needed blood meals. Scientists generally agree that local rat populations had to have died off first before the fleas would have jumped to other hosts. This means a lag time between the appearance of the pathogen in a community and the first local human victims. Bubonic plague passed via fleas from rats to people or person to person, which is why it seemed to premodern people that the plague was contagious. If one spent time around sick victims, the fleas abandoned the cooling bodies and found new hosts. And so a few cases of plague became an epidemic.

An unblocked flea or type of flea is fairly limited to passing along to humans germs that are located around the flea's oral cavity or that remain on the human's skin to be scratched subcutaneously into contact with the bloodstream. Relatively few bacteria enter via the unblocked fleas, but the blocked fleas, by unloading a glob of the bacteria at one regurgitation, are far more efficient.

The Human Disease

Once inside the human body the *Y. pestis* cells are too cool to produce the protective encapsulation that protects them from destruction, and many are killed outright by the defensive cells. Quickly, though, the survivors warm and acquire the valuable shells, while other antigens allow growth within host cells. Iron is taken from the surrounding environment and absorbed by the *Y. pestis*. The lymphatic system picks up some portion of the living *Y. pestis* plus debris from dead invaders and defenders and drains it all toward the closest lymph nodes. These are located in the neck behind the ears, under the armpits, and in the groin region. The living *Y. pestis* cells reproduce at a rate that doubles their mass every two hours. The encapsulation continues to protect them from destruction. They swell the nodes within four to six days after the initial infection. These become inflamed and hemorrhagic, very tender to the touch, a signal that much of the rest of the body, including blood and organs, has been infected. This swelling becomes visible in the nodes that are closest to the skin, forming what are called "buboes." There are also swellings deeper inside that are not at all obvious, though the pain is. In the late stages, septicemia is poisoned blood, which has poisoned the kidneys, spleen, and liver. Unless the body has recovered and developed antigens early in the process or the buboes opened outward without flooding the lymphatic system and bloodstream, the patient dies, essentially of toxic shock. If untreated, the destruction may heavily infect the lungs, causing secondary pneumonic plague, or remain traveling through the bloodstream and destroying organs, bringing on nearly certain death by secondary septicemic plague.

Meanwhile, the point of infection develops necrosis, lesions, swellings known as carbuncles, and other effects on the skin. Early symptoms mimic many diseases, with lethargy, headache, chills, nausea (up to 104°F), and fever 12 to 24 hours before the lymphatic swelling becomes common. The buboes and attendant pain typify the end game.

Modern patients recover without antibiotics in about 40 percent of cases. Untended cases develop into secondary pneumonic plague in about 15 percent of cases and in about 5 percent, secondary septicemic. An early antiplague vaccine was developed by the Russian Waldemar/Vladimir Haffkine in India after 1896 with limited success and serious side effects. Vaccine development is currently underway in light of contemporary study of the genome sequencing.

See also: Animals; Black Death: Debate over the Medical Nature of; Black Death: Origins and Early Spread; Bubonic Plague in North America; Clothing; Diagnosing Plague; End of Second Plague Pandemic: Theories; Fleas; Germ Theory; Pneumonic Plague; Rats and Other Plague Carriers; Septicemic Plague; *Yersinia pestis*.

References

Benedictow, Ole. *The Black Death: 1346–1353.* Rochester, NY: Boydell, 2004.

Gage, Kenneth and Michael Kosoy. "Natural History of Plague: Perspectives from More than a Century of Research." *Annual Review of Entomology* 50 (Jan. 2005): 505–528.

Marriott, Edward. *Plague: A Story of Science, Rivalry, Scientific Breakthrough and the Scourge that Won't Go away.* New York: Holt, 2002.

Scott, Susan and Christopher Duncan. *Biology of Plagues: Evidence from Historical Populations.* New York: Cambridge University Press, 2001.

Bubonic Plague in North America

Plague first appeared in North America during the Third Pandemic. In the U.S. territory, Honolulu, Hawaii, reported plague's arrival from the Far East in 1899,

Group of men standing outdoors around a makeshift table applying poison to bread used as rat bait during the San Francisco plague campaign, 1909. (Courtesy of the National Library of Medicine)

and an epidemic from December 1899 to March 1900 sparked 71 cases, of which 61 died. Mostly Chinese ethnics were victims, and antiplague measures, reflecting the new and evolving understanding of plague, were undertaken with a vengeance. It moved westward across the Pacific in one or more ships striking San Francisco, California, early in 1900. Initial cases were few, and again among the Chinese, leaving effective action suspended between local civic priorities and racism and the angry Chinese community supported by the federal government. Effective collective action was stymied until 1903, when the final case was reported. Then came the earthquake in April 1906 and a new round of plague cases in 1907, which were quickly tended to and the threat ended. All told, there were 280 cases with 172 deaths.

A ship from Brazil (infected in Santos in 1899; first known plague in the New World) carrying plague victims was quarantined in New York Harbor in 1899, saving that city, and a Japanese ship with victims was stopped before arriving in Seattle's Elliot Bay in 1900. In 1908, as the last human case was being reported in San Francisco, so was the first case of a disease carrying wild rodent, a squirrel in northern California. Despite slaughtering 700,000 wild rodents over the next decade, from this point, the United States can be said to have had a reservoir of infected wild mammals of various types (groundhogs, prairie dogs, squirrels, etc.). It has moved from its starting point in California just about due east some 1,250 miles over the past century.

Outbreaks of plague have never reached epidemic levels, but multiple cases have historically occurred. One began in New Orleans when a contaminated vessel from Cuba landed. Local health officials kept rats under control from 1912 to early 1914, but 31 human cases appeared later in the year. Swift action reduced that caseload to single cases in 1915 and 1916. In 1924, Los Angeles's Mexican community suffered from 33 cases of pneumonic plague and 8 of bubonic plague, with high death rates. The area was carefully cordoned off and both victims and rodents contained. Thereafter, U.S. cases numbered one or two on average per year. An isolated Navajo tribal meeting in 1965 resulted in 8 or 10 cases of bubonic plague from contaminated prairie dogs, but only one victim succumbed due to swift response by local health authorities.

Recently, American trends in recreation and residential choices have been developing in the American Southwest and encroaching on the plague reservoirs. Twelve states have plague foci, and in the so-called "four corners" region, roughly 15 percent of the land has been designated a "high risk" area for plague. As more people and their animals migrate, the number of cases will rise. Watchful public health and modern antibiotics quickly applied, however, should keep case fatalities near zero (though current case fatality rate is about 14 percent). In the 2000s, the United States has between 50 and 80 annual cases, of which 84 percent are bubonic plague. Increasing numbers of domestic cats are catching plague and bringing it home.

See also: Bubonic Plague; Rats and Other Plague Carriers; Third Plague Pandemic.

References

Chase, Marilyn. *The Barbary Plague: The Black Death in Victorian San Francisco*. New York: Random House, 2003.

Echenberg, Myron. *Plague Ports: The Global Urban Impact of Bubonic Plague, 1894–1901*. New York: New York University Press, 2007.

Marriott, Edward. *Plague: A Story of Science, Rivalry, Scientific Breakthrough and the Scourge that Won't Go away*. New York: Holt, 2002.

Bullein, William (d. 1576)

Apparently from Cambridgeshire, William studied medicine and may have earned an M.D. at a continental university. His first work (London, 1558/9) is titled *Gouvernemente of Healthe, wherein is uttered manye notable Rules for Mannes preseuacion, with sondry symples and other matters, no less fruiteful than profitable: Colect out of many approved authors. Reduced into the forme of a Dialogue for the better understanding of thunlearned. Whereunto is added a sufferain Regiment against the Pestilence*. He dedicated it to Sir Thomas Hilton, Captain of Tynemouth Castle near Newcastle. Since he later married Sir Thomas's widow, he seems to have spent much of his time in the north. In 1564/5, Bullein published the far more artful *Dialogue both pleasant and pietifull, wherein is a godly regiment against the Fever Pestilence*. He also produced one of the first English herbals, *The Book of Simples*.

Gouvernement of Healthe is a Galenist tract of a traditional sort, but his section on "pestilence" is more complex. Though "distempered air" and celestial bodies are God's tools, God is the ultimate cause, and prayer is the ultimate answer. For Bullein, the disease is as much moral and spiritual as it is physiological. He takes on the persona of a minister and analyzes the plague as a literal disease but also allegorically, its deeper and more important meanings being moral and faith-related. Physick, or medicinal remedies, is fine, but the best medicine is that prescribed by Jesus, St. Paul, and Moses. Social commentary is also present, as he contrasts urban filth, stench, crowds, and bad air and water with the purity of the natural countryside.

Bullein's *Dialogue* is a very different type of work. At the center is an *Everyman*-type morality play of a poor northerner who travels to London during plague. He is ill used by a number of such shady denizens as the doctor, the apothecary, the lawyer, a vile Catholic, and greedy Antonio. The cynical Mendicus ("liar") looks forward to the next plague, since the rich die, the evil die, and the suffering poor find peace. "Their loss is our luck: when they become naked, we are clothed against their wills." Even beggars make out well, acquiring "coats, jackets, hose, caps, belts, and shoes" (Bullein, 9). For Bullein, plague is a physical disease, but it is also a manifestation of the worst of fallen human nature and a metaphor for the diseased social body. Interspersed in the dialogue are recipes for remedies, good advice for diet, utopian dreams, and exhortations to prayer and good living. Whatever his background, Bullein has great feeling for the poor in the countryside who have been trodden down by their masters for generations. Urban poor, on the other hand, among whom the plague seems to originate and thrive, live in filth and squalor of their own making. They along with their urban environments are to blame when pestilence rages. Bullein is the first English writer to blend a physician's medical concerns with Protestant socio-political criticism, an amalgam that will characterize much Stuart-era plague literature.

See also: Metaphors for Plague; Morality Literature, Christian; Prayer and Fasting; Sin.

References

Boring, William C. "William Bullein's *Dialogue against the Fever Pestilence*." *The Nassau Review* 2 (1974): 33–42.

Grigsby, Bryon Lee. *Pestilence in Medieval and Early Modern English Literature*. New York: Routledge, 2004.

Healy, Margaret. *Fictions of Disease in Early Modern England: Bodies, Plagues and Politics*. New York: Palgrave, 2002.

McCutcheon, Elizabeth. "William Bullein's *Dialogue against the fever pestilence*: A Sixteenth-century Anatomy," in *Miscellanea moreana: Essays for German Marc Hadour*, edited by Clare M. Murphy and Mario di Cesare (Binghamton, NY: Medieval and Renaissance Texts and Studies, 1989), 341–359.

Caffa (Kaffa, Feodosiya), Ukraine

In 1266, the Mongol rulers of the Golden Horde ceded land along the Crimean coast to the Genoese and Venetians at Tana and to the Genoese alone at Caffa (also known as Kaffa and later changed to Feodosyia in the early 19th century). The Italians built walled settlements with warehouses for storing merchandise. It was a natural emporium for one part of the Silk Road. The Islamization of the Horde in 1313 raised resentment against the presence of Christian traders. In the early 1340s, the Kipchak Khan, Djanibeg, began maneuvering against the merchants. In 1343, a Venetian was charged with murdering a Tatar in Tana, and Djanibeg attacked both towns. Tana fell, but Caffa survived to undergo a second siege in 1345 to 1346. In its latter stages, a regional epidemic of plague struck the Mongols and "the European foreigners," according to both a Russian and an Italian account. Gabriele de Mussis reports in his chronicle that the Italians contracted the plague when the Mongols flung their plague corpses over the city's walls. As Europeans died, survivors boarded their ships and fled south, bringing the disease with them. Thus began the Black Death.

Though critics doubt the account's veracity, both Christians and Muslims would have believed that rotting corpses were themselves a cause of disease, including plague. According to ancient miasma theory, the corpses would "corrupt" the air that then poisoned the people. Such tactics were far from unknown among the Mongols. The more likely scenario is that from the Mongol camp,

rats with their infected fleas entered Caffa in various ways, sparking the epidemic.

Gabriele de Mussis of Piacenza died in 1356. He was a notary in Genoa who wrote of the plague's early ravages in Italy in his *Historia de morbo*, written shortly after the events. At one time, he was thought to have been an eye-witness to the events at Caffa, given that Genoese notaries would not have been strangers there. His account of the siege is, however, second hand, and the extant manuscript copy of his chronicle part of a later compilation.

See also: Black Death: Origins and Early Spread; Merchants; Miasma Theory.

References

Benedictow, Ole. *The Black Death, 1346–1353: The Complete History.* Rochester, NY: Boydell and Brewer, 2004.

Wheelis, Mark. "Biological Warfare at the 1346 Siege of Caffa." *Emerging Infectious Diseases* 8 (2002): 971–975.

Cairo, Egypt

Founded in the 10th century CE, 14th-century Cairo, nearby Fustat (Old Cairo), the port of Bulaq, and the vast cemeteries of Qarafa constituted the major Egyptian urban center to the south of Alexandria and the Nile River delta. It was described as the largest city west of China and may have had up to 600,000 inhabitants. Capital of the Turkic Mamluk Empire to 1517, afterward, Ottoman aristocrats called home this focal point of Red Sea–Nile trade and hajj, linking it more tightly with Istanbul and its expanding empire. Throughout the Second Pandemic, Cairo was a magnet for Muslims representing every corner of their world, from merchants to pilgrims, refugees to students.

Having crossed the Mediterranean from Constantinople to Alexandria in late 1347, the Black Death struck Cairo in late summer 1348 and ravaged the city. Its thousands of shops organized into 30 great markets were shuttered as owners fled or died. Many took lucrative jobs reciting prayers at the heads of processions or serving as corpse washers or carriers or gravediggers, the chronicler Al-Maqrizi reported. Corpses clogged the Nile and funeral processions the narrow, winding streets and alleyways. The young sultan, al-Nasir al-Hasan, fled in September to Siryaquz, setting a precedent for future rulers, but there is no sign of governmental breakdown. There was also little in the way of government action. Individuals prayed, fled, fasted, shared wealth as alms, and used what remedies they had. But Islam insisted on a certain resignation before God's inescapable will, teaching that the faithful would die as martyrs. Even so, a third to 40 percent of the city perished over eight months.

Demographic and economic devastation throughout Egypt immediately depressed Cairo's commerce and industries, as much of the wealth of the deceased passed to the Mamluk masters. With his share, Sultan al-Hasan undertook a huge worship and education complex in 1358: part economic stimulus, part memorial, part self-aggrandizement. Over the following 150 years, Mamluk Cairo suffered plague outbreaks in 55, with heavy tolls in 1363, 1367, 1381, 1388 to 1389, 1416, 1429 to 1430, 1438 (1,000 Mamluks died), 1444, 1449, 1459 to 1460 (1,400 Mamluks died), 1468 to 1469, 1476 to 1477, 1492, 1498, and 1505. Despite apparent recovery in the Black Death's immediate aftermath, structural economic weaknesses and political events drove Cairo into decline from the late 1380s. Between 1348 and 1420, tax revenues fell off 12 percent; the number of active looms dropped from 14,000 to 800 between 1388 and 1434. Factories and baths closed, tolls fell off; market official and chronicler Al-Maqrizi painted a bleak picture of Cairo's decline and of the terrible plague of 1438, in which another 90,000 died.

Despite an economic upturn and rebuilding program at mid-century, the population of Cairo-Fustat remained depressed into the 16th century. In 1517, Egypt fell to the Ottoman Empire. The largely parasitic Mamluks were replaced with diligent Ottoman officials, but power and influence shifted to Istanbul. Population remained about half of what it had been in 1347 as Cairo entered the 18th century, at least in part because of plague's continual recurrence. Its major hospital (*bimaristan*) was still the magnificent Hospital of Mansur Qala'un (1284–1285). The 16th-century Turks began borrowing some elements of European medicine, but they worked no better when transplanted in the east. More effective were such European public health measures as cordons and quarantines, which at least aided in bringing the Second Pandemic to a close in the 1840s.

See also: Allah; Arabic-Persian Medicine and Practitioners; Bimaristans; Demographic and Economic Effects of Plague: The Islamic World; Islam and Medicine; Islamic Religious Responses; al-Maqrizi, Muhammad; Mecca.

References

Abu-Lughod, Janet L. *Cairo: 1001 Years of the "City Victorious."* Princeton, NJ: Princeton University Press, 1971.

Borsch, Stuart. *The Black Death in Egypt and England.* Austin: University of Texas Press, 2005.

Dols, Michael W. *The Black Death in the Middle East*. Princeton, NJ: Princeton University Press, 1977.

Dols, Michael W. "The General Mortality of the Black Death in the Mamluk Empire," in *The Islamic Middle East, 700–1900: Studies in Social and Economic History*, edited by Abraham Udovitch (Princeton, NJ: Princeton University Press, 1981), 404–411.

Raymond, André. *Cairo*. Cambridge, MA: Harvard University Press, 2000.

Varlik, Nükhet. "Disease and Empire: A History of Plague and Epidemics in the Early Ottoman Empire (1453–1600)." Ph.D. dissertation, University of Chicago, 2008.

Canutus (Kanutus) Plague Tract

England's first and most popular 15th-century plague tract had its origins in the Latin tract of 1364 by Johannes Jacobi (Jean Jacmé). Jacobi was a royal and papal physician who served as Chancellor of Montpellier's Medical School. Shortly after 1450, a Scandinavian bishop, either Bengt Knuttson of Våsterås, Sweden, or Knud Mikkelsen of Viborg, Denmark, gave his name—Canutus—to an edition of Jacobi. Before 1500, the Latin *Canutus* had been reprinted 21 times across Europe and three times in London in 1483. In 1485, it was translated into *A Little Book for the Pestilence*, which appeared again in 1488, 1490, 1510, and perhaps 1536. Augustinian friar Thomas Paynell produced a second translation in the 1520s, *A Much Profitable Treatise against the Pestilence*.

Little Book opens with a list of plague "tokens:" morning rains, south winds, flies, thunderstorms, falling or blazing stars. The author then explains that either stars or terrestrial filth corrupt the air, creating poison that enters the body through open pores. In turn, sores release "smoke" that reinfects the air and those around. As prophylaxes, he recommends flight, washing with vinegar, eating two filbert nuts, and avoiding filth, south winds, baths, and rotting things. Aromatic fumigation helps clear the air and "living merrily" balances the humors.

See also: Consilia and Plague Tracts; John of Burgundy.

Reference

Pickett, Joseph. "A Translation of the *Canutus* Plague Treatise," in *Popular and Practical Science of Medieval England*, edited by Lister Matheson (East Lansing: Colleagues Press, 1994), 263–282.

Causes of Plague: Historical Theories

Modern medical science explains the historical plague in terms of bacteria carried by fleas that flee dying rats and find human hosts. Some of the fleas may have been human fleas that jumped from person to person, and sometimes the bacteria may have been transmitted by sneezing or coughing. Once in the human body, the bacteria reacted in one or more (today) predictable manners, either killing the victim or not. During the Second Plague Pandemic, no one came close to painting, let alone understanding, this picture. Instead, Western medicine—among Jews, Muslims, and Christians—remained tied to a model of epidemiology that was deeply rooted in classical Greek medicine and monotheistic religion. The answers to "What causes plague?" remained virtually unchanged from 1350 to 1750 and across cultures. Explanations were multiple and layered, which made perfect sense to cultures accustomed to Aristotle's teaching that all things have four "causes": final, efficient, material, and formal. Across the four centuries, we generally see God as the ultimate cause; very often using the celestial bodies as tools; combining their effects on the atmosphere with terrestrial sources of "corruption" in creating a miasma or corrupted air; and this entering the human body and poisoning it. Discussions of multiple causes were usually to be found in plague *consilia* and in later plague tracts that were generally written by physicians, though other written sources from chronicles to sermons and poetry reinforce the medical understanding. In *On the sources of health and sickness*, c. 1350, Greek physician Alexios Makrembolitès noted that ultimately, all elements work together because God is the source of the elements, humors, human bodies, and natural processes that maintain and destroy good health; he is the source of the good air and the bad.

Drawing heavily on Biblical precedents, medieval and early modern writers reflected the era's deep and literal religiosity. An outbreak as devastating and widespread as plague had to have its source in God. God hates sin and epidemic disease is one of his means of punishing transgressors. For the Christian, no person is without sin, so all plague deaths are justifiable. For the Muslim, the evil are punished with death and hellfire, but devout victims are brought directly to Paradise; again, there is no injustice. Writers had differing lists of the sins that brought on divine wrath, but it was generally accepted that the sin and guilt were communal. The earliest *consilia*, however, do not specify God as a cause. This could be because either the physicians expected their readers to understand the ultimate cause or they realized that the divine source was beyond medical analysis and treatment.

God's control of the celestial bodies and their ability to impact life on earth were givens by the 13th century. Ninth-century Muslim scientist Albumasar recognized the so-called Great Conjunctions of Saturn, Mars, and Jupiter as occurring in 20-year and major 240-year cycles. These he related to political and natural disasters on earth. Around 1250, University of Paris natural philosopher Albert the Great agreed with Albumasar but related the events to epidemic disease. When conjoined in such a zodiac water sign as Aquarius, Jupiter draws up corrupted vapors from the earth and Mars "ignites" them, creating miasma and pestilence that spreads through the air. The appropriate conjunction occurred on March 23, 1345, in the Aquarius sign. About one in three early plague *consilia* support this theory, but these are among the most influential, including those by Italian physician Gentile da Foligno and the often-copied medical faculty at the University of Paris. In Spain, Muslim physician Ibn Khatimah admitted that this influence was possible, but humans could know little and do even less about it. Ibn al-Khatib accepted the premise but noted that it was foreign to medicine and hence to his tract. Contemporary German author Conrad von Megenberg dismissed the Great Conjunction since it only lasted one to three years and the plague raged for five and because the planets' courses were quite regular, while plague spread haphazardly. Despite contradiction, some chroniclers, diarists, clerics, physicians, and scientists supported astrological causation down to the end of the 17th century. Almanacs helped keep popular imagination focused on celestial causation. Other purported celestial causes include comets' tails, eclipses, and lunar influences.

Following Hippocrates, Galen, and Avicenna, Western medical scholars long accepted that epidemics were a matter of miasma, "a venomous infection of the air . . .

the stench and filthy savors that corrupt the air we live in" (Thomas Phaer, 1544). For many like Conrad, earthly sources of stench, for example, rotting corpses, were plentiful. Corrupted air entered one's body through pores or inhalation, generating poison that sickened and usually killed. Healthy people with well-balanced humors could resist the poison, while the imbalanced were quite susceptible. Despite the miasma model, the infected could somehow spread the poison to other people, objects, and the space around them, which led scientists in the direction of plague atoms, seeds, and animalcules by the later 16th and 17th centuries.

See also: Almanacs; Astrology; Biblical Plagues; Christ; *Compendium of Paris*; Consilia and Plague Tracts; Contagion Theory; Earthquakes; Gentile da Foligno; Humoral Theory; Miasma Theory; Poetry, European; Sin.

References

Arrizabalaga, Jon. "Facing the Black Death: Perceptions and Reactions of University Medical Practitioners," in *Practical Medicine from Salerno to the Black Death*, edited by Luis Garcia-Ballester et al. (New York: Cambridge University Press, 1994), 237–288).

Chase, Melissa P. "Fevers, Poisons and Apostemes: Authority and Experience in Montpellier Plague Treatises," in *Science and Technology in Medieval Society*, edited by Pamela Long (New York: New York Academy of Sciences, 1985), 153–169.

Cohn, Samuel K. *Cultures of Plague: Medical Thinking at the End of the Renaissance*. New York: Oxford University Press, 2010.

Gottschall, Dagmar. "Conrad of Megenberg and the Causes of the Plague: A Latin Treatise on the Black Death Composed c. 1350 for the Papal Court in Avignon," in *La vie culturelle et scientifique à la cour des papes d'Avignon*, edited by Jacqueline Hamesse (Turnhout: Brepols, 2006), 319–332.

Keiser, G. R. "Two Medieval Plague Treatises and Their Afterlife in Early Modern England."

Journal of the History of Medicine and Allied Sciences 58 (2003): 292–324.

Cellites and Alexians

In 13th-century Dutch and lower Rhenish towns emerged small, leaderless groups of communally living, mendicant laymen dedicated to doing good works, including comforting the sick and dying and burying the dead. By 1350, they had a presence in Aachen, Antwerp, Cologne, Louvain, Mechlin, and Thienen. During plague outbreaks, they served the abandoned and dying when priests could not, burying corpses with dignity when others would not. Though no records of their early efforts survive, the few houses spawned many more—54 by 1520—as plague recurred. Suspected of heresy in the later 1300s, in the 1460s, Church authorities organized these brotherhoods into a religious order around the Rule of the Augustinian Canons. In Catholic cities, they continued their work, eventually adopting St. Alexius as patron saint and Alexians as their identity. In 1634, Jesuit Father Binet wrote that the Cellites "offer their services to those afflicted with the plague." In 17th-century Cologne, Cellites investigated and buried all of the plague dead, resulting in 1665 in the deaths of 22 of 23 local brothers. With plague's disappearance, Alexians rededicated themselves to aiding the mentally ill.

See also: Abandonment; Confraternities; Corpses; Friars (Mendicants).

Reference

Kauffman, Christopher. *Tamers of Death*. New York: Seabury, 1976.

Cemeteries. *See* **Mass Graves and Cemeteries**

Charlatans and Quacks

During the Second Pandemic (1347–1840s), the healing occupations in Europe underwent a process of professionalization. Since the 12th century, special medical schools had been training men to be specialists in the healing arts called *physicians* from the Greek, or *medici* from the Latin. Completion of a curriculum in medicine from a recognized school granted social status, privileges, opportunities for guild membership, and accountability for one's practice. Others practiced healing arts without formal training or status, including surgeons, apothecaries, midwives, and empirics. Each of these groups could claim special skills, and the first three usually training through apprenticeships.

Charlatans and quacksalvers treated the sick and dying and peddled medicines to keep one healthy but operated under no license to do so. The word *charlatan* derived from the Italian *ciarlare*, to chatter—presumably while gulling customers. The word *quacksalver* came from "quicksilver" or mercury, a substance used by some nontraditional healers. Though often tarred as frauds, their methods often differed little from those of the professionals. Medical school faculties and physician guilds had worked to limit charlatans' activities from long before the Black Death, and it remained an ongoing struggle. Demand for their services or products could be high, especially during epidemics, since their products were highly touted, fees usually lower, and availability readier than those of professionals. Their customers were generally of lower class than the physicians' clients. Charlatans were often itinerant, traveling to towns where epidemics were raging or professional presence thin, moving on when the crisis had passed or legal pressures mounted. This limited authorities' opportunity to punish the fraudulent. Seventeenth-century *mountebanks* were men who literally "mounted benches" from which they hawked miracle prophylactics and cures using high theater and stunts.

See also: Apothecaries; Empirics; Physicians; Surgeons/Barbers.

References

Gambaccini, Piero. *Mountebanks and Medicasters: A History of Charlatans from the Middle Ages to the Present.* Jefferson, NC: McFarland and Co, 2004.

Gentilcore, David. *Medical Charlatanism in Early Modern Italy.* New York: Oxford University Press, 2006.

Chaucer, Geoffrey (c. 1340/43–1400)

Geoffrey Chaucer was born to a respectable family and first appears to history as a page in London to Elizabeth de Burgh, Countess of Ulster, in 1357. In 1361, he was studying law at the Inns of Chancery, a term that was broken up by a second outbreak of plague. All told, he survived five bouts of plague, dying during the plague year of 1400. He lived most of his adult life on the fringes of royal society in London, wholesaling in the wine trade and, in 1375, serving as the Comptroller of Wool Customs and Subsidy for the Port of London, a highly placed and lucrative position. He performed some diplomatic tasks and perhaps visited Italy, where he may have become familiar with the tales in Boccaccio's *Decameron*.

Chaucer was an acute observer of humanity and a careful commentator on its foibles.

Fifteenth-century portrait of Geoffrey Chaucer (1343–1400). *The Canterbury Tales* is considered one of the greatest poetic works in English. It also represents the evolution of the English language in the late medieval period. (Library of Congress)

These traits are on display most clearly in his famed *Canterbury Tales*, whose earliest construction seems to have begun around 1385 and stretched out over the following decade. Like others of his class and time, Chaucer was dissatisfied with the postplague shift away from traditional values among all of the strata in society. In a rather idealized preplague world, there were clear expectations and people lived up to them. In the world in which he grew up, the rules seem to have changed, and for no reasons stronger than expediency. The pilgrims he sketches are usually subtle in their weaknesses—the physician is too friendly with the apothecary; the shipman knows the creeks in France through which he can smuggle goods—most of which are matters of greed

or sexual immorality. He is also subtle in his judgment of them, often using allusion and veiled reference rather than outright condemnation. If the plague was responsible for their moral decline, Chaucer soft-pedals it: the word appears nine times in the text, and six of these refer to a curse to moral evil, not the disease. Only the "Pardoner's Tale" is set during plague, with the three main characters swearing to "kill death" and ending up killing each other over "infected" gold. The plague also kills the hero of the "Knight's Tale" and provides the dead lady whom the protagonist laments in the poem *Le Songe Vert*.

See also: Boccaccio, Giovanni; Labourers, Ordinance and Statute of; Langland, William; Lollards; Merchants; Morality Literature, Christian; Peasants; Physicians; Poetry, European; Priests; Sin.

References

Beidler, Peter G. "The Plague and Chaucer's Pardoner." *Chaucer Review* 16 (1982): 257–269.

Robertson, D. W. "Chaucer and the Economic and Social Consequences of the Plague," in *Social Unrest in the Late Middle Ages*, edited by Francis X. Newman (Binghamton: Medieval and Renaissance Texts and Studies, 1986), 49–74.

Snell, William. "Parfit praktisour" or Quack? Chaucer's Physician and the Literary Image of Doctors after the Black Death." *Keio Hiyoshi Review of English Studies* 37 (2000): 117–136.

Ussery, Huling E. *Chaucer's Physician: Medicine and Literature in Fourteenth-century England*. New Orleans: Tulane University Press, 1971.

Chauliac, Guy de (Guido de Cauliaco; c. 1300–1367)

Guy is believed to have been born to a peasant family in Chauliac, France, but was patronized by the local lord of Mercoeur.

Guy studied at Toulouse and then Montpellier for his Masters in Medicine, which he earned in the 1320s. He taught for a while at Montpellier and at some point took clerical orders, perhaps becoming a priest. Further study took him to Bologna and then Paris, and by 1344, he was a practicing physician in Lyon. When plague struck Avignon, he was serving Pope Clement VI as physician and surgeon.

Guy later recalled that he suffered from plague at the papal court for six weeks in 1348. He refused to flee as a matter of pride, and perhaps because he was fairly new to the position. Other physicians did flee, he noted, which made little difference since they could not cure the sick if they had tried. Understanding plague to be caused in part by miasma, he had Clement sit between two large fires that were meant to cleanse the corrupted air. The prophylaxis worked, and Guy went on to serve the next two pontiffs. He may also have had a role in advising Clement on some of the many measures he adopted to deal with the epidemic.

After witnessing plague epidemics in 1358 and 1361, which he avoided by taking theriac, Guy wrote the masterful five-book *Inventory or Collection of Surgical Medicine* in 1363. Originally in Latin, by 1500, there were translations into French, Provençal, English, Italian, Dutch, and Hebrew. First printed in 1478—in French—it underwent 60 printed editions, including a French translation in 1580 by the head of Montpellier's faculty of medicine, Laurent Joubert, and 17 versions in the 17th century. As in his own practice, Guy sought to blend surgery and medicine rather than compartmentalizing them, as was the trend. With references to some 50 authors, including Greeks, Arabs, and contemporary Europeans, it is essentially a scholastic compendium. Book II Chapter 5 deals with the plague.

As in the *Compendium of Paris* of 1348, he credits the astrological conjunction of Jupiter, Saturn, and Mars in 1345 as the universal cause and miasmatic corruption of the atmosphere as proximate cause. He wrote that in the initial outbreak (January 1348–July 1348), victims suffered and died first from terrible three-day symptoms that included fever and bloody expectoration, and later victims had abscesses and buboes appear over five days, suggesting the difference between pneumonic and bubonic plague.

See also: Astrology; Bishops and Popes; Bubonic Plague; Clement VI, Pope; Consilia and Plague Tracts; Medical Education (1300–1500, Medieval Europe); Miasma Theory; Physicians, Court; Surgeons/Barbers.

References

Chauliac, Guy de. "On the Black Death," in *Medieval Medicine: A Reader*, edited by Faith Wallis (Toronto: University of Toronto Press, 2010), 419–421.

Chauliac, Guy de. *Inventarium sive Chirurgia Magna*. 2 volumes. Edited and translated by Michael McVaugh and Margaret Ogden. Boston: Brill, 1997.

Cohn, Samuel K. *The Black Death Transformed: Disease and Culture in Early Renaissance Europe*. New York: Oxford University Press, 2002.

Children

The Black Death (1347–1352) spared no demographic or social groups, but later plague visitations were said to have struck children especially hard. Chroniclers and other commentators repeatedly mention high death rates among children, and rare burial records show a dramatic increase in children after the initial strike. Historian

Samuel Cohn describes plague by about 1400 as "a disease largely of children" (212). An opponent of the conclusion that medieval epidemics were bubonic plague, he notes that since plague confers no immunity on survivors, the Black Death could not have been plague. This trend has been labeled a "supermortality of children." For example, 70 percent of Florentine plague victims in 1400 were "children." A study of Colyton, England, in the 1660s revealed that when both parents in a family survived, 23 percent of children still died on average. When the father alone died, 70 percent of children also did, and when the mother died, 90 percent of children did. On the other hand, premodern child mortality was very high even absent plague: a study of 17th-century France shows that while some 2,000,000 to 3,000,000 children died of plague, premature deaths from other causes were four to eight times higher. A typical demographer's table of Western premodern male death patterns shows that under normal circumstances, nearly a third of children died by their first birthday and half by age 10. This expectation of early death is reflected in the constant underreporting of childhood mortality during epidemics.

Children were most vulnerable while still in the womb. Reports of pregnant victims almost invariably mention the mothers' deaths, and all mention that of the fetus. Though midwives were sometimes hired by local authorities during epidemics, prenatal and neonatal help must have been nearly impossible to engage. From pest houses, we hear of mothers with infants, often still at the breast, and infants suckling from their dead mothers became a baroque-era visual topos, or theme in art.

The Colyton data suggest the tenuous situation in which children who survived an epidemic found themselves. A dead father meant that material support might dry up quickly, while a lost mother led to trauma, the severity of which depended in part on the child's age. Widows with children were often left with little on which to live, subject to abuse from in-laws and predators, who quickly married them for access to assets. Some cities' charitable institutions, for example, Florence's Or San Michele, shifted their monetary and in-kind donations from the poor generally to widows with children. So did wealthy benefactors and testators, who further insisted that the recipients be of good moral standing.

The principal strategy for protecting children was to send them away from the stricken cities to the presumably cleaner and safer countryside. The higher up the social ladder a family was, the more likely they were to have either country property of their own or family located away from plague's path. When fathers had to remain in a stricken city because of position or occupation, they often sent their families out as soon as they were assured the problem was plague. Children were also sent out of cities in carts driven by priests, schoolteachers, or other trusted men to places unknown, to rejoin their parents when—and if—God willed.

The greatest suffering took place among children left orphans by plague. Observers noted children in dire want and shock wandering the streets plaintively begging or huddled in alleyways, as if merely awaiting death. During the second wave of plague in 1363, Paris built the first orphans' hospital. Florence's famous Ospedale degli Innocenti was founded in 1410 (built by 1428; expanded to 700 beds by 1450) by Francesco Datini, a merchant himself orphaned in 1348. Heirless, he also established a foundation—*ceppo*—for abandoned ("thrown-away") children in his hometown of Prato. Testators targeted such facilities, which were increasingly run by lay boards rather than the Church.

Orphans like Datini relied on family friends and will executors to ensure that they received what the law and their fathers intended. While underage as wards, however, children required care, housing, and protection. Though a father's will might make clear provisions, deaths or chains of deaths could thwart even the best preparations, leaving children in the hands of relatives or the Church. As court cases show, "false friends" often emerged to claim kinship and ended up fleecing the young and vulnerable heir. Civil governments stepped in to defend victims of fraud and mischief, though against legitimate but abusive custodians there were few options.

Historians have noted a change in cultural attitude toward children that seems to be related to the repeated sweeps of plague. Put briefly, before the Black Death, the high rates of child mortality made parents less likely to bond closely with younger children. Women married young, and men married serially to ensure that—at least—the upper-class families would survive. The unpredictability and deadliness of plague, however, allowed for no such assurances. Children, especially males, who survived infancy came to mean more to their parents and took on a much higher social value as the very existence of a next generation was called into doubt by plague.

See also: Abandonment; Demographic Effects of Plague: Europe 1347–1400; Governments, Civil; Hospitals; Lazarettos and Pest Houses; Morbidity, Mortality, and Virulence; Poverty and Plague; Repopulation; Wills and Testaments; Women Medical Practitioners.

References

Cohn, Samuel K., Jr. *The Black Death Transformed: Disease and Culture in Early Renaissance Europe.* Oxford: Oxford University Press, 2002.

Hanawalt, Barbara. *Growing Up in Medieval London: The Experience of Childhood in History.* New York: Oxford University Press, 1993.

Nicholas, David. *The Domestic Life of a Medieval City: Women, Children and the Family in Fourteenth Century Ghent.* Lincoln, NE: University of Nebraska Press, 1985.

Orme, Nicholas. *Medieval Children.* New Haven, CT: Yale University Press, 2003.

China

In early November 2010, French scientists announced that a large and carefully conducted study of DNA mutations in *Yersinia pestis* "proved" that the plague-producing bacterium first appeared about 600 BCE in China. All later biovars originated from this initial strain, they claim. While an important insight, many plague scholars have long thought this to be the case, with Western visitations of the disease due to its being transported along the Silk Road during the Late Han period (sixth century CE) and again during the late Yüan era of the 14th century. Regarding the Black Death, was the initial reservoir in the Far East or nearer to the Crimea in southwest Central Asia? And if the latter, did it move eastward and spark an Asian pandemic as well as the West's Black Death?

The impediments to answering these questions are twofold. One is the ambiguity of Chinese terminology that might clearly identify a given epidemic outbreak as being plague; the second is the lack of sources, published or perhaps extant, that chronicle specific epidemics and their effects. In the early 1970s, historian William McNeill confidently claimed that his research links the Western Pandemic to Chinese outbreaks beginning in Hopei province in 1331 and a more general epidemic in the 1350s. He listed these in the Appendix to his 1975 *Plagues and Peoples*, noting that his source for the 14th century and beyond was a 1726 Chinese encyclopedic work. "Statistics" referred to in Xing Xiaochen's 1999 *History and Development of Traditional Chinese Medicine* (published by the Chinese Academy of Sciences) claim that during the 542 years of the Ming and Qing dynasties, 138 outbreaks of "epidemic febrile disease" (which would include plague) occurred; "over nineteen" between 1408 and 1643 (218). McNeill lists 79 epidemics over the same 235-year period, including the years 1408 and 1643. Beyond such discrepancies is identification of the epidemics or epidemic febrile diseases the records mention. To date, there have appeared no body of Chinese descriptions, whether lay or medical, of symptoms and other specific features of the disease(s). The recent DNA findings strongly suggest that at least some of the epidemics would have been plague, but specificity and certainty elude the scholar.

Equally opaque to historians are the effects of epidemics. Ninety percent of Hopei Province is said to have perished in 1331, and within a little more than a decade after widespread carnage in the 1350s, the Mongolian Yüan dynasty fell and the Ming began. The first figure is no doubt exaggerated and reminiscent of European death tolls reported in 1348 to 1350. Factors causing the Mongols' fall usually include 36 years of severe winters, continuous famines around mid-century, widespread and frequent droughts and floods, and unspecified epidemic disease. The hard-pressed populace revolted and drove out the Mongolians, though the role of disease is often minimized, and perhaps rightly so. One reason for the dearth of official information on epidemics may have been the popular notion that epidemics are the result of poor or corrupt government.

See also: Black Death: Origins and Early Spread; Bubonic Plague; Chinese Traditional Medicine; Mongols.

References

Bozhong, Li. "Was There a "Fourteenth-century Turning point"? Population, Land, Technology, and Farm Management," in *The Song-Yüan-Ming Transition in Chinese History*, edited by Paul Smith and Richard von Glahn (Cambridge, MA: Harvard University Press, 2003), 134–175.

Hymes, Robert P. "Not Quite Gentlemen? Doctors in Sung and Yüan." *Chinese Science* 8 (1987): 9–76.

McNeill, William. *Plagues and Peoples*. Garden City, NY: Anchor Press, 1975.

Twitchett, Denis. "Population and Pestilence in T'ang China," in *Studia Sino-Mongolica*, edited by Wolfgang Bauer (Wiesbaden: Franz Steiner Verlag, 1979), 35–68.

Chinese Traditional Medicine

The peoples of the area known historically as China had a rich and highly synthetic medical culture in ancient times. This was based largely on folk culture and practice. China's unification under the first emperors in the third century BCE created the mandate for a shared understanding of human health and illness. The classical expressions of this new orthodoxy—often called Chinese Traditional Medicine—were two pairs of texts: the divinely revealed *Inner Canon* and *Divine Husbandman's Materia medica* and the experiential *Canon of Problems* and *Treatise on Cold Damage Disorders*. Hundreds of commentaries reformulated or advanced the ideas in these texts, and hundreds of new texts supplemented the classics.

The *Inner Canon* lays out the fundamentals. Humans are microcosms that rely upon delicate balances of natural factors and fluids in the body for good health. Qi (chee) is the principle vital energy that fills the cosmos and courses through the human body. Usually this unimpeded flow helps in maintaining the proper balance of factors and fluids for good health. The principles that need to be balanced are known as yin and yang. Rather than such absolutes as body temperature or normal resting pulse rate, yin and yang are relative to each other and to the surrounding cosmos. Their imbalance results in symptoms and the imbalance itself is the pathological state. Addressing the imbalance of yin and yang by increasing the amount and freedom of flow of qi is vital. Drugs, either single ingredients or blends of several, serve many purposes: replenishing lacking blood qi; purging built up fluids; or unblocking blocked points of qi flow. The *Materia medica* originally contained 347 vegetable, animal, and mineral substances, but by the 16th century, this list had expanded to 1,900. These took the forms of pills, powders, sweetened syrups, and infusions and were the doctor's main tools. The classic *Treatise* outlined diagnosis and drug regimens for fever-producing diseases, a list greatly expanded in later centuries. Unblocking points of qi blockage is a major purpose of acupuncture, and burning certain aromatic substances on the inserted needles, known as moxibustion, enhances the effects and subsequent flow.

What the West calls plague, the Chinese would have labeled an epidemic febrile disease of one sort or another. Numerous Chinese medical texts address this type of illness from the point of view of the model briefly outlined above. Causation is never clear and included bodily imbalances of cold and warmth; unseasonable weather; exopathogens; "noxious factors;" in addition to the traditional "natural" factors blamed for fevers: wind, cold, summer heat, damp, dryness, and fire. Some even noted that traditional therapies had little effect on these deadly conditions. Shortly after the fall of the Yüan dynasty in 1368, the physician Wang Lu wrote in *Tracing the Origin of Medical Classics* that infectious epidemic fevers had to be distinguished from others. This differentiation was important in focusing attention on the illnesses that assaulted the Chinese people repeatedly over the succeeding 250 years.

One physician who benefited from this advice was the 17th-century Wu Youxing (Youke; also Yuhsing; fl. 1644). Epidemics of various types raged about him between 1641 and 1644, and he carefully observed how they differed in their onsets, courses, reactions to traditional remedies, and final outcomes. The result was his *Treatise on Pestilence* (*Wen Yi Lun*). Wu Youxing posited the existence of physical but invisible pathogens (li-qi) that enter the body from the outside through the mouth, nose, or hair tips through contact or the air. The greater the amount and virility of the pathogen will increase the likelihood of a dangerous outcome, just as the greater ability of the body to resist the "factor" with its own vital qi will decrease the likelihood. Natural forces or positive relational states of yin and yang, when well balanced in the body, will help block the pathogenic qi and maintain health. When poor diet, emotional states, or environmental factors throw off the balance, the body is weakened and the invasive bad qi accelerates the slide into sickness as it circulates in the body. This insight, derived from observation and reflection, ranks with that of Girolamo Fracastoro in Italy a century earlier.

Like Fracastoro, Youke had followers, who advanced his ideas on the etiology of febrile disease, its diagnosis, and theories on its treatment. These included the so-called "four major physicians of the Qing Dynasty:" Ye Gui (Xiang Yan; 1667–1746), Xue Xue (Piao; 1770–1761), Wu Tang (Jutong; 1758–1836), and Wang Shixiong (Mengying or Qianzhai; 1808–1866). Much of their work was practical treatment of patients and fine-tuning of Youke's theories. Without the microscope, however, Chinese medical science could go no further than Western medicine did with it.

See also: China; Contagion Theory; Fracastoro, Girolamo.

References

Benedict, Carol. *Bubonic Plague in Nineteenth-century China.* Stanford: Stanford University Press, 1996.

McNeill, William. *Plagues and Peoples.* Garden City, NY: Anchor Press, 1975.

Unschuld, Paul U. *Medicine in China.* Berkeley: University of California Press, 1988.

Xing Xiaochen, editor. *History and Development of Traditional Chinese Medicine.* Beijing: Science Press, 1999.

Christ

Christians are monotheists with a twist. Whereas Jews and Muslims, also monotheists, believe in and worship a single god (Yahweh, Allah), Christians understand God to consist of three distinct but inseparable persons: the Father, the Son (Jesus Christ), and the Holy Spirit. This is the Trinity, from tri-unity. Though a traditional belief, it was articulated at the Church Council of Nicea in 325. At the same council, the historical figure Jesus Christ ("the Anointed") was declared to be both fully God and fully human. What are accepted by believers as Jesus's teachings and actions are contained in the four biblical gospels. These are the bases for the Catholic and Orthodox Churches' sacraments, sacred rituals that include baptism, the Eucharist, Penance (confession of sins to a priest), and Last Rites, which includes taking of the Eucharist and one's last confession in preparation for death.

The gospels and biblical Apocalypse/Book of Revelation clearly teach that Christ is the "gateway" to heaven. His death by crucifixion was interpreted as a sacrifice that atoned for humanity's sinfulness and that made salvation possible for some. In this way, Christ is the Redeemer or Savior of humanity. He is also the perfect advocate for humanity before God the Father, a teaching of the final Apostle, St. Paul. On the other hand, Christ taught, "All judgment is given to me by the Father, that I might be glorified." Christ is the perfect judge who decides the fate of every human after death: damnation to hell or salvation and eternal life in heaven, as depicted in many church frescoes and sculptures as the Last Judgment. The Christian churches have always taught that Christ is at once an entity of perfect mercy and perfect justice, all loving, yet condemning many for their disobedience to God's laws (sinfulness). This balance has always been considered a mystery beyond human understanding, a matter of faith.

The role of Christ as saving/damning judge carried over into people's earthly lives as well. The Bible is a history book of God's punishment of living people for disobedience and sin. From expelling Adam and Eve from Paradise to the flood of Noah's time to the destruction of Sodom and Gomorrah to the plagues of Egypt and the conquest of sinful Jewish states, calamities have been interpreted as God's righteous punishment of people from individuals to nearly all of humanity. The end of time, too, would be preceded by great disasters, ordered by Christ and carried out by angels. Most early Christian voices declare Christ the judge also to be Christ the punisher.

Throughout the Second Pandemic, Christian clergy, physicians, and chroniclers agreed that a catastrophe as devastating as the plague was clearly under the control of Christ. His divine finger drew forth the poisonous miasmas by the action of the stars. Though writers often attributed causation simply to "God," prayers and paintings clarified the believers' meaning. In his call for prayers in July 1348, Archbishop Zouche of York in England clearly refers to Christ as both Almighty God, "kind and merciful," and as Savior to whom all should turn with their prayers. A month later, the Bishop of Bath and Wells (England) also called for prayers and penitence as plague approached, referring to Christ variously as God, Almighty God, Jesus Christ, and Lord. Another month passed and the Bishop of Exeter passed along a national call for prayers to the Lord, Lord God, and God Almighty, clearly identifying the last as the "son" of "the most Blessed and glorious Mary," clearly a reference to Christ.

In painted and printed art, the divine entity most often depicted as guiding the infliction of plague was Christ rather than the older, white-bearded divine Father or Holy Spirit (usually shown as a hovering dove). Christ often wears a burial shroud over his shoulder, a reminder of his sacrificial death and resurrection, and thus his role as savior. From Homer's *Iliad* through the first Pandemic, plague was identified with arrows falling from above. Throughout the Renaissance, angelic archers, sometimes joined by Christ himself, draw their bows as transfixed victims writhe below.

The logic of both plague art and calls for individual and communal prayers and repentance requires that Christ be able to be turned from his grim task by applications to his mercy and love. Throughout the Second Pandemic, Orthodox, Roman Catholic, and Protestant communities relied on Christ's mercy as they prayed to avoid or recover from pestilence. Catholics and Orthodox, however, also counted on the prayers of the saints in heaven, a source of spiritual aid rejected or denied by all Protestant groups. The English bishops' calls for prayers include the invocation of saints, including the Virgin Mary, Christ's mother, the Apostles, and saints especially associated with plague, for example, Sebastian, Roche, Rosalie, or Charles Borromeo. The power of the saints lay not in their own ability to affect epidemics directly but, rather, to invoke Christ's mercy on humanity's behalf. Christ may be the perfect advocate before the Father, but Christ himself was inflicting pestilence, and humanity felt the need for saintly advocates. Paintings dedicated to these saints often show them kneeling before Christ on humanity's behalf or as part of an entourage of holy friends flanking the Madonna with the vulnerable Christ-child on her lap.

See also: Apocalypse and Apocalypticism; Arrows; Art, Effects of Plague on; Bible; Causes of Plague: Historical Theories; God the Father; Plague Saints; Processions; Virgin Mary.

References

Bailey, Gauvin Alexander, et al., eds. *Hope and Healing: Painting in Italy in a Time of Plague, 1500–1800.* Chicago: University of Chicago Press, 2005.

Boeckl, Christine. *Images of Plague and Pestilence: Iconography and Iconology.* Kirksville, MO: Truman State University Press, 2000.

Lerner, Robert E. "The Black Death and Western Eschatological Mentalities." *American Historical Review* 86 (1981): 533–552.

Mormando, Franco and Thomas Worcester, eds. *Piety and Plague from Byzantium to the Baroque.* Kirksville, MO: Truman State University Press, 2007.

Pelikan, Jaroslav. *Jesus through the Centuries.* New Haven, CT: Yale University Press, 1999.

Chronicles and Annals

Annals are collections of historical information, descriptions, anecdotes, and tidbits organized roughly chronologically and with reference most often to a specific institution or locale. Chronicles are usually more narrative and interpretive in form, with a greater subjectivity and less tolerance for the merely remarkable or odd. Annals purport to record facts with little comment; chronicles attempt to make sense out of historical events and personalities. Medieval authors often used the terms interchangeably, however. By 1340, most of these historical records in northern Europe were being kept by canons, friars, monks, or other clergy, while northern Italian towns boasted lay jurists and notaries who had access to historical documents and acted as semiofficial chroniclers of the cities' political and social events. Along with official records, diaries, letters, journals, accounts, and medical advice, chronicles and annals constitute invaluable sources on medieval and early modern plague.

Annalists tended merely to record the fact that a sickness struck a particular area during a particular period. With plague, a rhetorically high death rate is sometimes appended, as is a comment on the source of the disease. Chroniclers, whether clerical or lay, begin here and expand in many descriptive and interpretive directions, depending on their interests, information, and experiences. Coverage might include "eastern" origins, moral explanations (sin and divine anger), physical or celestial causes, strange accompanying phenomena, the plague's universality, comments on symptoms or swiftness of death, numbers of victims, and such topoi as abandoned children or parents, physicians' ineffectiveness, and deserted fields and full cemeteries. Clergy might note their own high death tolls and such communal religious palliatives as processions. Many mention attacks on Jewish communities and the passage of flagellants. Death tolls are notoriously unreliable unless a monk is reporting on his community's losses. Such claims as "one in ten survived" or "100,000 perished" are clear exaggerations, but, as Horrox (3) reminds us, they are not without meaning. Such horrific figures are expressions of plague-induced terror.

Chroniclers continued writing through the 15th century, but the sense of horror of the 1340s seems left behind. Laconic references replace fuller descriptions, perhaps because plague's insistent return dulled sensitivities. Humanistically influenced histories have little to say, perhaps because their classical models—other than Thucydides—tended to avoid the low topic of disease.

The Arab world produced a few known chroniclers, for example, 15th-century Egyptians Muhammad al-Maqrizi and Ibn Taghri Birdi. From about 1500, such Ottoman court chroniclers as Selaniki Mustafa Effendi, recorded epidemics as irresistible expressions of the will of Allah. Much remains to be discovered and studied.

See also: Anti–Semitism and Anti–Jewish Violence; Flagellants; Jews; al-Maqrizi, Muhammad.

References

Cohn, Samuel K. *The Black Death Transformed: Disease and Culture in Early Renaissance Europe.* New York: Oxford University Press, 2002.

Conrad, Lawrence I. "Arabic Plague Chronologies and Treatises." *Studia Islamica* 54 (1981): 51–93.

Dale, Sharon, et al. *Chronicling History: Chronicles and Historians in Medieval and Renaissance Italy.* State College, PA: Penn State University Press, 2007.

Green, Louis. *Chronicle into History: An Essay on the Interpretation of History in Florentine Fourteenth-Century Chronicles.* New York: Cambridge University Press, 1972.

Horrox, Rosemary. *The Black Death.* New York: Manchester University Press, 1994.

Churches, Plague

Russian chroniclers report that when plague approached between 1390 and 1552, townspeople of Novgorod and Pskov built special votive churches (*obydennyie khramy*). Erected in 24 hours of fresh timbers and on "virgin soil," these temporary worship houses hosted special liturgies, and even Tsars Vasili III and Ivan IV had them built against the pestilence.

Elsewhere in Catholic Europe, communal and national governments and local Church authorities built churches either after vowing to do so (called ex voto) or spontaneously following epidemics. These combined communal thanksgiving for the plague's end with a view to spiritual prophylaxis. Often dedicated to local plague saints, whose advocacy convinced God to end the last plague, these structures helped remind the saints of the community's continued devotion. In London, monastic communities were established at the sites of East Smithfield cemetery (Cistercians, St. Mary Graces, 1350) and West Smithfield cemetery (Carthusian Charterhouse, 1371), a reminder of the importance of prayers for the dead to the Catholic Londoners. Florentines turned the city's grain storehouse into Or San Michele, dedicated to the angel whose sheathed sword signaled the end of a sixth-century Roman plague, and the Sienese built the memorial Capella della Piazza in 1352. In Ragusa, a dependency of Venice, a chapel dedicated to plague saint Sebastian (1465) proved popular and effective, so churches dedicated to plague saint Roche (1526) and the Virgin Mary (1533) followed. Venice herself has the most famous collection of plague churches. In 1478, the Scuole (confraternity) of San Rocco (St. Roche) was founded and his relics were brought to Venice in 1485. This sparked the building of the Church of San Rocco (Bartolomeo Bon, 1489–1508), which has long hosted a festival on his feast day (August 16). San Sebastiano followed immediately (1508–1548), and Andrea Palladio's Renaissance-style Redentore on the Giudecca, begun in 1577 (to 1592), followed a hard bout of plague that is still commemorated each third Sunday in July. On October 22, 1630, the plague-stricken Venetian government vowed to build Santa Maria della Salute, and Baldassare Longhena's great project began in 1631. Its floor rests on 1,200,000 oak and elm piles and announces in Latin "Whence the origin, thence the salvation." The same plague-fueled religiosity supported San Moisè (begun 1632) near San Marco. After the 1656 plague, Rome's Senate rededicated as a plague memorial Santa Maria in Campitelli, which housed a revered icon of Mary, and Naples's viceroy had Santa Maria del Pianto built (from 1662).

In the Empire, Rudolf II had Prague's St. Roch built (Giovanni Busi, 1602 on) after the 1599 epidemic on the grounds of Strahov Monastery above Hradčany Castle. Near Graz, Austria, the plague chapel at Stift Rein contained the gravestone of the parents of Emperor Maximillian II. One of Vienna's major sites is the Karlkirche (1713–1737), dedicated after the 1712 outbreak by Emperor Charles VI to Milan's archbishop Carlo Borromeo. Less grand is the plague church dedicated to Sts. Roche, Sebastian, and Fabian (1470) in Kranj, Slovenia. Lisbon's Igreja de São Roque (Jesuit Church of St. Roche) replaced a shrine built over a 1505 plague cemetery. In England, parish "plague churches" often stand alone, their plague-struck villages having been utterly depopulated or abandoned and relocated.

See also: Ex voto; Plague Memorials; Plague Saints; St. Roche; St. Sebastian; Virgin Mary.

Reference

Avery, Harold. "Plague Churches, Monuments and Memorials." *Proceedings of the Royal Society of Medicine* 59 (1966): 110–116.

Ciompi Revolt

In 1378, Florence, Italy, was in turmoil. Its population had rebounded but little from plague epidemics in 1348, 1363, and 1370 to 1371 and remained around half of its preplague apex of around 95,000 people. Florence's principal export industry was high-quality wool cloth, the production of which was multistage and required both skilled and semiskilled labor. At the lower end were the *ciompi* (CHAHM-pee), unorganized laborers whose postepidemic ranks were rather easily filled by immigrants. The international wool trade had been hard hit by the epidemics, and Florence's production had sunk from 100,000 cloths before 1348 to fewer than 24,000. Diplomatic issues, war, and increased taxes reduced production even further by July 1378. The *ciompi* organized and seized the civic government and the wool guild masters. They demanded a guild and guildhall of their own and a mandatory

annual production floor of 2,000 cloths per shop. The government crumbled, and for three and a half years, minor guildsmen governed Florence. In February 1382, city oligarchs struck back, executing *ciompi* leaders and intimidating their supporters. Historians often compare the *ciompi* revolt—its causes and aftermath—with the French Jacquerie (1358) and English Peasants' Revolt (1381). Most note the impact of rising social tensions fueled by plague, war, taxation, and the desire for a return to preplague conditions, real or imagined. Marxists celebrate these uprisings as early examples of rising lower-class consciousness and class revolution and decry the repressive reactions of late feudal and early capitalistic power structures.

See also: Demographic Effects of Plague: Europe, 1347–1400; Economic Effects of Plague in Europe; Florence, Italy; Jacquerie; Peasants' Revolt, English.

References

Cohn, Samuel K. "Popular Insurrections and the Black Death; a Comparative View." *Past and Present* 195 (2007): 188–204.

Crum, Roger J. and John Paoletti, eds. *Renaissance Florence: A Social History.* New York: Cambridge University Press, 2006.

Clement VI, Pope (1291/92–1352; r. 1342–1352)

Born Pierre Roger of lower nobility in Maumont, Corrèze, France, the future pope became a Benedictine monk and attended the University of Paris. A fine scholar and teacher, he was prematurely advanced on the University faculty. A strong supporter of the papacy, Pierre was appointed to a series of bishoprics: Arras (1328), Sens (1329), and Rouen (1330). In 1338, he was

A cameo of Pope Clement VI at Notre-Dame in Paris. When the Black Death broke out, Pope Clement VI stayed in Avignon supervising sick care, burials, and the pastoral care of the dying. (Library of Congress)

appointed a cardinal, and he was elected pope in 1342.

For three decades, the popes had resided in Avignon instead of Rome, and Clement helped make his Europe's finest court. He tolerated no challenge to papal authority. When plague struck Europe in late 1347, he directly ruled Avignon, Rome, and a swath of central Italy and was spiritual leader of all Catholics. Attempting to understand this new and horrifying phenomenon, he employed his astrologers to discern the celestial causes. After plague hit Avignon in February 1348, he ordered surgeon Guy Chauliac to conduct autopsies on victims to uncover its physiological secrets. As local spiritual leader, Clement preached against the sinfulness that had incurred God's wrath in the form of plague. Recognizing that many were dying without recourse to Last Rites, he removed the spiritual penalties from those who died without confessing their sins. Recognizing that many were disposing of corpses in the Rhône River instead of burying them in sanctified graves, he blessed the river and purchased additional land for mass cemeteries. Though he believed that crowds were a means of spreading infection, Clement imitated his predecessor Gregory I and sponsored a civic penitential procession, with barefoot flagellants from local confraternities.

As universal leader, Clement provided Catholics with a special mass for plague time. He also reacted very strongly against two movements spawned by the plague. One was the violence that destroyed Jewish communities in cities from Spain to northern Germany. Papal bulls in July and September 1348 condemned the violence, though to little effect. Clement, with the emperor, also condemned the later stages of the increasingly idiosyncratic flagellant movement. Finally, he declared 1350 to be a Jubilee Year, with special spiritual rewards for those who visited Rome as pilgrims.

See also: Anatomy and Dissection; Astrology; Bishops and Popes; Black Death (1347–1352); Flagellants; Jews; Mass Graves and Plague Cemeteries; Pilgrims and Pilgrimage; Processions; Sin.

References

Horrox, Rosemary. *The Black Death*. New York: Manchester University Press, 1994.

Wood, Diana. *Pope Clement VI: The Pontificate and Ideas of an Avignon Pope*. New York: Cambridge University Press, 1989.

Clothing

The relationship of clothing to the Second Plague Pandemic is complex. Everyone wore clothes, but most European Christian communities practiced minimal hygiene at best. Underclothing was either unknown or in its earliest stages, and bathing was rare, especially if plague was in the air. Most people had few if any changes of clothes, and these were rarely washed, especially in winter. They slept in their clothes, often an entire family in one bed, sharing all of the various bodily fluids, parasites, and pathogens the cloth may have absorbed.

From the time of Boccaccio's pig that died of rooting in contaminated rags, people feared cloth and miasma-exposed clothing. Atmospheric poison was believed to infiltrate or cling to cloth: the coarser, the more dangerous. Since plague fleas do find a home in cloth, their conclusions were not incorrect. When the rather isolated English village of Eyam blamed its 1665 outbreak on a package of clothes from plague-wracked London, they may well have been infested. On April 3, 1348, Florence passed a law banning people and goods from such infected places as Pisa and Genoa. Also in 1348, Pistoia, Italy, declared that any cloth brought into the city had to be incinerated in the main piazza. Commentators in 17th-century London echoed fears of buying any new clothing or even passing a clothier's shop. One specifically mentioned fur collars, and Londoner Samuel Pepys bought a new wig during the plague in 1665 but thought better of wearing it, since the hair might be a victim's.

Victims' clothing presented another issue. In some times and places, it was simply incinerated when the victim died or went to the pest house. Those who survived the pest house sometimes received a free shift or outfit. In 1348, Florence banned the sale or ownership of victims' clothing, but Dutch cities only suspended sales in used clothing until two months after a plague ended. In London, restrictions or bans were at the parish level. Rag pickers who supplied paper mills were also regulated during epidemics. Fumigating cloth and clothing was one answer to the wanton destruction by incineration, but how much was enough? One mark of official Islamic indifference is that victims' cloth and clothing were readily available in markets.

Prophylactic clothing could be simply a matter of shortening such gowns as priests' cassocks, as practiced in Barcelona and Milan, lest they stir up poisonous dust. One author recommended such "smooth" cloth as silk, taffeta, and satin, and cuffs and necklines that were tight, as well as changing clothes often, as did Archbishop Federigo Borromeo. Most distinctive were the "bird-suits" worn by physicians from the early 17th century. Invented in France, they became popular in Rome and Genoa and were required in Florence and Bologna during outbreaks. Covered by waxed or oil-cloth from head to feet, the doctor wore gloves, goggles, and a beak-like structure filled with aromatics to "filter" the air he breathed.

Sumptuary laws were also an effect of plague. Clothing was a signal of status, and many cities had to pass laws re-restricting use of certain rich materials or styles lest newly well-off lower classes be mistaken for their betters. This might include wearing ill-gotten fancy clothes of wealthy victims.

See also: Disinfection and Fumigation; Eyam, England; Miasma Theory; Physicians; Sumptuary Laws.

References

Byrne, Joseph. *Daily Life during the Black Death*. Westport, CT: Greenwood, 2006.

Hayward, Maria. *Rich Apparel: Clothing and the Law in Henry VIII's England*. Burlington, VT: Ashgate, 2009.

Nicholas, David. *The Domestic Life of a Medieval City: Women, Children and the Family in Fourteenth Century Ghent*. Lincoln, NE: University of Nebraska Press, 1985.

Compendium of Paris

As plague approached Paris in spring 1348, French King Philip VI called upon the College of Masters of the Medical Faculty of the University of Paris (49 Masters of Medicine) to prepare a medical *consilium* on the new and dreadful disease. A consilium was a standard medical report, generally requested of an expert, in which the causes, course, preventatives, and remedies of a given disease were laid out. Several plague *consilia* had already been written in Italy and southern France, but Philip wanted his recently installed medical faculty to create a definitive version. The *Compendium de epidemia* was their first known collective written effort. As the professors probably examined no victims, the vast bulk of their report was largely based on four classic medical sources—Aristotle, Hippocrates, Galen, and the Persian Avicenna—whose works informed any medical discussion of the day. The *Compendium* is thus very academic, reflecting the period's scholastic structure of teaching. The discussion of symptoms and course is purely speculative, missing the observations recorded in *consilia* of plague-experienced physicians. Nonetheless, this was perhaps the most influential medical tract of the period.

Though unmentioned, perhaps out of respect to the theologians, God used the celestial bodies to corrupt the atmosphere, creating a miasma that poisoned human victims. This effect was exacerbated by air-corrupting earthly "exhalations" and noxious vapors from rotting corpses and swamps. But God also provided medicine to protect and cure. The Masters accepted Galen's humoral theory of human health and sickness and laid out standard prevention and treatment regimens. To prevent contracting plague, maintain a diet that balanced the humors and avoid miasma by relocating or fumigating the air, they taught; and avoid strong passions that might overheat the body or cool it too much. Remedies were generally purgatives expected to rid the body of the disease and included phlebotomy, emetics, and other strong drugs.

Compendium's success was immediate. It was abridged, transformed into poetry, and translated into French and German, and many copies and versions still exist. Its less direct impacts on European medical plague literature for a century are also pronounced.

See also: Consilia and Plague Tracts; Galen and Galenism; Humoral Theory; Miasma Theory.

References

Getz, Faye Marie. *Medicine in the Middle Ages*. Princeton, NJ: Princeton University Press, 1998.

Horrox, Rosemary. *The Black Death*. New York: Manchester University Press, 1994.

O'Boyle, Cornelius. *The Art of Medicine: Medical Teaching at the University of Paris, 1250–1400*. Boston: Brill, 1998.

Confraternities

Confraternities were brotherhoods of Catholic laymen, usually in a town or city, who gathered for religious or charitable purposes. Though origins are rather sketchy, the early Franciscan movement from the mid-1200s emphasized a common and active Christian life that was at the heart of confraternal life.

Brothers could accept help when needed and a proper burial when the time came. While some confraternities were associated with particular occupations or guilds, most were not. Confraternities did, however, tend to specialize. In Italy, *laudesi* groups gathered to sing hymns in honor of the Virgin Mary; and *disciplinati*, dating back to 1260, met in dark places. Here they beat themselves or one another with flagella, multithonged whips, as a form of penance for the world's sin, giving rise to the flagellant movement. Other confraternities distributed charity to the needy, and some saw that abandoned corpses were buried.

During epidemics, the work of confraternities could be extremely important. From serving the needy refugees, widows, and orphans to collection and burial of corpses, public displays of flagellating penance (in hoods for anonymity), and participation in intercessory processions, brothers kept busy. Epidemics reduced their numbers, of course, requiring new and perhaps less committed members. Brothers can sometimes be seen in ex voto images of Mary, who protects them with her outstretched cape

See also: Cellites and Alexians; Ex voto; Flagellants; Friars (Mendicants); Poverty and Plague; Prayer and Fasting; Processions; Virgin Mary.

References

Banker, James R. *Death and the Community: Memorialization and Confraternities in an Italian Commune in the Late Middle Ages.* Athens: University of Georgia Press, 1988.

Marshall, Louise. "Confraternity and Community: Mobilizing the Sacred in Times of Plague," in *Confraternities and the Visual Arts in Renaissance Italy: Ritual, Spectacle, Image,* edited by Barbara Wisch and Diane Cole Ahl (New York: Cambridge University Press, 2000), 20–45.

Consilia and Plague Tracts

When a medical case required a second physician's expertise, the first requested a *consilium* from the better informed or more experienced colleague. The expert prepared a summary of what he knew of the case, what caused the condition, what developments the attending physician should be prepared for, what remedies should be used, and the likelihood of success. Both professionals shared the Galenic paradigm of health and disease and the *consilium* was a by-the-numbers response to professional query. A *tract* or *tractate* differed in that its author had not been consulted but rather was putting himself forward as an expert to a nonspecific audience. Their predecessors were *regimens* (rules) of health. They might be organized idiosyncratically, and the author might not be a practicing physician. Plague *consilia* disappear after 1348 in favor of the increasingly generic plague tracts, most of which were in fact penned by physicians and read like *consilia*.

When plague struck Europe in late 1347 and 1348, most medical practitioners recognized it as a new and terribly dangerous condition. The resulting *consilia* were directed to the disease rather than a specific patient's case. Physician Gentile da Foligno was a storied physician who was asked by medical guilds in Genoa, Naples, and his own Perugia to enlighten them. He provided causes, nature of the disease, prophylaxes, remedies, and medical school questions (*dubia*). The French king Philip VI required a *consilium* of the medical faculty at the University of Paris. The resulting *Compendium*, with its emphasis on astrological causation, became a template for French and German plague authors. Jacme d'Agramont, a lecturer at the University of Leida (Lerida) in Aragon, was asked by town authorities to produce a *consilium* for public use. The Catalan *Regiment de preservació de pestiléncia* of April 24, 1348, is directed specifically to "the benefit of the people" and not to physicians. He emphasized atmospheric miasma and presented pointed public preventative and remedial measures that required no specifically medical participation. Ultimately, he wrote, the best medicines were repentance and confession.

The second rounds of plague in the early 1360s invited new texts. Papal surgeon Guy de Chauliac included the equivalent of a short Latin plague treatise in his 1363 *Cyrurgia magna* or *Inventory or Collection of Surgical Medicine*. Translated into several European vernaculars and printed more than 60 times, it remained popular well into the 17th century. In 1364, papal physician and chancellor of Montpellier's medical faculty Johannes Jacobi wrote a Latin plague tract that appeared 90 years later in Scandinavia under a bishop's name as the *Canutus Tract*. The Latin text appeared in 21 editions before 1500 and in highly successful English versions as *A Little Book for the Pestilence* in 1485 and by Thomas Paynell as *A Much Profitable Treatise against Pestilence* in the 1520s. In or shortly after 1365, the Liège medical professor known as John of Burgundy wrote his own tract, of which 100 manuscripts survive in five languages. Only an English-language version was ever printed, but it remained current to 1580.

These classic texts continued the pattern: causes, course of the disease, preventative action, and remedies. The balance among these varied by the author's taste, also reflecting balances among humoralism, miasma theory, celestial causation, and divine anger. Printing made tracts cheaper and more widely available after 1450 and vernacular texts made them readable, though Latin works still appeared for professionals. From the mid-16th century, following tracts often replaced physicians' care, which was increasingly unavailable even in large cities and was in any case prohibitively expensive. In England, the genre became blurred as political and social criticism or calls for moral regeneration mimicked plague treatises during the late Tudor and Stuart periods. Yet the original genre continued to flourish. In France, for example, the epidemic at Marseille in 1720 to 1722 prompted more plague tracts than any comparable outbreak.

See also: Arabic-Persian Medicine and Practitioners; *Canutus* (*Kanutus*) Plague Tract; Chauliac, Guy de (Guido de Cauliaco); *Compendium of Paris*; Gentile da Foligno; Jews; John of Burgundy; Plague Orders and National Authorities.

References

Agrimi, Joel and Chiara Cristiani. *Les consilia médicaux*. Turnhout: Brepols, 1994.

Alexander, John. "Ivan Vien and the First Comprehensive Plague Tractate in Russian." *Medical History* 24 (1980): 419–431.

Barkai, Ron. "Jewish Treatises on the Black Death (1350–1500): A Preliminary Study," in *Practical Medicine from Salerno to the Black Death*, edited by Luis Garcia-Ballester, et al. (New York: Cambridge University Press, 1994), 6–25.

Cohn, Samuel K. *The Black Death Transformed: Disease and Culture in Early Renaissance Europe*. New York: Oxford University Press, 2002.

Cohn, Samuel K. *Cultures of Plague: Medical Thinking at the End of the Renaissance*. New York: Oxford University Press, 2010.

Fabbri, Christiane. "Continuity and Change in Late Medieval Plague Medicine: A Survey of 152 Plague Tracts from 1348 to 1599." Ph.D. dissertation, Yale University, 2006.

Henderson, John. "The Black Death in Florence: Medical and Communal Responses," in

Death in Towns, edited by Steven Bassett (New York: Leicester University Press, 1992), 136–150.

Mikołajczyk, Renata. "Examples of Medieval Plague Treatises from Central Europe." *Annual of Medieval Studies at the CEU* (1996–1997): 229–235.

Palazzotto, Dominick. "The Black Death and Medicine: A Report and Analysis of the Tractates Written between 1348 and 1350." Ph.D. dissertation, University of Kansas, 1974.

Singer, Dorothy W. "The Plague Tractates." *Proceedings of the Royal Society of Medicine* (History of Medicine) 9:2 (1915–16): 159–212.

Winslow, Charles Edward and M. Duran-Reynals. "Jacme d'Agramont and the First of the Plague Tractates." *Bulletin of the History of Medicine* 22 (1948): 747–765.

Constantinople/Istanbul

Constantinople was a hub linking the Black and Mediterranean Seas, Anatolia with the Balkans, and Asia with Europe. It thrived as the commercial, administrative, and religious center of the Eastern Roman—Byzantine—Empire. During the sixth-century reign of Justinian, Constantinople was struck heavily by plague, as witnessed and recorded by several sources. Repeatedly stricken, it always revived by drawing people and resources from its empire.

The Black Death arrived probably by ship from the Black Sea region in summer 1347. Emperor John VI Cantacuzenos, an educated aristocrat, was an acute observer of the epidemic that took his 13-year-old son's life. Though influenced by Thucydides' literary description of the Plague of Athens, he noted such differences as spread by contagion and through seaport cities. The city's suffering was also recorded by Nikephoros Gregoras and in a letter by Demetrios Kydones, who reported the multiplication of graves, deaths of friends, flight and abandonment, and the utter ineffectiveness of physicians. In Thessaly, John's cousin the governor died, which opened the region to Serbian invasion. The year-long epidemic took a terrible toll, though not the eight of every nine reported by Westerners. Constantinople suffered repeatedly during the following century, with sources listing at least 10 times between 1350 and 1400. Its position as the last vestige of the Empire and its maritime and overland trade meant that plague was regularly reintroduced from all sides.

Turkish military pressure swelled under Mehmet II, who conquered the isolated city of 50,000 in 1453. Henceforth the center of the Ottoman Turkish Empire, Constantinople revived as Istanbul, though slowly at first. Immigration quickened growth, which was in turn dampened by at least one or two percent loss to plague per year. Heavy epidemics hit between 1491 and 1503, especially in 1491 to 1493, according to the 16th-century historians Mustafa Ali and Hora Saadettin. Another round in 1511 to 1514 was followed by Turkish victories in Egypt, which tied Cairo and Alexandria directly to Istanbul, especially as a source of grain. Historian Nükhet Varlik notes that plague became essentially endemic in Istanbul from 1520 to 1529, 1533 to 1549, 1552 to 1567, and nearly continuously for the century's last three decades, with epidemics originating in the West. Daniel Panzac, however, locates reservoirs rather in the Hejaz (Mecca) and southern Russia.

Varlik attributes the increased frequency of outbreaks to Istanbul's new position at the center of an expansive and well-connected empire. Population growth in Anatolia, however, allowed Istanbul to replace its losses and maintain around 500,000 inhabitants down to 1800. Further outbreaks occurred in 1603, 1611 to 1613, 1647 to 1649, 1653 to

1656, 1659 to 1666, 1671 to 1680, 1685 to 1695, and from 1697 to 1701. Eighteenth-century Istanbul suffered 64 plague years, and from 1800 to 1850, another 30 years, until imperial quarantine and isolation procedures appear to have ended the cycle. Yet of 94 plague years in Istanbul from 1700 to 1850, 83 (88 percent) had population losses estimated at one percent or less, and only six years with losses greater than 5 percent (1705, 1726, 1751, 1778, 1812, and 1836).

Like Muslims elsewhere, Turks have been viewed as indifferent to plague's ravages, doing little to counteract it. Even prayer is only mentioned twice, around 1567, when Selim II called for services in Ayasofya (Hagia Sophia) Mosque, and again in 1592, when Murad III demanded two plus a procession. Varlik, however, reinterprets inactivity as resignation rather than indifference: God imposed the plague, and most outbreaks were light; plague death was release to paradise for the good Muslim and thus neither to be feared nor resisted.

See also: Arabic-Persian Medicine and Practitioners; Black Death (1347–1352); Cairo, Egypt; Islam and Medicine; Islamic Civil Responses; Islamic Religious Responses; Mecca; Merchants; Mongols; Public Health; *Ta'un*; Venice, Italy.

References

Boyar, Ebru and Kate Fleet. *A Social History of Ottoman Istanbul*. New York: Cambridge University Press, 2010.

Nicol, Donald. *The Reluctant Emperor: Biography of John Cantacuzenos, Byzantine Emperor and Monk, c. 11295–1383*. New York: Cambridge University Press, 1996.

Panzac, Daniel. *La Peste dans l'Empire Ottoman. 1700–1860*. Louvain: Editions Peeters, 1985.

Schamiloglu, Uli. "The Rise of the Ottoman Empire: The Black Death in Medieval Anatolia and Its Impact on Turkish Civilization," in *Views from the Edge*, edited by Neguin Yavari, et al. (New York: Columbia University Press, 2004), 255–279.

Shefer-Mossensohn, Miri. *Ottoman Medicine: Healing and Medical Institutions, 1500–1700*. Albany, NY: State University of New York, 2009.

Varlick, Nükhet. "Disease and Empire: A History of Plague and Epidemics in the Early Ottoman Empire (1453–1600)." Ph.D. dissertation, University of Chicago, 2008.

Contagion Theory

When the Black Death struck, Western medicine had two different theories of how one contracted a disease. Ancient humoral theory posited that disease was caused by an imbalance among the body's humors, attributable to a number of factors but especially diet. Equally ancient miasma theory blamed illness on "corrupted" air that entered the body and created a poison. Such poison could, some reasoned, affect humors, contributing to an imbalance. Neither humoralism nor miasma theory, however, easily admitted that an illness thus generated could be transmitted from a sick person to a well person. Nonetheless, common experience dictated that people with given symptoms often passed these along. Since Aristotelian philosophy could not accept action by one object on another at a distance, the mechanism was simply labeled *contagion*, from *contact*. The implication for avoiding disease was avoiding contact with the sick, which neither humoralism nor miasma theory dictated. This was passively achieved through flight and actively through isolation or expulsion of the sick person.

Pre–Islamic Arabs accepted contagion, which placed the spread of disease, including plague in the sixth and seventh centuries, in the hands of people and random events.

Islam's Prophet Muhammad believed all to be in God's (Allah's) hands, especially a force as powerful as plague. He taught that there was no contagion, but nonetheless never to enter or leave a plague-stricken area. Even so, some Muslims believed the air around a victim's head was similarly corrupted, and this mini-miasma could transmit disease. Spanish Arab physician Lisad ad-Din ibn al-Khatib experienced the Black Death and concluded that plague accompanied the plague-stricken, who transmitted it to others. Contagion was, he challenged, proven through the senses, research, and autopsies. Two decades later, the poet and physician Ali ibn Khatma al-Ansari wrote, again from his experience, that the sick transmit the identical disease to the well. These, however, remained minority opinions.

Both Christian physicians and civil authorities treated the Black Death as a transmissible disease. An anonymous physician of Montpellier claimed it was passed by sight, like basilisk poison; many wrote that poison was passed through tainted breath or emanation from pores. In the 1200s, despite humoralism and miasma, medical literature recognized 13 contagious diseases, and most were content later to add plague. Contagion gained support from the common observation that those who served the dead and dying, including priests, notaries, gravediggers, and doctors, readily died too. Laymen also noted that physical objects exposed to plague sufferers gained the ability to transmit the disease. Boccaccio's famous pigs rooted in "infected" clothing and quickly succumbed. The King of Aragon isolated both the sick and those who looted their "contagious" belongings. Milanese court physician Pietro da Tossignano warned in his *consilium* against moving to a place that had been struck, even after six months, since *reliquae* remain behind and will infect the

newcomer. The nature of such *reliquae* would remain a mystery.

As one epidemic followed another, miasma theory remained in place, but the recognized fact was that plague victims transmitted plague. Isolation of carriers through bans, pest houses, quarantines, shutting in, and later cordons sanitaires ignored miasma theory, while fumigation through localized disinfectant, neighborhood bonfires, and gunfire were attempts to redress corrupted air. Practice by authorities, however, outstripped the medical establishment's theory. Was the poison in the air or in the breath of the infected person? Or did the poisonous breath of the victim contaminate the atmosphere? Was touch necessary or was contact with the exhalations enough to transmit the disease? If the latter, then why did not everyone around the victim succumb or at least catch the plague?

The 16th century saw the revival of theories dating from the first centuries BCE and CE by the Romans Varro and Columella. Both posited that disease was caused by "animalcules," tiny, airborne animals that enter the human body through the nostrils and mouth. These insights remained dormant until early 17th-century microscopes revealed such animalcules, which led such men as Athanasius Kircher to theorize about living pathogens (1658). More typical was the thinking of men, for example, Girolamo Fracastoro (1546), who thought the airborne particles "seedlets," and Paracelsians, who openly attacked Galenism. Paracelsians insisted that disease was a matter of external occult forces, or perhaps tiny particles that entered and attacked specific body parts. No more organic were the "atoms" or "fomites" that physicians proposed: these, like odors, stuck to all surfaces, including the human respiratory organs and pores, and could be breathed out into a miniature miasma.

These notions led in three directions. In one, carriers were considered less victims than morally responsible transmitters of death. Plague and its victims were increasingly associated with poverty, filth, moral corruption, and social disorder. Societies accepted harsh actions against such vile creatures in order to protect society. The second, and contrary to the first, was the Calvinist predestination-inspired anticontagionism, which, like Islam, argued that all was in God's control. These "stoical Christians" saw as useless all attempts to battle plague, excepting repentance and trust in God. In England, from 1588, official plague orders forbade on pain of prison the undermining of contagionism and, by extension, such associated measures as quarantine, shutting in, and pest houses. In the third, physicians and authorities accepted a number of meanings of contagion, as with Girolamo Mercuriale (1577): transmission by direct contact of sick and well; infection by contact with fomite-contaminated objects; and infection by an unspecified pathogen through the air.

See also: Boyle, Robert; Fracastoro, Girolamo; Galen and Galenism; Germ Theory; Humoral Theory; Ibn al-Khatib, Lisad ad-Din; Kircher, Athanasius; Miasma Theory; Paracelsus and Paracelsianism; Public Health; Quarantine; Shutting In.

References

Carlin, Claire, ed. *Imagining Contagion in Early Modern Europe.* New York: Palgrave Macmillan, 2005.

Carmichael, Ann. "Contagion Theory and Contagion Practice in Fifteenth-century Milan." *Renaissance Quarterly* 44 (1991): 213–256.

Kinzelbach, Annemarie. "Infection, Contagion, and Public Health in Late Medieval and Early Modern German Imperial Towns." *Journal of the History of Medicine and Allied Sciences* 61 (2006): 369–389

Stearns, Justin. *Infectious Ideas: Contagion in Premodern Islamic and Christian Thought in the Western Mediterranean.* Baltimore, MD: Johns Hopkins University Press, 2011.

Cordons Sanitaires

Despite the general acceptance of miasma theory, during the Second Pandemic, observers noted that plague traveled with people. Whether pilgrims, armies, merchants, vagabonds, refugees, gypsies, or itinerant craftspeople, during plague outbreaks, people on the move were considered a threat to the safety of cities and, somewhat later, regions. Such people had to be kept out. Conversely, those who would leave a plague-infected area were expected to carry plague. Cities and regions experimented with isolating such areas and the people in them in hopes of stopping plague's spread, which led to the concept of *cordons sanitaires*, or health boundaries. Medieval walled cities and towns had limited access points—gates—that were easy to seal off from either inside or outside the walls. Unwalled suburbs, towns, and villages, let alone regions, presented many difficulties if passage in or out were to be banned effectively.

Travel bans to or from plague-stricken areas developed early and in Italy among the northern city-states. In January 1348, Lucca banned entry to anyone from Catalonia, Genoa, or the Romagna; in Visconti territories, Milan, Parma, and Padua denied access to any foreigners; and Venice restricted access to ambassadors. Bills of Health developed to aid in this process of discrimination, though documents could be forged and guards bribed. Seaports kept ships at anchor until their crews and cargoes were declared free of disease. In Portugal, when Coimbra suffered an epidemic in 1477 to 1479, officials in Oporto established a screen of soldiers between the cities in an attempt to isolate Coimbra. This went beyond normal procedures for denying entrance to anyone coming from a plague-stricken area. In 1486, Oporto walled up a street on which plague had been discovered, a technique used first in Milan in 1348 and later in many European cities.

The 16th century saw further developments. Quarantine facilities were placed in strategic places outside cities and ports to house those thought to have been exposed to the plague. In northern Italy, regional borders became more clearly established between the increasingly centralized powers centered on Milan, Florence, Venice, and Rome. Guard posts appeared at borders along major roads, along with quarantine facilities in some places. But miles of unguarded frontier stretched between these posts, making them more porous than effective. The Holy Roman Empire also established a geographical boundary between itself and the Turks to the south, at first along the southern frontiers of Croatia and Hungary. This *Militärgrenze*, or military border, was an early stage in what evolved two centuries later into a most effective health boundary, or in French, a *cordon sanitaire*. In the 17th century the cordon sanitaire became much more widely used by both civic and regional authorities. Such English towns as Sandwich (1610, 1644), Presteigne (1636), and most famously Eyam (1666) agreed to have themselves sealed off in return for regular delivery of bread for victims and survivors. Elsewhere, the application was more coercive. In 1629, the town of Digne, France, suffered plague deaths, and the surrounding towns posted armed guards around Digne as if besieging it. Digne's neighbors felt so threatened that

many advocated firebombing the unfortunate town to eradicate the disease. When a cordon was erected, as at Girona, Spain, in 1650, soldiers were often ordered to shoot anyone attempting to escape. Stakes marked the boundary line and exchange points were established, where money could be spent on food and other necessities. Potentially tainted coins were place on a "plague stone," often in the midst of a stream, or were washed in vinegar or passed through a flame for disinfection.

When the very serious plague of 1630 struck Bologna in May, the well-organized officials of the Grand Duke of Tuscany ordered a series of actions establishing a cordon sanitaire: travelers were required to show health passes or bills of health; each town was to have an officer in charge of these; on June 12, troops were posted to the northern border, camping no more than three miles apart; on the same date, all frontier residents were deputized to protect the border, to ring bells if any dared pass, and to follow any who did; at the gates of towns that still had walls, more and better-paid guards were posted. Florence still suffered; about 10 percent of its 70,000 residents died that summer. At Tuscany's southern border, papal guards delayed the passage of people and even mail (30 days): Florentine astronomer Galileo had to correspond through Genoa, which added 12 days to a postal journey. Papal guards stripped books of their covers, which were burned, and fumigated the pages with smoke before letting them pass. This process presented fateful delays to the publication in Rome of Galileo's seminal *Dialogue on the Two Chief World Systems*.

When plague struck Marseille in 1720, the Spanish erected a cordon with France, and the French army itself surrounded Provence with one quarter of all of its cavalry units and one third of its infantry. In the 18th century, Austria's *Militärgrenze* was formally transformed into a cordon sanitaire in 1710 and following the Peace of Passarowitz (1719) by imperial decrees (*Pestpatente*) of 1728, 1737, and 1770. It was directly controlled from Vienna by the Imperial Court War Council. Peasant soldiers served active duty for five months annually, guarding 1,000 miles of frontier with more than 100,000 mobilized men in 692 units by 1799. Many credit these efforts with ending the Second Pandemic.

See also: Bills of Health; Broadsheets, Broadsides, and Pamphlets; Civil Governments; Contagion Theory; Crime and Punishment; End of Second Plague Pandemic: Theories; Eyam, England; Flight; Lazarettos and Pest Houses; London, Great Plague of (1665–1666); Marseille, France; Plague Stone; Quarantine; Shutting In.

References

Christensen, Daniel. *Politics and the Plague in Early Modern Germany*. Saarbrücken: Verlag Müller, 2008.

Eckert, Edward. "The Retreat of Plague from Central Europe, 1640–1720: A Geomedical Approach." *Bulletin of the History of Medicine* 74 (2000): 1–28.

Rothenberg, Gunther. "The Austrian Sanitary Cordon and the Control of Bubonic Plague: 1710–1871." *Journal of the History of Medicine and Allied Sciences* 28 (1973): 15–23.

Slack, Paul. *The Impact of Plague in Tudor and Stuart England*. New York: Oxford University Press, 1990.

Corpse Carriers

"So many will lie dead in the houses that men will go through the streets crying 'Send forth your dead!' And the dead will be heaped on carts and horses; they will be piled and burnt. Men will pass through the streets crying aloud, 'Are there any dead?'" (Levine, 332). So warned Florence's religious reformer and prophet Girolamo Savonarola in the mid-1490s. Like most prophets, he spoke from experience as much as foresight. Throughout the Second Pandemic, cities had need of the "terrible men" who cleared away the human debris. Day after day the tumbrels, or carts, rolled behind the horses along their set routes, stopping all too often to retrieve a corpse left huddled in an alleyway, or to break into a house once occupied by the living to carry out the dead, or to allow a corpse to be dropped from a window onto the pile below. In Venice, men in barges called *piatte* plied the canals hooking floating corpses and calling out "*corpi morti!*" (dead bodies). People who withheld corpses from these collectors were liable to a heavy fine. Like scavenger animals, these men played a vital role in the urban ecology, removing the dead lest their putrefaction add to the miasma to which so many attributed the plague. William Dene in his *Rochester Chronicle* for 1348 lamented "no one could be found to carry the bodies of the dead to burial, but men and women carried the bodies of their own little ones to church on their shoulders and threw them into mass graves" (Horrox, 71). However terrible, corpse carriers saved survivors that last, soul-jarring errand.

Depending on the size of the city and the severity of the outbreak, the municipal gravediggers themselves might serve as corpse carriers, as at Barcelona in 1651. They were accompanied by a plague warden, who cleared the streets of onlookers as the tumbrels passed. At Pistoia, 16 men were elected to serve as "*becchini*" in 1348. These, like countless others across Europe who volunteered, received salaries, if they lived to

Seventeenth-century illustration of plague victims being collected and loaded on a cart in Rome. Note the becchini are smoking tobacco to purify the air. (Courtesy of the National Library of Medicine)

collect them. Like gravediggers, physicians, priests, and notaries, corpse carriers had continued contact with the dying and dead and stood an excellent chance of contracting the disease. With their vague notion of contagion, civil authorities often sequestered corpse carriers and gravediggers, forbidding them any contact with the healthy until after the end of an epidemic plus a quarantine period. Violating this ban was one of the typical crimes committed by these men. Others were directly related to their access to homes: assault, rape, theft, and vandalism.

Corpse carriers maintained their health the best they could, many wearing amulets or chewing nuts or other objects they believed would protect them. In 17th-century Milan, public health magistrates provided gravediggers and corpse carriers with sacks of powder to wear around the neck. They contained sulphur, arsenic, Palestinian incense, carnations, nutmeg, myrrh, radish leaves, ginger root, orange peel, peony leaves, mastic, and rue seeds and were believed to ward off airborne poisons. Others smoked pipes while on duty: the calming effect was joined to the belief that tobacco smoke counteracted and purified the miasma or poisoned air. Galen had warned against becoming depressed, as negative moods weakened one's resistance. In Barcelona, at least, the carriers took the advice, as tanner Miquel Parets noted in 1651: they "go about playing their guitars, tambourines, and other instruments in order to forget such great afflictions" (106). When such prophylactics failed and urban death tolls mounted, new recruits had to be found. Though they had to be even more closely supervised than earlier volunteers, galley slaves and prisoners of war who volunteered to serve were promised freedom by maritime cities, while other cities reluctantly utilized the denizens of their prisons.

See also: Civil Governments; Corpses; Crime and Punishment; Gravediggers; Lazarettos and Pest Houses; Mass Graves and Plague Cemeteries; Prisoners; Public Sanitation; Tumbrels.

References

Horrox, Rosemary. *The Black Death*. New York: Manchester University Press, 1994.

Levine, David. *At the Dawn of Modernity*. Berkeley: University of California Press, 2001.

Parets, Miquel. *A Journal of the Plague Year: The Diary of the Barcelona Tanner Miquel Parets, 1651.* Translated by James S. Amelang. New York: Oxford University Press, 1995.

Corpses

For most cultures, the dead human body is to be abandoned or disposed of as quickly as possible. Its rapid decomposition, especially in warmer, damper climes, is unsightly and nauseating in its stench. In medieval and early modern cultures, people confronted the dead far more often than we do today. Accidents were often fatal and the elderly usually died at home, where wakes and other prefunerary rituals were held. Unlike Jews and Muslims, Christians surrounded their houses of worship with corpses, symbolizing the spiritual community that survives death.

The horrors of plague were many, and most involved human corpses. Rotting corpses had long been blamed for generation of disease. A century before the Black Death, the knightly Sire de Joinville wrote of the "infectious smell" of battlefield dead that permanently sickened the living. Milan's Archbishop Federigo Borromeo opined during the 1630 epidemic, "without doubt the heaps of cadavers and the disgusting stench nourished and fed the contagion." In 1720, Marseille's Dr. Bertrand described the "infection arising from the mass of putrid corpses" that he believed supported the "impure particles" that caused plague. From 1348, many cities required special treatment of individual bodies: Venice banned exhibition of corpses and Pistoia required that they be sealed in a box so "the odors do not escape."

The volume of corpses produced during an epidemic strained society's capacities for handling them. Prefunerary, funerary, and burial customs and rituals were suspended. Respect for individuals disappeared as corpses were heaped on carts called tumbrels, carted off to mass graves, and dumped unceremoniously. In 1347, Southern Italians burned the bodies of refugees from plague-stricken Messina. In 1348, the pope blessed the waters of the Rhône River, into which hundreds of corpses had been dumped, only to reappear downriver. In 1349, Tournai forbade churchyard burials, effectively severing the sacred ties between living and dead. Since anyone could succumb to pestilence, every legal restriction on ritual, every chance encounter with a cadaver in the street was a personal encounter with one's own death, which could be as impersonal and unnoticed as any other's. But moralizing artists and poets never tired of using corpses as reminders of mortality and the vanity of earthly values, from cadaveral dialogues to "Triumphs of Death," "Meetings of the Three Living and Three Dead," and *memento mori* images.

From the pope in 1348 to 18th-century court officials in Vienna, Paris, and Moscow, orders went out to study corpses for better understanding of plague. Given the low level of physiological and even anatomical understanding, however, autopsies revealed little, except that examiners could also be infected.

See also: Anatomy and Dissection; Corpse Carriers; Danse Macabre; Funerals; Gravediggers; Lazarettos and Pest Houses; Mass Graves and Plague Cemeteries; Miasma Theory; Public Sanitation; "Three Living Meet the Three Dead;" Transi Tombs; Tumbrels.

References

Gordon, Bruce and Peter Marshall, eds. *The Place of the Dead.* New York: Cambridge University Press, 2000.

Halevi, Leor. *Muhammad's Grave: Death Rites and the Making of Islamic Society.* New York: Columbia University Press, 2007.

Park, Katherine. "The Life of the Corpse: Division and Dissection in Late Medieval Europe." *Journal of the History of Medicine* 50 (1995): 111–132.

Couvin, Simon de (Symon de Covino; c. 1320–1367)

Simon hailed from near Couvin in modern Belgium. He is believed to have studied theology in Paris from 1345 to 1355, but a later borrower of his work claimed he studied at Montpellier. He probably studied with parish funds from Couvin and was later made a canon at Liège's cathedral.

The Black Death struck while Couvin was in Paris, and he penned his only known work, the allegorical poem *Libellus de iudicio Solis in conviviis Saturni, seu de horrenda ille peste* (little book on the judgment of the Sun at the banquet of Saturn, or concerning the horrors of the plague), in 1349 to 1350. Like many theologians and physicians, Couvin was cross-trained in medicine and theology, and both are evident in the four-part, 1,132-line poem in hexameters. The long prologue (in Horrox) explains the astrological allegory. Saturn convokes the gods/planets for a banquet at which he lays out the case against humanity, which he claims is worse than in the days of Noah. Jupiter's defense of humans fails to sway the judge, the Sun, and a murderous plague is deemed fitting punishment. Saturn, Jupiter, and Mercury were to join (there was in fact an astronomical conjunction in 1345) together to carry out the sentence. Neither Juno's pleas nor physicians' remedies can help, though in Part Four, Couvin provides descriptions of the suffering and remedies. In fine, God punishes humankind through the agency of the planets, a mainstream medical belief of the day.

See also: Astrology; Black Death (1347–1352); Consilia and Plague Tracts; Poetry, European.

References

Friedman, John B. "Henryson's *Testament of Cresseid* and the *Judicio Solis in Conviviis Saturni* of Simon de Couvin." *Modern Philology* 82 (1985): 12 ff.

Renardy, Christine. "Un témoin de la Grande Peste: Maître Simon de Couvin, chanoine de Saint-Jean l'Évangéliste à Liège." *Revue belge de philologie et d'histoire* 52 (1974): 273–292.

Crime and Punishment

Crime incidence rose during times of plague because of both desperation and opportunity. Throughout the Second Pandemic, many believed that certain crimes (read: sins) angered God and prompted him to send the pestilence as punishment. Communities faced with the disease often passed new prohibitions or ramped up enforcement, including expelling prostitutes, vagabonds, and other unsavory characters. Though brothels were legal, in 1581, Seville's authorities rounded up 70—mostly innocent—women on suspicion of prostitution just before Holy Week as prophylaxis against plague.

Once plague struck, many towns and cities—more as time passed—enacted laws meant to minimize the damage the disease could wreak. Definitions of crime, seriousness of enforcement, and severity and types of punishment varied widely across time and space, but patterns are clear. Hiding the sick or corpses from authorities or burying corpses secretly was generally a criminal act. Laws forbade gathering in crowds or conducting funerals. When victims and their families were barricaded in their houses, they became criminals if they opened doors or windows or walked about without their wands or at times other than those designated by law. Outsiders who crossed the threshold for anything other than official business also broke the law. Possession, trading, or selling of clothing, bedding, furnishings, or other goods belonging to victims risked contagion and was usually punishable, more heavily if they were obtained by theft. Accepting or possessing merchandise from cities with which trade was barred due to plague also risked contagion and could result in strict punishment. Breaking cordons sanitaires or other plague barriers, whether entering or leaving a stricken area, usually bore heavy penalties. Though suspicion of witchcraft was rarely connected with plague, there were times when Jews, Gypsies, and others were charged with poisoning wells and even doorknobs.

Being sick but among the healthy risked contagion, as did being healthy and spending time among the sick or functionaries, for example, corpse carriers and gravediggers. Those who entered victims' houses to carry out the dead or to clean or fumigate were often charged with theft, bribery, physical violence, rape, dereliction of duty, and even murder through poisoning, smothering, or violence. Charges of necrophilia and witchcraft also attached to some of these intruders. Gravediggers, too, were charged with theft, murder, drunkenness, and mixing with the healthy. Civil and health board magistrates were subject to charges of flight, theft, negligence, bribery, and other forms of corruption.

Whether social disintegration was mild or intense, normal criminal activity increased, with miscreants taking advantage of the difficult times. Burglary, assaults, property crimes, theft, abandonment, and moral transgressions, for example, drunkenness, gambling, and fornication were noted, but often left unpunished, as authorities focused on threats to public health.

When plague had passed, new opportunities to break the laws appeared. Labor losses led to laws limiting wages, and these led to both outright violations and clever ways of skirting. Some of the newly wealthy expressed their changed economic conditions by aping the higher classes, an act often condemned by sumptuary laws. Disputed wills also led to fraud, cases of identity theft, and despoiling of young heirs.

Punishment in laws protecting public health could be brutal, involve torture, and be very public to enhance deterrence. Other jurisdictions conducted these measures outside of public view. This kept crowds down and reduced backlash against authorities. Capital punishment included hanging, decapitation, and firing squads. Such port cities as Seville, Venice, and Marseille punished lighter offenses with galley duty, while others imposed such plague-related duties as grave digging. Early in the 1581 outbreak, Seville had already hanged 45 thieves and sent 440 criminals to row in state galleys. Sixteenth-century Scotland leveled against plague-law breakers the penalties of branding, hanging, confiscation of all property, and eternal banishment, while Queen Elizabeth's *Plague Orders* of 1578 called for imprisonment or the stocks. Incarceration during an epidemic, however, was usually a death sentence. Often, the closure of royal, feudal, civil, and guild courts during an epidemic meant delay of judicial process and punishment.

See also: Civil Governments; Health Boards, Magistracies, and Commissions; Labourers, Ordinance and Statute of; Moral Legislation;

Public Health; Public Sanitation; Shutting In; Sumptuary Laws; Wands; Witches and Witchcraft.

References

Bowsky, William. "The Medieval Commune and Internal Violence: Police Power and Public Safety in Siena, 1287–1355." *The American Historical Review* 73 (1967): 1–17.

Shirk, Melanie V. "Violence and the Plague in Aragón, 1348–1351." *Journal of the Rocky Mountain Medieval and Renaissance Association* 5 (1984): 31–39.

D

Dancing Mania

People living under extremely strained conditions sometimes manifest unusual physical reactions to their stressed psychological states. Others in the stressed communities may acquire the same or similar physical patterns, as if by some contagion. Epidemics of uncontrollable dancing that took place for days and involved scores if not hundreds of people broke out in northwestern Europe in 1374, in 1463 in western Germany, and in Strasbourg during summer 1518. Joylessly, choreomaniacs (so dubbed by Paracelsus) rhythmically hopped about in trancelike states until their feet were stripped of skin and they dropped of exhaustion, only to recommence after restorative sleep. Contemporaries blamed demons, the anger of fourth-century martyr St. Vitus (hence "St. Vitus' Dance") or, following humoral medical notions, the accumulation and overheating of "excess blood" in dancers' bodies. Fifteen victims died daily, according to a chronicler of the Strasbourg epidemic, the best documented of the outbreaks. The Strasbourgeois responded predictably by corralling dancers and seeking to control the usual sources of heavenly anger, including drunkenness, prostitution, gambling, and blaspheming. Lasting several weeks, the mania subsided only after pilgrimage by the stricken to a local shrine to St. Vitus and much contrition for civic sinfulness.

From the viewpoint of modern social psychology, dancing mania seems to have been a reaction to very serious stressors in contemporary society. For Strasbourg, medical historian John Waller cites spiritual guilt, famine, interclass tensions, economic hardships, and, not least of all, recurrent and unpredictable plague. Choreomania's relation to the danse macabre theme in art and poetry remains unclear.

See also: Danse Macabre; Humoral Theory; Moral Legislation; Paracelsus and Paracelsianism; Pilgrims and Pilgrimage.

References

Midelfort, H. C. Erik. *A History of Madness in Sixteenth-Century Germany.* Stanford, CA: Stanford University Press, 1999.

Waller, John. *A Time to Dance a Time to Die: The Extraordinary Story of the Dancing Plague of 1518.* New York: Icon, 2008.

Danse Macabre

Totentanz. Danze macabre. Dança general de la Muerte. Dance of Death. A cast of the living joins hands with skeletal dancers who caper them off to the grave. From pope and emperor to peasant child and field hand, everyone joins the dance. An early version had death piping the tune while victims alone danced. The theme's origins remain uncertain. Once thought French, some scholars lean toward 13th-century Iberian roots. Painted versions appeared as early as 1312 (found in the Kligenthal Augustinian convent near Basel), accompanied by Latin verses and later in the vernaculars. About 100 versions of the motif are known, mostly from France, Spain, Germany, and Switzerland, arriving in England from France in the 1420s. As with Three Living Meet the Three Dead and

The Danse macabre or Dance of Death was popular into the mid-1500s and depicted skeletal Death dancing away a representative variety of social types, from pauper to pope. (Dover Pictorial Archives)

Triumph of Death motifs, the Danse predated the Black Death but gained popularity because of it.

The earliest use of the French term was in a 1376 poem by Jean le Fevre, who wrote after recovering from plague in 1374. One of the most influential versions was painted about 1424, with a poetic text on the wall of Paris's Cimitière des Innocents. It accompanied a 1408 version of Three Living Meet the Three Dead and remained until 1635. This text was the first version printed, in 1485 by Guyot Marchant in Paris. It also directly inspired the version painted about 1430 on the wall of Old St. Paul's Pardon Churchyard in London, a plague cemetery site. Poet John Lydgate translated the French poem for the fresco. It was titled "Dance of Machabray or Dance of Death" and disappeared in 1549.

While most that survive or are described have mixed companies, one French manuscript produced in the later 15th century featured women exclusively. The text was by Martial d'Auvergne and limited dancers' sins to covetousness and materialism rather than the fuller range usually displayed. Each has a clear occupation, including scholar, and each has a moneybag on her belt. The best-known printed version would be that by Hans Holbein the Younger (1524, 1538), whose skeletal figures accompany rather than dance with their victims.

The Danse was apparently also performed publicly, perhaps as part of religious drama. It certainly lent itself to a live interpretation, each "living" dancer disappearing in turn. Its theme of equality before death joined those of death's suddenness and unexpectedness. But while death chose its partner, the partner chose salvation or damnation. As with other plague themes, it was ultimately religious and hortatory: repent while you can!

See also: Art, Effects of Plague on; Death, Depictions of; "Three Living Meet the Three Dead;" Triumph of Death.

References

Eichenberg, Fritz. *The Dance of Death: A Graphic Commentary on the Danse Macabre through the Centuries*. New York: Abbeville Press, 1983.

Gertsman, Elina. *The Dance of Death in the Middle Ages*. Turnhout: Brepols, 2011.

Harrison, Ann Tukey. *The Danse Macabre of Women. Ms. fr. 995 of the Bibliothèque Nationale*. Kent, OH: Kent State University Press, 1994.

Holbein, Hans. *The Dance of Death. 41 Woodcuts by Hans Holbein the Younger. Complete Facsimile of the 1538 Edition*. New York: Dover, 1972.

Death, Depictions of

The later Middle Ages and the Baroque period of the 17th century reveled in cultural expressions that featured personified or metaphorical death. One such was the "vanitas" pictorial theme of the emptiness of worldly pleasures and pursuits, with its human skull, smoldering candlewick, and spilled glass of wine. Even in the Renaissance portrait, sitters sometimes featured a *memento mori*, such a reminder of death as a skull or a mirror with the faintest image of a skull.

Certain later medieval thematic ensembles featured death as a corpse, for example, the Three Living Meet the Three Dead, in which death in the form of three corpses of differing states of putrefaction greet three young men with the reminder that "what we are now you will soon be." The Danse macabre visual and poetic theme, rooted in the 14th century, features grinning corpses or skeletons joining hands with people from pope to peasant and dancing them away to the next world. In the Petrarch-inspired Triumph of Death, the universal punishment for Adam's sin is represented by an army of shrouded corpses or skeletons led by one of their own armed for battle. Defensive humankind include a doomed army of soldiers (Jean Colombe, 1485) or a variety of drinkers, lovers, and other oblivious victims (Brueghel, 1562). Death mows down the living with scythes or arrows. Giovanni di Paolo (1437) depicts death as a bat-winged mounted archer targeting the living and trampling the dead. The archer motif pretty clearly links death with the plague and the rider with the Four Horsemen of the Apocalypse. In at least one case, death rides atop a triumphal cart, brandishing its scythe. Related is another theme predating the Black Death, King Death. The crowned corpse in one case opens its chest to reveal squirming worms.

Earlier medieval death appeared as a snake or devouring beast or a small figure—often female—whom Christ defeats through his resurrection. Death was related to evil, sin, corruption, and the devil, and the idea was transmitted by having the devil seize the dying person's soul or fight for it with an angel. In the Spanish Revelaçion de un hermitanno (c. 1382), the soul in the form of a white bird berates its putrefying corpse until an angel saves the soul from a lurking demon. Some observers credit the Black Death with refocusing death away from its connection to sin, since all alike fell prey. In Dürer's famous woodcut, the exhausted "Knight" is accompanied by both Death and the Devil, neither standing for the other. Christ's triumph over death was replaced by death's triumph over humanity.

Death as a woman has roots both in Germanic culture and in Petrarch. In Petrarch's Triumph of Death, she appears draped in black cloth. German depictions, which may conflate death and the plague, have death as a hag or a young virgin (jungfrau) in a blue flame or an angel of death inspired by Exodus. An angel beats a woman carrying a scythe on the Vienna Pest Monument. The confusion of death and plague is even greater at the Lavaudieu monastery, in the Haute Loire, in a work dated to 1355: a hooded woman labeled "mors" (death) holds six arrows in each hand and is surrounded by dying figures.

See also: Arrows; Art, Effects of Plague on; Danse Macabre; "Three Living Meet the Three Dead;" Transi Tombs; Triumph of Death.

References

Camille, Michael. *Master of Death*. New Haven, CT: Yale University Press, 1996.

Cohen, Kathleen. *Metamorphosis of a Death Symbol: The Transi Tomb in the Late Middle Ages and the Renaissance*. Berkeley: University of California Press, 1973.

Guthke, Karl S. *The Gender of Death: A Cultural History in Art and Literature*. New York: Cambridge University Press, 1999.

Lindley, Phillip. "The Black Death and English Art: A Debate and Some Assumptions," in *The Black Death in England*, edited by W. M. Ormrod and P. G. Lindley (Stamford: Paul Watkins, 1996), 125–146.

Nyborg, Ebbe. "The Black Death as Reflected in Scandinavian Art and Architecture," in *Living with the Black Death*, edited by Lars Bisgaard and Leif Søndergaard (Odense: Southern Denmark University Press, 2009), 187–205.

Polzer, Joseph. "Aspects of the Fourteenth-Century Iconography of Death and the Plague," in *The Black Death: The Impact of the Fourteenth-century Plague*, edited by Daniel Williman (Binghamton, NY: Medieval and Renaissance Texts and Studies, 1982), 107–130.

Townsend, Eleanor. *Death and Art: Europe, 1200–1530*. London: Victoria and Albert Publishing, 2009.

Defoe, Daniel (1660–1731)

Daniel was born in 1660 to a London butcher named James Foe and added the "De" in 1703. The family presumably lived in London through both the Great Plague in 1665 (England's last) and the fire that destroyed much of the City in 1666. The Foes were Nonconforming with the Church of England and Daniel attended the Charles Morton's Newington Green Academy. Initially drawn to the ministry, Daniel joined the antiroyalist army for a brief time and engaged in several businesses. His poetry gained him acclaim and his defense of Nonconformist rights—and debt—landed him in jail several times. He was a controversial journalist contributing to several serial publications and, as a novelist, published *Robinson Crusoe* (1719) and *Moll Flanders* (1722) before penning *A Journal of the Plague Year: Being Observations or Memorials of the Most Remarkable Occurrences, As Well Publick As Private, Which Happened in London During the Last Great Pestilence* in 1722.

In 1720, the French Mediterranean port city of Marseille was stricken with the plague. The English government responded by preparing quarantines, port closures, and issuing Plague Orders as a precaution. Though England had gone 55 years without an epidemic of pestilence, the threat to London was very real. Several trends in the preparations disturbed Defoe, and these he addressed in several articles published between 1720 and 1722 and in his *Due Preparations for the Plague, As Well for Soul as Body*, which appeared a month before the *Journal*. *Due Preparations* draws on earlier plague experiences to guide citizens through any repeat of 1665. He wrote the *Journal*, however, as if it were a contemporary, first-hand account. He did not attach his own name as author but attributed it to "a Citizen who continued all the while [the plague lasted] in London." Its last page identifies the source as "H. F.," usually associated with Henry Foe, a London saddler who died when nephew Daniel was 14.

In the 1720s, Defoe was most concerned with opposition by the commercial interests, usually his allies, to the government's plan to impose quarantines and other measures that would interfere with free trade. Perhaps influenced by his uncle's stories of the epidemic or merely mindful that plague traps and slaughters the poor, Defoe desired above all to see England avoid the plague. His narrative densely interweaves broad themes—confusion, abandonment by the state clergy, divine causation and

A well-known novelist in Great Britain during the 18th century, Daniel Defoe wrote popular fiction works *Robinson Crusoe* and *Moll Flanders*. (Library of Congress)

protection—with perfectly reasonable detail and nuance. For many commentators, it is difficult to label the work as journalism, history, or historical fiction. Whatever his own memories and collected personal relations, Defoe was an assiduous collector of material related to the plague, from the Bills of Mortality to the contemporary plague tract *Loimologia* by Dr. Nathaniel Hodges just translated from Latin in 1722. Yet it is clearly a cautionary tale warning against the price to be paid for lack of vigilance, insisting that government officials remain in place to keep order and calling for the greater use of pest houses given the inequities of the practice of shutting in. However one wishes to view it, Defoe's *Journal* remains the greatest work in English—perhaps in any language—on the Second Pandemic.

See also: Hodges, Nathaniel; Lazarettos and Pest Houses; London, Great Plague of; Morality Literature, Christian; Shutting In.

References

Defoe, Daniel. *A Journal of the Plague Year.* Edited by Paula Backscheider. (Norton Critical Edition) New York: Norton, 1992. Also Digital Book Index.

Gilman, Ernest B. *Plague Writing in Early Modern England.* Chicago: University of Chicago Press, 2009.

Healy, Margaret. "Defoe's Journal and the English Plague Writing Tradition." *Literature and Medicine* 22 (2003): 25–44.

Dekker, Thomas (1570?–1632)

His name suggesting Dutch heritage, the English pamphleteer and playwright appears to history first in 1597. Between 1598 and 1602, Dekker authored eight plays for the London stage (Philip Henslowe's Admiral's Men) and collaborated on or produced another 17. All told, he had a hand in some 60 plays over his career, though none approaches the quality of his contemporaries Shakespeare, Marlow, or Jonson, with whom Dekker often quarreled. Cantankerousness and debt resulted in time spent in prison (seven years, 1512–1519).

When city authorities shut down London's theaters during the plague of 1603, Dekker began his second career as social critic. Like others of his generation, Dekker blamed the plague's ravages on divine retribution for human sin, especially on the part of the government. In 1603, he published anonymously *The Wonderfull Yeare 1603*, which set the tone for his seven plague pamphlets. His works are brutally realistic, bitingly satirical, and unstintingly critical of London society and its leaders. They echo the equally satirical and critical works of Thomas Nashe from the 1590s but outdo them in scope and construction. In *Wonderfull* (amazing) *Yeare*, Dekker traces the political shift from Tudor to Stuart and proceeds to make connections between individual and societal sin and punishment through plague. Political propaganda informs his description of new King James as Apollo, ironically both archer and healer. But it is physician James who will heal the country that has been punished for Elizabeth's sins. Dekker mixes prose and poetry, humor and cold criticism, and a range of journalistic styles, which takes him well beyond such contemporaries as John Davies and his highly descriptive "Triumph of Death" (1605) or Henry Petowe's "Londoners their Entertainment" (1604), which is far more religiously moralistic.

In 1604, Dekker published his plague pamphlets "Newes from Graves-End: Sent to Nobodie" and "A Meeting of Gallants at an Ordinarie." The first, mocking the city deserted by its leaders, who left "Mr. Nobody" behind, again mixes poetry and prose. He disdains medical advice since God alone is responsible, and his moral advice consists of a singular chord: repent lest the plague return. Dekker's "Gallants" meet and turn to boasting of their successes in promulgating war, famine, and plague. From this frame tale emerge a set of short stories *ala* Boccaccio's *Decameron*, but Dekker's are set during plague time. In 1606, Dekker's satirical "Seven Deadly Sinnes" appeared. The 1603 plague provides a backdrop but is not "on stage." A Petrarchan "trionfo" of Dekker's version of the Sins is wheeled into London, each in its chariot, each with its crowd of welcoming adherents. Fraud, Lying, Candle-Light (immoral acts hidden by night), Sloth, Apishnesse (stylish vanity), Shaving (sharp dealing), and Cruelty each appear in turn. All sins anger God, but those that harm the poor and disadvantaged, Dekker writes, unleash the plague.

London's 1625 plague inspired "Rod for Run-awaies" (1625), and a plague scare in 1630 prompted "London Looks Back" and "The Black Rod and the White Rod" (both 1630). "Run-awaies" is a reference to those who abandoned the city when plague struck, but Dekker's theme is essentially Malthusian. London was overpopulated and people lived in squalor, which led to famine, vice, sin, and the filth that spawned the plague. The epidemic itself was a "broom" that swept away "kingdoms of people, when they grow rank and too full." When plague threatened London in 1630, Dekker penned "London" and "Black Rod" as reminders of the horrors of 1625, "that dreadful scourge." He reiterated his warnings against reliance on physicians and medicines and his arguments against shutting the infected poor into their own houses to die (since there was no contagion): repentance was the only sure answer.

See also: Abandonment; Broadsheets, Broadsides, and Pamphlets; James I and VI Stuart, King; London, England; Malthusianism; Morality Literature, Christian.

References

Bower, Rick. "Antidote to the Plague: Dekker's Storytelling in *The Wonderful Year* (1603)." *English Studies* 73 (1992): 229–239.

Healy, Margaret. *Fictions of Disease in Early Modern England: Bodies, Plagues and Politics.* New York: Palgrave, 2002.

Porter, Stephen. *Lord Have Mercy upon Us: London's Plague Years.* Stroud, Gloucs, UK: Tempus, 2005.

Seargeant, Philip. "Discursive Diversity in the Textual Articulation of Epidemic Disease in Early Modern England." *Language and Literature* 16 (2007): 323–344.

De Mertens, Charles (1737–1788)

The Franco-Belgian physician was working in Vienna when called to Catherine the Great's Moscow in 1767. She had recently opened a well-endowed orphanage in a grand, new structure, but the children housed there were dying at enormously high rates. Valued for his expertise in inoculations, which he introduced in 1768, he was put in charge of the facility. In 1770, Moscow was suffering from what some considered plague deaths, while others in official circles denied pestilence. Western medical expertise was prized, and even though De Mertens had had no experience with plague, he was called to join the Commission for the Prevention of the Pestilential Infectious

Distemper, which included clerics and merchants as well as physicians like himself. He considered the disease caused by miasma but also deemed it contagious through tiny, microscopic pathogens. Early, in December 1770, he advocated a cordon sanitaire around the city both to prevent incoming infection and the exiting of any contagious people. The government was very slow in responding, but he placed the Foundling Hospital under strict isolation and thereby preserved the lives of 1,400 people by his count. But declaring plague entailed many restrictions, and commoners above all resented the official. They sacked his house during the plague riots on September 15, 1771.

De Mertens's *Treatise on the Plague* originated as part of a Latin pestilential fever text, published in Strasbourg in 1778. It was quickly translated into several languages, including German in 1779, French in Paris in 1784, and English in London in 1799. It was part of a debate among physicians and bureaucrats over the nature of the disease, its identification, and means of prevention. He advocated isolation of every case as early as possible. He preferred designated plague hospitals over shutting in of victims and families and stressed cleanliness, a hallmark of his success at the orphanage.

See also: Consilia and Plague Tracts; Miasma Theory; Moscow, Russia; Physicians.

References

Alexander, John T. *Bubonic Plague in Early Modern Russia: Public Health and Urban Disaster.* Baltimore, MD: Johns Hopkins University Press, 1980.

De Mertens, Charles. *Account of the Plague Which Raged at Moscow 1771.* London: 1799. Newtonville, MA: Oriental Research Partners, 1977. Facsimile.

Demographic and Economic Effects of Plague: The Islamic World

During the period of the Second Plague Pandemic, the Islamic world stretched from southern Spain across North, Central, and Eastern Africa, then east through Arabia to Indonesia and north through the Levant into Central Asia, Anatolia, and across Western Asia into Mughal India. It was an enormous area unified by Islam and knowledge of the Arabic language. Far from the unified Caliphate of the early Middle Ages, rulers included Mongols, Turks, Arabs, and native Africans. Yet goods and people tended to pass unhindered among the regions controlled by Muslims, which made for a very dynamic segment of the world.

The Black Death originated in Muslim territory north and east of the Black Sea and was transmitted south through trade and military campaigns, fanning out from south of the Black Sea. Ships took it to Egypt and caravans to Persia, Iraq, and Syria, while pilgrims, probably landing in the Hejaz, infected Mecca and southern Arabia. Central Africa, India, and Islamic Oceania were spared, but North African cities were stricken via land and sea routes, while Christian Spain probably spread the disease to what was left of Andalusia. The picture provided by such historical sources as Ibn Battuta, is one of massive devastation, with both cities and rural villages suffering terrible losses. Unfortunately, such records are rare and remain rare, especially once one moves away from the Mediterranean. Ships and large caravans would have transmitted the disease to larger settlements and port cities, while pilgrims, traders, soldiers, scholars, and refugees carried it to smaller villages. Civil and religious authorities famously did little if anything to prevent spread of the disease, though Muslim charity would have seen that victims were well cared for individually or in the bimaristans. Even so, sources are clear that death stalked the streets, which filled with corpses, as well as households whose members died together. If the much better European records are an indication, perhaps 50 to 60 percent of people in the affected areas died. Cairo, Islam's largest city, lost a reported 300 per day in early October 1348 and 3,000 per day a month later, for a total estimated at 200,000 dead of an initial population of perhaps 500,000.

Initially, prices rose dramatically for medicines and burial supplies, while food prices fell until reserves had been exhausted. As crops rotted in untended fields and animals fell to disease and predators, prices rose precipitously, and even breadbasket Tunisia had to import Sicilian wheat in 1350. Famines swept North Africa in the early 1350s. European markets dried up, skilled craftspeople of all types disappeared, and those who remained received inflated wages (by two or three times, studies suggest) and sales prices. In Egypt, this led to replacement of the silver *dirham* with copper (*fulus*), which was itself debased over time. Where the Mamluk aristocracy relied on the unstable and fief-like *iqta* system of landholding and exploitation of the peasantry, they were helpless to stop the plague-time and postplague rural hemorrhaging to cities as well as the reductions in production that followed depopulation. Most relied on oppression to maintain levels (further driving away labor), but the nonresident landholders had little real control over managers or labor. Necessary investment in the infrastructure (especially irrigation) dried up as these changed hands frequently with landholders' deaths. Originally in the sultans' hands, distribution of *iqtas* quickly became a matter of sale or exchange for cash, and the nonhereditary system began to disintegrate.

In Egypt, the plague returned in a cycle of seven-year reappearances, and similar patterns held elsewhere. By 1380, Cairo had seemingly recovered, but at the expense of the countryside, and only for a while. Plague in 1388 and 1389, insurrection, a change of dynasty (Barquq, 1382–1399), and the threat of Tamerlane around 1400 drove conditions down, a trend that continued through much of the 1400s. Despite repopulation through natural means, Egypt's population in 1400 may have been 60 percent what it was before the Black Death. Cairo had 66 sugar refineries in 1324 and 19 in 1400; Alexandria had around 13,000 weavers in 1394 and only 800 in 1434, a very low point. Revenues at Qatya toll station fell from 96,000 dinars in 1395 to a mere 8,000 a century later (from 350,000 in 1326).

To the north, what remained of the Byzantine Empire fell to the Turkic Ottoman Empire in 1453, bringing the major urban center of Constantinople/Istanbul into the Islamic ambit. When the Turks expanded southward to end finally the decrepit Mamluk regime in the Levant and Egypt (1517), they created a powerful Istanbul-Cairo axis of travel and trade that may have facilitated the spread of plague. No longer a besieged city, Istanbul recovered and thrived despite regular virulence of plague; Cairo, too, began to recover economically with new investments in building and in rural agriculture. Ottoman official records begin in the mid-16th century but suggest that growth was slow and discontinuous, though clearly stronger with the integration brought by Ottoman conquest. Plague recurrence was always weaker than in 1347 to 1350, but more frequent in some places, especially those associated with pilgrimage.

As Varlik points out, Ottoman rulers adopted some public health measures against plague but failed to establish the cordons, quarantines, and other isolation measures that seem to have relieved most of Europe. As a result, plague circulated through Islamic ports in the Mediterranean long after it had disappeared to the north. Varlik suggests that Ottoman officials got used to plague and thus took a more resigned view to its appearance. Insofar as its recurrence had little overall or cumulative effect on commerce or population, which seems to have been the case, it may not have been seen as worth the investment.

See also: al-Maqrizi, Muhammad; Black Death (1347–1352); Cairo, Egypt; Constantinople/Istanbul; Demographic and Economic Effects of Plague: The Islamic World; Demographic Effects of Plague: Europe 1347–1400; Demographic Effects of Plague: Europe 1400–1500; Demographic Effects of Plague: Europe 1500–1772; Demography; Economic Effects of Plague in Europe; Ibn Battuta, Abu Abdullah; Islamic Civil Responses; Mecca.

References

Al-Harithy, Howyda N. "The Complex of Sultan Hasan in Cairo: Reading between the Lines." *Muqarnas* 13 (1996): 68–79.

Ashtor, Eliyahu. *A Social and Economic History of the Near East in the Middle Ages*. Berkeley: University of California Press, 1976.

Biraben, Jean-Noel. *Les hommes et la peste en France et dans les pays européens et méditeranéens*. 2 vols. Paris: Mouton, 1975, 1976.

Borsch, Stuart. *The Black Death in Egypt and England*. Austin: University of Texas Press, 2005.

Boyar, Ebru and Kate Fleet. *A Social History of Ottoman Istanbul*. New York: Cambridge University Press, 2010.

Byrne, Joseph P. *Daily Life during the Black Death*. Westport, CT: Greenwood, 2006.

Dols, Michael W. *The Black Death in the Middle East*. Princeton, NJ: Princeton University Press, 1977.

Dols, Michael W. "The General Mortality of the Black Death in the Mamluk Empire," in *The Islamic Middle East, 700–1900: Studies in Social and Economic History*, edited by Abraham Udovitch (Princeton, NJ: Princeton University Press, 1981), 404–411.

Stearns, Justin. *Infectious Ideas: Contagion in Premodern Islamic and Christian Thought in the Western Mediterranean*. Baltimore, MD: Johns Hopkins University Press, 2011.

Tucker, William. "Natural Disasters and the Peasantry in Mamluk Egypt." *Journal of the Economic and Social History of the Orient* 24 (1981): 215–224.

Varlik, Nükhet. "Disease and Empire: A History of Plague and Epidemics in the Early Ottoman Empire (1453–1600)." Ph.D. dissertation, University of Chicago, 2008.

Demographic Effects of Plague: Europe 1347–1400

In 1969, Philip Ziegler accepted an average plague death toll in Europe of about 33 percent, or between 20,000,000 and 25,000,000; in the early 2000s, Benedictow presented an overall European population of around 80,000,000 and a plague death toll of about 60 percent overall in Europe, which is a total of about 48,000,000 dead. Percentages and numbers of plague deaths between 1347 and 1352 have been rising over the past decades as study after study refines and expands the numbers. After less than a decade to recover, Europe was swept again, though with tolls of 10 to 20 percent. About once per decade, the warning went out again, and again the graveyards filled, again at reduced rates of morbidity and mortality, but without the effect of allowing the local, national, or continental population levels to recover to preplague levels.

The contemporary estimates of losses can be wildly impossible, but then the medieval world was never much for statistics. Yet the initial numbers arrived at by using such proxies as wills, hearth tax bases, and special communities (monks, canons, hospital populations) tell the same story of devastation. In Catalonia, the Plain of Vic lost 439 of 643 hearths, or about 70 percent. In eight parishes near Montmelian, the number of hearths dropped from 303 in 1347 to 142 in 1350. In 10 Provençal localities, the number of households dropped from 8,511 to 3,839, or 54 percent. Abandoned English tenancies, guild list reductions, and clerical death rates tell the same story. No statistics to date provide details on age, sex, class, or occupation on any significant scales, and most observers noted that people dropped with equal ease, whether rich or poor, young or old.

During later plague outbreaks, however, observers note that women and children died at higher rates than men. If true, it may reflect the fact that women and children would have remained at home with rats and fleas while men were away from the sources of warmth and food. Despite the fact that there is no accepted immunity from the plague bacillus, except possibly in the very short term, survivors of one plague often survived subsequent epidemics, and overall death tolls dropped both absolutely and percentage-wise. It is likely that increasing numbers of people, hearing that plague was nearby, would have fled their homes for places where plague had or had not been—opinions on the matter differed. In other words, human populations began to adapt to the presence and patterns of plague.

Even so, demographically, Europe continued to decline, and the recurrences of plague kept recovery dampened, so the depression endured well into the 15th century.

Hainault had 27,203 hearths in 1365, a number that fell to 21,299 in 1406. In some areas, the trends differed from the norm, or at least the numbers did. Périgueux had 1,224 hearths preplague and only 850 by 1380 but had regained nearly half (1,233) by 1400. But had the definition of a hearth changed? And how many, on average, lived around a hearth in 1380 and again in 1400? To the last question, virtually every study must rely on guesses, estimates, or ranges, none of which is very satisfying.

See also: Abandonment; Black Death (1347–1352); Chronicles and Annals; Demographic and Economic Effects of Plague: the Islamic World; Demographic Effects of Plague: Europe 1400–1500; Demographic Effects of Plague: Europe 1500–1770; Demography; Dietary Regimens; Economic Effects of Plague in Europe; Epidemic and Pandemic; Famine; Flight; Morbidity, Mortality, and Virulence; Plague in Europe 1360–1500; Public Health; Repopulation; Third Plague Pandemic; individual cities.

References

Benedictow, Ole. *The Black Death 1346–1353: The Complete History.* Rochester, NY: Boydell & Brewer, 2004.

Christakos, George, et al. *Interdisciplinary Public Health Reasoning and Epistemic Modeling: The Case of the Black Death.* New York: Springer, 2005.

Noymer, Andrew. "Contesting the Cause and Severity of the Black Death: A Review Essay." *Population and Development Review* 33 (2007): 616–627.

Scott, Susan and Christopher Duncan. *Biology of Plagues: Evidence from Historical Populations.* New York: Cambridge University Press, 2001.

Wood, J. W., R. J. Ferrell and S. N. Dewitte-Avina. "The Temporal Dynamics of the Fourteenth-century Black Death: New Evidence from English Ecclesiastical Records." *Human Biology* 75 (2003): 427–448.

Demographic Effects of Plague: Europe 1400–1500

By 1400, older Europeans had experienced epidemics of plague about once every decade since 1347. High death rates and dampened fertility rates kept national population figures well below preplague numbers even where cities may have rebounded. While the blow of a 40- to 50-percent population loss devastated Europe during the 1350s, the 15th century, with its ongoing economic and demographic depression, is when the true postplague nadir was reached. By the end of the century, however, full recovery was underway.

The Netherlands suffered heavy losses in 1400 to 1401 and 1438 to 1439 of between 20 and 25 percent, though parts of England and Southern France may have lost as many as 50 percent during the same periods. Hainault's rural population dropped by about a third between 1349 and 1400 due to death and relocation. For nearly four decades, rural population rebounded, until powerful epidemics struck the Netherlands in 1438 to 1439, which, with recurrences, again reduced the rural population by about 30 percent down to 1479.

Florence had perhaps 100,000 inhabitants in 1340 but only 60,000 in 1401. This number fell even further, to 37,000 in 1427, and remained stagnant over the next half-century, with about 40,000 in 1480. Frequency of epidemics dropped between the first half (every 13 years on average) and the later second half (37 years), which made for more rapid growth. Verona, Italy, a thriving city in Venice's shadow, grew between 1425 and 1502 from 14,225 residents to 42,000, or 200 percent. Not only did the number of households increase, from 3,866 to 7,142, but the average household size grew from 3.68 to 5.89. Much of this increase, however, was later in the century.

Paris was stricken repeatedly during the 15th century: 1400 to 1401, 1412, 1416 to 1418, 1421, 1432, 1438 to 1439, 1448 to 1452, 1466 to 1468, 1471, 1478, 1481 to 1484, and 1499. From more than 200,000 inhabitants around 1330, it had fallen and was only half this figure in the early 1420s. During the first half of the century, refugees and other vicissitudes of the Hundred Years War kept local populations fluctuating. One Burgundian village had 53 hearths (roughly, families) in 1400, only 13 in 1423, 28 in 1436, and 42 in 1450. Périgueux had 1,224 hearths preplague and had lost many but reached 1,233 by 1400. Over the next five years, this dropped to 972 and, by 1455, down to 719. By 1430, Toulouse lost 42 percent of its 1405 population of 19,000. Over the four centuries between 1300 and 1700, France hit its lowest point between 1445 and 1470. In 1330, France's population was roughly 17,000,000, but by 1470, it was no more than 10,000,000, rising to 19,000,000 by 1700. In Aragon across the 15th century, Catalonia's population fell from 350,000 to 270,000 and Barcelona from 38,000 to 20,000, while Valencia rose from 40,000 to 75,000 from 1418 to 1483. The number of hearths in Catalonia dropped from 83,000 to 61,000 between 1378 and 1497, though complete villages did not vanish.

English villages continued to disappear, however, reaching a crescendo between 1450 and 1485, according to Hatcher. Cities continued to draw out rural folk, while others congregated in larger, stronger villages. Landlords also continued to convert arable land to pasture, eliminating villages, and to sell off large parcels to wealthier farmers who did not rely on villages. A study of Sussex County between 1450 and the 1490s shows continued population shrinkage. Canterbury suffered at least 13 plague epidemics in the 15th century, which may have accounted for one in five deaths. Experts in English population used to see national recovery beginning as early as 1450, 1430, or even 1400, but that turn has been pushed forward into the 16th century. Norway's late medieval population zenith was around 1300 at approximately 350,000. By 1450 to 1500, it had dropped by 64 percent to about 125,000, its stable low point until circa 1550. It would be 1650 before the preplague high would be achieved.

See also: Abandonment; Bills of Mortality; Chronicles and Annals; Demographic and Economic Effects of Plague: the Islamic World; Demographic Effects of Plague: Europe 1347–1400; Demographic Effects of Plague: Europe 1500–1722; Dietary Regimens; Economic Effects of Plague in Europe; Epidemic and Pandemic; Famine; Flight; Malthusianism; Morbidity, Mortality, and Virulence; Plague in Europe 1360–1500; Public Health; Repopulation; Third Plague Pandemic; individual cities.

References

Biraben, Jean-Noel. *Les hommes et la peste en France et dans les pays européens et méditerranéens*. 2 vols. Paris: Mouton, 1975, 1976.

Gottfried, Robert S. *Epidemic Disease in Fifteenth-Century England: The Medical Response and the Demographic Consequences*. New Brunswick, NJ: Rutgers University Press, 1978.

Harvey, Barbara. *Living and Dying in England, 1100–1540*. Oxford: Oxford University Press, 1993.

Hatcher, John. *Plague, Population, and the English Economy, 1348–1530*. London: Macmillan, 1977.

Poos, Larry. *A Rural Society after the Black Death: Essex, 1350–1525*. New York: Cambridge University Press, 1991.

Demographic Effects of Plague: Europe 1500–1722

Above all other diseases in Early Modern Europe, plague was "the pre-eminent arbiter of population growth rates to the mid-17th century. More than any other single factor, the comings and goings of bubonic plague determined whether and where population would grow, stagnate, or decline" (Flinn, 55). The 16th and 17th centuries saw the regime of recurrent plague slowly turn a corner until, by 1700, the disease had disappeared from all but the fringes of Europe. The widely accepted reason for this shift in trends is that Europe beyond Italy adopted (and adapted) many of the tools for dealing with plague first pioneered on the peninsula among the Renaissance city-states. While any given epidemic was no less deadly than any other since the Black Death, and many were worse, the frequency and geographic coverage of outbreaks were reduced considerably. Outside of the war-ravaged countryside of Germany during the Thirty Years' War (1618–1648), plague tended to become an urban phenomenon. This was due, at least in part, to the attempts by civic authorities to limit the plague's dissemination, a fool's errand during wartime. By 1500, Europe's population had reached preplague levels in some places, and regional population growth was now more easily replacing local losses. By 1700, Europe was little affected by plague.

Plague struck London in 1513, 1515, 1525, 1528, 1532, 1535, 1543 to 1548, 1558 to 1559, 1563, 1578, 1582, and 1593; and in 1603, 1625, 1630, and most spectacularly, 1665 to 1666. Despite an average of a plague per decade, London's population rose from 50,000 in 1500 to perhaps 200,000 in 1600 and 420,000 when plague last struck, killing 80,000. By 1701, it was 490,000. Clearly, London grew largely at the expense of England's smaller towns and countryside. The important Mediterranean port city of Marseille suffered in 1504 to 1508, 1524, 1527, 1530, 1546 to 1547, 1556, 1563, 1580 to 1582, 1586 to 1588, and 1598; and 17th-century epidemics in 1619, 1629 to 1630, 1640, 1649 to 1650, 1660, and 1664. After a hiatus of nearly 60 years, its final plague killed about half of its 100,000 residents between 1720 and 1722.

Of all the conflicts of the era, the Thirty Years' War had the greatest death tolls, with perhaps half of the German population dying of violence, typhus, smallpox, influenza, untended sexually transmitted diseases, famine, and plague. German Erfurt normally had about 13,000 citizens and buried 400 to 500 in a year. Due to plague, the death toll more than doubled in 1625 to 925; and in 1626, about one third of the citizens died (3,775). A decade later, the population swelled with refugees and plague struck. In 1635, gravediggers buried 1,542 citizens and 465 refugees (or other visitors); 273 citizens in November alone. Between 1635 and 1641, a total of 6,619 citizens and 4,485 refugees and others died from all causes.

During the 1630s, Europe more broadly suffered due to the expansion of the Thirty Years' War. From 1600 to 1670, France may have lost 2.5 million to plague, though perhaps 60 percent of these were between 1629 and 1635. For comparison, France lost about 14,000,000 to infant deaths from 1600 to 1670. On a local scale, the parish of Sulgen, Switzerland, covered about 20 square kilometers and had around 2,000 inhabitants. Between May and December, 1629, 801 died, a rate of 40 percent.

The war's spillover into Italy spread plague, as well as many other diseases, across the northern part of the peninsula despite the sophisticated systems of reporting and responding. Florence lost about 10 percent of its 70,000 residents, an estimated one third of Venice's much larger population succumbed, and 60,000 of Milan's 130,000 inhabitants died; recovery was stymied by recurrences. In 1630 to 1631 alone, according to a study of 13 Italian cities totaling 672,000 residents, 265,000 died, rates of 38 percent mortality and 50 percent morbidity. The same study shows that villages suffered higher morbidity than cities (66 percent to 50 percent). In 1630, in Poppi, Italy, of 22 families that had held offices over the previous 80 years, seven were wiped out. Outsiders married into depopulated elite families and quickly blended into the town's upper class, relying on their new wives' inheritances.

The second half of the 17th century also saw the last years of plague in most of Western Europe. Barcelona's final outbreak was in 1651 to 1653, with about half of the city's 40,000 population dying. Rome's scourge ended in 1656 with a modest death toll of 15,000 from a population of 120,000. The same epidemic struck Naples, killing perhaps half of the city's population of 300,000. Amsterdam's last and worst plague was in 1664 and it moved to London. Vienna, Marseille, Messina, and Moscow all suffered their last throes in the 18th century, and in each case, the losses were horrific. In each case, the outbreak was isolated and the city recovered quickly.

See also: Abandonment; Bills of Mortality; Black Death (1347–1352); Chronicles and Annals; Demographic and Economic Effects of Plague: the Islamic World; Demographic Effects of Plague: Europe 1347–1400; Demographic Effects of Plague: Europe 1400–1500; Dietary Regimens; Economic Effects of Plague in Europe; End of Second Plague Pandemic: Theories; Famine; Flight; Graunt, John; Malthusianism; Morbidity,

Mortality, and Virulence; Plague in Europe 1360–1500; Public Health; Repopulation; Third Plague Pandemic; individual cities.

References

Biraben, Jean-Noel. *Les hommes et la peste en France et dans les pays européens et méditerranéens.* 2 vols. Paris: Mouton, 1975, 1976.

Eckert, Edward A. *The Structure of Plagues and Pestilences in Early Modern Europe: Central Europe, 1560–1640.* New York: S. Karger Publishing, 1996.

Eckert, Edward A. "The Retreat of Plague from Central Europe, 1640–1720: A Geomedical Approach." *Bulletin of the History of Medicine* 74 (2000): 1–28.

Flinn, Michael. *The European Demographic System, 1500–1820.* Baltimore, MD: The Johns Hopkins University Press, 1981.

Houston, R. A. "The Population History of Britain and Ireland 1500–1750," in *British Population History from the Black Death to the Present Day*, edited by Michael Anderson (New York: Cambridge University Press, 1996), 95–190.

Slack, Paul. *The Impact of Plague in Tudor and Stuart England.* New York: Oxford University Press, 1990.

Demography

Demography literally means, "to record the people." As a modern social science, it seeks to define and analyze the characteristics of a given population, or definable group of people, at a point in time or over time. Characteristics might include size, proportions by sex or age categories, marriage or childrearing responsibilities, education levels, racial makeup, or socioeconomic class distribution. A snapshot in time, for example, a census, provides certain information, but a comparison of snapshots over time provides information about change. This leads to obvious questions about why changes occurred, the effects of changes on the population, and whether trends were/are long or short term. To study change over time, one would like a detailed baseline—all of the pertinent characteristics or data for a single year or other period at the beginning of the timeframe being examined.

Modern population statistics compiled by the apparatus of the modern state, for example, decennial censuses, tax records, or surveys, make demographic study of contemporary populations rather easy, especially in stable countries. Historically, the gathering of population data and study of it developed during the Second Pandemic in Europe, from the later Middle Ages to the end of the early modern period. Cities and regions began collecting data for several such reasons as taxation, military service, and food supply needs. The recurrence of plague made data on deaths particularly important, as an epidemic affected all of the above and added to public expenditures for health care and other costs. In addition, whether an area declared the presence of an epidemic became a major political and economic decision. When a declaration was made, fear gripped the populace; people fled; shops and markets closed; barriers to travel were erected; plague personnel were hired; and foreign trade stopped or was quarantined, depending on how sophisticated the locale's response mode was. The number of local plague deaths over a certain period of time was generally the key to determining whether appearance of disease was the beginning of a plague epidemic. Bills of mortality—records of deaths by cause and/or neighborhood—first developed in 15th-century Italian cities, were meant to do exactly that. Where they have survived, they are important to historical population studies of the era.

For the demographic historian (or historical demographer) reconstructing populations during the first 50 years of the Pandemic, however, the problems begin with the baseline. Simply, reliable preplague population totals, records of births, deaths, and migration in and out of a town or region do not exist. Historians have to use such proxies as diocesan clergy replacements, parish registries, guild members, or property tax payers. Such lists generally represent different years and served the purposes of those who compiled them. How many people did Europe have; or did Italy have; or did Tuscany have; or did Florence have in 1345 or 1347? The smaller the geographic unit, the smaller the ranges historians are comfortable with, but ranges—sometimes very wide ranges—are the best the careful demographer can do. To say that Florence had a population of 90,000 or of 100,000 in 1347 is to state an approximation, one often based on the statement of a historical source, for example, a chronicle or diary. Modern demographers often expend a great deal of energy studying a variety of such statements, as well as proxies and other data, with varying degrees of success.

How many died of the plague in Florence? How many fell ill and recovered? How many fled, never to return? How many fled and returned? How many immigrants moved in during or after the epidemic? From where did they originate? How many of each category were women? or children under 12? or elderly men? Such questions, even the first, cannot be answered with any reasonable level of precision. Even very late in the Second Pandemic, when deaths and causes of deaths were recorded, lists only included those who were carefully inspected, leaving out those who were dumped in rivers or mass graves or eaten by animals. Postmortem determinations of

cause of death were also unreliable, even when made by doctors, which was rare. "Signs of plague" did not necessarily mean plague, and a glance at a bill of mortality reveals the range of other causes of death noticed even during plague outbreaks. Demographers often seek a baseline of deaths or burials during the comparable season or month and attribute the additional deaths to plague.

Rather than the "truth" of exact numbers and rates and ratios, the demographer of the Second Pandemic has the "truth" of patterns and approximations. These were often as apparent to the people of the time as they are to the number crunchers of today.

See also: Abandonment; Bills of Mortality; Black Death (1347–1352); Chronicles and Annals; Demographic and Economic Effects of Plague: the Islamic World; Demographic Effects of Plague: Europe 1400–1500; Demographic Effects of Plague: Europe 1500–1722; Dietary Regimens; Economic Effects of Plague in Europe; Epidemic and Pandemic; Famine; Flight; Graunt, John; Malthusianism; Morbidity, Mortality, and Virulence; Plague in Europe 1360–1500; Public Health; Repopulation; Third Plague Pandemic.

References

Benedictow, Ole. *The Black Death 1346–1353: The Complete History.* Rochester, NY: Boydell & Brewer, 2004.

Benedictow, Ole J. *Plague in the Late Medieval Nordic Countries: Epidemiological Studies.* Oslo: Middelalderforlaget, 1992.

Beresford, Maurice and John Hulst. *Deserted Medieval Villages.* London: Lutterworth Press, 1971.

Biraben, Jean-Noel. *Les hommes et la peste en France et dans les pays europeens et mediteraneens.* 2 vols. Paris: Mouton, 1975, 1976.

Bisgaard, Lars and Leif Søndergaard, eds. *Living with the Black Death.* Odense: University of Southern Denmark Press, 2009.

Bowsky, William. "The Impact of the Black Death upon Sienese Government and Society." *Speculum* 39 (1964): 368–381.

Christakos, George, et al. *Interdisciplinary Public Health Reasoning and Epistemic Modeling: The Case of the Black Death.* New York: Springer, 2005.

Harvey, Barbara. *Living and Dying in England, 1100–1540.* New York: Oxford University Press, 1993.

Hatcher, John. *Plague, Population, and the English Economy, 1348–1530.* London: Macmillan, 1977.

Poos, Larry. *A Rural Society after the Black Death: Essex, 1350–1525.* New York: Cambridge University Press, 1991.

Scott, Susan and Christopher Duncan. *Biology of Plagues: Evidence from Historical Populations.* New York: Cambridge University Press, 2001.

Wood, J. W., R. J. Ferrell and S. N. Dewitte-Avina. "The Temporal Dynamics of the Fourteenth-century Black Death: New Evidence from English Ecclesiastical Records." *Human Biology* 75 (2003): 427–448.

Demons, Satan, and the Devil

Among premodern societies, the most commonly articulated cause for disease is malevolent spirits. In Vedic India (1200–800 BCE), *takman* caused fevers, especially pestilential fevers; *jinn* and *shayatin* of pre–Islamic Arabia spread contagious diseases; the Jew Jesus expelled evil spirits; and up to the Enlightenment, his Christian followers burned "witches" thought to work for Satan, the fallen angel who had God as a nemesis. Indian Ayurvedic medicine, founded between 200 BCE and 200 CE, rationalized much tradition but maintained a place for demons. The best-known Ayurvedic text, that of Susruta, categorized diseases as natural and supernatural (*adhidaivika*) and included a subset of diseases that were caused specifically by demons, the *daivabala* (cf. diabolical), which included pestilential fevers. Similarly, Chinese traditional medicine included a place for spirit possession and "demonic *qi*" (chee; a spiritual force or power) in explaining epidemic disease.

During the First Pandemic, Christian chronicler Pseudo-Zacharius wrote in Syriac that the plague was "a scourge from Satan, who was ordered by God to destroy men." Similarly, Agathias and John of Ephesus claimed that an angry God sent demons to inflict epidemic through possession, and healing required exorcism, the expelling of demons, by holy men. Contemporaneously, Muhammad was preaching that plague was God's will and not from malevolent spirits, or *jinn*; though Allah could certainly use *jinn* as agents.

The onset of the Second Pandemic (c. 1340s–c. 1840s) caught Christian Europe in a dark mood of guilt-induced penitence. Sicilian Michele da Piazza in Messina attributed the epidemic to "God's vengeance." People vainly hoped a cult statue of Mary "would drive the demons from the city and deliver it from the mortality." Presumably, the demons were inducing the sinful behavior that provoked God's ire rather than causing the disease directly. Michele clearly attributes the onslaught to the arrival of a Genoese ship with diseased sailors. Like Allah, the Christian God was sometimes believed to use demons as agents of his wrath, and some plague images display demonic archers delivering pestilence. The biblical story of Job, whom God allowed Satan to torment, was a reminder of the danger in second-guessing the Creator. Pestilence was almost unanimously attributed to an angry God, however, rather than Satan or the Devil, during the Pandemic's first two centuries.

In a rare case, 16th-century theologian Martin Luther attributed the plague of 1527 to "Satan's fury," expressing his faith that God would save their souls even if Satan "should devour our bodies." Early Stuart physician and astrologer Simon Forman in his plague essay (1607) noted that there were natural plagues brought on by the stars (planets), divine plagues prompted by human sin and wickedness, and devil-induced plagues. God either permitted or commanded these last, Forman wrote. The 16th century also saw the intensification of the devil's indirect role in causing plague by tempting people to sin. In their weakness, people ignored divine aid and fell into sin, which brought on divine wrath.

More directly, Satan was blamed for creating human minions who did his will directly by spreading plague. During the first epidemics of the late 1340s, this was laid at the door of Jews, who were suspected of poisoning wells or other "Christian" water supplies. In 1598, Dr. Arellano of Asti, Italy, claimed as the second cause of plague certain "wicked ones who diabolically spread their poisons through the world." This accusation, which eventually understood some plagues as resulting from a poisonous ointment applied to doorknobs, spread across Alpine territories in the 1500s and 1600s. It is no coincidence that the 16th and 17th centuries, despite the rise of scientific thinking and discovery, saw the greatest intensity of brutal persecutions of supposed witches, the servants of Satan.

See also: Arrows; Causes of Plague: Historical Theories; Contagion Theory; Crime and Punishment; Islam and Medicine; Jews; Jinn; Job; Sin; Witches and Witchcraft.

References

Closson, Marianne. "The Devil's Curse: The Demonic Origin of Disease in the Sixteenth and Seventeenth Centuries," in *Contagion in Early Modern Europe*, edited by Claire L. Carlin (New York: Palgrave Macmillan, 2005), 63–76.

Conrad, Laurence I. and Dominik Wujastyk, eds. *Contagion: Perspectives from Pre-Modern Societies.* Burlington, VT: Ashgate, 2000.

Naphy, William G. *Plagues, Poisons and Potions: Plague Spreading Conspiracies in the Western Alps c.1530–1640.* New York: Manchester University Press, 2002.

Diagnosing Plague

Determining whether a disease was plague, a pestilential fever, or another disease was of vital importance, especially when plague was not expected. Confirmation of plague could send a town into a frenzy of prophylactic activity; a false denial of plague could mean a deadly epidemic taking root with no preparation.

Physicians had no means of testing blood or pus for pathogens, and many such symptoms of plague as fever, delirium, and skin eruptions, are common to other conditions. Plague *consilia*, tracts, and even chronicles often contain lists of such visible symptoms, but these can be overwhelming. Around 1600, Italian physician Pietro Parisi noted that important "modern" experts listed from 15 (Ficino) to 52 (Ingrassia) plague symptoms.

But some symptoms were more important than others. In his 1636 *Physick for the Sicknesse*, Stephen Bradwell provided a guide for physicians and laypeople. After discussing fevers, pains, vomit, and "sinking spirit," he listed four "surest signs": tokens, or blue/purple spots from a flea-bite to a penny in size; blains, pus-filled blisters surrounded by redness that discharge, crust over, and reappear; blotches; the buboes in neck, armpits, and groin, in size from a nutmeg to a

A doctor attends to a plague victim while holding a sweet-smelling sponge over his nose and mouth. In the Middle Ages, it was believed that infection occurred by breathing in poison air. Fumigation and herb-soaked bundles held to the nose were thought to be deterrents to the spread of the disease. (National Library of Medicine)

"man's fist;" and carbuncles, enflamed pustules like the burns from hot coals. Two centuries earlier, in 1447, Michele Savonarola of Ferrara, Italy, provided a very similar list, including the tokens, discharging pustules, and buboes, along with fever, vomiting, and debilitation. During the first outbreak in the 1340s, however, observers noted the fever, along with various descriptions of spots and sores, at times without bubonic swelling in the lymphatic regions of neck, armpit, and groin. Sometimes the swellings preceded the spots, and sometimes it was the reverse.

One of the major problems in interpreting these descriptions is the range of terms used for spots, swellings, and other phenomena. Samuel Cohn found 22 different terms used in Milan alone for swellings of various types, including *bubo, aposteme, glandula, tumore, carbone, carbuncle, ant*, and *pustula*. Physicians had only their experience on which to rely when interpreting these "signs," since medical schools and major medical works provided no guidance. Sometimes plague *consilia* or tracts contained such descriptions as size, location, or softness of a swelling, which might help one's colleagues. Of course, cases of septicemic and pneumonic plague developed with such speed that usually swellings had no time to form.

Ingrassia, who studied in Padua, relates ironically that early during the Venetian epidemics of 1535 and 1555, "so many and excellent physicians" "maintained a great diversity of opinions" on whether several deaths were due to plague.

See also: Arabic-Persian Medicine and Practitioners; Bubonic Plague; Consilia and Plague Tracts; Ficino, Marsiglio; Ingrassia, Giovanni Filippo; Medical Education (1300–1500, Medieval Europe); Medical Education (1500–1700, Early Modern Europe); Pneumonic Plague; Septicemic Plague.

References

Byrne, Joseph P. *The Black Death*. Westport, CT: Greenwood Press, 2004.

Cipolla, Carlo. *Fighting the Plague in Seventeenth-Century Italy*. Madison: University of Wisconsin Press, 1981.

Cohn, Samuel K. *The Black Death Transformed: Disease and Culture in Early Renaissance Europe*. New York: Oxford University Press, 2002.

Dietary Regimens

During the Second Pandemic, the ruling medical paradigm, Galenism, insisted that proper diet, along with a balance of the others of the Hippocratic "six nonnaturals"—air, exercise and rest, sleep and waking, the passions, and repletion and evacuation—was key to maintaining the sound bodily constitution that would strengthen one against disease. Humoralism taught that constitutions were naturally hot or cold, moist or dry, and that foods shared the same qualities. For humoralists, disease was a matter of imbalance among the humors that shared these qualities. This could be redressed through consumption or avoidance of certain foods, as well as balancing the other nonnaturals, similar to the modern emphasis on diet and exercise.

Dietary regimens written by Christian, Jewish, and Muslim physicians laid these fundamentals out. They were rooted in ancient Greece, adjusted by Arab and Persian physicians, and delineated in Latin at the Medical School at Salerno in the 11th century (*Regimina salernitatis*). In the 14th and 15th centuries, these were often part of plague *consilia* and plague tracts, usually in the section devoted to preventative action. Beside "all in moderation," plague regimens advised avoiding activities that generated heat and moisture. Heat and moisture aided the process of putrefaction, which was believed to be the means by which the body was poisoned by miasmatic air. Included were fruits and vegetables; boiled, fatty, and fried meats; foods that were spicy, acidic, or bitter; milk; and fish. Foods that were "cold and dry," easily digested, and that flowed quickly through the body were good. Natural laxatives were also good, but these, like fruits, were often moist, so experts often differed over their use. Out were baths, sex (Muslims tended to allow moderation), and sweaty exercise, as were fear, anger, despair, sadness, and other passions that opened the body to pestilence. Encouraged were evacuating or purging excess humors through bleedings and cleansing bowel movements. Poet John Lydgate's 15th-century *Dietary* was as much about maintaining harmony in family and society as among humors.

See also: Consilia and Plague Tracts; Dietary Regimens; Galen and Galenism; Humoral Theory; Lydgate, John.

References

Nicoud, Marilyn. *Les regimes de santé au moyen Age: Naissance et diffusion d'une ecriture medicale (XIIIe-XVe siecle)*. 2 vols. Rome: École française de Rome, 2007.

Sotres, Pedro Gil. "The Regimens of Health," in *Western Medical Thought from Antiquity to the Middle Ages*, edited by Mirko Grmek (Cambridge, MA: Harvard University Press, 1998), 291–318.

Diseases, Opportunistic and Subsidiary

It is well known that diseases often break out in pairs or groups within a population and that premodern epidemics are more likely to present groups of diseases rather than singular ones. Scores of diseases afflicted the people who also suffered with the Second Pandemic's bubonic, pneumonic, and septicemic plague, and many of these appeared during plague epidemics. In some cases, an individual might have had two or more diseases, a condition made possible by the chronologically first attacking and weakening the immune system, easing the entry of the second and subsequent pathogens. In other cases, endemic diseases normally maintained at low incidence levels within the population were allowed to flourish. This could occur because of deaths of normal caregivers, parents, and medical practitioners; social disruption and fear that led to abandonment and flight; shutting in of whole families by authorities; or interruptions of food, safe water, and other necessities. Normal levels of medical attention, hygiene, and nutrition declined as weeks dragged on. Pathogens imported by outsiders (refugees, medical practitioners, merchants, soldiers, vagabonds, immigrants) found local immune systems shredded by malnutrition and low-level endemic illnesses, even in otherwise "healthy" individuals.

Disentangling these strands is virtually impossible, but given contemporary records, a modicum of sense can be made of them. Some diseases were easily distinguished from others. When the young and undernourished fell ill during plague times, it could very easily have been worms, pox, diarrhea, one of several fevers, dysentery, or tetanus. Contemporaries often remark on large numbers of children dying during epidemics, which some today ascribe to a syndrome specifically mixing smallpox with plague. Influenza did accompany plague in many cases, including northern Italy and Germany in 1387; London 1557 to 1559; and France in 1580. Carmichael points to flu pandemics in 1367, 1404, 1414, and 1427. Tuberculosis was a regular and major killer in 15th-century Tuscany.

During plague epidemics, authorities sometimes made certain assumptions that lumped diseases together. For example, in early modern France, officials were likely to assume plague deaths for all who died in pest houses; anyone claiming fever; and all who died while shut in with a plague victim. Some diseases could present like plague, confusing doctors who were content with quick examinations: scrub typhus, filarial orchitis, relapsing fever, typhoid, and glandular fever could produce buboes; anthrax, tularemia, diphtheria, *staphylococcus aureus, streptococcus pyogenes*, infectious mononucleosis, and lymphoma could look like bubonic plague, while any pneumonic condition could mimic pneumonic plague; and septicemic plague might be imitated by typhoid, meningococcal septicemia, and disseminated intravascular coagulation. Contagious diseases were sometimes treated with the same broad brush, including plague, leprosy, typhus (after 1477), malaria, dysentery, typhoid fever, smallpox, influenza, tuberculosis, and enteric diseases producing diarrhea.

New diseases included typhus, syphilis (from the 1490s), and the English Sweating Sickness in the 1550s. While these presented very differently from plague, they did occur simultaneously with it. Though the science of distinguishing groups of diseases (nosology) had to wait until the later 17th century, documents of all sorts seem to indicate that observers were very interested in accurately distinguishing and diagnosing plague and determining whether an outbreak was really an epidemic. By the 16th century, the cry "plague!" in a city came to mean contagion, isolation, flight, quarantines, expulsions, stoppage of trade, and other harsh means that seemed necessary. Bills of mortality that listed causes of death required often-untrained observers to make keen distinctions among diseases with similarly appearing outcomes. While no one can vouch for the accuracy of such determinations—indeed, many criticized them—they do indicate the culture's desire to be correct.

See also: Diagnosing Plague; Searchers.

References

Brockliss, Laurence and Colin Jones. *The Medical World of Early Modern France*. New York: Oxford University Press, 1997.

Carmichael, Ann G. *Plague and the Poor in Renaissance Florence*. New York: Cambridge University Press, 1986.

Cohn, Samuel K. *The Black Death Transformed: Disease and Culture in Early Renaissance Europe*. Oxford: Oxford University Press, 2002.

Lindemann, Mary. *Medicine and Society in Early Modern Europe*. 2nd edition. New York: Cambridge University Press, 2010.

Theilmann, John and Frances Cate. "A Plague of Plagues: The Problem of Plague Diagnosis in Medieval England." *Journal of Interdisciplinary History* 37 (2007): 371–393.

Twigg, Graham. *The Black Death: A Biological Reappraisal*. New York: Schocken Books, 1985.

Disinfection and Fumigation

In 1490, King John (João) II took drastic action with the Portuguese city of Évora, which had just been devastated by plague. He removed all people and let cattle roam the streets freely for several days; he then lit great fires in the streets and lesser ones in each home and, finally, whitewashed every wall and even the streets. Throughout the Second Pandemic, miasma theory insisted that "corrupted air" caused plague deaths and indicated that corrupted air needed to be purified and objects that were exposed to that air needed to be cleansed or destroyed. João believed his cattle were able to absorb poisonous vapors; fires would cleanse air with heat, aroma, and smoke; and whitewash would act as a disinfectant, neutralizing or covering any ambient poison. Admittedly, such a thorough, multivalent approach was rare.

Hippocrates, Galen, and Avicenna supported miasma theory, and Arabic physicians (Al-Kindi, ninth century, *On vapors that cleanse the air of pestilence*; Al-Timimi, 10th century, *The extension of life by purifying the air of corruption*) provided additional advice on how to counteract deadly air. When the Black Death struck, physicians in Spain, Italy, Germany, and France attributed the disease to miasma and made recommendations that echoed for centuries: personal sachets of herbal or mineral scents; bonfires outside and small fires inside, preferably with aromatics; exposure to fresh air; cleansing hard surfaces of poison residue; and baking or burning of victims' porous or soft items. The first was meant as prophylactic, the second was both prophylactic and a means of correcting corrupted air, and the last three cleaned up after plague had passed.

Filtering the air around a person's face was the simplest and most direct way of dealing with corrupted air. A small bag with a mixture of herbs, flowers, and spices could be held up to the nose and mouth periodically. Cardinal Wolsey used a hollowed-out orange with a vinegar-soaked sponge inside for the same purpose, or a clove-studded whole orange would do. Pomanders ("amber apples") were aromatic balls of amber or ambergris compounded with musk, aloes, camphor, and rosewater, or similar blends, worn around the neck. Poorer folk could substitute myrrh or mastic for the amber/ambergris. Both perfume and cologne (*eau de cologne*; *kölnische wasser*) were developed during the Second Pandemic as air correctives and to mask the stench of death. Contrarily, many believed the folk and alchemical wisdom: battle vile air with equally vile air. This led people to seek out tanning pits, cesspits, pig sties, any place that stank. French physician Ambroise Paré recommended living with an odiferous goat.

After 1600, tobacco smoked in pipes served as a portable fumigant, especially useful to doctors, corpse carriers, and gravediggers. It was a variation on burning aromatic dried herbs (savory, marjoram, mint), wood (ash, pine, juniper), incense, ambergris, and/or camphor on a brazier or grill in the rooms of a house. Pope Clement VI sat between two such fires in 1348, and Henry VIII had coal brought from northern England on which strong aromatics were burnt. Alfonso de Cordoba provided a recipe for a fumigant whose 21 ingredients include spikenard, sandal, ladanum, pepper, saffron, cardamom, and camphor. *Cautionary Rules for Preventing the Sickness* (London, 1665) recommended rose water and vinegar with bay leaves, rosemary, lemon peel, and cloves left to steam gently in a room.

When such measures failed, similar ones were applied to cleanse "infected" rooms. Leaving peeled onions about was one suggestion, as were firing guns, leaving dried toads or bowls of fresh milk about to absorb poison, and letting in birds to fly around soaking up bad air. Some places used such professional fumigators as trustworthy friars in Vienna (1712) or those in Florence who, in 1576, provided a locked-in family with a smoldering brazier that ignited the room, nearly killing all five. In 1562, Dr. Auger Ferrier suggested fumigating one's clothing each morning in aromatic smoke. At Ipswich, England, in 1579, the order was that "a load of weeds" be burnt in every infected house, and in Marseille, the poor were given sulphur to burn in 1720. To test fumigation's effectiveness, Bourg-en-Bresse in 1636 paid children—presumably orphans—to live in treated houses for 40 days. In 17th-century England, three sheep were left in a treated

room, their wool was washed, and the water fed to pigs. If the pigs died, more was needed.

Disinfecting was largely a matter of washing down rooms and their solid contents (wood, metal, pottery, glass) with some combination of astringents, sour wine, or rosewater. This was not to "kill germs" but to wash away poisonous miasma-deposited residue. In some times and places, all victims' "soft" belongings (clothes, bedding, cushions, books, leather) were merely fumed and left in open air; in others, they were incinerated. This practice led to thievery and the fear that fire rereleased the aerial poison. In 1665, London required coaches that had carried victims to be aired out for five to six full days. As for airing out houses, the Russian villages of Dimitrovka and Tverdokhleby had all windows knocked out and roofs removed.

From Novgorod (1352) to London (from 1563 to 1665 during plague years), European civil authorities had huge bonfires created to purify the atmosphere. Bonfires were one of the few nonreligious public actions of authorities in Islamic areas as well. Summer rains tended to curb their use.

See also: Arabic-Persian Medicine and Practitioners; Avicenna (Ibn Sina); Chauliac, Guy de (Guido Cauliaco); Clement VI, Pope; Consilia and Plague Tracts; Corpses; Health Boards, Magistracies, and Commissions; Miasma Theory; Prophylaxes; Public Health; Tobacco.

References

Cazes, Hélène. "Apples and Moustaches: Montaigne's Grin in the Face of Infection," in *Imagining Contagion in Early Modern Europe*, edited by Claire L. Carlin (New York: Palgrave Macmillan, 2005), 79–93.

Conrad, Laurence I. "*Ta'un* and *waba*: Conceptions of Plague and Pestilence in Early Islam." *Journal of the Economic and Social History of the Orient* 25 (1982): 268–307.

Riddle, John. "Pomum Ambrae: Amber and Ambergris in Plague Remedies." *Sudhoff's Archiv für Geschichte der Medizin und der Naturwissenschaften* 48 (1964): 111–122.

DNA and the Second Plague Pandemic

Deoxyribonucleic acid, or DNA, is the blueprint for building life. During the last decade of the 20th century and thereafter, scientists have been unrolling the schematics of organisms down to the level of identifying the highly specific DNA "fingerprint" so often used to prove or disprove criminal suspects on TV and in real life. By disassembling the individual pieces, scientists are just beginning to locate where along a strand of DNA lies the piece that dictates or influences certain traits of interest. To date, scientists study the DNA of *Yersinia pestis*, the plague bacillus, for two principle reasons.

One is to ascertain the presence or absence of plague DNA in the archeological remains of people who died during the Second Pandemic or other epidemics. Recently, scholars have used differences in the epidemiology of modern bubonic plague and the recorded patterns of the Second Pandemic to cast doubt on the identity of the pathogen and disease responsible for the Black Death and subsequent outbreaks. In 1998, a French team led by Michel Drancourt and Didier Raoult announced they had discovered plague DNA in tooth pulp of supposed plague victims. Skeptics attacked the choice of skeletal remains and cleanliness of the laboratory, and claimed that similar experiments yielded no such results. A much larger international study (Haensch, Bianucci, et al.) announced its positive findings in late 2010, but critics have yet to be heard from at this time.

The second DNA-related research area is locating the sources of virulence or lethality in pieces of *Y. pestis* DNA. By 2010, there have been advances in this area, which could answer numerous questions about why death tolls dropped during the Second Plague Pandemic and why modern bubonic plague acts differently from historical "plague." This determination might also allow for genetic research to lessen or counteract the threat posed by the bacillus today.

See also: Black Death: Debate over the Medical Nature of; *Yersinia pestis*.

References

Drancourt, Michel and Didier Raoult. "Detection of 400-year-old *Yersinia pestis* DNA in human dental pulp: An approach to the diagnosis of ancient septicemia." *Proceedings of the National Academy of Sciences* 95 (Oct. 27, 1998): 12637.

Drancourt, Michel and Didier Raoult. "Cause of Black Death." *Lancet: Infectious Diseases* 2 (2002): 459.

Haensch, Stephanie, Rafaella Bianucci, et al. "Distinct Clones of *Yersinia pestis* Caused the Black Death." *Public Library of Science Pathogens* 6 (2010, 10): e1001134, doi:10.1371/journal.ppat.101134.

Thomas, M., et al. "Response to Drancourt and Raoult." *Microbiology* 150 (2004): 264–265.

Wood, James and Sharon DeWitte-Aviña. "Was the Black Death Yersinial Plague?" *Lancet Infectious Diseases* (June 3, 2003): 327–328.

Doctors. See **Physicians**

Donne, John (1572–1631)

The poet and priest John Donne was born to a London ironmonger and his higher-class wife. John's father died early on and his mother married a successful physician, who provided for John's fortune. John studied law at Thavies Inn and Lincoln's Inn in London. Deprived of a position in the royal circle, however, he turned to the Anglican Church and was ordained in 1615. Donne rose to become Dean of (Old) St. Paul's cathedral in London, where his memorial remains today.

Donne weathered the plagues of 1593, 1603, 1610, and 1625. The first disturbed his second year at Lincoln's Inn, and the few remaining students elected him Master of Revels. He passed time writing poetry and letters in verse, which "dried" in him, "Grief which did drown me." His brother Henry, like John, having been raised a Catholic, had been arrested for aiding a Catholic priest and died of plague, unvisited and uncared for, in notorious Newgate Prison. By 1603, Donne had married and the couple lived at Pyrford, Surrey. They avoided the horrors of plague-struck London and briefly hosted the new king, James I, who was doing likewise.

The year 1610 found the Donnes in London, which John described as a "dead carcasse." Influenced by the suffering round about him, his poetic mood darkened and shifted to matters of death, mortality, and damnation. In November 1623, Donne suffered from relapsing fever and maintained a record of his experience, ordered reflections on imminent death. It inspired his "Meditations," collected in *Devotions upon Emergent Occasions* (1624). XVII famously reflects upon human mortality, human connectedness, and bells. "No man is an island," he wrote, and "never send to know for whom the bell tolls; it tolls for thee." Fleeing London in 1625, the Donnes only reached Chelsea, where they stayed at a fine house. They were hosted by Lady Magdalen Danvers, mother of poet George Herbert,

who proved to be an inspirational resource to the local poor and sick. Remounting St. Paul's pulpit in January, John railed against the "death wish" of those who lived hedonistically during plague; and to his smaller congregation at St. Dunstan's, he noted that the dead were literally all around them in the church, "Every grain of dust that flies here is a piece of a Christian," but that all share the promise of eternal life despite their suffering.

See also: Bells; London, England; Plague in Europe, 1500–1725.

References

Gilman, Ernest B. *Plague Writing in Early Modern England.* Chicago: University of Chicago Press, 2009.

Stubbs, John. *John Donne: The Reformed Soul: A Biography.* New York: Norton, 2007.

Doors

During plague epidemics, doors played important real and symbolic roles. In towns and cities, shut residential doors could indicate family members were sick, the residents had died, or the family had relocated. In certain cities like London and Amsterdam, residential doors marked with such symbols as a red cross, bundle of straw, and/or such a phrase as "Lord have mercy" told all a plague victim—and probably his family—was locked inside. Men with halberds guarded some doors to isolate such unfortunates even further. The fearful bolted their doors against miasma and against those who might take advantage of civic upset to rob or rape. At times, some Swiss and French feared their door handles had been smeared with plague poison. Too often, closed doors hid corpses whose presence was betrayed only by their stench; corpse carriers would use the doors themselves as stretchers to carry out the remains.

Closed shop doors reminded passersby of the economic hardship plague brought as it killed and scattered those who provided goods, services, employment, and alms. Ironically, the refugees themselves, however wealthy, found many closed doors as they fled: inns, churches, and even friends barred their entry. And finally, so highly symbolic was the pest house door, which swung so often in one direction only.

A mother with her child warily peers through a doorway into a plague-ridden house marked with a cross while, in the background, two men carry a dead body. (Courtesy of the National Library of Medicine)

Dublin, Ireland

The Vikings established *Dubh linn*, or "black pool," at the mouth of the Liffey River as a trading point around 1000 CE. The year 1169 saw Strongbow and his men arrive and harry the Irish, and his Plantagenet lord, Henry, arrived a few years later to make Dublin his seat of power. Plague entered the Isle through Drogheda and either Dublin or Dalkey and Howth, as Franciscan Brother John Clynn would have it in his *Annals of Ireland*, kept at St. Mary's Abbey in Dublin. Brother John's was the only record of Ireland's suffering, and he died at the work's close. Twenty-three of Dublin's Franciscans died, and 14,000 Dubliners, all told, wrote John, telling his readers more about what happened in Avignon than what he himself witnessed. The base population in 1348 has to be determined backward from John's number, with reasonable estimates running from 28,000 to 42,000 crammed within 44 walled acres and surrounding suburbs. Overcrowded wooden housing, poor personal hygiene, and streets teeming with filth that drew the king's rebuke made the city a fine home for the pestilential rats and fleas. Apart from Gaelic-speaking servants, most Dubliners would have been Anglo-Irish and English craftsmen, tradesmen, merchants, and landed colonial aristocrats. Outside of such port towns as Galway, Wexford, and Kilkenny lived the native Gaelic Irish in dispersed, low-density villages that were presumably spared much of the Black Death's horror.

Colonial life had rarely been secure, and many seem to have used the opportunities opened back in England—urban jobs, cheap land—as an excuse to abandon Dublin, further depleting the population. Rural Anglo-Irish built defensive Norman-style tower houses and began "going native," adopting Gaelic Irish clothing and customs as the English hold weakened. Edward responded by banning such native expressions in the Statutes of Kilkenny of 1365, after four rounds of plague (1348, 1357, 1361, and 1365). Another four rounds would complete the 14th century: 1370, 1383, 1390 to 1393, and 1398.

The 15th-century English wars and domestic problems preoccupied the government, and the Irish Pale (the region controlled by England) centered on Dublin shrunk to a patch 30 by 20 miles in extent by 1435. Sporadic plagues struck the port city, sweeping away administrators and tax collectors. During a 1534 outbreak, colonists' children sent away to rural schools were hijacked by rebels under "Silken" Thomas Fitzgerald. Parents organized and rescued their children and drove the rebels back from the Pale. In thanks for their aid, Henry VIII granted to the Dubliners the current site of Trinity College, then an Augustinian priory. In 1575, they decided to use it as a pest house site. Earlier facilities had been created from vacated leper hospices, including St. Stephen's, St. James's, and St. Lawrence's. When plague broke out in 1604 to 1605, another was established in St. George's Lane with a scant four-man crew. Twenty years later, Dublin authorities instituted quarantine procedures and sheds for crews and cargoes

See also: Demographic Effects of Plague: Europe 1347–1400 (and 1400–1500 and 1500–1772); Economic Effects of Plague in Europe; Friars (Mendicants); Leprosy (Hansen's Disease) and Leprosarium; Merchants; Nobility; Public Sanitation.

References

Houston, R. A. "The Population History of Britain and Ireland 1500–1750," in *British Population History from the Black Death to the Present Day*, edited by Michael Anderson (New York: Cambridge University Press, 1996), 95–190.

Kelly, Maria. *The Great Dying: The Black Death in Dublin*. Stroud, Gloucs, UK: Tempus, 2003.

Kelly, Maria. *A History of the Black Death in Ireland*. Stroud, Gloucs, UK: Tempus, 2001.

Moylan, T. K. "Vagabonds and Sturdy Beggars: Poverty, Pigs and Pestilence in Medieval Dublin," in *Medieval Dublin: The Living City*, edited by H. Clark (Dublin: Irish Academic Press, 1990), 192–199.

Earthquakes

From the beginning of the Second Pandemic, earthquakes have been associated with plague. Biblical passages predicted their concurrence, especially at the end of time (see Apoc/Rev: 6:12, 8:5, 11:13, 11:19, 16:18; Matt: 24:7; Mk 13:8; Lk 21:11). Chroniclers in the late 1340s noted news of great earthquakes in the East that preceded plague there: Italian notary Gabriele de'Mussis mentioned one in "the Indies" that "cast down whole towns." On January 25, 1348, eastern Austria was struck by a large tremor as many sources noted. William of Padua linked the subsequent epidemic directly to it, while Neuberg Abbey's Austrian recorder merely noted they occurred in the same year. A later 14th-century anonymous German commentator further developed the connection of earthquake and plague: "divine wrath" unleashed the quake, which released a "corrupt and poisonous earthy exhalation" that putrefied the atmosphere, creating miasma. The University of Paris's medical faculty (1348) speculated that rotting fish and animals killed by the quake corrupted the atmosphere or that "the escape of rottenness trapped in the center of the earth" was responsible. Later authors linked quakes to planetary conjunctions. Modern researchers dismiss these connections but will admit that tremors can disturb animal habitats in plague reservoirs such that infected rodents are displaced and may join uninfected colonies, creating a chain reaction that could lead to human plague cases.

See also: Apocalypse and Apocalypticism; Astrology; Causes of Plague: Historical Theories; *Compendium of Paris*; Miasma Theory.

References

Horrox, Rosemary. *The Black Death*. New York: Manchester University Press, 1994.

Rohr, Christian. "Man and Natural Disaster in the Late Middle Ages: The Earthquake in Carinthia and Northern Italy on 25 January 1348 and Its Perception." *Environment and History* 9 (2003): 127–149.

Smoller, Laura. "Of Earthquakes, Hail, Frogs, and Geography," in *Last Things: Death and the Apocalypse in the Middle Ages*, edited by Caroline Walker Bynum and Paul Freedman (Philadelphia: University of Pennsylvania Press, 2000), 156–187.

Economic Effects of Plague in Europe

Though the Black Death of 1347 through 1352 had an immediate and pronounced effect on the population and economy of Europe, the economic effects lessened over the following century and a half as the economy adjusted to the greatly decreased population, the virulence of the disease fell, and Europe's population rebounded. Locally, however, the combination of reduced production and commerce during epidemics with the sudden direct costs associated with increasingly complex antiplague efforts drained civic budgets. In the long run, the powerful European economies absorbed the local dislocations caused by plague and moved on.

The Black Death killed perhaps 50 to 60 percent of Europe's population, as many as 45,000,000 to 50,000,000 people. These included every walk of life, producers and consumers, urban and rural, poor and rich, skilled and unskilled, lenders who could no longer provide credit, and creditors who would never repay. Towns were stripped of craftspeople, professionals, and day laborers; rural communities lost heads of households as well as such skilled specialists as managers and blacksmiths. Taxpayers died or moved, leaving houses empty; peasants sought a fresh life in depopulated towns, leaving fields untilled or unharvested. Facing severe labor shortages, some landlords offered wages and special compensation to those who chose to work; others liquidated some or much of their holdings, turning serfs into tenants or day laborers and peasants into farmers. In northern Italy, urban merchants bought up land, established *mezzadria* (share-cropping) relationships with the workers, and shifted from subsistence to commercial production. Prices for agricultural goods, which had risen sharply after the plague, stabilized by the 1370s. Studies of art and architecture suggest a general decline in workshop skill and a shift toward simplicity on the part of patrons, especially those who rose from lower social classes. Survivors benefited from the redistribution of victims' wealth, eventually stoking demand and production, including more meat for the table. Greater disposable income meant demand for luxuries imported and domestic as well as investment in trade and regional commerce.

Many of these trends took several decades to establish themselves, while new episodes of plague struck roughly every decade. One of the major trends was concentration: depopulated parishes consolidated; wealth was now in fewer hands; farmers' average holdings (and buildings) grew in size; small villages disappeared in favor of larger neighbors; smaller towns stagnated as larger regional centers grew (at least in England); cities grew fastest of all, drawing large numbers from the countryside as laborers, apprentices, and servants. England in 1340 had between 2,000 and 3,000 licensed market towns, a number that shrank to 600 by 1550. The number of regional fairs increased as territorial lords sought to capture the benefits of the shrunken economy, but these became more specialized for the sake of economic efficiency. In many places, women entered the economy. Some replaced fallen husbands, others gained new skills as weavers or brewers, many earned their keep as servants. Insofar as they abstained from or delayed childbearing, they helped dampen demographic recovery.

Slow demographic growth combined with disease, war, and famine to keep Europe's economies depressed to the last decades of the 15th century. During the 16th century, European cities began rationalizing their responses to epidemics with isolation of the sick at home or in pest houses, quarantines of suspected victims and goods, improved recordkeeping, and the regulation of public gatherings. Economic effects centered on the cities affected and the networks of towns and trading partners dependent upon them. The very declaration of plague in a city made it a pariah, with central governments creating cordons, ports closing, commerce halting, and those who could fleeing the city. This led to famous cases of long delays in officially admitting the presence of plague and possibly prolonging the agony. Victims and the poor went unprovided for unless private charity or taxes from neighboring areas could be tapped. The Italian ideal of public health required public expenditures on extraordinary medical supplies and personnel, hospitals or pest houses, security details, inspectors, corpse collection and burial, food for those isolated, and materials and wages for house cleaners and fumigators. Normal markets for food and other necessities collapsed, forcing nearby or central governments to provide for survivors, further distorting markets. Some locales resorted to brutal expulsions of the poor or even plague victims to lower their costs. Once an epidemic had ended, however, cities tended to rebound very rapidly as businessmen returned, trade resumed, and rural folks flocked to replace the servants and workers who had been left behind to fend for themselves or die. An important exception was Venice, which lost one-third of its people in the midst of the Thirty Years' War and its own decline.

Some historians understand that plague had broad economic effects across Europe, at least down to 1500. Some believe that the redistribution of wealth in Europe drove up the demand for eastern luxuries and thus sparked the drive for Asian suppliers via the Atlantic. On the other hand, at least one believes that plague delayed European exploration of Africa's coast—and thus Atlantic expansion—at least half a century. Manorialism as an economic system collapsed in part because of the increased opportunities for peasants and the pressures on landlords. Some labor-saving devices may have been invented or spread because of the high cost of labor, but most agricultural advances came before or after the plague's heyday. The printing press, often pointed to, steadily grew in output after the crisis in labor had subsided.

See also: Black Death (1347–1352); Demographic and Economic Effects of Plague: the Islamic World; Demographic Effects of Plague: Europe 1347–1400; Demographic Effects of Plague: Europe 1400–1500; Demographic Effects of Plague: Europe 1500–1722; Dietary Regimens; Economic Effects of Plague in Europe; Epidemic and Pandemic; Famine; Feudalism and Manorialism; Plague in Europe 1360–1500; Public Health; Repopulation; individual cities.

References

Aberth, John. *From the Brink of the Apocalypse: Crisis and Recovery in Late Medieval England.* New York: Routledge, 2000.

Aers, David. "Justice and Wage-labor after the Black Death: Some Perplexities for William Langland," in *The Work of Work: Servitude, Slavery, and Labor in Medieval England*, edited by Allen J. Frantzen and Douglas Moffat (Glasgow: Cruithne Press, 1994), 169–190.

Braid, Robert. "Behavioral Economics, the Black Death and the Labor Market," in *Living with the Black Death*, edited by Lars Bisgaard and Leif Søndergaard (Odense: University of Southern Denmark Press, 2009), 135–159.

Byrne, Joseph. *The Black Death.* Westport, CT: Greenwood, 2004.

Cantor, Norman. *In the Wake of the Plague: The Black Death and the World It Made.* New York: Harper, 2001.

Carmichael, Ann G. *Plague and the Poor in Renaissance Florence.* New York: Cambridge University Press, 1986.

Dodds, Ben and Richard Britnell. *Agriculture and Rural Society after the Black Death: Common Themes and Regional Variations.* Hatfield, Herts., UK: University of Hertfordshire Press, 2008.

Epstein, Steven. "Regional Fairs, Institutional Innovation and Economic Growth in Late Medieval Europe." *Economic History Review* 2nd ed. 47 (1994): 459–482.

Huppert, George. *After the Black Death: A Social History of Early Modern Europe.* 2nd ed. Bloomington: Indiana University Press, 1998.

Mate, Mavis E. *Daughters, Wives and Widows after the Black Death: Women in Sussex, 1350–1535.* Rochester, NY: Boydell Press, 1998.

Platt, Colin. *King Death: The Black Death and its Aftermath in Late-medieval England.* Toronto: University of Toronto Press, 1996.

Stone, David. "Plague, Population and Economic Decline in England in the Later Middle Ages." *Economic History Review* 50 (1997): 640–656.

Thirsk, Joan. *Alternative Agriculture, A History: From the Black Death to the Present Day.* New York: Oxford University Press, 1997.

Economic Effects of Plague in Islam. *See* **Demography and Economic Effects of Plague: Islamic World**

Empirics

Deriving their label from the Greek word for "experience," empirics were medical practitioners who had not graduated from one of Europe's recognized medical schools. Instead, they depended on informal apprenticeships and their own experience of the healing arts. Unlike the ministrations of charlatans and quacks, empirics' treatments were usually considered effective. Though they often differed little from degreed doctors in their understanding of the human body, sickness, and methods of treatment, their lack of formal education usually meant local authorities could not license them. Virtually all Jewish doctors, women practitioners, and Paracelsians were considered empirics. In 1598, the Parlement of Paris formally defined empirics as those practitioners not approved of by the Faculty of Medicine.

These healers remained popular throughout the era of the Second Pandemic. Licensed physicians were relatively rare, usually expensive, and often shunned the lower classes. Elizabethan England had an average of one physician per 100 parishes; London in 1600 boasted one per 4,000 residents; in the 17th century, rural Tuscany had one per 10,000 and Russia a total of 100, none of whom served plague patients. When plague struck, physicians had a tendency to flee with their well-off clients, leaving a vacuum for service often filled by unlicensed healers. Dependent on popular acceptance, empirics took the chances that physicians tended to forego. A royal decree of 1542 protected "honest" English practitioners from harassment by licensed physicians. Rural folk relied regularly on local healers, Tuscan peasants shunning physicians sent to treat them during the epidemic of 1630. Licensing bodies tended to ignore these breaches, sometimes granting licenses to especially effective healers. In July 1589, Jewish physician David de Pomis of Rome petitioned Pope Sixtus V for a license in recognition of his uncompensated services to the state during the recent epidemic.

Both empirics and much of the public were convinced that the theories underlying professional medicine were incorrect, at least as they pertained to plague. Paracelsians with their chemical medicine provided the clearest alternative to official Galenism, but the true empirics set theory aside and relied on observation and their own experience of symptoms and the effects of various remedies. Recognizing the superiority of experiential over learned medicine, beginning in the later 16th century, empirics began empowering common folk by publishing self-help guides from broadsheets to books. Perhaps best known in English are Nicholas Culpepper's publications of the 1650s, especially his *Herbal*.

See also: Charlatans and Quacks; Medical Education (1300–1500, Medieval Europe);

Medical Education (1500–1700, Early Modern Europe); Paracelsus and Paracelsianism; Physicians; Physicians, Court; Physicians, Town; Remedies, External; Remedies, Internal; Women Medical Practitioners.

References

Gottfied, Robert. *Doctors and Medicine in Medieval England, 1340–1530*. Princeton, NJ: Princeton University Press, 1986.

Lingo, Alison Klairmont. "Empirics and Charlatans in Early Modern France: The Genesis of the Classification of the Other in Medical Practice." *Journal of Social History* 19 (1986): 583–604.

Park, Katherine. *Doctors and Medicine in Early Renaissance Florence*. Princeton, NJ: Princeton University Press, 1985.

Wooley, Benjamin. *Heal Thyself: Nicholas Culpepper and the Seventeenth-century Struggle to Bring Medicine to the People*. New York: Harper Collins, 2004.

End of Second Plague Pandemic: Theories

Bubonic plague retreated from Europe between the mid-17th and mid-18th centuries. It did so in a series of major urban outbreaks, each proving to be its last appearance in the host country: Naples, 1656; Amsterdam, 1664 to 1665; London, 1665 to 1666; Vienna, 1712; Marseille, 1720 to 1722; Moscow, 1770 to 1772. Russia's western frontier experienced sporadic outbreaks up to the 1810s and the Ottoman Empire major epidemics into the 1840s. Ironically, only a few decades passed before the Third Plague Pandemic began in central China.

The reasons plague died out in the West remain elusive. Some scholars have adopted a single-factor answer to the question, but more admit the likelihood of the interaction of several causes. For those content merely to list the most likely factors, these fall into two very broad categories: biology and human activity. Biological answers come in several varieties: one or more of the organisms involved (humans, rodents, fleas, *Y. pestis*) changed significantly; or new, natural relationships between two or more of the organisms emerged. From the pandemic's outset, people attempted to avoid or defeat the disease, from the individual's level to that of the nascent nation-states. Most measures were developed early and used often to little effect. Despite the concurrence of the Renaissance and Scientific Revolution, medicine and public health relied on Galenism, humoral theory, and miasma theory and only vague notions of contagion throughout the pandemic.

Natural Causes. The simplest and most elegant explanation would be that the *Yersinia pestis medievalis* biovar—the Second Pandemic's plague germ—mutated very rapidly to become far less virulent, perhaps even to become its *Yersinia enterocolitica* or *Y. pseudotuberculosis* cousins. The rats stopped dying off during epizootics and the fleas remained with their live, rodent hosts; any human hosts would suffer far less as well. But there is no evidence to support this theory; the tapering off would have taken longer and been far more gradual; and with so many human hosts, there was no real advantage to the mutation. Might the presence of *Y. pseudotuberculosis* have cross-immunized Westerners against *Y. pestis*? Researchers recognized such a possible effect but have determined that once in the human body, *Y. pestis* in every form creates an inhibitor that neutralizes other Yersinia bacteria, making cross-immunization unlikely.

Few theories credit changes in the carrier fleas, but several feature the *Rattus rattus*. Some time ago, historians credited the replacement of black *Rattus* with the less flea-pleasing brown *Norvegicus*, which prefers to live away from people. The brown rat does appear in Europe, but after plague's disappearance, in the 18th century (London, 1727; Paris, 1753). Also, *Rattus* did not disappear but has coexisted alongside its new neighbor. Some credit global cooling of the Little Ice Age, which reached low points in the later 17th century, with disrupting the rats' habitats and reproductive cycles, perhaps lowering the population below that needed to sustain epizootics. Others posit that rats may have gained powerful resistance or immunity to the pathogen, but again there is no evidence, and the pattern of disappearance would have been gradual rather than sudden. A last theory suggests that *Y. pestis* never had a reservoir among European fleas and rats, and each epidemic was freshly imported. Stop the imports, stop the epidemics.

Was human biology responsible? Plague seems to confer a rather brief state of immunity on its survivors, but nothing lasting. Widespread mutations may have created strong resistance or immunity among enough people to reduce the percentage of susceptible population significantly. Again, however, the pace of decline is too quick to credit genetics without clear evidence.

Human Action. Fighting plague was an exercise in experiment and observation. Nothing in humoral theory, miasma theory, astrology, or religious explanations outfitted Western authorities and medical practitioners to avoid, prevent, treat, or cure the disease. Modern scholars recognize that some measures may have had a slight effect—fumigating clothing may have driven off fleas, bonfires may have frightened rats—but the effects were minor and incidental, not intended and dramatic. More than any theory, the observation of "contagion," or at least its effects, may well have played an important role in taming plague, at least on a local level.

Perhaps as powerful, if not more so, were environmental changes unrelated to plague programs.

Advances in personal hygiene did occur over the Second Pandemic, which would have disrupted the fleas' human habitats. Bathing, the use of soap, and laundering clothing became more widespread and frequent. Nutrition tended to improve as well, perhaps increasing resistance at the margins. Scholars used to credit the Great Fire of 1666 with ending London's string of plagues, but the conflagration barely touched the most wretched and plague-producing neighborhoods around the City. Rebuilding in brick, tile, and slate is credited with dissuading the return of rats who thrived in thatch and plaster structures. Of course, cheap housing remained in place across Europe, only slowly being replaced with inhospitable stone. The slums of Naples were legendary, yet plague ceased there very early on. Soviet historian V. N. Fyodorov claimed that most Central and Eastern European plague was focused among squirrels and that the expansion of cultivation in the 17th century disrupted their habitats and ended plague. Ecological disruption tends to disseminate plague, however, not dampen it. One economic trend that may have played a role is the shift of major trade routes from the Mediterranean to the Atlantic and beyond. Insofar as the southern and eastern Mediterranean was the main source of reinfection, the shift reduced the risk of plague importation.

This effect of this shift would have been reinforced by intentional policies adopted by European seaports or nations with seaports. In general, if authorities can isolate plague carriers for a long enough period, then the threat of infection is greatly reduced. If a ship approaching a port has or has had cases of plague among its crew or passengers and the ship is diverted to an isolated landing place where crew, passengers, cargo and even rats are quarantined—traditionally a 40- (*quaranta* in Italian) day period—then the disease should be contained. Problems occurred if the disease remained an epizootic among rats that would disembark and infect those on land. Sequestering all ships from suspect ports was one way to enhance quarantine's effectiveness. But ships could run up false flags, authorities accept bribes, and smugglers unload along lonely coastlines.

Land routes from Turkish and Russian lands presented a special problem to Central and Western Europe. Frontiers were long, rugged, and sparsely populated. Rural folk often benefited from helping border jumpers. While governments sought to control access across their borders, they were hard pressed to do so effectively. Russia and later Prussia attempted to control border crossings, but with little success. Maneuvering Russian border units were notorious for sparking plague outbreaks rather than controlling them. The Empire, later Austria, maintained a formally militarized border against the Turks from the early 16th century. From the early 18th, it reinforced this line by settling troops, setting up formal passageways and checkpoints with quarantines. This cordon sanitaire apparently worked very well at keeping plague at bay. Of course, this system postdates most of the terminal outbreaks of plague (Naples, 1656; London, 1665, etc.), so it can hardly be credited with earlier effects.

Kari Konkola presents an intriguing if not entirely satisfying theory in noting the appearance of white arsenic as pest control from the later 17th century. Use of the substance against rats had nothing to do with plague, since no one understood the role rats played. It was, rather, a matter of general cleanliness and sanitation. Arsenic was a byproduct of industrial-scale metals mining and was used in glassmaking and pharmacologically. Konkola estimates that one site in Austria produced 300 to 400 tons per year. It is effective and tasteless and was both available and cheap. Konkola thinks the pattern of retreat reflects what one would expect with the reduction in rodent numbers that would preclude further epizootics. No epizootic, no epidemic.

See also: Bubonic Plague; Cordons Sanitaires; Little Ice Age; Morbidity, Mortality, and Virulence; Public Health; Public Sanitation; Quarantine; Rats and Other Plague Carriers; Shutting In; *Yersinia pestis*.

References

Appleby, A. B. "The Disappearance of the Plague: A Continuing Puzzle." *Economic History Review* 33 (1980): 161–173.

Bayliss, J. H. "The Extinction of Bubonic Plague in Britain." *Endeavour* 4 (1980): 58–66.

Byrne, Joseph P. *Daily Life during the Black Death.* Westport, CT: Greenwood Press, 2006.

Christensen, Peter. "Appearance and Disappearance of the Plague: Still a Puzzle?" In *Living with the Black Death*, edited by Lars Bisgaard and Leif Søndergaard (Odense: University Press of Southern Denmark, 2009), 10–21.

Eckert, Edward A. "The Retreat of Plague from Central Europe, 1640–1720: A Geomedical Approach." *Bulletin of the History of Medicine* 74 (2000): 1–28.

Konkola, Kari. "More Than a Coincidence? The Arrival of Arsenic and the Disappearance of Plague in Early Modern Europe." *History of Medicine* 47 (1992): 186–209.

Rothenberg, Gunther. "The Austrian Sanitary Cordon and the Control of Bubonic Plague: 1710–1871." *Journal of the History of Medicine and Allied Sciences* 28 (1973): 15–23.

Scott, Susan and Christopher Duncan. *The Return of the Black Death.* Hoboken, NJ: Wiley, 2004.

Slack, Paul. "The Disappearance of Plague: An Alternative View." *Economic History Review* 2nd ser. 34 (1981): 469–476.

Epidemic and Pandemic

Diseases come in many forms. Obesity is caused by an individual's behaviors and possibly genetics; diabetes may be triggered by obesity and diet or by genetics; black lung is brought on by breathing atmospheric coal dust; and cancers have genetic, environmental, and behavioral components. Infectious diseases are those in which carriers, who have the disease, transmit the pathogens, or germs that cause the disease, to otherwise healthy people. This might be by direct contact with the carrier's skin, or blood, saliva, or other bodily fluids; or the contact might be indirect, as when a carrier sneezes airborne droplets containing the pathogen in the presence and proximity of other people. Contact, or contagion, might also be through materials exposed to pathogens that remain active, for example, a sick person's clothing or bedclothes, that are brought into close contact with a healthy person who contracts the disease. With the common cold or influenza (flu), the carrier either directly or indirectly infects others. Many diseases, however, require an intermediary, or vector, for example, contaminated water, food, or an insect to transmit the disease from the carrier to the victim. In such cases, such environmental conditions as humidity and temperature can play a major role in the likelihood of transmission because these factors can affect the vectors by inactivating, killing, or interrupting reproduction habits.

A disease is endemic when it is present within a human population at a level that is considered normal, stable, and nonthreatening. The stability is often attributed to behavioral immunization, the adoption of habits that minimize the risk of infection, for example, the use of insecticide or good hygiene or the avoidance of known threats or vectors.

Individual and group immunity may also be bolstered by exposure to the pathogen naturally in nonlethal doses or artificially through vaccination. Exposure stimulates the body's production and employment of the natural cellular defenses that control or destroy the intruding pathogens. An epidemic occurs when one or more of these patterns is broken and new cases increase rapidly. An epidemic may also occur when a new pathogen or a new variation of a pathogen is introduced into a human population, as when Europeans first encountered New World Natives. The weakening of individual immune systems by poor diets or concurrent illnesses or the adoption of habits or relocation to areas conducive to contraction of the pathogens may also increase the likelihood of catching the disease. Changes in the pathogen may make it more or less destructive (virulence) or more or less easily contracted. We see this every year with the predictions as to which strains of flu will be dominant and which new strains are waiting in the wings. We also talk somewhat loosely of an epidemic of obesity or smoking, for example, which are not contagious, because case rates have multiplied very rapidly over some period of time.

The increases in numbers or percentages of new cases per week or month or the numbers killed over a period of time by a pathogen defines an epidemic; but this number may be as political as it is epidemiological. The number(s) chosen is usually the point at which expensive and frightening extraordinary public health efforts go into effect, and so it cannot be set too low; if it is set too high, then attempts at containment will be in vain.

A pandemic is a wide-scale epidemic of a given disease. An epidemic may last a few weeks or months, but a pandemic will last years; an epidemic will strike a city or region, but a pandemic will affect a continent or, given modern transportation, the world. The 19th century saw several cholera pandemics, each lasting less than a decade or so, and in 1918 to 1920, the Influenza Pandemic (Spanish Flu) killed perhaps 20,000,000 worldwide. We speak of the First, Second, and Third Plague Pandemics. The First—the Plague of Justinian—struck the Mediterranean and possibly northern Europe and was characterized by epidemics every few years over nearly three centuries of the early Middle Ages. The Second is the period of recurring epidemics from 1347 to 1850 (or 1666 or 1712 or 1722) and included all of Europe and most of the Muslim world. The Black Death (1347–1353) was itself a pandemic within the Second Pandemic, as it left little of the Christian and Muslim worlds untouched and lasted six years. The Third Plague Pandemic began in East Asia, probably China, and is considered by some to be ongoing (though others end it about 1950).

See also: Black Death (1347–1352); Bubonic Plague; Bubonic Plague in North America; Fleas; Germ Theory; Justinian, Plague of (First Plague Pandemic); Morbidity, Mortality, and Virulence; Rats and Other Plague Carriers; Third Plague Pandemic.

References

Magnus, Manya. *Essentials of Infectious Disease Epidemiology*. Sudbury, MA: Jones and Bartlett, 2008.

Snodgrass, Mary Ellen. *World Epidemics*. Jefferson, NC: McFarlane, 2003.

Watts, Sheldon. *Epidemics and History: Disease, Power and Imperialism*. New Haven, CT: Yale University Press, 1997.

Ex voto

Catholic ex voto images are those created after having made a vow to God or saints.

More telling than the style or theme is the intent of the patron or purchaser: thanksgiving, hope, love, or devotion. Paintings, statues, banners, prints, wax body parts, even churches dedicated to a protecting or healing saint or to God may be considered ex voto: a tangible offering to the spiritual figure. The hopeful or thankful could be simple individuals, religious brotherhoods, families, town councils, kings or popes, and the works generally appeared in public for inspiration. The object's imagery is generally associated with the spiritual entity and the reason for hope or thanks. Local patron saints, plague saints like Roche and Sebastian, the Virgin Mary and Child, or several of these together, and scenes of saintly intercession during a plague or of biblical plagues or scenes of healing or resurrection mark plague ex votos. Failure to give thanks through an ex voto could have dire consequences.

See also: Art, Effects of Plague on; Bible; Biblical Plagues; Broadsheets, Broadsides, and Pamphlets; Plague Memorials; Plague Saints; Prayer and Fasting; Virgin Mary.

References

Boeckl, Christine. *Images of Plague and Pestilence: Iconography and Iconology*. Kirksville, MO: Truman State University Press, 2000.

Mormando, Franco and Thomas Worcester, eds. *Piety and Plague from Byzantium to the Baroque*. Kirksville, MO: Truman State University Press, 2007.

Expulsion of Victims

One way for a town to deal with the victims of plague was to expel them from the city. As early as 1348, Uzerche, France, expelled unfortunate victims, and Pistoia's plague ordinances called for "the sick" to be removed from the city: destination unclear. Presumably, the fear was contagion. On January 17, 1374, Milan's lord Bernabò Visconti informed his deputy (*podestà*) in Reggio that during an epidemic, priests were to inform on all plague victims to the searchers, who would have them expelled beyond the city walls. Some could occupy huts, and others merely live "in the woods," "until [they] either die or recover" (Horrox, 203). The means was draconian and the effect chilling and inhumane, but the Visconti understood the threat that plague carriers represented. Harsh communal isolation had preserved Milan in 1348 and again in 1360, and the Dukes' control over the capital and its dependents was unquestioned.

By 1400, the Milanese were constructing tiny extramural *mansiones* for victims, a step toward pest houses. In part, this reflected the resistance to housing the sick in hospitals and, in part, it recognized that having the contagious sick wandering the countryside only spread the disease further. Plague authorities developed pest houses and isolation of the sick in their own homes, which theoretically obviated the need to ban victims. Yet Florence did so in 1498 and Troyes in 1497, as, no doubt, did many cities. Overcrowding of facilities was one excuse, but the ritual power of "cleansing" that expulsions represented was another powerful motive. As much as anything, frustration drove the Florentine officers, who drove the sick from their hospital beds and out the city gates, threatening any who returned with excruciating torture. As a contemporary diarist commented, "It was a brutal thing and a harsh remedy."

By 1500, plague had long been associated with strangers—Gypsies, Jews, vagabonds—who also found themselves expelled when plague threatened. Even a city's native poor became targets for harsh treatment as the Second Pandemic entered its third century. In September 1539, the Venetian Council of Ten noted that Milan had expelled "poor persons suspected of carrying the plague" and ordered that these be barred from entering Venice. Venice then acted in kind, banishing 4,000 to 5,000 beggars and other recent immigrants, many of them to service on the city's galleys. As with the next-mentioned group, whores, there were moral and sanitary as well as medical elements to these bans. The same combination appeared again 90 years later as Venice prepared for civic religions processions. In June 1630, they paid off with state alms the poor who were loitering along the parade route. On October 22, Venice again targeted beggars near a processional route, transporting them to the island monastery of San Lazzaro dei Mendicanti. The same day, the Council vowed to build the votive church of Santa Maria della Salute.

But Italy was not alone in the practice. As plague loomed, Seville in 1581 tried to protect the city by shipping out all people ill of indefinite diseases to "houses of cure." Dartmouth, England, had practiced a similar prophylaxis in 1563 with all who were sick and poor. In 1585, 350 of the poorest folk of Pont-à-Mousson were banned to fend for themselves. Local Jesuits, however, provided bread and wine twice weekly to them over a two-month period.

See also: Contagion Theory; Governments, Civil; Lazarettos and Pest Houses; Leprosy (Hansen's Disease) and Leprosarium; Moral Legislation; Poverty and Plague; Public Health; Public Sanitation; Shutting In.

References

Carmichael, Ann G. *Plague and the Poor in Renaissance Florence*. New York: Cambridge University Press, 1986.

Pullan, Brian. "Plague and Perceptions of the Poor in Early Modern Italy," in *Epidemics and Ideas*, edited by Terence Ranger and Paul Slack (New York: Cambridge University Press, 1992), 101–123.

Eyam, England (1666)

As plague raged in London in 1665, the provinces prayed they would be spared. The small village of Eyam, in Derbyshire, with its roughly 400 souls, remained blessed until late summer 1665. Pestilence arrived, it was said, in a load of London cloth, and the tailor receiving it was the first to die. Some villagers fled, and their spiritual leader, 26-year-old William Mompesson, and his wife sent their children away. Mompesson convinced the remainder that if all stayed in their homes and those outside the village sealed them off from all personal contact, then they could isolate the disease to their families and spare thousands of others. Most remained, living off of the charity provided by neighboring villagers who agreed not to cross a line—a cordon sanitaire—between the infested, suffering Eyam and the outside world. Of course, the people of Eyam could not cross either, under severe penalties. For 14 months, the plague raged, killing some 260—including Mrs. Mompesson—and leaving about 100 survivors in various states of shock. Though they established a pest house, many died in their homes and were buried by their relatives. As local poet Mary Howitt wrote:

The dead are everywhere!
The mountainside; the plain; the woods profound;
All the lone dells—the fertile and the fair,
Is one vast burial ground.

The Parish Church of St. Lawerence, Eyam. (StockPhotoPro)

Today, many original buildings remain, and Eyam itself is a plague memorial, with an annual church service in commemoration of the community's self-sacrifice.

See also: Cordons Sanitaires; London, Great Plague of; Plague Memorials; Quarantine; Shutting In.

References

Slack, Paul. *The Impact of Plague in Tudor and Stuart England*. Boston: Routledge and Kegan Paul, 1985.

Wallis, Patrick. "A Dreadful Heritage: Interpreting Epidemic Diseases at Eyam, 1666–2000." *History Workshop Journal* 61 (2006): 31–56.

F

Famine

"First dearth, then plague," went the old saying from the Second Pandemic. Some historians have related the two causally; others deny any causal connection, claiming random coincidence when an epidemic follows a period of famine. While remaining apart from this controversy, this short entry will provide some food for thought.

During the late medieval and early modern periods, about one year in every six suffered famine in any given area of Europe. Food shortages affected not only people but the commensal rat populations as well. Scarcity could drive them further afield than usual, could weaken their own immune systems, leading to faster and more frequent die-offs, or could lead to stronger but infected populations replacing weakened, local ones.

Italy and Spain both suffered dearth in 1347, and plague broke out in 1348 and thereafter. Europe suffered its worst famines sine 1317 in 1438 to 1440, and plague broke out in 1439. Poor harvests lead to food shortages and rises in prices. People in susceptible categories are malnourished, with attendant weakened immune systems and resistance to disease. Endemic diseases (plague?) become epidemic. This "common sense" picture has been challenged by studies of grain prices—a proxy for dearth—and has been found wanting. In general, epidemics of plague broke out independently of environmental factors. They also killed indiscriminately: rich and poor died proportionately, though their diets no doubt differed markedly. Jordan saw the possibility of a long-term effect: that famines around 1320 nutritionally weakened children, who grew into the susceptible adult victims of 1348 to 1350.

Epidemics did lead to localized food shortages, at least to the 16th century. Rural epidemics killed off and weakened workers at just the time of year all hands were needed for harvest. Crops were left to rot or feed animals. The healthy fled to stay that way, often moving to towns that were seeking laborers. Towns that were stricken also suffered food shortages as providers refused to trade with the unfortunates behind their walls. With the flight of the well-off, the poor were left to fend for themselves. Around 1400, European observers began associating plague with the poor, especially perceived filthiness and immoral habits, but poor nutrition went largely unnoticed. The single biggest factor in contracting plague is access to the infected rat fleas, and while the development of one's immune system may be a factor in the likelihood of mortality, it does not stave off fleas.

See also: Bubonic Plague; Diseases, Opportunistic and Subsidiary.

References

Aberth, John. *From the Brink of the Apocalypse: Crisis and Recovery in Late Medieval England*. New York: Routledge, 2000.

Cunningham, Andrew and Ole Peter Grell. *The Four Horsemen of the Apocalypse: Religion, War, Famine and Death in Reformation Europe*. New York: Cambridge University Press, 2000.

Jordan, William Chester. *The Great Famine: Northern Europe in the Early Fourteenth Century*. Princeton, NJ: Princeton University Press, 1996.

Ó Gráda, Cormac. *Famine: A Short History.* Princeton, NJ: Princeton University Press, 2009.

Fernel, Jean (c. 1497–1558)

Born to a well-off furrier in Montdidier, France, Fernel studied locally and went on to graduate in philosophy and rhetoric from the University of Paris. With family support, he continued his own studies until forced to choose a career. Returning to Paris, he completed the Doctor of Medicine in 1530. After teaching for several years, he turned to writing. Fernel was a trained Galenist, but he developed refinements in the classical model that addressed the admitted weaknesses in the model's treatment of such "contagious" diseases as plague.

He laid the groundwork with his *Physiologia* (1542–1554), a Galenic textbook of the first order, followed by *On the Hidden Causes of Things* (1548), in which he specifically tackled contagious and infectious diseases. Bypassing humoral effects, Fernel saw these diseases as assaults on the body as a holistic system, though the precise mechanisms remained occult (hidden). Equally problematic was the matter of apparent interpersonal transmission. He posited that both worked in ways similar to alchemical processes, or the effects of magnetism on metals, or the stars on human lives (astrology). The resulting explanation was unsatisfying, however, even for him. Ironically, his inability to reform Galenism underlined its problems and led to further erosion of its dominant position in the era of Fracastoro and Paracelsus.

See also: Contagion Theory; Fracastoro, Girolamo; Galen and Galenism; Humoral Theory; Paracelsus and Paracelsianism.

References

Forrester, John M., translator, and John Henry, editor. *On the Hidden Causes of Things* [Jean Fernel]: *Forms, Souls and Occult Diseases in Renaissance Medicine.* Boston: Brill, 2005.

Feudalism and Manorialism

Feudalism and manorialism, if one chooses to accept their existence, developed in ninth- and 10th-century Europe as the Carolingian Empire disintegrated. Feudalism organized the upper echelons of Western European society around the exchange of military service for landholding and the benefits of the products of that land. The resulting hierarchical system produced the political terrain on which central authorities (kings, emperors) were heavily beholden to their vassals (dukes, counts, barons, bishops), who marshaled the knights who controlled the countryside and rode into battle. In feudalism, kings usually had authority and respect but little power to enforce their will. Manorialism refers to the economic relationships that supported the knights on their landholdings, or manors. The landlords needed labor to grow and harvest crops, and the agricultural laborers (peasants, serfs) needed access to land and security on it to grow food for themselves and their families. Custom and tradition going back centuries set the terms for manorial relations, which locally had the force of law. The laborers performed the necessary agricultural work and additional tasks (road and common building repair, for example) while the landlord provided necessary tools, seed, horses, and such less tangible goods as defense and justice within the village, all of which was determined by custom.

From the late 11th century, depending where one was in Europe, these systems had begun to change and disappear. Many of the traditions remained, but several powerful forces were undermining the balances that had been struck. Rapid population growth and the growth of towns and cities made peasant labor less valuable; agricultural innovation made crop yields higher per acre and created surpluses that were soaked up by new markets in towns; the circulation of money increased, so that land was proportionally less important as a form of wealth; taxes collected in cash replaced in-kind payments, which provided society's rulers more flexibility in developing their resources; monarchs often allied with cash-generating townspeople to reduce their reliance on nobles and the Church; and aggressive monarchs gained power by fighting and diplomacy, marriage, and centralizing their authority over royal armies, courts of justice, and revenue-producing activities.

By the mid-1300s, both feudalism and manorialism had changed radically from their classic forms. Of all the developments, three factors stand out: population growth, money, and cities. When the Black Death struck, the three factors were altered and combined to accelerate the decline of feudalism and manorialism. First, populations dropped suddenly and precipitously. Though upper classes as well as workers died away, the huge proportion of workers in society— no fewer than 85 percent in most areas— weighted their losses. The value of labor rose, and the chaos of the era meant easier escape from village life to depopulated towns. Though monarchs sought to stabilize the situation by passing laws against raising wages or reducing village customs, landlords and urban craftsmen incentivized workers by raising their incomes and reducing their obligations. The value of the land, too, dropped as the cost of labor rose, driving large landholders, including monasteries and bishops, to sell off portions of their holdings or to shift production away from crops to sheep or other commercial animals (enclosing).

The continued rise in importance of markets continued to support the rise of a powerful middle class, especially in Italy, England, and the Netherlands. Traditionally, this class played no role in either feudal relations or manorial economics, which tended to be self-supporting. Plague tended to concentrate money and other resources in the hands of fewer, while it reduced the numbers of individuals or "hearths" that could be taxed by central authorities. Slowly in France and Spain, more rapidly in England, a rural middling class emerged—*yeoman* in England—that helped dissolve both the feudal ties that had organized rural society and the manorial custom that had anchored it. They acquired the land from those desperate to sell and worked it with a contractual labor force rather than "captive" villagers. In England, the slightly higher gentry class also consolidated land and worked it with salaried labor and became the monarchs' tool for stabilizing the countryside as justices of the peace, sheriffs, and coroners and represented the countryside as elected members of the House of Commons.

Towns continued to profit from rural depopulation as each epidemic raised the need anew for new day laborers, apprentices, and servants. Though population growth reached a self-sustaining level across Europe by around 1500 and, through the century, led to large population gains in much of it, each urban epidemic opened the doors for rural migration. Where urban development was thin, as in Catalonia and parts of Central and much of Eastern Europe, the old feudal elite could and did maintain a much tighter control over their peasants. The initial waves of plague brought tighter restrictions and heavier duties on those lucky enough to have survived. The lack of a well-developed cash market for peasants' rural produce meant fewer options for the laborers and little leverage with their landlords. The result was a retrenchment, with the promise of punishment and retribution; in parts of Poland, it is even referred to as refeudalization. In 1525, peasant resentment in Germany led leaders to grab onto Martin Luther's idea of Christian freedom and demand its application. They violently killed landowners and seized property, demanding release from what they considered both traditional manorial burdens and novel impositions. Eventually spurred on by Luther, both Catholic and Protestant authorities soaked the soil in peasant blood, slaughtering entire communities; all told, perhaps as many as 100,000 fell victim.

See also: Bishops and Popes; Economic Effects of Plague in Europe; Labourers, Ordinance and Statute of; Nobility; Peasants; Yeoman Farmers and Gentry.

References

Britnell, R. H. "Feudal Reaction after the Black Death in the Palatinate of Durham." *Past & Present* 128 (1990): 28–47.

Byrne, Joseph P. *Daily Life during the Black Death*. Westport, CT: Greenwood, 2006.

Hilton, Rodney. *Class Conflict and the Crisis of Feudalism: Essays in Medieval Social History*. London: Hambledon Press, 1985.

Poos, Larry. *A Rural Society after the Black Death: Essex, 1350–1525*. New York: Cambridge University Press, 1991.

Ficino, Marsiglio (1433–1499)

Humanist, Platonist, priest, and sometime physician, Marsiglio (Marsilius) Ficino was born to a Florentine surgeon, Ficino, who served Cosimo de'Medici. Marsiglio received training in medicine but turned to humanist studies of Greek and Latin literature while at the Medici court. He specialized in Plato and translated many of the Greek philosopher's works, as well as producing his own, for example, the *Platonic Theology*, which blends Christianity and Platonism. He was ordained a priest in 1473.

Florence had experienced plague in 1439, 1449, 1450, 1456, and between 1464 and 1468. During or shortly after the plague outbreak of 1478/1479, Ficino wrote, in Italian, his *Consiglio contro la pestilentia*, which was published in 1481 and published in Latin in 1518. It remained an authoritative text for nearly three centuries. He meant it to be a practical guide for the benefit of his fellow Tuscans—laymen and practitioners alike—hence his use of the vernacular. Relying heavily on the early *consilium* of Gentile da Foligno, Ficino nevertheless trimmed away a good deal of the speculative material typical of the genre. Also missing is an explicit role for divine causation, though he admits to the epidemic's celestial source. Russell estimates that 95 percent of the tract is preventatives and treatments, the latter including many surgical procedures. Ficino also specifies certain amulets and talismans derived from his study of ancient occult sources and relies on current applications of astrology to medicine.

See also: Amulets, Talismans, and Magic; Astrology; Consilia and Plague Tracts; Florence, Italy; Gentile da Foligno; Physicians.

References

Biow, Douglas. *Doctors, Ambassadors, Secretaries: Humanism and Professions in Renaissance Italy*. Chicago: University of Chicago Press, 2002.

Katinis, Teodoro. *Medicina e filosofia in Marsilio Ficino: Il Consilio contro la pestilenza*. Rome: Edizioni di storia e letteratura, 2007.

Russell, Paul A. "Ficino's *Consiglio contro la pestilentia* in the European Tradition." *Verbum, Analecta neolatina* 1 (1999): 85–96.

First Plague Pandemic. *See* Justinian, Plague of

Flagellants

When Jesus was being prepared for his crucifixion, the Roman guards scourged him with a flabellum, a whip of many leather strands, each of which ended in a dumbbell-shaped piece of lead. In the later Middle Ages, monks and other Christians—most often males—who sought to imitate physically the flagellation and suffering of Jesus did so by beating themselves with whips (*flagella*) or by joining groups who carried this ritual out on each other. Their idea was that such pain and suffering would help atone for their sinfulness and that of their communities; it was a form of self-imposed penance. The revival movement of 1260, known as the Great Alleluia, popularized the practice, and local church authorities organized many practitioners into parish penitential confraternities, alongside those formed for praise and for service to the needy. Known as *disciplinati* in Italy, after the discipline-inducing whip they used, these anonymous flagellant groups met in secret, often at night, and with clerical supervision, often by a Franciscan friar. The practice spread across much of Europe and is still evident in Spanish towns and villages. During the epidemic of 1576, 1,000 hooded *disciplinati* accompanied Archbishop Charles Borromeo's penitential procession through Milan.

The Black Death, understood as a punishment for sin, markedly increased participation in flagellant confraternities. The Franciscan-sponsored group in Florence, for example, normally added six or seven new members per year, but in 1348, 106 joined. During the same year, 109 members died, some on the day of their admission. The year 1349 saw 36 join and 1350 another 20. In 1350, there were 134 members, though only 26 of these had been enrolled as of June 1348.

Gherardus of Cosvelde, a scholar in Münster, Germany, cast the horoscope for another flagellant movement spawned by the Black Death. It would, he claimed, be from "the east," a product of natural mania, not divine inspiration, powerful but hypocritical and false, ending suddenly and infamously. This was a movement of thousands of men of all statuses who took to the roads of central Europe for 33-day stints of itinerant group flagellation. Originating in Austria (or perhaps Hungary or Northern Italy), the penitential processions moved from town to town in Germany and the Low Countries, singing vernacular hymns or silently praying while on the road. They halted in town squares to give a dramatic performance of beating one another on the back while praying. Witnesses relate that the barefoot flagellants wore only a long skirt and hood, leaving the wounds and scars on their torsos very visible. The whipcords were tipped with sharp metal bits that drew copious blood that is described as spattering the walls, roads, and bystanders. Some treated this blood as they would a holy relic and the penitents as holy men.

Clerics, on the other hand, disdained the "arrogant," self-proclaimed martyrs for their lack of clerical leadership. Unless the Church sanctioned and led these processions, they were little more than mockeries of the Church. Fears arose that some of the lay leaders were heretics or at least displaying heterodox tendencies. Some witnesses reported anticlerical preaching and assaults and claims that

acbiti anno predito qi in die ceperuut compati persoms et
accumptions uirgins glos penteure condolere et deo gra
ose venerunt a uilla brugen tias reddere super tanta peni
si arater. cc. hominre. quasi hora rencia quam grauissimam re

Flagellants in the Netherlands town of Tournai, 1349. Flagellants, known as the Brothers of the Cross, scourging themselves as they walk through the streets in order to free the world from the Black Death. (Ann Ronan Pictures/StockphotoPro)

processors recognized only the authority of God. Others noted that some flagellants considered their blood to be as holy as that shed by Christ. A few recorded statements seem to link the flagellants with apocalypticism, their extreme activities helping to bring about the world's end.

Holy Roman Emperor Charles and the University of Paris's Theology Faculty urged Pope Clement to condemn the movement, which was seen as preying on common people's fears, instilling false hopes, and stirring up trouble. Spurred by the personal report of the Flemish Benedictine Jean de Fayt, on October 20, 1349,

the pope complied through the bull *Inter sollecitudines*. In this, he linked the movement to anti–Semitic activity, including reports of murder in Frankfurt and Cologne. He wrote that they seemed "not in the least afraid to shed the blood of Jews." Contemporaries sometimes linked the presence and even preaching of flagellants to outbreaks of violence against Jews and Jewish communities in Germany and the Low Countries. While this is far from improbable, modern studies tend to conclude that while both flagellant appearances and pogroms preceded local epidemics as social prophylaxes, there seem to have been few causal connections.

In 1350, the movement appears to have broken up and gone underground in Thuringia. Lübeck, Erfurt, and Strassburg had refused entry to the flagellants, and other towns increasingly complied with the pope's bull to suppress the activity. One modern scholar estimates that the year-long movement touched perhaps a million lives.

See also: Anti–Semitism and Anti–Jewish Violence before the Black Death; Anticlericalism; Apocalypse and Apocalypticism; Bishops and Popes; Black Death (1347–1352); Chronicles and Annals; Confraternities; Prayer and Fasting; Processions; Sin.

References

Cohn, Norman. *The Pursuit of the Millennium.* New York: Oxford University Press, 1990.

Henderson, John. "The Flagellant Movement and Flagellant Confraternities in Central Italy, 1260–1400." *Studies in Church History* 15 (1978): 147–160.

Kieckhefer, Richard. "Radical Tendencies in the Flagellant Movement of the Mid-Fourteenth Century." *Journal of Medieval and Renaissance Studies* 4 (1974): 157–176.

Nohl, Johannes. *The Black Death: A Chronicle of the Plague.* Translated by C. H. Clarke. London: George Allen and Unwin, 1926; reprinted Yardley, PA: Westholme Publishing, 2006.

Ziegler, Philip. *The Black Death.* New York: Harper and Row, 1969.

Fleas

The bubonic plague bacterium *Yersinia pestis* is most readily carried from victim to victim in the foregut of the rat fleas *Xenopsylla cheopis* and *Nosopsyllus fasciatus*. *X. cheopis* is a small, wingless flea that moves by jumping, normally four inches, three when engorged with bacteria. It clings with tiny hooks on its legs and prepares to feed by piercing its host's skin with two organs called maxillary laciniae. Blood is siphoned from the host's small vein (venule) into the foregut (proventriculus) and then gut, where the flea digests its sanguine meal. When the rat host has *Y. pestis* in its bloodstream, these bacteria are taken in by the flea along with the blood. This pollutant, however, is usually kept isolated in the foregut rather than being digested. Here the bacteria reproduce, multiply, and eventually may block passage of fresh meals into the digestive system. The hungry flea will pierce its host numerous times or change hosts, trying to clear its foregut by regurgitating masses of bacteria and other infected material into the venules. If enough is cleared to allow successful feeding, some of the regurgitated material is likely to be redrawn into the foregut, reinfecting the flea or adding to its bacterial count. The flea may also defecate onto the host's skin feces that contain bacteria that survived digestion; this may be introduced subdermally by scratching. The blocked flea will remain infectious (and alive) for up to six weeks, averaging about 17 days. If the flea is not blocked, it does not infect. Infection requires a minimum of 25,000 bacteria, an amount passed only through regurgitation. Human infection through insect regurgitation is very rare, the only other known case being the sandfly's transmission of the pathogens responsible for Leishmaniasis.

X. cheopis prefers high relative humidity and temperatures within the range 13° to 34°C; adults will hibernate when temperatures drop further. They range in length from 1.5 to 4 millimeters and, when healthy, will live about one year. They prefer to live on rodents, but humans will do when rat hosts die off. A typical rat will host around a dozen fleas, keeping the population down by grooming. A dying rat, foregoing grooming, may host 50 to 100 fleas. Fleas have been found to survive on grain debris away from blood meals for several weeks, so flea transmission of plague absent rats is possible. Blood meals are necessary for reproduction, however, as are temperatures between 20° and 25°C.

Thirty-one species of flea can be vectors of plague, though none is as efficient as *X. cheopis*. Some scholars attribute the widespread nature of the Black Death to its spread by the versatile, multihost flea, *Pulex irritans*. Attracted to humans, *P. irritans* seems much better fitted to northern climates, where *X. cheopis* is far less comfortable, and infrequent changes of bedding and clothing minimized disturbance. Not subject to blockage and regurgitation, *Pulex* could only infect by means of the bacteria on its siphoning organs, which in any single case would be far below the critical mass needed for infection. Supporters suggest that sheer numbers of infectious bites would make up for nonregurgitation, but critics reply that human blood sources would have to be septicemic for *Pulex* to pick up the bacteria. Studies of modern plagues show a limited role for *Pulex*.

The problems apparent in flea transmission have led many to seek other explanations for the nature and spread of "plague" during the Second Pandemic.

See also: Animals; Black Death: Debate over the Medical Nature of; Bubonic Plague; Pneumonic Plague; Rats and Other Plague Carriers; Yersin, Alexandre; *Yersinia pestis*.

References

Benedictow, Ole. *The Black Death 1346–1353: The Complete History*. Rochester, NY: Boydell & Brewer, 2004.

Eisen, R. J., et al. "Early-Phase Transmission of *Yersinia pestis* by Unblocked Fleas as a Mechanism Explaining Rapidly Spreading Plague Epizootics." *Proceedings of the National Academy of Sciences of the USA* 103 (2006): 15380–15385.

Gross, Ludwik. "How the Plague Bacillus and its Transmission through Fleas Were Discovered: Reminiscences from My Years at the Pasteur Institute in Paris." *Proceedings of the National Academy of Sciences of USA* 92 (1995): 7609–7611.

Marriott, Edward. *Plague: A Story of Science, Rivalry, Scientific Breakthrough and the Scourge that Won't Go away*. New York: Holt, 2002.

Moseng, Ole Georg. "Climate, Ecology and Plague: The Second and the Third Pandemic Reconsidered," in *Living with the Black Death*, edited by Lars Bisgaard and Leif Søndergaard (Odense: University of Southern Denmark Press, 2009), 23–45.

Flight

"Flee quickly, far away, stay long." This plague-time advice is echoed throughout the Second Pandemic, by physicians no less than common folk. If plague spread by some form of contagion or local miasmic poisoning or psychic stress from plague horrors increased vulnerability (as Galenists believed it did), the advice matches the theory. If plague is simply God's will, no distance will separate one from his fate. In 1564, a Catholic magistrate in Lyon, France, noted predestinarian Calvinists who refused to flee died "in heaps."

Muslims wavered between Galenic—and common-sense—recommendations to flee plague-stricken areas and religious laws against flight. Flight seemed to challenge Allah's will and omnipotence; to remain was to submit in the spirit of Islam. Muhammad in the Hadith counseled "Neither flee nor enter a region where plague is found." Since Muhammad lived during the Plague of Justinian and rejected contagion theory, scholars have argued whether the rule is merely pragmatic or religious in nature. In 639, Muhammad's successor Caliph 'Umar relocated his army away from a plague-stricken area in Syria, a precedent for licit flight.

Records for such cities as Cairo show that while the court and many residents often fled, crowds of villagers entered the cities, fleeing their homes and, presumably, the plague. This historically voiceless multitude may have been seeking food, wages, alms, spiritual strength at shrines, doctors, medicines, or amulets, not foreseeing urban conditions. Their relocation probably helped spread plague, added to the urban death tolls, and exaggerated rural tolls while further depopulating the food-producing countryside from Spain to Iran.

In *Decameron* (1352), Boccaccio's 10 aristocratic storytellers flee Florence's plague to relax in a suburban villa. He emphasizes that there is nothing they can do in the city; medical advice of the day clearly recommended avoiding upsetting scenes. Monarchs and their entourages fled to royal rural retreats; aristocrats to villas, country houses, and estates; bishops to episcopal manor houses; merchants to the houses of friends, family, and partners. In 1374, Gualberto Morelli hosted more than 20 relatives in his home in Bologna. In 1390 and 1400, Tuscan merchant Francesco Datini sought out accommodations abroad as pestilence threatened his native Prato. He rented a house in Pistoia in 1390 and, following many other Tuscans, moved family and employees to Bologna in 1400. Letters from those left behind in Prato chronicle the carnage in litanies of victims.

In 16th- and 17th-century England, even the wealthy fleeing London had trouble finding rural accommodations. Fear of contagion led innkeepers to remove signs, villages to post guards against refugees, and farmers to deny travelers food and roust those sleeping in their barns. Poet John Donne wrote of Londoners carrying enough money to buy an entire village dying alone on its outskirts. Children, or mothers and children, of the higher classes were often sent away early in an epidemic. William Bullein described in his *Dialogue* "wagons, carts and horses fully loaded ... " He also noticed that refugees feared each other as much as rural folks feared them as sources of contagion.

Among the working and lower classes, some could flee to family in nearby villages, and others occupied abandoned seasonal huts and sheds outside of town. When the wealthy fled, they generally took their money with them, which meant both tax receipts and charity plummeted. Businesses closed and fired employees, families dismissed servants, and the once-working poor joined the urban indigent. Finally, the flight of certain civic officials—who were sometimes fined for desertion—and clergy, notaries, and physicians presented issues of professional ethics: should doctors follow their fleeing rich patients or remain to tend the sick? In England, at least, professionals' flight left behind such marginal figures as medical empirics and dissenting clerics, whose reputations and popularity rose.

See also: Abandonment; Anticlericalism; Chronicles and Annals; Civil Governments; Consilia and Plague Tracts; Contagion Theory; Jonson, Ben; Muhammad the Prophet; Pastors, Preachers, and Ministers; Physicians; Priests; Repopulation.

References

Aberth, John. *Plagues in World History.* New York: Rowman and Littlefield, 2011.

Conrad, Lawrence I. "'Umar at Sargh: The Evolution of an Umayyad Tradition on Flight from the Plague," in *Story-Telling in the*

Framework of Non-fictional Arabic Literature, edited by S. Leder (Wiesbaden: Harrassowitz, 1998), 488–528.

Dols, Michael W. *The Black Death in the Middle East*. Princeton, NJ: Princeton University Press, 1977.

Luther, Martin. "Whether One May Flee from a Deadly Plague," in *Luther's Works*, Vol. 43, edited and translated by G. K. Wienke (Philadelphia: Fortress Press, 1968), 115–138.

Florence, Italy

Florence is nestled among the Tuscan hills at what was the lowest bridgeable point on the Arno River. Its bridge served the busy medieval highway between Rome and France, and its ports at Livorno and Pisa carried raw wool to Florentine carders and back out to sea as fine woolen cloth. Its commercial success became financial power with the growth of banking, though this suffered disaster when the English king reneged on large loans in the 1340s. Ruled loosely by German emperors, the city was a republic and sometimes, in fact, as the Medici family ruled first *de facto* (1434–1492) and then as dukes and grand dukes of Tuscany from 1512.

The Black Death struck Italy's third largest and wealthiest city in March 1348. Its approach prompted leading citizens to hasten public sanitation regulations. People from infected areas were banned, as was the sale of victims' clothing and other goods. By April 11, measures had proven ineffective, and the city established a special committee to direct antiplague activities, one of Europe's earliest. It discussed establishing a new hospital, monitoring the spread of plague, and targeting the most needy with charity. The various fates of the roughly 100,000 residents were brilliantly described by poet and raconteur Giovanni Boccaccio in the Introduction to his *Decameron* and recorded less literarily by the Villanis and other observers. The disease killed for about seven months, during which death tolls rose to perhaps 1,000 per day. By October, the population had been cut roughly in half.

In-migration from the countryside helped Florence rebound, but epidemics recurred in 1363 and during each decade into the 1420s. Even though average death tolls dropped from that of 1348, social and economic pressures were exacerbated by plague and kept Florence's estimated population numbers depressed (60,000 in 1401; 37,000 in 1427; 40,000 in 1480) and helped spark the Ciompi Revolt in 1383. Epidemics recurred an average of every 13 years during the first half of the 15th century and an average of every 37 years during the second. Florence's "Books of the Dead," or *Libri della Grascia morti*, were a type of bills of mortality kept by the Grain Office until the later 18th century. Based upon parish burial records, from 1424, cause of death was required for each entry. The government experimented again with a temporary health commission in 1448 and, in 1464, made plans to build a pest house for plague victims. The 200-bed hospital of Santa Maria Nuova, which served plague victims, established and ran the 26-bed extramural pest house of San Bastiano from the 1470s to June 1527. Henceforth it was run by the new, permanent five-member health magistracy established by the Medici duke and called the Ufficiali di Sanità.

Florence's last major bout with plague occurred in 1630 to 1633 during the Thirty Years' War. It probably crossed the Alps in 1629 with invading troops and ended up killing some 280,000 over several years. In Florence, the epidemic killed about 7,000, or 10 percent of the city's population and was well documented and well handled by overwrought authorities. Florence's health magistracy oversaw all of the duke's Tuscan territory and coordinated efforts at providing medical care and appropriate isolation in pest houses. Such success as there was led to the *concerto*, an agreement among Italian cities and territories to monitor and share information on pestilential outbreaks and prepare accordingly.

See also: Boccaccio, Giovanni; Ciompi Revolt; Health Boards, Magistracies, and Commissions; Lazarettos and Pest Houses; Public Sanitation.

References

Calvi, Giulia. *Histories of a Plague Year: The Social and the Imaginary in Baroque Florence.* Berkeley: University of California Press, 1989.

Carmichael, Ann G. *Plague and the Poor in Renaissance Florence.* New York: Cambridge University Press, 1986.

Cipolla, Carlo. *Public Health and the Medical Profession in Renaissance Florence.* Cambridge: Cambridge University Press, 1976.

Day, William R. "The Population of Florence before the Black Death: Survey and Synthesis." *Journal of Medieval History* 28 (2002): 93–129.

Henderson, John. "The Black Death in Florence: Medical and Communal Responses," in *Death in Towns*, edited by Steven Bassett (New York: Leicester University Press, 1992), 136–150.

Park, Katherine. *Doctors and Medicine in Early Renaissance Florence.* Princeton, NJ: Princeton University Press, 1985.

Tetel, Marcel, et al., editors. *Life and Death in Fifteenth Century Florence.* Durham, NC: Duke University Press, 1989.

Fracastoro, Girolamo (1478–1553)

The physician, humanist, and poet was born to an old, aristocratic family whose seat was near Verona, Italy. Fracastoro was tutored by his father and then sent to the University of Padua. He studied philosophy, with special emphasis on natural philosophy and medicine, earning his degree in medicine in 1502. He stayed in Padua, teaching logic, then anatomy, joining Padua's College (guild) of Physicians in 1505. When the university closed in 1508, he returned to his estate and practiced medicine in Verona. In 1530, he finished publication of his famed poem *Syphilis*, which he began during a retreat from plague in 1510. In it, he allegorized the origins of the new disease in humanist fashion, providing a name for "the French (Neapolitan) disease." Fracastoro also provided the first clinical description of typhus, and a few years before Copernicus, he published on the cosmos's heliocentricity—he may have known the Polish priest in Padua. Moving to Rome in the 1530s, Fracastoro became the personal physician of Pope Paul III.

Paul III named Fracastoro one of two Chief Medical Officers for the landmark Council of Trent (1545–1563). The city sits astride one of the main Alpine passes, between Venice and Innsbruck, Austria, and was quite prone to the importation of plague. Correctly reading the signs, Fracastoro strongly advised moving the Council, which the pope did in 1547. Perhaps spurred by these responsibilities, Fracastoro published his *On contagion and contagious diseases* in Venice in1546. Written in 1538 and revised in 1542, *De contagione* underwent 10 editions by 1600, though its influence was delayed until later in the 17th century.

Fracastoro was a Galenist who accepted humoral theory, but he rejected explanations based on either miasma or occult ("hidden") processes. He noted that specific diseases seemed to spread by people who had those diseases, just as seeds from a given plant produced copies of that plant. The "seedlets," or *seminaria*, that he postulated were living things, though not the animalcules or germs of later generations. These enter the human body and reproduce, eventually attacking organs and inducing life-threatening "putrefaction." "Sympathy," or similarity, between two entities draws them together. New diseases, as were both plague and syphilis, are created by astrological forces in the celestial realm and descend to earth, where they reproduce and spread like broadcast seeds. Fracastoro noted three types of contagion: when an infected person touches another; when a person handles items on which the seminaria—known in this case as fomites (kindling)—have settled; and through meeting the glance of an infected person, along the "rays" of sight. Fracastoro rejected medical responses that sought to reduce miasmas: at the heart of prophylaxis and treatment had to be blocking the entry of seminaria, stopping their propagation, or expelling them once taken in. He also advocated drying powders to clear up putrefaction in the body.

Most of Fracastoro's ideas were not new—the Romans Galen and Lucretius had suggested the possibility of "seedlets"—but he developed and organized them in a way that was a mark of medical humanism. His insistence on a purely material cause of disease, plague included, places him in the front ranks of the early Scientific Revolution. His impact was limited in the absence of the microscope and the growth in the influence of Paracelsus among physicians. Protestants mistrusted the papal physician's conclusions, and it would be the German Jesuit Athanasius Kircher (1602–1680) who continued Fracastoro's work.

See also: Contagion Theory; Kircher, Athanasius; Medical Humanism; Paracelsus and Paracelsianism; Scientific Revolution.

References

Biow, Douglas. *Doctors, Ambassadors, Secretaries: Humanism and Professions in Renaissance Italy.* Chicago: University of Chicago Press, 2002.

Cohn, Samuel K. *Cultures of Plague.* New York: Oxford University Press, 2010.

Nutton, Vivian. "The Reception of Fracastoro's Theory of Contagion: The Seed that Fell among Thorns." *Osiris* 2nd ser. 6 (1990): 196–234.

Pantin, Sabelle. "Fracastoro's *De contagione* and Medieval Reflection on 'Action at a Distance': Old and New Trends in Renaissance Discourse on Contagion," in *Imagining Contagion in Early Modern Europe*, edited by Claire L. Carlin (New York: Palgrave Macmillan, 2005), 3–15.

Friars (Mendicants)

Also known as mendicants (beggars), friars (brothers; from Latin *frater*) were male members of five Catholic religious orders: Order of Preachers or Dominicans; Order of Little Brothers or Franciscans; Augustinians; Carmelites; and Servites. Each order also had a women's branch, but since these communities were usually cloistered, or closed off in a monastic setting, these nuns played far less of a role during plague than their brethren. These orders were founded during the high Middle Ages to meet the spiritual needs of an increasingly complex European society. Though they lived in communities and according to their founders' rules, friars were unlike monks in that they took on ministries among the people, especially urban populations. They served as teachers, preachers, and health care providers, and ordained friars administered the sacraments. Even moderate-sized towns had churches belonging to each of the orders, which were frequented by townsfolk drawn to Franciscan humility or the Dominicans' preaching acumen. Independent of local bishops, mendicants were often in competition with parishes and among themselves, usually locating their churches as distant from one another as possible. Catholics were essentially taxed to support the local parishes and diocese clergy, but they chose to provide for the friars, who had taken vows of poverty, chastity and obedience, like monks but unlike the diocesan priests. Often better educated than parish clergy in the era before mandatory seminaries, friars enjoyed reputations for being better preachers and pastors and wiser counselors than their parochial rivals. Men joined the orders knowing they could be sent far away as missionaries, to university for years of education, or to serve injured humanity in a leprosarium. They were inspired by their founders' visions and, by the time of the Black Death, by more than a century of tradition.

Friars suffered more during the first outbreak of plague than other religious groups because they actively served the physical and spiritual needs of the suffering and they lived together in convents. When priests, they provided last rites, and all witnessed last wills and testaments, served as nurses, tended the dying, and buried the dead, exposing themselves to the deadly plague fleas. Some suffered and recovered, but many more succumbed. Of 140 Dominicans in the university town of Montpellier, only seven survived; of 160 at Maguellore in Languedoc, likewise only seven remained. Tuscan Dominicans fared better, with 78 of around 150 surviving in Santa Maria Novella's convent, and smaller numbers remaining in Pisa (57), Siena (49), and Lucca (39). Thriving Italian Franciscan communities lost 60 brothers and 40 nuns in Florence, 50 friars and 30 nuns in Venice, 100 brothers in Bologna, and 30 in and around Ferrara. As these raw numbers suggest, we rarely

know how many resided in any of these houses at the time. When we do have base figures, as for Llanthony Augustinian priory in Gloucester, England, where four of 30 survived, the numbers prove profound. While many of these data come from contemporary accounts, others were recorded later, for example, those of the English Augustinian Henry Knighton of Leicester, who wrote in the 1390s. He noted that at Avignon, all of his Augustinian brethren died, and at Marseille, only one of 150 Franciscans, "which is the way it should be." Though interpreted as a snide slam against the rival order, Knighton's comment could just as well mean that the friars should have given up their lives in service to God's people.

Plague's immediate impact on the orders was devastating. Victims included leaders, teachers, and models for the next generations, and the depletion was widely felt. The intellectual elites were the Dominicans, who now had to admit boys as young as 10 to 14 years of age to the adult world of spiritual formation. At the 1376 Chapter General meeting, after two or even three more epidemics across much of Europe, the complaint was recorded that few of the novices were even literate and few proved a good fit for the order. The leaders decided that, nonetheless, a large portion of their income had to support the novices and their education.

If personnel were a problem, funding generally was not. During epidemics, the pious and the frightened contributed through their wills, and afterward, those who had witnessed the mendicants' sacrifices attached themselves more firmly still, often switching support from the parishes and monasteries. Envious bishops, abbots, and clergy complained, but Pope Clement himself rebuked them: "This money was properly gained. While so many of the parish priests took flight and abandoned their parishioners, the mendicants cared for and buried them."

During subsequent outbreaks, mendicants continued to be noted for their high level of selfless service. In Catholic countries, better-organized cities relied on brothers to participate in processions and other rituals, administer pest houses, and help in plague hospitals and recuperation facilities. Bishops like Charles and Federigo Borromeo of Milan could trust the local convents to supplement the efforts of their diocesan clergy in supplying physical and spiritual aid to the myriad victims each epidemic claimed.

See also: Bishops and Popes; Confraternities; Flagellants; Monks, Nuns, and Monasteries; Priests; Processions.

References

Byrne, Joseph P. *Daily Life during the Black Death.* Westport, CT: Greenwood Press, 2006.

Harper-Bill, Christopher. "The English Church and English Religion after the Black Death," in *The Black Death in England*, edited by W. M. Ormrod and P. G. Lindley (Stamford, UK: Paul Watkins, 1996), 79–124.

Montford, Angela. *Health, Sickness, Medicine, and the Friars in the Thirteenth and Fourteenth Centuries.* Burlington, VT: Ashgate, 2004.

Webster, Jill. *Els menorets: The Franciscans in the Realms of Aragon from St. Francis to the Black Death.* Toronto: Pontifical Institute of Mediaeval Studies, 1993.

Funerals, Catholic

Distinctive Christian funerary rites are older than the Roman catacombs. Following Jewish tradition and practice, Christians treated the corpse with respect, cleaning and anointing it, wrapping it in a shroud, and placing it in the earth. Prayers and hymns of hope for salvation of the deceased differed across the growing Christian world, but the promise of eternal life and bodily resurrection deterred cremation or other deliberate forms of destruction. Mourning accompanied interment, but the Church sought to minimize this since the good Christian should have gone on to his or her heavenly reward, while no one should mourn the inveterate sinner now burning in hell.

Medieval theology developed purgatory, which has been understood as the temporary cleansing place of most departed souls. By the Black Death, funeral rites had developed around this and several other insights. Purgatory meant that prayers for the dead could shorten their time in purgatory and were thus a form of charity. This extended to the

A 16th-century German woodcut showing the Catholic priest officiating over a burial in a church. (Courtesy of the National Library of Medicine)

living who took part, as the soul that finally reached heaven—now a saint—could serve as an advocate before God for those left behind. Funerals that drew many participants meant many pray-ers "storming heaven" with requests on behalf of the deceased. Among a community's poor, this could mean a small stipend and a good meal, as stipulated in the departed's will. Another insight was that each participant would one day share the deceased's fate—both physical and spiritual. Inclusion of the magnificent poem *Dies irae*, with its terrifying depiction of the world's last moments, marks the eschatological function of the Requiem Mass: one day, all will be judged for eternity as the just Judge metes out divine justice.

Typically, a deceased member of any community would have had family, friends, guild, or confraternity prepare his body for burial and sponsor a showing at home of the corpse, at which visitors might pray and discuss the departed in a spirit of shared melancholy. After two or three days, a procession led by a priest and acolytes with cross and candles would transport the body to the church for either a full Mass for the Dead or an abridged funeral blessing and homily. Burial was usually in or near the same church and might be witnessed by the family alone. In many cultures, this sober ritual was followed by a more festive meal, perhaps held in the street at long tables with benches.

Civil concerns for plague's contagion and the medically debilitating effects of melancholy caused authorities to reduce rituals to a bare minimum. No bells were to remind folks to pray, no processions were to gather, and no meals were to be held. Churches were often closed to even private services, and churchyards and vaults in churches rapidly filled to overflowing. Bishops assured

their flocks that burial in consecrated ground would continue, but when corpse carriers began literally carting off the dead to mass graves, any certainty of spiritual peace left as well. Final communion, confession, and blessing at the deathbed—known as last rites—without which no Catholic could bear to die, also disappeared from many communities as priests died, fled, or feared such duties. "The living were overwhelmed by the dead" (Daniell, 193). Sudden, unpredictable death was troubling enough, but denial of the normal and expected rituals of passage to the next world made plague death terrifying.

See also: *Ars moriendi* (*The Art of Dying*); Books of Hours; Confraternities; Corpse Carriers; Corpses; Funerals, Muslim; Funerals, Protestant; Governments, Civil; Guilds; Health Boards, Magistracies, and Commissions; Individualism and Individual Liberties; Mass Graves and Plague Cemeteries; Processions; Public Health; Purgatory; Reformation and Protestantism; Wills and Testaments.

References

Banker, James R. *Death and the Community: Memorialization and Confraternities in an Italian Commune in the Late Middle Ages.* Athens: University of Georgia Press, 1988.

Daniell, Christopher. *Death and Burial in Medieval England.* New York: Routledge, 1997.

Harding, Vanessa. *The Dead and the Living in Paris and London, 1500–1670.* New York: Cambridge University Press, 2002.

Houlbrook, R. A., ed. *Death, Ritual and Bereavement.* New York: Routledge, 1989.

Rowell, Geoffrey. *The Liturgy of Christian Burial: An Introductory Survey of the Historical Development of Christian Burial Rites.* London: Alcuin Club/S.P.C.K., 1977.

Strocchia, Sharon T. *Death and Ritual in Renaissance Florence.* Baltimore, MD: Johns Hopkins University Press, 1992.

Funerals, Muslim

Medieval and early modern Muslim funerary customs blended pre–Islamic cultural practices and prescriptions of Hadith and Sharia Law. The principal objective was to place the body into the earth as quickly as possible, yet with the dignity owed the living person. Preparation for death usually meant acquisition of a shroud or three (men) or five (women). Its quality reflected the lifetime status of the person, and many believed they would greet Allah at judgment dressed in it. The corpse was washed, or rubbed with sand when water was scarce, by one's spouse, same-sex relatives or companions, or by a community specialist. It was beautified and anointed with camphor on the knees, palms, feet, and forehead, points that had touched the ground during prayerful prostration. Whether corpses ritually defiled those that touched them was an important question that came to be answered in the negative.

Prayers for the souls of the dead were acceptable, since Allah's mercy could always be invoked, but no services were held in mosques. This could differ during plague time, however, as one source describes a double row of coffins from mihrab to main door in Cairo's al-Hakim mosque. In this case, community prayer took the place of groups of mourners for individuals.

Bodies were carried on biers, hard to come by during epidemics, to the graveyards in procession, with women wailing and men stoic. Bystanders often joined, as it was considered a charitable act. Graveside, participants were separated by sex and prayed standing up, in rows as they would in a mosque. When plague struck, corpses were often abandoned to rot or accompanied to the grave by tiny groups of friends or relatives. Where cemeteries were well organized, an imam might pray over the bodies laid to rest. At least some Muslims believed the soul lived on in its grave awaiting judgment, even visiting neighbors, which must have made the idea of mass graves unbearable. The disruption to normal rituals was mitigated by Islamic teaching that those struck down by plague were equivalent to martyrs on jihad, gaining immediate access to paradise.

See also: Allah; Corpses; Funerals, Catholic; Funerals, Protestant; Islamic Religious Responses; Muhammad the Prophet.

References

Dols, Michael. "The Comparative Communal Responses to the Black Death in Muslim and Christian Societies." *Viator* (1974): 269–287.

Halevi, Leor. *Muhammad's Grave: Death Rites and the Making of Islamic Society.* New York: Columbia University Press, 2007.

Funerals, Protestant

Europe's 16th-century Protestant Reformation took place in the midst of the Second Pandemic. The single movement of Martin Luther in Germany and Scandinavia paralleled or spawned similar challenges to Catholicism in France (Calvinist Huguenots), Switzerland (Calvinism), the Holy Roman Empire (Anabaptist groups and Dutch Calvinism), England (Calvinist Puritanism and dissenters), and Scotland (Calvinist Presbyterianism), to mention the major denominations. Despite their variety, Protestant churches shared many features related to death and burial, especially in rejecting Catholic traditions.

Rejecting the spiritual power and necessity of sacraments, Reformers generally did away with last rites. Rejecting purgatory,

Protestants eliminated prayer for the dead, replacing it with prayer for the survivors and a call for repentance. The Mass in general was considered idolatrous and eliminated, as was any reliance on the advocacy of saints. Anniversary masses and other rituals thought to aid the departed also disappeared. The dead were no longer considered part of the spiritual community, as Catholics saw them, and for the more extreme reformers, funerals were essentially about disposal of corpses. What ceremony took place was stripped of holy water, incense, a cross, candles, acolytes, Latin hymns, and a priest. Christian burial was simplified, with perhaps vernacular psalms sung and a sermon proclaimed for the benefit of those present. The horrors of hellfire and the bliss of heaven remained, as did the fearful judgment, but the deceased were on their own: no human agency could affect their fate. Lutheran and Calvinist ideas of predestination underscored this teaching.

For Protestant Christians, the deathbed was for showing one's spiritual strength and organizing one's final affairs. A pastor's presence might help strengthen the dying and help the family with grieving, but it played no role in changing a person's spiritual fate. The same was true of the graveside ritual. Though the tradition of processing to the grave was usually preserved, the community gathered to support the family and gain spiritual strength from hymn singing and the sermon. Upper-class individuals, however, still merited expensive and lavish processions, what Restoration Anglican Samuel Pepys called "the Show," while members of guilds were also treated well by their brethren. Postburial feasting and distribution of charity also survived. In general, Anglican guidelines remained closest

to Catholic, retaining elements of ancient ritual, while Calvinists moved furthest away from Catholic practices. In Scotland, Presbyterian John Knox forbade singing, Scripture reading, and even preaching, since sermons were for Sundays.

When plague epidemics forced towns and cities to restrict ceremonies and even collect and dump bodies of victims, Catholics were horrified by denial of spiritually necessary ritual and prayers. Protestants, with no need for either, however, could face their ends with less anxiety. Though fear of death itself—with the attendant sense of impending loss and separation, regrets, and possibility of hell fire—might remain, it mattered relatively little whether one died and was buried ceremonially or alone; lowered lovingly into a marked grave in one's parish graveyard or carelessly cast into a mass burial pit by hired brutes. Human sensitivities meant that the living ultimately cared, however, and few were indifferent to the terrors of sudden collapse and death, a meaningless interment, and an anonymous grave.

Nonetheless, as Gittings points out, the normal took on greater meaning during epidemics. Bans on church or churchyard burials or gatherings for funeral sermons and civic collection and disposal of corpses violated norms of decorum. While not damaging to victims' souls, such disruptions undermined community solidarity and violated emerging traditions.

See also: *Ars moriendi* (*The Art of Dying*); Corpse Carriers; Corpses; Funerals, Catholic; Funerals, Muslim; Governments, Civil; Guilds; Health Boards, Magistracies, and Commissions; Individualism and Individual Liberties; Mass Graves and Plague Cemeteries; Processions; Public Health; Reformation and Protestantism; Wills and Testaments.

References

Gittings, Clare. *Death, Burial and the Individual in Early Modern England*. London: Croom Helm, 1984.

Harding, Vanessa. *The Dead and the Living in Paris and London, 1500–1670*. New York: Cambridge University Press, 2002.

Houlbrook, R. A., ed. *Death, Ritual and Bereavement*. New York: Routledge, 1989.

Koslofsky, C. M. *The Reformation and the Dead: Death and Ritual in Early Modern Germany, 1450–1700*. Basingstoke: Macmillan, 2000.

Rowell, Geoffrey. *The Liturgy of Christian Burial: An Introductory Survey of the Historical Development of Christian Burial Rites*. London: Alcuin Club/S.P.C.K., 1977.

G

Galen and Galenism (129 CE–c. 216)

Galen of Pergamum (Pergamon) was the great Roman exponent of the medical ideas of Hippocrates and his school. Galen's scores of writings transmitted these and his own ideas and observations through late antique, Byzantine, Persian, and Arabic translators, compilers and commentators, into medieval Latin medical textbooks and beyond. So-called Galenism provided the dominant Western medical paradigm until the 18th century.

Galen's Pergamum in modern Turkey was a center of Greek Hellenistic culture. Though Roman since 133 BCE, Greek remained the language of education and the streets. Galen's father was an architect well connected to the upper classes. Galen began study of medicine in Pergamum, known for its dedication to the healing god Aesculpius. He continued in Smyrna, Corinth, and at the great intellectual center of Alexandria, Egypt. He left Alexandria, returning to Pergamum in 157. Here he treated wounded gladiators and the city's pagan priesthood. Arriving in Rome in 162, his reputation preceded him and he served the emperor's family and other aristocrats. A pandemic—smallpox or measles?—struck in 166, and Galen returned to Pergamum. He was recalled to treat a Roman army stationed in Aquileia in northeastern Italy. He avoided the subsequent campaign and spent his remaining years in Rome and other parts of Italy, with eastern Mediterranean excursions difficult to reconstruct.

As a Hellenistic scholar and practitioner, Galen borrowed eclectically from medical traditions that suited him best. It happened that was the system of humoralism, experientialism, and case studies associated with fifth-century BCE Hippocrates and his followers, who compiled the so-called Hippocratic corpus. Based on his experiences and long study, Galen wrote scores of medical works and commentaries on the corpus. But Galen shaped his empiricist Hippocrates with the help of Aristotelian rationalism and first principles, lest he fall into the camp of his competitors, the pure empiricists. This balance, perhaps more than any characteristic of Galen's approach, endeared him to future generations. Physiologically, Galen was a humoralist who aligned the four humors with the four qualities, four elements, and three organs (the spleen was later added). The Hippocratic doctrine of the naturals, nonnaturals, and contranaturals provided Galen a basis for logical health regimens and treatments of diseases. These were the result of humoral imbalances that could be redressed by depleting or replenishing the body's excesses or superfluities.

Galen taught through his own writings and later digested works in compilations and such encyclopedias as that by late fourth-century Oribasius. Alexandria became a center for Galenic teaching, drawing students from throughout the classical world. After the Arabs' conquest of the city in the 640s, Galen's influence flowed through the Islamic world in Arabic translations culminating with those of the ninth-century Syriac Hunain ibn

One of the most influential thinkers to spring from the Roman Empire, Galen of Pergamum was a Greek physician whose writings formed the basis of the European medical canon down to the 19th century. (Courtesy of the National Library of Medicine)

Ishaq in the ninth century. They also underlay the medical works of the early 11th-century Persian Avicenna, most importantly his encyclopedic *Kanon* or *Qanon*. These largely Galenic works shaped Islamic medicine to the 18th century.

When the Christian West began absorbing Latin translations of Arabic medical works in the late 11th century, it was not only the authority of the ancients for which they were appreciated, but also the emphasis on the practitioner's personal observations and experience. Nonetheless, the humoral paradigm reigned supreme, and its development in European universities peaked in the 1300s. As plague repeatedly savaged the Western world from 1347, medical scholars and practitioners (usually the same) reconciled Galen's humoralism with epidemic-inducing miasmas and the astrological influence of celestial bodies. This only strengthened Galenism into the 16th century. Renaissance humanist scholarship and printing led to the replacement of derivative Arab works with Galenic and Hippocratic editions in their original Greek, beginning in 1500, which further strengthened the Galenic paradigm. Ironically, the Renaissance is known as much for its emphasis on one's own experience and observation as for its reliance on the ancients. Galenism had atrophied as a model but was unassailable. Early proponents of contagion and germ theory had to treat with Galen, as did empirics, who eschewed any theory and claimed to rely entirely on experience. Paracelsus and his alternatives to humoral theory presented a challenge, especially in Protestant countries, but in 1600, the University of Paris medical faculty rededicated itself to Galenism. They also took 30 years to accept Harvey's circulation of the blood. Despite the discoveries of the Scientific Revolution, there was no medical equivalent of the Copernican Revolution before the end of the Second Pandemic.

See also: Arabic-Persian Medicine and Practitioners; Avicenna (Ibn Sina); Dietary Regimens; Hippocrates and the Hippocratic Corpus; Humoral Theory; Medical Education (1300–1500, Medieval Europe); Medical Education (1500–1700, Early Modern Europe); Medical Humanism; Miasma Theory; Paracelsus and Paracelsianism.

References

French, Roger. *Medicine before Science: The Business of Medicine from the Middle Ages to the Enlightenment.* New York: Cambridge University Press, 2003.

Nutton, Vivian. *Ancient Medicine.* New York: Routledge, 2004.

Pormann, Peter E. and Emilie Savage-Smith. *Medieval Islamic Medicine*. Washington, DC: Georgetown University Press, 2007.

Temkin, Owsei. *Galenism: The Rise and Decline of a Medical Philosophy*. Ithaca: Cornell University Press, 1973.

Wear, Andrew. "Medical Practice in Late Seventeenth- and Early Eighteenth-century England: Continuity and Union," in *The Medical Revolution of the Seventeenth Century*, edited by Wear and Roger French (New York: Cambridge University Press, 1989), 294–320.

Gentile da Foligno (c. 1275–1348)

Gentile was born in Foligno or Perugia, Italy, to a Bolognese physician. He probably studied medicine in Bologna, perhaps under Taddeo Alderotti, the era's greatest medical educator. He married and had four children, two of whom became physicians. He practiced in Bologna until 1322, moving to Siena to help establish a medical school. When this failed, Gentile became lecturer and civic physician in Perugia, which remained his home until his death. He wrote learned commentaries on Galen, the *Articella*, and Avicenna's *Canon* (considered authoritative to 1520), and by 1348 was probably northern Italy's best-known physician.

In later 1347 and early 1348, Gentile addressed Europe's earliest plague *Consilia* to the authorities in Genoa, Naples, and Perugia. In the copy to Perugia, *Consilia contra pestilentiam*, he claims to write for the honor of the university, whose medical faculty had requested the work, and "for the common benefit of all" (Arrizabalaga, 269). Indeed, much of his advice is aimed not at individuals, as with typical medical *consilia*, but at community leaders. He recommends that Perugia's College (guild) of Physicians meet with "some good men" to "make arrangements for preserving the health of the people of the city" (271).

Gentile's *Consilia* consisted of four parts: causes of plague, prophylactic suggestions, remedies, and "dubia," or exercises for medical students. As for cause, he considered astrological forces but set them aside. Clearly, poisonous vapors, or miasma, were at work introducing poison into the body, where it settled around heart and lungs, putrefying these organs and killing the individual. A Galenist, he accepted the importance of nonnaturals but downplayed the role of humoral imbalance. Once contracted, he believed, poison was passed on to others through "contagious conversation." This theory had clear implications for avoiding or preventing the spread of plague: stay away from corrupted or potentially corrupted air; purify local corrupted air with fumigation; and avoid those with the disease. Flight to disease-free places helped with points one and three, and burning wood, aromatic substances, or herbs helped purify the local atmosphere. Flight also helped correct one's emotional state. When upset, fearful, or angry, one becomes susceptible to plague. Gentile treated Galen's other nonnaturals similarly (balanced diet, ample sleep, moderate exercise, minimal sexual activity, purging, bleeding, etc.). His *consilia* includes specific remedies, for which he provided recipes, as well as theriac and cordials with powdered gemstones, and cupping and cauterization of buboes to draw off poison. Gentile died June 18 in Perugia, probably of exhaustion.

See also: Consilia and Plague Tracts; Dietary Regimens; Galen and Galenism; Humoral Theory; Medical Education (1300–1500, Medieval Europe); Miasma Theory; Physicians; Public Health.

References

Arrizabalaga, Jon. "Facing the Black Death: Perceptions and Reactions of University Medical Practitioners," in *Practical Medicine from Salerno to the Black Death*, edited by Luis Garcia-Ballester, et al. (New York: Cambridge University Press, 1994), 237–288.

Bonora, F. and G. Kern. "Does Anyone Really Know the Life of Gentile da Foligno?" *Medicina nei secoli* 9 (1972): 29–53.

French, Roger. *Canonical Medicine: Gentile da Foligno and Scholasticism*. Boston: Brill, 2001.

Germ Theory

Modern medical science spends an enormous amount of time and other resources seeking to understand the "germ," since it is understood today to be the principle agent of most human diseases. The germ never acts alone in producing a disease but is a necessary if not sufficient part of the equation. Also required is the living human; the germ must be able to enter the human's body in such a way and at such an entry point that is conducive to the germ's survival and reproduction; the human's immune system must be incapable of containing and eliminating the germ and its threat; the threshold quantity of germs needed to overcome the immune system must be present; and the human must not take any effective element to her body, for example, an antibiotic, that would thwart the germ. *Germ*, of course, is a nontechnical term for microscopic biological entities (microbes) that includes certain bacteria, viruses, and fungal spores and is stretched sometimes to inorganic toxins.

During the Second Pandemic, this theory—fact, as far as we are concerned—was unknown by any culture's science. In part, this was because the germs or microbes are too tiny to be seen, but mainly because the various traditions provided more or less satisfactory explanations of how disease worked. In the West, this is collectively known as Galenism, after the Greco-Roman physician. For Galen, good health meant a proper balancing of bodily fluids or humors, and disease resulted from an imbalance of these. Imbalances resulted from a number of factors from exercise to emotional state and such matter taken into the body as food, water, or poison. Regarding plague, Galenists understood that the body was poisoned by a malignant condition of the atmosphere, a miasma. What they did not understand is why it seemed that people "caught" the disease from other people and things. Towns from Dublin to Moscow reacted in ways that indicated they believed that certain people suffering the disease could transmit it to others. These people were shut in their homes, refused entry, expelled, quarantined, and generally shunned. But what could they have been transmitting?

In the 16th century, physicians began theorizing about the means and method of transmission. Some thought it might be an occult, or hidden, power like magnetism at work. Galenist Girolamo Fracastoro outlined his belief in seedlets or *seminaria* in his *De contagione* (1538). Just as seeds reproduce the plant that produced them, so these produce a particular disease in any set of people. His was an idea that echoed notions held by Galen as well as other classical Romans Lucretius, Columella, and Varro, whose works were being studied by the humanistically inclined. The last two wrote about tiny animals, or *animalcules*, that entered a person's body from the air through the nose or mouth. A third model came from the Paracelsians of the later 16th century, who privileged tiny inorganic particles that attacked specific body parts, producing specific symptoms. The development of the microscope made the existence of such organisms and particles and their study a reality. Jesuit priest Athanasius Kircher did this with the "little worms" he discovered and published in the 1650s, but he was overshadowed by the flashier studies of waterborne organisms by Robert Hooke. The Second Pandemic was fading quickly by this time, and interests shifted.

The 18th century saw little movement in the direct connection of microbial entities and diseases. Carl Linnaeus and François de la Croix, however, advanced physicians' understanding of the nature and relations of diseases through their organizational systems of genera and species. This suggested that diseases were specific reactions of the human body to specific pathogens, the underlying notion behind vaccination, variolation, and inoculation as treatments for smallpox. In the early 19th century, advances in the study of cadavers and patients led to finer distinctions among diseases and variations of disease types. But it was the discovery of plant and then animal cells as the building blocks of life (1838, 1839) that sent biological and medical researchers to their microscopes in search of the tiny germs that others had posited. In the 1850s, Prussian physician and researcher Rudolph Virchow came to understand disease as a matter of cellular-level activities: pathogenic—harm-causing—microorganisms, or germs, invade the body and attack it on a cellular level.

There was a powerful logic and mounting evidence for this germ theory, including John Snow's discovery of cholera pathogens in London's water supply (1854). Yet this theory remained a theory as many medical school-trained physicians and researchers retained humoralism and miasma theory as their working models. Because neither adequately explained contagion, these scientists were often labeled anticontagionists and associated with the sanitarian movement to "clean up" cities and their teeming populations. Two microbiologists, Robert Koch in Germany (trained as a pathologist) and Louis Pasteur in France (a chemist), working separately but with state-of-the-art laboratories and brilliant associates, finally demonstrated that germ theory was valid. Pasteur's famous broth experiment showed that his organic material, when exposed to the air, attracted microorganisms that caused it to putrefy and cloud up. His work with a silk worm disease disclosed the responsible pathogen. Koch developed (but rarely applied) several rules or postulates for proving the effect of an outside germ, starting with the need for a researcher to isolate the germ from all other organisms. He was able to isolate the tuberculosis pathogen and his colleagues several others. When plague broke out in Hong Kong in the 1890s, Koch's student Shibasaburo Kitasato and Pasteur's student Alexandre Yersin independently studied victims, and one or both isolated the bacterium *Yersinia pestis*.

See also: Contagion Theory; Fracastoro, Girolamo; Galen and Galenism; Humoral Theory; Kircher, Athanasius; Kitasato, Shibasaburo; Koch, Robert; Miasma Theory; Paracelsus and Paracelsianism; Pasteur, Louis; Yersin, Alexandre; *Yersinia pestis*.

References

Cook, Harold J. "From the Scientific Revolution to the Germ Theory," in *Western Medicine: An Illustrated History*, edited by Irvine Loudon (New York: Oxford University Press, 1997), 80–101.

Cunningham, Andrew. "Transforming Plague: The Laboratory and the Identification of Infectious Disease," in *The Laboratory Revolution in Medicine*, edited by Cunningham and Perry Williams (New York: Cambridge University Press, 1992), 209–244.

God the Father

The Christian conception of God is mono-theistic, but it is less simply monotheistic than either Judaism or Islam. The Christian divinity is a single God with three distinct persons: the Father, the Son (Jesus Christ), and the Holy Spirit. Admittedly difficult to accept, let alone understand, this is a mystery of the faith that is simply meant to be accepted through faith. Though the major Christian creed states, "all things were made" through Jesus Christ, the Father is typically associated with creation. Human beings and the world in which we live our daily lives were designed and brought into being by the Father.

Early medieval Western Christianity ignored much of the classical inheritance, including the rational structure of Galenic medicine, replacing it with folk healing and reliance on divine intervention. Arab and scholastic medicine from the 12th century privileged human reason and reestablished much of what had been lost. But it was neither classical nor Arab; rather, it was elements of these within a Christian matrix in which God rules the universe, his creation, in ways made understandable to humans through their faith and reason. On an important cultural level, medicine had to admit that God created human beings and the body; God created all medicines and other treatments when the body fails, and these are discoverable through human use of reason; God had long sent healers from Adam to Jesus to Galen to repair the damage done by sin to fleshly bodies; God also created diseases, though humans bring them down on themselves by sin; and finally, God ultimately knows the outcome of every case of illness, since the supernatural works through the natural in this world.

As the medical profession developed into the 14th century, physicians generally admitted to the above while further admitting that their purview was the body and their model was that of Aristotle and Galen. Willing to admit that God played a huge role, their role was to do their best with what God had given them. The onset of plague in the late 1340s began to change things. While most medical writing all but ignored a divine role, physicians no less than theologians attributed a phenomenon so all-encompassing, so deadly, so seemingly arbitrary to God at work through nature. In the Bible, Jesus says that "all judgment" is given to him by the Father, and Christians took that to mean the judgment of people in this world as well as final spiritual judgment after death. Divine justice and righteous divine anger at humanity's sinfulness began and continued the regimen of plague, generally seen as conducted by Jesus Christ rather than by the Creator. Christ the Judge hurls the arrows from on high and receives the prayers for mercy from saint and sinner alike.

At the same time, the belief was that nothing happens unless willed by the Father. But this begs the classic question of human free will: if all that happens is willed by God, then is free will—and guilt for sin and righteous punishment—a sham? How could a just God punish disobedience if he willed it? Popularly reduced to a mystery, a matter of faith, the Christian God was seen, indeed, to respond to human behavior: first in allowing punishment of sinfulness with plague, then—for prayers, penitence, contrition—allowing clemency by lifting the scourge, as he had lowered the flood waters for Noah.

By the 17th century, the Christian landscape had become variegated, but the themes were familiar. Calvinists and some Lutherans accepted divine predestination as well as the mission of the physician; Lutheran Paracelsians rejected "pagan" Galenism and saw their medical innovations as divinely inspired reform; atheists attributed all to nature; and traditionalists watched as the Father worked through the nature he created.

See also: Allah; Causes of Plague: Historical Theories; Christ; Paracelsus and Paracelsianism; Reformation and Protestantism.

References

Cohn, Samuel K. *Cultures of Plague: Medical Thinking at the End of the Renaissance*. New York: Oxford University Press, 2010.

French, Roger. *Medicine before Science: The Business of Medicine from the Middle Ages to the Enlightenment*. New York: Cambridge University Press, 2003.

Kocher, Paul. "The Idea of God in Elizabethan Medicine." *Journal of the History of Ideas* 11 (1950): 3–29.

Gold

Gold is like the sun: eternally gleaming, pure, and cleansing. Thanks to the impact of medical alchemists, during the Second Pandemic many believed in gold's prophylactic and/or medicinal properties. It could rebalance unbalanced humors and counteract poisons thanks to its perfect balance and purity. Alchemists sought the means of producing it more for a universal remedy than for coinage, and physicians from Gentile da Foligno (d. 1348) on sought the proper solution of gold in alcohol, rosewater, or barley water. Potable (drinkable) gold was the goal: *aqua vitae*, the water of life. Gold's incorruptible qualities derived directly from the sun, many believed, and this was the vital force that could cure plague, itself produced by corruption. Paracelsians, emphasizing mineral rather than organic therapies, heightened interest in

medicinal gold from the later 16th century. One could also wear gold or hold a gold coin in one's mouth as protection. Queen Elizabeth's gold "angels" were thought to be alchemically produced and thus very effective: "keep it always in your mouth when you walk out or any sick persons come to you," wrote John Allin in 1665.

See also: Alchemy; Prophylaxes; Remedies, Internal.

Reference

Crisciani, Chiara. "Black Death and Golden Remedies," in *Regulation of Evil*, edited by Agostino Paravicini Bagliani and Francesco Santi (Sismel: Galluzzo, 1998), 7–39.

Governments, Civil

Late medieval Europe was a sea of villages dotted with larger towns and a handful of cities. Some towns and cities were ruled by their feudal lords, while others had gained a large degree of self-governance from theirs. Florence, Venice, and Milan were virtually independent and controlled small empires of their own, but urban affairs had become sophisticated enough to necessitate bourgeois expertise even where royal governors made most decisions. From 1347 on, plague was a localized phenomenon: the battle was fought at the smallest local jurisdiction. Until the 16th century, "national" governments were generally too weak to command necessary resources. Even Renaissance new monarchs and their successors, who often attempted to act kingdomwide, were unable or unwilling to fund or enforce their own dictates. Through most of the Second Pandemic, fighting plague fell to local functionaries, parishes, and councils.

Council governments were variously formed of local nobility or guildsmen, sometimes with two—larger and smaller—bodies making and enforcing laws and policies. As plague approached, the concern was usually for protecting the city. Sanitation and moral laws were enforced or reenacted to keep the level of sin and stench—both blamed for plague—at minimum levels. Laws sanctioning trade with plague-stricken areas and requiring quarantine of foreigners and their goods took a toll on the local economy and were far from popular. When residents began to fall ill, the council was often the body that had to decide whether and when to enact the full range of emergency measures, usually relying on those utilized last time. This key decision was usually made after consultation with local physicians or, if it existed, the council-created health board. Even experts could disagree, however, which could postpone action for precious weeks.

Between the 14th and 17th centuries, urban governments developed a wide range of responses to epidemics, all of which had their costs. Among the earliest was restriction on gatherings, including funerals, out of fear of contagion. Civic regulations forbade public displays, often with increasing strictness as epidemics progressed. They minimized the use of church bells and wearing of black by mourners and required that graves be at least six feet deep. City councils and local Catholic clergy often quarreled when the former sought to forbid or limit religious processions whose participants sought God's forgiveness and mercy: did the spiritual benefits outweigh the risks of contagion?

As deaths mounted, councils had to hire guards, corpse carriers, gravediggers, street cleaners, executioners, and public health personnel, including physicians, surgeons, and nurses, and purchase many medicines from the local apothecaries. As personnel died off, replacements had to be recruited, which could be nearly impossible when an entire region suffered. Councils also had to negotiate for pay and perks with the knowledge that many would not live to collect. From at least the 16th century, towns and cities established, outfitted, manned, and financed pest houses, quarantine facilities, and convalescent hospitals for survivors. Some of these duties fell to health board members, but many of these died and had to be replaced or were members of the council as well, as in Habsburg Spain. The councils also had to negotiate with the outside world, whether seeking support from the monarch or negotiating for shipments of wheat for starving residents.

Council efforts were met with varying public responses, from grudging obedience to quiet disobedience to open hostility. When an epidemic ended the council went to work cleaning up filth, punishing malefactors, attracting new residents, borrowing funds, and paying bills.

See also: Bells; Crime and Punishment; Economic Effects of Plague in Europe; Gravediggers; Health Boards, Magistracies, and Commissions; Lazarettos and Pest Houses; Moral Legislation; Public Health; Public Sanitation; Taxes and Public Finance; individual cities.

References

Alexander, John T. *Bubonic Plague in Early Modern Russia: Public Health and Urban Disaster.* Baltimore, MD: Johns Hopkins University Press, 1980.

Barron, Caroline. *London in the Later Middle Ages: Government and People, 1200–1500.* New York: Oxford University Press, 2004.

Bowsky, William. "The Impact of the Black Death upon Sienese Government and Society." *Speculum* 39 (1964): 368–381.

Carmichael, Ann G. "Plague Legislation in the Italian Renaissance." *Bulletin of the History of Medicine* 57 (1983): 508–525.

Cook, Alexandra Parma and Noble David Cook. *The Plague Files: Crisis Management in Sixteenth-Century Seville*. Baton Rouge: University of Louisiana Press, 2009.

Graunt, John (1620–1674)

Born to a London haberdasher (clothier), John was apprenticed to a fellow guildsman. From 1641, he developed his own business and proved to be very successful. He served in guild and civic offices and became well connected within London society. Discrimination following his conversion to Catholicism and losses during the Great Fire (1666) bankrupted him in his later years.

Graunt's civic-mindedness and acute business skills combined with the mathematical spirit and optimism of the Scientific Revolution. These led him to study London's bills of mortality as a shopkeeper examines inventories or other commercial accounts. Creating mortality tables instead of lists, rationalizing and recategorizing causes of deaths, he sought general factors that explained patterns he could now discern from the previously muddled data. Though some of his assumptions were incorrect (e.g., London's population size) and conclusions traditional (avoid night air and animals; shut in victims), his methods advanced the new science of statistics and helped found the fields of demographics and epidemiology. He set a new standard for recordkeeping and noted regularities in human populations, for example, women's longer life spans. In 1662, Graunt published his *Natural and Political Observations of the Bills of Mortality*, a book of fewer than 100 pages. For this, the young Royal Society made him a fellow and subsidized publication of one of the four editions that appeared before Graunt's death. He also published a compilation of London's death records during London's Great Plague (1665): *London's dreadful visitation, or, A collection of all the bills of mortality for this present year*. With contemporaries, Graunt believed that knowledge was power and that a better-informed state could create better conditions for all.

See also: Bills of Mortality; Demographic Effects of Plague: Europe 1500–1722; London, England; Scientific Revolution.

Reference

Rusnock, Andrea. *Vital Accounts: Quantifying Health and Population in Eighteenth-Century England and France*. New York: Cambridge University Press, 2002.

Gravediggers

Before 1347, those who dug graves did so in churches and churchyards and were considered vital to the parish life. In such cities as Florence, they were even associated with physicians' or apothecaries' guilds. Tipping them with the deceased's clothing was customary in Tuscany to ensure deep and quick burial.

During the Black Death, these men were quickly overwhelmed as bodies piled up, and open land or spaces in church walls and floors disappeared. These parish servants died off early, especially if they assumed plague victims' flea-infested clothing. Even before the horrors of mass graves, families handed their deceased loved ones to strangers whose lack of sympathy and gruffness were considered necessary to their survival. Within a single epidemic season, several generations of gravediggers completed their grim tasks and passed on to join their clients. In Avignon, the second generation were mountain men thought to be immune to the valley's "miasmatic air," a belief quickly belied. Thereafter, condemned prisoners were offered freedom for their service. In Mediterranean port cities, galley slaves were often impressed into service.

As deaths mounted, urban communities created large cemeteries with no ties to neighborhoods or parishes. These were located beyond city walls and represented the alienation of the dead, whose presence was no longer welcome within. Gravediggers received communal wages and were purposely isolated for fear of contagion. Living together in huts, they ate, drank, and gambled at community expense. Whether they worked beside corpse carriers or did that job too, the two merged in people's imaginations. They were feared as nearly monstrous men whose dire duties had eaten away at their humanity. In later years, moralists noted their greed and immorality in dealing with the dead and their possessions. Most cheered at the thought that the infected goods they stole would lead to the thieves' own deaths.

That gravediggers considered themselves immortal is also recorded many times. They certainly knew they held a unique position in society during an epidemic. In Montelupo, Italy, in 1631, two gravediggers used "arrogant words" with the mayor, refusing to do their job until back pay was provided. Knowing of high death rates among gravediggers, officials often withheld pay while expecting service. Threatened with galley service, these threatened to toss corpses in front of the mayor's house, and they did bury corpses beside a nobleman's house. Tortured violently, they continued to refuse until the mayor died of plague; him they happily buried.

As a function of increased concern for public sanitation, governments exercised greater control over burial sites and practices. New regulations mandated the depths of graves, the use of lime or other agents to increase decomposition and reduce odors, shrouding, and use of coffins.

See also: Corpse Carriers; Corpses; Crime and Punishment; Governments, Civil; Mass Graves and Plague Cemeteries; Parish; Public Sanitation.

References

Byrne, Joseph P. *Daily Life during the Black Death*. Westport, CT: Greenwood, 2006.

Calvi, Giulia. *Histories of a Plague Year: The Social and the Imaginary in Baroque Florence*. Berkeley: University of California Press, 1989.

Graves. *See* **Mass Graves and Plague Cemeteries**

Gregory the Great, Pope (r. 590–604)

Gregory was born into one of sixth-century Rome's best families. He was educated as well as could be at that turbulent time and entered urban public service. By 573, Gregory was urban prefect, but in 574, he retired to his own monastic house on Rome's Caelian Hill. Five years later, Pope Pelagius sent him to Constantinople as papal legate, and in the 580s, Gregory served as deacon and papal secretary.

When Pelagius died of plague in February 590, Gregory was elected to replace him. The epidemic savaged Rome, and Gregory was convinced it was their sins that had brought it upon them. Gregory immediately held processions of intercession and thanksgiving to placate God. Eighty people are said to have died during one, but a

One of the greatest and most influential popes of the early Middle Ages, Gregory the Great, also known as Saint Gregory I, is recognized as one of the fathers of the Catholic Church. His papacy spanned the years 590 to 604. (Library of Congress)

miracle, reported only much later, supposedly convinced him of their efficacy. As they prayed and processed, they had a vision of St. Michael the Archangel atop Hadrian's Mausoleum, sheathing his plague sword. Soon the plague stopped.

But Gregory did more. He used the crisis of plague to urge conversions of polytheistic or Arian Lombards and Romans, and he composed a mass for plague dead. He is also credited with making St. Sebastian the third patron saint of Rome, after Peter and Paul, and widening the cult of Sebastian. Gregory appears as a plague saint from the later 15th century, and his mass, treatment of Sebastian, and successful processions set important precedents for the Second Pandemic.

See also: Justinian, Plague of (First Plague Pandemic); Plague Saints; Popes; Processions; Rome, Italy; St. Michael the Archangel.

References

Boeckl, Christine. *Images of Plague and Pestilence: Iconography and Iconology.* Kirksville, MO: Truman State University Press, 2000.

Markus, R. A. *Gregory the Great and His World.* New York: Cambridge University Press, 1997.

Grindal, Edmund (1519–1583)

Grindal studied theology at Magdalen and Christ's College, Cambridge; he was named Master of Pembroke College in 1549. He became a staunch supporter of the Calvinist Puritanism that grew up in response to the conservatism of Henry VIII and the Catholicism of Mary Tudor. He spent much of the latter's reign in Strasbourg, where such ideas circulated freely. In 1558, Elizabeth took the throne and soon appointed scholarly Matthew Parker, her late mother's chaplain, Archbishop of Canterbury. Parker was a very moderate Anglican with a conservative historical sense that clashed with Grindal's radicalism. Nonetheless, Grindal was appointed Bishop of London, a Puritan hotbed, then Archbishop of York, where he could openly oppress Roman Catholics. He attained Canterbury in 1575 upon Parker's death thanks to the aid of Lord Burleigh.

Bishop Grindal worked closely with Parker, who generally lived in London, when plague hit the city in 1563. Grindal's approach to directing the diocese's prayer life, however, reflected Geneva rather than tradition. Freshly written prayers were printed and recited at daylong church services on Wednesdays and

Fridays, at which seven approved set sermons were read; public fasts and personal prayer brought the ritual home. He also produced special prayer pamphlets for home use by shut-ins and prayers thanking God when plagues ended. Unlike some ecclesiastical authorities, Grindal understood the dangers of congregating during plague time, supporting small neighborhood gatherings and civic restrictions. Most of his liturgical regimen was curtailed under his successor in 1593.

In Calvinist fashion, he detested theaters and plays, using moral and public health concerns to ban their performances at least temporarily. Religious dramas of any kind were banned outright, and companies of players had to seek patrons from among the aristocracy.

Parker-style religious moderates on one side and strictly predestinarian Calvinists on the other opposed much of what Grindal advocated. Moderates, including the queen, feared a drift into religious radicalism. For the rock-ribbed anticontagionists whose God had predetermined each person's fate, prayer and fasting were always good things, but expecting God to alter his course or that personal or civic precautions might save a single soul was tantamount to blasphemy.

See also: Bishops and Popes; Contagion Theory; London, England; Prayer and Fasting; Reformation and Protestantism.

References

Collinson, Patrick. *Archbishop Grindal, 1519–1583: The Struggle for a Reformed Church.* Berkeley: University of California, 1979.

Nicholson, William. *The Remains of Edmund Grindal.* New York: Johnson Reprint Corp., 1968.

Guilds

The European guild (*societas, compagnia, collegium, universitas*) was a local organization of business owners or masters in the same or similar trades, crafts, or professions. Rooted in ancient Rome and established by Roman Law, they revived in medieval towns from the 12th century. Each guild had a charter recognizing its rights to control the quality, output, pricing, wage scales, education, and inspection of its members, as well as determining a set of officers, dues, fines, and other organizational matters. Guild statutes laid out the specific rules and regulations and were updated every few decades to keep pace with local change. Only the masters were guildsmen (sometimes but rarely guildswomen). The independent journeymen they hired, the apprentices who worked for and learned from them under contract, and the shopboys who were too young to be apprentices had no specific representatives, though the guild statutes set and monitored their numbers, age ranges, education, work conditions, wages, and eventual entry into the guild as masters themselves. Guilds were highly conservative, restricting entry to reduce competition, setting prices high and wages low to support the masters. They kept their own records and held their own courts to enforce contracts or punish statutory infractions. Well-developed cities, including Paris, Barcelona, London, Hamburg, and Dutch and English trading centers and Italian city-states, had several dozen guilds, sometimes divided into greater and lesser. Greater guilds might include physicians, goldsmiths, apothecaries, bankers, long-distance merchants, lawyers, and judges; lesser guilds represented the building trades, cloth production and sales, local businessmen, artists and craftsmen, and even second-hand clothiers. Florence and other city-republics were ruled by governments (communes) on which sat only guildsmen. Royal or imperial officials often used the guilds as means of enforcing economic and other governmental laws, as the ancients Romans had.

When plague struck a town or city, its guilds were directly affected. Among the dead were guild masters, journeymen, and apprentices, as well as suppliers and consumers. Relatively wealthy guild masters often fled to another town. While they might take a couple of apprentices—depending on the occupation—they would more likely leave all but family and a few servants behind. Most of these would be left to their own devices as long as the epidemic lasted. The partially trained teen-aged apprentices might rejoin their birth families or join together to live as they could amid the chaos and misery. Journeymen could theoretically relocate rather easily, but many chose to remain where they were. Guild records show that meetings were still held a month or more into an outbreak, but attendance was inevitably low and official business slight, so most probably suspended meetings rather quickly.

Some guilds did remain active during epidemics, or at least their members did. Carpenters pounded together coffins and chandlers provided candles for funerals and processions as long as these were tolerated. Guildsmen usually provided food and drink to sustain survivors, and, of course, physicians, surgeons, barbers, apothecaries, notaries, and some lawyers were needed to see to the medical and legal needs of the dying and those they left behind. These practitioners died at greater rates than others because of their greater exposure to the pathogen.

Guilds and groups of guilds reacted in many different ways to their postplague positions. Sons sometimes inherited their fathers' positions as guild masters, appearing in the Elizabethan-era guild rolls as new masters "by patrimony." In many towns, this was a norm, but plague often dislocated family strategies. When father and heir apparent both died, then a younger son with no occupational interests would inherit the business, liquidate it, and begin a new venture. Guilds that had suffered a large loss of masters needed to raise journeymen to these positions as rapidly as possible. Rules governing length of service or age were either ignored or rewritten into new statutes. In other cases, the depleted group of masters took advantage of the drop in competition and refused to promote journeymen, creating local discontent and some violence. While some apprentices and journeymen who had been let go returned to their masters at the old pay and other conditions, the more savvy realized that they could leverage their scarcity for better wages and conditions. In London after 1349, journeymen gathered in "brotherhoods" in attempts to create labor monopolies. In the face of the English Statute of Laborers, this was clearly illegal, and many were prosecuted by the crown. Guilds and guild-run governments also resisted these pressures. One way was to bring in new apprentices from out of town, which readjusted the supply of labor. Young locals naturally resented and sometimes rebelled against this tactic. In London, the Grocers' Company required that all masters take back their local apprentices after the 1563 epidemic before they brought in cheaper "foreigners," and in 1603, London aldermen recommended masters take in poor children from Christ's Hospital before they apprentice "foreign" children.

But hiring on unskilled children hardly made up for the enormous loss of skills and experience that the plague had wrought. Young men might train for a decade or more before they were considered skilled craftsmen, and art historians have noted declines in artistic quality as due, in part at least, to losses of painters, sculptors, and masons during the decennial returns of plague in the later 14th century. University masters and clerical recruiters across Europe also lamented this diminished pool of the bright and the ambitious.

See also: Apothecaries; Art, Effects of Plague on; Ciompi Revolt; Confraternities; Economic Effects of Plague in Europe; Flight; London, England; Merchants; Notaries; Physicians; Processions; Repopulation.

References

Britnell, R. H. "The Black Death in English Towns." *Urban History* 21 (1994): 195–210.

Carmichael, Ann G. *Plague and the Poor in Renaissance Florence*. New York: Cambridge University Press, 1986.

Nightingale, Pamela. *A Medieval Mercantile Community: The Grocers' Company and the Politics and Trade of London, 1000–1485*. New Haven, CT: Yale University Press, 1995.

Pelling, Margaret. *Medical Conflicts in Early Modern London: Patronage, Physicians, and Irregular Practitioners 1550–1640*. New York: Oxford University Press, 2003.

Pullan, Brian. "Wage-earners and the Venetian Economy, 1550–1630," in his *Crisis and Change in the Venetian Economy in the Sixteenth and Seventeenth Centuries* (London: Methuen, 1968), 146–174.

Health Boards, Magistracies, and Commissions

Health boards and similar bodies developed in Europe as a direct result of the Second Pandemic. Prior to 1348, when medical emergencies arose, authorities requested advice of individual physicians, physicians' guilds, and medical school faculties, who responded with *consilia* or other forms of recommendations.

In March 1348, Venice's Major Council appointed three of its members to study the plague and instruct the government how to avoid and prepare for the epidemic. They were charged with conserving residents' health and eliminating the region's "corruption," or sources of miasma. This temporary commission recommended typical sanitation laws, extramural burial of plague corpses, and denial of entry to suspect ships and people. The Senate passed most of these in July, lifting them two years later. Florence's government passed a flurry of prophylactic sanitation laws beginning in January, 1348, and in April appointed an ad hoc commission of eight prominent citizens to oversee its efforts. Nearby Siena acted similarly, appointing a three-man commission. In Perugia, physician Gentile da Foligno in his plague *consilium* recommended that a panel of citizens work with physicians to manage the emergency, but to no avail. In fact, for more than two centuries, health commissions and boards consisted solely of non-medical practitioners.

Despite four additional epidemics sweeping Italy to 1400, no advances were made on the initial emergency arrangements. In 1399/1400, the Visconti dukes of Milan appointed a single administrator to combat plague. By 1424, a commissioner was enacting plague ordinances in the duke's name; a document from 1437 mentions a commissioner "for contagion." By 1450, the commissioner oversaw a physician, surgeon, barber, notary, two horsemen, three footmen, an officer for recording bills of mortality, a carter (for corpses), and two gravediggers. In 1408, Barcelona experimented with a public health committee of 12, with three representing each of the social estates (elites, merchants, high and low guildsmen); Majorca waited until 1471. During the plague of 1448, the Florentine *Otto di Guardia* ("eight custodians") were charged for three months with preserving health and avoiding contagion. The poor and poor victims specifically were their charges, and they provided bread, 40 women and 20 men to visit and inspect the sick, 200 beds for plague victims in Santa Maria Nuova hospital, and four physicians and four surgeons to serve their medical needs. In 1494, a commission (*balìa*) of five was active keeping plague out from March to September. With both plague and syphilis threatening, Florence appointed yet another commission of Officials for Disease in March 1496. Florence's first permanent health magistracy was created in 1527. The five members appointed a superintendant, chancellor, and notary. Under Cosimo I de' Medici, only noblemen could be members. In 1485, Venice finally created a permanent health magistracy, the *Provveditori alla Sanità*, to act continuously to protect Venice from plague; Milan quickly followed. During epidemics, *Provveditori* had broad law-making powers over all traditional health and sanitation matters; by 1540, its authority was extended over poor relief, prostitution, and suppression of begging, and by 1550, over Jews, physicians, drugs, and hospitals. Its success was notable: no major plagues occurred in Venice between 1577 and 1630, and the Dutch government carefully studied its techniques.

The 16th century saw the further development and spread of these offices. In 1523, Perugia created a plague magistracy of three men over age 60 with five assistants, one representing each of the city's quarters. They passed and enforced sanitation laws, restrictions on foreign trade, ordinances restricting the poor and vagabonds, providing charity, limiting funerals, and appointing 20 security police. Milan's Duke Francesco II Sforza replaced his commissioner with a five-man board presided over by a senator. Three were administrators, and two were physicians recommended by Milan's College (guild) of Physicians. The addition of physicians to the board was a true advance. French cities followed the Italian lead slowly, apparently pioneered by Brignoles (1460), Carpentras (1474), nearby Avignon (1479), and Marseille (1472). By 1600, all French cities had royal commissions. The Empire lagged further, Vienna receiving its director of health only in 1585.

Such Spanish cities as Barcelona and Seville, continued to appoint emergency commissions, usually of civil magistrates, who advised the royal governor, whose word was law—in the king's name. The ruler could empower the commission to enact laws in his name. Where magistracies developed, as in Italian states, they wielded lawmaking and judicial power that broadened in scope over time: forcible expulsion, isolation, or committal to a pest house; seizure and destruction of clothing and other property; restrictions on travel and trade; invasive inspections; additional taxation; draconian penalties for what seemed, to many, petty crimes. Crises of public health required powerful coercive measures. Such capitals as Florence, Venice, and Milan had jurisdiction over their towns and villages, and magistracies appointed health officers to enforce their legislation. By 1600, their activities usually alienated locals, unleashing despair, resentment, and outright opposition. Other, palliative measures, for example, provision of health professionals, medicines, and food, also under the magistracies' purview, hardly tipped the balance.

During the 1630 epidemic, Florentine health magistrates appointed agents who were to inspect all dwellings of the poor, clean and paint them to limit sources of "corruption," and restuff old mattresses or provide new ones. The magistracy included a canon of the Cathedral who oversaw the provision of the sacraments—presumably especially the last rites—in both city and countryside. He was also to see that the rural clergy was treated satisfactorily by the urban authorities, since clergy cooperation was vital in reducing community tensions.

See also: Bills of Health; Expulsion of Victims; Governments, Civil; Lazarettos and Pest Houses; Mass Graves and Plague Cemeteries; Miasma Theory; Plague Orders and National Authorities; Public Health; Public Sanitation; Quarantine.

References

Carmichael, Ann. "Plague Legislation in the Italian Renaissance." *Bulletin of the History of Medicine* 57 (1983): 508–525.

Cipolla, Carlo. *Public Health and the Medical Profession in Renaissance Florence*. New York: Cambridge University Press, 1976.

Cook, Alexandra Parma and Noble David Cook. *The Plague Files: Crisis Management in Sixteenth-Century Seville*. Baton Rouge: University of Louisiana Press, 2009.

Heaven and Hell

Medieval Judaism, Christianity, and Islam taught that after life on earth, one's soul lived on eternally in either heaven (Paradise) with God, or hell, a place of suffering and torment reserved for the faithless or disobedient to the revealed divine will. Religious doctrines and rituals were believed to have spiritual effects, directing the way toward eternal bliss and lessening the likelihood of damnation. Christian and Muslim understandings of spiritual salvation and punishment were the most developed. Christian depictions of hell, lorded over by Satan and illumined only by flames of perdition, filled prayer books and decorated church walls across Europe; among poets, Dante Alighieri of Florence best captured the pain and loss suffered by the damned in his *Divine Comedy*. Heaven was more difficult to capture in the imagination, though Dante and others tried.

During plague outbreaks, many of the rituals felt necessary or helpful for a proper entry into heaven were suspended, including those related to the deathbed, funeral, and burial. The sudden death reportedly associated with plague left many unprepared for death and unable to summon the necessary clergy. Islam taught that Allah treated righteous Muslims, who had lived according to Koranic dictates, and died of plague, as he treated those who had died as martyrs. Good Muslims had nothing to fear from plague, since Paradise was explained in largely physical terms, a place of unending pleasures. Unending torment awaited the immoral and the faithless (infidel). Plague was thus a warning to remain faithful, and a reminder that God eternally punishes the sinner and the enemies of Islam.

The Christian doctrine of purgatory, a spiritual "place" where souls suffer for their sins as purification for ultimate heavenly residence, was unique to Catholics and well developed by 1347. This teaching allowed the Church to compel acquiescence in its sacramental and moral life without outright condemnation of those who fell short. Suffering during one's earthly life was also considered cleansing of spiritual guilt, as lepers had long been taught. Plague sufferers, too, were believed to suffer less in the afterlife, especially if they had repented of their sins before life's end. Suspensions of death rituals—last rites at bedside, a funeral mass and procession, burial in consecrated ground—accompanied many epidemics, and bishops, including popes, declared certain loopholes or dispensations for those who died of plague unprepared. Indulgences granting full remission of penalties for sins were directly linked to one's participation in confession, intercessory masses or processions, however, and to one's true sorrow (contrition). Early modern Protestants saw no value in rituals and generally understood that one's afterlife was entirely in God's hands. Rejecting purgatory, their view of God's justice and mercy was at once bleak and reassuring.

See also: Allah; *Ars moriendi* (*The Art of Dying*); Funerals, Catholic; Funerals, Muslim; Funerals, Protestant; God the Father; Islamic Religious Responses; Mass Graves and Plague Cemeteries; Purgatory; Reformation and Protestantism.

References
Camporesi, Piero. *The Fear of Hell*. University Park, PA: Penn State University Press, 1990.

McDaniell, Colleen and Bernhard Lang. *Heaven: A History*. New York: Vintage, 1990.

Henry VIII, King of England (1491–1547; r. 1509–1547)

Henry was the second son of Henry VII Tudor, victor of Bosworth Field and the Wars of the Roses. When his father died in 1509, the well-educated Henry assumed the throne. Though the court was wherever the king was, London's Westminster was England's capital. It was swelling with unfettered growth and suffering almost annual plague, a disease Henry feared obsessively. As nearby refuges, he had Windsor and Woodstock, purchased Hunson Manor in Hertfordshire, and likewise seized Thomas Cardinal Wolsey's estate at Hampton up the Thames in the 1530s.

Breaking with tradition, Henry rode horseback instead of walking in ceremonial processions from St. Paul's to Westminster to avoid contagion. When he and the court "progressed" through the provinces to visit his towns and nobles, routes were carefully chosen to avoid plague. In 1517, he disappeared in the Thames Valley to escape contact with people, but Wolsey, Chancellor since 1515, remained in London. In January 1518, he issued the first English royal plague regulations. These ordered houses with victims to be identified, their inhabitants to carry wands while on the street, and basic sanitation measures to be carried out at taxpayers' expense. Later in 1518, Wolsey established the Royal College of Physicians as a sort of board of medical experts and, the following year, the first bills of mortality. Henry put no trust in these, as he banned visitors from Christmas at Eltham in 1525 and watched as Anne Boleyn and Wolsey contracted and recovered from the plague in 1529. Two years later, he relocated the court to Greenwich, but not before paying the supposedly susceptible poor to leave.

Here he probably had northern English coal and aromatic brush and wood burnt for fumigation. Henry had infant daughters Mary and Elizabeth baptized privately to lessen exposure. He postponed Jane Seymour's 1536 coronation, personally avoided Edward's birth at Hampton Court in 1537, and then had Edward baptized privately.

As part of his Reformation, he closed several Church-run hospitals (most reopened under Mary) and established Regis professorships in medicine at Oxford and Cambridge. His religious changes also profoundly altered how English people dealt spiritually with the plague.

See also: Bills of Mortality; Flight; London, England; Plague Orders and National Authorities; Reformation and Protestantism.

References

MacCullough, Diarmaid, ed. *The Reign of Henry VIII: Politics, Policy, and Piety.* New York: St. Martin's, 1995.

Slack, Paul. *The Impact of Plague in Tudor and Stuart England.* New York: Oxford University Press, 1990.

Hippocrates (c. 460–c. 360 BCE) and the Hippocratic Corpus

"The Father of Medicine" was born into the clan of traditional healers—the Asklepiads—on the Greek island of Kos. Little is known of his career as a medical practitioner, and modern scholars do not attribute any systematic medical work to him. There is, however, a body of some 70 medical writings, the Hippocratic Corpus, formerly attributed to him, though probably written by contemporaries and followers over several centuries. They share a rejection of supernatural causation of illnesses and an embrace of natural factors in prevention, diagnosis, prognosis, and treatment of disease. These works demonstrate a reliance on the practitioner's experience over theory. Hippocrates accepted the humoral theory of his day but stressed the roles of diet and environment in the course of most diseases. The Hippocratic physician was a professional whom the patient could trust. Through his acquired experience, he interpreted the individual case history, providing a reliable diagnosis and prognosis and prescribing a fitting regimen of treatment.

Hippocrates's followers developed and spread his message and practice. Scholars studied his works at the great Library at Alexandria, and his greatest ancient student was the Roman Galen. A few key Hippocratic works were translated into Latin in Ravenna, Italy, from at least the sixth century and into Arabic from the ninth by Hunayn ibn Ishaq and his circle in Baghdad. The Arabic-Persian absorption of Hippocrates came with commentaries as well as translations, and both found their way into Latin from the later 11th century. From the medical school at Salerno, Italy, came the *Articella*, which included the Hippocratic *Aphorisms* and *Prognosis*, and, later, the *Regimen*. Translations into Latin directly from the Greek appeared from the 12th century and were replaced by humanistic versions in the 1480s. In 1526, the first Greek edition of the full Hippocratic Corpus was printed in Venice, a milestone in humanistic medicine.

Despite the role that divine intervention played through most of the Second Pandemic, Hippocratic medicine and the Hippocratic physician remained the medical ideal and model. As medical schools and guilds developed in the 13th and early 14th centuries, they produced and regulated physicians grounded in Hippocratic rationality, empiricism, and pragmatism. Though contemporary medical theories of pestilence included powerful astrological and theological components, plague *consilia*, tracts, and practice centered on the natural processes of the physical body, its constitution, diet, and environment. Hippocratic authority, bolstered by Aristotelian natural philosophy and Galen's fine tuning, led many decision makers to adopt practical programs of prevention and melioration, even if the Greek miasma and humoral models distracted scientists from finding the true nature of the disease and effective means of combating it.

See also: Arabic-Persian Medicine and Practitioners; *Articella*; Galen and Galenism; Medical Humanism; Humoral Theory; Medical Education (1300–1500, Medieval Europe); Medical Education (1500–1700, Early Modern Europe).

References

French, Roger. *Medicine before Science: The Business of Medicine from the Middle Ages to the Enlightenment.* New York: Cambridge University Press, 2003.

Jouana, Jacques. *Hippocrates.* Translated by M. B. DeBevoise. Baltimore, MD: Johns Hopkins University Press, 1999.

Smith, Wesley. *The Hippocratic Tradition.* Ithaca, NY: Cornell University Press, 1973.

Hodges, Nathaniel (1629–1688)

The English physician and public health pioneer was born to a rural vicar but educated at Oxford's Christchurch College. Hodges was a first-rate practitioner who worked in London's Red Lyon Court and enrolled in the City's College of Physicians. He was a traditionalist who accepted Galenic humoralism and the prerogatives of the professions against Paracelsians, quacks, empirics, and unscrupulous apothecaries who peddled dangerous drugs. After great success early, he fell into alcoholism and debt, dying in prison.

During London's Great Plague of 1665 to 1666, Hodges stayed in the City and was chosen to serve on the emergency public health committee alongside another physician, two aldermen, two sheriffs, surgeons, and apothecaries. He advocated for stricter quarantines, a ban on lethal drugs, and more effective police measures against criminals. Recognizing medical science's limitations, he opted for pragmatic official actions to mitigate the epidemic's effects. In 1672, Hodges published his experiences, observations, and conclusions in his Latin *Loimologia; or, Historical Account of the Plague in London in 1665: with Precautionary Directions against the like Contagion*. It was translated and published in 1720 as Marseille's plague epidemic threatened. Novelist Daniel Defoe relied heavily on Hodges's horrifically graphic details and his rejection of such extreme measures as shutting in whole families. Hodges straddled the causal line between miasma theory and Athanasius Kircher's *animalcules* but limited his discussion to "natural and obvious Causes" and precautions and remedies they seemed to dictate. Dismissing astrology, he decried the superstition and fears that drove people to panic and desperate measures. *Loimologia* is thus practical and useful; an important text in the early history of epidemiology and public health.

See also: Defoe, Daniel; Health Boards, Magistracies, and Commissions; Kircher, Athanasius; London, Great Plague of; Physicians; Physicians, Town; Public Health; Shutting In.

Reference

Moote, A. Lloyd and Dorothy C. Moote. *The Great Plague: The Story of London's Most Deadly Year*. Baltimore, MD: Johns Hopkins University Press, 2004.

Hospitals

The Latin *hospes* can mean either guest or host, and the institution named *hospital* appears to have been an invention of Christian charity. Places of healing existed in the ancient, pre–Christian world, but this was only one function of the early hospitals. These served the poor, pilgrims, orphans, the elderly, the mentally ill, the incapacitated, and paying residents; some specialized and others were of a general nature. The earliest may have been the leprosarium at St.-Claude from 460; Arles opened the Maison Dieu to all poor sick in 503, and in 506, the regional Council of Agde required each diocese to have such a place of succor. Muslims developed the bimaristan and Jews in Europe had their own hospitals from at least 1210 (Regensburg). By the later Middle Ages, they were Christian institutions run like monasteries and often by religious, with funding from pious layfolk (either cash or rent-producing lands).

Such large cities as Paris, Florence, or London had several hospitals by the mid-14th century but also had set aside leprosaria for fear of contagion. Early plague victims were housed in hospitals, but almost immediately, concern for contagion created the felt need for segregation. Some hospitals established special wards for plague patients; some had their residents cleared out to make room for exclusively plague patients. The need for specialized plague facilities that could handle huge influxes of patients for relatively short periods and that had ample burial areas surrounding was felt by the 16th century and

Napoleon visits plague victims at a hospital in Jaffa during his Egyptian Campaign, 1799. Napoleon, accompanied by his officers, touching the armpit bubo presented to him by one of the sick. In front of him, an Arab doctor is caring for another sick man, while a blind man struggles to approach the general. (Courtesy of the National Library of Medicine)

provided for in only a few areas. Most hospitals normally served a population of chronic, continuous, and noninfectious residents, while plague called for acute treatment of multitudes every decade or so. One common answer was to shut victims inside their houses with their families until the disease had run its course. But those without proper houses, the indigent, diseased refugees, expelled servants, and apprentices, had need of care, and charity could not leave them to the streets.

Even in typical times, many hospitals were overcrowded—Paris's Hotel Dieu averaged three to a bed in the 14th century. Pest houses, when available, quickly filled to hellish overflowing and additional quarters were all too often needed. The more authoritarian rulers of the 16th and 17th centuries had few qualms about pressing monasteries, hospitals, almshouses, and other large buildings into service. They seemed reluctant, however, to provide more hospital space, despite growing demand even in their capital cities.

See also: Bimaristans; Lazarettos and Pest Houses; Leprosy (Hansen's Disease) and Leprosarium; Physicians.

References

Henderson, John. *The Renaissance Hospital: Healing the Body and Healing the Soul.* New Haven, CT: Yale University Press, 2006.

Horden, Peregrine. *Hospitals and Healing from Antiquity to the Later Middle Ages.* Burlington, VT: Ashgate, 2008.

Marmoy, Charles F. A. "The Pesthouse, 1681–1717: Predecessor of the French Hospital." *Huguenot Society of London Proceedings* 25 (1992): 385–399.

Park, Katherine. "Healing the Poor: Hospitals and Medical Assistance in Renaissance Florence," in *Medicine and Charity before the Welfare State*, edited by Jonathan Barry and Colin Jones (New York: Routledge, 1991), 26–45.

Presciutti, Diana Bullen. "David Michael D'Andrea, Civic Christianity in Renaissance Italy: The Hospital of Treviso, 1400–1530." *Medieval Feminist Forum* 44 (2008): 149–152.

Swettinburgh, Sheila. *The Role of the Hospital in Medieval England: Gift-giving and the Spiritual Economy*. Dublin: Four Courts Press, 2004.

Humoral Theory

The belief that within the human body there circulated four vital humors is found first among the fifth-century BCE Greeks. Often conceived of as fluids (though never defined as such), blood, phlegm, and yellow and black bile were thought to correspond to the four elements—air, water, fire, and earth—of which all things including the body are made, and the four qualities of wet, dry, hot, and cold. Blood corresponded to air and was hot and moist; phlegm corresponded to water and was cold and moist; yellow bile corresponded to fire and was hot and dry; and black bile corresponded to earth and was cold and dry. The ancients also connected the humors to the four temperaments: sanguine, phlegmatic, choleric, and melancholic. Later, medical astrologers linked the whole lot to zodiac signs and seasons. More than anything else, the humors made the human a true microcosm, or miniature cosmos.

Health depended upon a balance of the humors, which might differ with age, sex, activity level, emotional state, diet, and other factors both natural and behavioral. Sickness meant humoral imbalance (*cacochymia*), which was medically treated with diet, rest, exercise, medicines, and elimination of excess humors or of toxins that cause the imbalance. Natural elimination included urination, defecation, sweating, ejaculation, spitting, vomiting, blowing one's nose, or menstruation; induced elimination included enemas and bleeding or bloodletting. Foods and medications were understood to be hot, cold, dry, or wet, and their consumption or avoidance could help redress the imbalance. In the Latin West, calefactives warmed the body, infrigidatives cooled it, humefactives moistened, and dessicatives dried it, mollificatives softened, lubrifactives lubricated, stupefactives calmed the mind, and purgatives helped purge excesses and impurities.

Humoral theory and the practices based upon it were logical, natural, and flew in the face of superstition and religious healing. Hippocrates worked within its framework and Galen developed it further, as attested to by his many writings. The Byzantine East and Islamic worlds inherited Galen and humoralism, and the West slowly reabsorbed it through Arabic-Persian filters, especially those of Hunayn, Ibn-Ishaq and Avicenna. Fascinated likewise by Ptolemy's *Tetrabiblos*, the Muslims joined humoralism to astrology, providing the connection between celestial movements and terrestrial health. Galen and humoral medicine stood at the center of the curricula of the Christian West's new medical schools. When plague struck Italy in 1347, physicians from Baghdad to Ireland relied on humoral theory and practice.

From the start, plague provided problems that contradicted humoral principles. So many caught it at once that it clearly was not a matter of individual humoral imbalances. It seemed to spread by contact, or contagion, which implied some external toxin: the Galenic miasma! But while everyone breathed, not everyone contracted plague; so some had to be more and some less susceptible. The Galenic physician wanted to see those possessed of a well-balanced complexion stave off the fever and buboes, but the vigorous died alongside the weakling. Throughout the Second Pandemic, physicians, officials, hospitals, and medical schools treated plague as an atmospheric toxin that entered some bodies, sickening them by "virulent putrefaction" of the humors and killing them by suffocation of the heart. Purgation, including drugs and bleeding, might expel the poison, but humoralism had little else to offer by way of remedy.

Challenges to the humoral model of therapy came from Christian and Muslim writers, who denied man's ability to thwart God's will. From the mid-16th century, Paracelsians, or chemical physicians (iatrochemists), emphasized the importance of mineral rather than organic balances and treatments. Paracelsus himself correctly discerned that the pagan model was incorrect and interfered with true understanding of human physiology. Yet humoralism persisted into the 19th century, despite Renaissance, Scientific Revolution, and Enlightenment: a testament to its explanatory value if not its efficacy in treating disease.

See also: Astrology; Bleeding/Phlebotomy; Galen and Galenism; Hippocrates and the Hippocratic Corpus; Miasma Theory; Paracelsus and Paracelsianism.

References

Arikha, Noga. *Passions and Tempers: A History of the Humours*. New York: Ecco, 2007.

Pormann, Peter E. and Emilie Savage-Smith. *Medieval Islamic Medicine*. Washington, DC: Georgetown University Press, 2007.

Rawcliffe, Carole. *Medicine and Society in Later Medieval England*. Stroud, Gloucs, UK: Sutton, 1997.

Siraisi, Nancy. *Medieval and Early Renaissance Medicine*. Chicago: University of Chicago Press, 1990.

Hundred Years War (1337–1453)

Medieval Europe's most protracted armed conflict began a decade before plague struck. As vassals of French kings, England's monarchs had long held large portions of what is today France. In 1328, France's last Capetian King died without a clear heir, the French nobility accepting his nephew Philip Valois. Isabella, Queen of England and mother of young Edward III, was daughter of King Louis X, and her party pressed for Edward once he reached legitimate age. The resulting dynastic war ravaged the French countryside and drained English coffers.

In August 1346, Edward destroyed a strong French army at Crécy but was too weakened to continue. By late 1347, Philip was preparing a counterattack against England itself. In early 1348, Black Death struck France and, soon after, England. Cities lay prostrate, manpower disappeared, and tax bases shrank. By 1355, French coinage had lost 70 percent of its value. Between 1347 and 1355, the kings agreed to three truces. The French worked hard to maintain military discipline and unit strengths and revised pay scales upward. The war continued, commanders learning to pause when plague was noted nearby and to avoid areas where disease was present. The war's length was no doubt prolonged by resource depletion caused by recurrent plague coupled with unrealistic plans and expectations on both sides. Battles were few; most of the damage to France was the result of English armed companies living off the land between formal skirmishes. To some degree, these roving bands spread plague along with many other diseases among villages and towns, some wandering as far afield as Tuscany. Mustering of troops together for campaigns from across Western Europe also presented opportunities for exchange of diseases, though no army is known to have been crippled by plague.

See also: Armies.

Reference

Allmand, C. T. *The Hundred Years War: England and France at War.* New York: Cambridge University Press, 1988.

I

I promessi sposi (1827)

Alessandro Manzoni (1785–1873) was born near Lake Como to a conservative aristocrat and liberal mother, daughter of Enlightenment reformer Cesare Beccaria. Thrilling to revolutionary trends, Alessandro moved to Paris in 1805, wrote nationalistic poetry, and drifted from Catholicism. His religious convictions revived after he married. In 1810, the couple moved to Milan, where he wrote religious poetry and studied history, penning his historical novel, *The Betrothed*, between 1821 and 1823 (published 1827; revised and republished 1840). It is considered Italy's national novel.

Aimed at popular rather than aristocratic readers, it combines Romanticism and faith with liberal Italian nationalism. The romance between Lombards Renzo and Lucia is set circa 1630 against the chaotic Thirty Years' War, Spanish occupation, and plague. Initially thwarted by the lustful desires of Don Rodrigo, their love survives flight, separation, imprisonment, and lives as refugees. Like the powerful men who stand between them, plague is an important character. Morally neutral, it both separates and brings the lovers together, threatens their lives, but is overcome in the awful setting of Milan's lazaretto. Scenes borrowed from Archbishop Borromeo's *La peste di Milano* and other sources gain life and dimension as Renzo climactically searches the hecatomb for his beloved.

See also: Borromeo, Federigo; Lazarettos and Pest Houses; Milan, Italy; Thirty Years' War.

Reference

Manzoni, Alessandro. *The Betrothed*. Translated by Bruce Penman. New York: Penguin, 1972.

Ibn al-Khatib, Lisad-ad Din (1313–1374)

Al-Khatib's father's family was among the early Muslim settlers in Andalusia, as the Arabs called Spain. His birth name was Loja and his father served the local ruler as chief minister (*vizier*). He studied medicine in Granada and entered the service of Yusuf I around 1341. He was working as a secretary under the *vizier* when the man died of plague in 1349. Al-Khatib replaced the *vizier* and continued to serve Yusuf and then his successor Muhammad V from 1354. In 1359, Muhammad was ousted, and Al-Khatib followed him to Morocco. Muhammad returned to power and the pair returned to Granada in 1362, but a decade later, Al-Khatib's enemies had him imprisoned for heresy, where he was strangled.

Though educated to be a physician, Al-Khatib would only have served at court, and his 19 known writings show a wide range of interests. He seems to have penned his plague tract, "A Very Useful Inquiry into the Horrible Sickness," while in exile (1359–1362), having lived through at least two epidemics. Not surprisingly, Al-Khatib was a Galenist who accepted the need to maintain a balance of the humors. He believed women and children to be more susceptible to plague because of their humoral makeup.

From observation, he concluded that those who had been exposed to the plague and lived seem to have acquired a certain resistance or immunity. He also noted that groups that remained isolated from the disease did not contract it, which seemed to suggest that the cause was neither miasma nor divine will. Though cognizant that Muhammad definitively declared that there is no contagion, there is only Allah's will at work, Al-Khatib stated unequivocally, "The existence of contagion is well established through experience, research, sense perception, autopsy, and authenticated information, and this material is the proof" (Dols, 93). Clearly, he observed, plague follows the plague-ridden. He also distinguished bubonic from pneumonic plague and declared pneumonic to be the most infectious. He defended his position by explaining that sacred texts had to be read allegorically when they clearly contradict human experience. Further, he condemned as murderers those who ignored those who ignored contagion, forbade flight, and forced people to remain congregated as murderers. Alone among known Muslim physicians of the day, Ibn al-Khatib placed his own experience and reason above the received wisdom.

See also: Arabic-Persian Medicine and Practitioners; Contagion Theory; Islam and Medicine.

References

Campbell, Anna Montgomery. *The Black Death and Men of Learning*. New York: Columbia University Press, 1931.

Dols, Michael W. *The Black Death in the Middle East*. Princeton, NJ: Princeton University Press, 1977.

Ober, W. B. and Alloush, N. "The Plague at Granada 1348–1349: Ibn Al-Khatib and ideas of Contagion," in *Bottoms Up!: A Pathologist's Essays on Medicine and the Humanities*, edited by W. B. Ober (Carbondale: Southern Illinois University Press, 1987): 288–293.

Ibn Battuta, Abu Abdullah (1304–1368)

Ibn Battuta was born into a family of Muslim legal scholars in Tangier, Morocco. Pursuing the same profession, he studied at home until he was 20. At this point, he set out on the required hajj, or pilgrimage to Mecca. He returned 24 years later on the heels of the Black Death.

He recorded many details of his 24-year journey in his *Book of Travels*. As a pilgrim and a scholar, Ibn Battuta was entitled to support from the Muslim communities through which he traveled. He sought out and studied with prominent scholars, visited Mecca several times, traveled to India, where he served as a judge for eight years, filled the same role in the Maldive Islands, and claimed to have been in Beijing. In January 1348, Ibn Battuta reached Baghdad from southern Arabia.

He headed for home in the spring, stopping at Damascus and Aleppo in Syria. Here news of the plague reached him for the first time. He heard of incredible death tolls exceeding a thousand per day in Gaza. Moving south, he stopped in Homs, which suffered 300 casualties on the day of his arrival. Returning to Damascus in July, he reported the city losing 2,400 victims per day. Nonetheless, after a three-day fast and prayers God lifted the outbreak. Leaving quickly, Ibn Battuta began the hajj to Mecca again, stopping in Jerusalem and Gaza. In the former, his host was celebrating the apparent end of the epidemic. Gaza they found depopulated due to the prior outbreak there. A fellow judge informed him that only 60 of 80 notaries remained alive, and daily death tolls of 1,100 emptied the streets and houses. In Egypt, evidence of the plague was everywhere. At Abu Sir, he stayed in a hospice room with an old holy man who did not survive the night. His informants in Alexandria reported 1,080 daily deaths and in Cairo, 21,000. All of the scholars with whom he had earlier studied were dead. He completed his hajj and traveled back to Tangier late in the year. Unbeknownst to him, his mother had died of plague shortly before his arrival.

See also: Black Death (1347–1352); Cairo, Egypt; Mecca; Pilgrims and Pilgrimage.

References
Dols, Michael W. *The Black Death in the Middle East*. Princeton, NJ: Princeton University Press, 1977.

Ibn Battuta. *Voyages of Ibn Battuta*. Volume 4. Hakluyt Society #178. Cambridge: for the Hakluyt Society, 1994.

Ibn Khatimah, Abu Jafar Ahmed (1323?–1369)

Abu Jafar Ahmed ibn Ali ibn Muhammad ibn Ali ibn Khatimah was a Muslim born and educated in Almeria in the Muslim-controlled southern Spanish kingdom of Granada. He was a legal scholar and poet as well as an educated physician who worked among his fellow Almerians for much of his life. Ibn Khatimah was well known in high circles and friend and rival of Almeria's other great physician, Ibn al-Khatib. He was the author of at least three dozen works, among them the *Description of and Remedy for the Plague*. The Black Death had stricken Almeria in early June 1348, and soon 70 victims were dying each day. It was a busy port and the first Andalusian city to suffer the epidemic. Ibn Khatimah wrote in its midst after six months of tending its victims, in February 1349. Though trained as an orthodox Galenic physician, he claims to have written from his experience rather than authorities, who had never encountered such a phenomenon. The tract's format is a series of 10 questions with answers; his main point seems to be the reconciliation of medicine with Islamic teaching on contagion, especially in Question 8.

His tract posits three causes for the disease: astrological events, meteorological (seasonal) irregularities, and putrefaction of matter that "changes" (poisons) the air. The air is poisoned locally by putrefaction, thanks to the weather and decaying matter (manure, corpses, plant matter, etc.), and is not universal. Once in the body, the poison attacks the heart, creating a fever, and then spreads to other parts; the opposite, Ibn Khatimah contended, to all other forms of disease. Particles of the poison can deposit themselves on textiles and be absorbed into the body. The breath of the infected can also "infest the air" around her. While Ibn al-Khatib insisted that plague was contagious, Ibn Khatimah avoided such a declaration for religious reasons. Despite understanding that mechanisms for random contagion existed and operated in nature, he had to admit that Allah, and not chance, directed the disease to the chosen victim.

See also: Arabic-Persian Medicine and Practitioners; Consilia and Plague Tracts; Contagion Theory; Ibn al-Khatib, Lisad ad-Din; Islam and Medicine; Miasma Theory; *Ta'un*.

References
Campbell, Anna Montgomery. *The Black Death and Men of Learning*. New York: Columbia University Press, 1931.

Dols, Michael W. *The Black Death in the Middle East*. Princeton, NJ: Princeton University Press, 1977.

Individualism and Individual Liberties

When a society is under threat from some outside force, the members of the society may have to give up some of their freedom, rights, or liberties in the name of handling the threat. Every society must make decisions regarding the lengths to which it is willing to go to protect itself at the expense of individuals. A military threat might entail paying higher taxes, drafting young men, or increasing security measures. Serious modern public health risks might require access to otherwise private medical records, restrictions on travel, quarantine or isolation, or unwanted but such mandatory medical procedures as vaccinations. During the Second Pandemic, plague killed by the thousands, and this called for drastic measures. Late medieval cities had broad police powers, and these were broadest where the government was most absolute. In general, European governments gained power and authority over time and became more willing to use more extreme measures. Run by the pragmatic Visconti dukes, Milan in 1348 escaped all but a few plague cases by taking drastic measures: traffic in and out of the city was stopped and those who showed signs of disease were walled up in their homes with their families. Over time, even politically liberal cities and states legislated greater impositions in the name of curtailing contagion: such religious ritual gatherings as funerals and churchyard burials were banned in favor of unceremonious mass burial; plague hospitals and pest houses were provided for poor victims, who were forcibly moved to these places; the Visconti method of shutting up sick people and their families in their own homes was widely used; symptomless family members

were forced to undergo quarantine; private property—from one's residence to clothing and retail stock—could be seized and cleansed or burnt without compensation; and poorer and not-so-poor victims could be expelled from the city. Each such action was an assault on previously understood freedoms. Apart from the occasional published criticism and local rioting against forced isolation, there was little in the way of opposition to state measures that trampled traditional liberties for the sake of the common good.

When the prospect of seizure and transport to a pest house or anonymous burial in a mass grave had subsided, many reacted in ways that emphasized their individuality. Will makers specified burial places, epitaphs, and personal memorials more regularly and with greater detail than before; they demanded accurate likenesses, once a prerogative of the wealthy; they endowed chantries to pray for their souls; and they decorated churches and chapels with an eye toward God's favor. Whereas earlier medieval piety often revolved around the "contempt for the world" ascetic theme inherited from the monastic tradition, the threat of sudden and unexpected death seems to have sparked or accelerated a tendency toward validation of the natural world typically associated with the Renaissance. The death of friends was lamented, and the Petrarchan validation of self in which his lamentations were embedded evolved quickly in the hecatombs that gave rise to humanism. At the same time, the redistribution of wealth from the dead to the survivors gave a wider circle of people the ability to rise above anonymity.

It is well known that during the later 14th century, the search for worldly fame began to supplant anonymous humility. Was this unreasonable in the face of familial extinction and plague cemeteries? Historian Samuel

Cohn suggests that worldly remembrance and spiritual salvation were not antithetical but became "tied inextricably together" in northern Italy, especially after the second round of plague in the 1360s. The initial shock dissipated as the threat receded and people gave thanks for having survived. But when the "mortality" returned, people sensed a new order was beginning. It was neither the end of the world nor a one-time explosion of God's wrath, and each person stood before it alone.

See also: Art, Effects of Plague on; Corpse Carriers; Corpses; Funerals, Catholic; Lazarettos and Pest Houses; Mass Graves and Plague Cemeteries; Shutting In.

References

Cohn, Samuel K. *The Cult of Remembrance and the Black Death*. Baltimore, MD: Johns Hopkins University Press, 1992.

Meiss, Millard. *Painting in Florence and Siena after the Black Death: The Arts, Religion, and Society in the Mid-fourteenth Century*. Princeton, NJ: Princeton University Press, 1951.

Ingrassia, Giovanni Filippo (Gianfilippo; 1510–1580)

Known as the "Sicilian Hippocrates," Ingrassia was born near Palermo and educated there in medicine by Giovanni Battista di Pietra. He moved to Padua's medical school, where he befriended the gifted anatomist Andreas Vesalius. Ingrassia graduated in 1537, disappeared from the record, and appeared in Naples in 1544. Here he held the chair in anatomy and medicine, gaining renown as a teacher and anatomist. In 1556, Philip II of Spain, which controlled Naples and Sicily, appointed Ingrassia *protomedicus* of Palermo and, in 1563, head physician for all of Sicily and surrounding islands. In both positions,

he served as chief medical inspector of pharmacies, hospitals, and physicians' credentials. He continued his medical research program, distinguishing scarlet fever from chicken pox and making important discoveries regarding the human skeleton. Considered by some to be the founder of legal medicine, in Palermo Ingrassia established Sicily's first Board of Health and Sanitary Code.

When plague threatened from North Africa in 1575, Ingrassia began his *Information (Informatione) on pestiferous and contagious disease*, a landmark plague tract that would swell to more than 550 pages and reach the printer the following year. As *protomedicus*, Ingrassia actively battled the epidemic by recommending action to the Spanish governor: quarantines, isolation of the sick, new hospitals, and precautions to keep plague workers healthy. His Health Board collected and provided unprecedented—for Sicily—data Ingrassia used in his lobbying with Spain. All this found its way into *Informatione*. Dedicated to Philip II, it opens by blaming the plague on God's wrath but quickly shifts to the pragmatic. He relates his evidence for the epidemic being "plague" and not another "fever" and proceeds with a chronological account of the plague's arrival, spread, and effects. His emphasis is on his professional point of view and what the situation demanded of the public authorities: even massacring all cats and dogs. "Part Five," published in 1577, contains his program of public health measures against a future epidemic. For example, he planned a new pest house (*lazaretto*) from location to each room's layout to the necessary financing. Though his activism may not have been unprecedented, his chronicling of the plague as a public health emergency was a foundation stone for epidemiology.

See also: Consilia and Plague Tracts; Epidemic and Pandemic; Vesalius, Andreas.

References

Byrne, Joseph P. *Daily Life during the Black Death*. Westport, CT: Greenwood Press, 2006.

Cohn, Samuel K. *Cultures of Plague: Medical Thinking at the End of the Renaissance*. New York: Oxford University Press, 2010.

Islam and Medicine

At the time of the Black Death, the religion of Islam affected the lives of millions across a swath of Eurasia and Africa from Spain to India. *Islam* refers to the willful "submission" of each Muslim to Allah (God) and the teaching revealed to Muhammad His Prophet and embodied in the Koran. Muslim teaching is further informed by the Hadith, a body of teachings and actions attributed to Muhammad that shed light on a multitude of issues not clearly delineated in the Koran. Together, these sources inform sharia law in its four schools or traditions. The law and will of Allah dominate every aspect of a Muslim's life, and Islam tends to be a deterministic religion in which God is responsible for all that happens.

Health and sickness certainly would fall under God's purview, and indeed there is a strand of thought that teaches full reliance on God's will alone. But Islam emerged from Arabia and a set of folk medical traditions and matured in the presence of learned, scholarly medicine with roots in ancient Greece. The result was a complex, multifaceted healing tradition that blended religious imperatives with talismans and magic while absorbing and often further developing sophisticated medical theories and practices. There was a clear dividing line between the practitioners of Greek Galenic medicine and the religious experts who taught and judged according to Prophetic Medicine, by which the more spiritual approach came to be known. Even so, those who followed Galen were expected to respect and adhere to the Prophetic traditions as well. For the most part, this worked, since the Koran and even Hadith had relatively little to say about medical issues. In fact, the accepted principle was that God sent the disease, the doctor, and the remedy.

As Pormann and Savage-Smith point out, the vast scope of the Black Death created a "fault line" (58) between the medical professionals and the religious authorities, who began writing plague treatises according to the Muslim traditions, especially the Hadiths. Perhaps the single greatest issue revolved around whether disease is spread only according to the will of Allah or the mechanism of random contact (contagion) operates to propagate epidemic disease. The implications for advice and treatment, and for matters of public health, were quite real.

Islam also supported the charitable healing facilities known as bimaristans. Probably modeled on Christian monastic and urban hospitals, bimaristans were privately funded and established by people of high class and wealth, sometimes the leaders of society. Not merely for the poor, these were elegant structures with multiple purposes including surgery, acute and chronic care, pharmacy, education, prayer, and often the enshrining of the patron.

See also: Allah; Arabic-Persian Medicine and Practitioners; Bimaristans; Contagion Theory; Galen and Galenism; Ibn al-Khatib, Lisad-ad Din, Islamic Religious Responses; Jinn; Muhammad the Prophet; *Ta'un*.

References

Pormann, Peter E. and Emilie Savage-Smith. *Medieval Islamic Medicine*. Washington, DC: Georgetown University Press, 2007.

Shefer-Mossensohn, Miri. *Ottoman Medicine: Healing and Medical Institutions, 1500–1700*. Albany: SUNY Press, 2009.

Ullmann, Manfred. *Islamic Medicine*. Edinburgh: Edinburgh University Press, 1978.

Islamic Civil Responses

The urban portion of the Islamic world at the time of the Second Plague Pandemic was among the most civilized and well organized in the world. Urban space may have seemed chaotic, but it followed the logic of a culture that eschewed wheeled conveyances, developed in intense heat and sunlight, and imposed strict social regulations usually based on religious precepts. Government was imposed from above and supported by a sophisticated bureaucracy and court. The Muslim God was omnipotent and brooked no opposition, working his will through natural forces and supernatural jinn.

When plague struck Muslim urban centers, there was a level of acceptance and, perhaps, resignation that was quite different from that of Christian cities. Where Christians were quite active—even frenetic—in both the spiritual and material world, seeking any way possible to avoid the disease, Muslims seemed content to accept God's will. Islamic society had officials, for example, the physicians who oversaw medical education, the judges or qadi, and hisba who oversaw the marketplaces, but neither records nor observers depict their active organizing of the stricken communities. The wealthy and powerful did tend to flee, despite the Prophet's teaching neither to enter nor leave an unhealthy place. Those left behind did react to the disasters by maintaining social order and some level of hygiene; endless private parades to and from the great cemeteries passed in silence or mournful wailing, but no one organized civic disposal of victims.

Islam accepted both God's will and miasma as causes of plague, and the religion specifically taught that there was no contagion. Much of what the Christian world did to protect itself from plague was based on the idea of contagion, even if no medical theory supported it. Quarantine, isolation, and other measures may have been carried out sporadically, but religious authorities would not allow a policy contrary to doctrine. In addition, since God promised that the faithful who died would be blessed with a martyr's afterlife, even to pray that Allah lift the plague was a sacrilege in many circles.

Sixteenth-century Turkish authorities seem to have been more active than their predecessors, with Selim II calling for communal prayer in 1567 and Murad II twice in 1592, along with religious processions and the freeing of prisoners. As Varlik's research shows, the sultans adopted a more Westernized version of the state and the ruler's obligation to the public welfare. Regulations on physicians, burials (gypsy gravediggers and the use of lime), water supplies, public sanitation, public baths (40 built from 1540 to 1588; to be closed during epidemics), and monitoring of death tolls replaced civic inaction as contagion theory made inroads.

See also: Allah; Arabic-Persian Medicine and Practitioners; Cairo, Egypt; Constantinople/Istanbul; Contagion Theory; Governments, Civil; Islam and Medicine; Islamic Religious Responses; Miasma Theory.

References

Aberth, John. *Plagues in World History*. New York: Rowman and Littlefield, 2011.

Borsch, Stuart. *The Black Death in Egypt and England*. Austin: University of Texas Press, 2005.

Dols, Michael W. "The Comparative Communal Responses to the Black Death in Muslim and Christian Societies." *Viator* 5 (1974): 269–287.

Kharmi, Ghada. "State Control of the Physician in the Middle Ages: An Islamic Model," in *Town and State Physicians in Europe from the Middle Ages to the Enlightenment*, edited by Andrew Russell (Wolfenbüttel Forschungen 17: Herzog August Bibliothek, 1981), 63–84.

Varlik, Nükhet. "Disease and Empire: A History of Plague and Epidemics in the Early Ottoman Empire (1453–1600)." Ph.D. dissertation, University of Chicago, 2008.

Islamic Religious Responses

Islam is not a monolithic religion but one with variations among believers and sects. When plague entered the Muslim world in the 1340s, it was doing so for the second time, since Muhammad had defined Islam in the midst of the First Plague Pandemic. Islam considers God to be the originator and director of all things, including such a great medical crisis as plague. As inheritors of the Hippocratic and Galenic schools of rationalistic medicine, Muslims also understood plague and other epidemics as natural crises to which humans can respond naturally in the hope of avoiding or curing the disease. Muslims, like Christians, attributed the ultimate cause of plague to God and immediate causes to God's natural tools, for example, celestial alignments, miasma (atmospheric poison), or diet. At the same time, some Islamic teachers taught that God gave people both diseases and the means of dealing with them, and others that God's will was not to be challenged. Was it challenging God to flee, have oneself bled, or take medicines in hope of avoiding the disease? Muhammad had said never to enter nor leave an area where plague was found,

which appears to forbid the first, but what of the other prophylaxes or remedies?

These were not fine points of theology but terribly practical matters. If the legal teacher Ibn Hajar al-Asqalana was correct, then one would do nothing. He taught that plague is not death to a true Muslim but eternal life; it is a mercy that introduces the faithful to Paradise. One should not question God or flee either physically or spiritually through prayer seeking avoidance. Nor should one seek to protect one's community by prayer on its behalf: this is really rebellion against the will of God. Thus the religious teachers and judges: submission (*islam*) meant just that.

But this flew in the face of human nature and defied the human ability to direct prayer to God and to contend with a disease that had natural causes. We do not have the type of evidence that tells us what individuals believed as Muslims before their God, but we do have quite a bit of evidence of personal and communal activity that defied al-Asqalana's teachings.

Poets, chroniclers, and travelers described the communities they saw as transfigured by popular fear and sadness and the omnipresence of death. We read little of divine mercy and much of prayers for mercy and forgiveness. Whatever the teachers said of the plague's not being punishment, the popular reaction belies. Individuals took up the ancient practice of wearing talismans, stones, and amulets, incantations and inscriptions that were thought to have power against the spirits (*jinn*) whom some believed to be spreaders of the disease. In Cairo, men sat alone on street corners reciting prayers of supplication and on behalf of the dead. But personal prayer also meant seeking the spiritual strength to accept God's will, whether it meant life or Paradise. Visionaries claimed Muhammad told them to say particular prayers. Observers noted greater attention to matters of normal ritual purity in people's private lives, and extraordinary fasting was both recommended and undertaken.

Shi'ite Muslims venerated saints and shrines associated with them, and many had recourse to these through prayer and visitation. None of these, however, was the equivalent of a Christian plague saint. Such holy men and women presumably had the good will of Allah and might persuade him on behalf of their devotees. Shi'ites also had a strong tradition of faith healing, among other miracles, and directed themselves accordingly.

But most observers noted the group activities that either appeared or intensified because of the plague. Devout prayer at the local mosque several times a day became the norm as shops closed and regular activities ceased. Friday prayer and sermon were very important gatherings as people noted who had disappeared during the previous week. But there were also long processions of penitent Muslims in Cairo, Damascus, and even Constantinople. Funerals for dozens at a time were held—against custom— in mosques. After, each small procession wended its way to the huge extramural graveyards, carrying the corpse on whatever panel of wood was available. On a smaller scale, a family would process alone to the cemetery, where they would pray and wait for a gravedigger to accommodate their loved one. Return visits were not unusual since some Muslims believed that souls of the dead remained present.

See also: Allah; Amulets, Talismans, and Magic; Cairo, Egypt; Constantinople/Istanbul; Funerals, Muslim; Islam and Medicine; Islamic Civil Responses; Jinn.

References

Akasoy, Anna. "Islamic Attitudes to Disasters in the Middle Ages: A Comparison of Earthquakes and Plagues." *Medieval History Journal* 10 (2007): 387–410.

Dols, Michael W. *The Black Death in the Middle East.* Princeton, NJ: Princeton University Press, 1977.

Dols, Michael W. "The Comparative Communal Responses to the Black Death in Muslim and Christian Societies." *Viator* 5 (1974): 269–287.

Halevi, Leor. *Muhammad's Grave: Death Rites and the Making of Islamic Society.* New York: Columbia University Press, 2007.

Perho, I. *The Prophet's Medicine: A Creation of the Muslim Traditionalist Scholars.* Studia Orientalia 74. Helsinki: Finnish Oriental Society, 1995.

Islip, Simon (d. 1366)

The future Archbishop of Canterbury was born at Islip near Oxford, and he attended Oxford, gaining degrees in Canon and Civil Law. Before the Black Death, he served in many English church positions, including legal counsel to the bishops of Lichfield, Lincoln, and London. In the 1340s, he was a royal chaplain in London and a member of Edward III's royal council.

In 1348, Archbishop John Stratford of Canterbury, leader of the Church in England, died, and John Ufford (Offord) quickly replaced him but was never consecrated. When Ufford died in 1349, famed Oxford theologian and natural philosopher Thomas Bradwardine replaced him. Bradwardine died only 40 days after his consecration, on August 26, 1349. A month later, Islip was formally elected and consecrated on Christmas. He had to rebuild the English Church in the plague's wake. Islip immediately wrote to his peers ordering thanksgiving prayers and processions. He then toured the country on a visitation to determine the nature and extent of damage. The Archbishop's treasury had been depleted by high expenses, low revenues, and huge exactions sent by Ufford and Bradwardine to the pope, and Islip refilled it.

His biggest concern was for the clergy. Large numbers of pastors had died, and bishops had done what they could to replace them with qualified men, but many remained half-literate and otherwise unprepared. He founded an Oxford College for monks, but it remained attached to Christchurch. More troubling were the many cases in which pastors abandoned their congregations to serve as beneficed "mass-priests" for wealthy donors, whose wills called for thousands of commemorative services. The easy work paid well, and Islip railed against the priests' greed and laziness and sought to limit stipends. A stroke during the epidemic of 1363 rendered him mute.

See also: Anticlericalism; Bishops and Popes; Priests.

Reference

Horrox, Rosemary. *The Black Death*. New York: Manchester University Press, 1994.

Issyk Kul, Kyrgystan

In 1885, at a settlement site located south of Lake Issyk Kul (Balkhash), Russian archeologists led by Daniel Chwolsen excavated two cemeteries belonging to medieval Nestorian Christians. They found graves of 650 people identified by 330 stone markers dating from 1186 to 1349, when the settlement was presumably abandoned. One hundred six of the corpses were buried in 1338 to 1339, and the markers representing about 10 of them mention "pestilence" or "plague" or "epidemic," depending on the translation from Syriac. Since Issyk Kul is located along the classic Silk Road, which under Mongol domination connected China with the West, some historians have long wanted to interpret the spot as the oldest known link in the spread of the Black Death that reached Europe in 1347. In 2009, the area underwent a plague reservoir research study by the International Science and Technology Center.

See also: Black Death: Origins and Early Spread; Mass Graves and Plague Cemeteries.

References

Norris, John. "East or West? The Geographic Origin of the Black Death." *Bulletin of the History of Medicine* 51 (1977): 1–24; and his remarks in 52 (1978), 112–120.

Thacker, T. W. "A Nestorian Gravestone from Central Asia in the Gulbenkian Museum, Durham University." *Durham University Journal* 59 (1967): 94–107.

J

Jacquerie

In 1358, a decade after the Black Death swept through France, members of the French lower classes rose up violently against their lords in a short series of attacks known collectively as the Jacquerie. These events, constituting the most important French uprising before the Revolution, were limited to the Ile-de-France, Picardy, and the Beauvaisis and to the two weeks from May 25 to June 10. Neither the regions nor insurgents involved were suffering; rather, they were relatively well off, though the "Jacques" were angered and ashamed by French reverses during the Hundred Years War. Failure of the French aristocracy and crown to protect adequately the laboring class and its land led to the violent revolt that was, in turn, violently repressed.

While historians today express a wide variety of views of the participants and their motives, none directly involves the Black Death. Some, however, point to the social tensions created by the huge losses in life. On the one hand, if the Jacques were from among the better-off rural elements in 1358, then their positions may well have improved because of the redistribution of resources following the epidemic. Seeing these gains threatened by English armies and noble incompetence could have proven intolerable. This was combined with increased taxation, in large part to support the threatened French military cause, a burden now spread over far fewer hearths due to the disease. Since sources reflect only upper-class voices, causation remains largely conjectural.

See also: Ciompi Revolt; Economic Effects of Plague in Europe; Hundred Years War; Peasants; Peasants' Revolt, English.

References

Cohn, Samuel K. *Lust for Liberty: The Politics of Social Revolt in Medieval Europe, 1200–1425*. Cambridge, MA: Harvard University Press, 2006.

Mollat, Michel and Philippe Wolff. *The Popular Revolutions of the Late Middle Ages*. Translated by A. L. Lyttonsells. New York: Allen and Unwin, 1973.

James I and VI Stuart, King (1566–1625)

When England's Queen Elizabeth died without issue in the spring of 1603, the crown went to the king of Scotland, James VI. He had lived through several plague epidemics before 1603, and when it visited London on the eve of his scheduled coronation, he changed course. Leaving Holyrood Castle in Scotland on April 5, he and his entourage arrived at Greenwich near London and immediately relocated to royal Windsor, arriving on July 25. They later approached London as far as Westminster but were barred from entry—like all others—by the Lord Mayor. Courtiers had acquired the plague, and it followed them to Hampton Court, and then Richmond, Woodstock near Oxford, Southampton, Winchester, and Salisbury. He finally made his royal entry into his new capital in March, 1604.

Not surprisingly, among his earliest royal acts was a set of changes to the Plague Orders of 1578, which had been in effect during 1603. For 25 years, areas hit by plague had to generate their own relief to support poor (plague?) victims. James's initiative extended the responsible area, first to five miles around the stricken area and then to the surrounding hundred and later county. "Reasonable" weekly taxes would help pay expenses the local governments incurred. His system endured for more than two centuries. Following Scots' models, his second initiative gave English officials some of the harshest penalties in Europe for ignoring statutory isolation of the sick. Those plague victims who avoided isolation and appeared in public were to be considered felons and subject to execution by hanging. Though many were beaten, none are known to have been executed.

Though skeptical of medicine, James's medical interests led him to patronize the London College of Physicians and shift public policy away from loose acceptance of empirics and charlatans as substitutes for licensed practitioners. He fancied himself a healer and expressed this as both metaphor—he would heal an unhealthy body politic—and literally, as in his campaign against tobacco use. As early as 1604 (Jamestown founded 1607), James wrote his *Counter-blaste to Tobacco*, expressing disgust with its filthiness and probably vile effects on people's health. His biggest problem was, however, that people came to see tobacco as a prophylactic against the plague, chewing and smoking it in great quantities during epidemics. James also famously wrote a work on demonology, as one with both an interest in and genuine fear of witches and sorcerers. He dismissed such popular medical notions as the belief that a touch by royalty could cure such skin diseases as scrofula. Even so, he carried out the ritual touchings since they reinforced his charisma and strengthened his hand in his new kingdom.

Ironically, plague in 1625 ushered out James' reign as it welcomed his son, ill-fated Charles I.

See also: London, England; Nobility; Plague Orders and National Authorities; Tobacco.

References

Pady, D. S. "The Medico-psychological Interests of King James I." *Clio Medica* 19 (1984): 22–31.

Slack, Paul. *The Impact of Plague in Tudor and Stuart England.* New York: Oxford University Press, 1990.

Jewish Treasure Hoards

In late 1348 and early 1349, when both plague and anti–Jewish violence threatened Jewish communities in German cities, some Jewish families hid their coins and other precious metalware in or around their homes. When they died or fled suddenly, these caches were left behind. Several of these "hoards" have been found, studied, and displayed, providing important insights into late medieval Jewish life and culture. Major finds have been in Weissenfels (1826), Marbach (1862), Colmar (1863), Basel (Switzerland; cemetery; 1937), Münster (1951), Cologne (1953), Jülich (1953), Lingenfeld (1969), Środa Śląska (near Wrocław, Poland;1988), and Erfurt (1998).

The Colmar collection may have belonged to a pawnbroker or goldsmith who hid it during the January 1349 pogrom. The owner in 1863 found it in the wall of the house on the old Judengasse and much of it was sold to Paris's Musée de Cluny. Today the collection consists of 333 coins of various mints and about 50 pieces of jewelry and other precious metalwork. The most recently discovered hoard, found beneath the west wall of

43 Michaelstrasse in Erfurt (1998), has about 10 times the bulk of the Colmar collection: 3,141 coins (all *gros tournois*) and more than 600 metal objects. The most poignant pieces are those associated with Jewish ritual, including wedding rings and *kidduch* wine cups. Erfurt's ancient synagogue, the oldest one intact in Germany, houses the collection as a memorial to the Jewish community utterly massacred on March 2, 1349. At Lingenfeld, some 2,500 coins were recovered, Münster produced 1,941 coins and assorted jewelry, and Środa Śląska a crown that may have been pawned by Emperor Charles IV.

See also: Jews; Plague Memorials.

Reference

Descatoire, Christine, ed. *Treasures of the Black Death*. London: The Wallace Collection, 2009.

Jews

Historians estimate that in 1340, about 1 percent of Christian Europe's population was Jewish. For matters of convenience, culture, religion, and safety, they tended to live in neighborhoods as communities led by their religious teachers or rabbis. Historians long argued whether Jewish communities suffered proportionally fewer plague deaths than did Christian ones during the Black Death due to Jewish patterns of diet and cleanliness; or both groups suffered more or less equally, as many contemporary sources indicate and most modern historians agree. The pattern is probably less a matter of religion than of class and location within the community. Jews were often restricted in their dealings with Christians, which may have isolated them somewhat from the rats and fleas.

Jewish Physicians. Different countries and regions had their own laws governing Jews, and usually these placed disabilities on both individuals and their communities. For example, those who wished to serve as physicians were generally prohibited from university education, outside of Italy. Apart from epidemics, Jewish doctors were forbidden to treat Christian patients or they had to have a license or a Christian as a partner. Even so, Jewish physicians were prized for their skills and knowledge, whether formally educated or not. Many town physicians in Italy were Jews, especially after the Black Death, and mendicant convents—including the Franciscan base in Assisi in the 1360s—hired Jewish healers. Governments after the Black Death eased restrictions on Jewish physicians: Venice allowed nighttime movement outside of the Ghetto, and Rome lifted the requirement for distinctive clothing in 1360. There was, however, backsliding on the part of governments, including Rome's papal license requirement to treat Christians after 1450. In northeastern Spain before the persecutions and expulsions of the 1390s, Jews constituted an estimated 20 to 30 percent of medical personnel. Their freedom of movement and from distinctive clothing and taxation and other privileges drew the dangerous envy of Christian competitors and courtiers. Iberian royal courts regularly drew Jewish intellectuals and experts, including doctors, advancing and rewarding them ahead of Christians.

During the plague years, Jewish physicians and rabbis kept largely silent about the epidemics. Barkai points out that religious authorities were silent on plague and Jewish physicians largely limited themselves to translating Christians' works into Hebrew (including those of Gentile da Foligno, Velasco de Taranto, John of Burgundy, and 15th-century Antonio Guaineri). The earliest

Burning of the Jews of Nuremberg, a woodcut in Hartmann Schedel's *Nuremberg Chronicle*, 1493. Despite the protests of Pope Clement VI, over 60 large and 150 small Jewish communities were destroyed. (Courtesy of the National Library of Medicine)

known Italian plague tract by a Jew is Venetian physician David de Pomi's *Brevi discorsi*. In 1589, David had to petition Pope Sixtus V for a license to treat Christian patients regularly, pointing out that during the previous plague, he had done much for the state, caring for and seeing to victims while receiving no reward. Many could have repeated his claim.

The Poisoning Libel and the Black Death. The most notorious episodes of anti–Jewish behavior during the Black Death were the leveling of poison libels and subsequent attacks on Jewish communities from Spain to Holland. The plague's virulence, movement, and terrible nature led many to conclude that it was a form of poison. An Aragonese royal official reported the popular belief that pilgrims were poisoning water supplies, and 11 Carcassonne beggars convicted of carrying poison were brutally executed. Physicians Jacme d'Agramont and Alfonso de Cordoba wrote in their plague *consilia* that action by evil men—probably meaning Jews—spread poisonous vapors. Though Gypsies, Muslims, sorcerers, nobles, lepers, and foreigners received blame, Jews bore the brunt of suspicion and maltreatment. The earliest "confession" to poisoning was in Geneva, by a "Jew of Savoy" supposedly working for a rabbi. Many interrogations and forced "confessions" followed.

Attacks on Jewish communities both preceded and followed local epidemic outbreaks. A week before Easter, 1348, following the local plague, 40 Jews in the port city of Toulon, France, were murdered as they slept, their corpses dragged to the streets and violated. In May, the Jewish communities of Carcassonne, Narbonne, and La Baume were slaughtered; Barcelona's Jewish quarter was plundered on May 17; in Tárrega, 300 were murdered; and in tiny Cervera, 18 fell to angry mobs. The libels and massacres followed lines of communication eastward and northward. In September, Zürich expelled and banned all Jews forever, while in January 1349, Basle slaughtered its 600 Jews by burning them alive, then baptizing their 130 children. Pope Clement VI condemned the violence, perhaps to some effect. Emperor Charles IV and Austrian Duke Albrecht II forbade anti–Jewish violence while granting immunity to the attackers and planning how to divide the spoils from destroyed communities. The German rulers' attitude was complex, reflecting the notion that the Jewish communities were imperial or royal property whose goods and persons were Charles's to dispose of as he would.

Cohn has recently demonstrated that the perpetrators were not among the lowest working classes but of the upper strata, often legitimating their murders and destruction with court proceedings. Insofar as debt was a motivation—and the pope as well as others believed this—the debtors were of the upper classes. Even so, Cohn sees little evidence of economic motivation. Friars and flagellants may have played a role in inciting violence, but the procedures undertaken seem to have been carefully planned and conducted. Since the massacres often preceded epidemics in German cities, they may have been prophylactic: kill the impious Jews and God will soften the plague.

In later 1348 and 1349, thousands were executed by fire and the sword in scores of German and Dutch town squares. Half of Strasbourg's Jews were incinerated alive while the other half fled or were banished; Speyer's cornered Jews gathered in their synagogue and took their own lives, as did those of Worms. Despite their horrors, "hardly a trace" (Raspe, 471) of these events appears in Jewish sources, our knowledge coming almost exclusively from oddly unmoved Christian sources.

As if plague were not bad enough, these assaults made refugees of many of the survivors, and following decades saw further expulsions of entire Jewish communities. For example, in Alsace there were 60 Jewish communities before the plague and half as many a few years after. The flow of Jews was eastward, to Poland and Russia; Hungary's Jewish population quadrupled between 1348 and 1490, and Poland's quintupled. Anti–Jewish activities continued but with little or no direct connection to plague. Traditional religious libels, economic perceptions, taxation matters, or antiroyalist antipathy against the "king's Jews" motivated these later bigots.

See also: Anti–Semitism and Anti–Jewish Violence before the Black Death; Black Death (1347–1352); Flagellants; Jewish Treasure Hoards; Physicians; Poisoning and Plague Spreading.

References

Aberth, John. *The Black Death: The Great Mortality of 1348–1350.* New York: Bedford, 2005, 138–159.

Barkai, Ron. "Jewish Treatises on the Black Death (1350–1500): A Preliminary Study," in *Practical Medicine from Salerno to the Black Death,* edited by Luis Garcia-Ballester et al. (New York: Cambridge University Press, 1994), 6–25.

Cohn, Samuel K. "The Black Death and the Burning of Jews." *Past & Present* 196 (2007): 3–36.

Foa, Anna. *The Jews of Europe after the Black Death*. Berkeley: University of California, 2000.

Graus, Frantisek. *Pest, Geissler, Judenmorde: Das 14. Jahrhundert als Krisenzeit*. Göttingen: Vandenhoek und Ruprecht, 1987.

Guerchberg, Sèraphine. "The Controversy over the Alleged Sowers of the Black Death in the Contemporary Treatises on Plague," in *Change in Medieval Society: Europe North of the Alps, 1050–1500*, edited by Sylvia Thrupp (New York: Appleton-Century-Crofts, 1965), 208–224.

Havercamp, Alfred. "Die Judenverfolgungen zur Zeit des Schwarzen Todes im Gesellschaftsgefüge deutscher Städte," in his *Zur Geschichte der Juden in Deutschland des späten Mittelalters und der frühen Neuzeit* (Stuttgart: Hierseman, 1981), 27–93.

Horrox, Rosemary. *The Black Death*. New York: Manchester University Press, 1994.

Mentgen, Gerd. "Die Pest-Pandemie und die Juden Pogrome der Jahre 1348–1350/1," in *Heiliges Römisches Reich Deutscher Nation 962 bis 1806* (Dresden: Sandstein Verlag, 2006), 298–309.

Raspe, Lucia. "The Black Death in Jewish Sources: A Second Look at Mayse Nissim." *Jewish Quarterly Review* 94 (2004): 471–489.

Shatzmiller, Joseph. *Jews, Medicine, and Medieval Society*. Berkeley: University of California Press, 1994.

Toch, Michael. "The Formation of a Diaspora: The Settlement of Jews in the Medieval German *Reich*." *Aschkenas: Zeitschrift für Geschichte und Kultur der Juden* 7 (1997): 55–78.

Jinn

In Arabic culture, jinn (or *djinn*) are malevolent, generally invisible but, when manifested, shape-shifting spirits. Many blamed them for plague. Originating in the pre–Islamic worldview, jinn appear in the Koran and were thus absorbed into multiethnic Islamic culture. In popular culture, the jinn, as opposed to angels, had their own wills and capriciously intervened in human affairs. This seemed, however, to contradict the omnipotence of Allah, and orthodox Muslims ascribed apparent capriciousness to divine will.

According to the Hadith-based Prophetic Medicine, jinn could cause disease. Though very mobile, they were territorial and vengeful. Foul odors indicated their presence, linking them with miasma theory of plague. Illness on a wide scale, or epidemic, was considered the assault of an army of jinn. Disease resulted from the "prick" or "sting" of a jinn's spear or arrow. Legal scholar Muhammad al-Manbiji in his *Report on Plague* (1363–1364), attributed epidemics to Allah's will as implemented by stabbing jinn and not to miasma. In his 1431 Hadith-based plague tract, Ibn Hajar al-'Asqalani interpreted plague as a source of martyrdom at the hands of jinn who stabbed and created an entry point for the miasmic poison. Amulets made of silver, gunpowder, or tar by holy men or women (marabouts) could keep jinn away. Alum inscribed with jinn names "laghigh, baligh, talugh" and placed on a bubo drove away the alum-hating spirits. Mystical Sufi healers exorcized jinn through music and wild dancing, which drew them into their own bodies, which they believed to be immune.

See also: Allah; Amulets, Talismans, and Magic; Arrows; Causes of Plague: Historical Theories; Islam and Medicine; Islamic Religious Responses; Muhammad the Prophet.

References

Dols, Michael W. *The Black Death in the Middle East*. Princeton, NJ: Princeton University Press, 1977.

Ibn Qayyim al-Jawziyya. *Medicine of the Prophet*. Translated by Penelope Johnstone. Cambridge: Islamic Texts Society, 1998.

Job

In the biblical Book of Job, the title character is described as the most righteous of men, faithful to God, and divinely well rewarded for adhering to God's will. To prove Job's virtue, God allows Satan to rain misfortune upon Job up to death itself. Though poor, diseased, and utterly confused, Job remains faithful, and God ultimately rewards him with a second family and greater wealth. For Jews, Christians, and Muslims, Job represented the innocent person who suffers at God's hands; Job's sores and boils echoed buboes and plague sores. The story reminded people that suffering was not always punishment, and people could not always understand God's actions. Though an Old Testament figure, some Christians considered Job a plague saint (others a patron of syphilitics)—San Giobbe in Italy. Just as God restored Job's health, people who were stricken or whose loved ones were prayed that Job's fate might be theirs. Though rare, there are depictions of disease-ridden Job and the occasional church dedicated to him (e.g., Venice, 1450). These date after 1350 and may have served as ex votos.

See also: Ex voto; Plague Memorials; Plague Saints.

John of Burgundy (c. 1338–1390; also Johannes de Burgundia, Burdeus, La Barba, Burgoyne)

John was a physician and professor of medicine in Liège (then in Burgundy) who wrote a very influential plague tract during or after the 1365 epidemic. Organized in typical fashion—causes, prevention, remedies—it is heavily influenced by medical astrology and avoids religious moralizing. French surgeon Guy de Chauliac's *Cyrurgia magna* (1363) seems to have influenced the section on causation. Composed in Latin in both longer and shorter formats, there are also English translations and English glosses added to several Latin texts. English versions appear in both prose and meter and generally emphasize remedies over causes or preventatives. Remedies are also standard for the period: diet, bloodletting, expensive theriac, and cheaper herbs and compounds.

More than 100 manuscripts of Latin, English, French, Dutch, and Hebrew versions survive. Fifteenth-century medical authors liberally borrowed from John's work. The Norman physician Thomas Forestier adapted it to the outbreak of the English Sweat around 1485. Oxford surgeon John Stipse translated and edited it around 1472, claiming the remedies worked on him; John Thornton incorporated an abridged version in his leechbook, *Liber de diversis medicinis*; and in 1475, Dominican Thomas Moulton produced an often reprinted (to 1580) redaction, the only printed edition (*The Mirror or Glass of Health*). Thornton's work eliminated academic elements of John's original text, addressing the needs and resources of common folk rather than colleagues or wealthy clients.

See also: Astrology; Causes of Plague: Historical Theories; Consilia and Plague Tracts; Leechbooks; Remedies, External; Remedies, Internal.

Reference

Keiser, G. R. "Two Medieval Plague Treatises and Their Afterlife in Early Modern England." *Journal of the History of Medicine and Allied Sciences* 58 (2003): 292–324.

Matheson, Lister M. "Médecin sans Frontières? The European Dissemination of John of Burgundy's Plague Treatise." *ANQ* 18 (2005): 17–29.

Jonson, Ben (1572–1637)

Playwright and poet Ben Jonson was born in London to a minister and his wife, who remarried a bricklayer when Ben's father died. Though educated at Westminster School, Ben early on engaged in bricklaying and military service before becoming an actor in London. As author, his first success was *Every Man in His Humor*, produced in 1598.

Jonson experienced plague in London in 1578 and 1593 and, a decade later, lost his son Benjamin, aged seven, and probably infant Joseph to pestilence. Away from London, probably seeking patronage, when the children died, he lamented Benjamin's loss in the 12-line elegy "On my first sonne." Joseph and his fate are nowhere mentioned. Plague touched Jonson again in 1606, when it took his very close friend, courtier John Roe. In 1619, Jonson discussed both deaths with William Drummond, noting that Roe died in his arms. This implied that Jonson disobeyed the 1604 *Plague Orders*, which forbade visitation of the plague-stricken. Some read the scene as a righting of the wrong done to young Benjamin: Roe received the "good death" of which Jonson deprived his son. Jonson's Epigrams #26, 32, 33, and 34 refer to Roe's passing.

Jonson's comedy *The Alchemist* of 1610 is set—uniquely for the era's plays—in the same year's pestilential London. The homeowner has fled to avoid plague, leaving his house in servants' hands. These lend it to a pair of rogues "confecting" the alchemical Philosophers' Stone, the cure-all that promises untold wealth. The merciful owner returns early and disrupts the scam, in what became one of the time's most popular plays.

See also: Abandonment; *Ars moriendi (The Art of Dying)*; Dekker, Thomas; Flight; London, England; Shakespeare, William.

References

Martin, Mathew. "Play and Plague in Ben Jonson's *The Alchemist*." *English Studies in Canada* 26 (2000): 393–408.

Phillips, Patrick. "Fleshes Rage: Ben Jonson and the Plague." Ph.D. dissertation, New York University, 2006.

Ross, Cheryl L. "The Plague of the Alchemist." *Renaissance Quarterly* 41 (1988): 439–58.

Justinian, Plague of (First Plague Pandemic)

Eight centuries before the Black Death, a series of bubonic plague epidemics swept across the Mediterranean, parts of Europe's interior, and the British Isles. Often named for Justinian I, Byzantine Emperor during whose reign it began, given its 200-year length, the series is also labeled the First Plague Pandemic. Though little archeological or archival evidence marks its passage, the literary remains of monks, bishops, travelers, and the odd lawyer and court official make it clear that the early medieval world was devastated. Their descriptions of sufferers often clearly indicate the presence of buboes, and both individuals' experiences and the movement of the disease parallel those of the Second Pandemic. Researchers have determined that 18 distinct waves of plague washed over some portion of the Western world during the two centuries, more frequently early on, less so in its later stages. As with the Second Pandemic, the first appears to have been spread by human activity, including caravan movements, shipping, army maneuvers, and flight of refugees from ravaged areas.

Though some eyewitnesses clearly relate the horrors of huge death tolls, mass graves, and depopulated countrysides, modern scholars debate the demographic and economic effects of the waves and of the pandemic as a whole. Some contemporaries provide impossibly high death figures that modern interpreters adjust to an overall effect of about 33 to 40 percent of a given population. Though Greek physicians were influenced by the clinical medical theories of Hippocrates and Galen, most of the Christian and, after the 620s, Muslim populations saw God's hand at work, as amply demonstrated in Scripture. Muhammad laid down guidelines that held through the Second Pandemic: only infidel victims are punished, the faithful are martyrs; neither flee nor enter a plague zone; there is no contagion; and amulets may repel plague-spreading spirits. Though individual Byzantine Christians feared the Apocalypse was nigh and sought out churches, shrines, astrologers, saints, and holy people, Church leaders organized no communal responses. In the Western Christian world, leaders were more proactive, leading special liturgies, processions, fasts, and pilgrimages, parading miracle-working icons through cities, and honoring such saints as Sebastian. In Rome, Pope Gregory I famously led such a procession after which the Archangel Michael was seen in the sky sheathing his plague-dispensing sword.

Historians credit this pandemic with aiding the rise of Islam and its medical science, the Slavic entry into the Balkans, the Lombard invasion of Italy, and the popularity of Christian monasticism. Memory of the pandemic's horrors and of their ancestors' responses, however vague, shaped the reactions of the generation of 1347 to 1352.

See also: Arabic-Persian Medicine and Practitioners; Constantinople/Istanbul; Flight; Gregory the Great, Pope; Islam and Medicine; Mecca; Muhammad the Prophet; Prayer and Fasting; Processions; St. Michael the Archangel; St. Sebastian.

References

Little, Lester K., ed. *Plague and the End of Antiquity: The Pandemic of 511–750.* New York: Cambridge University Press, 2006.

Rosen, William. *Justinian's Flea.* New York: Viking, 2007.

Stathakopoulos, Dionysios. *Famine and Pestilence in the Late Roman and Early Byzantine Empire.* Burlington, VT: Ashgate, 2004.

K

Kircher, Athanasius (1602–1680)

Athanasius was born to a well-educated German civil servant who sent his son to study with the Jesuits in nearby Fulda. The precocious lad entered the novitiate in Paderborn and was ordained a priest in 1628. Kircher taught mathematics and biblical languages in Jesuit schools. In 1634, he was appointed Mathematician to the Emperor in Vienna, but a series of adventures landed him in Rome at the Roman College of the Society of Jesus instead. He held the Chair of Mathematics, carrying out and publishing a widely varying series of studies in such areas as astronomy, Egyptology, optics, physics, natural history, and mathematics. His early work in microscopy has led some to consider him the "father of bacteriology."

When plague struck Rome in spring 1656, Kircher interrupted work on subterranean studies to pursue pestilential phenomena. In 1658, he published his 250-page study *Scrutinium Physico-Medicum Pestis*, which saw four reprintings and a German translation in 1680. Influenced by Fracastoro, alchemy, and Paracelsian iatrochemistry (chemical medicine), Kircher considered plague to be caused by tiny, invisible seeds that were spontaneously generated by rotting corpses and other putrid sources. Using magnifying lenses no stronger than 32X, he viewed tiny "worms" in victims' blood, probably part of the structure of the blood cells themselves. As he saw it, these airborne *vermiculi* were breathed into the lungs, from which they reached the heart via the vena cava. Here, Kircher believed, they produced the damage evidenced by the plague-stricken. "Seeds" spread naturally and by the exhalations of victims. Galenic medicine was a failure, and the only sure answer to plague was flight, though cleanliness could not hurt. He admitted the value of religious amulets but attributed their success to the devil rather than God. Toad amulets, however, were full of a poison that absorbed vermiculi through sympathetic action. They also had rough skin like plague victims and ate worms (*vermi*) like those in the victim's stomach. Kircher was a pioneer in his bio-medical use of early microscopes but was quickly overshadowed by Robert Hooke's *Micrographia* (1665) and the studies by Anton van Leeuwenhoek.

See also: Amulets, Talismans, and Magic; Boyle, Robert; Causes of Plague: Historical Theories; Miasma Theory; Paracelsus and Paracelsianism; Toads; Van Helmont, Joan Baptista.

References

Findlen, Paula, ed. *Athanasius Kircher: The Last Man Who Knew Everything*. New York: Routledge, 2006.

Godwin, Joscelyn. *Athanasius Kircher: A Renaissance Man and the Search for Lost Knowledge*. New York: Thames and Hudson, 1979.

Kitasato, Shibasaburo (1852–1931)

Born on Kyshu, Japan, Shibasaburo attended Tokyo University, earning his doctorate in biology. Kitasato learned German and with Japanese state funding became the first non–German to study with Robert Koch (1885–1892). He quickly absorbed Koch's techniques and made important strides in microbiology, studying cholera, diphtheria, and typhoid fever and isolating the tetanus germ. He left Berlin in 1892, having received the title Professor, the first non–German to be so honored. In Tokyo, Kitasato reigned as the preeminent microbiologist and established his own laboratory on the German model.

When plague struck Hong Kong in 1894, Governor William Robinson sought professional aid. No one knew what caused the disease, but Koch's germ theory suggested it was a microscopic organism. Kitasato responded, arriving in early June with two colleagues, three assistants, and trunks filled with scientific equipment. Local authorities were honored to host the distinguished scientist, and Kitasato enjoyed the role. They were given deluxe quarters and ample space for a makeshift pathology laboratory near a plague hospital. Unlike his Swiss/French rival, Alexandre Yersin, who arrived several days after Kitasato, the Japanese were provided with ample corpses for autopsy. In fact, Kitasato bribed the colonial authorities to deny Yersin access to corpses. While Yersin decided to study the bacteria he found in dead victims' buboes, the Japanese searched victims' blood and organ tissue. Yersin's logic was correct: with bubonic plague, bacteria do collect in the swollen lymph nodes known as buboes. Kitasato claimed success first, however, and his British hosts conveyed the news to Britain's premier medical journal *The Lancet* (July 7). Kitasato's formal report, like his laboratory method, followed Koch's "postulates" to the letter, but he was incorrect. Yersin correctly identified the nonmotile bacillus that would not take a stain—later labeled *Pasteurella pestis*—as plague's causal agent. Kitasato's candidate readily took a stain, which placed it in a different category of bacterium. Even so, Kitasato has often been considered the codiscoverer of the plague germ.

In later years, Kitasato facilitated important discoveries in dysentery and worked to curb the pneumonic plague in Manchuria. His laboratory eventually evolved into Kitasato University.

See also: Bubonic Plague; Germ Theory; Koch, Robert; Third Plague Pandemic; Yersin, Alexandre; *Yersinia pestis*.

References

Howard-Jones, N. "Was Shibasaburo Kitasato the Co-discoverer of the Plague Bacillus?" *Perspectives on Biological Medicine* 16 (1973): 292–307.

Marriott, Edward. *Plague: A Story of Science, Rivalry, Scientific Breakthrough and the Scourge that Won't Go away.* New York: Holt, 2002.

Koch, Robert (1843–1910)

Born to a mining engineer and his wife in Clausthal, Germany, Robert was a precocious but self-disciplined child with an interest in biology. He studied medicine at the University of Göttingen, where he was exposed to anatomist Jacob Henle's theory that infectious diseases were caused by microscopic, parasitic organisms rather than miasmas, imbalanced humors, or God's wrath. Koch earned his doctorate in 1866 and then spent six months studying chemistry in Berlin, where he absorbed Rudolf Virchow's new ideas. Considered the father of cellular pathology, Virchow understood disease as the negative effect of microbial pathogens on the cellular structures of human organs. Koch worked briefly in Hamburg's General Hospital before establishing his own practice. After holding several positions, Koch served as Wollstein's District Medical Officer (1872–1880).

In this capacity, Koch began his study of anthrax, a disease of both man and animal. Though the anthrax bacillus had earlier been

Koch was, with Louis Pasteur, a founder of modern microbiology. (Courtesy of the National Library of Medicine)

isolated, its role in producing the disease had not been proven. He conducted his landmark research in his home laboratory. Koch demonstrated that germs isolated from diseased farm animals caused disease in mice inoculated with the matter. He also showed that the bacillus retained its ability to cause disease even after being bred in a neutral culture for several generations. Perhaps more important than his findings were the research laboratory procedures or protocols he pioneered or improved, including cell staining and photography. Publication of his findings in 1876 gained him notoriety, and he expanded his work to bacterial infections of wounds, a significant work on which he published two years later. In 1880, Koch was called to Berlin to serve in the Imperial Health Office, where he had access to a professional laboratory and well-trained colleagues. He developed his methods still further and laid down "Koch's postulates," four benchmarks that ensured a given pathogen causes a particular disease: (1) the suspect microbe must be found in every case of the disease; (2) the microbe must be isolated and grown in a laboratory environment outside the known host; (3) when inoculated with the isolated microbe, a healthy host must develop the particular disease; and (4) an identical microbe must be isolated from the new, diseased host.

In rapid succession, Koch isolated the tuberculosis bacillus and the vibrio that caused the 19th century's great pandemics, cholera. Further, he designed measures for countering cholera epidemics based upon his understanding of the pathogen and its interaction with human communities. In 1891, Koch became director of Berlin's new Institute for Infectious Diseases, where he worked with such luminaries as Paul Ehrlich and Emil von Behring, and plague researchers Shibasaburo Kitasato and Alexandre Yersin. In his later years, Koch contributed to research on malaria, tuberculosis, rinderpest, sleeping sickness, and serology, receiving the Nobel Prize for Physiology or Medicine in 1905.

See also: Germ Theory; Kitasato, Shibasaburo; Pasteur, Louis; Simond, Paul-Louis; Yersin, Alexandre.

References

Brock, Thomas D. *Robert Koch: A Life in Medicine and Bacteriology.* Washington, DC: AMS Press, 1999.

Gradmann, Christoph. *Laboratory Disease: Robert Koch's Medical Bacteriology.* Translated by Elborg Forster. Baltimore, MD: Johns Hopkins University Press, 2009.

L

Labourers, Ordinance and Statute of

When the Black Death struck England, it eliminated perhaps half of the country's labor force in both towns and rural areas. Elementary economics dictated that the value of the remaining workers rise, and employers quickly responded by raising wages, improving working conditions, and adding in-kind benefits, for example, food and drink. King Edward III and Parliament responded rapidly to this blow to the competitive edge of landowners and employers. On June 18, 1349, they promulgated the Ordinance of Labourers in letters to the Sheriff of Kent and the Bishop of Winchester. It ordered all wages and work arrangements to be rolled back to what they had been in 1346 "or five or six years earlier." Landowners and employers were to oversee enforcement, which included imprisonment for refusal to work. Two years later, the "Statute of Labourers" addressed holes in the Ordinance. Hiring had to be made openly and without secret side deals. All men and women under age 60 had to work, and suspected shirkers were to be denied alms. Also punishable was excessive movement in search of higher wages. Enforcement was now to be by local aristocrats, including constables, bailiffs, and justices. During the first decade, 671 justices served just to hear cases under the Statute. In 1352, 7,556 people were fined in Essex County, of whom 20 percent were women. Aragon (Cortes of Saragossa, 1350), Castile (Cortes of 1351), and Portugal (laws of 1349 and 1350) similarly regulated prices and wages in favor of employers and consumers in the face of plague-induced inflation.

Historians have long argued over the English laws: were they enforced? were they effective? Clearly there was official abuse and corruption, and this injustice added fuel to the working class's resentment, which flared violently in 1381. The knights were co-opted to serve the royal purpose on a local level, further draining feudalism of its particularism and replacing incipient market freedom with royal paternalism. As late as 1389, Essex County alone saw 791 annual fines levied under the Statute.

See also: Feudalism and Manorialism; Peasants; Peasants' Revolt, English.

References

Cohn, Samuel K. "After the Black Death: Labour Legislations and Attitudes towards Labour in Late-Medieval Western Europe." *Economic History Review* 60 (2007): 457–485.

Ormrod, W. Mark. "The Politics of Pestilence: Government in England after the Black Death," in *The Black Death in England*, edited by Mark Ormrod and Phillip Lindley (Stanford, UK: Paul Watkins, 1996), 147–181.

Poos, Larry R. "The Social Context of the Statute of Labourers Enforcement." *Law and History* 1 (1983): 27–52.

Langland, William (c. 1325–after 1388)

The life of one of England's greatest poets remains lost to those who seek it. The

C-version of *Piers Plowman* provides a short autobiographical sketch of Langland, but little of substance. He claims home schooling and his dialect suggests Worcestershire. He knows London and its ways quite well, and he appears to have been a cleric. He was probably mature when plague first struck in 1348 and grew to hate the societal corruption that followed in its wake. He blended this antipathy in his great *Piers Plowman*; the first, or A, version of which is dated to between 1360 and 1370, the second to around 1380, and the final C-version to around 1390. The B-version is usually considered the most critical.

In the wake of the Black Death and subsequent plagues, clergy of low-class origins entered service ill prepared and far too anxious to make money as mass-priests who served wealthy clients rather than as rural pastors or in poor urban parishes. Many actually left poor parishes for easy and lucrative positions, abandoning parishioners without leadership and teaching, to fall prey to evil and sinfulness. To Langland, Sloth is a 30-year old priest who does not know the Lord's Prayer. The resulting lazy, greedy, and gluttonous peasants—"shirkers" and "wasters"—abandon their old habits of hard work and become no better than beggars, despite the great need for workers. Postplague (illegal) high wages further corrupt the once virtuous class, who are now being punished by Hunger. Physicians, too, are corrupted by the need for their services and high fees. They are ineffective and yet profiteers, no better than harlots, and shown sending to Liar for help with their examination of urine. Langland characterizes them as irrational but greedy "apes" and sly, deceptive "foxes." Langland even criticizes women who survive the plague and then refuse their duty to repopulate the earth.

The poem becomes apocalyptic in the C-version, wherein the Anti–Christ has arrived and right and wrong are reversed. Only the plague makes this reversal clear to humanity, and by punishing the wicked helps correct the survivors. Right living—including knowing one's traditional place in the social hierarchy and remaining content in it—and repentance are the only sure correctives to society.

See also: Chaucer, Geoffrey; Economic Effects of Plague in Europe; Feudalism and Manorialism; Labourers, Ordinance and Statute of; Morality Literature, Christian; Peasants; Physicians; Poetry, European; Priests; Sin.

References

Aers, David. "Justice and Wage-labor after the Black Death: Some Perplexities for William Langland," in *The Work of Work: Servitude, Slavery, and Labor in Medieval England*, edited by Allen J. Frantzen and Douglas Moffat (Glasgow: Cruithne Press, 1994), 169–190.

Grigsby, Bryon Lee. *Pestilence in Medieval and Early Modern English Literature*. New York: Routledge, 2004.

Papka, Claudia R. "The Limits of Apocalypse: Eschatology, Epistemology, and Textuality in the *Commedia* and *Piers Plowman*," in *Last Things: Death and the Apocalypse in the Middle Ages*, edited by Carolyn Walker Bynum and Paul Freedman (Philadelphia: University of Pennsylvania Press, 2000), 233–256.

Robertson, Elizabeth and Stephen H. A. Shepherd, eds. *William Langland: Piers Plowman*. New York: Norton, 2006.

Languages: Vernacular and Latin

The Latin phrase *post hoc ergo propter hoc* means just because something happens before something else, it follows that the first caused the second. For students of history, this connection is a seductive one. Historians remind us that many trends in Europe's society and economy had been active before

1347 and the role of the Black Death or recurrent plague was to intensify or accelerate these, not to cause them. "Plague caused 'X'" seems much more satisfying than "'X' was an ongoing phenomenon whose development was affected to some degree by the plague." The shift away from Latin and other languages for certain purposes toward the use of local vernaculars for these same purposes is a phenomenon accelerated by plague-related trends.

The 14th century saw many trends that expanded the use of written vernaculars. Urbanization, literacy, and bourgeois recordkeeping; cheap paper and spectacles; patronage of vernaculars by such rulers as Alfonso X; vernacular preaching and writing by Franciscans; the desire for such written records as land deeds in the common language; and the Black Death. For the English-speaking student, the best example is the shift away from Old English, Latin, and Anglo-Norman/French to the Middle English of Chaucer. From 1066 until the mid-14th century, English had been developing from heavily Germanic Old English or Anglo-Saxon into several dialects of Middle English. Traditionally popular literature as well as records of all kinds had been kept in the French dialect of the invaders of 1066 as the illiterate underclass retained their evolving spoken English. Education in English was sporadic in the early 14th century, but it slowly replaced education in French in the larger towns and cities. The Hundred Years War with France, beginning in the 1330s, may well have fuelled English nationalism and fostered literature in English. The Black Death may well have killed off French-speaking teachers as some have claimed, but for some reason in 1362, French was banned from the law courts, and Parliaments in 1362, 1363, and 1364 were opened in English. Grammar master

John Cornwall stopped teaching translation from Latin to French and began teaching translation into English sometime after 1350. By 1385, educator John of Trevisa noted the trend: teachers leave French and teach Latin using English. This was an effect, as well, of the dissemination of landholding in England to lower classes—due in part to the Black Death—who had no use for French.

Latin in England suffered as French did, though for different reasons. French had already taken over large segments of record-keeping, leaving Latin largely to the universities and Church. Yet even the Church was challenged by the demand for devotional literature in English and the Lollard insistence on Scripture in English. Since no one was raised with Latin as a home language, all had to spend years studying it under teachers. The supply of these in the Church declined with high clerical death tolls and the new call for chantry priests. The Dominicans, among others, from the 1360s lamented the poor language preparation by their university-bound novices. In Florence, a similar pattern: in 1356, Ser Andrea Lancia was told to translate all Florentine statutes from Latin into Italian. In the 15th century, diplomatic language was all to be Italian. The period also saw the translations of Roman classics into Italian: Landino's *Pliny* and Boccaccio's *Livy*.

Other signs appeared where plague had struck. The Bishop of Armagh preached his only vernacular sermon in a Carmelite church in Drogheda on March 25—New Year—1349. In colonized Ireland, Anglo-Irish declined to nonexistence in favor of a resurgence of Gaelic. With Dublin's decline as an English cultural center—due to flight back to England after 1350—even the old settler families' attachment to Gaelic culture had to be limited or reduced by the Statutes of Kilkenny in the 1370s.

In northern Castile, the use of Galician-Portuguese among poets and others disappeared quickly after 1350, to be replaced by Castilian. The work of poet Alfonso Alvarez de Villasandino shows the trend, as his early work was Galician-Portuguese and his later Castilian. Devotional translations and adaptations in Spanish vernaculars also appeared after 1350, including the prose catechism of Bishop Gutiere de Toledo of Oviedo in the 1380s and Pero López de Ayala's translation of *In moralia Job* by Pope Gregory I (c. 600).

See also: Boccaccio, Giovanni; Chaucer, Geoffrey; Gregory the Great, Pope; Hundred Years War; Yeoman Farmers and Gentry.

References

Kelly, Maria. *A History of the Black Death in Ireland.* Stroud, Gloucs, UK: Tempus, 2001.

Lindley, Phillip. "The Black Death and English Art: A Debate and Some Assumptions," in *The Black Death in England*, edited by W. M. Ormrod and P. G. Lindley (Stamford: Paul Watkins, 1996), 125–146.

Lazarettos and Pest Houses

The pest house (Dutch *pesthuis*; German *Pesthaus*), or lazar house (*lazaretto, lazaret* derived from Lazarus in the New Testament), was a facility in which plague victims suffered until they recovered or died. Local governments provided these to isolate the sick from the healthy and to establish some modicum of care for victims. Established because of the same nebulous fear of contagion that had led to leprosaria, they likewise reflected the Christian virtue of charity and the civic virtue of concern for the poor. Unlike hospitals or leprosaria that usually had endowments or flows of alms and continuous residents, pest houses only operated during plague epidemics and relied on civic funding and creative management for their expenses.

Among existing structures pressed into temporary service were hospitals or wings of hospitals, leprosaria, poorhouses, monasteries and convents, Spanish inns known as *corrals*, pilgrim hospices, and even agricultural workers' huts or lean-tos in fields and forests. Larger cities, for example, Dubrovnik, Venice, Amsterdam, and most famously Milan, built special facilities for plague victims, putting the spaces to use in other ways in normal years. All too often, pest houses consisted of groups of cheap, temporary huts—"hovels," "cabins," "tents," "booths," even "cages"—erected when plague struck and destroyed or disassembled and stored for the next epidemic.

Though Geertruidenburg, Holland, may claim the oldest *pesthuis* in Europe (1356), scholars usually credit the Venetian territory of Dubrovnik with having built the first on the Isle of Mljet in 1377. Growth as a Venetian emporium led to a second *pesthuis*, established on the Isle of Supetar in 1429. Venice built itself an isolation hospital for plague victims in 1403 and ordered construction of the much larger Lazzaretto (Vecchio) two decades later. The port city of Marseille had a plague facility in 1383, and Milan experimented with clusters of small, extramural *mansioni* in 1399. Milan's duke established a plague hospital in a villa at Cusago in 1451, and work began on its huge Lazzaretto di San Gregorio in 1488. This prompted Florence to set up its first lazaretto at San Bastiano in 1494. The German cities of Ulm and Überlingen are said to have had *Pesthäuser* from about the same time.

The 16th century saw the spread of the institution, but as in the 15th century, the politics of each city determined the outcome. In 1562, Barcelona's authorities took over the Dominican convent of Angels vells to serve as a lazaret. Seville's first pest house (1568) was a large extramural rooming house (*corral*) built around a central courtyard. Utrecht and Ghent established their first in 1567 and 1582, Palermo its *cubba* in 1576 to 1577, and Paris its never-finished copy of Milan's in 1580. Oxford, Newcastle, and Windsor had pest houses after the 1603 epidemic, by order of King James I, but London still had little more than "cabins in the fields" when plague struck in 1625. Oddly, the capital remained grossly underserved even in 1665 to 1666, when all five houses together could hold only 600 patients. The Tudors and Stuarts relied heavily on shutting-in policies, though new plague orders in 1666 mandated a pest house in every English town. Copenhagen built its first in 1619, and after 1625, they were mandated for Danish cities by royal decree. Amsterdam's first dates to 1636, while Florence and Barcelona added new facilities in 1630 and 1651 respectively. In 1630, Cambridge constructed 40 "booths" for the sick.

The provision of a pest house was the sure sign that authorities recognized the presence of plague. Once they chose the site or sites, they needed to hire staff. Because of the dangers, the employers needed to use high wages, perks, for example, free housing, and even compulsion to get compliance. The civic physician often served as administrator, while junior doctors tended victims. At least one barber-surgeon, an apothecary, and often a midwife for pregnant victims assisted. These professionals were well paid, at least those who lived to collect. Cheaper were such aides as a cook, gravedigger, guards, carriers, laundresses, a nurse or two, a notary for will making and recordkeeping, and a clergyman (paid in Protestant countries). In some places, Catholic confraternities provided labor, especially visiting the sick and burying the dead. Food, fuel, medicines, disinfectants and

fumigants, bedding, and candles had to be purchased in what were often tight markets. Financing differed in form across time and region: almsgiving in some Catholic areas; parish rates (taxes) in England; the civic fisc or royal treasury; levies on guilds or Jewish communities. But health boards and city councils were never prepared for the expenses. Records reveal that at times, administrators literally begged door to door for necessities.

Conditions in pest houses differed from place to place and time to time during an epidemic. Small, permanent, and well-staffed facilities may have been tolerable during the early stages of an outbreak, while supplies were fresh, the staff hopeful, and the premises reasonably clean. Over time, the victim counts mounted, beds came to hold several instead of one, and blankets on stone floors replaced mattresses. The stench of stricken humanity permeated the walls, floors, and bedding, rising with summer temperatures. Overworked and increasingly calloused staff went through the motions, knowing that most would die without comfort or solace. Dying mothers brought their infants, who fed on hired wet nurses when orphaned; when the nurses died, nanny goats provided the neonates' last few meals. One of the most chilling descriptions of a pest house is that of Milan's in 1630 by Alessandro Manzoni, in his 19th-century *I promessi sposi*, considered Italy's national novel. No less so are the eyewitness accounts of administrators and clerics, for example, Milan's Archbishop Federigo Borromeo, on whose work Manzoni relied.

Dedicated facilities were inevitably overcrowded: Lyons' held up to 4,000 patients, and huts were built for the excess. In 1630, Florence's San Miniato had 82 beds for 412 female patients, or five per bed, while the men's quarters had 93 beds for 312. Milan's huge lazaretto held up to 10,000 at one time in 1629 and teemed with 15,000 the following year. Mortality rates are difficult to find, but it seems clear that survival was more prevalent in smaller, well-supplied places. Pistoia's (Italy) two pest houses served 1,198 victims in 1630 to 1631, of whom 607 reportedly died, for a mortality rate of just over half. Similar figures between 50 and 60 percent seem to hold for those in Florence, Empoli, Trent, and Prato in 1630 to 1631. By contrast, Ukraine's pest houses lost 76 to 80 percent of their residents during the 1770s.

As with other harsh measures imposed by authorities during epidemics, pest houses often drew resentment and sometimes violent opposition. Many hated the fact that their loved ones were carted off to hellholes to await near-certain death; most feared the same fate for themselves. Clearly, wealthy victims had options, whereas the poor were warehoused to suffer and die. Many decried the inadequate administration and lack of resources that plagued a lot of facilities, and women patients complained of being abused or even violated. As a result, families hid away the sick; patients fled or were secreted out; patients and family members assaulted staff; and in 18th-century Hungary, pest houses were sporadically ransacked. In Temesvár, an angry mob could not get at the pest house itself, so they ignited surrounding houses, hoping to raze the hated structure. Such interference with plague officials was intolerable and met with harsh measures. An image of Rome in 1656 shows gallows beside the lazaretto; a pair of German patients escaped to a barn, which the authorities immediately burned to the ground with them inside; in 1631, Norwich established special prisons for violators, and in 1666, they set up a whipping post and stocks at the pest house.

Early modern pest houses often had post–plague-era lives. Some remained refuges for victims of such diseases as syphilis, smallpox, or cholera. Others served as convents, poorhouses, quarantine quarters, warehouses, or inns. Utrecht's Leeuwenberg Gasthuis ("guesthouse") was once its *pesthuis*. Still, others remain as memorials or museums.

See also: Causes of Plague: Historical Theories; Defoe, Daniel; Governments, Civil; Health Boards, Magistracies, and Commissions; Hospitals; *I promessi sposi*; Individualism and Individual Liberties; Lazarus; Leprosy (Hansen's Disease) and Leprosarium; Physicians, Town; Poverty and Plague; Public Health; Quarantine; Shutting In; individual cities.

References

Byrne, Joseph. *Daily Life during the Black Death*. Westport, CT: Greenwood, 2006.

Calvi, Giulia. *Histories of a Plague Year: The Social and the Imaginary in Baroque Florence*. Berkeley: University of California Press, 1989.

Christensen, Daniel. *Politics and the Plague in Early Modern Germany: Political Efforts to Combat Epidemics in the Duchy of Braunschweig-Wolffenbüttel during the Seventeenth Century*. Saarbrücken: Verlag Müller, 2008.

Cipolla, Carlo. *Fighting the Plague in Seventeenth-Century Italy*. Madison: University of Wisconsin Press, 1981.

Cook, Alexandra Parma and Noble David Cook. *The Plague Files: Crisis Management in Sixteenth-Century Seville*. Baton Rouge: University of Louisiana Press, 2009.

Pullan, Brian. "Plague and Perceptions of the Poor in Early Modern Italy," in *Epidemics and Ideas*, edited by Terence Ranger and Paul Slack (New York: Cambridge University Press, 1992), 101–123.

Lazarus

Two Gospel characters named Lazarus gave hope to epidemic victims. One was Mary and Martha's brother and friend of Jesus, who raised Lazarus back to life and gave hope to all who followed him (John 11:1–34). The other was the parable's suffering, sore-covered foil to wealthy "Dives," who was damned for ignoring the wretch. Suffering Lazarus was saved, as would have been Dives had he aided Lazarus while alive (Luke 16: 19–31). This moral warned the rich, heartened the suffering, and was popular during the Middle Ages. Believed to have been a leper, from the 11th century, "St. Lazarus" became associated with leper-houses (lazarets, lazarettos, lazzaretti, lazar-houses). As leprosy declined and plague struck, facilities for plague victims adopted the name and in parts of Europe St. Lazarus (St. Lazaire, San Lazzaro) emerged as a plague saint. Images of both "Christ Raising Lazarus" and "Dives and Lazarus" served for veneration and as ex voto offerings.

See also: Ex voto; Lazarettos and Pest Houses; Leprosy (Hansen's Disease) and Leprosarium; Plague Saints; Poverty and Plague.

Reference

Hopkins, Andrew. "Combating the Plague," in *Piety and Plague from Byzantium to the Baroque*, edited by Franco Mormando and Thomas Worcester (Kirksville, MO: Truman State University Press, 2007), 137–151.

Leechbooks

In medieval England, vernacular books that contained recipes for medicines and means of medical treatment were called leechbooks (healer-books; in Germany, *Arzneibücher*). Written as early as Anglo-Saxon times, Middle English versions after 1350 came to incorporate sections on preventing and remedying plague. Rather than reflecting elite medicine, these were popular texts developed for common folk. Some, like that of

John Thornton, might include an abridged vernacular version of a professorial plague tract, but most of the physician's jargon and packaging would have been removed. Medicines utilizing herbs, flowers, roots, beer, honey, and other commonly accessible materials were preferred over expensive apothecary-prepared compounds and exotic elixirs. One recipe for an ointment to soothe a plague bubo includes honey, duck grease, turpentine, soot, treacle, egg yolks, and scorpion oil (to draw out the poison). With a dearth of physicians (perhaps 60 in the 15th century) and an increasingly literate commons, England clearly profited from such self-help books.

See also: Consilia and Plague Tracts; Empirics; John of Burgundy.

Reference

Gottfried, Robert. *Epidemic Disease in Fifteenth-Century England*. New Brunswick, NJ: Rutgers University Press, 1978.

Leprosy (Hansen's Disease) and Leprosarium

During the middle ages, one of the most dreaded of all diseases was leprosy, today known as Hansen's disease. The *Mycobacterium leprae* is usually overwhelmed by the body's immune system, but sometimes the bacteria and the immune response combine to produce terrible damage to the victim's skin and nervous system. In early 14th-century Europe, those labeled lepers were not uncommon. Scripture and custom dictated that they were to be shunned, even expelled from towns, at least in part because they were associated with lust, hypersexuality, rape, and seduction. Leprosy was believed to be a personal curse from God, often punishment cast on children of promiscuous parents. Christian

From a 15th-century broadside on the care and treatment of leprosy patients. (Courtesy of the National Library of Medicine)

charity and pity led to the provision of special facilities for lepers, the earliest being the first recognized Christian hospital, built in fourth-century Caesarea by St. Basil. Leprosaria, like the monasteries on which they were modeled, insisted on chastity among residents, who were taught that their physical suffering on earth helped reduce their spiritual time in purgatory. Leprosaria, also called lazarettos, lazar houses, or lazarets after Biblical Lazarus, were provided by wealthy or communal patrons and located along roads outside city gates to facilitate the begging by which residents supported themselves. There may have been as many as 19,000 of these houses in 13th-century Europe.

Plague was blamed on collective rather than personal guilt for sin, but the plague

victim's agony and awful disfigurement paralleled those suffered by lepers. Like lepers, plague victims were shunned and often abandoned even by family, and for similar notions of contagion. Across Europe, authorities transformed the idea of long-term leprosaria into the acute, short-term plague hospital or pest house. Even the name *lazaretto* stuck to the new care facilities, which eventually came to be associated with poor plague victims. In a sense, Europeans' experience with leprosy paved the way for their reactions to plague.

The widespread presence of *Yersinia pestis* and related *Yersinia pseudotuberculosis* may have served to lessen the prevalence of *Mycobacterium leprae* among Europeans during the Second Plague Pandemic. Indeed, leprosy's incidence dropped significantly, though plague-inspired sanitation improvements and other communal efforts may have played their part.

See also: Expulsion of Victims; Lazarettos and Pest Houses; Lazarus; Purgatory; Sin.

References

Ell, Stephen. "Plague and Leprosy in the Middle Ages: A Paradoxical Cross-immunity?" *International Journal of Leprosy and Other Mycobacterial Diseases* 55 (1987): 345–350.

Palmer, Robert. "The Church, Leprosy and Plague," in *The Church and Healing*, a volume of *Studies in Church History* 19 (1982): 79–99.

Rawcliffe, Carole. *Leprosy in Medieval England*. Rochester, NY: Boydell, 2006.

Li Muisis, Gilles (Le Muisit; 1271/72–1353)

Abbot Gilles began life as son of a Tournai (Belgium) merchant, who had him educated in local schools and briefly at Paris. Young

Gilles became a monk at Saint-Martin of Tournai in 1289, showing an aptitude for administration. He rose to become prior in 1330 and abbot the following year. He took pleasure in French poetry, mathematics, and astrology, and was a first-rate record-keeper, known for his precision. Gilles went blind in August 1348 and began dictating everything he knew of Saint-Martin's history and moralizing prose and poetry. He also began a journal or chronicle of events from 1346, when his cataracts first appeared.

Gilles was 78 when the Black Death reached northeastern France in 1349. In late 1348, he had provided a short entry in his *Chronicle*, in which he mentioned storms, unhealthy air, and "great [sexual] immorality" as background to the epidemic. Gilles related the Kaffa story, Europe's importation of pestilence from the east, and its advance northward from Mediterranean ports. He recorded reports of extensive depopulation and sudden death and provided his sources. In 1350, Gilles provided a longer and more reflective section with details on his observations. He began with a local astrologer's prediction of disasters in and after 1345, relating this to Jewish poison libels and Christian pogroms. Reports of Asiatic epidemics follow, as do those of southern European flagellants and more on atrocities against Jews. He then shifted to Tournai: the bishop's flight and death and city government proclamations requiring quick and deep burial and limiting funeral rites, encouraging marriage of concubines, and banning gambling and sales on the Sabbath. Later legislation (September 21) banned tolling bells, black mourning garb, and funeral gatherings altogether. Gilles provided chronological signposts: the bishop died June 11; the death rate soared after August 29 and began to abate in November; fatalities spiked at Christmas. He also noted the patterns of mortality: all were susceptible,

though the better off apparently died more frequently, as did priests and parish officers who visited the dying, and domestic animals. Finally, Gilles mentioned civic pilgrimages to Hennegau and Soissons to invoke St. Sebastian, the plague saint whose relics graced local churches.

See also: Black Death (1347–1353); Chronicles and Annals; Flagellants; Funerals, Catholic; Jews; Kaffa; Monks, Nuns, and Monasteries; St. Sebastian.

References

Guenée, Bernard. *Between Church and State: The Lives of Four French Prelates in the Late Middle Ages.* Translated by Arthur Goldhammer. Chicago: University of Chicago Press, 1991.

Horrox, Rosemary. *The Black Death.* New York: Manchester University Press, 1994.

Little Ice Age

In 2006, a Dutch study concluded that millions of trees that had been allowed to grow on farmlands abandoned during the 14th and 15th centuries had soaked up so much carbon dioxide that the climate cooled and thus began the Little Ice Age (a term coined in 1939 by French scientist François Matthes). The farmland would have been abandoned because of the deaths of millions of agricultural workers during the Black Death and succeeding plagues. Whether or not the Dutch were correct, it is a fact that a cooling trend gripped much of Europe from about 1300 to about 1850. The prior warming period had released the Vikings, led to the colonizing of Iceland and Greenland, and supported tremendous population growth throughout Europe prior to the Black Death. There is no reason to link the shorter growing times and wetter seasons with the onset of plague epidemics, though the cooling trend may have helped bring them to a close. London's last and "Great" plague, however, struck right after brutally cold temperatures, imported most likely from Amsterdam, which had shared canal-freezing weather. One possible effect of the onset of cold weather may have been that Mongols traversing western Central Asia may have traveled normally quieter southern routes, disrupting local foci of plague-enzootic rodents and unleashing epidemics. Another is that rodents exposed to the cold may have sought out warmer habitations or locales. The fact is that no clear relationship between climate change and the causes or course of the Second Pandemic has been established.

See also: Famine; Mongols; Rats and Other Plague Carriers.

References

Duncan, Kirsty. "The Possible Influence of Climate on the Bubonic Plague in Scotland." *Scottish Geographical Magazine* 108 (1992): 29–34.

Fagan, Brian. *The Little Ice Age: How Climate Made History, 1300–1850*. New York: Basic Books, 2000.

Lollards

The Oxford scholar and Lutterworth parish priest John Wyclif (Wycliffe; 1324–1384) experienced the Black Death and its aftermath first-hand. While many Catholic clergy comported themselves heroically during the plague and continued to serve the survivors, all too many others fled when the epidemic raged, refused to return after it had ended, or were replaced by ill-prepared, even if well-meaning, substitutes. As one dedicated to Scripture and his Christian flock, Wyclif developed the same revulsion that animated some monks, friars, and even bishops. His university studies had prepared him to question the very fundamentals of the Christian Church, while the plague exposed its glaring weaknesses. His preaching became radical, he began writing tracts that embodied his new insights, and he gained followers who spread them by itinerant preaching. These, and later followers, became known as Lollards, a name of uncertain derivation.

Known as the Morningstar of the (later) Reformation, Wyclif laid out the alternative to Catholic organization and practice that developed as Lutheranism and Calvinism in the 16th century. His ideas also traveled to Bohemia, thanks to the English Queen, where they sparked the radical movement named for its leader, Jan Hus. Wyclif and the Lollards began with the Bible, accepting it as sole source of authority and insisting that all have access to it in the vernacular. The ordained priesthood in all of its forms was to be replaced by a priesthood of believers, any of whom could preach. Rome was an abomination, as demonstrated by the immorality of Avignon and recent schism; all wealth in the Church's hands was to be redistributed among the people; monasticism was not biblical and thus a fraud. Faith alone, and not works, saved one's soul, and all sacraments were bogus excepting baptism and the Eucharist, which were clearly established in Scripture. The only church a believer needed was the local pastor and congregation: all higher organization was parasitic, corrupt, and misled the people. It was truly a radical program, and developed over the 1370s. Most historians do not directly tie it to the peasants' revolt of 1381, but in 1382, the Church condemned Wyclif and his followers. Young King Richard refused to execute his subject, and Wyclif died naturally. His movement went underground at least until the 1440s, perhaps until the Anglican Reformation in the later 1520s. Some believe Chaucer's simple and devout Parson reflects the Lollard ideal.

See also: Anticlericalism; Bishops and Popes; Chaucer, Geoffrey; Langland, William; Languages: Vernacular and Latin; Peasants' Revolt, English; Priests; Reformation and Protestantism

References

Evans, R. G. *John Wyclif: Myth and Reality.* Downers Grove, IL: IVP, 2006.

Somerset, Fiona, et al., editors. *Lollards and their Influence on Late Medieval England.* Rochester, NY: Boydell, 2009.

London, England

Romans built London at the lowest bridgeable point on the River Thames, the longest southern river in England. Well situated for Continental trade, by the 14th century, it was a merchant bastion of wharves and warehouses with royal bookends of the Tower of London and Westminster Abbey and Palace. The Roman mile-square heart was simply The City, a densely packed core with 113 parishes and 113 churches. Suburbs and so-called liberties had grown up all around The City, which was governed by aldermen representing the 24 City wards, one of whom served as Lord Mayor. By the 1340s, London was England's commercial and cultural center, seat of royal and legal administration, usual home of the archbishops of Canterbury, leaders of the English Church, and England's largest city, with around 50,000 densely packed souls. Another 30 to 40,000 lived in the surrounding towns and villages. True to its Roman origins, all roads led to London.

In the late summer or fall of 1348, plague arrived in London via the road from Bristol through Oxford as well as river port traffic. By June 1349, an average of 290 victims were dying per day. Tax assessment records indicate that about a third of London's wealthiest perished (from all causes), and about the same percentage of the city's grocers. Half of Westminster Abbey's monks and their abbot died, as did some 100 Franciscan friars. The need for consecrated burial ground outstripped the tiny urban churchyards, and two new cemeteries were established north and east of The City. Together they held some 12,400 corpses. Guild leaders died off and were replaced, including a third of the City aldermen. All told, perhaps 40 percent of London's population perished. In the aftermath, courts labored to protect orphans and legacies and, in 1349 tried to impose the Ordinance of Labourers by listing acceptable wages, charges, and prices. Since stench was credited with causing plague, in 1349, London's filth and lack of adequate sanitation prompted King Edward III to order the aldermen to cleanse the city. He repeated the command in 1361 when the disease returned.

Like other European urban centers, London initially recovered rather quickly with influxes of men and women from surrounding rural areas. Epidemic plague returned 18 times between 1369 and 1485 for at least 27 affected years. In 1373, St. Bartholomew's Hospital was granted a cemetery, and later St Paul's Cathedral yard came to serve as burial ground. The City's population remained depressed during the 15th century: around 40,000 in 1400 and only 50,000 in 1500, following a heavy outbreak in 1498 to 1500.

Plague struck London in 1513, 1515, 1525, 1528, 1532, 1535, 1543 to 1548, 1558 to 1559, 1563, 1578, 1582, and 1593. Yet the 16th century saw Renaissance London's population grow to 200,000 at the same time its royal administrators—especially the Privy Council—began to emulate Continental governments. This began in 1518 with the establishment of the College of Physicians of London; also, Chancellor Thomas Wolsey ordered that plague victims be shut in their houses and that these be clearly marked, and that London taxpayers support antiplague measures with special levies. The year 1519 saw the first use of bills of mortality, by which the government could monitor deaths, a tool regularized in 1563. Between 1547 and 1553, five hospitals were founded or refounded as Anglican institutions. In 1549, St. Paul's was cleared of human remains, 1,000 cartloads of which were relocated to extramural Finsbury Fields, and two decades later a new cemetery appeared near Bethlehem (Bedlam) Hospital. In 1563, public bonfires to cleanse the air were first mandated, in 1564, theaters were first closed during an epidemic, and in 1578, royal Plague Orders collecting royal regulations of all sorts for epidemics were first published as broadsides. Though the royal will included a proper pest house, London's leaders dragged their heels. In 1580, English quarantine of a ship's crew and cargo was first noted.

Plague interrupted coronations at Westminster Abbey for Elizabeth in 1558 (8,000 victims estimated), James I in 1603 (35,104), and Charles I in 1625 (41,313). London's population was exploding, but all efforts to control growth failed. London's first comprehensive sanitation regulations, Statute of the Streets, dates to the early 1600s, but poor housing, overcrowding, and poverty negated intentions and focused blame for plague on the city's burgeoning poor. A rich moral literature of social, political, and religious criticism emerged with each epidemic in the 1590s and 17th century (1604 to 1610: around 15,000 plague deaths, 1629 to 1636: more than 12,000, 1647: 3,597, and 1665 to 1666), culminating with Daniel Defoe's retrospective *Journal of the Plague Year* in 1722. Together

epidemics claimed at least 190,000 lives between 1603 and 1666, London's last plague year, while its population continued to grow, to 375,000 in 1650 and 490,000 in 1700. Yet plague measures remained rudimentary by Continental standards, Plague Orders being little changed since 1578. This despite provision of a blueprint for action prepared by French doctor Theodore de Mayerne, the Queen's Physician in the 1630s. One exception was quarantine and its strict enforcement by the Royal Navy.

See also: Bills of Mortality; Black Death (1347–1352); Dekker, Thomas; Donne, John; Eyam, England; Grindal, Edmund; Henry VIII, King of England; London, Great Plague of; London's East Smithfield Plague Cemetery; Morality Literature, Christian; Plague Orders and National Authorities; Searchers; Shakespeare, William; Shutting In; Sydenham, Thomas; Wither, George.

References

Barron, Caroline. *London in the Later Middle Ages: Government and People, 1200–1500*. New York: Oxford University Press, 2004.

Caraman, R. P. *Henry Morse: Priest of the Plague*. London: Longmans, Green & Co, 1957.

Champion, Justin A. I., ed. *Epidemic Disease in London*. London: Centre for Metropolitan History Working Papers Series 1, 1993.

Harding, Vanessa. *The Dead and the Living in Paris and London, 1500–1670*. New York: Cambridge University Press, 2002.

Porter, Stephen. *Lord have Mercy upon Us: London's Plague Years*. Stroud, Gloucs, UK: Tempus, 2005.

Shrewsbury, J. F. *History of Bubonic Plague in the British Isles*. New York: Cambridge University Press, 1970.

Slack, Paul. *The Impact of Plague in Tudor and Stuart England*. New York: Oxford University Press, 1990.

Wilson, F. P. *Plague in Shakespeare's London*. New York: Oxford University Press, 1999.

London, Great Plague of (1665–1666)

English officials watched with trepidation as Amsterdam was stricken with plague in 1663 and 1664. Port exclusions and quarantine orders were kept close at hand, not least because by March 1665, the Dutch and English were at war. Naval supplies administrator Samuel Pepys, whose famous diary guides one through London's Great Plague, first noted the disease on April 30, 1665, and a second time on May 24. Between 1649 and 1665, annual plague deaths in the London Bills of Mortality had reached 36 only once. An especially warm early June tripled this in one week; recorded plague deaths reached 267 a week later. The royal court at Westminster fled on June 29 for Syon House at Isleworth. They stayed here until leaving for Hampton Court on July 9; two weeks later, they relocated to Salisbury, and from September 23 to January 27, they remained at Oxford.

By mid-June, the wealthier were fleeing in the thousands, while the poorer sort and dedicated public servants, like Pepys, remained. George Monck, Duke of Albermarle, ran the city with the aid of the Earl of Craven and the Lord Mayor for 1665, Sir John Laurence. Maintaining the peace, securing property, and keeping the sick isolated were among their chief concerns. Parish officials, however, did most of the work: hiring personnel to seek out the sick and dead, shutting in the former, burying the latter, and recording all of it. The Bishop of London administered parish funding, which reached £600 per week by high summer. Parishes had different levels and types of need. Well-off St. Dunstan West spent a total of £149 in 1665, with a quarter for poor relief and nearly that for, respectively, nursing and burials. By contrast, poor St. Margaret's Westminster spent £1,232, with 80 percent going for poor relief. The flight of the wealthy left beggars and vicars alike without supporters, and servants and apprentices found themselves left behind or simply abandoned to fend for themselves. Ironically, those who fled often found themselves unwelcomed along hostile roads, their wealth of no use against the yeomans' fear of contagion.

Across the summer, the tolls rose, empty streets and boarded shops a constant reminder of the devastated city. An average of 350 people died per week, with a high point of 8,000 victims during a single September week. Outlying parishes, with their poorer and less mobile denizens, suffered most. Stepney and Whitechapel together lost more than all 97 City parishes taken together. On September 11 alone, Stepney officials buried 154 corpses. Plague pits for mass burials appeared in suburban parishes, and pest houses finally appeared in Soho and on the site of modern Westminster Cathedral. Taken together, deaths in pest houses in 1665 totaled 312, or .0045 percent of the year's total plague deaths. By comparison, 10 percent of Norwich's 1665 plague deaths occurred in pest houses. Public outcry and learned opinion prompted royal officials in the May 1666 Book of Orders to insist that whenever possible, the sick be taken to pest houses to spare their family members.

The summary Bills of Mortality reported 68,956 plague deaths in 1665. December saw plague deaths drop away and Londoners return, a stream that became a flood in January. The new year produced scattered reports of plague deaths, especially in the spring, for a total of 1,800 plague burials. All told, as many as 75,000 to 80,000 plague deaths may have occurred, given the vagaries of the era's recordkeeping (under-reporting, lack of dissenter reports, children) out of a population of perhaps 400,000. Yet London recovered rapidly and England would not see the Great Plague's like again.

See also: Bills of Mortality; Defoe, Daniel; Flight; Lazarettos and Pest Houses; London, England; Pepys, Samuel; Plague Orders and National Authorities; Quarantine; Shutting In.

References

Bell, Walter George. *The Great Plague in London in 1665*. New York: AMS Press, 1976.

Champion, Justin A. I. *London's Dreaded Visitation: The Social Geography of the Great Plague in 1665*. London: Historical Geography Research Paper Series 31, 1995.

Moote, A. Lloyd and Dorothy C. Moote. *The Great Plague: The Story of London's Most Deadly Year*. Baltimore, MD: Johns Hopkins University Press, 2004.

Porter, Stephen. *The Great Plague*. Stroud, Gloucs, UK: Sutton, 1999.

London's East Smithfield Plague Cemetery

Beneath London's Royal Mint complex lies the best-studied mass gravesite from 1348 to 1350. Located outside the Roman wall near the Tower of London, the site was originally a sand and gravel quarry. When plague struck in late 1348, Bishop Ralph Stratford founded West Smithfield plague cemetery to the north, and John Corey (Cory), agent of the Black Prince, purchased the quarry site and had it consecrated on April 12, 1349. The two cemeteries supplemented the churchyards and church vaults traditionally used for burials. A wall with gatehouse was erected to keep scavengers out, and at some point, a chapel for memorial prayers and services was erected. In 1350, King Edward III established the Cistercian monastery of St. Mary Graces adjacent to the burial area. The cemetery itself may have been used during subsequent plague outbreaks, but this is unclear.

Excavations (1986–1988) revealed two long trenches for mass burial: one 125 meters long, 2 meters wide, and .75 meters deep with 102 corpses, and the other 67 meters long, 2 meters wide, and 1.25 meters deep with 242 individuals buried, stacked as many as five deep. Corpses were carefully laid out rather than dumped, with small bodies wedged between larger for highest efficiency. About 10 percent of those in trenches had wooden coffins, the insides of which were often scorched, perhaps to control stench. Men outnumbered women 1.8:1, and most ranged from age 26 to 35. Experts estimate that East Smithfield cemetery contained 2,400 individual and trench burials, or about 3 to 5 percent of London's population.

See also: Corpses; Gravediggers; London, England; Mass Graves and Plague Cemeteries; Plague Memorials.

References

Gowland, R. L. and A. T. Chamberlain. "Detecting Plague: Palaeodemographic Characterization of a Catastrophic Death Assemblage." *Antiquity* 79 (2005): 146–157.

Grainger, Ian, et al. *The Black Death Cemetery, East Smithfeld, London*. London: Museum of London, 2008.

Luther, Martin (1483–1546)

Martin Luther was born to a Saxon miner who wanted his son to become a lawyer. Instead, Martin found his way into the Catholic Augustinian Order of friars. While he earned

Martin Luther was a 16th-century German theologian who brought on the Protestant Reformation by demanding changes in the Catholic Church. (Library of Congress)

his doctorate in theology, was ordained, and gained pastoral experience, Luther wrestled with his Catholicism but never his Christianity. Between 1517 and 1522, he debated and was excommunicated by the Church, establishing his own variant in Wittenberg and effectively beginning the Reformation.

Luther's pastoral side shone when plague struck Wittenberg on August 2, 1527. On the 10th, his lord and employer, John the German Elector of Saxony, insisted that Luther and other Wittenberg university faculty and students flee for Jena, but Luther and pastor Johannes Bugenhagen refused, remaining in the city to tend to the sick and dying. Luther's house became a hospice, but neither his nor Bugenhagen's family suffered loss. At roughly the same time, plague hit Silesian Breslau, prompting debate among

Lutherans there over whether a Christian should flee before plague. They contacted Luther through their leader Johann Hess and Luther responded belatedly in November with a 14-page German pamphlet, "Whether One May Flee from a Deadly Plague." Published immediately, it underwent 19 reprintings. Essentially, he wrote that public officials have a moral duty to remain, as do those with obligations to others—parents, masters, neighbors—who do not or cannot flee. The steadfast in faith should remain and do what they can to aid the suffering, he stated, since none can flee God's judgment. This must be done in humility, however, and not to tempt or test God. He concludes with a few remarks about burials and cemeteries that helped direct the unfolding Protestant tradition.

See also: Flight; Pastors, Preachers, and Ministers; Reformation and Protestantism.

Reference

Leroux, Neil R. *Martin Luther as Comforter: Writings on Death.* Boston: Brill, 2007.

Lydgate, John (c. 1370–1450)

Monk and poet John Lydgate was born in the wake of England's third plague visitation (1369). Lydgate village was near the town and half-millennium-old monastery of Bury St. Edmunds, and John joined the 80 or so monks in 1385. He studied in their school and 2000-book library and probably spent some time at Oxford University. Ordained a priest in 1397, John entered royal circles as a poet and was provided a sinecure as prior at Hatfield Regis (1423–1434). He traveled to Paris with Henry V and Duke Humphrey (1426–1429) and spent time in London and at court in Windsor (1429–1434). Considered a royal counselor, John spent his last years at Bury.

Arguably the greatest English poet between Chaucer and Shakespeare, John Lydgate was essentially a poet for hire to England's high nobility. His output was huge and varied, often reworking forms, themes, and characters from French, Italian, or classical originals. His works associated with plague are also varied. The Galenic *A Dietary*, a regimen of health in time of plague in iambic pentameter, is the only such prescriptive work from 14th- or 15th-century England apart from the derivative *Canutus* tract. He avoided religion and metaphysics and emphasized physical and social harmony and balance for physical and social health. While in Paris, he copied the *Danse macabre* text at Les Innocents and reworked it into English, adding characters and a plague motif: "cruel death . . . which slayeth alas, by stroke of pestilence both young and old, of low and high estate." His "Legend of Petronilla," daughter of St. Peter and a plague saint, emphasizes the virtue of patience in suffering from sickness and pestilence and was written for her feast day (May 31), probably during the plague year 1434. "How the Plague Was Ceased" is a short, uninspired reworking of the St. Sebastian story from the northern Italian plague of 680. Finally, he wrote two Latin prayers dedicated to the Virgin Mary during plague time, the supplication *"Stella celi extirpavit"* ("be our shield from stroke of pestilence") and, more glorifying than beseeching, *"De Sancta Maria contra pestilenciam."*

See also: *Canutus (Kanutus)* Plague Tract; Danse Macabre; Dietary Regimens; Languages: Vernacular and Latin; Monks, Nuns, and Monasteries; Plague Saints; Poetry, European; St. Sebastian; Virgin Mary.

References

Bühler, C. F. "Lydgate's Rules of Health." *Medium Aevum* 3 (1934): 51–56.

Byrne, Joseph. *The Black Death*. Westport, CT: Greenwood, 2004.

Grigsby, Bryon Lee. *Pestilence in Medieval and Early Modern English Literature*. New York: Routledge, 2004.

Schirmer, Walter F. *John Lydgate*. Westport, CT: Greenwood, 1961.

Magic. *See* **Amulets, Talismans, and Magic**

Malthusianism

English clergyman, scholar, and pioneer of modern demography Thomas Malthus (1766–1834) lived in the postplague era of rapid population growth, early industrialization, and urbanization. It was also a time of optimism about the human condition and hope in new sciences, both natural and social. Malthus saw things differently, however, and in his 1798 *Essay on the Principle of Population* warned of the inevitable crisis accompanying unchecked human population growth. Quite simply, he posited that population grew at a geometric rate (2:4:8:16:32) while the human food supply only grew arithmetically (2:3:4:5:6). At some point in a growth period, humans outstrip their food supplies and starve. Historical—and future—famines were the result of natural processes that reduced the population to a sustainable level. The Irish potato famine of the later 1840s seemed to confirm Malthus's theory. Nature had other means of limiting population growth, Malthusians mused, including human aggression (war) and epidemic disease.

The idea that plague was nature's (or God's) check on population growth was expressed many times during the Second Pandemic. In 1658, Genoese priest Antero Maria wrote that plague was God's way of both punishing sinners and "ordering the universe;" Genoa's population had grown tremendously and plague was God "shaving its beard." Carlo Cipolla found a group of Italian "naturalists" or "proto–Malthusians" in 16th- and 17th-century Italy: in 1580, Bartolomeo Paschetti compared plague to "floods and fires that Nature uses to rid the world of a superfluity of people" (278). Seventeenth-century English playwright, moralist, and plague pamphleteer Thomas Dekker called this theory the self-flattery of people who want to avoid the consequences of sin.

Some modern historians and social scientists, too, have seen the Black Death of 1347 to 1352 as a kind of Malthusian check. Population in Europe and the Near East had grown rapidly, especially in the 13th century, and had hit its "natural limit" by the 1340s. Widespread and prolonged famines in the late 1310s and 1340s took their tolls, but further population growth and overexpansion required further culling, especially from swelled cities and marginal croplands. Norman Cantor writes of Europe's "classic Malthusian situation" in the 13th and 14th centuries. Famine and warfare were nature's answers to the "Malthusian maelstrom" and created a "particularly adverse context" for plague (198–199). Harvard's David Herlihy wrote that although he had embraced Malthusianism early on, his subsequent studies swayed him against its determinism and plague's inevitability. Philip Ziegler in *The Black Death* (1969) briefly describes the Malthusian model but questions its validity and warns against positing limited theories of causation.

See also: Black Death: Origins and Early Spread; Bubonic Plague; Dietary Regimens; Little Ice Age; Poverty and Plague; Virgin Soil Disease.

References

Cantor, Norman. *In the Wake of the Plague.* New York: Free Press, 2001.

Cipolla, Carlo. "The Plague and Pre-Malthus Malthusians." *Journal of Economic History* 3 (1974): 277–284.

Morineau, Michael. "Malthus: There and Back from the Period Preceding the Black Death to the 'Industrial Revolution.' " *Journal of European Economic History* 27 (1998): 137–202.

Marseille, France

Situated at the mouth of the Rhône River, Marseille was the principle French port on the Mediterranean Sea. It was an international meeting point between ships of maritime Aragon and Italy between Sicily and Genoa. Barges sailed up the Rhône bringing Mediterranean goods into the French interior and back down laden with French merchandise.

Marseille was the hub of Provence, at which all of the region's major roads met, and the gateway to Avignon, home of popes in 1348 and beyond.

The Genoese who brought the plague back from the Black Sea supposedly deposited it in Marseille. Plague did break out in early November 1347, remaining at low levels until February 1348, when it raged until August. Despite a death toll reckoned today at 40 percent (at the time as 80 or 90%), records of notaries show surprisingly little disruption in government and the public life of the city. French historian Biraben notes epidemics returning in 1361 and 1374, after which Marseille built a pest house and quarantine facilities (1383). The city established a health commission in 1472, but plague returned in 1476, 1483 to 1485, 1490, and 1494. The city grew in size and traffic during the 16th century, and plagues followed repeatedly: 1504 to 1508, 1524, 1627, 1530, 1546 to 1547,

Vista down a long boulevard in Marseille in 1720, with plague victims in the foreground and along the boulevard. (Courtesy of the National Library of Medicine)

1556, 1563, 1580 to 1582, 1586 to 1588, and 1598. After a respite, they continued in 1619, 1629 to 1630, 1640, 1649 to 1650, 1660, and 1664.

After more than 50 years without an epidemic, the cargo ship *Le Grande St. Antoine* docked on May 25, 1720, and Western Europe's last great plague epidemic began. The disease spread as rapidly and widely as it did because in its earliest stages, medical personnel disagreed over its nature. While some recognized it as plague, others dismissed it as "pestilential fever," a diagnosis friendly to the mercantile community that dearly wanted to avoid a general quarantine. By late July, the truth was out and circulating; in the meantime, thousands circulated in and out of Marseille before any sort of cordon was positioned. Marseille's plague became that of Provence. Provincial military officials established guards and a cordon to limit travel even as many of the physicians of the College insisted the plague was miasmatic and not contagious. A contingent of Montpellier physicians appeared and agreed locally that the disease was plague and not a malignant fever, but they officially reported the opposite, adding to the confusion. The hospital Hôtel Dieu was chosen to house poor victims, but the staff died, and for six weeks at the epidemic's height, there were only tents.

Royal authority was finally activated when, on September 12, the Regent appointed the Chevalier de Langeron to take over from the dithering and ineffective local councilmen. Royal aid made food, doctors, and medicines available and royal troops established a sound cordon sanitaire (October 3), and the following day a proper lazaret opened at the poorhouse of La Charité. Seven hundred convicts were put to work clearing away and burying corpses that littered streets and had been stuffed in church basements and storerooms

within the walls. By late October and November, the epidemic was winding down in the city even as it raged in the environs, thanks to the initially weak efforts at containment. In the end, around half of Marseille's population of 100,000 died, and as many in such towns as Avignon, Apt, and Lourmarin. Surrounding such countries as Spain, Piedmonte, and England effectively used cordons and quarantines to limit the epidemic's effects.

See also: Bertrand, Jean-Baptiste; Cordons Sanitaires; Defoe, Daniel; London, England; Mead, Richard; Quarantine.

References

Biraben, Jean-Noel. *Les hommes et la peste en France et dans les pays europeens et mediteraneens.* 2 vols. Paris: Mouton, 1975, 1976.

Naphy, William G. and Andrew Spicer. *The Black Death and the History of Plagues, 1345–1730.* Stroud, Gloucs, UK: Sutton, 2001.

Sheppard, T. F. *Lourmarin in the Eighteenth Century: A Study of a French Village.* Baltimore, MD: Johns Hopkins University Press, 1971.

Smail, Daniel Lord. "Accommodating Plague in Medieval Marseille." *Continuity and Change* 11 (1996): 11–41.

Mass Graves and Plague Cemeteries

Disposal of plague victims' corpses proved a major problem for local governments and Church authorities. This became evident during the 1347 to 1352 pandemic and remained an issue into the 18th century. In the earliest known instance, in 1347, residents of Catania in southern Italy decided to burn the corpses of refugees from plague-stricken Messina, and to do so outside town walls. Venice, too, resorted to incineration during the epidemic of 1575 to 1577, prompting one observer to mention the resulting "clouds

A mass burial of plague victims, who are being thrown into a pit in Holywell, Wales, 1665. (Courtesy of the National Library of Medicine)

of smoke" over the Lazaretto Vecchio. While other cities no doubt did the same, the fear of miasma, of the fires releasing toxic elements back into the atmosphere, kept most cities at most times pursuing other solutions.

Dumping corpses into rivers or the sea presented problems of downstream pollution and rotting corpses being washed back ashore during high tides. Traditional burial in ground or within the fabric of a church remained most common. In Catholic and some Protestant countries, ground had to be consecrated or blessed for the deceaseds' souls to find true rest. Though simple enough, it meant reporting all places of burial to Church authorities. Burial also had to be deep—contemporary statutes for

Pistoia and Tournai specify about six feet—to insure against miasmic odors seeping upward and predation by dogs and other scavengers. Burial in coffins was also desirable, but victims fell so rapidly, in such numbers, and often without family to provide for them, that such a demand was deemed unreasonable.

Fourteenth-century chroniclers agree that churches, where burials in walls and under the pavement had long taken place, had filled up, and even churchyards sported mounds covering local victims. Burial in one's own parish church or graveyard was desirable both for the proximity to family and friends on Judgment Day but also as a reminder to the community to pray for one's soul lest it linger in Purgatory. Giovanni Boccaccio is among the first to mention that rather than being carried to the specified resting place, bodies were often tossed into the nearest grave.

Records of the Black Death are replete with stories of authorities having to purchase and consecrate large tracts of land for mass burials after the normal venues had filled up. Despite having blessed the Rhône River to receive the dead, early in 1348, Pope Clement in Avignon purchased and consecrated a large field near Notre-Dame des Miracles. By March 14, an anonymous chronicler wrote, 11,000 bodies had been deposited there. Clement also ordered the consecration of a new cemetery in Dublin, which one credulous source said held 50,000 corpses. Other bishops also allowed graveyard consecration by proxy. York's Archbishop ordered at least seven, for a total of 11 new or expanded cemeteries in his diocese in July and August 1349. Klosterneuberg's annalist reports that Viennese church burials were forbidden because of the "stench and horror." Between May 31 and September 29, five large and deep pits dug in God's Field outside the city received the local dead. Gabriel de' Mussis noted that Piacenza quickly ran out of space, so bodies were placed in pits dug into piazzas and colonnades. On April 18, 1349, Worcester's bishop informed his deans that the cathedral's graveyards were full, and corpses would henceforth be buried in the cemetery of St. Oswald Hospital. Tournai created two new cemeteries, and Pirano in Istria bought three gardens for burials. French towns required royal permission to establish or expand graveyards and the National Archive preserves many requests. Perhaps the best-known plague cemeteries are London's East and West Smithfield sites. Bishop Ralph Stratford bought No Man's Land to the west, consecrated it, built a chapel, and surrounded it with a wall to exclude animals. Clergyman John Corey similarly developed the eastern site, on which the Royal Mint is located.

Commentators throughout the Second Pandemic note the chilling practice of using public corpse carriers to collect the dead and cart them to the new mass burial sites. Statutes often specify the collections take place after dark, which made them less visible, yet more terrifying. Records grow increasingly literary over time, and writers lingered on plague-pit scenes with their horrible smells, the bits of putrefying human anatomy scattered here and there, the half-buried and unburied, eyes staring blankly or missing, and limbs akimbo. While such descriptions emphasize the chaotic dumping of bodies with no attention to their positioning, others depict careful, ordered placement, as one early Italian put it: like layers of cheese in lasagna. Modern excavations in London and elsewhere also find order rather than chaos in mass graves, leading one scholar to remark that one could not distinguish normal from plague-time burials. At East Smithfield, however, up to five bodies were carefully placed atop one another; given

their common death dates, this would not have normally occurred.

In 1418, Parisian gravediggers excavated five huge pits at Holy Innocents Cemetery, four at Trinity, and others as land availability permitted, each of which was said to hold about 600 corpses. Dutch cities of Amsterdam (1601), Zwolle (1602), and Leyden (1635, 1639) resorted to digging burial pits on the ramparts protecting the cities. As plague lingered in Marseille in 1720, one burial trench measured 140 feet long, 52 feet wide, and 14 feet deep. London Metro's Piccadilly Line had to make a wide curve around a very dense boneyard beneath a corner of Hyde Park. Mass graves were often associated with pest houses and plague hospitals, located outside of town and away from family and home. This "alienation of the dead" may have inspired greater attempts at individuation, especially in burial, during typical/normal times. Denied normal funeral rites that delayed burial for several days, and given the medical ravages of plague, stories of people being buried alive or awaking in plague pits were not uncommon. In 1665, London's William Austin wrote that gravediggers were wise to leave pits uncovered for a while, lest the unthinkable occur.

Tudor authorities emptied St. Paul's Cathedral churchyard of its dead, sending 1,000 cartloads of bones north to Finsbury (Bunhill or Bone-Hill) Fields for proper burial. Like other plague cemeteries, Bunhill became the graveyard for religious minorities. Between 1665 and 1852, an estimated 123,000 more were laid to rest here. Paris's famous catacombs date from the 1780s, when the public Cemetery of the Holy Innocents was emptied of 15,373 cartloads of corpses and thousands of bones. Some plague cemeteries became homes to religious orders, as with London's Charterhouse at West Smithfield, and later others were reserved as plague memorials.

See also: Corpse Carriers; Corpses; DNA and the Second Plague Pandemic; Gravediggers; Individualism and Individual Liberties; London's East Smithfield Plague Cemetery; Plague Memorials; Tumbrels; individual cities.

References

Daniell, Christopher. *Death and Burial in Medieval England*. New York: Routledge, 1997.

De Boe, Guy and Frans Verhaeghe. *Death and Burial in Medieval Europe*. Zellik [Belgium]: Instituut voor het Archeologisch Patrimonium, 1997.

Harding, Vanessa. "Burial of the Plague Dead in Early Modern London," in *Epidemic Disease in London*, edited by J. A. I. Champion (London: Centre for Metropolitan History Working Papers Series 1, 1993), 53–64.

Harding, Vanessa. *The Dead and the Living in Paris and London, 1500–1670*. New York: Cambridge University Press, 2002.

Hawkins, D. "The Black Death and the New London Cemeteries of 1348." *Antiquity* 64 (1990): 637–642.

Mead, Richard (1673–1754)

Born to and home schooled by English Nonconformist minister Matthew Mead, Richard attended Universities of Utrecht (Netherlands, Arts, 1689), Leiden (Netherlands, Medicine, 1692), and Padua (Italy, M.D., 1695). Returning to Stepney, he became a Fellow of the Royal Society (1703) and began work in St. Thomas's Hospital, London. Mead acquired an Oxford University M.D. (1707), joining the College of Physicians in 1708. He attended dying Queen Anne and the young George II, and by 1720, he was London's premier physician.

When plague threatened in 1719, Secretary of State James Craggs commissioned directions for protecting Britain, which had not suffered since 1666. As Marseille began its ordeal in 1720, Mead's *A Short Discourse concerning Pestilential Contagion and the Methods to be Used to Prevent It* appeared in seven editions, a greatly expanded eighth being produced in 1722, and a ninth in 1744. The fourth edition—November 25, 1720—contains 59 pages and is divided into two major sections. The first explains plague in largely Galenic terms, though Mead envisioned it as "contagious particles drawn in with the air we breathe." The second was further divided: how to prevent plague's import into Britain, and how to cope if it arrived. For prevention he advised quarantines, lazarettos, cordons sanitaires, and destruction of suspect goods, especially hair, feathers, fur, and textiles. Opposed to shutting in, Mead recommended isolation of the sick and suspect miles outside cities, burning of tainted property and houses, and public sanitation. Though it became the basis for Government responses, Mead's pragmatic work drew fire from anticontagionists and opponents of such commercial barriers as quarantines.

See also: Causes of Plague: Historical Theories; Cordons Sanitaires; Lazarettos and Pest Houses; London, England; Marseille, France; Prophylaxes; Public Health; Public Sanitation; Quarantine; Shutting In.

References

Zuckerman, Arnold. *Dr. Richard Mead (1673–1754): A Biographical Study*. Urbana: University of Illinois, 1964.

Zuckerman, Arnold. "Plague and Contagionism in Eighteenth-century England: the Role of Richard Mead." *Bulletin of the History of Medicine* 78 (2004): 273–308.

Mecca

Located in the Hijaz region of southwestern Arabia, Mecca has long been a commercial center for the caravan trade as well as the principal destination of Muslim pilgrims. In

630, Islam's Prophet Muhammad cleansed the shrine known as the Ka'aba of its hundreds of idols and dictated that henceforth it would be visited at least once in each adherent's lifetime. Inland rather than a port, pilgrims arrived on foot at the end of a caravan or at Jiddah on maritime voyages and began their return journeys similarly. Six major routes converged on the city. By the 1340s, Mecca was also a center for religious scholarship, drawing students from throughout the Islamic world to its madrasas.

Though in the 19th century English traveler Richard Burton was told that nearby Medina had never been struck by plague, Mecca suffered repeatedly. In 1348, surprised by Allah's apparent ire, locals blamed the presence of Jews in the Holy City. Regular sea traffic—both religious and commercial—through Jiddah to Mecca and back continually refreshed the plague's presence, and at least one plague historian recognizes the Hijaz as a plague reservoir by the early Ottoman period (from 1517). Ottoman domination brought Mecca into a much larger political world, which meant stronger and more regular ties to the Black Sea, Anatolia, Istanbul, Mesopotamia, the Levant, Greece, and the Balkans. Much traffic passed through Alexandria and Cairo, Egypt. Ottoman leaders built three additional hospitals in Mecca for sick pilgrims and residents, two in the 16th century and another in 1679, but little else was done to stem the plague's recurrence until the 19th century.

See also: Bimaristans; Ibn Battuta, Abu Abdullah; Islam and Medicine; Islamic Civil Responses; Muhammad the Prophet; Pilgrims and Pilgrimage; *Ta'un.*

References

Dols, Michael W. *The Black Death in the Middle East.* Princeton, NJ: Princeton University Press, 1977.

Shefer-Mossensohn, Miri. *Ottoman Medicine: Healing and Medical Institutions, 1500–1700.* Albany: SUNY Press, 2009.

Medical Education (1300–1500, Medieval Europe)

When the Black Death struck Europe in 1347, medical practitioners were utterly unprepared for a disease as deadly, fast moving, and widely spread as plague proved to be. This was due in large part to the newness of the disease—despite its ravages as Justinian's Plague—but also in part to the nature of medical training and education before and during the initial phases of the Second Pandemic.

Medieval medical education took place in monasteries and in such early cathedral schools as Rheims and Chartres as part of the liberal arts curriculum. Italy gained the first medical school during the 11th century at Salerno, south of Naples, an institution heavily influenced by Jewish and Muslim scholarship. Here the heavily Galenic *Articella* was compiled during the 1100s as the earliest and longest-lived Latin medical textbook. Before 1340, schools were established in Montpellier, Paris, Perugia, Bologna, Avignon, with medical degrees still a part of the liberal arts programs at Oxford and other northern universities. Typically, grammar or Latin school prepared the student for university, in which he matriculated in the arts at age 14 or 15. Around 20, he earned his master's and then spent five years earning the medical licentiate with additional study for the doctorate. The curricula were filled with Latin abridgments of and commentaries on classical Galen and Hippocrates and both personal and derivative works of Arabic-Persian scholars, especially the 10th-century *Kanon* of Avicenna and works of Averroes. The prescribed texts were read to students and commented upon with little else to support a physician's education. Anatomical education was crude and available at few universities. Only in Italy was surgery a curricular staple, in large part thanks to Bologna's interest in forensic medicine. The result was a physician with years of Aristotelian natural philosophy, Galenic humoralism, and Hippocratic non-naturals but no clinical experience.

Between 1350 and 1500, very little happened to improve medical education. The plague's only effect was to spur more medical schools and the addition of astrology to the curriculum (Paris from 1371 to 1538; Montpellier from at least 1400; Bologna from 1400 to about 1500; also Krakow, Erfurt, Leipzig, and Vienna). Belief in the influence of the stars on human health has deep roots, and even Paris's medical faculty blamed a celestial conjunction for the Black Death in 1348.

The emperor founded Vienna's university in 1365 for imperial students, but its medical school had to wait 35 years. His postplague university in Prague graduated only Balthasar de Marcellinus de Tuscia before 1409. Taken together, 15th-century German universities saw only 20 to 30 new medical students, and most universities had but a pair of professors, for theory and practice. From 1390 to 1500, only Paris graduated French M.D.s, and only an average of fewer than three per year. In the 15th century, Oxford only produced 40 medical doctors while graduating 500 Doctors of Divinity.

See also: Anatomy and Dissection; *Articella*; Astrology; Avicenna (Ibn Sina); Contagion Theory; Empirics; Galen and Galenism; Hippocrates and the Hippocratic Corpus; Medical Education (1500–1700, Early Modern Europe); Physicians.

References

Arrizabalaga, Jon. "Facing the Black Death: Perceptions and Reactions of University Medical Practitioners," in *Practical Medicine from Salerno to the Black Death*, edited by Luis Garcia-Ballester, et al. (New York: Cambridge University Press, 1994, 237–288.

Bullough, Vern L. *Universities, Medicine and Science in the Medieval West*. Burlington, VT: Ashgate, 2004.

Demaitre, Luke. "Theory and Practice in Medical Education at the University of Montpellier in the Thirteenth and Fourteenth Centuries." *Journal of the History of Medicine and Allied Science*s 30 (1975): 103–123.

French, Roger. *Medicine before Science: The Business of Medicine from the Middle Ages to the Enlightenment*. New York: Cambridge University Press, 2003.

McVaugh, Michael. "Surgical Education in the Middle Ages." *Dynamis* 20 (2000): 283–304.

O'Boyle, Cornelius. *The Art of Medicine: Medical Teaching at the University of Paris, 1250–1400*. Boston: Brill, 1998.

Siraisi, Nancy. "The Faculty of Medicine," in *A History of the University in Europe*, Volume 1, edited by Hilde de Ridder-Symoens (New York: Cambridge University Press, 1992), 360–387

Medical Education (1500–1700, Early Modern Europe)

By 1500, the plague had been ravaging Europe for 150 years. Yet little had changed in how medical practitioners were trained to deal with the disease on either an individual or a communal basis. In 1500, medical schools continued to teach the theories and practices associated with Hippocrates, Aristotle, and Galen in their Arabic garb. From the early 16th century, however, intellectual and societal trends affected medical education both directly and indirectly. Even

An interior view of an anatomical theater in which a dissection is in progress, 1574. (Courtesy of the National Library of Medicine)

so, such phenomena as the Renaissance, Reformation, and Scientific Revolution and improvements in training had little impact on the profession's ability to explain or alleviate the plague.

A number of factors, including humanism, printing, inclusion of surgical elements, anatomical education through dissections, medical botany, pharmacy, and the beginning of clinical teaching affected 16th-century medical education. Medical humanism shifted the focus away from older translations of and Arab commentaries on classical Greek medicine. Instead, new translations and editions of the original works of Hippocrates and Galen superseded the derivative texts, but the old paradigms of humors and miasmas remained. Printing made both the older and newer

scholarship cheaper and more readily available but also gave voice to medical alternatives, including Paracelsian and vernacular self-help texts. Anatomical education through dissections and elements of surgery had long been a part of medieval Italian medical education but became more frequent and moved north in the early 1500s. For example, Paris included surgery in 1506 and Montpellier in 1514. Educational dissections had long been carried out in the west, but under strict limitations. Anatomical theaters appeared first in Italy in the 1520s, then in Montpellier (1556) and Paris (1617). In the 1540s, Andreas Vesalius challenged anatomical teaching by his own hands-on demonstrations and through his beautiful (if often inaccurate) printed texts and plates.

The Western pharmacopoeia remained largely organic, but what had been the apothecaries' secrets were increasingly laid before medical students. The classical Dioscorides wrote in his manual of some 600 plants and their properties; between Islamic connections and New World discoveries, the 17th-century manual had 6,000. Paris began pharmaceutical lectures in 1538 and Montpellier around 1550, and the latter had a botanical garden by 1593. These gardens began in Padua, Italy, by Francesco Bonafide in 1545, spreading to Bologna (1568), Leiden (1577), and Paris (1591). Judged by some historians to be the most important innovation of the period, precepting or clinical education also had its roots in Italy. Before 1250, Emperor Frederick II required doctors trained at Salerno to have been apprenticed to a practicing physician. The requirement fell away until Giambattista da Monte and Francesco Frigimeliga began walking through San Francesco Hospital in Padua with their students. The practice was taken to Leiden by Jan van Heurne of Utrecht, whose son Otto regularized it at Caecilia Hospital by 1636.

In 1500, there were about 80 universities in Europe, but fully fledged medical schools were far fewer. Rome had added the Collegium Medicorum with a dozen professors in the 1460s, and Venice its prestigious University of Padua with 15 faculty members. England's first medical faculty appeared in 1423 and quickly disappeared, only to reappear in 1518. Henry VIII bolstered medical education with his humanistic Regius Professors of Physic, one each at Oxford and Cambridge. Paris and Montpellier remained the major French medical schools with three minor provincial programs among 15 universities. These were so tough that no degrees were conferred between 1500 and 1509, and only Avignon conferred degrees (nine) over the following decade. By 1665,

nine French medical schools were producing an average of 68 graduates per year, and in 1700, 19 French medical schools were licensed. Standards were lowered and innovation had stagnated—except in those German schools where Paracelsian chemical medicine was being taught. Much of the energy of the 17th-century medical schools was spent consolidating the changes of the 16th. But what of the advances in physiology (Harvey), technology (microscopy), theory (empiricism and scientific method) that were so vital to early modern science? That would be for the 18th century to digest.

See also: Anatomy and Dissection; Astrology; Galen and Galenism; Medical Education (1300–1500, Early Modern Europe) Medical Humanism; Paracelsus and Paracelsianism; Physicians; Scientific Revolution; Surgeons/Barbers; Vesalius, Andreas.

References

Brockliss, Laurence and Colin Jones. *The Medical World of Early Modern France.* New York: Oxford University Press, 1997.

Cohn, Samuel K. *Cultures of Plague: Medical Thinking at the End of the Renaissance.* New York: Oxford University Press, 2010.

O'Malley, C. D. *The History of Medical Education.* Berkeley: University of California Press, 1970.

Medical Humanism

A defining feature of the Renaissance was humanism. In natural philosophy and medicine, humanists sought to replace the West's medieval knowledge base founded on haphazardly recorded experience, Christian teachings, and classical writings filtered through Arab and Persian scholarship. They believed ancient Greeks and Romans possessed wisdom and experience superior to their own and that mastering them would advance their own theory and practice. Long the subject of medieval and Islamic commentaries, the medical giants Hippocrates and Galen, and lesser lights like the botanist Dioscorides, could be read directly thanks to widespread mastery of Greek and the printing press.

Around 1490, the movement to replace medieval Arab and scholastic medicine with its Hellenic (Greek) sources began at the University of Padua, Europe's premier medical school. Alessandro Benedetti had spent time in the Venetian Greek territories, and upon returning to Padua to teach in 1490, he railed against all but the pure classical Greeks. Niccolò Leoniceno, part of a pro–Hellenic circle at Ferrara, published *On the errors of Pliny* (1492) as a challenge to both direct observation and reliance on error-ridden derivative medical scholarship. He helped with the first Greek edition of Galen, his *Method of Healing*, in nearby Venice (1500). Venice's Aldine Press also published the first complete Greek editions of Galen (1525) and of Hippocrates (1526). English physician Thomas Linacre studied in Padua in 1492 and went on to translate Galen's *Method* into Latin, which underwent 30 printings from 1519 to 1598. Accurate and critical printed translations of Greek classics into elegant Latin were as important to the movement as expert and critical editions of Greek originals.

Though instrumental in reducing reliance on Aristotle and Avicenna and promoting experiential (clinical) education, medical botany, and anatomical studies, medical humanism contributed little of use in understanding or fighting plague. Some medical humanists, for example, Janus Cornarius of Marburg, wrote plague tracts, but none advanced the boundaries. One possible nexus, however, is with so-called civic humanism, rooted in the works of Romans Cicero, Cato, and Seneca. Its emphasis on a citizen's duty to community may have helped shape the new emphasis on public health found in Italian plague tracts of the 1570s.

See also: Anatomy and Dissection; Arabic-Persian Medicine and Practitioners; Galen and Galenism; Hippocrates and the Hippocratic Corpus; Medical Education (1500–1700, Early Modern Europe); Vesalius, Andreas.

References

Bylebyl, Jerome L. "The School of Padua: Humanistic Medicine in the Sixteenth Century," in *Health, Medicine, and Morality*, edited by Charles Webster (New York: Cambridge University Press, 1979), 335–370.

Nutton, Vivian. "Humanist Surgery," in *Medical Renaissance of the Sixteenth Century*, edited by Andrew Wear, et al. (New York: Cambridge University Press, 1985), 75–99.

Medicine and Islam. See **Islam and Medicine**

Merchants

By the mid-14th century, Jewish, Christian, and Muslim merchants were playing an indispensable role in circulating raw materials, finished products, and foodstuffs throughout Europe, North Africa, the Middle East, and beyond. Ships, barges, and caravans transported the goods of the great international merchants, while those with smaller horizons and capitalization ran urban shops, plied the roadways, or moved from one fair to another. Larger operators often diversified their activities by participating in such business as cloth production, retail sales, and banking, while trade on every scale was lubricated with such developments as insurance, bills of credit, *commenda* contracts, and more stable currencies. The major Tuscan figure Francesco Datini, who was orphaned in 1348 and survived five subsequent epidemics, belonged to numerous Florentine merchant guilds and had offices with partners in Prato, Florence, Genoa, Milan, Barcelona, Majorca, Avignon, and Bruges. Early capitalists, men like Datini reinvested their profits in further ventures, sometimes building great fortunes. Even when the businessmen stayed at home, their agents and cargoes moved far and wide.

Merchants and international trade played important roles in traditional explanations for the importation of plague into the West from Asia and then within the West. Scholars who attribute the origins of plague to China or eastern Central Asia usually hypothesize that it moved westward with trade caravans into the lands of the Golden Horde. Genoese and Venetian merchants supposedly underwent infection during a siege of their trading posts at Caffa. Fleeing, they brought pestilence with them into Constantinople, the Mediterranean, and Europe. Likewise, Muslim merchant seamen imported plague from Constantinople to Alexandria, Egypt, from which others spread it to the Middle East and westward across Africa. Though merchants were not the only ones to travel by ship—clerics, pilgrims, emissaries, soldiers, slaves, and refugees did so as well—merchants and their cargoes probably played the largest role in transmitting ship-borne plague.

Merchants suffered in numerous ways from the Black Death and subsequent outbreaks. They and their families were often victims, of course, but many, including Datini, fled as plague approached, leaving behind servants, partners, and much wealth in homes, shops, and warehouses. This usually meant spending money without a return and always presented the threat of thievery,

plunder, or destruction. Retail merchants often closed up shop, whether they fled or not, halting their income and depriving their customers of their wares. Civic officials were quick to associate plague's spread with commercial traffic and sought to control it accordingly. Long-distance merchants risked having cargoes delayed, fumigated, quarantined, or even destroyed while en route, and destination cities could simply turn the transports away from their docks or gates. Even a few carts or pack animals might bring the pest with them. Stocks of goods could sit in shops or warehouses for months as plague raged around.

In the wake of an epidemic, merchants tended to fare better than other occupations. Towns and cities often recovered rather quickly as men and women from smaller settlements and rural areas arrived to take advantage of higher wages. Prices of many goods rose as customers flocked to long-closed shops and markets. Surviving merchants also profited from prices inflated by the deaths of competitors, at least in the short run. At first in Italy and elsewhere over time well-heeled merchants bought up much of the agricultural property sold off by increasingly impoverished noble families and bishops. Freed from ancient feudal restrictions, merchants established multiyear contractual arrangements with laborers while providing land, seed, and equipment. This sharecropping—*mezzadria* in Italy—was the agricultural equivalent of the "putting out" system of production developing simultaneously in Europe. Ownership of land, long associated with the nobility, satisfied the social aspirations of many ambitious and wealthy middle-class merchants.

Despite adherence to the early capitalistic norm of continual reinvestment of capital, in wills, many wealthy merchants in Catholic countries invested in their salvation with generous gifts ranging from contributions to local charities to the establishment of great foundations. Some of these were related directly to needs exacerbated by plague, for example, hospitals and educational colleges to restock depleted teaching ranks. The childless Francesco Datini (d. 1410) set aside a tidy sum to establish an orphanage in Florence, the Ospedale degli Innocenti, and the bulk of his wealth funded a new foundation (Ceppo) for orphans and "castaway" children in his hometown of Prato. Perhaps spurred by fears of the anonymity of solitary death and mass graves and fearful of spiritual punishment for economic sins (profiteering, usury), Catholic merchants also invested in chapels, altars, altarpieces, fancy grave markers, memorial stained glass windows, and other intergenerational reminders of their earthly passage.

By the later 17th and 18th centuries, the control of long-range commerce by means of cordons sanitaires and quarantines, especially those that controlled traffic between Western Europe and the Muslim world—in ports and along the southern Austrian border—was so effective it may have stifled the importation of plague and ended the Second Pandemic. As with earlier efforts, these were met with resentment, bribery, and smuggling, but the authorities seem to have won out.

See also: Black Death: Origins and Early Spread; Caffa (Kaffa, Feodosiya), Ukraine; China; Cordons Sanitaires; Demographic and Economic Effects of Plague: the Islamic World; Flight; Guilds; Jews; Peasants; Quarantine; Servants, Household; Sin.

References

Bolton, James. The World Upside Down: Plague as an Agent of Economic and Social Change," in *The Black Death in England*, edited by M. Ormrod and P. G. Lindley (Stamford: Paul Watkins, 1996), 17–77.

Borsch, Stuart. *The Black Death in Egypt and England*. Austin: University of Texas Press, 2005.

Nightingale, Pamela. *A Medieval Mercantile Community: The Grocers' Company and the Politics and Trade of London, 1000–1485*. New Haven, CT: Yale University Press, 1995.

Udovitch, Abraham, Robert Lopez, and Henry Miskimin. "England to Egypt, 1350–1500: Long-term Trends and Long-distance Trade," in *Studies in the Economic History of the Middle East*, Vol. III, edited by M. Cook (New York: Oxford University Press, 1970), 93–128.

Mercuriale, Girolamo (1530–1606)

Girolamo Mercuriale was born in Forlì and was educated locally. He studied for his doctorate in philosophy and medicine in Venice, graduating in 1555. Mercuriale returned to Forlì, where he practiced medicine. In 1562, he entered the service of Cardinal Alessandro Farnese in Rome. The year 1569 saw Mercuriale's appointment to the chair of practical (humanist) medicine at Padua, which he held until 1587. He attended Emperor Maximilan II in Vienna in 1573, and when an epidemic re-emerged in Venice in 1576, he led several Paduan physicians to Venice to advise its health board, the Provveditori alla Sanità.

The Provveditori believed the relatively few plague-like deaths suffered into June 1576 were the plague that had struck Trent, Mantua, and Padua and had already killed more than 3,700 Venetians in 1575 and early 1576. On their authority, public health actions were undertaken, including isolation decrees, preparation of lazarettos, and transportation for victims. Mercuriale and his colleagues examined the sick and victims' records and concluded on June 7 that the illness was a malignant fever but not plague. They reasoned that both were symptomatically similar but that Venice's malady was restricted to the poor and produced very few victims. The Paduans advocated stopping all public health measures designed for plague, since thousands of residents were fleeing the city from fear. On June 10, the two sides debated before the Doge and other leaders, who accepted the Paduans' explanation. Preparations stopped and Mercuriale and his allies ostentatiously traveled about, meeting victims and seeking to assuage fears. But Mercuriale's star fell as corpses piled up from June into July. Local opinion turned on the arrogant Paduans, who were blamed for preventing important measures and spreading plague through their visitations. Typically pugnacious, Mercuriale responded that God had inspired their understanding and actions. He wrote an eight-page report defending his position that the epidemic was pestilential fever, not plague, and belatedly recommending fumigation and isolation.

To bolster his reputation, Mercuriale lectured on plague at Padua in early 1577 and immediately published his lectures as a 114-page book, *De pestilentia*.

See also: Health Boards, Magistracies, and Commissions; Medical Humanism; Physicians; Venice, Italy.

References

Nutton, Vivian. "With Benefit of Hindsight: Girolamo Mercuriale and Simone Simoni on Plague." *Medicina e Storia* 11 (2006): 5–19.

Palmer, Richard J. "Mercuriale and the Plague of Venice," in *Girolamo Mercuriale*, edited by Alessandro Arcangeli and Vivian Nutton (Florence: Olschki, 2008), 51–65.

Metaphors for Plague

Measures by a government against the occurrence or spread of a disease might be a military "campaign," "assault," or "defense." The disease itself may "attack," "invade," "outwit," "defeat," or "retreat." Such language is metaphorical and speaks to our attitude toward a pathogen and its effects: it is a type of enemy that "wages war" on our health and even lives. Similarly, the struggle could be a chess match or other sport or the onset of a storm. Famously, Homer had Achilles unleash an epidemic in the form of a torrent of arrows upon the Greek camp outside Troy. The visual symbol of the arrow remained associated with epidemic disease and, during the Second Pandemic, specifically with plague. Verbally, *arrow* played the same role, along with many other terms that referred to plague, and *plague* came to acquire many referents of its own.

Arabic poetry treated plague as a cup of poison, an invading army, a sword or arrow, a predatory animal, a bolt of lightning, or a suddenly striking snake. Al-Wardi of Syria, himself a victim, called it a lion, a silkworm, a storm, a king, and a murderous lover. For the Turkish chronicler Selaniki Mustafa Effendi (d.c. 1600), the disease was "fire" or "burning," possibly a reference to the attendant fever or to a cleansing effected by the disease in society. The burning created smoke, which was the sorrow felt by the survivors. Plague was also "the blessed," a personification who executes the divine will of Allah and invites an official to dine.

In Germany, plague was a red-scarved virgin, an "evil stepmother of the human race," a spectral, bluish flame that poisoned doors and windows as it flitted across a community. More than a mere metaphor, this highly visual image embodied very real fears. Plague was also an unhealed wound, a raging dog, poison itself, horsemen, a devouring cloud, a new deluge (flood of Noah's day), death itself, and, of course, an invading enemy. In Scandinavia, oral tradition personified plague as a headless man with a shovel astride a three-legged horse, a wheel of fire, a black cloud, or a boy and girl with a spade and rake. Many Christians treated it as a scourge (whip), a tool of divine punishment. Jacobean playwright Thomas Dekker labeled plague "a Tragedie" that was performed in the streets; yet it was a foreign disease, "a Spanish Leaguer, or rather like stalking Tamburlaine." Arrows having gone out of style, plague was a "cannon," "dart," or "bullet" aimed at the community. Later in the 17th century, Londoners spoke of plague's "visitation" as if some mad and bloodthirsty relative had stopped by to chat. In 1575, Venetians suffered from a terrible epidemic and referred to the city having lost its virginity and having become a "dirty whore" in the process.

In its turn, plague came to stand for those things that destroyed or brought sorrow, an archetypal disaster, especially wrought upon a community. It was "contagion" that turned good people into evil ones, and a plague, like heresy, that turned people from truth to death. Hell's association with the stench of brimstone carried over to the plague-stricken city's deadly miasma. Illness of the body became a metaphor for illness of the body politic: immorality, social imbalance, heresy. When Shakespeare's Mercutio famously curses "a plague o' both your houses," he is being equally descriptive of the "plague" that already affects the two. Catholics lamented the plague of Protestantism and Reformers condemned the plague of Papistry. Like plague, they reasoned, such movements were contagious, infectious, and lethal. On a more intimate level, plague was also individual moral failing and sickness and equally spiritually lethal. Caught from others via contagion or from the poisoned communal atmosphere—moral miasma—the spiritual corruption killed the soul, though plague killed only the body.

See also: Arrows; Dekker, Thomas; Miasma Theory; Morality Literature, Christian; Poetry, European; Poisoning and Plague Spreading; Sin.

References

Goodman, Ailene Sybil. "Explorations of a Baroque Motif: The Plague in Selected Seventeenth-century English and German Literature." Ph.D. dissertation, University of Maryland, 1981.

Gordon, Daniel. "Confrontations with the Plague in Eighteenth-century France," in *Dreadful Visitations*, edited by Alessa Johns (New York: Routledge, 1999), 3–30.

Healy, Margaret. *Fictions of Disease in Early Modern England: Bodies, Plagues and Politics.* New York: Palgrave, 2002.

Lindow, John. "Personification and Narrative Structure in Scandinavian Plague Legends." *Arv. Tidskrift för Nordisk Folksminnesforskning* 29/30 (1973/1974): 83–92.

Miasma Theory

When someone became ill, Hippocrates's followers blamed his or her diet, constitution, or accident, but when many became ill together, it had to be due to something all shared: the air. Air can have many things suspended in it, from dust and smoke to pleasant smells, and it is taken directly into the body. Bad smells stem from rotting, spoiled, or putrid things, and smells can bring on nausea. When Hippocrates blamed bad air—*miasma*—for epidemic disease, he was being commonsensical. Galen followed him in attributing widely spread diseases to the atmosphere, and the great Avicenna added support in his *Canon*, following such fellow Arabic thinkers as Al-Kindi (d.c. 870) and Al-Timimi (d. 990).

Arabic astrology helped explain how air became corrupted by positing celestial causes for miasma. By 1347, the picture had become more complex. Spanish physician Ibn Khatimah admitted the possibility of starry or planetary influences but noted that the "how" was missing. He proposed seasonal weather irregularities that drew up dangerous southern "vapors" and agreed that "putrid contamination" from great sources of stench—stagnant water, piles of unburied corpses (as after a battle or during an epidemic), human filth—could also corrupt air. Once corrupted, the air coated everything with its poison, permitting infection by contact. His Italian contemporary Gentile da Foligno blamed southern airs but also such local sources as vapors from long shut-up water wells, caves, ponds, animal corpses, and even long shut-up rooms. His German contemporary, Konrad von Megenberg, blamed earthquakes—and God who caused them. The earth enclosed poison gases that were released through cracks and corrupted air. Alfonso de Cordoba fell prey to contemporary poisoning libels: cosmic forces began the pestilence, he thought, but its prolongation was due to deliberate poisoning of food, air, and water by evil people. It took a non-physician to dismiss miasma theory based on his own experience of plague: Florentine chancellor Coluccio Salutati, who lost a slave and favorite son to pestilence. Whatever its weaknesses, miasma theory held the field until the 20th century.

Arabic-Persian medicine understood that once in the body, the poison created a humoral imbalance, with the excess humors being deposited in buboes. Christian physicians imagined it entered via lungs or pores, moved to the heart, and putrefied it, thus killing the victim. Humors played a role in maintaining one's level of resistance to the poison. By the 17th century, many pictured the miasma as a cloud of poisonous atoms that coated everything.

See also: Avicenna (Ibn Sina); Disinfection and Fumigation; Galen and Galenism; Gentile da Foligno; Hippocrates and the Hippocratic Corpus.

References

Arrizabalaga, Jon. "Facing the Black Death: Perceptions and Reactions of University Medical Practitioners," in *Practical Medicine from Salerno to the Black Death*, edited by Luis Garcia-Ballester, et al. (New York: Cambridge University Press, 1994): 237–288.

Cipolla, Carlo. *Miasmas and Disease: Public Health and the Environment in the Pre-industrial Age*. Translated by Elizabeth Potter. New Haven, CT: Yale University Press, 1992.

Dols, Michael W. *The Black Death in the Middle East*. Princeton, NJ: Princeton University Press, 1977.

Milan, Italy

The broad Lombard plain has long been dominated by Milan, as have important Alpine passes between Italy and Northern Europe. In the 14th century, it was an aggressive imperial city-state ruled by the Visconti dukes, one of the two or three largest Italian cities. It had grown wealthy through cross-alpine commerce and that which moved east and west through the Po Valley but also on such finished metalwork as weapons and armor.

Given its central position and high level of traffic, one would expect a catastrophe in 1348. In fact, Milan was but lightly brushed: Sienese chronicler Agnolo di Tura reported a mere three city families having been affected. The ducal government guarded every gate and screened every visitor, and when plague nonetheless appeared, the families were tightly sealed (shut in) in their homes. Similar prophylactic measures seem to have worked during the 1360 epidemic, but despite continued attention and experimentation, Milan suffered thereafter. Duke Giangaleazzo tried expelling all sick from subject Reggio in 1374, and extramural huts (*mansiones*) were provided to house victims, an early form of pest house. When plague approached the duchy in 1399, Milanese towns were cut off from contact with the capital; fairs and other gatherings were forbidden; victims and families were isolated in *mansiones*, and their houses fumigated. Later, hospitals were designated; victims were forcibly gathered and conveyed in carts. From 1424, a permanent ducal health commissioner oversaw this increasingly wide range of measures, including death registries with cause of death, from 1452. From 1468, Milanese authorities diagnosed each death and plotted geographic patterns, a century ahead of others.

The Villa at Cusago became a plague hospice in 1447 and, in 1451, a plague hospital that served many of the epidemic's 30,000 dead. During plague year 1468, authorities agreed to build a monumental lazaretto, San Gregorio, which was substantially completed two decades later, following the devastating epidemic of 1485. Following plagues in 1503 and 1523, it functioned fully in 1524. Truly dreadful but well chronicled plagues struck in 1576 to 1577 and 1629 to 1630, the latter brought by troops from the north. Archbishops Charles and Federigo Borromeo, uncle and nephew, actively led efforts to alleviate suffering. Charles built chapels and led processions, while Federigo did much the same and recorded his observations for posterity. Two centuries later, novelist Carlo Manzoni penned Italy's "national novel," in which the 1630 plague is a virtual character thwarting the protagonists. In 1629, San Gregorio hosted 10,000 plague victims and held another 15,000 at one time in 1630. From 1629 to 1636, Milan lost 60,000 of a population of 130,000.

See also: Borromeo, St. Charles (San Carlo); Borromeo, Federigo; Expulsion of Victims; Health Boards, Magistracies, and Commissions; *I promessi sposi*; Lazarettos and Pest Houses; Public Health; Shutting In.

References

Carmichael, Ann G. "Contagion Theory and Contagion Practice in Fifteenth-century Milan." *Renaissance Quarterly* 44 (1991): 213–256.

Carmichael, Ann G. "Epidemics and State Medicine in Fifteenth Century Milan," in *Practical Medicine from Salerno to the Black Death*, edited by Luis Garcia-Ballester, et al. (New York: Cambridge University Press, 1994), 221–247.

Cohn, Samuel K. *Cultures of Plague: Medical Thinking at the End of the Renaissance*. New York: Oxford University Press, 2010.

Giussano, Giovani Pietro. *The Life of St. Charles Borromeo, Cardinal Archbishop of Milan*. 2 vols. New York: Burns and Oates, 1884; facsimile edition of Vol. 1 by Bibliolife, 2010.

Pasi Testa, Antonia. "Alle origini dell'Ufficio di Sanità nel ducato di Milano e principato di Pavia." *Archivio storico lombardo* 102 (1976): 376–386.

Mongols

The Mongol peoples were united under Genghis Khan (Chinggis; c. 1167–1227) in the 13th century and created an empire that stretched from the western steppes to the Pacific Ocean. Mongols ruled China as the Yüan Dynasty to 1368 and established western khanates that organized central and western Asia under the great hordes. They reestablished direct contact between China and the Western states of Islam and Christendom along the famed Silk Road, bringing a *Pax Mongolica* (Mongolian peace) to the vast area.

Scene depicting the capture of a Chinese town by 13th-century Mongol leader Genghis Khan; from the 14th-century Persian manuscript *Jami al-Tavarikh*. The Mongols and their successors used brutal warfare to maintain their huge empire. (Corel)

the Crimea. Mongols controlled this area as well, in the form of the Golden Horde of the Kipchak Khanate. The story of the Mongol siege of Caffa is told elsewhere, but Schamiloglu believes the Horde as a whole lost 20 to 45 percent of its population from the 1330s over the next few decades. Just as China left a scant record of its troubles, so, too the Horde provides nothing definitive about the role of disease. It is clear, however, that the problems of Janibeg and his army metastasized, creating "great trouble" for the Golden Horde, its leadership, and military. Four western Turkic tribes—"cousins" of the Mongols—were devastated by the 1380s, leaving a vacuum for four tribes further east to migrate and settle as central authority disintegrated. One of the winners in this reshuffling was the Ottoman Turks of northeastern Anatolia, named for their leader Osman (d. 1326). This also allowed for the rise of the great Temur the Lame (Tamerlane; c. 1325?–1405), who carved out an empire stretching from Ankara to Moscow to Delhi to Damascus.

As Mongolian influence ebbed from its western frontiers, plague no doubt traveled to and through Mongol populations, but to date, records have not disclosed the details.

See also: Black Death: Origins and Early Spread; Caffa (Kaffa, Feodosiya), Ukraine; China; Issyk Kul, Kyrgystan.

References

Liu Xinru. *The Silk Road in World History.* New York: Oxford University Press, 2010.

McNeill, William. *Plagues and Peoples*. Garden City: Anchor Press, 1975.

Schamiloglu, Uli. "Preliminary Remarks on the Role of Disease in the History of the Golden Horde." *Central Asian Survey* 12 (1993): 447–457.

Schamiloglu, Uli. "The Rise of the Ottoman Empire: The Black Death in Medieval Anatolia

At least one and probably several foci of bubonic plague lay under the Mongols' control, and one or more of these were probably responsible for the Second Pandemic. A very recent genetic study appears to demonstrate that plague (*Yersinia pestis*) originated in China, and there is no reason that a reservoir would have relocated away from the region. Activity from this source may well have contributed to the disruption and chaos that led to the downfall of the Yüan a scant two decades after the Black Death began to the west. It also appears that a plague reservoir existed in the Black Sea region, in or near and Its Impact on Turkish Civilization," in *Views from the Edge*, edited by Neguin Yavari, et al. (New York: Columbia University Press, 2004), 255–279.

Monks, Nuns, and Monasteries

Both Orthodox and Roman Catholic churches support male and female monasticism. Since the third century, men and women have abandoned lay society to pursue lives of prayer and self-support, closed away physically and symbolically in the cloister. Western monks followed the Rule of St. Benedict or that of St. Augustine, while St. Basil's Rule dominated Eastern monasticism. Women were strictly cloistered, while men had greater freedom to travel about, but only on monastery or related business. Though monasteries lost the near monopolies they had centuries before in education and health care, most cared for their own sick, and some remained centers of scholarship by the 14th century. Such monastic rituals as last rites and funerary services shaped the layperson's sacrament of last anointing and funeral services, from tolling of bells and fumigation with incense to the apocalyptic hymn *Dies irae*.

Monastic infirmaries were models for early hospitals, and as freestanding hospitals began appearing in the West in the 11th century. They were often staffed by religious men and women, especially nuns, who also staffed many leprosaria. By the later 16th century, special orders of nuns dedicated to helping the sick began to emerge (e.g., in France Daughters of Charity, 1633; Sisters of St. Joseph, 1630; Sisters of Providence, 1656; and Sisters of Charity of Notre Dame, 1682). During the Second Pandemic, such dedicated Catholic men and women played a limited but expanding role in tending plague victims. During plague time, from

around 1500, large monasteries, for example, Florence's San Miniato and Barcelona's Angels vells, were commandeered to serve as pest houses to which victims were sent to recover or die. Resident religious could choose to remain or relocate. Protestantism, however, disavowed monasticism as unbiblical and un–Christian, relying on paid—if no less dedicated—hospital staff.

Monasteries tended to be better built, cleaner and more hygienic, and better supplied with food and medical supplies than typical residential situations. When plague broke out across Christendom in 1347 to 1352, however, religious suffered at least as consistently as other Europeans. At Barcelona's Santa Maria de Ribes, a single monk survived and elected himself abbot. Florence's Santa Maria degli Angeli lost 21 monks in 1348, with the remaining seven ill at year's end. Westminster Abbey lost half of its monks and its abbot; the isolated abbey of Newenham lost 20 of 23 Cistercians; Honiton in Devon 23 of 26; and Meaux's Cistercians lost 33 of 43 brothers, five having been buried on a single day in August. The nearly hermetic Carthusian Order normally lost about 100 brothers per year, but over 1348 to 1350, they lost 900; though Petrarch's brother Gherardo lived to bury all 34 of his fellows. Historian J. C. Russell estimated that overall, English monasteries lost 45.1 percent of their populations. Monastic records tend to be more trustworthy than most, since they had long been excellent record-keepers and annalists. Dozens of European monks kept notes on the Black Death, though monastic records rapidly drop off after 1350.

Monasteries suffered from declines in recruiting and financial support, in having to close shrunken monasteries, and in labor shortages and falling land values. The Muslim Al-Maqrizi noted that Christian monasteries around Natron in Egypt fell from more than 100 to seven; and not one new monastery or house of canons appeared in Ireland between 1348 and 1539. Benefactors shifted from monks to friars, many of whom were active among the sick and needful. Women were now expected to procreate rather than languish unfruitfully within the cloister. Abbots and abbesses sold off large portions of their estates that now had fewer inmates to support and fewer dedicated laborers to work them.

Some monastic communities did well, especially when gifted with chantries, thousands of masses, or colleges. Bishop Henry Chichele founded All Souls, Richard Fleming Lincoln College, and later Archbishop Simon Islip a college at Christchurch, all at Oxford. In Russia, early 15th-century rural monasteries burst into large-scale economic enterprises in the vacuum left by peasant deaths.

See also: Anticlericalism; Chronicles and Annals; Friars (Mendicants); Hospitals; Peasants.

References

Harvey, Barbara. *Living and Dying in England, 1100–1540: The Monastic Experience.* New York: Oxford University Press, 1993.

Langer, Lawrence. "Plague and the Russian Countryside: Monastic Estates in the Late Fourteenth and Fifteenth Centuries." *Canadian American Slavic Studies* 10 (1976): 351–368.

Mode, Peter. *The Influence of the Black Death on the English Monasteries.* Winasha, WI: George Banta; reprint LaVergne, TN: Kessinger Publishing, 1916/2009.

Platt, Colin. *King Death: The Black Death and its Aftermath in Late-medieval England.* Toronto: University of Toronto Press, 1996.

Moral Legislation

God unleashed plague as a punishment for sin. Throughout the Second Pandemic, Christians and Muslims understood divine displeasure to be the fundamental cause of this scourge, which killed the wicked and the seemingly good alike. Christian governments clearly believed that by clamping down on sinful behavior, both individually and as communities, God would be mollified and plagues would be less virulent or frequent or perhaps even cease.

Islamic Shariah law had strong moral components, especially regarding alcohol and sexual activity, but the idea that changes in behavior would affect the divine will was far less accepted among Muslims than Christians. Enforcement of Shariah was in any case desirable, but new laws were not, so most evidence suggests that Muslim authorities usually intensified compliance rather than creating novel statutes. An interesting exception was in Cairo in 1438, when the sultan became convinced that an epidemic was due specifically to illicit fornication and prostitution. He argued with his council but issued an edict forbidding all women, excepting old women and slaves, from entering the streets. The penalty was death, even though it meant they could not participate in public funerary activities. Commentator Ibn Taghri Birdi thought this both ineffective and immoral and noted that the sultan died soon after.

Governments in Christian-majority countries regularly passed laws against sexual sins and drunkenness, but also gambling, blaspheming, heresy, swearing, vagrancy, and even attending the theater. Such legislation was often prophylactic, meant to dissuade God from punishing the specific community, given that it was displaying repentance and a change to a more acceptable life. In Catholic cities, this was often accompanied by communal expressions of contrition and cries for mercy in the form of fasts, processions, vigils, or special masses. Protestant governments were less uniform in response, but fasts, prayer services, and sermons were common. A moral component also defined the relationship between religious majorities and minorities. Early on, "toleration" of Jewish subcommunities in Christian cities was defined as repugnant to God by anti–Semitic preachers, which led to violence and anti–Jewish legislation. This pattern was repeated in both Catholic and Protestant cities as toleration of the "other" was declared to be immoral and a source of God's anger. Religious minorities were disfranchised, forbidden to worship, or even expelled in the name of pleasing God. Expulsion followed the older custom of rousting prostitutes, homosexuals, heretics, drunks, gamblers, vagrants, and other public sinners.

Passage or enforcement of moral laws during an epidemic had a dual purpose. One was to convince God to lift the plague; the other was recognition that particular immoral acts helped physically spread plague. The drunk's disruptiveness, the prostitute's sexual promiscuity, the gamblers' or theater-goers' gatherings: all provoked concerns for public health as well as religious scruples.

By the mid-16th century (at least), governments were using plague-time moral legislation as a means of social control for its own sake. Increasingly, the plague was identified with the poor and poverty, and the poor and poverty with vice and immorality. Many Protestant states absorbed care for the poor from the Catholic authorities, blending plague prophylaxis with measures meant to keep the potentially dangerous lower classes in their places. For example, early slum clearance in London helped control "miasma" but also broke up tightly packed communities of the discontented. Catholic governments, too, reduced the role of Church authorities and organizations in supporting and controlling the "shameless" poor, and moral legislation was a common tool. In freer regions, critics responded that, if anything, the new, rougher handling of the powerless angered God more than their own misbehavior, and so it was the pitiless regimes that prompted divine wrath and plague.

See also: Anti–Semitism and Anti–Jewish Violence before the Black Death; Expulsion of Victims; Governments, Civil; Morality Literature, Christian; Poverty and Plague; Processions; Prostitutes; Public Sanitation; Sin; Sumptuary Laws.

References

Carmichael, Ann G. "Plague Legislation in the Italian Renaissance." *Bulletin of the History of Medicine* 57 (1983): 508–525.

Dols, Michael W. *The Black Death in the Middle East.* Princeton, NJ: Princeton University Press, 1977.

Slack, Paul. *The Impact of Plague in Tudor and Stuart England.* New York: Oxford University Press, 1990.

Morality Literature, Christian

Throughout the Second Plague Pandemic, Christian authors produced moral works that were meant to evoke from their readers a spiritual response, which would manifest itself in a change of habits and ways of life. Some of this was merely a matter of personally "putting away sin," while some was an exhortation to change society in line with Christian virtues. These works took many forms: poems, epigrams, sermons, dialogues, medical tracts, pamphlets, broadsheets, and letters. The appearance of this literature was spurred by growing popular literacy, the printing press, the confessional debates of the 16th century Reformation, and the growing self-reliance of literate people in religion and medicine.

Christianity has traditionally required both spiritual transformation and action that manifests the "new man." From the Gospels forward, these have been twin themes in moral literature. By the 14th century, the calls to do good, gain eternal life, and avoid damnation were typical topics in popular culture. Plague, however, reframed the issues. Unexpected death on an unprecedented scale was now quite real and not left to the end of time. The reasoning was that God's anger with sinful humankind was the ultimate cause of the plague. Sin was no longer merely a matter of one's own spiritual fate but of everyone's in this world as well. Even medical literature from the 14th century on recognized God's role in the plagues the writers sought to treat and often began by recommending amendment of life and preparation for death as a medical matter. Body and soul were inextricably intertwined until death separated them, so morality was as much a matter of body as soul.

Socially critical literature, for example, that by William Langland or the author of "Dives and Pauper: A Warning To Be Ware" is less direct in its approach. Such works often attack a single sin as the chief culprit: in the biblical Dives's case, it was his greed. This adds a dimension: not only does the sin of greed anger God, cause plague, and condemn Dives, but it also undermines society by forcing the pauper to live miserably. Like much moral literature, such stories served as mirrors into which the members of society were to look to see whether they had the same fate coming. More explicitly egalitarian were poems connected with such themes as the Three Living Meet the Three Dead and the Danse macabre. The three dead, putrefying corpses remind the three dandies "we were once what you are now; you will

soon be what we are now." In the Danse, popular in many languages well into the 16th century, skeletal Death takes away to the grave each unsuspecting character, from innocent child to pope. Every verse is a reminder of the debt owed by each to death, the timing of the payment known to Death alone. In the "Disputacion betwixt the Body and Worms" from the early 14th century, the lowly worms feeding on the decayed flesh explain Nature's case that all must die and all must eat.

The 16th-century Reformation created a new sense of personal commitment, responsibility, and guilt. From the Lutheran, Radical, or Calvinist view, individuals chose or rejected Christ and his true church. Collective sin (wicked monks or immoral clergy) was still seen to anger God and help cause plague, but individual sinfulness and need for repentance became a renewed theme. Klairmont claims that "most" French plague tracts of the era were outfitted with biblical references and calls to personal reform of life. Calvinism spurred this new sensibility but also begged the question, if plague is a matter of predestination, then of what use is medical intervention? Such works, along with German Lutheran sermons, were readily translated and sold among the English. Healy finds a trend among English literary works to treat disease in a more moralized, allegorized, and spiritualized manner especially from the 1550s. Miles Coverdale borrowed the German Osiander's 1534 sermon on whether to flee during plague time; the Augustinian Thomas Paynell took an earlier French tract and Englished it as "A Much Profitable Treatise against the Pestilence." In his *Haven of Health* (1584), Thomas Cogan emphasized that "fear of God" had to accompany the proper prophylactic diet, just as a temperate diet was itself a sign of godliness. Cogan was no preacher but a physician turned grammar school teacher. In 1531, Bristol's bishop Paul Bush produced *Certain ghostly [spiritual] medicines necessary to be used among well disposed people to eschew and avoid the common plague of pestilence.* "Recipes" for plague nostrums appearing in broadsides called for such ingredients as faith, hope, and charity, and penance applied to the affected spirit.

The focus shifted from about 1590 in London from exhortations to individual moral rectitude to collective responsibility and action. William Muggins addressed "you heads of London's City" in *London's Mourning Garment* (1603) to eschew vice and embrace reform for the city's good. Homilies printed by James Godskall in 1603 presented an "Arke of Noah" in which London survivors could still find refuge and safety; and a set of plague recipes that remedied soul and body. Calvinist Thomas Dekker also published several famous tracts addressed to Londoners that were matters of social criticism (official corruption, middle-class greed, working class laziness) as well as moral exhortations to repentance.

Finally, moralists from Spain to Germany began to rail against the moral failings of the poor. In his "Dialogue," Englishman William Bullein condemned the "sluttish, beastly people that keep their houses and lodgings unclean," linking filth with both moral failing and physical disease. Plague epidemics seemed to begin among the poor and to strike them the hardest, so reformers, moralists, and officials alike preached better habits and the abandonment of overcrowded tenements, gambling, prostitution, and the other vices of the poor.

See also: Broadsheets, Broadsides, and Pamphlets; Consilia and Plague Tracts; *Danse Macabre*; Dekker, Thomas; Langland, William; Poetry, European; Poverty and Plague; Reformation and Protestantism; Sin; "Three Living Meet the Three Dead."

References

Byrne, Joseph P. *The Black Death.* Westport, CT: Greenwood, 2004.

Healy, Margaret. "Discourses of the Plague in Early Modern London," in *Epidemic Disease in London*, edited by J. A. I. Champion (London: Centre for Metropolitan History Working Papers Series 1, 1993), 19–34.

Klairmont, A. "The Problem of the Plague: New Challenges to Healing in Sixteenth-century France." *Proceedings of the Annual Meeting of the Western Society of French History* (1977): 119–127.

Morbidity, Mortality, and Virulence

When epidemiologists study the effect of a disease on a human population, they are interested in a wide range of factors relating to the disease agent or pathogen; to its carrier; to the human population exposed to the pathogen; and to the environment in which the population is living. Morbidity and mortality are measures—usually expressed in rates or percentages—of the disease's effects on the population. Morbidity measures the occurrence of the disease and mortality the occurrence of death related specifically to the disease. There are several ways of defining each, depending upon the questions the researcher asks.

The incidence of a disease is the number of people in the population or a portion of it (children, clergy, whites) who become clinically ill with the disease *for the first time* (new cases) during some specific period of time divided by the number in the population *or portion* during the same time who were at risk for the disease. A related measure is prevalence, which is the *total* number of cases of the disease at a given point or over a specific time period divided by the total population. Today, morbidity rates are usually expressed as cases per 100,000 since the populations tend to be so large and the number of cases of a given disease so small. Premodern data on plague are usually expressed in percentages.

Mortality is the measure of the number in the population who die of *all causes* divided by the number in the population. As with other rates, the numerator and denominator must measure the same kind of population. In other words, the denominator must include only those who were susceptible to the disease. For many diseases, only a portion of the population is susceptible or of interest to the researchers (women, coal miners), and the denominator must include only those people. With historic plague, for which there were no long-term immunity or other known resistance factors, the population is in fact the total population. Plague mortality, then, is the number of plague deaths divided by the entire population over some period of time. A related and important but different term is *case fatality rate*, which is the number of deaths divided by the number of cases of the disease reported. Such numbers are almost impossible to obtain during the Second Pandemic, since notice was recorded when people died and were buried. The one locale where such data were recorded and some survived was plague hospitals and pest houses, especially in Italy. The assumption was that those recorded being brought in were suffering from plague—though that was not the case and officials knew it—and therefore those who needed burial were all plague victims. The resulting figure is an indication of the disease's lethality. Yet the number of variables affecting this number was large: the extent of overcrowding in the facility; the level of care provided; the degree of hygiene maintained; the time of year; and so on.

Virulence is related directly to the pathogen rather than to the population affected. It is a descriptive term indicating the ability of a pathogen to produce a disease and can be indicative of either morbidity or mortality. A "highly virulent" pathogen may cause a low (or high) morbidity rate with a high case fatality rate, meaning that those who get the disease have a good chance of dying; virulence can be a matter of lethality. High virulence might also mean a large number of cases of the disease with few or with many resulting deaths, meaning that the population is highly susceptible to contracting the disease; virulence may not be a measure of lethality.

Morbidity on any meaningful level is impossible to measure during any Second Pandemic epidemic because there was either no or inconsistent and unreliable reporting and recording of cases of illness across a given population. The closest might be a convent or monastery that tended its own sick and was able to distinguish plague from other diseases. On the other hand, scholars produce many mortality figures: from those taken directly from chronicles and other contemporary documents to carefully reconstructed numerical pictures drawn from various types of records and statistically reapplied across a population. Of course, all of these records and extrapolations have their problems, many of which are discussed elsewhere in this volume. Our current tools of statistics gathering and our expectations from them are modern, though with roots in the 17th century. As with other attempts to use modern tools with historical phenomena, the result is often frustrating.

Finally, case fatality rates and virulence in general are of interest because virulence in general seems to drop off immediately after the Black Death despite recurrences roughly once a decade. One reads repeatedly of children dying in high proportions in the later 14th century. By the 16th century, intervals between episodes in a given place were getting longer. By the later 17th century, the disease was disappearing from Europe altogether. To what extent might these changes have been due to changes in the nature of the pathogen? Might its virulence have weakened to allow for greater survival of the pathogen? If pathogens are too lethal and kill off their hosts, then they do not last long.

See also: Bills of Mortality; Chronicles and Annals; Demographic and Economic Effects of Plague: the Islamic World; Demographic Effects of Plague: Europe 1347–1400; Demographic Effects of Plague: Europe 1400–1500; Demographic Effects of Plague: Europe 1500–1770; Demography; Epidemic and Pandemic; Social Construction of Disease; Virgin Soil Disease.

References

Benedictow, Ole. *The Black Death 1346–1353: The Complete History.* Rochester, NY: Boydell & Brewer, 2004.

Christakos, George, et al. *Interdisciplinary Public Health Reasoning and Epistemic Modeling: The Case of the Black Death.* New York: Springer, 2005.

Moscow, Russia

In the 14th century, the Grand Duchy of Muscovy was beginning its rise to control the core of the future Russian state. The merchant centers of Pskov and Novgorod to the north and west, with their closer proximity to the Baltic Sea, were weakened by the recurrent plagues that began in 1352. Russian chronicles describe the same disease the West had suffered earlier—three days of intense pain, the coughing of blood, and nearly inevitable death—and the crowded churches and cemeteries that resulted. Novgorod's Orthodox bishop traveled west to lead processions in Pskov but soon died of the disease. It seems to have moved eastward from Poland and from Pskov to Novgorod, further east. From there, the plague turned southward along well-traveled trade and communication routes. Moscow tasted the bitter cup in 1353, losing its Grand Prince Semen Ivanovich, his two sons, and his brother Andrei. Moscow's bishop, the Metropolitan Feognost, may have also died of plague. The Muscovite aristocracy suffered terrible losses, seriously weakening its ascendancy.

Pskov and Novgorod were repeatedly stricken beginning in 1360 (1363–1365, 1387–1390, 1403, 1406–1407, 1414, 1417, 1419–1420 and so on). Thereafter, the intervals widened. Novgorod recorded claims of cannibalism in 1421 to 1424 as plague joined with famine, and 15,396 registered burials over two years of plague in 1507 to 1508. Expelling the sick and foreign and shutting their gates after them seemed their only recourse. Moscow was able to avoid the plague much more successfully, suffering only in 1365 to 1370, 1425, 1570 to 1571 (a major epidemic joined by a Tatar siege producing a reported 250,000 dead), 1654 to 1655, and the great epidemic of 1770 to 1772. The huge distances involved certainly helped insulate the growing city, but from the 16th century, records show Moscow's officials utilized such Western prophylactic tools as expulsion, restricted entry, isolation, and military cordons and organized these into national plague orders. Once the disease got inside, however, there was very little done other than flight and prayer.

By the mid-18th century, under the German Tsarina Catherine the Great, the enlightened ways of the West had penetrated further, but Russia still relied solely on prophylaxis. Moscow had about one physician for every 10,000 people; most of its protection depended on military sealing of the western and southern borders, along which epidemic plague recurred at least every eight years. In 1770, this was breached along a front with Turkey, and Moscow paid the price as military maneuvers brought plague to the interior. The earliest deaths were recorded in November 1770, but there was disagreement about their cause. Imperial and commercial interests wanted desperately to avoid the steps dictated by a decree of plague, for example, travel bans, trade restrictions, quarantines, and limitations on religious services, as well as such reactions as flight, hoarding, and avoidance of the city of 250,000.

For foreign consumption, the state press denied the epidemic even as it raged through the city in 1771; even such foreign diplomats as the British Ambassador took the same line. Meanwhile, by the summer of 1771, half the population had died or fled, leaving a city of mostly servants behind. Medical officers, including the French director of the city's orphanage, Charles De Mertens, worked closely with authorities to battle the plague, but all believed the disease to be miasmic, which limited their responses. In September 1771, thousands of frightened and frustrated members of the lower classes rioted over rumors of state actions, including the removal of an important religious icon. Tensions and confrontations lasted more than three weeks. Leaders demanded church burials, opening of public baths, and pardons, among other things, and matters reached a crescendo between September 15 and 17. Leaders were executed, 78 rioters were killed by soldiers, and hundreds were jailed. Nonetheless, as a result, quarantine conditions improved, baths were opened, 6,000 houses were fumigated, and Catherine established a Commission for the Prevention and Treatment of the Pestilential Infectious Distemper (still not "Plague"), which included merchants and clergy. The experience led to closer care of the frontier cordon and to the first partition of Poland between opportunistic Prussia and Austria and a sorely wounded Russia.

See also: Armies; Cordons Sanitaires; De Mertens, Charles; Miasma Theory; Quarantine.

References

Alef, Gustave. "The Crisis of the Muscovite Aristocracy: A Factor in the Growth of Monarchical Power." *Forschungen zur osteuropäischen Geschichte* 15 (1970): 15–58; reprinted in his *Rulers and Nobles in Fifteenth-century Muscovy* (London: Variorum) same pagination.

Alexander, John T. *Bubonic Plague in Early Modern Russia: Public Health and Urban Disaster.* Baltimore, MD: Johns Hopkins University Press, 1980.

De Mertens, Charles. *Account of the Plague Which Raged at Moscow 1771.* London: 1799. Newtonville, MA: Oriental Research Partners, 1977. Facsimile.

Dolgova, S. R. "Notes of an Eyewitness of the Plague Riot in Moscow in 1771." *Soviet Studies in History* 25 (1987): 79–90.

Kowal, Areta O. "Danilo Samoilowitz: An Eighteenth-century Ukrainian Epidemiologist and his Role in the Moscow Plague (1770–72)." *Journal of the History of Medicine and Allied Sciences* 27 (1972): 434–446.

Prokhorov, M. F. "The Moscow Uprising of September 1771." *Soviet Studies in History* 25 (1987): 44–78.

Muhammad the Prophet (570–632)

Muhammad was born into the mercantile-class Banu Hashim family within the powerful

Q'raysh clan in Mecca in the Hijaz region of the Arabian Peninsula. He married the wealthy and older Khadija, who managed a thriving caravan enterprise. In 610, Muhammad began receiving divine revelations via the Angel Gabriel regarding the reform of the monotheistic religions of Judaism and Christianity. Eventually, these were collected into the *Quran*, or *Recitation*. The reformed religion of the one God, Allah (God), would replace the supposedly corrupted Bible with the *Quran* and accept Muhammad as the final and greatest of prophets. Adherents were to submit to the will of Allah as preached by the Prophet and in the Quran, and so the true religion was named Islam, or Submission to God. Muhammad's small movement left Mecca for Medina in 622 (the Hijra), where Muhammad served as social and religious reformer and political leader. Once hostile and polytheistic Mecca submitted to Muhammad and his fiercely monotheistic movement in 630, it became the focal point of the Hajj, the pilgrimage required of all Muslims, or followers of Islam.

Muhammad wrote nothing, so his life and teachings were recorded in literary collections known as Hadith. As he lived during the Plague of Justinian, he provided his followers with several specific teachings regarding plague as well as much about health and sickness in general. This, as well as Arabian tradition, Quranic teaching, and commentary on all three, formed the basis of "Prophetic Medicine" (*al-tibb al-nabawi*). More theological than medicinal in the Greek sense, the tradition produced two compendia in the 14th century, by the theologians Ibn Qayyim al-Jawzziya (d. 1350) and Shams al-Din al-Dhahabi (d. 1348), both of whom were students of Ibn Taymiyah (d.1318), who directly opposed Greek rationalistic medicine with that of the Prophet. During the Second Pandemic, numerous physicians and theologians produced plague tracts based on prophetic medicine.

At root, Muhammad had three principal teachings regarding plague. First, it is Allah's direct intervention in the lives of individuals. For the faithful Muslim, it is a mercy, since he or she will enter Paradise as a martyr. For the infidel, plague is punishment for faithlessness and sin; he or she is damned and, thus, the punishment is just. Second, since plague is directed by Allah alone, there is no contagion or random infection. And third, one should neither enter into nor seek to leave a place stricken by plague. Since he denied contagion, this could only mean that to do so would be an inadvisable challenge to Allah.

See also: Allah; Consilia and Plague Tracts; Contagion Theory; Islam and Medicine; Islamic Religious Responses; Mecca.

References

Conrad, Laurence I. "Epidemic Disease in Formal and Popular Thought in Early Islamic Society," in *Epidemics and Ideas*, edited by Ranger and Slack (Cambridge: Cambridge University Press, 1992), 77–99.

Ibn Qayyim al-Jawziyya. *Medicine of the Prophet*. Translated by Penelope Johnstone. Cambridge: Islamic Texts Society, 1998.

Pormann, Peter E. and Emilie Savage-Smith. *Medieval Islamic Medicine*. Washington, DC: Georgetown University Press, 2007.

N

Naples, Italy

The ancient Greek colony of Neapolis grew into Italy's greatest port city. Throughout the Second Pandemic, however, it remained in Spanish hands as the capital of the Kingdom of Naples, or simply Il Regno. Though the large Kingdom was relatively underdeveloped and poor, the colonial capital boasted a flourishing aristocracy and well-patronized church. Its government was, however, for much of the period, a colonial government, which meant that much decision making was delayed and ultimately in favor of the distant rulers rather than the inhabitants.

In May or June 1348, plague appeared in the city and savaged it. Subsequent records are somewhat sketchy, but it returned in at least 1349, 1382, 1400, 1422, 1428, 1456, 1458, 1478, 1481, 1493, 1495 to 1497, 1504, 1522, 1526 to 1529, and 1575. By comparison with the increasing levels of organization and infrastructure in the major cities of northern Italy, Naples was quite backward; the same is true of comparisons with such major Spanish centers as Seville and Barcelona. State action was all but unknown, and what little existed was reactionary rather than preventive. In 1587, the Brothers Hospitaller of Saint John of God built the lazaretto connected to Sta. Maria della Pace in the form of a great hall 30 by 180 feet and, for good ventilation, a frescoed ceiling 36 feet from the floor.

Major epidemics occurred in 1624 and 1646, and Naples's final and most deadly attack of plague occurred in 1656 to 1657. In 1652, northern Italian cities had created a network that pledged early warning and joint action against commerce or communication with plague-stricken areas, and they wanted Naples (and Rome) to join. Naples could not promise to act against Spain's interests and stayed out. Four years later, the slaughter began. Lacking adequate facilities as an average of more than 1,000 died daily between May and August, the authorities—which included the Viceroy Garcia de Avellaneda y Haro, count of Castrillo, and a venal two-man health magistracy—decreed that the sick were to remain shut up in their homes with their households under pain of death. Public health measures failing, the devoutly Catholic officials tried exposition of holy relics, processions, and vows to patronize paintings of plague saints to soften God's wrath. Galley slaves buried the dead and clergy died dutifully bringing the sacraments to the suffering. Four hundred of 600 Neapolitan Dominicans died, as did most of the 160 Franciscans and 190 Capuchins in the city. In the end, an estimated half of the city of 300,000 perished.

See also: Art, Effects of Plague on; Ex voto; Plague Saints; Processions; St. Januarius (San Gennaro); Shutting In.

References

Clifton, James. "Art and Plague at Naples," in *Hope and Healing: Painting in Italy in a Time of Plague, 1500–1800*, edited by Gauvin Alexander Bailey (Chicago: University of Chicago Press, 2005), 97–117.

Gentilcore, David. "Cradle of Saints and Useful Institutions: Health Care and Poor Relief in the Kingdom of Naples," in *Health Care and Poor Relief in Counter-Reformation Europe*,

Plague in Naples, by Micco Spadara, 1656. This painting makes clear the devastation the plague caused in this major Italian port. (Courtesy of the National Library of Medicine)

edited by Ole Grell, Jon Arrizabalaga, and Andrew Cunningham (New York: Routledge, 1999), 131–150.

Lopez, Pasquale. *Napoli e la peste, 1464–1530*. Naples: Jovene Editore, San Juan, 1989.

San Juan, Rose Marie "Corruptible Bodies and Contaminating Technologies: Jesuit Devotional Print and the 1656 Plague in Naples," in *Imagining Contagion in Early Modern Europe*, edited by Claire L. Carlin (New York: Palgrave Macmillan, 2005), 107–123.

Narwhal/Unicorn Horn Powder

Pulverized unicorn horn was claimed to be a common component in pricier potions prepared to combat plague. Its effectiveness was guaranteed by its antiquity as a medicine and by its presumed purity in counteracting poison. Only a virgin, it was said, could approach the mythical animal, which figures prominently in medieval art and literature. Simon Kellaway wrote in 1593 that half a dram mixed with half a dram of angelica root would expel plague poison and promote sweat. He also insisted on its purity. To test it, he made a circle of the powder and placed a spider in it; if the spider remained still—charmed—the powder was potent. Contemporary French physician Ambroise Paré also conducted experiments, claiming success against spider, toad, and scorpion venoms. A half-century later, scientist Athanasius Kircher admired its "efficacy and admirable virtue" but believed it the product of a horned fish (narwhal) rather than a unicorn.

See also: Apothecaries; Remedies, Internal.

Reference

Wilson, F. P. *Plague in Shakespeare's London.* New York: Oxford University Press, 1999.

Nashe, Thomas (1567–1601)

Thomas was born to the local curate in Lowestoft, Suffolk. The family later moved near Thetford, and Thomas attended St. John's College, Cambridge, with financial aid. He graduated with a bachelor's degree in 1586, quickly proceeding to London to make his way in the world of letters. He became a critic and pamphleteer involved in several of the day's major literary issues.

Plague in 1593 brought out Nashe's sense of human impotence in the face of God's wrath. Yet he seems to have felt all lives are tragic, and grace through faith and repentance alone can save one. Like others, he raised this to a social level, blaming the plague on such of London's collective sins as immorality by all classes and the wealthy's inhumane treatment of servants and the poor. Though no Puritan, his works often sound the same note. In 1593, he fled London and produced "Unfortunate Traveler," in which he shifted the scene to Papal Rome, and "Christ's Tears over Jerusalem." His sole play, an allegorical comedy that is a forerunner to Jacobean masques in form, was also first performed in 1593. "Summer's Last Will and Testament" on the surface treats the passage of time from one season to the next, but the context of one's own passage through plague from life to death underlies the work. Its most famous portion, the poem "Litany in Time of Plague," often appears alone in anthologies. Published in 1600, the last lines appear on at least one popular broadside of the day:

> None from his darts can fly;
> I am sick I must die:
> Lord have mercy on us!

The final line was the very text painted on the front doors of London houses whose inhabitants were suffering from plague.

See also: London, England; Morality Literature, Christian; Poetry, European.

References

Brown, Georgia, editor. *Thomas Nashe.* Burlington, VT: Ashgate, 2011.

Nashe, Thomas. *The Unfortunate Traveler and Other Works.* Edited by J. B. Steane. Harmondsworth: Penguin, 1972.

Nobility

The landed aristocracy in Europe and the Islamic world's rulers were far from immune to the slaughter of the waves of plague that constituted the Second Plague Pandemic. Their diet was richer, their houses often built of stone and tile rather than thatch, and their access to medical care better than those of the commoners, but they were just as likely to die from the fleabite as anyone.

The noble's real advantage was mobility. Over each generation, the aristocratic classes had the ability to follow the ancient advice to flee quickly and far and stay away. They often possessed multiple residences, and servants and retainers were used to absences the family would take for all sorts of reasons. The well off could also benefit from the hospitality of friends and family in areas through which the plague had passed or that seemed out of its path. Royalty regularly set the tone by removing court when the pestilence approached. Plague attacked Dijon, Burgundy, in 1414. The duchess retired to Auxonne, leaving orders that no one from Dijon "should presume to come" to Auxonne since she and her children were there to escape the pestilence. Henry VIII was especially prone to run with court in tow. Coronations, for example, those of England's Elizabeth and James I, were postponed for as long as six months with the guest of honor on the lam; and Charles II rewarded with inscribed silver plate the noble servants who remained behind during London's Great Plague—while the king was away, of course.

As monarchs developed their courts and bureaucracies, nobles often played key roles as administrators. This was especially true in Spain and Spanish Naples, where nobles had direct control over cities or regions when epidemics blazed. The supposed natural qualities of these men and the acquired judgment and leadership skills often put them in good stead with both the rulers and the leaders of communities affected. Some even had knowledge of medicine, which was not even beneath a king. In the *Weisskunig*, written for Emperor Maximilian I in the early 16th century, the young ruler is told medicine is usefully studied for healing souls, as an antidote to sorcerers, to help him maintain a proper diet and therefore health, and as a tool against poisoning and illness. The last would, of course, have included plague. At the end of the century, Emperor Rudolf II in Prague supported alchemists who promised him the secret of making gold, which he wanted less for its monetary value than as an antidote to the plague. Obtaining the so-called philosopher's stone would have been a public boon, since he could cure or prevent all cases of pestilence. Aristocratic women across Europe took healthcare seriously, tending to their own extended families as well as aiding the servants and villagers as a matter of noblesse oblige.

In the 14th century, nobles often suffered heavily from the economic and social effects of the recurring plague. Their status, wealth, and power rested in their lands, and these needed people laboring on them to make them productive. During and after the epidemics, people fled their villages: some out of the supposed path of the epidemic, others to the nearest large city that would need fresh infusions of labor, both men and women, and still others rejoined family in distant villages. The rural economy had been contracting for decades by the 1340s, and the plagues exacerbated the situation. Dislocations of people and redistributions of wealth through deaths in general meant fewer hands on the land, and the necessary abandonment of land that was marginal. Landlords, especially the larger ones, saw their rents from productive land drop, as they had to negotiate with workers. They sold off where and what they could to a growing class of independent farmers or to merchants who sought diversification or the cachet that went with land. Feudal seigneurship was increasingly replaced with cash relationships and rents. These transformations were far from uniform across the map: while England fostered the yeoman farmers, Eastern Europe witnessed a retrenchment of the landed nobility, who imposed new and more stringent terms on the peasant classes.

Finally, the upper classes had traditionally lived through their bloodlines. The suddenness of death, its ability to eliminate a bloodline in a week or two, and the threat of the mass grave made aristocrats especially conscious of memorialization through funerary rituals and monuments. Johan Huizinga's classic study of the 14th and 15th centuries, *The Waning of the Middle Ages*, highlighted the cult of the individual as people faced death and expressed this in extravagant tomb sculpture and other forms of display.

In Islamic Egypt before 1517, the nobles or aristocracy were the Mamluks, slaves from the Black Sea region whose civil and military roles were repaid with *iqtas*, grants of supposedly productive land with the people who worked the land. These changed hands with the holder's death, and in 1430, one such had nine holders over just a few days. The landlords never had dynastic claims, nor did they set down roots or invest much, which, along with the large numbers of plague deaths in the class, meant that the *iqtas* and the infrastructure that sustained them were left to decay. This process only ended with the Ottoman victory.

See also: Art, Effects of Plague on; Demographic and Economic Effects of Plague: the Islamic World; Feudalism and Manorialism; Flight; Henry VIII, King of England; Individualism and Individual Liberties; James I and VI Stuart, King; Peasants; Plague Orders and National Authorities; Transi Tombs; Women Medical Practitioners; Wills and Testaments.

References

Alef, Gustave. "The Crisis of the Muscovite Aristocracy: A Factor in the Growth of Monarchical Power." *Forschungen zur osteuropäischen Geschichte* 15 (1970) 15–58; reprinted in his *Rulers and Nobles in Fifteenth-century Muscovy*, London: Variorum, 1983.

Bavel, Bas van. *Manors and Markets: Economy and Society in the Low Countries, 500–1600*. New York: Oxford University Press, 2010.

Borsch, Stuart. *The Black Death in Egypt and England*. Austin: University of Texas Press, 2005.

Christensen, Daniel. *Politics and the Plague in Early Modern Germany: Political Efforts to Combat Epidemics in the Duchy of Braunschweig-Wolffenbüttel during the Seventeenth Century.* Saarbrücken: Verlag Dr. Müller, 2008.

Cohn, Samuel K. *The Cult of Remembrance and the Black Death*. Baltimore, MD: The Johns Hopkins University Press, 1992.

Kelly, Maria. *A History of the Black Death in Ireland*. Stroud, Gloucs, England: Tempus, 2001.

Platt, Colin. *King Death: The Black Death and its Aftermath in Late-medieval England*. Toronto: University of Toronto Press, 1996.

Notaries

The notary was the nexus of most continental medieval legal systems and the public. While lawyers were the university-trained legal experts whose advice was eagerly sought and dearly bought, the notary was the workhorse who produced the day-to-day legal documents that lubricated urban communities. Their tradition was rooted in ancient Roman law and never quite died out in the Mediterranean region. Their importance grew with the revival of Roman law and urban life in the 11th and 12th centuries. Notaries generally trained under master notaries and utilized guides to legal forms, for example, the *Ars notariis*. Notaries had their own guilds or were subordinated to lawyers or judges in theirs. They served guilds, foundations, and Church and civil authorities as record-keepers, letter writers, and archivists, and often maintained urban chronicles or annals of important events. They served the general public by recording business contracts, marriage arrangements, gifts *inter vivos*, and wills, and often moonlighted as Latin teachers or copyists before the printing press.

When plague struck a city, the services of the notary became vital. An important part of one's good death, throughout the Second Pandemic, was to provide for one's family—and, in Catholic regions, for one's soul—through the preparation of a last will and testament. This involved the physical presence of several witnesses, often a clergyman, and a notary who recorded the instructions of the testator. In normal times, this could take place in one's home, a church, a mendicant convent, or a monastery. Often, wills were dictated or updated while on one's deathbed. During an epidemic, notaries were often at the bedside along with the physician, clergyman, and often an apothecary, all of whom exposed themselves to the deadly bacterium. In Bologna in 1348, some 200 notaries remained to record wills, though only a few did the bulk of the work. In July, 185 notaries filed these documents, but in August, the number dropped to 89. Some no doubt fled, others died, and still others refused to risk contagion. In Orvieto, two dozen died, leaving a mere seven to carry on when plague had passed. Siena's archive contains only one notarial record-book that spans the 1348 epidemic period, and the Sienese government allowed clergy to act as notaries. Perpignan lost 58 percent of its 117 legal professionals, and the French royal court one third. Toulouse licensed 97 new notaries in the fall of 1348 and another 108 in 1349. Similar patterns of notarial losses appear in guild lists and other records throughout the Second Pandemic, though percentages fell as overall death tolls fell. In Italy, at least, later legal experts and civic authorities reduced the burden on notaries by decreasing the number of required witnesses—which often included other notaries—or allowing women to serve as witnesses; granting the right to hear dictation through a doorway or window; and allowing will making without a notary but with witnesses and a priest.

Notaries also played key roles in civic governments and later health magistracies and boards. During the plague of 1630 to 1631 in the well-organized Grand Duchy of Tuscany, notaries (along with armed guards) accompanied the all-powerful commissioners-general who ensured that public health laws were being observed and enforced. Some notaries took up the task of recording events during plagues in chronicles or annals. Much of the early material from Italy, however, is second-hand or official. Samuel Cohn notes that only from 1576 do Italian notaries record their own experiences of plague for posterity. The broadening of literacy and the growth of centralized bureaucracies limited the roles and the importance of the roles notaries played during and after the 16th century.

See also: *Ars moriendi (The Art of Dying)*; Chronicles and Annals; Guilds; Health Boards, Magistracies, and Commissions; Wills and Testaments.

References

Cohn, Samuel K. *The Cult of Remembrance and the Black Death.* Baltimore, MD: The Johns Hopkins University Press, 1992.

Reyerson, Kathryn L. "Changes in Testamentary Practice at Montpellier on the Eve of the Black Death." *Church History* 47 (1978): 253–269.

Smail, Daniel Lord. "Accommodating Plague in Medieval Marseille." *Continuity and Change* 11 (1996): 11–41.

Wray, Shona Kelly. *Communities and Crisis: Bologna during the Black Death.* Boston: Brill, 2009.

Nurses

Historically, nurses may be identified as medical personnel who directly tended the daily needs of the sick. In Catholic settings, such institutions as hospitals, hostels, leprosaria, and pest houses were staffed with unmarried women—lay or nuns—who dedicated their lives to the charitable activity of nursing. In communities, certain women were skilled in healing arts and tending the dying and were called upon when needed. Some aided "professional" physicians, surgeons, and apothecaries by changing bandages, administering medicines, and collecting urine. Such skills and knowledge as "attendants," "helpers," "assistants," or "comforters" possessed came experientially and informally, as nurses had neither schools nor guilds.

During the Second Pandemic, numerous orders of Catholic nursing nuns sprang up, their members staffing plague facilities, augmenting the efforts of doctors and surgeons. As professed religious women, they also provided spiritual comfort. Rome's Oblates of Mary (1425) was the first order of uncloistered nuns whose members could work directly with the sick in the streets and in their homes. Spurred by later 16th-century Catholic Reform and examples of such saints as Catherine of Siena, Catherine of Genoa,

Charles Borromeo of Milan, and the Jesuit Aloysius Gonzaga, who died tending Rome's plague victims in 1591, nursing orders multiplied in the 1600s. Protestant countries, however, disbanded orders and relied on paid assistants, volunteers, or even patients. Since the well-off had their physicians and servants, or fled, plague facilities were largely for the poor, and staffing these was more a matter of social policy than of Christian charity. In England and the Netherlands, older women were even hired by cities to visit housebound poor victims of plague as "comforters" or "scrubsters." The English term *nurse* first appeared between 1640 and 1660.

See also: Bimaristans; Cellites and Alexians; Empirics; Hospitals; Lazarettos and Pest Houses; Monks, Nuns, and Monasteries; Physicians; Public Health; Witches and Witchcraft; Women Practitioners.

Reference

Donohue, Patricia. *Nursing, The Finest Art.* New York: Mosby, 2010.

P

Paracelsus (1493–1541) and Paracelsianism

Theophrastus von Hohenheim, who later adopted the Latin form of his native town, Paracelsus, was a rebel. Son of a Swiss physician and educated haphazardly in arts and medicine, he may have obtained a doctorate in medicine from the University of Verona in 1526. He practiced and taught medicine for a short time in Basel, but in his frustration with and rejection of Galenic medicine, in 1528, he publicly burned a copy of Avicenna's *Canon*, echoing his hero Martin Luther's famous burning of Canon Law. Never settling down, Paracelsus combined religious and medical reform, expecting the literal apocalypse and societal upheaval.

Paracelsus replaced Galenic medicine, with its humors and organic dietary regimens, with a chemical model of human physiology, emphasizing the roles of three "principles" he named sulphur, mercury, and salt. Roots of this approach went back through Albertus Magnus to Arab medical alchemy. Paracelsus understood diseases to be disorders of specific bodily organs caused by external *semina* (seeds) rather than humoral imbalances. Chemical medicines, prepared in essentially alchemical manners, provided the surest remedies. Paracelsus's medical writings are quite complex and often confusing, however; replete with the jargon of alchemist and astrologer, they often obscure his meaning and ultimately fall back on God as cause and only certain cure of disease.

In 1529, he experienced plague in Nördlingen. The resulting tracts were the German *Two Books on the Plague*, and the Latin *Three Books on the Plague*. He also treated plague at Sterzing, Austria, in 1534. In hope of obtaining a position, he quickly composed a fairly traditional plague tract—*On the Plague in Sterzing*—in which he nonetheless condemned the advice of surgeons past and contemporary. He failed to get the job. This contained references to his unfailing plague amulet he called zenexton. The book was published in French in 1570, and his followers sought the formula well into the next century.

Paracelsians—chemical physicians—provided an alternative medicine to the university-trained physicians' and threatened the medical profession. Paracelsians believed that "like cured like" (poison fights poison), rather than Galen's "fight an illness with its opposite" ("cool" foods cure fever). Since plague was poison, patients needed either internal remedies made with chemically depleted poisons (a huge target for critics), or amulets, plasters, and other external remedies that contained poisons. Drinkable gold (*aurum potabile*) was an elusive formula many thought could cure even plague. Europe's medical establishments considered Paracelsians empirics, though they often served as court physicians. Their willingness to avoid theory for "what works" according to observation and experiment was one thread in the Scientific Revolution.

See also: Alchemy; Amulets, Talismans, and Magic; Astrology; Causes of Plague: Historical

Renaissance magician, physician, alchemist, Hermeticist, and philosopher, Paracelsus (Theophrastus Bombastus von Hohenheim). (Library of Congress)

Theories; Empirics; Galen and Galenism; Gold; Van Helmont, Joan Baptista.

References

Grell, Ole. *Paracelsus: The Man and His Reputation, His Ideas and Their Transformation*. Leiden: Brill, 1998.

Webster, Charles. *Paracelsus*. New Haven, CT: Yale University Press, 2008.

Williams, Gerhild S., et al., editors. *Paracelsian Moments*. Kirksville, MO: Truman State University Press, 2003.

Parets, Miquel (1610–1661)

Miquel was born to a Barcelona tanner and adopted his father's craft. In 1631, he took his deceased father's place as a guild master. In the same year, he stood guard on the city's walls lest the plague in Milan ravage Barcelona. Civic-minded and involved in Barcelona's political life, Parets maintained a city chronicle from 1626 until 1660. For the year 1651, his tone and focus changed as he chronicled his own experiences and observations of the devastating Catalonian plague (1651–1653). The result is the longest popular first-hand treatment of a plague from the Second Pandemic.

Parets's viewpoint is that of the commoner in the streets, subject to rumor and myths about plague, but detached from the medical practitioner's concerns for theories of cause and treatment regimens. Though no cleric, Parets takes the moralist's stance in denouncing the corrupt, greedy, and self-preserving when their actions place many others at risk. His observations are fresh and unaffected by literary conventions, which make their echoes of other plague histories all the more compelling. His wife suffered and died of plague, but her sisters abandoned her to suffer alone. Only money could buy charity. He also lost three of his four children, though he carefully notes that only one clearly died from plague. Parets comments on extraordinary religious measures taken by churches and the diocese: liturgies, processions, adoption of a plague saint, even details on the dispensing of the sacraments. But at the center of the narrative lies the suffering: terrible to endure, horrifying to observe, yet cleansing and ultimately ending, thanks to God's mercy.

See also: Abandonment; Barcelona, Spain; Flight; Plague Saints; Processions.

Reference

Parets, Miquel. *A Journal of the Plague Year: The Diary of the Barcelona Tanner Miquel Parets, 1651*. Translated by James S. Amelang. New York: Oxford University Press, 1995.

Paris, France

Paris was the symbolic capital of the French kings, the seat of Europe's premier university, and the center of the French church. The Seine River connected Paris to the sea and Roman roads stretched out in all directions. Its administrators and aristocrats controlled the fertile Île de France, whose cartloads of food and other goods lumbered into the city of 200,000. In 1348, it was at the center of the Hundred Years War, whose English men-at-arms harried the countryside when not defeating French chivalry. Paris's university medical faculty composed one of the earliest plague tracts (*Compendium*), outlining understanding of the disease that approached Paris in June 1348 through Roissy and St. Denis. On August 20, the plague's earliest cases were discovered and the disease quickly spread. Death tolls rose rapidly into the fall, tapered off during the winter's cold, and savaged the inhabitants again until the fall of 1349. Religious processions wound through the ancient streets, but the bishop himself succumbed. Strict laws against blasphemy were imposed lest God continue his wrath: on first offense, they cut off a lip; on second, the other and 1/3 of the tongue disappeared. The Cemetery of the Holy Innocents filled up, though bones were dug up and deposited in its charnel house. The Hôtel Dieu carried out 500 corpses per day at the plague's height, filling its cemetery. Trinité hospital in 1350 added a plague graveyard 4,500 square meters in size. The Hôtel Dieu used this space in 1416 to 1418 for 9,224 plague corpses. One would expect the death toll to be near the 40 or 50 percent suffered in other large cities, but the chronicler at the Monastery of St. Denis claimed only 25 percent or 50,000 dead.

In the 1360 to 1363 epidemic, people noticed that children and the well-off seemed to be overrepresented, and Paris's first orphanage was established in 1363. Some demographers claim this also kept the population stunted for a generation or more, though migration from rural areas should have made up for the losses. From 1350 to the 1530s, Paris was stricken an average of every 11 years, though many cases were relatively light: 1366 to 1369, 1374, 1379, 1387, 1400 to 1401, 1412, 1416 to 1418, 1421, 1432, 1438 to 1439, 1448 to 1452, 1466 to 1468, 1471, 1478, 1481 to 1484, 1499, 1500, 1510, 1519, 1522 to 1523, and 1529 to 1533. That of 1416 to 1418 was especially bad, prompting a local diarist to claim 100,000 had been buried. The year 1510 saw the earliest marking of the houses of plague victims to warn visitors away, and in 1531, the government codified a set of antiplague measures from establishment of a health board to shutting in victims and quarantining suspects. Lawbreakers were to be hung and all their goods confiscated (leaving their families nothing). In 1496, the need in Paris for a plague hospital or lazaretto like Milan's was recognized, and reiterated in 1531. One was begun in 1580 but never finished; that of St. Louis was finally completed in 1612.

Between 1536 and 1670, the average time between epidemics grew to about 15 years: 1544 to 1546, 1548, 1553 to 1555, 1560 to 1562, 1566 to 1568, 1577, 1580 to 1581, 1583 to 1586, 1595 to 1597, 1603 to 1604, 1606 to 1608, 1612, 1618 to 1619, 1623 to 1631, 1636, 1638, 1652, and 1668. Major pandemics occurred in France in 1583 to 1586, 1595 to 1597, and 1628 to 1630 during the Thirty Years' War. The last few outbreaks seem to have been lighter, perhaps because of strict measures strictly enforced by an absolutist government. Young Louis XIV's minister Jean-Baptiste Colbert worked with the municipal officials and the chief judicial body, the Parlement of Paris, to impose bans on trade and travel, quarantines, and shutting in. They preemptively expelled visitors hailing from areas where plague was known to have been but decided to hold the local fair on the grounds that it was better to inspect and seize infected goods and people than prohibit the market and have contraband smuggled or snuck in.

See also: Children; *Compendium of Paris*; Hundred Years War; Lazarettos and Pest Houses; Plague Orders and National Authorities; Quarantine.

References

Brockliss, Laurence and Colin Jones. *The Medical World of Early Modern France*. New York: Oxford University Press, 1997.

Harding, Vanessa. *The Dead and the Living in Paris and London, 1500–1670*. New York: Cambridge University Press, 2002.

O'Boyle, C. "Surgical Texts and Social Contexts: Physicians and Surgeons in Paris, c. 1270 to 1430," in *Practical Medicine from Salerno to the Black Death*, edited by Luis Garcia-Ballester, et al. (New York: Cambridge University Press, 1994), 156–185.

Trout, A. P. "The Municipality of Paris Confronts the Plague of 1668." *Medical History* 17 (1973): 418–423.

Parish

The parish is the smallest subdivision of a Christian diocese. Centered on a church served by one or more priests, it is both a geographically bounded area and a worshipping community. A late-medieval rural parish might include several villages and scores of square miles, being served by a single priest. Around London, for example, parishes covered 20 to 100 acres and served 1,200 to 4,500 parishioners; inside the square-mile City of London, there were 100 parishes of between 1 and 12 acres in extent, each serving an average of 300 adults in 1548. Bishops administered parishes and appointed clergy, and active participation in parish life was expected of each parishioner. Most sacraments were administered through the parish and most Christians chose to be buried in the parish churchyard or even the church itself. Though a resident might choose to worship with friars, at the bishop's cathedral, or in a monastic chapel, she was no less tied to and expected to support her parish. In cities, several parishes made up a neighborhood and several neighborhoods a "quarter," so the parish was also a unit of civic identity and administration.

The pandemic of 1347 to 1352 altered the ecclesiastical landscape as priests and parishioners died, villages disappeared, and parochial and diocesan incomes dropped. In 1300, the English county of Hampshire had 54 parishes and 33 in 1400; only 2 had closed before 1348. In 1349, Canterbury's parish of St. Mary de Castro absorbed the remnants of neighboring St. John's. Between 1349 and 1400, Winchester diocese eliminated 19 parishes by consolidation and Norwich 29; Winchester lost a further seven between 1400 and 1500. Consolidation could enrich surviving parishes, however, with bequests, burial fees, new family chapels, or ex voto offerings. Priests promoted during an epidemic may have been found wanting, but some wealthy families dedicated scholarships and even schools for clerical education.

Despite their administrative importance, medieval parishes tended to keep poor records. Some individual cities, in Italy for example, required burial records from the 15th century, but it took Catholic authorities at the Council of Trent to require universal parochial registration of marriages, baptisms, and burials from about 1600. In 1538,

English Chancellor Thomas Cromwell ordered parish records of marriages, baptisms, and burials, and Denmark's royal government ordered parish-level death registration from the 1540s (few survive). Queen Elizabeth placed responsibility for plague-time corpse removal, attendance on shut-in plague victims, and general relief of the poor in the hands of parish authorities who appointed "viewers, searchers, keepers, watchers, surveyors, collectors, providers, deliverers, and such like officers of men and women" (St. Andrew Holborn, London, 1584).

See also: Bills of Mortality; Bishops and Popes; Borromeo, St. Charles (San Carlo); London, Great Plague of; Priests; Searchers.

References

Davies, R. H. "The Effect of the Black Death on the Parish Priests of the Medieval Diocese of Coventry and Lichfield." *Bulletin of the Institute of Historical Research* 62 (1989): 85–90.

French, Katherine L. *The Good Women of the Parish: Gender and Religion after the Black Death.* Philadelphia: University of Pennsylvania Press, 2008.

Gyug, Richard F. *The Diocese of Barcelona during the Black Death: The Register Notule communium 15 (1348–1349).* Toronto: Pontifical Institute of Medieval Studies, 1994.

Henderson, John. "The Parish and the Poor in Florence at the Time of the Black Death: The Case of San Frediano." *Continuity and Change* 3 (1988): 247–272.

Pasteur, Louis (1822–1895)

The key to unlocking the secrets of plague and preventing or curing it lay in the rejection of traditional disease models and their replacement with an accurate, scientific understanding of germ theory and its implications. Divine intervention, miasma, humoral imbalance, and Paracelsian *semina* and iatrochemistry remained viable explanations of plague until pioneers in microbiology, especially Louis Pasteur and German Robert Koch, discovered, proved, and demonstrated the existence and nature of germs and their roles in human disease. Though neither worked directly with plague, their students applied the new methods and models and determined what caused plague and explored ways of preventing and curing it.

Born in Dôle, France, young Louis was first drawn to art at Paris's École Normale Supérieure. Later, he turned to chemistry, a science still linked to biology and medicine. Between 1849 and 1867, Pasteur taught chemistry at the Universities of Strasbourg

France's Louis Pasteur was a 19th-century scientist who, with German Robert Koch, is credited with founding the field of microbiology. His research into bacteria and disease revolutionized contemporary understanding of microorganisms. (Library of Congress)

and Lille and directed the sciences at the École Normale Supérieure. He taught at the Sorbonne (1867–1888), founding his own Pasteur Institute for microbiological research in 1888.

Early work with crystals led him to fermentation. He proved that yeast was not an inorganic catalyst but an organism whose metabolism transformed sugar into alcohol. Wild yeasts are airborne and may spoil good wine unless kept out of solutions by airtight seal. This further showed that what people had believed to be spontaneous generation of organic material was really the work of invisible, airborne germs. He translated his findings to diseases in the late 1850s and agreed to work on a disease of silkworms, which were vital to the French silk industry. In the 1870s, Pasteur and Koch independently studied anthrax, both an animal and a human disease. Pasteur isolated the bacterium and determined that it multiplied in each host, which explained the effects of contagion. This turned the corner for germ theory. The questions now were which germs caused which diseases and how these might be counteracted. For the latter, Pasteur turned to Edward Jenner's innovation of vaccination. He prepared weakened strains of the pathogen, whose introduction into the animal or person triggered a protective immune response without threatening the host. He succeeded in creating vaccines for anthrax (1881) and, famously, rabies (1885).

See also: Germ Theory; Koch, Robert; Third Plague Pandemic; Yersin, Alexandre.

References

Debré, Patrice. *Louis Pasteur.* Translated by Elborg Forster. Baltimore, MD: Johns Hopkins University Press, 1998.

Geison, Gerald L. *The Private Science of Louis Pasteur.* Princeton, NJ: Princeton University Press, 1995.

Pastors, Preachers, and Ministers

Pastors (shepherds), preachers, and church ministries predated the 16th-century Reformation and are rooted in the Bible. In redefining the Christian church away from its Catholic form and traditions, however, most reformers adopted new names for their congregational leaders or clergy. With Luther's doctrine that each person is his or her own priest, that is, there is no intermediary between people and God, the Catholic (and Orthodox) title *priest* was disposed of among continental Protestants (Lutherans, Calvinists, and Radicals of various stripes). In England, the Anglican Church retained the priesthood and episcopacy, but sects affected by Calvin and the Radicals, for example, Puritans, Baptists, and Separatists, accepted Luther's rejection of an ordained priesthood.

Despite its variety, Protestant clergy was married, more or less well educated, and generally accepted as leaders by some form of ordination ritual. Unlike Catholic priests, Protestant clergy possessed no special graces or spiritual powers, nor did they confer grace on congregants through the sacraments or other rituals. In most communities, they did baptize and preside at the Eucharistic ceremony often renamed the Lord's Supper, two "sacraments" recognized by many reformers. They also played ceremonial (not sacramental) roles at weddings and at deathbeds, reading appropriate passages of Scripture for benefit of the participants and bystanders. Protestants rejected the Catholic ideas that spiritual benefits derived from participation in sacraments, other good deeds, or such rituals as blessings, processions, or prayers made to saints. They rejected the idea that living people could communicate with saints in heaven, including the traditional plague saints and even the Virgin Mary, and the very existence of Purgatory. While the preacher or minister did represent the Christian community to the individual, he did so as a teacher, exhortator, counselor, and comforter, and not as a man possessed of sacred authority and power.

The early Protestant clergy's authority was charismatic and reinforced by the fact that congregations usually chose their pastor rather than having him appointed by a bishop or patron (except among the Anglicans). When plague struck early in the process of congregational reform, local Catholics often blamed the epidemic on God's anger with the impiety of religious challenge and change. Reformers logically and eloquently responded that God's anger was more probably stirred by Catholic resistance to godly change, since pestilence had savaged Catholic Europe for nearly two centuries. In the age of pamphleteering, the two sides could make their cases and good Christians take their stands. Many early reformed clergy were itinerant, moving from town to town planting their denomination's ideas in pioneer communities and then moving on. Some of these took advantage of epidemics to preach openly in town squares or fields. Surrounded by suffering and death, they warned of divine wrath and the need for true repentance and change of life. The passing earthly torments of plague paled beside the eternal horrors of damnation, they stressed. Though such preaching had traditionally been the trade of fiery friars, these men were often engaged in the physical ministration to the sick and dying. In any case, friars had long been planted and supported locally, and service was expected of them.

The clearest examples of Protestant clerics making headway during epidemics come from England, which tolerated a wide diversity of religious identity. From 1348, the established clergy—whether Catholic or Protestant—had been slammed for taking flight during plague. Pope Clement VI had upbraided fearful parish priests, and reformer Martin Luther openly disobeyed a direct order to abandon plague-stricken Wittenberg. Despite the dangers, most Christian leaders expected their clergy to remain in place as long as their aid was needed. Nonetheless, in regions with state churches, the clergy often acted in a correspondingly secularized manner. With no need to confer last rites or funerary blessings or hear last confessions, Anglican and Lutheran clergy often followed their richer parishioners out of town when plague lowered. London pharmacist William Boghurst wrote of the Great Plague (1665–1666) that "the divines (Anglican clergy)" always advise flight and condemn those who stay for "provoking God." We read reports of heightened (and welcomed) dissenter and other sectarian clerical activity, sometimes in the very churches abandoned by the established clerics. Communal Christian life went on despite pestilence. In a 1666 report from Southampton, the French Huguenot (Calvinist) pastor Couraud noted having baptized "a little English child named Nicholas" in July 1665 and two other "English" children in November. The local Anglican priest Bernert had taken ill and to the countryside, abandoning his flock. Couraud continued that in December, he had performed several English marriages in the parish church of St. John, "the English clergy having deserted the congregations because of the plague." Criticism, however, never rises to the level of anticlericalism, no doubt because there were viable options among the many sects.

As a believer might say, only God knows the balance between the faithful pastors and the fearful ones. Many died, having been infected while comforting the dying in their homes or in pest houses. In 1666, in Eyam,

England, pastor Mompesson famously convinced his plague-stricken flock to remain isolated in their village to prevent broadcast of the disease. Two-thirds of his flock died, including Mrs. Mompesson, whom he buried with his own hands. Leadership often exacts a price, and in plague time, a terrible price.

See also: Anticlericalism; *Ars moriendi (The Art of Dying)*; Donne, John; Eyam, England; Flight; Funerals, Protestant; Henry VIII, King of England; London, England; London, Great Plague of (1665–1666); Luther, Martin; Parish; Priests; Reformation and Protestantism; Sin.

References

Reinis, Austra. *Reforming the Art of Dying: The Ars Moriendi in the German Reformation (1519–1528)*. Burlington, VT: Ashgate, 2007.

Rowell, Geoffrey. *The Liturgy of Christian Burial: An Introductory Survey of the Historical Development of Christian Burial Rites*. London: S.P.C.K., 1977.

Slack, Paul. *The Impact of Plague in Tudor and Stuart England*. Oxford and New York: Oxford University Press, 1990.

Taylor, J. "Plague in the Towns of Hampshire: The Epidemic of 1665–1666." *Southern History* 6 (1984): 104–122.

Peasants

In the initial plague outbreaks, peasants tended to die in what appear to be similar percentages to members of the upper classes and with townsfolk. Since they constituted perhaps 80 to 90 percent of the population, however, their absolute numbers were enormous. Across the vast area affected by the Second Pandemic, the plagues had varying effects on the conditions and options of these workers, dependent largely on previous trends and economic conditions. Over time, however, plague seems to have focused on European urban centers rather than rural areas, sparing much of the countryside by the 17th century. In Islamic areas, the picture is less detailed but seems clear.

Peasants, as used in this entry, were no monolithic class, but people with varying levels of mobility, income and wealth, and specialized skills. At the lowest end were serfs who were tied to their villages, subject to traditional rights and obligations, and dependent on their landlords for equipment, justice, defense, and other necessities. Though not allowed by custom and law to relocate, many who were dissatisfied used the chaos of the epidemics to escape to better landlords or to towns. Though probably limited in skills, villagers often included a miller, blacksmith, carpenters, masons, and many who made perfectly good day laborers, as well as women who might make fine servants. Above serfs were free peasants who presumably had more wealth and normally more options. They had the rights, defined in agreements or contracts, to leave or renegotiate the terms of their leases. Though not owning land outright, many used the depressed land market following plague to buy when strapped landlords were selling, or at least acquiring more land by lease at very favorable terms. These were the aspirants to the yeoman class in England, for example. Landlords and tenants depended on occasional or seasonal labor, a need filled by several types of workers, from rented-out serfs to small-time tenants who enhanced their income by hiring out.

In Western Europe, the plague depopulated the countryside not only by killing people by the millions but also by killing townsfolk, whose replacement entailed drawing from the rural population. Exact numbers or percentages are always problematic, but tax registers drop over time, and such proxies as rises in wages, reductions in cultivable areas sown, and the disappearance of villages, as well as petitions, letters, court records, and other written testimonies, indicate that declines were heavy and repeated through much of the 15th century.

With the drop in labor supply, the price of labor rose virtually everywhere there was a cash economy. English studies show that on the Bishop of Winchester's estates, in real terms, salaries tripled, and laborers at Tavistock Abbey saw their wages double between 1334 and 1385. A broader study of southern England discovered that agricultural wages rose between 50 and 100 percent from 1348 to 1375, then flattened out to about 1410, rose again about a third until 1550, and steadily thereafter. Initial rises in wages and prices led kings in England (Statute of Labourers) and Spain to try to limit these, with mixed results (in Essex in 1389, 791 fines were levied). Rising wages, falling demand for agricultural produce, and reductions in cultivable acreage led to declines in rents that forced many landlords to sell off or lease out even more land. In Brandenburg, rents dropped nearly a third between 1375 and 1450. At St.-Germain-des-Pres, they fell from 84 *livres* per acre in the later 1300s to 32 *livres* between 1461 and 1483, and even more precipitously at Beaufor, Normandy: 142 *livres* per acre in 1397, 112 in 1428, 52 in 1437, and 10 in 1444. Of course, war and famine also did their parts.

In much of Western Europe, serfdom had been waning long before the Black Death with the growth of towns and the money economy. Where these forces of change were weak or limited elsewhere, as in Eastern and part of Central Europe and Catalonia, the local landlords were able to keep a lid on rural aspirations. In the face of plague, the lords tended to increase their demands on their peasants and avoid negotiations favorable to them. The situation was similar in Islamic lands for which we have records. Under the Mamluks in the Levant and Egypt, the peasants lived in villages under customary laws and whose ownership changed hands frequently. Hired administrators rather than the social aristocrats managed the properties and people, with an emphasis on keeping the peace and keeping profits high at minimal investments. Concern for the welfare of the peasants, either individually or as a class, was neither a matter of religion nor of landholders' interest. Rural unrest was a constant, especially in Egypt. This only began to change when the Ottoman Turks conquered Mamluk territories (1517) and redistributed the land. In northern Italy, where serfdom was rarely a factor, much land fell onto the market at low prices and was acquired by urban entrepreneurs. They tended to be rational in their exploitation of the land and often let land through a sharecropper-type contractual arrangement known as *mezzadria*. Italian *contadini* often combined this with early examples of the "putting out" system—in both cases putting capital directly in the hands of workers. The spinning, weaving, or other tasks provided additional capital to peasants during seasonal down times while helping businessmen keep production high in times of labor shortages. Entrepreneurial control also meant a greater emphasis on multiple crops and cash crops over mere subsistence farming and rationalized methods that minimized labor intensity.

Concentration of wealth in fewer peasant hands and longer-term declines in prices of food and other commodities meant a rising standard of living for peasants across much of Europe. Some villages or village managers invested in tools: Maillane in Provence had 40 draft animals in 1430 and more than 200 in 1471 thanks in part to the greater availability of meadowland. Pictures, contracts, and probate inventories indicate better-designed and constructed implements.

Peasants replaced maslin, rye, and chestnut flour with wheat for bread, and dredge and barley for oats in brewing, added more meat to their diets, and acquired more utensils and clothing and higher-quality housing that owners kept in better condition in order to protect their investments and retain workers.

While one cannot say that all migration to European towns after epidemics was from rural areas, this replacement was a drain on the countryside. For example, the German Hansa towns of Lüneburg, Hamburg, and Lübeck had numbers of new citizens averaging (1317–1349) 29, 59, and 175 respectively; in 1351 the numbers jumped to 95, 108, and 422. At the same time, cultivated acreage dropped precipitously across Europe, especially among the most marginally valuable and thus most recently cropped lands. On individual manors in England, losses might reach 60 to 70 percent, and studies of southern Jutland (Denmark) show overall figures of 50 percent. Entire villages disappeared as peasants died or moved. Some consolidation of small with larger settlements had occurred earlier, but the Black Death and subsequent plagues had terrible effects. Between 1,300 and 2,000 English villages were abandoned between 1350 and 1500. Around Pola in Istria, only 11 of 72 villages remained by 1371; in Castile, the Bishop of Palencia reported that 82 of 420 settled areas disappeared between 1348 and 1350 due to plague, war, and famine. Some of these were victims of their landlords' desire to rationalize land use, abandoning labor-intensive and less commercially profitable farming for pasture. Pre–Mamluk Fatimid Egypt had around 10,000 villages, a number reduced to 2,170 by 1435. Egyptians fled to cities after epidemics for the same reasons Europeans did.

See also: Black Death (1347–1352); Bishops and Popes; Economic Effects of Plague in Europe; Famine; Feudalism and Manorialism; Jacquerie; Labourers, Ordinance and Statute of; Langland, William; Nobility; Peasants' Revolt, English; Repopulation; Yeoman Farmers and Gentry.

References

Bailey, Mark. "Peasant Welfare in England, 1290–1348." *Economic History Review* NS 51 (1998): 223–251.

Borsch, Stuart. *The Black Death in Egypt and England.* Austin: University of Texas Press, 2005.

Byrne, Joseph P. *Daily Life during the Black Death.* Westport, CT: Greenwood, 2006.

Dyer, Christopher. *Everyday Life in Medieval England.* New York: Hambledon Continuum, 2000.

Freedman, Paul. *Origins of Peasant Servitude in Medieval Catalonia.* New York: Cambridge University Press, 1991.

Ladurie, Emmanuel LeRoy. *The French Peasantry, 1450–1600.* Translated by Alan Sheridan. Berkeley: University of California Press, 1987.

Rösener, Werner. *Peasants in the Middle Ages.* Trans. by Alexander Stützer. Urbana: University of Illinois Press, 1992.

Scott, Tom. *The Peasantries of Europe: From the Fourteenth to the Eighteenth Centuries.* New York and London: Longman, 1998.

Tucker, William. "Natural Disasters and the Peasantry in Mamluk Egypt." *Journal of the Economic and Social History of the Orient* 24 (1981): 215–224.

Peasants' Revolt, English

Also known as the Great Rising of 1381, this landmark event had complex roots, including the Black Death. The plague killed much of England's laboring class, empowering survivors to bargain from strength with employers and landlords. Royal reaction limited this effect severely, however, with the Ordinance of Labourers (1349) and

Statute of Labourers (1351). Resentment among working classes both rural and urban grew with enforcement that fined and jailed thousands each year for decades and gave greater control to local landowners. By 1381, military losses in France and levies of poll (head) taxes to support the war—three between 1377 and 1380—fueled social tensions and peasant discontent with decaying manorialism. Some leaders, like clergyman John Ball, preached radical egalitarianism.

Violent action erupted on May 30, 1381. Led by village elites and disaffected townsmen, mobs of Essex peasants attacked manor houses and abbeys, killing and destroying records of tenancy, dues, and customs. Violence and destruction rapidly spread to Kent and northward across England. Kent's uprising took center stage, moving north from Canterbury to Rochester to London. Here, on June 15, leaders John Ball, Wat Tyler, and Jack Straw dramatically confronted young King Richard II after armed groups had ransacked the Temple (with its legal records) and the Savoy Palace and executed Canterbury's Archbishop Sudbury and other officials on Tower Hill. Tyler was killed in Richard's presence, other leaders captured, and many followers led out of London, only to be hunted down when order had been restored to the capital. Throughout England, aristocratic reaction was brutal.

See also: Ciompi Revolt; Economic Effects of Plague in Europe; Feudalism and Manorialism; Hundred Years War; Jacquerie; Labourers, Ordinance and Statute of; Peasants.

References

Dunn, Alastair. *The Great Rising of 1381.* Stroud, Gloucs., UK: Tempus, 2004.

Platt, Colin. *King Death: The Black Death and Its Aftermath in Late-medieval England.* Toronto: University of Toronto Press, 1997.

Pepys, Samuel (1633–1703)

Born to a London tailor, Samuel was educated at St. Paul's School and Cambridge. He entered the service of a well-off cousin and by age 27 had risen to Clerk of the Acts to the Navy Board. By diligence and skill, Pepys ascended in the bureaucracy that was creating Britain's Royal Navy. From his appointment as Clerk in 1660 until 1669, Pepys maintained an intimate journal or diary in which he recorded personal matters and matters of state from his ailments and attempted cures to illicit sexual dalliances (he was married) and problems at the office and at court.

Pepys lived in London through most of the Great Plague of 1665/6, having sent his wife away to nearby Greenwich. He continued his diary, noting the steady increases in plague deaths and considering remedies. Plague acts as background noise that empties the streets and closes the shops and wells up in chance encounters with the random corpse or shut-up house. In a letter to Lady Carteret (September 4), he noted that he remained in London "til the nights are grown too short to conceal the burials of those that died the day before . . . til I could find neither meat nor drink safe, the butcheries being everywhere visited [by the plague], my brewer's house shut up, and my baker with his whole family dead of the plague" (De le Bédoyère, 46). But England was at war with Holland, ships and sailors needed tending, the royal court was away, and Pepys the bureaucrat was on the job. His diary, as his days, is filled with Navy business, and he moved about London with diminishing apprehension, noting his dull reaction to seeing yet another corpse. Such sights only reminded him that he needed more prophylactic tobacco. He noted public fasts but avoided attending church, whose swollen churchyard made him nervous. Pepys and wife returned from Greenwich on January 7, later receiving a gift of specially engraved plate from King Charles, grateful for those who stayed in London and served.

See also: Bills of Mortality; Flight; London, Great Plague of; Tobacco.

References

De le Bédoyère, Guy, ed. *The Letters of Samuel Pepys.* Rochester, NY: Boydell Press, 2006.

Moote, A. Lloyd and Dorothy C. Moote. *The Great Plague: The Story of London's Most Deadly Year.* Baltimore, MD: Johns Hopkins University Press, 2004.

Pepys, Samuel. *The Diary of Samuel Pepys.* Edited by Robert Latham and William Matthews. 11 vols. Berkeley: University of California Press, 2000. Also Digital Book Index.

Pest Houses. See Lazarettos and Pest Houses

Pestilence. See *Black Death, Plague,* and *Pestilence* (Terms)

Petrarch, Francesco (1304–1374)

Francesco was born near Florence into a notarial family that later moved to papal Avignon. Though his father wanted him to pursue law, Francesco dropped out, joined the lower clergy, and made his way as a secretary at the papal court. He developed his gifts as a poet and promoted himself by circulating copies of his work. He also immersed himself in classical Latin literature and was, by many accounts, the first Renaissance humanist. Intellectually, he rejected his own time of materialism, war, and corruption and embraced a golden ancient past he could only dimly perceive.

He was in northern Italy when the Black Death struck in 1348. The disease mowed down many close friends, including his muse, Laura, who had dominated his poetic program for two decades. With the death of Cardinal Giovanni Colonna ("column"), he lost his principal patron and supporter. Petrarch's brother Gherardo was a Carthusian monk, all of whose brothers died as Gherardo comforted them. Petrarch's grief and depression were deep, and he expressed them in letters and poetry, including "Ad te ipsum." This haunting work recalls coffin-filled churches, the multitude of graves, and the "dear ones" who left this world without honor. Earlier he had written long poems in Latin on the *Triumph of Cupid* and *Triumph of Chastity*; now he set out to pair the *Triumph of Death* with *Triumph of Fame*. *Death* would have a long life, especially as a pictorial theme, and *Fame* sparked a revival of the classical ideal of the individual, a major Renaissance motif.

The arrogance of physicians coupled with their inability to remedy plague sufferers drew Petrarch's wrath on a number of occasions. They make extravagant claims and simply cheat the sick whom they watch die. Like most, he blamed the plague on the "crimes" of humanity. Should the crimes end, so would the suffering, he wrote in 1367, "but it is never really gone. Just when it seems to be over, it returns and attacks once more those who were briefly happy" (Watkins, 218).

See also: Individualism and Individual Liberties; Physicians; Triumph of Death.

References

Carlino, Andrea. "Petrarch and the Early Modern Critics of Medicine." *Journal of Medieval and Early Modern Studies* 35 (2005): 559–582.

Watkins, Renee Neu. "Petrarch and the Black Death: From Fear to Monuments." *Studies in the Renaissance* 19 (1972): 196–223.

Wilkins, Ernest H. "On Petrarch's 'Ad te ipsum' and 'I' vo pensando.' " *Speculum* 32 (1957): 84–91.

Physicians

Physician is derived from the Greek word for nature and referred to those who studied and worked to cure the ills of the physical human body. The Latin equivalent, *medicus*, found its way into English *medicine*, but not as a label for practitioners. In the Middle Ages, both were used, with the distinction being that the *physicus* was the intellectually trained theoretician and the *medicus* handled patients' problems. Medical school training founded on university credentials by the 13th century emphasized the theoretical over the practical and the physician over the mere practitioner. By the mid-14th century, the educated physicians were generally separated from the master-trained surgeons —who typically dealt with hands-on tasks from phlebotomy to bone setting and cutting for stones—and apothecaries (druggists), each group having its own guild in a city. Beginning in later 13th-century Italy, physicians also formed local boards called colleges. Unlike guilds, colleges contained only university-educated practicing physicians who sought to restrict entrance into the profession, to set and uphold standards of conduct, distinguish true physicians from such nonprofessionals as empirics, and advise civil authorities. Colleges in university cities also served on the faculty and examined graduates. London established its College only in 1518, under the influence of Italian-educated Thomas Linacre. Like others, London's insisted on education in and the practice of Galenic medicine only.

The clothing identifies the person as a "plague doctor" and is intended as protection. Descriptions indicate that the gown was made from heavy fabric or leather and was usually waxed. The beak contained pungent substances like herbs or perfumes, thought at the time to purify the air and helpful in relieving the stench. The person also carries a wand to keep patients at a distance. (Courtesy of the National Library of Medicine)

When the Black Death struck between 1347 and 1352, physicians died in large numbers due to their contact with the sick and their fleas: Montpellier's entire faculty; 20 of 24 in Venice; 6 of 8 in Perpignan. When visiting a victim's home, they took the pulse, estimated the fever, and examined urine and possibly excrement. There was little they could do, however, other than provide some comfort with such opiate-containing drugs as theriac. With fear of contagion, doctors began distancing themselves from patients by doing what they could at arm's length or even from another room or outside a window. The distinctive plague-doctor's suit developed during the 17th century covered the practitioner from head to feet with stiff oilcloth, goggles, and a "beak" stuffed with aromatics that supposedly purified the air. A wand, ancient symbol of the healer, was often required by authorities for identification. Physicians also served in plague hospitals and pest houses as they became more common. Despite the suit—and other personal prophylactics—many had to be coerced into what was commonly considered a fatal undertaking.

The expansion of medical education ensured that the number of physicians increased from the 14th century, but physicians remained rare. For example, Elizabeth's 9,000 English parishes shared 814 licensed physicians; wealthy London had about one physician for 4,000 residents. By comparison, contemporary Barcelona had one for every 1,450, Venice 1:2,222, and Lyons 1:4,143. The wealthy and urban had best access.

Like clergy and lawyers, physicians were often vilified. They were arrogant yet ineffective; they charged too much; they knowingly defrauded their patients; they made or kept people sick in order to empty their wallets. They were mocked for their Latin "gibberish" and dependence on astrology. William Langland lumped them in with harlots and whores, and manuscripts depict them as irrational apes or prevaricating foxes. The poet Petrarch considered them pretentious for placing their skill before faith, yet ignorant of their business since they were so ineffective during the plague. Physicians themselves agreed, from Guy de Chauliac in 1363 (they "did little or nothing . . . almost all died") to London's Richard Blackmore, who lamented that even "the most sagacious and inquisitive physicians" had yet to find a cure in 1721. When wealthy doctors accompanied their wealthy clients to healthier locales, they were accused of fleeing their duties to the unfortunates left behind. Sometimes disaffection became violent and physicians were attacked and even killed, especially when they supported or enforced harsh antiplague measures.

Yet the profession retained its prestige throughout the Second Pandemic and beyond. Early on this may have been because plague tolls dropped from their mid–14th-century highs: certainly physicians took credit for their remedies or treatments. As intervals between outbreaks widened in the 15th through 17th centuries, the profession likewise took credit. But more important was the burnishing of the profession by its own efforts. Physicians in Spain and Italy retrenched by becoming official *protomedicati* (a town's or region's chief medical official, appointed by noble or royal authority), commanding obedience and respect. They exercised power through local colleges and health boards and touted the high standards they demanded. Aside from rebels like Paracelsus, physicians aspired to and enjoyed upper-class status. With their shared Galenic education, they presented a phalanx against empirics and other practitioners, a front supported by increasingly authoritarian 16th- and 17th-century governments.

See also: Anatomy and Dissection; Arabic-Persian Medicine and Practitioners; Astrology; Charlatans and Quacks; Consilia and Plague Tracts; Diagnosing Plague; Diseases, Opportunistic and Subsidiary; Empirics; Health Boards, Magistracies, and Commissions; Hospitals;

Medical Education (1300–1500, Medieval Europe); Medical Education (1500–1700, Early Modern Europe); Petrarch, Francesco; Physicians, Court; Physicians, Town; Prophylaxes; Surgeons/Barbers; Women Medical Practitioners.

References

Brockliss, Laurence and Colin Jones. *The Medical World of Early Modern France*. New York: Oxford University Press, 1997.

Cipolla, Carlo. *Public Health and the Medical Profession in Renaissance Florence*. New York: Cambridge University Press, 1976.

Cohn, Samuel K. *Cultures of Plague: Medical Thinking at the End of the Renaissance*. New York: Oxford University Press, 2010.

Gentilcore, David. *Healers and Healing in Early Modern Europe*. New York: Manchester University Press, 2003.

Grell, Ole Peter. "Conflicting Duties: Plague and the Obligations of Early Modern Physicians towards Patients and Commonwealth in England and The Netherlands." *Clio Medica* 24 (1993): 131–152.

Jacquart, Danielle. "Theory, Everyday Practice, and Three Fifteenth-century Physicians," in her *La Science médicale occidentale entre deux renaissances (XIIe s.–XVe s.)* (Aldershot: Variorum, 1997), 140–160.

O'Boyle, C. "Surgical Texts and Social Contexts: Physicians and Surgeons in Paris, c. 1270 to 1430," in *Practical Medicine from Salerno to the Black Death*, edited by Luis Garcia-Ballester, et al. (New York: Cambridge University Press, 1994), 156–185.

Pelling, Margaret. *Medical Conflicts in Early Modern London: Patronage, Physicians, and Irregular Practitioners 1550–1640*. New York: Oxford University Press, 2003.

Physicians, Court

The health of rulers, their families, and especially their heirs has been a major concern of monarchies from ancient China and Egypt to the present. Traditionally, the era's physicians best known for their knowledge, skill, loyalty, and discretion served the dynasty. A position at court marked the apex of one's career but was far from stable, as even one slip could seal one's fate. Following the Byzantine and Persian examples, Muslim caliphs and later sultans employed the finest medical men of their day, while monastic healers tended to European rulers, sometimes doubling as court chaplains. With the development of the medical profession in the 13th century, kings, popes, and emperors hired formally trained physicians, often several at a time. They were compensated with salary, room and board, fancy clothing, horses, and other perks and were rewarded for special service with gifts ranging from jewels to landed estates. Lower-ranking royal surgeons handled the manual aspects of treatment and care, from shaving to bloodletting to bone setting.

Throughout the Second Pandemic, court physicians recommended flight as the principal prophylaxis against plague. They also mandated and oversaw prophylactic dietary regimens and warned against behaviors thought to bring on the disease. In the 16th and 17th centuries, monarchs and many nobles became patrons of first humanist and then Paracelsian "chemical" medicine. The latter appealed to Protestant German nobles and the Catholic convert French King Henry IV, who had 35 closet Paracelsians at court around 1600. His successor Louis XIII employed between 80 and 100 Paracelsians and Galenists. Many court physicians published on plague and public health, including Guy de Chauliac, Alonso de Chirino of Castile, Ambroise Paré, Richard Mead, and Gilbert Skeyne, whose *Brief Description of the Pest* for King James VI was the first Scots medical book. Thomas de Mayerne, who tended Queen Henrietta Maria, prepared an insightful, detailed, but never acted upon report on public plague prophylaxis for Charles I in 1631. During London's Great Plague in 1665, three of Charles II's personal physicians stayed to tend the poor; all survived.

See also: Avicenna (Ibn Sina); Chauliac, Guy de (Guido Cauliaco); Clement VI, Pope; Galen and Galenism; Henry VIII, King of England; James I and VI Stuart, King; Mead, Richard; Paracelsus and Paracelsianism; Physicians; Surgeons/Barbers.

References

Lamont-Brown, Raymond. *Royal Poxes and Potions: The Lives of Court Physicians, Surgeons and Apothecaries.* Stroud, Gloucs., UK: Sutton, 2001.

Nutton, Vivian, ed. *Medicine at the Courts of Europe, 1500–1837.* New York: Routledge, 1990.

Physicians, Town

The development of formal medical education in the West led to professionalization of medicine. These trends accompanied the growth of towns and increased sophistication of civic life, especially in 13th-century Italy. Beginning with the contractual, salaried hiring of Ugo Borgognoni of Lucca in 1214, Bologna provided professional health care at civic expense for all soldiers, residents, and injured rural folk who came to town. Bruges, Milan, and Venice appointed salaried community doctors in the later 1200s; Milan had three in 1288. By 1324, Venice had 13, and 18 when the Black Death struck; Ragusa's first was in 1301. The earliest known German *stadtärtzen* were appointed by Wismar in 1281 and Munich in 1312. France's earliest known public physician appeared in 1288. Over the next two centuries, 15 percent of French physicians would serve in public positions. They had to be resident and were expected solely to practice medicine. As doctors became more plentiful, public physicians most often tended the poor, often aided by a paid surgeon and midwife.

The position spread widely after 1348, and in 1431, Emperor Sigismund decreed that all imperial cities employ at least one physician. When plague struck, communal physicians were expected by custom and contract to remain and tend the sick. When they fell ill or died, the authorities did what they could to replace them. In October 1348, Orvieto Doctor Matteo fu Angelo was paid four times the salary of his predecessors. Others received free housing, immediate citizenship, and free meals in addition to inflated salaries. Volunteers were often third-rate physicians, students, or even empirics. As rulers gained public health apparatus and jurisdiction over civic health, they mandated service during epidemics, which physicians equated to death sentences. The alternative was to do without while waiting: Châlons-sur-Marne went without a doctor from 1440 to 1443.

During epidemics, town physicians experienced the same range of horrors all caregivers did. Most were required to visit the sick in their homes, hospitals, jails, and even pest houses. They examined urine and feces, felt pulses and body temperatures, and prescribed treatments, especially painkillers and purgatives. In smaller towns, they were often also placed in charge of pest houses, working a primitive triage with admissions, declaring and recording the dead and the recovered, and providing medicines.

Basel's city physician in 1610 to 1611, Felix Platter, conducted a very early epidemiological study. As it unfolded, he followed its path, and at the epidemic's end, he had a full census taken by assistants of every household: number of residents, of plague deaths, and of those who recovered. He determined about one-third of patients recovered.

See also: Apothecaries; Arabic-Persian Medicine and Practitioners; Governments, Civil; Health Boards, Magistracies, and Commissions; Islamic Civil Responses; Jews; Physicians; Public Health.

References

Cipolla, Carlo. *Public Health and the Medical Profession in Renaissance Florence.* Cambridge: Cambridge University Press, 1976.

Gentilcore, David. *Healers and Healing in Early Modern Europe.* New York: Manchester University Press, 2003.

Russell, Andrew, ed. *The Town and State Physician in Europe from the Middle Ages to the Enlightenment.* Wolfenbüttel: Herzog August Bibliothek, 1981.

Pilgrims and Pilgrimage

There are certain places on earth to which Christians and Muslims are drawn by tradition. The routes there and the places themselves have been made sacred by the historical or continuing presence of Jesus, Muhammad, or one of their holy followers. For all Muslims, Mecca has pride of place, while Medina and Jerusalem follow. Shi'ite Muslims recognize numerous holy men as saints, and annual processions to their tombs dot the calendar. Christians venerate Jerusalem, Bethlehem, and other sites in the "Holy Land" for their roles in Jesus's life. For most Catholics, Rome, with its connections to Sts. Peter and Paul and a host of martyrs, was much closer and safer to visit. Compostella had the body of St. James (Sant'Iago), Venice those of Sts. Mark and Roche, Soissons St. Sebastian, and Canterbury

St. Thomas Becket. Most regions in Europe also had sites of minor or local importance, for example, Walsingham, Peterborough, and Holywell in England or Assisi and Loreto in Italy. Many visitors paid their respects during special festivals on the saint's day, but pilgrims from long distances flowed to major sites from spring through fall. Christian pilgrims may have been sent by their confessors as penance or have undertaken the trip as fulfillment of a vow ("protect me from the plague, Mary, and I will visit your shrine at Chartres").

Such promises were no doubt very common during plague epidemics. Also common were local, communal trips to powerful shrines. As late as 1678, imperial physician Paul de Sorbait led such a group from Vienna to Mariazell, some 50 miles away. In 1350, leaderless groups, "an enormous number of people ... flocked to the monastery of St. Peter at Hennegau, when it was discovered that there were relics of St. Sebastian in a shrine there," Belgian Abbot Gilles Li Muisis tells us (Horrox, 54). He also noted that pilgrims "of every social class [and] from all parts of France" flocked to St. Medard Church in Soissons to venerate St. Sebastian's relics. When plague stopped, so did the flow of pilgrims. While we know Sorbait's group contracted plague and spread it with them, we can assume that the mixing of folk at Hennegau or Soissons can only have had the same effect. As with religious processions within cities, these were dangerous for the crowds they drew, but more so as they traveled through potentially plague-ridden countryside.

Pope Clement VI almost cancelled the Jubilee Year (1350), which was certain to draw tens of thousands of pilgrims to Rome for special spiritual benefits. He relented, as pestilence seemed to recede; the spiritual benefits would outweigh the physical risks, he reasoned from Avignon. In some ways it replaced the Flagellant movement he had just condemned. Ironically, pilgrims were seen as rootless strangers and sometimes suspected of poisoning wells or otherwise spreading plague on purpose. Some did spread disease, of course, though not on purpose.

See also: Flagellants; Mecca; Plague Saints; Processions; Rome, Italy; Virgin Mary.

Reference

Horrox, Rosemary. *The Black Death.* New York: Manchester University Press, 1994.

Plague in Europe, 1360–1500

The pestilence of the Black Death returned in the late 1350s and early 1360s from its beginnings in 1347. Any relief felt at the end of the first wave was now washed away as people came to realize that the epidemic was not a one-time event. People also realized that plague's return was not the catastrophe its first appearance was. Whereas the disease had moved quickly and systematically across the countryside from south to north like some enormous scythe, it now merely appeared, killed, and moved on in one or more directions. The few areas spared the first time now paid their dues, while many locales were left untouched. Death tolls (by percentage) were much lower, despite few efforts to prevent plague's appearance and no medical advances. Some physicians claimed successes in healing the suffering, but all attributed it to God. In Italy, most of the north felt the scourge in 1357 to 1358, except Tuscany. In 1360, plague struck Buda (16,000 killed), Bohemia, Norway, Uri (Switzerland), and—in Istria—Pirano, Grisignana, and Capodistria; in

1361, the Netherlands endured the "Plague of the Children," England suffered, as did southern France and much of northern Italy, though Tuscany was again spared until 1363. Tuscan international merchant Francesco Datini lived through epidemics in each decade from his being orphaned in 1348 to his (natural) death in 1410. In 1390 and 1400, he carefully considered his options and made his plans to relocate his business and family away from the plague's path, in both cases to where the plague had been. Such predictability was not found everywhere: records of Carpentras in the Comtat Venaissin in southern France make no mention of plague from 1395 to 1468; from 1468 to 1501, there are 16 notices of its presence, or once every two years.

Plague's recurrence over its first century fit a pattern of every 6 to 12 years in any given urban place, or about two to four times in a generation. After 1480, the pattern changed, with returns spread out to every 15 to 20 years. During the later 1300s, the countryside continued to lose population due to death and relocation to cities, which might help explain why rural areas were often spared after 1400. Less easily explained are the remarks by many commentators that later 14th- and 15th-century epidemics claimed a disproportionate number of women and children. Some dismiss this as a function of diet, despite the improvements since 1348, while others attribute it to their presence in the household where the rats and fleas were most comfortable. Some scholars also claim that low levels of "endemic"—which would actually have to be enzootic—plague had settled in across much of Europe, combining with severe bouts of cold weather and famine (Little Ice Age), especially in the 1430s and 1460s, to depress repopulation.

And depressed repopulation was. In most European locales studied, the 15th century was the post–Black Death low point for population. While larger cities retained stable or growing populations, it was only at the expense of the smaller towns and countryside, from which many villages disappeared and in which many consolidated to survive. The later 14th century saw many manorial lords sell off their holdings or turn to other forms of tenancy in the face of severe labor shortages. Cultivated land that was difficult to work was quickly abandoned as well-off peasants accumulated their holdings, while landlords turned large tracts from cultivable to pasture. Even where lords were not oppressive by custom, as they were in Eastern Europe and Catalonia, the falling rents and high labor costs squeezed the landholders, who, in turn, squeezed the lower peasant classes. Tax revenue, too, fell off, leading to fresh exactions and repressions in France and England (at war since 1327). These sparked rural uprisings including the French Jacquerie and English Peasants' Revolt. In cities, rising conditions led the wool workers (*ciompi*) of Florence to revolt, demanding guild status and political representation.

In Islamic regions stricken by plague, both rich and poor suffered, though the poor took it hardest. As in Europe, most cities recovered as resources were reshuffled among the land and business owners. In Mamluk Syria and Egypt, the peasantry was hardest hit, as they depended on their landlords for much. The military aristocracy did little to improve the agrarian infrastructure when conditions were good and did less under the stress of plague. Workers abandoned the land to disuse, decay, and depredation as they relocated to labor-starved cities. Between 1350 and 1500, conditions rose and fell, with an increasing tendency to rural unrest and violence. Finally, after 1500, the Ottoman Turks fell on the Mamluks and seized the Levant and Egypt,

ameliorating the worst of the region's economic conditions.

Northern Italy stood apart from both northern Europe and the Islamic world in its attempts to organize defenses against the occurrence or spread of plague. Florence, Venice, and Milan were large and generally prosperous cities that controlled the old counties (*contadi*) around them, including networks of subordinate towns. Each was located strategically for commercial traffic, and each produced industrial goods that had wide markets. Each had a great deal to lose with each passage of the plague, and each had the wealth and strength of government to experiment with antiplague tools. Most of what the rest of Europe would later adopt was developed in northern Italy. Quarantine, plague hospitals, lazarettos, bills of mortality, bills of health, commissions and boards of health, shutting in, cordons sanitaires, expulsion: all were developed first among the Italian city-states in the 14th and 15th centuries. Reasons for this may be sought in the Renaissance ideals of the age, the combination of small states with much wealth and powerful governments, the commercial bases of these cities, or the small distances separating the players and the need for innovation and cooperation to survive.

See also: Black Death (1347–1352); Demographic and Economic Effects of Plague: the Islamic World; Economic Effects of Plague in Europe; Plague in Europe, 1500–1725; individual cities.

References

Borsch, Stuart. *The Black Death in Egypt and England*. Austin: University of Texas Press, 2005.

Byrne, Joseph P. *The Black Death*. Westport, CT: Greenwood Press. 2004.

Carmichael, Ann G. *Plague and the Poor in Renaissance Florence*. New York: Cambridge University Press, 1986.

Cohn, Samuel K., Jr. *The Black Death Transformed: Disease and Culture in Early Renaissance Europe*. Oxford: Oxford University Press, 2002.

Dols, Michael W. *The Black Death in the Middle East*. Princeton, NJ: Princeton University Press, 1977.

Gottfried, Robert S. *Epidemic Disease in Fifteenth-Century England: The Medical Response and the Demographic Consequences*. New Brunswick, NJ: Rutgers University Press, 1978.

Horrox, Rosemary. *The Black Death*. New York: Manchester University Press, 1994.

Naphy, William G. and Andrew Spicer. *The Black Death and the History of Plagues, 1345–1730*. Stroud, Gloucs, England, 2001.

Nutton, Vivian, ed. *Pestilential Complexities: Understanding the Medieval Plague*. Supplement #27 to *Medical History*. London: Wellcome Trust for the History of Medicine, 2008.

Platt, Colin. *King Death: The Black Death and its Aftermath in Late-medieval England*. Toronto: University of Toronto Press, 1996.

Poos, Larry. *A Rural Society after the Black Death: Essex, 1350–1525*. New York: Cambridge University Press, 1991.

Twigg, Graham. *The Black Death: A Biological Reappraisal*. New York: Schocken Books, 1985.

Walløe, Lars. *Plagues and Population: Norway, 1350–1750*. Oslo: University of Oslo, 1995.

Ziegler, Philip. *The Black Death*. New York: Harper and Row, 1969.

Plague in Europe, 1500–1725

The early modern period of the Second Plague Pandemic is marked in Europe by an intensification of communal efforts to prevent the occurrence of the disease and/or to lessen its effects. Borrowing from Italian city-states, increasingly powerful nation-states in Spain, England, France, and Scandinavia began collecting data on disease and imposing uniform regulations for use during epidemics, including cordons, quarantines, and other forms of isolation. Plague affected large swaths of the continent in 1522, 1564, 1580, 1586, 1599, 1604, 1625, 1630, and 1636; northern areas of Germany, the Netherlands, and England suffered most in 1498, 1535, 1543, 1563, 1589, 1603, 1625, 1636, and 1664 to 1666. During the Thirty Years' War (1618–1648), plague had an almost constant presence in German states that were ravaged by one foreign army after another. Thereafter, major urban epidemics (Rome, Naples, Amsterdam, London, Vienna, Marseille, Moscow) marked the end of the Pandemic in one state after another.

By 1520, important portions of the Islamic world, especially the eastern Mediterranean Basin, had been conquered by the Ottoman Turks. Influenced by the West, they brought a more aggressive approach to avoiding plague but fell short of adopting many of the tools that seem to have ended the scourge in Europe. Islamic ports in the Mediterranean would continue to suffer recurring outbreaks into the 1840s.

Between 1400 and 1530, Europe had changed radically. Fully a third of feudal France had belonged to England but was now largely united and led by a powerful monarch. England lost its continental territories, save Calais, and suffered a civil war but had gained an effective and accepted dynasty—the Tudors—that had just declared its own Christian church (1529). The monarchs of Castile and Aragon united their thrones, creating Spain, ousted the last Muslim monarch in Iberia, and were sponsoring the conquest of the Western Hemisphere. Religious dissatisfaction in Germany erupted into the Reformation, establishing "Protestant" churches and communities that essentially redefined the Christian Church and brought Germany to the brink of civil war. Destructive Habsburg

(Spanish and Imperial) and French armies crisscrossed Italy in their campaigns for control of Naples, and in 1527, Lutheran troops sacked Rome.

The French attack on Naples in 1494 was a harbinger of a new regime of disease. However syphilis had made its way to Naples, here it was firmly planted among Italians, French, and Spaniards, who spread the pox as they returned home. Like plague 150 years earlier, it was transported throughout the Mediterranean by ships visiting Naples. Other diseases, too, took their place beside plague as major killers in Europe, at the same time that plague epidemics were becoming less frequent, less severe, and more localized. The same national governments that organized, equipped, fed, and directed increasingly huge armies—which generally spread disease—began to take it upon themselves to direct antiplague efforts at home. Authorities collected data on those who died, and bills of mortality were used as signals when such a city as London had more cases than normal. Health boards and magistrates appeared, as did plague hospitals and pest houses. Stricken individuals were by law shut in their homes at government expense; ships, crews, and cargoes were quarantined; victims' property was seized and disinfected or destroyed; barriers or cordons appeared around neighborhoods, villages, or even whole cities to reduce the disease's exposure. Shakespeare's theaters were shut down to curb both contagion and immorality.

Though mainstream medicine came nowhere near explaining plague, contagion theory moved forward with the ideas of 16th-century physician Girolamo Fracastoro (who also named syphilis) and his 17th-century followers. Almost all public health measures—aside from removing sources of stench and igniting gunpowder and bonfires to clears miasmas—were founded on the idea of contagion. Yet despite the scientific revolution and although microscopes appeared by the 1620s, the tiny creatures they revealed remained unconnected to plague until the late-19th century. Miasma remained the default explanation.

Increasingly, the urban poor, with their lack of cleanliness, sanitation, and decent diets and their growing numbers, overcrowding, and objectionable habits, came to be the focus of much official attention during the 16th and 17th centuries. The newly compiled records showed that epidemics often began in poor quarters of a city, spreading outward through vile odors or contagion. Plague-stricken poor were dealt with by isolation in their neighborhoods, and when that failed, often by expulsion or dispatch to the pest house. Waves of plague- and poison-spreading libels returned for the first time since the Black Death between the 1530s and 1640, though Jews tended to be spared the calumny and witches caught the unwelcome attention.

In war-torn regions, disease-ridden refugees often swelled walled cities, reducing the food supplies and living in nightmarish conditions. When such a place became the target of a siege, the exits were sealed and Death took its toll in earnest. The Habsburg-Valois Wars (1494–1559), the German civil wars of religion, the French civil wars of religion (1562–1598), the Dutch Rebellion (1566–1609), the Thirty Years' war (1618–1648), the English Civil War (1642–1649), and numerous smaller conflicts disrupted societies, caused famines, spread diseases, and killed far more among the civilian populations than among soldiers. France, relatively untouched by conflict after 1600, nonetheless suffered an estimated 750,000 to 1,150,000 plague deaths between 1628 and 1631. The city of Amiens between 1582 and 1669 suffered 19 plague epidemics, an average of once every 4.5 years. Second only to infant death, plague was France's main killer between 1600 and 1670.

The regime of war ended temporarily in 1648, and plague's regime ended in most of Europe over the next few decades. Trade rather than war continued to spread plague, however: London's Great Plague of 1665 came via Amsterdam and returned to the continent—a cordon sanitaire saved Paris; southern Spain was hit hard between 1679 and 1682; Buda, Prague, Belgrade, and Vienna suffered between 1679 and 1682, the last losing 76,000 people; many Baltic ports lost a quarter of their populations between 1708 and 1711, and Marseille suffered a terrible blow, probably via a poorly quarantined cargo ship in 1720. Strict quarantines, personal isolation, and a regional military cordon utilizing much of the French army prevented a wider outbreak.

See also: Almanacs; Armies; Bills of Health; Bills of Mortality; Borromeo, St. Charles (San Carlo); Contagion Theory; Cordons Sanitaires; Defoe, Daniel; Demographic and Economic Effects of Plague: the Islamic World; Demographic Effects of Plague: Europe 1500–1722; Economic Effects of Plague in Europe; End of Second Plague Pandemic: Theories; Health Boards, Magistracies, and Commissions; Islamic Civil Responses; London, Great Plague of (1665–1666); Marseille, France; Medical Education (1500–1700, Early Modern Europe); Moscow, Russia; Poverty and Plague; Public Health; Quarantine; Reformation and Protestantism; Scientific Revolution; Thirty Years' War; Vienna, Austria; Wills and Testaments.

References

Alexander, John T. *Bubonic Plague in Early Modern Russia: Public Health and Urban Disaster.* Baltimore, MD: Johns Hopkins University Press, 1980.

Bailey, Gauvin Alexander, et al., eds. *Hope and Healing: Painting in Italy in a Time of Plague, 1500–1800.* Chicago: University of Chicago Press, 2005.

Byrne, Joseph P. *Daily Life during the Black Death.* Westport, CT: Greenwood, 2006.

Calvi, Giulia. *Histories of a Plague Year: The Social and the Imaginary in Baroque Florence.* Berkeley: University of California Press, 1989.

Christensen, Daniel. *Politics and the Plague in Early Modern Germany: Political Efforts to Combat Epidemics in the Duchy of Braunschweig-Wolffenbüttel during the Seventeenth Century.* Saarbrücken: Verlag Dr. Müller, 2008.

Cipolla, Carlo. *Fighting the Plague in Seventeenth-Century Italy* (Merle Curti Lectures, 1978.) Madison: University of Wisconsin Press, 1981.

Cohn, Samuel K. *Cultures of Plague: Medical Thinking at the End of the Renaissance.* New York: Oxford University Press, 2010.

Cook, Alexandra Parma and Noble David Cook. *The Plague Files: Crisis Management in Sixteenth-Century Seville.* Baton Rouge: University of Louisiana Press, 2009.

Dobson, Mary. *Contours of Death and Disease in Early Modern England.* New York: Cambridge University Press, 1997.

Eckert, Edward A. *The Structure of Plagues and Pestilences in Early Modern Europe: Central Europe, 1560–1640.* New York: S. Karger Publishing, 1996.

Frandsen, Karl-Erik. *The Last Plagues in the Baltic Region, 1709–1713.* Copenhagen: Museum Tusculanum Press, 2010.

Healy, Margaret. *Fictions of Disease in Early Modern England: Bodies, Plagues and Politics.* New York: Palgrave, 2002.

Moote, A. Lloyd and Dorothy C. Moote. *The Great Plague: The Story of London's Most Deadly Year.* Baltimore, MD: Johns Hopkins University Press, 2004.

Naphy, William G. *Plagues, Poisons and Potions: Plague Spreading Conspiracies in the Western Alps c.1530–1640.* New York: Manchester University Press, 2002.

Slack, Paul. *The Impact of Plague in Tudor and Stuart England.* Oxford and New York: Oxford University Press, 1990.

Plague Churches. *See* Churches, Plague

Plague Memorials

There are two principal ways that Europeans have memorialized plague and its victims: the creation of monuments by survivors and the preservation of places and things associated with historical outbreaks.

Throughout the Second Pandemic, the simplest folk and the best-educated physicians agreed that God both sent and stopped epidemic disease. During outbreaks, many, especially among Catholics, made vows to God or saints. Survivors often fulfilled these vows with ex voto tokens from small wax figures to statues, painted altarpieces, and decorated chapels dedicated to God's mercy or the saints credited with having obtained it. Communities and civic governments also made vows whose fulfillments might be in the form of churches, crosses, or tall memorial columns. Similar religious works were also commissioned by thankful survivors who had not made vows, and only the circumstances of their creation, when known, can distinguish ex votos from other artistic offerings. Some memorial paintings featured scenes of contemporary suffering; more typical were iconic portraits of the Virgin Mary, often with the Christ Child, and other plague saints. During subsequent outbreaks, these portraits could acquire reputations for spiritual powers that made them focuses for prayer and supplication. Simpler extant memorials consist of wall plaques or even graffiti noting the awful year: on the north wall of St. Mary Ashwell, Hertfordshire, someone painted in Latin, "The first plague [was] in 1350 minus one."

More spectacular were the open-air *Pestsäulen* (plague columns) found scattered

The Marian Plague Monument in the Town Square of Českî Krumlov, The Czech Republic. Built in 1715–17 to commemorate a visitation of the plague in 1680–82, it features a fountain surrounding a column atop which stands the crowned Virgin Mary holding the infant Jesus. Around the column base are statues of four local traditional protective saints: Václav, Vitus, John the Evangelist, and Thaddeus Jude in the upper row; and plague saints Francis Xavier, Sebastian, Cajetan and St. Roche in the lower. (Courtesy of Benjamin Jones)

through the former Holy Roman Empire from Ljubliana (Slovenia) to Trier (Germany). Dating largely from the 17th century and products of Catholic Reformation spirituality and Baroque aesthetics, these memorials feature statues of plague saints, the Virgin and Child, angels soaring, and death overcome. As communal expressions, these commemorate both the sorrow generated by often huge death tolls and the joy at the conclusion of a specific epidemic. The most famous *Pestsäule* is that in Vienna. An ex voto dedicated by Emperor Leopold I to victims of the 1679 epidemic, it evolved over 14 years. Paul Strudel's final design is a pyramidal upwelling of clouds with angels, surmounted by a gilded level featuring Christ and a sunburst. It is located in front of the city's Karlskirche (Charles-church), itself an ex voto dedicated to the Milanese archbishop and plague saint Charles Borromeo. Other notable plague columns are in Budapest and Szentendre, Hungary; Trier, Germany; Linz and Baden, Austria; Telc, Mikulov, and Kutna Hora, Czech Republic; Banska Stiavnica and Kremnica, Slovakia; and Naples, Italy. Outdoor *Pestkreuze* (plague crosses) are more common, generally dating from the 1600s. That in Schönberg, Bavaria, commemorates the 1648/49 epidemic and its 63 local victims. In the summer of 2009, the old dilapidated cross was replaced in a communal ceremony. *Pestkreuz* may also refer to a grisly crucifix carved before 1348 but utilized during epidemics.

Maintaining—and restoring—a soaring plague memorial, which often dominates a town's main square, is one way a modern community manifests it connections with historical plagues. Another is the acknowledgment and preservation of plague sites. Most extensive and best known is the village of Eyam in Derbyshire, England. Eyam's self-sacrifice in 1666 is commemorated in its houses, graves, church, and other communal sites. Each August, a communal liturgy and procession revisit the village's death. More commonly, preservation applies to pest houses and graveyards or sites of mass graves. Dutch towns of Maastrict, Gouda, and Utrecht retain their *pesthuizen*, and Germany's Halle, Passau, and Werne their *pesthäuser*. After 1350, Erfurt's 11 long trenches filled with 12,000 plague corpses were marked by a memorial plaque, as was London's 13-acre West Smithfield cemetery. Here a Carthusian charterhouse (monastery)

was established (1371) to mark, guard, and pray for the purported "50,000" interred plague victims "besides many others thenceforth." Lisbon's 1505 mass cemetery was marked with a shrine to St. Roche (built 1506–1515), which was replaced by the Jesuit church of São Rocque (1555–c. 1595). Today a park, Rouen's Aître de St. Maclou was a mass cemetery opened after 1348, surrounded in the 1520s by the remaining half-timbered charnel house. Helsinki's (Finland) Plague Park (Ruttopuisto) abuts the city's oldest church and marks the mass grave of 1,185 victims of the 1712 epidemic; a modern marble stele commemorates the 652 residents of Porvoo, Finland, who died in an earlier stage of the same outbreak.

A final type of ex voto memorial is represented by the famous Oberammergau (Bavaria, Germany) Passion Play, still performed every 10th year since 1634.

See also: Borromeo, St. Charles (San Carlo); Churches, Plague; Ex voto; Eyam, England; Lazarettos and Pest Houses; Mass Graves and Plague Cemeteries; Plague Saints; Virgin Mary.

References

Avery, Harold. "Plague Churches, Monuments and Memorials." *Proceedings of the Royal Society of Medicine* 59 (1966): 110–116.

Boeckl, Christine. *Images of Plague and Pestilence.* Kirkville, MO: Truman State University Press, 2000.

Plague Orders and National Authorities

When the Second Pandemic began in Europe, it was viewed not as a universal tragedy but as a local event. As long as taxes were paid, monarchs and their minions paid little attention to plague outside their courts. Slowly, notions of contagion and Renaissance ideas of public utility spurred centralized coordination. By the 16th century, postfeudal national governments began issuing guidelines or laws for local authorities when plague threatened. Between 1500 and 1720, regional French *parlements* usurped local governments, acting with greater resources and a broader viewpoint. Often, they appointed and oversaw local plague commissions or sanitary boards, ensuring regional uniformity of response and cooperation among local jurisdictions. In the Empire, occasionally updated imperial letters patent known as the *ordo pestis* organized previous ad hoc instructions and imposed local Italian models of communal plague precautions and antiepidemic activity.

Authorities in Denmark and England had done very little during epidemics, but after 1500, royal action imposed and outlined expected activities. English antiplague edicts began with Henry VIII. In 1518, Chancellor Thomas Wolsey created the Royal College of Physicians, linking crown and medical profession. He also issued orders to local constables and aldermen regarding sanitation and victim isolation. In 1578, Elizabeth had royal expectations drawn up in a *Book of Orders*, which was updated and re-released by the Privy Council during plague years in 1592, 1593, 1603, 1609, 1630, 1636, 1646, and, with radical revisions, in 1666. These nonstatutory regulations were accompanied by *Advice* by the College of Physicians on personal prophylaxis and therapy. In 1630, these *Orders* were linked to *Orders* on poverty and food scarcity.

See also: Health Boards, Magistracies, and Commissions; James I and VI Stuart, King; Public Health.

Reference

Slack, Paul. "Books of Orders: The Making of English Social Policy, 1577–1631." *Transactions of the Royal Historical Society* 5th ser. 30 (1980): 1–22.

Plague Saints

For Roman Catholics and Orthodox Christians, saints are those Christians who have died, been saved by God, and surround him in Heaven. They are aware of the living on Earth, can hear them and respond, and may intercede with God on behalf of those who request it. God willing, they may also intervene in lives, appearing in visions, as voices, or in miracles. Catholic art and literature have long celebrated saints and their activities.

Certain saints became associated with occupations, places, or specific human needs. Catholic towns generally had one or more "patron" saints who protected the city: often a local saint and a major figure, for example, Mary or an Apostle, whose relics the cathedral held. When plague struck, these patrons became advocates to whom individuals, groups, and the full community turned for help. Saints Sebastian and Roche were universal "plague saints" to whom people across Europe prayed for protection. Local figures, for example, Nicholas of Tolentino in Tuscany and Rosalia in Palermo, acquired status as plague saints due to plague-time traditions of supernatural aid.

See also: Art, Effects of Plague on; Borromeo, St. Charles (San Carlo); Christ; Confraternities; Ex voto; Gregory the Great, Pope; Heaven and Hell; Lazarus; Plague Memorials; Processions; St. Januarius (San Gennaro); St. Nicholas of Tolentino; St. Roche; St. Rosalia; St. Sebastian; Virgin Mary.

References

Dormeier, Heinrich. "Saints as Protectors against Plague: Problems of Definition and Economic and Social Implications," in *Living with the Black Death*, edited by Lars Bisgaard and Leif Søndergaard (Odense: University of Southern Denmark Press, 2009), 161–186.

Schiferl, Ellen. "Iconography of Plague Saints in Fifteenth-century Italian Painting." *Fifteenth Century Studies* 6 (1983): 205–225.

Plague Stone

When isolating a plague-struck community or larger area, authorities had to make some arrangements for delivering messages and charity and selling such necessities as food and drugs. Direct contact with those being isolated was forbidden, and any coins coming as payment from a plague area were considered contaminated. Though rarely documented, there is evidence that such landmarks as large flat stones in fields or cleared woodlands served as points of contact. Goods and messages would be left by the healthy and retrieved by members of the isolated community. This might happen at predetermined times, or a signal might be given. In Penrith, England, and Thun, Switzerland, coins used for payment by the infected were left underwater in flowing streams on specific, large, concave stones. The rushing water was believed to have the power to cleanse tainted money.

See also: Cordons Sanitaires; Disinfection and Fumigation; Eyam, England; Quarantine.

Reference

Byrne, Joseph. *Daily Life during the Black Death*. Westport, CT: Greenwood Press, 2006.

Plague Tracts. See Consilia and Plague Tracts

"Plagues" in the West, 900–1345

Low population densities between the First and Second Plague Pandemics mitigated against widespread infectious disease outbreaks, but localized epidemics were precursors to the Black Death. Neither communal nor medical responses to these were noteworthy, leaving few precedents for confronting late medieval plague. Identifying specific diseases from contemporary literary descriptions is always risky business, and without a clear medical paradigm in Christian Europe, descriptions are very problematic. Communication being limited, early chroniclers could have little idea how widespread any illness was. Medical theory and practice were more advanced in Muslim-dominated areas, as was communication, making their records somewhat more reliable. Identifying specific diseases, however, remains difficult. In 1056 to 1057, a major pandemic swept the Middle East according to Ibn Hajar, and another, more limited, struck Egypt and Syria in 1063. Evidence suggests an epidemic in Egypt and Syria in 1142 to 1143 and more probably in Egypt, the Hijaz, and Yemen in 1157. Egypt suffered again in 1200 to 1202, 1236 to 1238, and 1273 to 1274; Syria and Egypt may have suffered an early epidemic of plague in 1258 to 1259. Russian chronicles mention localized epidemics in Novgorod, Vladimir-Suzdal, Smolensk, Pskov, and Tver between 1158 and 1344 but offer no help in identifying the culprit. Western European records are no more helpful. Diseases caused "great mortality" among urban residents, especially in the

Mediterranean region, and swept away battalions of Crusaders and other armies (cities and armies being the two great concentrations of people). Some scholars insist that plague played its role in some of these episodes, though typhus, influenza, malaria, and even smallpox are far likelier candidates.

See also: Diseases, Opportunistic and Subsidiary; Famine; Justinian, Plague of (First Plague Pandemic); Leprosy (Hansen's Disease) and Leprosarium; Virgin Soil Disease.

References

Bray, R. S. *Armies of Pestilence: The Effects of Pandemics on History.* Cambridge: Lutterworth Press, 1998.

Hays, J. N. *The Burden of Disease.* New Brunswick: Rutgers University Press, 1998.

Pneumonic Plague

Pneumonic plague is caused by the *Yersinia pestis* bacterium, which is the same bacterium that causes bubonic plague. The two diseases are essentially the same, except that while in bubonic plague the destructive action of the pathogen does not directly interfere with the lungs, pneumonic plague is characterized by the bacteria's presence in the lungs. This makes pneumonic plague more lethal than bubonic plague and allows it to be spread directly from person to person, unlike bubonic plague.

There are two types of pneumonic plague, primary and secondary. Secondary results from the spreading of flea-injected bubonic plague from the lymphatic and circulatory systems to the lungs. Typically, an abscess filled with the toxic material will form and burst, forcing the victim to cough

out some of the material, along with blood from the damaged tissue. Primary pneumonic plague results from a bystander breathing in the pathogen resulting from a sufferer's coughing or sneezing. Normal speaking can scatter bacteria up to two meters from the source, while an unobstructed sneeze may double that range. The *Y. pestis* is immediately absorbed into the mucous and the lining of the lungs themselves. Because the bacteria had just been in a human body, it will have developed the protective envelope that resists the body's defenses and allows for very rapid reproduction and multiplication. Even so, a period of incubation takes several days.

If the pneumonic plague is secondary, early symptoms of infection will be similar to those of bubonic plague: lethargy, chills, headache, nausea, and fever, but pulmonary distress will quickly set in. In both primary and secondary pneumonic plague, pulmonary distress is distinguishing. A cough and chest pains will be followed by asthma-like shortage of breath and the coughing up of blood or blood-coated sputum. Medieval doctors and chroniclers mention this specific symptom as the sign of certain death. Blood pressure will drop rapidly and shock will set in with the inability of the body to provide blood to its cells. Asphyxia, cyanosis, and coma are common in late stages.

Plague historians have found pneumonic plague a very tantalizing alternative to bubonic plague in explaining the characteristics of many outbreaks during the Second Plague Pandemic. It would go far in accounting for the respiratory symptoms mentioned by observers, it seems that it would account for the rapid and distant spread of plague, and it seems to make rat epizootics much less necessary. In some cases, rats might be done away with entirely. This is especially useful to Scandinavian historians, who have otherwise to work with winter outbreaks and rats and fleas that do not take well to the cold. Combinations of bubonic and both primary and secondary pneumonic plague are certainly possible in epidemic conditions, a compromise that appeals to a number of historians.

One problem is that even pneumonic plague in the context of modern railways in 1910 and 1911 in rather cold Manchuria did not produce the high death rates of the Black Death. While it was certainly contagious, only .4 percent of the population died during this epidemic. One factor limiting contagion was probably that prostration came early in the contagious phase, reducing the time and number of contacts a victim might have. A constant in plague studies is the possibility of changes in the pathogen that account for greater infectivity and lethality in the past and less in its current forms. Unfortunately, while studies of *Y. pestis* DNA may shed light on changes over time, it will be impossible to distinguish skeletal cases of bubonic from pneumonic plague.

See also: Black Death: Debate over the Medical Nature of; Black Death: Origins and Early Spread; Bubonic Plague; Morbidity, Mortality, and Virulence; Septicemic Plague; Third Plague Pandemic; *Yersinia pestis*.

References

Gamsu, Mark. "The Epidemic of Pneumonic Plague in Manchuria 1910–1911." *Past & Present* 190 (2006): 147–183.

Gani, Raymond and Steve Leach. "Epidemiologic Determinants for Modeling Pneumonic Plague outbreaks." *Emerging Infectious Diseases* 10 (2004): 608–614.

Gorbach, Sherwood L., et al. *Infectious Diseases*. 3rd edition. New York: Lippincott, Williams & Wilkins, 2004.

Orent, Wendy. *Plague: The Mysterious Past and Terrifying Future of the World's Most Dangerous Disease*. New York: Free Press, 2004.

Poetry, European

In the immediate wake of the Black Death, poets laid out their major lines of response. Paris's Simon de Couvin and Prague's Heinrich von Mügeln anthropomorphized the astrological Great Conjunction of 1345 that many blamed for the plague. Others set medical advice to verse, as in a French version of the *Paris Compendium* and John Lydgate's 15th-century "Diet and Doctrine for the Pestilence." Among others, the Italian Petrarch and the Welshman Llywelyn Fythan lamented their beloved dead, and Bishop Richard Ledrede of Ossory (Ireland) versified his lament for the loss of virtue and goodness with the plague: "Everywhere rapine flourishes, hatred, and arson ..." Into Latin sermons, English preachers embedded short English "preachers' tags," poems recited in vernacular to serve as memory aids or proof texts to be remembered by the faithful. Many of these were translations from Latin. The great Rheims composer Guillaume Machaut used the plague as a frame tale for a poem of courtly love, "*Le jugement dou Roy de Navarre*." Among Spanish court poets, fear and misery replaced chivalric confidence and bravado; the epic disappeared, replaced by the simpler and more emotional ballad. Pero López de Ayala penned *Rimado de palacio*, a versified vernacular court confessor's manual and *Art of Government* with reflections of the Great Schism of 1378.

Later poems follow similar lines, often borrowing from prior works, for example, Olivier de la Hayes's 1425 verse treatment of the Paris *Compendium* (3,600 octosyllables), translations from Latin prayers in *Ars*

Moriendi, and translated meditations on death. Poetry also accompanied illustrations of the *Danse macabre*, the Three Living Meet the Three Dead, and "The Body and the Worms," all treatments of the suddenness and inevitability of death.

The 16th century produced versified plague chronicles, as that of Padua in 1555 by the Piedmontese Christoforo Baravalle. Samuel Cohn found 15 verse narratives from 1576 to 1578, which included such elements as praise for boards of health and descriptions of the postplague celebrations. The Italian Plague of 1576 seems especially rich, as many poems survive, including a Vatican collection of five sonnets on plague remedies and a Verona book with 35 plague poems, none by known physicians. Some serve as introductions to prose plague tracts. The French *Elegiae de Peste* by Dr. Jean Ursin is a deluxe collection of 16 moralizing poems dedicated to Cosimo de' Medici that is considered the first collection of plague verse.

Elizabethan and Stuart Londoners produced a rich literature of plague poetry that often linked the author's personal grief to that of a personified London, who laments her lost children. Others chastise sinful Londoners whose behaviors brought on God's punishment, like Old Testament prophets. Some allegorize, others describe horrors quite literally, and others rely on the memories of their readers. Notable examples include Bartholomew Chappell's "A Warning Voice" (1593), the works of Thomas Dekker (1603 to 1625), John Davies's "Triumph of Death" (1609), John Taylor's "The Fearefull Summer" (1625 and 1636), and George Wither's *Britain's Remembrancer* (1628). London's Great Plague of 1665 produced Thomas Clarke's "Meditations in My Confinement," John Tabor's "Reflections on the Pestilence," and William Austin's "The Anatomy of the Pestilence."

The plague of 1720 to 1722 in Marseille also spawned many poems in France and England, most eminently forgettable.

See also: Apocalypse and Apocalypticism; *Ars moriendi* (*The Art of Dying*); Astrology; Broadsheets, Broadsides, and Pamphlets; Chaucer, Geoffrey; *Compendium of Paris*; Couvin, Simon de; Danse Macabre; Donne, John; Langland, William; Languages: Vernacular and Latin; Lydgate, John; Morality Literature, Christian; Nashe, Thomas; Petrarch, Francesco; Poetry, Islamic; Shakespeare, William; Triumph of Death; Wither, George.

References

Anselment, Raymond. *The Realms of Apollo. Literature and Healing in Seventeenth-Century England*. Newark: University of Delaware Press and Associated University Presses, 1995.

Cerquiglini-Toulet, Jacqueline. *The Color of Melancholy: The Uses of Books in the Fourteenth Century*. Baltimore, MD: Johns Hopkins University Press, 1997.

Cohn, Samuel K. *Cultures of Plague: Medical Thinking at the End of the Renaissance*. New York: Oxford University Press, 2010.

Colin, William. *A Poet at the Fountain: Essays on the Narrative Verse of Guillaume de Machaut*. Lexington: University of Kentucky Press, 1974.

McDonald, William C. "Death in the Stars: Heinrich von Mügeln on the Black Plague." *Mediaevalia* 5 (1979): 89–112.

Wenzel, Siegfried. "Pestilence and Middle English Literature: Friar John Grimestone's Poems on Death," in *The Black Death: The Impact of the Fourteenth-century Plague*, edited by Daniel Williman (Binghamton, NY: Medieval and Renaissance Texts and Studies, 1982), 131–159.

Poetry, Islamic

Long before they turned to Islam, the Arab people prized poetry as the height of human expression. The Koran itself was recorded as a type of poetry, as were most types of communication. Often poetic passages were embedded in prose texts on contemporary narrative, history, or even medicine. During the initial outbreak of the Black Death, the most important passage was by eyewitness Ibn al-Wardi (d. 1349) of Aleppo, Syria, the *risalah al-naba an'alwaba* ("an essay on the report of the pestilence") from his chronicle *Tarikh*. At least four manuscript copies exist of this descriptive narrative of the plague's progress through Muslim lands. It "struck," "cleansed," "uprooted," "reviled," ravished," "humbled," and "triumphed." Though orthodoxly Muslim, the poem attributes the plague to Allah's "wrath" and "punishment" and ends in a prayer for His mercy. Several later Muslim historians quoted from it, and it remains an important historical source.

Other poetic descriptions of the Black Death are collected in manuscripts in Cairo and London: a contemporary epistolary account of plague in Egypt; a few quoted verses of Ibrahim al-Mimar from Cairo; and a description of the Black Death in Syria and Palestine, featuring Damascus. The pattern of poetically expressing horror, sadness, and religious resignation and hope during epidemics continued in the Islamic world through the Second Pandemic.

See also: Black Death (1347–1352); Islamic Religious Responses; Poetry, European.

References

Byrne, Joseph P. *The Black Death*. Westport, CT: Greenwood Press, 2004. Reprints Dols' translation and plague poem recorded by Muhammad ibn Sasra (c. 1390).

Dols, Michael W. 1974. "Ibn al-Wardī's Risā-lah al-naba' 'an al-waba,' A Translation of a Major Source for the History for the Black Death in the Middle East," in *Near Eastern Numismatics,*

Iconography, Epigraphy and History, edited by Dickran Kouymjian (Beirut: American University of Beirut Press, 1974), 443–455.

Dols, Michael W. *The Black Death in the Middle East*. Princeton, NJ: Princeton University Press, 1977.

Poisoning and Plague Spreading

From the first outbreak of plague in 1347 until the late 1600s, Europeans echoed fears and accusations of poisoning and of the disease being spread deliberately. As people sought to understand the strange patterns of epidemic death, Jews, gypsies, lepers, witches, Satanists, thieves, vagabonds, Protestants, corpse carriers, foreigners, pilgrims, caregivers, Muslims, and simply the malevolent were suspected and sometimes tried; hundreds were executed. Some were thought to have spread deadly ointments on door handles, others to have poisoned civic wells, and still others to have directly poisoned individuals through food or medicine. Poisonings ranged from corpses or dead animals in wells to spider and toad venoms, while plague could be spread by infected clothing or unguents made with plague-victims' pus.

Before 1347, poison libels had been cast at anti–Christian Jews, lepers, and gypsies. Famous cases of well poisoning arose in Bohemia in 1161, Vienna in 1267, and around France in 1321. With the Black Death came both claims and the usual scapegoats. In Buda, Hungary, Christian physicians accused rival Jewish doctors of poisoning their patients, and in Visby, several "foreigners" were burned for well poisoning in 1350. In 1348, paupers and beggars were dismembered and burned in Narbonne for possessing poison and failing to disclose its source; nearby physician

Jacme d'Agramont commented approvingly, and Rheims poet and musician Guillaume Machaut opined that God's pestilential wrath was aimed at well-poisoning Jews. In September 1348, 11 South German Jews confessed to well poisoning and were executed. At the same time, a Geneva court extracted a confession from a Savoyard Jew that a rabbi had given him poison to contaminate wells, cisterns, and springs, "so as to kill and destroy the whole of Christianity." Despite the objections of physicians, nobles, and even the pope, the claims spread and fueled the anti–Semitism that destroyed many German Jewish communities.

Jewish poisoning libels ceased after about 1350, but scapegoats emerged again and again, often under torture. Genevan pest house attendants and a priest were executed for spreading plague in 1530. Officials in Milan blamed Jews for spreading plague with ointment-soaked cloths in 1576, but the carpenter Gianbattista Casale knew to blame "certain renegade Christians" from Turkey for the crime. Famous French physician Ambroise Paré wrote that in Lyons, 1565, thieves smeared doors and walls of rich people's homes with excretions from carbuncles and buboes. In 1545, 56 people were prosecuted in Geneva, of whom 19 were executed and 16 banished. In 1570, Genevan authorities sentenced convicted plague-spreaders to be burned alive until only ashes remained.

After the Milanese epidemic of 1630, Archbishop Federigo Borromeo wrote of the "many" who went into the pest house, presumably to gather pus "with the intention of poison smearing." He reported that they poisoned prayer books, cookies for children, holy water basins, and even plague prophylactics. He ascribed demonic influence, hunger, desperation, and misery as some of their motivations. Borromeo faulted the Milanese

government for spending too much time tracking these people down, though they appear repeatedly in his own book.

See also: Anti–Semitism and Anti–Jewish Violence before the Black Death; Contagion Theory; Crime and Punishment; Jews; Milan, Italy; Social Construction of Disease; Wills and Testaments.

References

Guerchberg, Sèraphine. "The Controversy over the Alleged Sowers of the Black Death in the Contemporary Treatises on Plague," in *Change in Medieval Society*, edited by Sylvia Thrupp (New York: Appleton-Century-Crofts, 1965), 208–224.

Naphy, William. *Plagues, Poisons and Potions: Plague Spreading Conspiracies in the Western Alps c.1530–1640.* New York: Manchester University Press, 2002.

Popes. *See* Bishops and Popes; Clement VI, Pope; Gregory the Great, Pope

Population. *See* entries beginning with *Demographic* and *Demography*

Poverty and Plague

In the manorial system, peasants may have been materially poor, but they had direct access to the most important means of production: the land. Poverty in the later Middle Ages and early modern periods will be understood as applying to those who had neither this access nor a reasonably steady income apart from the land in villages, towns or cities. Poverty increased across Europe alongside urbanization and monetization during the high Middle Ages and was all too common by the mid-14th century. The poor were far from homogenous, however, and before the Black Death, some societies had begun to distinguish the religious poor (friars), the "shamefaced poor"—widows with children, those born with physical defects, those crippled in the course of life or work, the mentally weak, and those who had temporarily fallen on bad times—from the shameless poor who were able-bodied but preferred to beg or otherwise seek support. The plague spurred this development as resentment—and legal penalties—increased against skulkers, vagabonds, vagrants, beggars, and others who refused to work despite the labor shortages brought on by huge death tolls.

Jewish, Christian, and Muslim societies had long accepted the duty of supporting the truly poor, almsgiving being one of the pillars of Islam and a means of gaining grace among Catholics. Preachers often linked almsgiving with pleasing God and thus avoiding the plague. Feeding and caring for the poor had traditionally been one of the functions of monastic houses, but in cities, confraternities and even civic governments increasingly usurped this role. Reformed cities of the 16th and 17th centuries secularized poor relief, though Anglican England left it in the hands of the parishes. During plague times, the public fisc suffered from income starvation just as new expenses for plague-related services and goods rose steeply.

When plague struck, the poor were disadvantaged in several distinct ways. Sometimes the civic government expelled them, along with prostitutes and other undesirables. With few or no resources beyond their immediate community, they would often seek shelter in nearby woods or workers' huts, making do as best they could. In other cases, the poor remained as the wealthy fled to the countryside or other towns. The poor suffered through the epidemic without the financial support provided by the wealthy. Many wills, however, include higher-than-usual gifts for the poor in recognition of this systemic problem. Many people entered the ranks of the unemployed poor as bosses sickened, died, or shut up shop and left. Servants, too, found themselves on the street when their employers fled without them or died. As early as 1348, some observers noticed that the plague epidemic seemed to originate in the poorer areas of towns. Eventually, many cities experimented with cordons sanitaires that surrounded such a neighborhood and sealed the disease inside, theoretically.

While none associated plague with rats, many understood plague to be generated by filth and stink. Not surprisingly, these were characteristic of poorer residential areas and those in which butchers, tanners, fishmongers, and other unsavory occupations were located. As the 14th century produced one more plague outbreak after another, authorities came to conclude a direct correlation between poverty and the disease. Since God was widely considered to be the cause of plague and sin the irritant that induced God to act, the (im-)morality of the poor (drunkenness, gambling, thievery, fornication, sloth) became an issue of public health and public legislation. Though the poor who moved between cities during epidemics were often believed to be plague carriers (despite miasma theory), expulsion of "beggars" and other poverty-stricken folks increased in frequency. In September 1539, the Venetians barred entry to poor people who had been expelled from Milan and, in turn, expelled or enslaved in its galley fleet between 4,000 and 5,000 beggars and others who had arrived in Venice recently. After this prophylactic move, they turned against the city's whores. In 16th- and 17th-century Central Europe, many cities established depots where the poor would gather during plagues to receive food and alms. This was a way of estimating the extent of poverty as well as a means of controlling those who were needful.

As early as 1348, Florence established a central alms distribution center at the civic grain storehouse of Or San Michele. The Florentine aristocrats understood the power of the organized lower class and sought to keep its members satisfied if not happy. With so many civic leaders dead or absent and governments barely operating, urban unrest could flare and leave a city gutted or in ashes. Such uprisings as those by the Ciompi in Florence and peasants in France and England made the point. So pity often gave way to fear as a motivator.

Finally, in most towns, some poor folk found new jobs when plague struck. The initial increase in funerals beckoned the poor as mourners and processors. The sudden need for corpse carriers, gravediggers, searchers, guards, fumigators, house cleansers, and other plague specialists absorbed some percentage of the otherwise unemployed. Many of these positions allowed the unscrupulous to steal and cheat and enrich themselves at the expense of victims and survivors, and many were tried and punished for just such crimes.

See also: Abandonment; Ciompi Revolt; Cordons Sanitaires; Corpse Carriers; Crime and Punishment; Demographic and Economic Effects of Plague: the Islamic World; Dietary Regimens; Diseases, Opportunistic and Subsidiary; Economic Effects of Plague in Europe; Expulsion of Victims; Funerals, Catholic; Gravediggers; Jacquerie; Labourers, Ordinance and Statute of; Langland, William; Moral Legislation; Peasants' Revolt, English; Searchers.

References

Carmichael, Ann G. *Plague and the Poor in Renaissance Florence.* New York: Cambridge University Press, 1986.

Epstein, P. R. "Commentary: Pestilence and Poverty—Historical Transitions and the Great Pandemics." *American Journal of Preventive Medicine* 8 (1992): 263–265.

Grell, Ole Peter and Andrew Cunningham, eds. *Health Care and Poor Relief in Protestant Europe, 1500–1700.* New York: Routledge, 1997.

Henderson, John. *Piety and Charity in Late Medieval Florence.* Chicago: University of Chicago Press, 1992.

Pelling, Margaret. *The Common Lot: Sickness, Medical Occupations and the Urban Poor in Early Modern England.* New York: Longman, 1998.

Pullan, Brian. "Plague and Perceptions of the Poor in Early Modern Italy," in *Epidemics and Ideas*, edited by Terence Ranger and Paul Slack (New York: Cambridge University Press, 1992), 101–123.

Prayer and Fasting

God was the source of plague, God was believed to hear and, within limits, answer prayers. This is deeply embedded in Hebrew Scripture, the Christian Old Testament, and therefore informs Judaism, Christianity, and Islam. Fasting, signaling repentance, was common to monotheistic traditions. Denial of food was seen as a means of mild suffering and self-discipline of the body. Since God desires that people reject sin and turn toward his mercy and love, fasting and penitential prayer were powerful signs of contrition and correction of life. Since for Christians plague was divine wrath manifested against the unrepentant and infidel, the repentant and faithful felt compelled to act.

Prayer

For most, prayer is a monologue addressed to God. It may be silent, spoken, or sung, articulated in words or "heart-felt," memorized or spontaneous, part of a ritual or not, addressed individually or as a group. Traditionally, a given prayer has one of several themes, including praise and worship acknowledging the divine attributes (power, goodness, mercy, etc.); acknowledgement of and contrition for one's own sin; request for divine aid or favor for oneself or another; love and thanksgiving in general or for reputed aid or favor; or desire for salvation.

Catholic and Orthodox Christians also acknowledge the value of prayer directed to Christian saints who have joined God in Heaven. Doctrinally correct prayer requests that the saint pray to God with the same intention as the earthbound pray-er, to intercede with God on behalf of the supplicant. The famous "Hail Mary" directed to Jesus's mother ends "pray for us sinners, now and at the hour of our death." Popular Christianity often attributed greater powers to the saints themselves, however: to destroy enemies, protect travelers, or heal illnesses. Church leaders recognized that just as God performed miracles through such biblical figures as Moses or the Apostles, God might act on prayers directed to saints. As Protestantism developed in its several forms, adherents rejected such "unbiblical" accretions.

In plague-wracked Catholic Europe, prayer was expected less of the average parishioner than of monks and nuns. At Barcelona in 1650, the bishop ordered monastic communities to pray for the city's safety. Communal lay prayer at special liturgies and processions supplemented masses, confessions, and last rites that included a final confession. Such set prayers as the Rosary could be said by an individual or a crowd if led by a cleric. Protestants stressed individual and group prayer, though church services normally occurred once a week, whereas daily mass was typical in well-manned urban Catholic churches. In August 1624, Calvinist Leyden's civil authorities demanded that two churches be open for prayer services on Wednesdays and Thursdays. Twelve years later, the Dutch States General ordered a day of prayer devoid of drinking, golf, ballgames, and other "vanities." In Elizabeth I's England, Anglican services were added on Wednesdays and Fridays. Edmund Grindal, her Bishop of London, thought it "meet to excite and stir up all goodly people . . . to pray earnestly and heartily to God, to turn away his deserved wrath" (Cunningham and Grell, 291). He recommended daily family prayer gatherings, with specific petitions for divine forgiveness, mercy, and assistance. Suggested prayers were often printed in pamphlets or on broadsides. Muslim prayers during plague time seem to have reiterated one's submission to Allah's will with reliance on his infinite mercy.

Fasting

In normal times, Catholics fasted penitentially on Fridays and throughout Lent, but for Protestants, communal fasts—dictated by civil or royal authorities—were held only at special times, during wartime, a famine, or plague. These were often linked to special church services (i.e., sermons) that might last all day.

See also: Allah; Almanacs; Amulets, Talismans, and Magic; *Ars moriendi* (*The Art of Dying*); Bible; Bishops and Popes; Books of Hours; Christ; Consilia and Plague Tracts; Demons, Satan, and the Devil; Ex voto; Flagellants; Funerals, Catholic; God the Father; Heaven and Hell; Monks, Nuns, and Monasteries; Plague Saints; Processions; Purgatory; Reformation and Protestantism; Sin; Virgin Mary.

References

Bailey, Gauvin Alexander, et al. eds. *Hope and Healing: Painting in Italy in a Time of*

Plague, 1500–1800. Chicago: University of Chicago Press, 2005.

Cunningham, Andrew and Ole Peter Grell. *The Four Horsemen of the Apocalypse: Religion, War, Famine and Death in Reformation Europe*. New York: Cambridge University Press, 2000.

Dols, Michael W. *The Black Death in the Middle East*. Princeton, NJ: Princeton University Press, 1977.

Horrox, Rosemary. *The Black Death*. New York: Manchester University Press, 1994.

Priests

In Catholic, Orthodox, and Anglican Christianity, priests were men who were ordained in a special, sacramental ritual by a bishop, who oversaw a district (diocese). Ordination made one an aide to the bishop, armed with the spiritual powers and authority to administer most of the seven sacraments and usually given the duties of overseeing the parishes into which the dioceses of Europe were divided. These priests were diocesan clergy, and most had "cure of souls," or the responsibility of leading the spiritual life of his parish community (baptizing, hearing confessions, saying mass, preaching, witnessing and blessing marriages, providing last rites to the dying, and performing funeral masses) along with teaching and counseling. A village or group of villages would have its own pastor (lit. "shepherd"), and a town would normally have several parishes and several priests per parish. Large cities would have a score or more parishes and perhaps hundreds of diocesan clergy.

Diocesan priests also handled administrative duties, served in hospitals or other church institutions, or merely used their status to obtain an income (sinecure). Other men also became priests, including most abbots and some members of monasteries,

A Catholic priest administers last rites to plague victims during the 17th century. To die without a priest's ministrations was a Catholic's great fear. (Courtesy of the National Library of Medicine)

many friars, and all Jesuits (founded in 1540). All bishops, including the pope, had to be priests. Normally one rose to the status of priest through promotion according to time and experience, though this could be short-circuited in times of need.

When plague struck a Catholic area, priests were burdened with extraordinary duties. The numbers of sick parishioners multiplied, and the parish priest had a duty to visit each one. Those on their deathbeds needed comforting as well as the sacrament of Extreme Unction or the Last Rites. Proper preparation for death included one's last confession and communion, anointing with holy oil, and special prayers at bedside. At an epidemic's high tide, priests exposed themselves to plague victims many times each day. While some took prophylactic measures—hearing confession through a candle flame to purify the victim's breath, using a long spatula to serve communion, or doing both from outside through a window—the risks of infection were high. Bishops who could ill afford to lose their clergy often eased the burden by reducing the required rituals or offering all who died in good conscience or true contrition for their sins a plenary indulgence. The 16th-century Council of Trent (1545–1563) acted similarly, reducing the number of anointings from five to one and, if the bishop had granted a plenary indulgence, only final communion was necessary. Priests also served in pest houses and hospitals, as celebrants at funeral masses, and at the graveside while these services were allowed. They also continued to say mass and hear confessions from the healthy and participate in religious processions. No doubt, the most dedicated were among the first to succumb.

When a parish priest died, a vacancy opened and the bishop or archdeacon had to fill it as soon as possible. This could take months for a rural parish (Canon Law allowed six months), longer if the diocesan leaders had died. Men were rushed through promotion to ordination or moved among parishes, in turn opening new vacancies. Studies of English bishops' registers for 1348 to 1349, in which these changes were recorded, suggest clerical death rates of 40 to 77 percent, averaging around 50 percent. In Barcelona, it was at least 40 percent, and the vacancy rate was 15 times normal; Vienna's cathedral the Stefansdom lost 54 clergy in 1349; and the Bishop of Marseille died along with all of his cathedral clergy (canons). During later plagues, the numbers were not necessarily as dramatic, but the high rates continued. In Iceland, Skálholt diocese lost 97 of 100 clergy in 1402 and 60 percent of new clerics two years later;

and in one 15th-century plague, 86 percent of the clergy of Hólar diocese died. Modern scholars have to be careful, however, since every relocation of a priest creates a new vacancy, so the number of vacancies does not equal the number of clergy deaths. Some registers are clearer than others when recording data.

In the rush to fill vacancies, bishops ordained younger, less experienced and less well-educated men. Both new and established clerics were also drawn to new, well-paying jobs as chaplains and chantry priests, privately hired by wealthy individuals to pray and say (chant) the mass on behalf of the dead. The draw was acute since the incomes of many parishes fell dramatically with parishioner deaths. Fourteenth-century Archbishops of Canterbury tried to limit rises in English clerical wages or stipends with mixed effects. Some priests took multiple jobs (pluralism) and were often away from one or more of their posts (absenteeism). Friars, bishops, and even the pope attacked diocesan clergy for these abuses and for flight during plague time and were among the priests' harshest critics. Regular folk, too, who had often had negative things to say about priests, ratcheted up their complaints, increasing anticlericalism across Europe. From Boccaccio to the Reformation, the drumbeat of unprepared, under-dedicated, immoral, and greedy priests could be heard across Europe. Yet by 1500, Europe had never had so many priests serving Christians' spiritual needs. For Reformers, every person was his or her own priest, and, except among Anglicans, "priests" were replaced with pastors, ministers, preachers, or elders. Catholic leaders strengthened their priesthood through the Council of Trent's demands for better education and episcopal (bishops') oversight.

England had its established Anglican priesthood and bishops, but also its dissenters who had been heavily influenced by the Radical Reformation and Calvinism. When plague tested the dedication of London's 17th-century clergy, the Anglican priests often fell well behind the Puritans, Quakers, and other nonconforming preachers in meeting the needs of all Londoners, a trend that softened the line between the official and minority religious communities.

See also: Anticlericalism; *Ars moriendi* (*The Art of Dying*); Bishops and Popes; Christ; Friars (Mendicants); Funerals, Catholic; Lollards; Parish; Pastors, Preachers, and Ministers; Purgatory; Reformation and Protestantism.

References

Aberth, John. "The Black Death in the Diocese of Ely: The Evidence of the Bishop's Register." *Journal of Medieval History* 21 (1995): 275–287.

Dohar, William J. *The Black Death and Pastoral Leadership: The Diocese of Hereford in the Fourteenth Century.* Philadelphia: University of Pennsylvania Press, 1995.

Martin, A. Lynn. *Plague? Jesuit Accounts of Epidemic Disease in the Sixteenth Century.* Kirksville, MO: Sixteenth Century Journal Publishers, 1996.

Moran, JoAnn Hoeppner. "Clerical Recruitment in the Diocese of York, 1340–1530: Data and Commentary." *Journal of Ecclesiastical History* 34 (1983): 19–54.

Wood, J. W., R. J. Ferrell and S. N. Dewitte-Avina. "The Temporal Dynamics of the Fourteenth-century Black Death: New Evidence from English Ecclesiastical Records." *Human Biology* 75 (2003): 427–448.

Printing

When Johannes Gutenberg combined the elements that became the printing press, he began a revolution in communication. Mechanically reproduced books, booklets, pamphlets, broadsides, and broadsheets in various sizes replaced laboriously hand-copied works from Bibles to rowdy ballads. Manuscripts with scribal errors gave way to well-proofread definitive editions; reproduction costs fell. Beautiful and accurate illustrations in the Renaissance style could be wedded to text. Along with urban schools and the Bible-centered Reformation, printing helped make literacy much more evident in 1550 than it had been in 1350. There would be not only a market for learned or technical materials but also for popular works from satires to do-it-yourself manuals.

Among medical professionals, printing meant the availability of a wide range of medical literature, from such old textbooks as the *Articella* and Mondino's *Anathomia* to Vesalius's groundbreaking *Epitomes*. Plague tracts, *consilia*, and regimens (diets) could now be written for a very broad audience. If in Latin, international sales to other professionals were likely; if vernacular, then sales nearer to home among a broad audience. Medical humanists published purer versions of the classical Greeks, giving Galenism a boost, while Paracelsians spread the new and competing iatrochemical philosophy—and its remedies for plague—by printing Paracelsus's works as well as their own.

Broader literacy meant new markets for popular moral literature; such writers as physician William Bullein and playwright Thomas Dekker produced it. Self-help books on medicine, astrology, and even alchemy appeared from the 16th century, as did recurring almanacs, with astronomical data and predictions of such disasters as plague. The literate citizen had never been better able to forego the physician's expensive services in favor of published remedy recipes and details on treating buboes.

Governments increasingly used the press to circulate important information quickly and cheaply. Bills of Mortality appeared in England from 1514 and, later, on a weekly basis so that interested parties could watch the ebb and flow of the disease and make important decisions accordingly. Royal, ducal, and municipal warnings and plague orders were circulated rapidly and accurately when printed, and suggestions and commands of local health boards and magistracies appeared more authentic and official when in print and posted. Bills of health were increasingly printed forms signed by the appropriate authority. These licenses to travel were more uniform and harder to counterfeit than hand-scripted ones.

The Catholic Church printed and circulated prayer sheets with petitions to plague saints or Mary accompanying their images. Printed vernacular "lives" of such plague saints as Charles Borromeo and Rosalie helped spread their cults among Catholics. Protestant religious authorities also circulated prayer sheets, pamphlets on "good dying," and regulations for keeping fast days. Anglican bishops and Continental ministers published sermons and exhortations to repentance.

See also: Alchemy; Almanacs; *Ars moriendi (The Art of Dying)*; Astrology; Bills of Health; Bills of Mortality; Broadsheets, Broadsides, and Pamphlets; Consilia and Plague Tracts; Morality Literature, Christian; Prayer and Fasting.

References

Anselment, Raymond. *The Realms of Apollo. Literature and Healing in Seventeenth-Century England*, Newark: University of Delaware Press and Associated University Presses, 1995.

Eisenstein, Elizabeth L. *The Printing Revolution in Early Modern Europe*. New edition. New York: Cambridge University Press, 2005.

Prisoners

Kings had prisons for those who displeased their majesties; the Church imprisoned blasphemers, heretics, and its own criminal clergy. Cities generally kept criminals and debtors, those who could not meet their financial obligations, under lock and key. Such Mediterranean seaports as Marseille and Venice kept prisoners of war and convicts as galley slaves, oarsmen who were often chained to their posts even when in port. Conditions in medieval and early modern jails and prisons were close to inhumane at best. Lack of sanitation, poor-quality food and water, little sun or light, and overcrowding were common complaints. Many died of diseases brought in by new inmates or from the vile conditions themselves, and some of these were dissected by local medical students.

When plague struck, few considered the plight of the prisoners, trapped as they were in their cells. Given the prevalence of rats in cells, one would think that the incarcerated would be among the first to die. Yet in Florence's Stinche Prison, the death rate was quite low during the plague's first year. Those elsewhere did not fare as well, as plague routinely ran through the populations. Worse, perhaps, was the decline of conditions as the city authority structure broke down, as it often did. If a key administrator took ill or died, the inmates could be left without food or water for days or weeks. English playwright and moralist Thomas Dekker pled fervently on behalf of London's inmates in 1625, especially debtors. Like prisoners elsewhere, Fleet Prison's petitioned Parliament under habeas corpus to be released lest they die like dogs. The committee denied the request, saying they feared the lot would escape. Eleven years later, debtors from Fleet and King's Bench were released under a writ of habeas corpus and taken in custody to places in the country. Real criminals had to remain and suffer.

During the horrendous epidemic of 1575 to 1577, Venetian authorities opened their jails and prisons, releasing prisoners, many of whom went to work on Venice's pest house facilities. In Marseille in 1720, the designated corpse carriers had all died and the convicts who powered the coastal galleys were put into service. Seventy percent of the 696 died.

See also: Corpse Carriers; Corpses; Gravediggers.

References

Bertrand, Jean Baptiste. *A Historical Relation of the Plague at Marseilles in the Year 1720.* New York: McGraw-Hill, 1973.

Geltner, Guy. *The Medieval Prison: A Social History.* Princeton, NJ: Princeton University Press, 2008.

Processions

Religious processions have long been means of making the secular sacred. Urban routes, roads to shrines, and city walls were rededicated to the divinity or divinities or saints, and participants, too, were sacralized. Processions elicited divine attention and instilled hope in the community. When Christian processions included a sacred destination, holy icon, or the Eucharist, vital spiritual bonds were re-established. Jewish, Christian, and Muslim funeral processions to graveyards were signs of respect for the deceased and reminders of one's own mortality. Shiite Muslims placed faith in annual and special processions to saints' tombs and shrines as powerful places from which prayer rose to Allah.

When plague struck Rome in 590, new Pope Gregory could imagine no better way of pleading with an angry God than processing through the streets, demonstrating communal repentance, and stopping at the major churches. It worked, setting a precedent for Christians throughout the Second Pandemic. Prophylactic, or preventive, processions took place as plague approached a city or region. Organized by a bishop, abbot, or rural priest, clergy would lead behind a relic, icon or crucifix, penitential hymns would be sung, and prayers would be said. In larger cities, people would line up hierarchically by social, civic, or guild status or in such lay religious groups as confraternities. The point was to pray to God directly, and indirectly through saints, that God would spare his people.

During plagues, many wanted to hold processions, but the fear of spreading the disease in crowds kept governments from allowing them. Even funeral processions were banned once epidemic was declared. Yet in Brescia, Italy, in 1469, civil authorities deliberated and authorized a procession, "since from the said solemnity and devotion to it liberation and health are to be hoped for rather than greater infection" (Palmer, 96). London's Lord Mayor defied the Privy Council's ban during the 1625 plague and allowed the funeral procession of the militia captain, which included 244 troops and crowds of viewers. The end of plague often called for a procession of thanksgiving by the survivors. Many of these ended at the sites of future plague churches or memorials.

Processions of penitential flagellants and devotees through the Rhineland in 1348 to 1349 acquired a menacing aspect as they lost clerical leadership and turned hostile toward Jews. Pope and emperor eventually banned them. The prophylactic Bianchi movement of summer 1399, which organized northern Italians into three-day pilgrimages of prayer and reconciliation, maintained its clerical leadership and integrity but failed to halt the deadly plague of 1400.

See also: Allah; Bishops and Popes Christ; Confraternities; Contagion Theory; Danse Macabre; Flagellants; Funerals; Gregory the Great, Pope; Islamic Religious Responses; Plague Saints; Public Health; Virgin Mary.

References

Byrne, Joseph P. *Daily Life during the Black Death*. Westport, CT: Greenwood, 2006.

Horrox, Rosemary. *The Black Death*. New York: Manchester University Press, 1994.

Slack, Paul. "Responses to Plague in Early Modern England," in *Famine, Disease and the Social Order in Early Modern Society*, edited by Walter R. Schofield (New York: Cambridge University Press, 1989), 167–187.

Prophylaxes

Prophylaxes are quite simply preventive measures. They may be taken by an individual, group, or community. This entry is concerned with the actions recommended for and taken by individuals to avoid plague during the Second Pandemic. These were rooted in current understandings of human physiology and the plague as a disease. Across the Western world, people blended Galenic medicine, miasma theory, astrology, religion, and folk beliefs in adopting prophylaxes. Depending on their time, place, education, faith, class, and options, individuals often adopted a range of prophylaxes, each of which was meant to create a barrier against plague. Suggestions for these were not difficult to obtain. Medical *consilia* and physicians' tracts throughout the era contained prophylactic recommendations, as did later printed almanacs, leechbooks, broadsides, pamphlets, sermons, and religious tracts. Official bodies for example, England's Privy Council, Colleges of Physicians, and Faculties of Medicine published lists of favored actions in orders, *consilia*, and handbooks. Published works tended to be recycled from one outbreak to the next, so the range of advice tends to be rather narrow, and there is little in the way of evolution from 1348 to the 18th century.

Among Christians, lists of prophylaxes often begin with the universally accepted ultimate source of plague, God. Prayer, invocation of saints, repentance, amendment of life, acts of charity, fasting, participation in religious liturgies and processions: Catholics had a wide range of preventive measures. Such plague saints as Roche and Sebastian received special attention. Protestants saw fewer religious options since they denied the value of most "Papist" rituals, though prayer, fasting, sermon-going, amendment of life, and Bible study were acceptable. Bombarding God with Christian piety was thought to have the potential to turn away God's wrath and his pestilence, except among predestinarians. Muslims, too, prayed and processed, though religious leaders and their plague texts stressed acceptance of Allah's will and discouraged "bargaining."

Christians, Muslims, and Jews were heirs of the Hippocratic and Galenic medical traditions. Though neither Greek knew bubonic plague, their advice on dealing with epidemics and epidemic diseases—heavily influenced by 10th-century Arabic commentary until the 16th century—was the gold standard. Hippocrates favored an environmental approach, locating one's house strategically to avoid southern winds and stagnant water bodies, and sealing it against miasmas. Environmental humidity and stench had long been associated with putrefaction and the production of poison air (miasma), which led many to clean up, relocate, or treat local cesspits and other producers of foul odors. Cleansing of the air through fumigation was another way to defeat miasma: burning incense or aromatic woods, firing guns, maintaining a bonfire, as Pope Clement did, censing one's clothing with aromatic smoke, and even smoking tobacco. Since miasmas were or produced poisons, amulets, talismans, pomanders, dried toads, charms, jewels, gold medallions, and other poison-repelling or poison-absorbing objects were recommended and worn. The famous physicians' "bird suit" was another attempt to limit contact with the environment.

From Galen's well-developed humoralism and his concept of the "nonnaturals" sprang many recommendations. Maintenance of well-balanced humors through a diet that was more "dry" than "humid" and moderation in sexual activity and exercise topped most lists. Adequate sleep and regular evacuation of the bladder and bowels kept the body functioning properly. With the threat of plague, special diets (regimens), purgatives, and bleedings could help keep the humors balanced. Gentile da Foligno followed Galen in urging his readers to remain tranquil and avoid fear, wakefulness, wrath, worry, and other disruptive emotions that overheat the body and mind. Conversely, fresh air, sweet smells, music, hope, and good conversation strengthened the heart, as Boccaccio's tale-spinners demonstrated after fleeing plague-stricken Florence. Indeed, flight from pestilential areas was a very common preventive response, as was avoidance of the sick or of crowds or facilities where they might be. Though Muhammad had forbidden Muslims to flee their homes when plague struck, many did.

See also: Alchemy; Amulets, Talismans, and Magic; Causes of Plague: Historical Theories; Consilia and Plague Tracts; Dietary Regimens; Disinfection and Fumigation; Flight; Galen and Galenism; Hippocrates and the Hippocratic Corpus; Humoral Theory; Islam and Medicine; Islamic Religious Responses; Miasma Theory; Prayer and Fasting; Processions; Purgatives.

References

Dols, Michael W. *The Black Death in the Middle East*. Princeton, NJ: Princeton University Press, 1977.

Nohl, Johannes. *The Black Death: A Chronicle of the Plague*. Translated by C. H. Clarke. Yardley, PA: Westholme Publishing, 2006.

Sotres, Pedro Gil. "The Regimens of Health," in *Western Medical Thought from Antiquity to the Middle Ages*, edited by Mirko Grmek (Cambridge, MA: Harvard University Press, 1998), 291–318.

Prostitutes

Sexual intercourse outside of marriage has long been considered sinful by most Christians. Larger towns and cities of late medieval and early modern Europe had some laws or regulations related to the control of this type of activity. Prostitution, perhaps surprisingly, was tolerated in many larger urban centers, especially port cities that had a constant influx of strangers. Providing licensed brothels kept sailors and other traveling men from seeking sexual release—welcomed or not—among the townswomen. A brothel kept the working women relatively safe and off the streets and could be taxed. The poorest plied their trade on the streets, and the best off were the equivalent of modern "call girls," who serviced the wealthy and preferred to be known as courtesans. Even before the introduction of syphilis in the 1490s, prostitutes and their often-foreign customers exchanged parasites and pathogenic germs on a most intimate scale.

But bodily cleanliness and spread of diseases bothered the civic officials little by comparison with the moral issues involved in tolerating or even subsidizing prostitution. Since plague clearly came from God, and God was punishing sin, and sexual sins were considered to be among the most common, many concluded that sexual sins brought on the plague. While preachers could preach against personal immorality to little or great effect, the very presence of professional sex workers seemed to mock divine law. In Tuscany, San Bernardino railed against prostitution and homosexual activity from the pulpit and street corner, blaming plague visitations on the official toleration of both. In 1403, Florence banned prostitutes from walking the streets, though the brothels remained. In 1421, Florentine officials clamped down on female monasteries that had gained reputations for unwholesome behavior rather than piety, and in 1432, they outlawed sodomy (male homosexual behavior). Venice tightened its regulations in 1486 and such cities as Perugia, Siena, and Mantua also issued several generations of moral legislation. Smaller towns often expelled their whores and other sexual offenders at the first hint of plague. Officials and townspeople conflated sweeping out these "filthy people" with improving physical sanitation as prophylaxis against plague: just as physical stench was a cause and sign of miasma, moral stench fired God's wrath, and both meant plague. For a civic body not to address the presence of prostitutes was often considered a breach of one's official duty, and Church leaders were among the first to speak out. As official malfeasance was also sinful, official toleration of vice was doubly blameworthy.

Over time, prostitutes tended to be grouped together with vagabonds, vagrants, and the poor more generally as being somehow responsible for plague, which often began officially in the poorer quarters.

See also: Governments, Civil; Moral Legislation; Sin.

References

Carmichael, Ann G. *Plague and the Poor in Renaissance Florence*. New York: Cambridge University Press, 1986.

Richards, Jeffrey. *Sex, Dissidence, and Damnation*. New York: Routledge, 1994.

Public Health

The modern idea that that the community or even nation-state is responsible for protecting and promoting the health of its citizens was pioneered during the Second Pandemic. Some of its features, for example, hospitals and leprosaria, professionalization of medical practitioners, and concern for sanitation, predate 1347, but it was the Italian city-states of the 1300s and 1400s and the emerging nation-states of the 1500s and 1600s that innovated and created the constellation of attitudes, tools, and organizations we loosely label historic public health.

Before the Black Death, various impulses drove the development of early public health tools. Hospitals were a charitable Christian reaction to human suffering. Founding, supporting, and even working in these quasimonastic facilities were literally good for the soul and means of salvation. A combination of revulsion and pity spurred the establishment of leprosaria, which also used a monastic model for isolating the diseased. Vague notions of contagion mixed with fears of ritual uncleanliness. In the 14th century, the profession of physician was in its infancy, shaped by elite university education and social organization in urban guilds. Surrounded by empirics, charlatans, surgeons, midwives, and cunning men and women, physicians defined themselves apart by their formal training, book learning, and command of contemporary medical theory. They were the experts on sickness and health whom popes, kings, emperors, nobles, and city councils sought out and who composed Latin *consilia* and medical tracts in which their expertise was displayed. Finally, early urban sanitation laws were meant to alleviate aesthetic problems as well as remove sources of potentially miasmatic stench. Marginalizing noxious businesses, controlling trash and filth, penning pigs and other animals, and paving streets were important steps toward civilization.

When the Black Death struck, Europe was ill prepared but not unprepared. Though some Italian cities instituted ad hoc committees to expand and reinforce sanitation laws, disconnect the city from potential foreign sources of disease, and institute extramural burials, it took decades for Venice or Florence to establish health boards or magistracies whose purpose was to prepare for, monitor, and fight epidemic outbreaks. Yet the idea of a fully empowered magistracy that could make and enforce its own laws threatened many power structures. The Spanish crown and French *parlements* retained their authority over local plague commissions or boards, while the English Privy Council only acted by promulgating plague orders to local constables and councils. In place of a board, English parishes were required to appoint a variety of officials from searchers to guards and rakers.

Whether established by city councils, health magistracies, or central governments, the range of tools for fighting plague expanded. Increasingly, medical professionals were consulted and even appeared on health magistracies, further enhancing their civic stature. Influenced by religious guilt as well as miasma and contagion medical theories, authorities developed and repeated patterns of response. Repentance both personal and communal was stressed in prayers and services, in Catholic processions and Protestant sermons and days of fasting. Moral legislation banning gambling, prostitution, and drunkenness, or expelling the sinners, was considered as vital as clearing drains and removing animal carcasses. Contagion theory suggested bills of health, quarantine, shutting victims in, extramural pest houses, burning infected goods, cordons sanitaires, and bans on assembly. Miasma theory suggested fumigation, bonfires, and most sanitation laws. Practical exigency dictated mass burials, draconian legal penalties, and hiring of communal health personnel. Never before had so much and so varied public activity been directed toward issues of a community's health. Each of these measures, and many more, were developed, applied, borrowed, tweaked, argued about, dropped, and tried again as they migrated outward to Europe from Italy.

Along with tools and institutions developed attitudes supportive of public health activity. Plague recurred across nearly four centuries, but religious and medical theories attached to it remained essentially static. People fled, prayed, were bled, and shunned victims in 1348 and in 1771. But public action developed around the expanding power of the state and its increasing willingness to interfere in traditional areas of personal liberty. The idea that communal safety and health outweighed economic interests, access to religious worship, and freedom of movement was slow in coming but did parallel the growth of absolutism and state control.

Aristotle in his *Politics*, Machiavelli in his *Prince*, and Hobbes in his *Leviathan* emphasized the public good over individual liberty. As authorities came to see plague's association with the poor, with their filth, their supposed low morals, and overcrowded living conditions, measures were aimed increasingly in their direction, reducing something of the sting felt by the better off. Yet if national authorities in England, Holland, France, and even the Habsburg Empire learned anything about reducing the threat of plague, it was to prevent its importation on a regional or national level, adopting the strictest of cordons and quarantines in ports and along borders. The social cost of inattentiveness was simply too high.

See also: Bimaristans; Contagion Theory; Governments, Civil; Health Boards, Magistracies, and Commissions; Hospitals; Individualism and Individual Liberties; Lazarettos and Pest Houses; Mass Graves and Plague Cemeteries; Miasma Theory; Physicians, Town; Plague Orders and National Authorities; Poverty and Plague; Public Sanitation; Quarantine; Shutting In.

References

Alexander, John. *Bubonic Plague in Early Modern Russia: Public Health and Urban Disaster.* Baltimore, MD: Johns Hopkins University Press, 1980.

Bowers, Kristy Wilson. "Balancing Individual and Communal Needs: Plague and Public Health in Early Modern Seville." *Bulletin of the History of Medicine* 81 (2007): 335–358.

Christensen, Peter. " 'In these perilous times:' Plague and Plague Policies in Early Modern Denmark." *Medical History* 47 (2003): 413–450.

Cipolla, Carlo. *Cristofano and the Plague: A Study in the History of Public Health in the Age of Galileo.* Berkeley: University of California Press, 1973.

Greenberg, S. J. "The 'Dreadful Visitations': Public Health and Public Awareness in Seventeenth-century London." *Bulletin of the Medical Library Association* 85 (1997): 391–401.

Kinzelbach, Annemarie. "Infection, Contagion, and Public Health in Late Medieval and Early Modern German Imperial Towns." *Journal of the History of Medicine and Allied Sciences* 61 (2006): 369–389.

Lindemann, Mary. *Medicine and Society in Early Modern Europe.* Second edition. New York: Cambridge University Press, 2010.

Slack, Paul. "Responses to Plague in Early Modern Europe: The Implications of Public Health." *Social Research* 55 (1988): 433–453.

Public Sanitation

Later medieval Europe's cities were filthy places. From the later 13th century, Italian civic governments passed laws regulating waste disposal, street sweeping, and the location of such noxious businesses as tanners and fish sellers, but it was an ongoing battle. Bologna did so in 1245, Pisa in 1287, and Florence in 1319 and 1324. Cambridge authorities passed a series of statutes against public filth from its chartering in 1267; London's streets began to be paved under Edward I, and Dublin's from 1329. Yet most cities suffered from animal waste (commonly dogs, cats, horses, chickens, and pigs), human waste, garbage, and wastewater in streets and byways. Runoff sewers and streams drained filth into rivers, polluting water downriver and groundwater, both of which were sources of drinking water. Where cesspits existed, they were often ignored and badly maintained, overfilled and overrunning when it rained. Butchers were sometimes relegated away from city centers by guild and civic regulations, but disposal of their waste materials was a constant problem. Three decades before the Black Death, the Florentine law regulating animal slaughter provided the rationale that attendant "pestiferous exhalations" "provoked illness" among residents. Indeed, there was a clearly established relationship between filth and disease: stink putrefied the air and the resulting miasma caused disease in humans.

This understanding was central during and after the Black Death's initial shock. As plague threatened, cities, for example, Florence and Pistoia, immediately passed laws against "corruption and infection of the air." In March 1348, Florence ordered removal from the city or suburbs of "any putrid thing or things and infected persons (!) and similar things" (Henderson, 143) that might cause corruption or infection. Sanitation was also about keeping potential sources of infection out by banning newcomers and goods from, in Pistoia's case, Pisa and Lucca. Pistoia also banned crowds at funerals or burials and gatherings after funerals and insisted corpses be sealed in coffins and buried at least six feet deep to prevent stink. They also passed new laws relocating tanners out of town and forcing butchers to keep fresh meat away from corrupting stench. Plague-stricken Hereford's authorities in 1349 removed the main market from near the cathedral to a mile outside the city walls. This was to protect buyers and sellers from the miasma in the town, to protect edibles from infection, and to keep outsiders from entering the town. In 1349, London's civic leaders petitioned King Edward III to force the Lord Mayor to enforce existing sanitation laws to keep the filth under control, a sign that little was being done in the capital.

In the wake of the 1347 to 1352 pandemic, many towns and cities passed laws regulating human and animal waste, garbage removal, noxious businesses, burial practices, such immoral practices as prostitution and gambling (which were thought to anger God and cause his wrath), covering cesspits and drains, and paving major streets and squares. From 1354, London's butchers were to locate along the Thames (from 1361 specifically at Stratford and Knightsbridge), and Florence's on the Ponte Vecchio (bridge), so they could easily dispose of offal. Similar laws affecting Londoners appeared in 1353, 1356, 1357, 1362, 1366, and 1370. Reappearance of plague in the 1360s and 1370s underlined the need for sanitary vigilance.

During the 15th century, old sanitation laws piled up in reenactments, but enforcement and innovation seem to have waned. With the appearance of stronger central governments in 16th-century Spain, France, Italy, and England came renewed attention to public sanitation. London's Bill of Sewers of 1535 banned waste from city sewers and required "rakers" to collect human waste from each house every Monday, Wednesday, and Friday morning; later daily. Oath-bound "scavengers" oversaw the rakers, who were paid from collections from neighborhood householders. Between 1555 and 1600, the government of Verona, Italy, passed at least 282 sanitation ordinances: all but four from 1575 on. The royal government closed virtually every bathhouse in France, since bathing opened pores to miasmatic infection and could lead to illicit sex. Meanwhile, plague came increasingly to be identified with the poor and the disordered lives many of them lived. Vagabonds and beggars had long been targets of "sanitation" legislation, but by the later 1500s, the connections seemed more obvious. During London's epidemic of 1603, Thomas Lodge in his *Treatise on the Plague* linked poverty, vice, filth, sin, and plague. In 1604, England's new Stuart king pulled together the poor law, the plague ordinances, and criminal law so that sanitation meant social control.

The 1500s and 1600s saw demographic revival after the late medieval population crisis. People flocked to Europe's burgeoning cities despite plague and other diseases, crowding together in dense warrens and straining attempts to control urban growth and sanitation. When plague struck, governments tried to enhance civic cleanliness, but the combination of filth, corpses, scavengers, discarded belongings of plague victims, and inattention to septic matters was often overwhelming. As Tuscan inspectors found in 1622, rural villages were no better off. Their reports chronicle open cesspits and sewers, pigs and sheep living in family quarters or wandering the streets at will, butchers dumping offal in pits under their houses, and streets covered with human and animal waste. However ineffective, Europe's plague-driven attempts led toward more successful sanitation regimens in the 18th and 19th centuries.

See also: Crime and Punishment; Expulsion of Victims; Governments, Civil; Health Boards, Magistracies, and Commissions; Miasma Theory; Moral Legislation; Public Health; Sin.

References

Biow, Douglas. "The Politics of Cleanliness in Northern Renaissance Italy." *Symposium* 50 (1996): 75–86.

Byrne, Joseph P. *Daily Life during the Black Death*. Westport, CT: Greenwood Press, 2006.

Cipolla, Carlo. *Miasmas and Disease: Public Health and the Environment in the Preindustrial Age*. Trans. by Elizabeth Potter. New Haven, CT: Yale University Press, 1992.

Henderson, John. "The Black Death in Florence: Medical and Communal Responses," in *Death in Towns*, edited by Steven Bassett (New York: Leicester University Press, 1992), 136–150.

Sabine, Ernest. "Butchering in Mediaeval London." *Speculum* 8 (1933): 225–253; and "City Cleaning in Mediaeval London." *Speculum* 12 (1937): 19–43.

Purgatives

Galenic humoralism, miasma theory, and Paracelsianism recommended induced purging of the body for both prophylaxis and remedy. It could help rebalance humors or expel poisons, or both. Purgatives were treatments, usually internal, that aided vomiting, sweating, urinating, and defecating. Natural laxatives were well known, but apothecaries and medical practitioners had a wide rage of laxatives, diuretics, and suppositories. England's Privy Council recommended a simple laxative suppository of boiled honey and powdered salt. To induce sweat, they suggested butterbur, valerian root, and sorrel boiled together and again with vinegar and sugar. For the same purpose, Dr. Simon Kellawaye in 1593 prescribed a half-dram of unicorn horn mixed with a half-dram of angelica root, and the Portuguese king's physician used a complex recipe that started with a wine-drunk badger and added gold, pearls, and coral, cinnamon, cloves, and myrrh. Many early "patent medicines," for example, Anderson's Scots Pills (1630s to 1916), were purgatives, whose effectiveness was always evident to the patient. Because of purging's often-unpleasant olfactory effects, the apothecaries who usually administered these carried perfumes.

See also: Apothecaries; Dietary Regimens; Humoral Theory; Narwhal/Unicorn Horn Powder; Prophylaxes; Remedies, Internal.

Reference

Mullett, Charles F. *The Bubonic Plague and England*. Lexington: University of Kentucky Press, 1956.

Purgatory

In Roman Catholic theology, God prepared Hell as an eternal resting place for unrepentant sinners and Heaven as an eternal resting place for those who please God with their faith and well-led lives. The Bible provides evidence for both. Unlike Orthodoxy or Protestantism, medieval Catholicism declared a third destination, never explicitly mentioned in Scripture. In it are souls of those who died without having repented adequately of their sinfulness but whose sins were not serious enough to warrant eternal damnation. A soul enters Purgatory upon death and remains in anguish and torment until purged, cleansed, and made worthy of Heaven. All in Purgatory are destined for salvation and life in Heaven and thus live in hope; and time in Purgatory is limited. At the Last Judgment, Purgatory will be emptied and never occupied again. Dante Alighieri presented Purgatory magisterially in the second book of his *Divine Comedy*, "Purgatorio," depicting it as a mountain reaching toward the heavens.

Catholics have sought to avoid Purgatory by the development of their faith; by participation in Church life, the sacraments, and good works; and especially by a properly conducted end of life, including the sacrament of Extreme Unction (Last Anointing, today Sacrament of the Sick). The oral Confession of one's sins and statement of heartfelt contrition to the priest, part of Extreme Unction, was a last chance to repent and eliminate or reduce time in Purgatory. Prayers on behalf of the deceased's soul were (and are) also considered useful for shortening time in Purgatory, though of no use to those condemned to Hell.

In wills after 1350, testators often paid for large numbers of prayers and masses to be said on behalf of their souls, usually by monks or clergy. This spiritual insurance hedged against one's own family—and natural advocates—being erased by plague.

Throughout the Second Pandemic, anxiety surrounded the unavailability of priests to perform last rites. Sudden or unexpected death, death in a foreign place, abandonment at the time of death, death in a pest house or while shut up in one's own house: all might occur in the absence of the clergy's final ministrations and the all-important final Confession. Experiencing a "good death" was not only a personal concern, but one shared by far-away family and loved ones, whose letters sometimes express relief or fear over news of a good death or its lack. Almost as serious was the plague-time curtailment or abolition of Catholic funeral rituals, during which participants prayed for the salvation of the deceased's soul, that it might "rest in peace." Personal and family memorials, especially family chapels in Catholic churches, provided mechanisms for avoiding postmortem anonymity and increasing the likelihood of prayer.

See also: Abandonment; *Ars moriendi* (*The Art of Dying*); Funerals, Catholic; Heaven and Hell; Priests; Sin; Wills and Testaments.

References
Cohn, Samuel K. *The Cult of Remembrance and the Black Death*. Baltimore, MD: Johns Hopkins University Press, 1992.

LeGoff, Jacques. *The Birth of Purgatory*. Trans. by Arthur Goldhammer. Chicago: University of Chicago Press, 1984.

Quarantine

To quarantine something or someone, or to place someone or something in quarantine, is to isolate him, her, or it from infectious conditions and for a set time period to determine whether the person or thing has a suspected disease. Though sometimes applied loosely, it is not isolation of the diseased or isolation of an area suspected of disease. It is prophylactic rather than remedial. During the Second Pandemic, once someone was determined to have plague, he or she was placed in a plague hospital or pest house to either recuperate or die. Once past the crisis, the victim might be moved to a convalescent facility. If the suspect had merchandise and/or animals, these would also be isolated in clean air for set periods. A ship seeking to enter a port might also have itself, its crew, and/or its cargo quarantined if its departure had been from a plague-stricken city or if port authorities did not trust the certification of health provided by the captain. Stricken sailors would be treated like residents, and cargo would be subjected to fumigation or other cleansing or destruction to prevent contagion. The practice reflected both the miasma theory of the day, since both cleansing and quarantine of people was to be done in clean, "uncorrupted" air, and the vaguer sense of contagion, since it was important to isolate the suspect from the healthy. Facilities were near but set apart from normal human activity, outside city walls, along cordons sanitaires or regional boundaries, or on islands near port facilities.

The Adriatic port city of Dubrovnik (Ragusa) instituted the earliest known practice of quarantine in 1377 on the advice of its town physician Jacob of Padua. Independent of Venice since 1358, it had developed an extensive trade network in the eastern Mediterranean and suffered six epidemics in 30 years. The law of July 27, 1377, was meant to protect the city while only minimally interfering with commerce. The period was to be 30 days, and "purification" facilities were provided on the island of Mrkan and in the town of Cavtat for those hailing from places reported to have plague. When plague appeared in Dubrovnik again in 1391 and 1397, authorities strengthened policies and replaced officials. Marseille provided the second known example in 1383. Authorities there opted for 40 (*quaranta*) days, which gave the practice its name. There are various modern explanations for the number—for example, the biblical 40 days or years for ritual purification or Hippocrates's notion that the 40th day was the critical day in the course of a disease—but the term itself originated in the 15th century.

Genoa and Venice may have had some similar practice as early as 1380, though evidence is clear only from the 15th century. Despite opposition from commercial interests, the practice spread because it made sense. By the 16th century, jurisdictions treated the required time period variously. In southern German cities, textiles had to be aired in quarantine for one year, since bad air or pestiferous matter might hide in the weave, while hard, smooth objects needed only two weeks. People with no known plague contacts required two weeks' isolation, while known exposure meant four weeks, more if the epidemic were virulent.

Henry VIII's plague orders of 1543 required the full 40-day isolation for those who had had contact with plague victims. In 1625, Dublin officials built two wooden houses for quarantine near the port. Passengers had to undergo a 20-day quarantine, while suspect goods required 30 days of airing.

With the consolidation of regional and national authorities in the 16th and 17th centuries, quarantine became a more effective tool in the fight to avoid plague. It worked with bills or certificates of health and cordons sanitaires to lessen the likelihood that plague would be imported or that potentially "contagious" victims would wander about. Though quarantine interfered with commerce, these effects tended to be limited to the incoming ship or merchant and his immediate customers. In 1664, Dutch sailors quarantined in East Anglia rioted, but sneaking past or bribing authorities and smuggling in goods at night were more common responses. When plague lurked, Danish cavalry patrolled their beaches, arresting Dutch smugglers, seizing their goods, and burning their vessels.

Where central and local authorities had little incentive and poor organization, quarantine measures had little effect. They required living quarters, food and fuel, honest guards, and records of arrivals, cargoes, deaths, and releases. Those who fell ill needed separate quarters, and those released had a right to all of their belongings. Western European countries tended to have the resources and institutions to organize and enforce quarantine, whereas Russia and the Turkish Empire lacked these advantages. German cities, ravaged by the Thirty Years' War, simply kept outsiders out, denying shelter to desperate refugees. In 1635, Erfurt's council took pity and let these folk occupy a poorhouse outside the walls as a sort of quarantine. Some states were late adopting quarantine: the Duchy of Braunschweig-Wolfenbüttel waited until 1680. Germans without health passes were quarantined eight days, and those from "infected" areas the full 40. Villagers were to provide guarded quarantine huts for any locals who traveled to disease-ridden areas.

And so the practice spread. Istanbul and Tunis utilized it from at least 1700, and in 1771, even Starodub in Ukraine had "(a) quarantine station of straw huts and dugouts . . . in a remote forest." England's system grew more sophisticated with its worldwide trading network, reinforcing increasingly stringent quarantine acts with outright bans on ships from known plague ports. In 1713, noncompliance was punished with forfeiture and in the 1720s, with death.

See also: Governments, Civil; Contagion Theory; Cordons Sanitaires; Merchants; Miasma Theory; Plague Orders and National Authorities; Public Health; Shutting In.

References

Borodi, N. K. "The Quarantine Service and Anti-epidemic Measures in the Ukraine in the Eighteenth Century." *Soviet Studies in History* 25 (1987): 24–32.

Christensen, Peter. "Appearance and Disappearance of the Plague: Still a Puzzle?" In *Living with the Black Death*, edited by Lars Bisgaard and Leif Søndergaard (Odense: University Press of Southern Denmark, 2009), 10–21.

Sehdev, P. S. "The Origin of Quarantine." *Clinical Infectious Diseases* 35 (2002): 1071–1072.

Slack, Paul. *The Impact of Plague in Tudor and Stuart England.* New York: Oxford University Press, 1990.

R

Rats and Other Plague Carriers

In 1898, French medical researcher Paul-Louis Simond discovered that bubonic plague bacteria were transmitted between black rats by fleas. This revealed for the first time a major piece of the ancient puzzle, though Simond was ridiculed and it would take another 16 years for the full picture to develop. Bubonic plague is a disease of animals that, under certain circumstances, involves the human community. Rats and other rodents play key roles in the plague cycle, both isolated in the wild and among humans. Though certain types of fleas are the actual carriers of the bacteria (*Yersinia pestis*), the fleas live and dine on the skin of rats and other rodents. An infected flea inserts its feeding tube through a rodent's skin and regurgitates the bacteria that had been reproducing in its foregut before it can draw out its blood meal. The newly infected rat has the bacteria circulating in its blood system, on which other, noninfected, fleas now feed. Having ingested the infected blood, the fleas now host the bacteria, which reproduces in dozens of foreguts. Meanwhile, the rodent's immune system attempts to fight off the infection, becoming warmer with fever and usually cold with death. Its fleas seek the moderate body temperature of a healthy rat and the process starts anew. When a rodent colony can maintain this cycle indefinitely, it is called an enzootic. This is most likely due to high levels of immunity or resistance among the rodents. Resistance or immunity to plague seems to be a matter of the individual animals and not the genus or species. Some individuals seem naturally immune, some survivors seem to have at least short-term, antibody-mediated immunity conferred, while cross-immunity may be conferred by such pathogens as *salmonella, tularemia,* and *Yersinia enterocolitica.* When many colony members in a region have reached this stage, zoologists speak of a reservoir or focus of plague. Today, people who catch plague usually do so by intruding on such an area and disturbing the infected animals, and this was probably true historically.

When the disease threatens the existence of a colony, zoologists consider this an epizootic, an animal version of an epidemic. If isolated and undisturbed, the rodents, fleas, and bacteria will die off. If near other colonies or other animals that could sustain the fleas, the infected fleas will abandon the dying rodents for fresh, if less tasty, pastures. When the new host is a human, we have a case of plague; when it is thousands of people, we have an epidemic.

Humans are slobs and rats are scavengers that clean up after them. Rats and other rodents living in the wild are called sylvatic, and those that live in close proximity to humans are commensal; literally, they share a table. The roof, fruit, house, alexandrine, or simply black rat (*Rattus rattus*) was a common resident among medieval and early modern people and was the principal host of the primary plague bacillus-carrying flea, *Xenopsyllus cheopis.* Studies of black rat behavior note that they are timid creatures that prefer obscurity, close quarters, and ready food supplies. Artificial nesting preferences include thatched roofing (which could be several feet thick), barn straw and hay, and grain storage receptacles. Typical medieval housing tended to be dark, warm, dry but humid, soft-walled, accessible, and littered with food scraps.

R. rattus reaches sexual maturity at four months and can produce several litters per year of up to nine young per litter (20–30 pups per year). Life spans are about two years and a generation lasts about a year. Typically, more than 90 percent of a colony will die off in the course of a year under normal conditions. With the importation of infected fleas, of course, the rate approaches 100 percent. Even so, recent work utilizing computer modeling has shown that plague may remain enzootic in a large colony for up to a decade before fleas are forced to find human hosts; this cycling may persist for up to a century. Though comfortable as a loner, over a lifetime, a black rat is unlikely to travel more than 200 yards from its nest, though it would be driven much farther when hungry or when it found itself on a cart loaded with grain or other foodstuffs. It is also a good sailor.

Since massive rat die-offs are necessary for fleas to jump to human hosts, one would expect to find evidence of these in the historical literature, art, or archeology. That such evidence is scant and ambiguous helps sustain those who believe that Second Pandemic pestilence is not modern bubonic plague. They also consider the rats' behavioral patterns and doubt that they can account for the rapid and wide spread of plague between 1347 and 1352, even with human agency.

The *Rattus* genus has around 120 species, including the brown or wharf rat, *Rattus norvegicus*, whose arrival in Europe circa 1700 was once thought to have had a role in bringing Europe's plagues to an end (it arrived too late). But if *R. rattus*'s Scandinavian cousin makes a poor carrier, numerous more distant relatives around the world are known to carry fleas that carry *Y. pestis*: among these are giant marmots, susliks, ground squirrels (typical carriers in the southwestern United States), desert gerbils, tarbagans, meriones, and wild guinea pigs. Some 300 species of carriers have been identified.

See also: Animals; Black Death (1347–1352); Black Death: Debate over the Medical Nature of; Bubonic Plague; Bubonic Plague in North America; Fleas; Simond, Paul-Louis; *Yersinia pestis*.

References

Davis, David. "The Scarcity of Rats and the Black Death: An Ecological History." *Journal of Interdisciplinary History* 16 (1986): 455–470.

Hendrickson, Robert. *More Cunning than Man: A Complete History of the Rat and Its Role in History.* New York: Kensington Books, 1983.

Karlsson, Gunnar. "Plague without Rats: The Case of Fifteenth-century Iceland." *Journal of Medieval History* 22 (1996): 263–284.

Keeling, M. J. and C. A. Gilligan. "Metapopulation Dynamics of Bubonic Plague." *Nature* 19 (October, 2000): 903–906.

McCormick, Michael. "Rats, Communications and Plague: Toward an Ecological History." *Journal of Interdisciplinary History* 34 (2003): 1–25.

Moseng, Ole Georg. "Climate, Ecology and Plague: The Second and the Third Pandemic Reconsidered," in *Living with the Black Death*, edited by Lars Bisgaard and Leif Søndergaard (Odense: University of Southern Denmark Press, 2009), 23–45.

Reformation and Protestantism

The Reformation of the 16th century was a series of religious movements that divided the Roman Catholic Church and established numerous Christian variations collectively known as Protestant churches. Because of the depth of influence of the Catholic Church in late medieval and early modern European culture, its division and redefinition had major social, political, cultural, and economic effects that helped usher in the modern age.

Although anti–Catholic dissent and anti-clericalism as well as attempts at Church reform long predate the 16th century, the activities of the disaffected Catholic priests Martin Luther in German Saxony and Huldrich Zwingli in Switzerland set the Reformation in motion. Both men took the Bible very seriously (*sola scriptura*) and decided that the Catholic authorities did not and that the Church had strayed from proper belief and practice. Catholics taught that the grace from God, which Scripture says is necessary for salvation and eternal life with God, is in part mediated through one's participation in the Church's sacraments as well as the performance of good actions. Luther and Zwingli taught that God freely dispensed grace to whomever he pleased to grant faith (*sola fide*) and that one's actions, even those commanded by Scripture, had no effect on one's salvation. Nor could saints interfere in one's life, even as intercessors. Luther emphasized God's power by denying free will and claiming that one was predestined to heaven or hell (reformers dismissed purgatory as myth), a position later popularized by John Calvin and his followers. Luther and Zwingli also taught that ordained priests had no special sacramental powers and that all people were priests (priesthood of all believers), and they renamed congregational leaders ministers and pastors (shepherds). Luther retained bishops, since they are scriptural, but Zwingli denied any practical church hierarchy. Both also renounced the Pope and most of the traditions that unified the Catholic Church around him, Canon Law, and earlier Church councils. Luther's movement took hold in northern Germany and Scandinavia, being adopted as the state church in most of these territories.

Zwingli died in battle at Kappel in 1531 but spawned the Radical Reformation in Germany and laid the foundation for the success of Frenchman John Calvin. Radicals split off from Zwingli's rather slow approach to reform and insisted on baptizing only faith-attesting adults (hence the pejorative "Anabaptist," or rebaptizer), like modern Baptists. They preached living in radical separation from the world—like the Amish or Hutterites—pacifism, and self-sacrifice as a mark of love for God. They often lived in tight rural communities according to the roots of communal life (*radices*) laid out in Scripture (Acts 2:42–47), often suffering persecution for their idiosyncratic ways. They condemned the traditional trappings of church ritual and power, urging simplicity of life and death.

John Calvin was a Catholic French law student who was influenced by these unfolding movements while at the University of Paris. He adopted many of the ideas advanced by Luther and Zwingli and others who, in turn, had been influenced. Exhibiting a well-disciplined mind, Calvin welded together what he considered the reformed reform movement into his doctrinal *Institutes of the Christian Religion* and the *Ecclesiastical Ordinances*, which laid out a reproducible church organization that could be copied almost anywhere. A second-generation reformer, Calvin was also a universal or international reformer whose influence would be felt from Ireland to Poland. He accepted the standard reformed or Protestant (a term specifically referring to Lutherans who "protested" against a decision by the 1529 Imperial Diet of Speyer against religious toleration) positions: sola fide, sola scriptura, priesthood of all believers, Luther's predestination, rejection of Catholic tradition, ritual, and hierarchy. But unlike the Swiss and Germans, Calvin established an Academy at which reformers from all of Europe gathered to absorb the *Institutes* and learn the

Ordinances. He and his successors also added a sense of mission that was new, and this sense brought his followers into religious conflict with many of Europe's powers. Almost always in the minority, Calvinists challenged Catholic authority in France, the Netherlands, and Scotland, and eventually against the Anglicans in England and Ireland.

The Anglican Church emerged in the wake of King Henry VIII's divorce from Katherine of Aragon. Henry renounced the authority of the pope, Clement VII, who stood in his way, and had Parliament declare him Head of the Church of England. Though Henry famously abolished monasticism and veneration of saints, he retained most of the ancient Catholic framework, including clergy and sacraments. Under his son Edward and his daughter Elizabeth, the Anglican Church took a turn to the Calvinist, especially at the hands of the Puritans, who sought to purify the Church of its "Catholic" trappings. This resulted in a nervous cohabitation of a "high" church supported by the state, with its cathedrals, priests, candles, sacraments, and incense, and a protestantized "low" church with simple services and emphasis on Scripture, along with many small sects, usually reflecting native and continental religious radicalism (Baptists, Quakers, Separatists). Eventually, Parliament, dominated by the Puritans, went to war with the Crown and its generally Anglican supporters among the upper classes in the English Civil War (1642–1649). On the continent, the last major religious war was the Thirty Years' War (1618–1648), which began as a conflict between the Catholic Empire and its Protestant states and their allies.

While these developments had no effect on plague apart from its spread during wartime, they did reshape the cultural landscape. Because of their emphasis on Scripture, literacy rose in many Protestant areas, spurring demand for medical books as well. Organized health care, once church-run, fell into the hands of the state or civic groups, secularizing hospitals and pest houses. Protestant (broadly defined) churches and regions lost their interceding saints and shrines, and thus their ex votos and other art, their grace-inducing sacraments (including last rites), their processions (usually), and the clergy and monastics who led them. Believers' prayers, whether for the dead or for themselves, seemed to have lost influence in light of predestination. Death-bedside, funerary, and burial practices changed, and what remained often lost meaning. God was still the dispenser of plague onto a sinful humankind, but sin now included joining or toleration of other Christian sects.

See also: Anticlericalism; *Ars moriendi* (*The Art of Dying*); Bishops and Popes; Demons, Satan, and the Devil; Ex voto; Funerals, Catholic; Funerals, Protestant; Henry VIII, King of England; Hospitals; Luther, Martin; Paracelsus and Paracelsianism; Pastors, Preachers, and Ministers; Plague Saints; Prayer and Fasting; Priests; Purgatory; Sin; Thirty Years' War.

References

Grell, Ole Peter and Andrew Cunningham, eds. *Health Care and Poor Relief in Protestant Europe, 1500–1700.* New York: Routledge, 1997.

Grell, Ole Peter, and Andrew Cunningham, eds. *Medicine and the Reformation.* London: Routledge, 1993.

MacCulloch, Diarmaid. *The Reformation: A History.* New York: Vintage, 2004.

Remedies, External

Remedies or cures were meant to aid the healing of plague patients. Doctors generally used several treatments, as no single course could claim success. Galenic medicine with its emphasis on balancing the humors privileged internal treatments. Miasma and early contagion theory tended to overlap Galenism from the beginning of the Second Pandemic. "Poison" entered the body from the air or "contact," or was generated by miasma. Poison might be counteracted by internal medicines, purging, and bleeding, but many doctors trusted topical treatments that would draw the poison out through the skin. Some were also used prophylactically, since they placed a barrier between poison and body.

Since victims whose buboes (the swellings under the skin) naturally suppurated, or discharged, had a fairly high rate of survival, many doctors lanced, cauterized, cut out, or cupped the swellings, following venerable Arab advice. In nonsterile conditions, however, infections often set in. Following the same theory, as late as 1665, London's College of Physicians recommended pressing the anus of a live, plucked chicken or pigeon on the bubo until it dies, to "draw out the poison." Ointments of a wide array of herbs, minerals, roots, turpentine, honey, and other ingredients were worked into cloth plasters and placed on opened buboes for the same purpose. Folk medicine, alchemy, and Paracelsian medicine agreed that poisons could attract poisons, so amulets, bezoar stones, toads, or alchemically prepared arsenic and antimony were also placed on the skin, worn suspended from ribbons, or mixed into poultices.

See also: Amulets, Talismans, and Magic; Apothecaries; Armenian Bole; Bezoar Stones; Broadsheets, Broadsides, and Pamphlets; Charlatans and Quacks; Consilia and Plague Tracts; Empirics; Gold; Islam and Medicine; Leechbooks; Narwhal/Unicorn Horn Powder; Paracelsus and Paracelsianism; Toads.

References

Holland, B. K. "Treatments for Bubonic Plague: Reports from Seventeenth-Century British Epidemics." *Journal of the Royal Society of Medicine* 93 (2000): 322–324.

Riddle, John M. "Pomum Ambrae: Amber and Ambergris in Plague Remedies." *Sudhoff's Archiv für Geschichte der Medizin und der Naturwissenschaften* 48 (1964): 111–122.

Remedies, Internal

Physicians tended to agree that once (and however) caught, plague acted as a poison in the human body. While they did not understand plague, they did understand poison, and most emphasized ridding the body of the deadly matter. Galenists who continued to see disease as humoral imbalance stressed foods, drinks, and oral medications that redressed the imbalance: coolants (vinegar, cucumbers, oranges), warmers (ginger, garlic, cloves, honey), moisteners, dryers, stupefactives for pain, and purgatives, lubricants, and softeners to aid elimination of troublesome humors and poison. Prescribed treatments or changes in treatments followed careful diagnosis and determination of which type of rebalance was needed. The "cool, moist" nature of plague usually had to be counteracted by its opposite. Such counter-poisonous herbs as valerian and verbena were mixed in syrups or cordials to aid drinkability.

Folk medicine, alchemy, and, later, Paracelsianism, stressed "fighting poison with poison." Theriac and mithridatum were considered effective drugs because they contained snake poison; such alchemically prepared poisonous metals as mercury and antimony supposedly worked for the same reason.

Alchemists sought the elusive philosopher's stone, which some believed a universal remedy. Meanwhile, they claimed success turning base metals into gold, which many considered a plague prophylactic and remedy.

When gold was dipped into rosewater, juices, syrups, wine, and other drinks, these "absorbed" some of the sun's cleansing energy that made gold the perfect metal and an antidote to plague's poison. Since this used none of the gold, it was ideal for poorer folk. For really poor folk, Gentile da Foligno suggested barley water in which gold had soaked. Turning gold into gold-water (*aurum potabile*) was a goal of many alchemists and Paracelsians, though most settled for gold powder suspended in a cordial. Friar John of Rupiscissa thought strong alcohol made a better vehicle, but the problem remained. Powdered emerald, pearl, sapphire, and other gems also found their way into cordials that were supposed to fight the poison with the occult power of the stone.

Apothecaries, Paracelsians, and alchemists developed their own proprietary recipes for sale in pill, powder, or potion form. These were advertised on posters and in almanacs, plague tracts, and pamphlets, and sold from inns, coffee houses, and apothecary shops. In England, the 1624 Statute of Monopolies protected the secret recipes of such offerings as Anderson's Scots Pills and Countesse of Kent's Powder. In 1720, the French King bought the recipe for Alkermes plague remedy and dispatched it to plague-stricken Marseille. It had little effect.

See also: Alchemy; Apothecaries; Armenian Bole; Bezoar Stones; Broadsheets, Broadsides, and Pamphlets; Charlatans and Quacks; Consilia and Plague Tracts; Diagnosing Plague; Dietary Regimens; Empirics; Gold; Islam and Medicine; Leechbooks; Narwhal/Unicorn Horn Powder; Paracelsus and Paracelsianism; Purgatives; Syrups and Electuaries; Theriac and Mithridatum.

References

Eamon, William. "Plagues, Healers, and Patients in Early Modern Europe." *Renaissance Quarterly* 52 (1999): 474–486.

Nohl, Johannes. *The Black Death*. Yardley, PA: Westholme, 2006.

Pormann, Peter E. and Emilie Savage-Smith. *Medieval Islamic Medicine*. Washington, DC: Georgetown University Press, 2007.

Repopulation

The Black Death killed indiscriminately. Urban centers were emptied of nearly half their inhabitants; some rural villages lost so many as to become unsustainable and disappeared from history as survivors sought new homes. While the dead could not be raised, they could be replaced, at least locally and in the long run. This meant natural population replacement through births and the reshuffling of population through migration. Europe's growing cities had always drawn new denizens from the countryside, and this now had to be developed into an art. Landlords seeking laborers also tried to strike better deals than their competitors. Nonetheless, cycles of plague and other natural threats combined with national legislation to limit replenishment and growth for decades after 1350. By 1500, plague was largely confined to cities, which readily drew new residents from rapidly growing rural areas, making repopulation far less important an issue.

Christian Europe expected births to occur within families, discouraging sinful fornication and resulting illegitimacy. Post–Black Death observers commented on the rush to marry or remarry and the inappropriate matches to which some widows gave themselves. Westminster monk John of Reading wrote in 1365 that "shameless widows . . . rushed into the arms of foreigners . . . and kinsmen" (Horrox, 87) and of brothers marrying sisters. Bachelors with sketchy intentions sought out widows with wealth, and widowed mothers sought good men with resources to help them raise children. Men who had lost wife and children needed to begin families anew, especially if they had also lost blood relations who could carry on their families. Chronicler Jean Venette remarked, "After the end of the epidemic ... the men and women who stayed alive did everything to get married."

Modern scholars tend to agree that marriages spiked following the Black Death and later epidemics. Parish records are very scarce, but many have used that of Givry in Burgundy (France) to make their point. This town of about 2,000 souls in 1347 averaged 17.5 marriages between 1336 and 1341. In 1348, when plague struck and killed about 700, there were none. The following year, 86 couples were wed. In 1350 and 1351, the numbers dropped to 33 and 22 respectively. In Vic, the same pattern held: 23 annual marriages between 1338 and 1347; none in the summer of 1348; but 73 in 1349, 39 in 1350, and only 6 in 1351. Florentine records show that Tuscans followed the same pattern well into the 15th century. As far along as the later 17th century, immediately after epidemics, French widows and widowers remarried at rates three times normal years. All marriages, of course, did not result in children. Even so, from 1350 to 1500, levels of fertility seem to have been relatively high in much of Europe, which means the low national population recovery rates resulted from high mortality rather than fewer births.

Young women of status usually required dowries to contract a marriage, and post-plague cities developed schemes to provide these for the less fortunate. In 1425, Florence established the *Monte delle doti*, a fund into which fathers contributed with the promise of 250 percent return after 7.5 years or 500 percent after 15. By 1433, 864 young girls had been enrolled. Over 150 years, it

served some 25,000 prospective brides. Testators, too, increasingly supported marriage with funds for dowries, expecting spiritually useful prayers in return. By 1376, 12 percent of Sienese wills included dowry bequests, and by 1500, it was 75 percent. Though often generous, Tuscan merchant Francesco Datini (1335–1410) refused to fund dowries during epidemics, since the girls might soon die and provide him no benefit.

The Church had always taught the value of large families, and (celibate) preachers, for example, San Bernardino of Siena, made passionate pleas for reproduction. Illicit sex had been widely ignored before 1350, but preachers, confessors, and legislators took up the cause of sex only for procreation by condemning contraception and hounding prostitutes, homosexuals, and other fornicators. Lay gifts to monasteries and nunneries dropped off during the later 1300s, as if to discourage the communities of celibates. Letters of parents—for example, Florentine Alessandra Strozzi (b. 1408)—to unmarried sons encourage them to marry early and well for the sake of the family and republic. Surviving spouses also contributed to population rebounds since plague-induced fear releases hormones and neuro-chemicals that trigger the instinct for survival, which increases levels of dopamine and testosterone that stimulate the sex drive.

To encourage settlement in plague-ravaged Orvieto, Italy, and its countryside, the city council in 1349 granted all immigrant foreigners automatic citizenship rights with no duties to pay taxes or imposts or serve in the army for 10 years. Venice gave immigrants with families full citizenship after only one year; and the Archbishop of Auch gave patents of nobility to Italian merchants who settled in his diocese. In 1351, the Margrave of Moravia granted new settlers in Brno and Znojmo full tax exemption. Cities lost no time in innovating ways to draw useful people, men and women, to fill the new gaps in the labor forces. Immediate citizenship, tax and service exemptions, free housing, high wages, business subsidies, and immediate guild membership were among the perks offered. Large cities with populous countrysides had few problems generating immigration, but rural folk could not replace skilled artisans and professionals.

Nor could rural agriculture easily suffer such depopulation. Rural no less than urban resettlement concerned many authorities. Individual landlords, too, from archbishops to feudal nobles and newly landed merchants, needed peasant labor and offered new villagers free housing, improved living and working conditions, and a larger portion of the annual crops.

Recurring plague kept regional populations from returning to preplague levels until about 1500. Government action—unintentionally—also delayed recovery. In Castile, widows had to wait the traditional six months before remarrying, despite pleas of local officials to the king in 1351. Siena passed wage and price controls twice in 1348 and again in March 1350, which kept wages and immigration low. The Ordinance and Statute of Labourers in England and similar legislation elsewhere deprived landlords and employers of incentives to draw new workers or settlers.

See also: Black Death (1347–1352); Demographic and Economic Effects of Plague: the Islamic World; Demographic Effects of Plague: Europe 1347–1400; Demographic Effects of Plague: Europe 1401–1500; Demographic Effects of Plague: Europe 1501–1722; Economic Effects of Plague in Europe; Governments, Civil; Islamic Civil Responses; Labourers, Ordinance and Statute of; Merchants; Moral Legislation; Peasants; Taxes and Public Finance.

References

Anderson, Michael, ed. *British Population History: From the Black Death to the Present Day.* New York: Cambridge University Press, 1996.

Benedictow, Ole. *The Black Death 1346–1353: The Complete History.* New York: Boydell and Brewer, 2004.

Byrne, Joseph P. *Daily Life during the Black Death.* Westport, CT: Greenwood, 2006.

Livi Bacci, Massimo. *The Population of Europe: A History.* Translated by Cynthia and Carl Ipsen. New York: Blackwell, 1999.

Rome, Italy

Mid-14th-century Rome was not the Eternal City of the ancient emperors nor the splendid pile of Renaissance and Baroque popes and their entourages. It was a withered vine living by the relics of saints and the extortion of rapacious *signori*. Gone was the wealth and powerful attraction of the papal court, gone to Avignon some 40 years. This backwater of perhaps 20,000 inhabitants existed to serve pilgrims, who probably brought the plague in mid-1348. Clear spikes in the number of last wills occur in June and July, which implies its arrival in April. We know little about Roman life with plague, but on August 17, 1349, Pope Clement VI in Avignon published *Unigenitus Dei Filius,* in which he announced the Jubilee Year of 1350. Those who visited Rome as devout pilgrims during the year acquired special spiritual graces. Tens of thousands took to the roads, no doubt spreading plague to some extent along the way.

The next recorded epidemic was in 1389, after the papacy had returned to Rome, and the third occurred in the Jubilee Year of

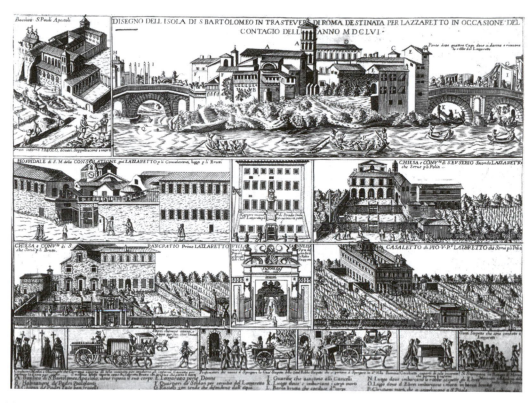

Vignettes of Rome during the plague of 1656: eight views are of buildings used as plague hospitals, and six views show fumigation activities, as well as funerals and processions resulting from the plague. (Courtesy of the National Library of Medicine)

1400, when much of Italy was suffering. As the Renaissance city began rebuilding itself, it weathered the plague in 1435, 1448 to 1450, 1457, 1468, 1476, 1478, 1480 to 1481, 1485, 1493 to 1494, and 1499 to 1500. In January 1449, Pope Nicholas V declared the Jubilee, which again drew tens of thousands to Rome in 1450. Plague forced the city to close its gate and bridges, and 200 are said to have died in the crush to cross the Sant' Angelo Bridge. Epidemics struck the city in 1503 to 1505, 1522 to 1527—an especially deadly year associated with the sack of the city by the Lutheran troops of Emperor Charles V—1529, and 1591.

Rome's last and deadliest plague was in 1656, when the city's population was around 120,000. The terrible outbreak in Naples made its way to Rome, but the papal administration was far better prepared than the Spanish colonial officials. Pope Alexander VII and his older brother Mario Chigi stayed in Rome and worked together to employ what were cutting-edge measures. The very effective Cardinal Girolamo Gastaldi, who was in charge of the newly established Congregation of Health and effectively controlled and coordinated all official responses, aided them. Communication with the Kingdom of Naples was strictly forbidden. Gates were closely guarded, and all travelers underwent quarantine. Large religious gatherings were banned, and those who had been shut up in their homes were removed to lodgings at

Sant'Eusebio. Lazarettos were also established at the Tiber Island and at Isola di San Bartolomeo. The Jewish Ghetto was sealed off, requiring Christians to carry buckets of fresh water to the residents. Bills of mortality kept track of plague deaths, and new plague orders and other announcements were posted on broadsides to inform the public. Alexander and the Congregation ruled the situation with wisdom and an iron fist; the result was that just about 15,000 plague deaths occurred, or about 12.5 percent of its population. At about the same time, Venice, Naples, and Genoa each lost an estimated 50 percent of their populations, and London's Great Plague of 1665 to 1666, 70,000 or more perished.

See also: Bishops and Popes; Governments, Civil; Individualism and Individual Liberties; Lazarettos and Pest Houses; Naples, Italy; Plague Orders and National Authorities.

References

Jones, Pamela. "Serving the Poor Sick with Humility from the Lazaretto of Milan to the Hospitals of Rome: Andrea Commodi's *San Carlo Borromeo Venerating the Holy Nail* (c. 1621–22) in the Church of San Carlo at Catinari," in her *Altarpieces and Their Viewers in the Churches of Rome from Caravaggio to Guido Reni* (Burlington, VT: Ashgate, 2008), 13–73

Liebowitz, J. O. "Bubonic Plague in the Ghetto of Rome (1656). Descriptions by Zahalon and by Gastaldi." *Koroth* 4 (1967): xxv–xxvii.

Magnuson, Torgil. *Rome in the Age of Bernini.* Vol. 2. New Jersey: Humanities Press, 1986.

San Juan, Rose Marie. *Rome: A City Out of Print.* Minneapolis: University of Minnesota Press, 2001.

S

St. Januarius (San Gennaro; d. c. 305)

In the later third and early fourth centuries, the Roman emperor Diocletian vigorously persecuted Christians as scapegoats for the empire's many problems. Januarius was the bishop of Benevento, south and east of Rome, who was decapitated in Pozzuoli on the Bay of Naples. His relics were taken to Naples, and San Gennaro became one of many Neapolitan patron saints. His cult gained favor when two vials of his blood began to liquefy and redry three times each year beginning in 1382. During plague in 1527, authorities made a vow, and, in fulfillment, later built the saint's ex voto chapel in the cathedral for the blood and other relics. In 1631, San Gennaro was said to have protected Naples from an earthquake, gaining a public "spire" akin to a plague memorial. During the epidemic of 1656, officials had San Gennaro painted beside Mary and other local saints above four city gates as protectors of the city.

See also: Ex voto; Naples, Italy; Plague Memorials; Plague Saints.

Reference

Clifton, James. "Art and Plague in Naples," in *Hope and Healing: Painting in Italy in a Time of Plague, 1500–1800*, edited by Gauvin Bailey, et al. (Chicago: University of Chicago Press, 2005), 97–117.

St. Michael the Archangel

One of four members of the highest order of angels, Christians credited Michael with having led the obedient angels against Lucifer and those rebel angels who separated themselves from God. In a perhaps related function, Michael is the guide of departed souls to heaven, lest they fall prey to Lucifer's (Satan's) minions.

He was also said to have been God's instrument in causing biblical plagues, including that in I Chronicles 21:15–16. In a clearly derivative story regarding the First Pandemic, during a Roman votive procession, Pope Gregory I grasped the success of his communal ritual because he saw St. Michael poised over the Mausoleum of Emperor Hadrian sheathing his sword of judgment and punishment. The scene appears in plague art, including the Limbourg Brothers' *Belles Heures* (c. 1411), and other books of hours. The mausoleum retains the name Castel Sant'Angelo (Castle of the Holy Angel) and is topped by a gilded statue of Michael (1752). Michael occasionally appears at Christ's side, sword drawn, in depictions of the divine source of plague.

See also: Books of Hours; Gregory the Great, Pope; Justinian, Plague of (First Plague Pandemic); Processions.

Reference

Boeckl, Christine. *Images of Plague and Pestilence: Iconography and Iconology*. Kirksville, MO: Truman State University Press, 2000.

St. Nicholas of Tolentino (1245–1305)

Young Nicholas was named for St. Nicholas of Myra by his Tuscan parents and played at being a hermit. At age 18, he joined the Augustinian Order of Catholic friars and was ordained a priest in 1270. Though preferring to live as a hermit, he also served as a chaplain to the sick and was notable as a preacher and healer in the area around Tolentino. After his death, in need of a popular Augustinian saint, his order presented Nicholas as a miraculous healer and a worthy advocate before God on behalf of the plague-stricken. They lobbied for his canonization as a saint, which occurred only in 1446. He was recognized for his moral purity and his dedication to repentance and was declared a protector of souls in Purgatory. Only locally was Nicholas reverenced as a plague saint, however, and he appears in a number of Florentine paintings as a miracle worker and plague saint. Often depicted with Saints Sebastian and Roche, Nicholas is identifiable by the lily he carries.

See also: Plague Saints; Purgatory.

Reference

Boeckl, Christine. *Images of Plague and Pestilence: Iconography and Iconology.* Kirksville, MO: Truman State University Press, 2000.

St. Roche

Second only to St. Sebastian, St. Roche (Rocco, Roch) was Europe's universal plague saint. Supposedly born in Montpellier, while on pilgrimage to Rome, he aided plague victims at Aquapendente, Tuscany. On his return, he contracted the plague in Piacenza and was cured with the help of a dog and an angel. At Montpellier, authorities jailed him as a spy, and he died in prison. He is depicted as a young pilgrim with floppy hat, pilgrim's scallop shell, staff, and dog, often exposing the bubo on his upper thigh.

A confraternity near Constance dedicated itself to him, which may have influenced the Council of Constance in 1414 to approve his cult, though he was formally canonized a saint in 1629. Published "Lives" came later (Francesco Diedo's Milan 1479, Venice 1480, Vienna and Nuremberg 1482). After the 1477 epidemic, Venetians established the Scuola (Confraternity) of San Rocco, and Roche's body was moved from Montpellier to Venice in 1484. It rests in an urn on the main altar of the Church of San Rocco. Recipient of extravagant gifts, by 1500, the confraternity became one of Venice's six Scuoli grandi and a center of religious culture, charity, and mutual aid. Roche's cult spread across Europe, celebrated in paintings, woodcuts, statues, and stained glass, in houses, chapels, and churches. His devotees sought his aid before God with prayers, vows, hymns, and invocations that God might spare them from plague and plague death as he had spared Roche.

See also: Art, Effects of Plague on; Christ; Confraternities; Ex voto; Plague Memorials; Plague Saints; Prayer and Fasting; Processions.

References

Boeckel, Christine. "Giorgio Vasari's "San Rocco Altarpiece": Tradition and Innovation in Plague Iconography." *Artibus et Historiae* 22 (2001): 29–40.

Worcester, Thomas. "Saint Roch vs. Plague, Famine, and Fear," in *Hope and Healing*, edited by Gauvin Alexander Bailey (Chicago: University of Chicago Press, 2005), 153–175.

St. Rosalia

Rosalia was a Norman noblewoman of Palermo, Sicily, who shunned marriage and became a hermit on Mount Pellegrino, near the city. After her death circa 1160, a small cult grew up around her cave, and she gained

The grotto of St. Rosalia in Sicily, Italy. After her death circa 1160 a small cult grew up around her cave and she gained minor fame as a plague saint. (Art Directors.co.uk/Ark Religion.com/StockPhotoPro)

minor fame as a healing saint. During the plague of 1624, a hunter discovered her bones, and following a heavenly voice, he took them to Palermo. The city paraded them through the city praying for Rosalia's intercession, and soon the plague ended. She became the city's plague saint; soon paintings appeared of her interceding with God: kneeling, dressed as a Franciscan with a rose crown and skull representing plague dead. Local Jesuits began an annual procession that still occurs each July and spread her cult to Rome, Paris, and Antwerp. She is buried in her chapel in Palermo's cathedral.

See also: Art, Effects of Plague on; Christ; Confraternities; Ex voto; Plague Saints; Prayer and Fasting; Processions.

Reference

Bailey, Gauvin Alexander. "Anthony van Dyck, the Cult of Saint Rosalie, and the 1624 Plague in Palermo," in *Hope and Healing: Painting in Italy in a Time of Plague, 1500–1800*, edited by Bailey et al. (Chicago: University of Chicago Press, 2005), 118–135.

St. Sebastian

Tradition claims that Sebastian was born in Narbonne, Gaul, about 256 CE. He entered the Roman army and became an officer but also converted to Christianity. In Rome in 288, he was executed with arrows for being Christian. Nursed back to health by St. Irene, he returned to Emperor Diocletian's court and was bludgeoned to death. His bones were collected and kept for a time at San Sebastiano Church near Rome. His martyr cult began in 654 or 680 during the Plague of Justinian.

Sebastian's initial survival made him the quintessential plague saint. Like a lightning rod, he absorbed divine plague arrows meant for people, asking God to forgive them and lift the epidemic. While asking and waiting, Catholics had thousands of images created, praying before these both prayers of the heart and composed petitions. In March 1511, a young Venetian boy prayed every night to Sebastian to keep his merchant father safe, while down the canal, the patrician Sanudo family cherished a relic of Sebastian they credited with having always preserved them from plague. From cottages to royal palaces, images of nearly-nude Sebastian bristling with anywhere from two arrows to dozens hung in places of honor. In Normandy alone, 254 remaining images from private and church sites have been catalogued. In thanks for spiritual intercession, communities across Europe built ex voto chapels and churches dedicated to Saint Sebastièn or San Sebastiano.

See also: Arrows; Art, Effects of Plague on; Christ; Ex voto; Plague Memorials; Plague Saints; Prayer and Fasting.

References

Gelpi, A. P. "Saint Sebastian and the Black Death." *Vesalius* 4 (1998): 23–30.

Mormando, Franco and Thomas Worcester, eds. *Piety and Plague from Byzantium to the Baroque*. Kirksville, MO: Truman State University Press, 2007.

Talvacchia, Bette. "The Double Life of St. Sebastian in Renaissance Art," in *The Body in Early Modern Italy*, edited by Julia Hairston and Walter Stephens (Baltimore, MD: Johns Hopkins University Press, 2010), 226–248.

Scientific Revolution

Scientific Revolution refers to a collection of discoveries, inventions, theories, writings, and institutional foundations that took place between about 1600 and 1750. These replaced existing systems of explanation—often rooted in antiquity and religion—that had long accounted for nature and natural phenomena and served as a foundation for further developments in what properly came to be known as science.

The interest in the natural world prompted by the Renaissance and geographic discoveries led early pioneers to challenge long-held beliefs. In the 1540s, Nikolaus Copernicus shattered traditional geocentric cosmology by showing that placement of the sun at the universe's center explained celestial motion more elegantly and accurately. Andreas Vesalius's hands-on anatomical studies and publications began the eclipse of Galenic anatomy, and Paracelsus's iatrochemical experiments challenged Galenic therapy and expanded the range of medical treatments. In order to take its place in Western culture, however,

science required a methodology that reassured practitioners and the public of the accuracy of its findings. In the early 1600s, Francis Bacon, Galileo Galilei, and Rene Descartes contributed to the modern understanding of scientific method by insisting that observations and experiments be carefully carried out and repeated and that findings be replicable by other scientists. Descartes's contributions to mathematics insured that methods and results of inquiry would be quantitatively based and expressed; Galileo's discoveries with his improved telescope spurred the invention of more and better instruments of measurement and discovery; and Bacon's emphasis on sharing findings led to the founding of scientific societies and publications.

Despite biological and medical discoveries and advances during the 1600s, little was added to the understanding of plague. New theories of its nature (tiny animal or spore) and means of spread were difficult to support, even with the new microscope, and had little practical effect. Throughout the Second Pandemic, Galenic medicine remained the dominant model and miasma the principal medical explanation of plague.

The Scientific Revolution's emphases on experience (empiricism) and rational action for the betterment of society (Bacon) did, however, affect the ways in which communities and authorities dealt with epidemics. Setting aside traditional miasma theory, from the beginning, observers noted that plague seemed to spread through some form of contagion, and many antiplague efforts relied on this new model. Though such innovations as health boards, bills of health, bills of mortality, quarantine, and isolation of infected areas predate the 1600s, the new science demanded that these be evaluated and applied systematically. Difficult to do while plague raged, the discipline of public health grew out of the many publications arguing the efficacy of some official app-roaches, condemning others, and proposing still more, the nexus of personal experience and public action.

See also: Bills of Mortality; Boyle, Robert; Fracastoro, Girolamo; Galen and Galenism; Graunt, John; Kircher, Athanasius; Miasma Theory; Paracelsus and Paracelsianism.

References

Cipolla, Carlo. *Faith, Reason, and the Plague in Seventeenth-Century Tuscany.* New York: W. W. Norton & Company, 1981.

Henry, John. *The Scientific Revolution and the Origins of Modern Science.* New York: Palgrave Macmillan, 2008.

Jacob, Margaret. *The Scientific Revolution.* New York: St. Martin's, 2010.

Searchers

Plague victims died in many different places and under many circumstances. Corpses of family members or members of religious communities or those in hospital would have been buried or given over for burial to corpse carriers. Many, however, died alone, from solitary widows to sick servants expelled from their employers' households and the otherwise poverty-stricken, vagrant, or abandoned. Their corpses might be found in sheds or back alleys, in shut-up houses, or lying openly in the street. As cities began to collect plague statistics in the 15th century, officials called searchers were tasked with inspecting a given neighborhood or parish, seeking out the dead, determining cause of death, and reporting their findings to parish or civic authorities. These figures provided the foundation for bills of mortality and were considered more reliable than burial reports from parish clergy. Once pest houses were established, searchers also made determinations of who became an inmate and who remained free.

In Catholic countries, friars often served as searchers who also brought spiritual comfort to the dying they found, and in 16th-century Seville, the city's aldermen did. In Anglican England, parishes gave these positions to "sober ancient women" who were paid small salaries from parish funds. Like corpse car-riers, these female searchers were suspected of (and sometimes tried for) crimes, including being bribed to hide plague deaths, theft of victims' goods, and even murder. The credi-bility of these amateurs was questioned from the 16th century on: how were they to deter-mine whether an illness was plague? As late as 1720, while plague ravaged Marseille, London's Dr. Richard Mead decried searchers as "ignorant old women" who should be replaced by "understanding and diligent men" whose findings would be confirmed by physicians.

See also: Bills of Mortality; Corpse Carriers; Corpses; Friars (Mendicants); Lazarettos and Pest Houses.

Reference

Munkhoff, Richelle. "Searchers of the Dead: Authority, Marginality, and the Interpretation of Plague in England, 1574–1665." *Gender and History* 11 (2002): 1–29.

Second Plague Pandemic (1340s–1840s)

The Second Plague Pandemic is the half-millennium series of recurring bubonic, pneumonic, and septicemic plague epidem-ics in Western Eurasia and North Africa, which lasted from the 1340s through the 1840s. The initial pandemic, which struck the entire region between 1347 and 1352, is known as the Black Death and may have killed as much as 40 percent of the population. It may also have stricken late Yüan China. Though quality and quantity of records differ across time and among regions, it seems that plague first hit rural and urban areas indiscriminately and with a frequency of once a decade for any given locale. Over time, plague became an urban disease with less frequent but virulent "visitations." By the mid-17th century, one by one, major cities began suffering their final epidemics, trailing off with London (1665–1666), Vienna (1712), Marseille (1720–1722), and Moscow (1770–1772). Plague continued to circulate among Mediterranean Ottoman ports until the late 1830s, kept at bay by European cordons sanitaires and quarantines.

See also: Black Death (1347–1352); Demographic and Economic Effects of Plague: the Islamic World; End of Second Plague Pandemic: Theories; Plague in Europe 1360–1500; Plague in Europe 1500–1725.

References

Aberth, John. *Plagues in World History.* New York: Rowman and Littlefield, 2011.

Byrne, Joseph P. *Daily Life during the Black Death.* Westport, CT: Greenwood Press, 2006.

Septicemic Plague

Septicemic plague is a form of bubonic plague and is caused by the introduction of the *Yersinia pestis* bacterium into the human body. This generally occurs when a feeding flea inserts its tube into the epidermis, puncturing a venule or tiny vein. If the flea is an infected *Xenopsylla cheopis*, then its digestive tract should be blocked by a glob of the *Y. pestis* bacteria. In this case, the flea regurgitates the glob into the victim to clear its digestive tract.

Once in the body, a large amount of this is normally picked up by the lymphatic system. Upon entering the body, the temperature of the bacteria is that of the cold-blooded flea, about 26°C. As they warm in the new host, the bacteria that survive the initial onslaught by the immune system develop protective envelopes that allow these cells to be taken through the body but not destroyed by it. Normally, most of this is deposited in the lymph node near the back of the neck, the armpits, or the groin, whichever is closest to the point of infection. As the protected bacteria multiply, they swell and inflame the node. If it is near the surface, it will become noticeable as the bubo of bubonic plague. If it is deeper in the body, its swelling will not usually be visible.

Septicemia, or blood poisoning, occurs in one of two ways. In primary septicemic plague, the flea deposits the bacteria directly into the bloodstream without interference from the lymphatic system. The rapidly multiplying *Y. pestis* quickly makes its way to body organs, including the heart, liver, kidneys, and spleen. The onset is sudden and severe, with fever spiking to 40 to 42°C as internal hemorrhaging begins. Without the participation of the lymphatic system, the lymph nodes do not swell, as they really do not have the time.

In secondary septicemic plague, the bacterial and other material is picked up largely by the lymphatic system and deposited in the nodes. These, however, are overwhelmed and may rupture, and much of the still lethal material finds its way into the bloodstream. The circulatory system then distributes the still-reproducing cells among the organs. In many ways, the final stage of bubonic plague is really a matter of septicemia and toxic shock. Because the lungs may become infected, coughing and sneezing may spread toxic material and thus make the patient contagious.

The clinical symptoms parallel those of bubonic plague, but with greater severity, for example, higher fever, more violent nausea, vomiting and diarrhea, greater discomfort, and delirium. Also, manifestations of the internal hemorrhaging appear more readily on the skin, discoloring large patches and producing more pustules. Drug treatment is identical to that for bubonic plague, but in the case of primary septicemic plague, it is needed more readily.

Cases of septicemic plague are about 5 percent of modern plague cases and probably appeared during the Second Plague Pandemic. This would explain some of the symptoms observed at the time that do not match bubonic plague. Since both are caused by *Yersinia pestis*, however, with only skeletal remains and DNA, it would be impossible to tell cases apart.

See also: Black Death: Debate over the Medical Nature of; Bubonic Plague; Pneumonic Plague; *Yersinia pestis*.

References

Gorbach, Sherwood L., et al. *Infectious Diseases*. 3rd edition. New York: Lippincott, Williams & Wilkins, 2004.

Sebbane, Florent. "Role of the *Yersinia pestis* Plasmogin Activator in the Incidence of Distinct Septicemic and Bubonic Forms of Flea-borne Plague." *Proceedings of the National Academy of Sciences of the USA* 103 (2006): 5526–5530.

Servants, Household

The fates of household servants in plague time were as varied as those of any other group, but their positions within households shaped their experiences in certain ways. Trusted servants were often sent from country estates or villas into local towns or large cities on errands of various sorts, and if plague were about and their urban contacts put them at risk, they could return home with the fleas that spread the disease. In an urban setting, daily errands might also cause servants to contract plague before other family members. Their living quarters, while with the family, tended to be in undesirable parts of the residence, outbuildings, or attics, where rats and fleas were at home. When servants caught the plague early in an epidemic, they could be cared for tenderly, but in cities where shutting in of victims and families was mandated, they could just as easily be hidden away until recovering or dying. If the latter, the corpse was likely to be dumped or hastily buried away from its former home.

If a family stayed in a plague-stricken town, the servants usually remained. They would be exposed to the disease as they did their chores. If the family were shut in, so were the help. If the family decided to flee, they could take the servants with them, release them to make their own arrangements, or require that they stay behind to guard property or even handle financial matters. These last had to be very trustworthy since they now had complete control over what was often great wealth. Ben Jonson's comedy *The Alchemist* is set in just such a situation: and when the cat was away, the mice did play. Of course, leaving servants behind could be as good as signing their death warrants, and it could not have been a decision lightly made. Yet the City of London was said to have been a city of servants during 17th-century epidemics, and many may well have lived it up. In the wake of an epidemic, demand for servants would have increased dramatically, drawing in young women and men from the countryside. Given the blow to the overall labor pool in a given area, wages would have risen, making domestic service even more attractive.

See also: Abandonment; Economic Effects of Plague in Europe; Flight.

Reference

Byrne, Joseph P. *Daily Life during the Black Death*. Westport, CT: Greenwood, 2006.

Shakespeare, William (1564–1616)

Playwright and poet William Shakespeare was born in Stratford-on-Avon during a plague year to Mary and John, a glover, wool merchant, and money lender. Educated locally through grammar School, sometime in the 1580s, William married, then moved to London to pursue an acting career. This he extended into troupe management and authorship of many of the best-known plays in English.

Shakespeare's life was often touched by plague. He lost two infant sisters, Joan and Margaret, and seven-year-old Anne, his 27-year-old brother Edmund, and his own son Hamnet in 1596. Three grandsons also succumbed to pestilence. Both Elizabethan and early Stuart authorities regularly closed theaters after plague deaths reached epidemic proportions, stifling demand for actors and new plays alike. Troupes that stayed together received royal patronage or toured provincial venues. Like Thomas Dekker and Ben Jonson, Shakespeare used downtime to seek patronage among the younger aristocrats and pen poetry, including his 154 sonnets (published in moderately pestilential 1609 but written before). Across Shakespeare's career, these times included September 1592 to June 1594; July 13, 1603, to Easter Monday 1604; and 1608 to 1610. He published *Venus*

Hailed as the greatest writer in Western literature, Great Britain's William Shakespeare dominated the London theatrical world in the late 16th and early 17th centuries. Many of his plays reflect the plague's recurring presence in the city. (Perry-Castaneda Library)

and Adonis and *The Rape of Lucrece* during the first break, emerging as a celebrated poet with these, his first published works. During the second, Shakespeare's The King's Men traveled with their new, eponymous patron, performing on several occasions.

Among Shakespeare's plays, only *Romeo and Juliet* (1596) is set during a plague epidemic. Plague searchers lock up Friar John and his vital message for Romeo in Mantua. Modern scholars point to other tragedies set in metaphorically diseased, morally corrupted settings, often courts. "Something is rotten in Denmark" characterizes *Hamlet*'s Elsinore Castle (published 1603), where gathers a "foul and pestilent congregation of vapors." At Macbeth's court (1603), "violent sorrow seems A modern ecstasy: the dead man's knell Is there scarce ask'd for who, and good men's lives Expire before the Flowers in their Caps, dying, or ere they sicken." Celestially stirred up miasmas—the stuff of plagues—appear in a number of plays: "a planetary plague, when Jove Will o'er some high vic'd City, hang his poison In the sick air" (*Timon of Athens*, IV:iii); "When the planets In evil mixture to disorder wander, What plagues, and what portents, what mutiny . . . Divert and crack, rend and deracinate The unity, and married calm of States Quite from their fixtures" (*Troilus and Cressida*, I:iii); and in Lear's curse (III:iv), "Now all the plagues, that in the pendulous air Hang fated o'er men's faults, light on thy Daughters." Cleopatra's curse, "The most infectious pestilence upon thee!" (*Antony and Cleopatra*, II:v), has echoes throughout the period's dramas.

See also Jonson, Ben; London, England; Metaphors for Plague.

References

Barroll, John Leeds. *Politics, Plague, and Shakespeare's Theater: The Stuart Years*. Ithaca: Cornell University Press, 1991.

Forbes, T. R. *Chronicle from Aldgate: Life and Death in Shakespeare's London*. New Haven, CT: Yale University Press, 1971.

Harris, Jonathan Gil. *Sick Economies: Drama, Mercantilism and Disease in Shakespeare's England*. Philadelphia: University of Pennsylvania Press, 2004.

Wilson, F. P. *Plague in Shakespeare's London*. New York: Oxford University Press, 1999.

Shutting In

As plague approached Milan in spring 1348, the duke and his councilors decided on two courses of action. First, deny entrance to the city to anyone from any place suspected of plague; and, should plague appear in the city, immediately isolate cases in their own homes. It worked. According to Agnolo di Tura, only three families suffered, and Milan avoided the fate of most urban areas. The principle behind shutting in was the vague notion of contagion: that contact with victims could make others sick. Though this seemed to contradict contemporary miasma theory, civic officials were interested in results, not philosophical arguments.

Depending on local regulations, the residents of the house in which a plague victim was found could be required to remain in the house for a set period as a kind of quarantine. Some Dutch cities allowed relatives a choice to stay or leave and even to walk about the streets at certain times if they stayed. Most regulations required strict isolation, with doors and windows barred or nailed shut and only one opening left for passage of food and other necessities. This was often a second-story window, with supplies delivered in a basket on a rope. Even keyholes were sealed. Life inside must have been hellish. If the victim died, she probably did so without medical aid or spiritual comfort, though Catholic cities usually allowed for last rites. The corpse would be bundled off—having been lowered or dropped out of the second story window—with none of the requisite rituals, since family remained locked in. The blend of fetid odors would have been augmented with smoke from fumigation, the recognition of miasma theory. To counteract corrupted air, families would burn wool, tar, resins, perhaps incense or herbs, or discharge gunpowder; in poorer homes, old shoes or leather scraps. This would mix with body odors, candle smoke, cooking smells, and uncollected human waste. If additional cases of plague appeared inside, these would have to be tended by the family, with medicines delivered at civic expense. Those who escaped faced draconian penalties including immediate execution, as governments became increasingly authoritarian.

Houses were marked in various but clear ways to keep the curious away. In Utrecht in 1467, plague house doors had a 9-by-18-inch white linen sheet hung. Sixteenth-century Dutch cities hung bundles of straw or straw wreaths on doors; at The Hague, they had "P.P." (Dutch for plague present) painted; and Roermond required affixing tin sheets painted with the name Jesus. In 1518, Henry VIII's chancellor Cardinal Wolsey required a painted red cross and the hopeful phrase "Lord have mercy on us" painted or erection of a 10-foot pole with a bundle of straw, perhaps to aid Dutch visitors. In 1521, London experimented with a T-cross—St. Anthony's symbol—on blue or white paper as a sign; in 1578 and 1592, a large red circle with "Lord have mercy on us." Less easily removed were the red wooden crosses nailed to doors in July 1593, and the oil-painted, 14-by-14-inch red crosses of May 1603. In 17th-century Italy, cities ordered red or white crosses, or a cross and "*sanità*" (health) painted on the front door.

Lengths of isolation also differed. In Leicester, England, survivors could only leave after a period of two months after the death of the last victim (1563); in London (1568), it was 20 days; in 18th-century London, one month. In 1557 in Holland, after a victim's death, the family could immediately leave the house or choose to remain isolated in it for another full six weeks.

Guards or warders patrolled these houses to ensure compliance, usually at community expense. Other expenses included padlocks, bars or spikes, medical personnel, medicines, food, fumigation material, and fuel for cooking. The number of houses shut up during a given epidemic could be rather large, as 17th-century records begin to show. In 1631, Pistoia, a town of about 8,000 residents, shut up 125 houses; nearby Prato, with about 6,000, shut up 208 houses. In 1604, 20 percent of Salisbury, England's, population was shut in (411 houses with 1,300 people); small Stone, Staffordshire, had to support 115 families, and Nantwich, Cheshire, 55, all at local expense. Lowestoft, Suffolk, lost 600 dead by November 1638 of a population of about 5,000, but had 263 infected families shut in at a weekly expense of £200.

Resistance to being shut in is clear from stories of escaped victims or family members, but of greater interest, perhaps, is the debate in European society over the appropriateness of the practice. Dutch humanist Desiderius Erasmus recognized the harshness of the practice but balanced it with the lives supposedly saved. Others, especially in contentious England, advocated the use of pest houses and hospitals and "murder" of family members, though the practice came to be seen as unconscionable, given that simple quarantine would accomplish the same goal. The anonymous 1665 tract *Shutting Up Infected Houses* crisply judged: "Infection may have killed its thousands, but shutting up hath killed its ten thousands." Playwright and moralist Thomas Dekker noted that the wealthy fled while the poor were cruelly shut up; others opined that God must become angry at so uncharitable a practice and continue visitation of plague as punishment. The practice continued during London's Great Plague (1665), but when plague threatened from Marseille in 1720, the critical chorus rose up. Novelist Daniel Defoe decried it because people escaped; imprisoning the well with victims was inhumane and "medically outrageous;" and the asymptomatic wandered freely about spreading infection. At the same time, Dr. Richard

Bradley, though accepting contagion, condemned shutting in as inhumane and plain murder.

See also: Contagion Theory; Governments, Civil; Health Boards, Magistracies, and Commissions; Individualism and Individual Liberties; Lazarettos and Pest Houses; Public Health; Quarantine.

References

Byrne, Joseph P. *Daily Life during the Black Death*. Westport, CT: Greenwood Press, 2006.

Cipolla, Carlo. *Fighting the Plague in Seventeenth-Century Italy*. Madison: University of Wisconsin Press, 1981.

Slack, Paul. "Metropolitan Government in Crisis: The Response to Plague," in *London: 1500–1700: The Making of the Metropolis*, edited by A. L. Beier and Roger Finlay (New York: Longman, 1986), 60–81.

Signs of Plague

Chroniclers, physicians, and other plague authors often noted occurrences in nature (signs) that they believed were related to a later plague outbreak. Some of these portents were deemed to be divine warnings, others were linked to natural causes of the epidemics, and still others were interpreted as accompanying phenomena, perhaps with occult or hidden connections to disease. A given commentator was likely to report several signs for a given epidemic. Forewarning of plague presented obvious advantages to a community. People could flee, take prophylactic measures, or repent and pray; and authorities could avoid deadly delays in declaring plague or the costs of a false declaration (panic, flight, economic disruptions). Interest in signs remained high throughout the Second Pandemic.

Due to astrological and religious beliefs, people first looked to the skies. Traditionally, such celestial changes as a new star or comet portended some major change for mankind, usually for the worse. Certain astrological alignments of planets and zodiac constellations were thought to have a similar, even causative effect. God might create a new star or send a comet as warning, but the "moist" or "dry" nature of a planet or zodiac sign directly affected floods or droughts on earth, they believed. "The Great Conjunction" of 1345 was interpreted, retrospectively, as a portent of the Black Death. Miasma theorists saw causation: the celestial bodies created cracks in the earth's surface through which the poisonous underground miasmas entered the atmosphere. Anomalies in the atmosphere were also noted as plague signs, especially by followers of Hippocrates's environmental theory of epidemics. Unseasonal warmth or coolness, storms, mists or cloudiness, unusual rainfall, and constant southern winds fostered humid conditions that directly led to putrefaction, another supposed cause of poisonous miasmas. The *St. Alban's Chronicle* noted that in the plague year 1391, "for almost six weeks [after July 10] thick mists prevailed from about noon every day. Sometimes they lasted all day and night . . . " (p. 912).

Closer to home, earth-opening quakes were both portent and cause, as were floods that left putrefying moisture across the land. Henricus of Bratislava theorized that corruption of the earth's interior forced such burrowing animals as mice and snakes to surface in large numbers. Signs included the unusual presence of snakes, toads, lizards, worms, and such insects as locusts. Birds and larger animals flee the region ripe for plague or act in bizarre ways: in 1634, a Bavarian cat caught a rare albino sparrow, and plague followed. Putrefaction also caused birth defects in lower animals—possibly the sparrow, too. Francis Bacon reported the appearance of long-tailed toads in ditches near London just before the plague of 1625. Plants could also be affected by putrefaction before people: large numbers of fungi, for example, toadstools or withering blights, were clear warnings.

See also: Astrology; Causes of Plague: Historical Theories; Miasma Theory.

References

Cooke, W. G. "Fiery Drakes and Blazing Bearded Light." *English Studies* 61 (1980): 97–103.

Goldstein, B. *Levi ben Gerson's Prognostication for the Conjunction of 1345.* Philadelphia: American Philosophical Association, 1990.

Simond, Paul-Louis (1858–1947)

Paul-Louis Simond was born in Beaufort-sur-Gervanne, France, to a Protestant cleric and his wife. Educated at the Bordeaux School of Medicine and Pharmacy, Simond entered the Naval Medical Corps. While pursuing his doctorate in Medicine, he directed a leper colony in French Guyana, contracted yellow fever, and wrote a prize-winning thesis on leprosy in Guyana (1887). Between 1890 and 1896, Simond worked as a member of the Colonial Health Corps on smallpox vaccinations in Indochina, compiled oceanographic data, and gathered medical histories of Chinese locales near the Indochinese border. In 1896 to 1897, he studied microbiology and worked in the Pasteur Institute under Elie Metchnikoff.

In March 1897, the Institute asked Simond to relocate to Bombay (now Mumbai), India. Alexandre Yersin, another Pasteurian, had begun a vaccination campaign during an Indian bubonic plague epidemic; Simond was to relieve Yersin and continue research. Treatment successes were limited, and

Simond contracted malaria. After a short rest, he went to Karachi (now Pakistan), where he became very interested in the means of transmission of the bacillus Yersin had discovered. Yersin had noted that rats died of plague, and field researchers blamed dried rat and human excrement absorbed through breathing, eating, or open skin sores. Simond noticed on new plague patients small pustules resembling infected insect bites. Within the blisters, he discovered plague bacilli in large numbers and theorized that these were the bite locations of some pathogen-carrying insects. Rejecting cockroaches, he turned to the fleas that fed on the very rats—and people—that died of plague. He captured some of these fleas and discovered large concentrations of the *Yersinia pestis* pathogen in them. Japanese researcher Masanori Ogata made the same discovery at the same time but did not connect it to plague transmission, which Simond did: infected fleas carried the pathogen from rat to rat and rat to person. He tested his theory on rats in Karachi, and on June 2, 1898, he proved rat-to-rat transmission of the bacillus via fleas. Later in the year, the Pasteur Institute published Simond's results after relatively few tests, but the wider scientific world remained skeptical. Simond left plague research for mosquito-spread yellow fever.

Attempts to repeat the experiment failed until 1903, when J.-Constantin Gauthier and A. Raybaud confirmed that fleas were necessary for transmission. Exactly how the fleas acquired, carried, and deposited the bacteria remained unknown until 1914. A. W. Bacot and C. J. Martin of the British Lister Institute determined that fleas fed on the blood of both infected rats and humans, drawing the bacteria into their foregut or proventriculus. Here, the bacteria multiply until the flea vomits them into its next blood host. The cycle was complete.

See also: Bubonic Plague; Fleas; Pasteur, Louis; Rats and Other Plague Carriers; Third Plague Pandemic; Yersin, Alexandre; *Yersinia pestis*.

References

Crawford, Edward A. "Paul-Louis Simond and His Work on Plague." *Perspectives in Biology and Medicine* 39 (1996): 446–458.

Simond, Marc, et al. "Paul-Louis Simond and His Discovery of Plague Transmission by Rat Fleas." *Journal of the Royal Society of Medicine* 91 (1998): 101–104.

Sin

In the revealed, monotheistic religions of Judaism, Christianity, and Islam, sin is the transgression of God's will. God's will is known through the sacred texts of Hebrew Scripture, the Bible, and the Koran. Each source makes clear that God will punish the transgressors, either in this life or in the afterlife. But God is merciful and will save from damnation those who reject sin and submit to his will. As the Bible makes clear, however, God also punishes communities that fail to live according to his will. This included his own people, the biblical Hebrews or Jews, whom he chastised by military defeat and pestilence. Their collective falling away, or that of their leadership, was punished collectively, a notion that had deep roots when plague epidemics struck Europe, Africa, and the Near East.

To unlock the mystery of plague, understanding God's will was as important to medieval and early modern leaders as understanding germ theory and its implications is to ours today. For Muslims, who saw both the believer and the infidel fall to the pestilence, the epidemics were punishments only for the faithless, who suffered here and were damned. For the faithful Muslim, death by plague was a type of martyrdom that sent one directly to Heaven. The faithless and disobedient needed to repent if possible and, in any case, throw themselves on Allah's mercy. Christian individuals and communities assumed that the most common sins, not necessarily the most egregious, were the sins that unleashed divine wrath. In general, such punishments as leprosy or smallpox were considered individual punishments for individual sins, while plagues, famines, and military defeats were chastisements for communal sins. These needed to be identified if individuals were to be warned against them and communities to act against them.

In medieval Europe, the Ten Commandments and the Seven Deadly Sins provided a good starting point. Honoring God, the Sabbath, and one's parents and refraining from violence, thievery, lying or fraud, sexual immorality, and envy were expected of all Christians. Gluttony, sloth, anger, drunkenness, lust, envy, and greed were at the heart of many sermons and religious tracts and, for Catholics, formed the heart of reflection before confession.

Lust had a special place in medieval thinking. Sexual desire for someone other than one's spouse was sinful in itself. Heterosexual intercourse outside of marriage by two unmarried persons was simple fornication. If the two carried on as if they were married, it was concubinage, a sin especially associated with unmarried Catholic priests. Intercourse involving at least one otherwise married person was adultery, a very serious offence for which Hebrew Scripture prescribed stoning. And there were prostitutes, often tolerated by civic authorities for purely practical reasons, and rapists, whose class often determined their punishment. Finally, homosexual activity, generally called sodomy, was far from unknown. Ill-disciplined monasteries for both men and women had this charge hurled at them, as did never-married men, especially those with whom younger men and boys worked as apprentices or students. While lust in its various forms was a personal sin, its toleration was a communal one. When plague threatened, both moral legislation and moral lessons appeared. Priests, bishops, preachers, and ministers thundered from pulpits and in print about personal reform and chastised authorities who allowed notorious sexual sinfulness. City councils closed bordellos and expelled sex workers from their cities, and bishops intervened in lax monasteries. To the extent that plague conditions themselves unleashed sexual aberrations, as suggested by Boccaccio and commentators since, authorities could blame an outbreak's duration on the people's ongoing licentiousness.

Public moral failing also came in many other forms. Public intoxication, which easily led to violence or accidents, and gambling were two that were commonly punished more strictly as plague approached. Theaters, at least in England, drew the ire of religious authorities, and London's were often shut down during plague times. Apart from being venues for contagion, theatre going was associated with sinful behaviors of many types, from sexual activity to drunkenness and thievery. An Elizabethan preacher at St. Paul's reasoned: sin causes plague; plays lead to sin; so plays lead to plague. In 1584, the London city council reported to the royal Privy Council, "To play in plague-time is to increase the plague by infection; to play out of plague time is to draw the plague by the offending of God" (Mullett, 99).

In 1348 to 1349 and again from the 1520s, some Christian religious zealots concluded that God was punishing communities that tolerated, respectively, Jews or the wrong type of Christian. Brutal assaults on Jewish communities from Spain to the Rhineland were justified by some with the excuse that God was or will be punishing Christians for allowing Jews to live in their midst. Christianity's divisions in the Reformation allowed for cross-blaming. Where reforms had taken hold, the Catholic holdouts were to blame; since Catholic authorities considered Reformers heretics and thus enemies of God, their toleration by Catholic civil authorities could bring down God's wrath. Blasphemers who insulted God, Antitrinitarians who disbelieved, witches, any who were suspected of collusion with Satan, and anyone who swore and misused God's name publicly were also subject to expulsion if not death when the community was threatened.

Sinful or immoral leadership carried more weight than immoral followers. Apart from failing to set good examples, the opportunities for graft, injustice, corruption, and general abuse of power or authority made church, civic, and national leaders susceptible to sin and suspect of it.

See also: Allah; Bible; Biblical Plagues; Christ; God the Father; Islamic Religious Responses; Moral Legislation; Morality Literature, Christian; Prayer and Fasting; Processions.

References
Allen, Peter Lewis. *The Wages of Sin: Sex and Disease, Past and Present.* Chicago: University of Chicago Press, 2000.

Horrox, Rosemary. *The Black Death.* New York: Manchester University Press, 1994.

Delumeau, Jean. *Sin and Fear: The Emergence of a Western Guilt Culture 13th–18th Centuries.* Translated by Eric Nicholson. New York: St. Martin's Press, 1990.

Mullett, Charles F. *The Bubonic Plague and England.* Lexington: University of Kentucky Press, 1956.

Social Construction of Disease

Social construction recognizes that disease is not merely a biological fact but is an artifact of societal interpretation. Diseases have meanings. Homosexuality used to be considered a disease; catching a cold and catching herpes are somehow different. A human pathogen, for example, the *Yersinia pestis* bacillus, outside of a host is merely an organism. A person who is otherwise "healthy" and without the *Y. pestis* inside has no disease. Place the *Y. pestis* inside the person, allow for some time for nature to take its course, and one has disease. Or did the disease begin at the point of infection? Does it end when the symptoms disappear or when the last pathogen is dead or when the host is dead? When explaining the reasons why a person is suffering symptoms, does one say, "God is angry;" "God is merciful;" "The planets are aligned in a rare pattern;" "You are a sinner;" "The air around you has putrefied;" "You live in filthy and overcrowded conditions;" "Your humors are out of balance because of your poor diet;" "You have breathed in a poisonous animalcule;" or "It is a random event?" Does the caregiver recommend prayer for society? Joy? Stoical resignation? Spiritual repentance? Moving away? Eating less fish? Expelling the poison with theriac? Or other medical treatment? The biological fact remains the same: person with symptoms caused by pathogen; the explanations—meaning—and recommendations many.

Today, the "reason" and the recommendation would be couched in medical terms and medical terms only: you have plague and you need an antibiotic. And when told the patient had camped out in a high-risk plague zone in the hills of New Mexico despite warnings, does the caregiver proclaim a judgment? Does this fact affect the course of treatment? Or the likelihood of recovery? Or even the attitude of the caregiver? No, no, and maybe. But why maybe? In large part because our society values

personal responsibility and she was irresponsible; or because we still value the word of authority and she ignored it. Because she was, at least in part, responsible for contracting the disease; she should not have gone into the high-risk zone. Perhaps she even deserved it.

In the Middle Ages, people were comfortable with multiple explanations for why things were the way they were, in part because Aristotle taught that everything had four causes, from material to a purpose. God—the stars—the air—internal poison—all were connected, not only without competing but, some would say, all necessary for the disease to appear. Society understood that the supernatural was real, that the planets and stars had power over human affairs, that nature had been created to maintain itself, and that medicines could aid the body's health. In medieval society, disease was not just only the organism and host, but there wasn't even an organism.

One of the most powerful ways that communities interpreted plague was through religious and moralistic lenses. Christians understood God to be angry with humankind and to be lashing out in the tradition of the Bible's Old Testament. Muslims ascribed the same role to Allah but interpreted it as punishment only for the faithless; faithful Muslims would be taken directly to Paradise. Christians often felt the need to pinpoint the causes of God's wrath, and these shifted as they exposed social tensions. At various times, people blamed personal immorality, runaway priests and doctors, corrupt authorities, Jews, heretics, those who ignored the poor, the poor, gypsies, and the greedy rich. By the later 16th century, the emphasis was less focused on personal responsibility than on social responsibility, especially in England. Plague was increasingly seen as a disease of the poor, there was a stigma attached to it, moralists railed against the lack of virtue, and the poor were blamed. Since a particular and marginalized group was the one at fault *and* largely suffering, society could feel good about using stringent and almost punitive measures for treating those labeled as suffering from the disease.

This also related to the social creation of scapegoats on whom social frustrations were piled in hope of relief. During the Black Death, it was the Jews on whom the burden fell: Many believed that the Jews were responsible, either as reasons for God's wrath or as poisoners of Christian wells and other water supplies. Even though water played no role in any medical explanation of plague, the popular imagination conjured the furtive outsider with the pocket-sized bag of poison. Two centuries later, the "poisoners" reappeared in the popular imaginations of some in Milan, Savoy, and Switzerland, with alleged poisoners said to be smearing doorknobs with deadly grease made with bubo pus from pest house patients, as Milan's Archbishop Federigo Borromeo attested in 1632. This was a common theme during plague times: First human sin angered God; then the depravity of a whole class with its filth and bad habits fostered the epidemics; and then the diabolical agents of destruction used the vile stuff of the disease to spread the disease. And yet these were not chronological divisions, clearly showing periods of dominance, but, like polyphonic musical themes, they intertwined over time, appearing as societies needed them.

See also: Allah; Anti–Semitism and Anti–Jewish Violence before the Black Death; Christ; Morality Literature, Christian; Poisoning and Plague Spreading; Poverty and Plague; Prayer and Fasting; Sin.

References

Gilman, Ernest B. *Plague Writing in Early Modern England*. Chicago: University of Chicago Press, 2009.

Kiheung, Kim. *Social Construction of Disease*. New York: Routledge, 2006.

Vora, Setu K. "Living with the Plague." *Emerging Infectious Diseases* 10 (2004): 956–957.

Sumptuary Laws

In premodern times, one's socio-economic class was an important part of his or her identity. Dress and other forms of display were meant to reflect accurately class or status or station in life. To dress or act above or below one's station was at least unseemly or at worst a form of fraud. Even today, it is illegal to wear priestly vestments or a police uniform if one is not entitled to. Sumptuary laws were laws that forbade people within a community to dress or act publicly above their station. These predated the Black Death, and such examples as England's earliest in 1337 (refined 17 times and repealed in 1604) stated as their purpose to protect English cloth trade against luxuries from abroad; to maintain apparent status; to stop people from squandering their wealth; and to lessen the likelihood of pridefullness. Certain types of cloth and furs, certain expensive dyes, and certain styles of clothing were restricted to the aristocracy and forbidden to even wealthy bourgeois.

One form of show or display that was bound by decorum was ritual associated with funerals. Mourners wore special black clothing; beeswax candles and expensive incense were burned; dozens of mourners were paid to process to the graveyard; a lavish feast might be provided, and so on. As plague mowed urban populations down, city governments forbade elements of such rituals or simply the rituals themselves to keep people from bankrupting themselves and to prevent jealousy and depression. In September 1348, widows alone were allowed to wear mourning clothes. Florence's authorities passed laws limiting funerary display in 1374, but, between 1384 and 1392, made money selling 233 exemptions.

The plague also left many with greater disposable income or with access to (dead) wealthy people's clothing, whether by purchase or theft. In 1349, Siena forbade all but families of knights, judges, and physicians from wearing expensive and lavish clothing, since "many pretended to a station higher" than their own. In 1363, one of Edward's reiterations of the 1337 laws specifically mentions "outrageous and excessive apparel," linking it to people acting "against their estate [status]" and "impoverishment." The preservation of society itself was seen as dependent on maintaining clear lines between classes. In this way, sumptuary laws, especially regarding clothing, were directly related to attempts by monarchs to return workers' pay scales to preplague levels.

In later centuries, the issue of false class display faded in favor of cost and morality. In 17th-century Europe, lavish but ephemeral expenditures smacked of vanity and worldliness, as unfashionable in Catholic Spain as Calvinist Holland.

See also: Clothing; Economic Effects of Plague in Europe; Funerals, Catholic; Funerals, Protestant; Labourers, Ordinance and Statute of; Merchants.

References

Crane, Susan. *The Performance of Self: Ritual, Clothing and Identity during the Hundred Years War.* Philadelphia: University of Pennsylvania Press, 2002.

Hayward, Maria. *Rich Apparel: Clothing and the Law in Henry VIII's England.* Burlington, VT: Ashgate, 2009.

Ruiz, Teofilo. *Spain's Centuries of Crisis, 1300–1474.* New York: Wiley-Blackwell, 2007.

Schama, Simon. *Embarrassment of Riches: An Interpretation of Dutch Culture in the Golden Age.* New York: Vintage, 1997.

Surgeons/Barbers

The distinction between the surgeon who manipulated the human body and the physician who observed, diagnosed, and prescribed medicines was neither classical nor Arabic but a Western Christian one. It is generally explained by emerging professionalization of the physician in the 12th century and the papal prohibition (1163) against clerics spilling human blood, as in phlebotomies, wound treatments, or surgery. This split was further realized in the establishments of surgeons or barber-surgeons' guilds, beginning in Paris around 1215 and again in 1271. Even with high professional standards for surgeons, the Medical Faculties kept them separated from and inferior to physicians, who were considered masters of medical theory. First mention of a guild in England was 1306; in 1376, the king required examination and licensing; and in 1540, the Company of Barber-Surgeons was established. In most places, surgeons were inferior in status to physicians, but Edinburgh's Guild of Barber-Surgeons, founded in 1505, ran the School of Medicine. Italian schools long recognized surgery as an academic discipline, and many received M.D. degrees in both *physic* and surgery. Their professional emphasis on anatomy helped the subject emerge as a medical specialty during the 16th century, which in turn increased their own social status.

The plague, its demands on medical practitioners, and the flood of empirics and charlatans may well have played roles in new testing, licensing, and organizing of surgeons and distinguishing the less skilled barbers, who shaved, pulled teeth, and performed minor surgical tasks. Throughout the Second Pandemic, barbers and surgeons strove for higher status against the entrenched physicians. During epidemics, the far more numerous surgeons (263 in London in 1641) were indispensable medical practitioners: they located the sick and identified plague, gave phlebotomies as treatment, administered medicines, and tended the sores and other manifestations of plague. They tried to draw bad humors by cupping and cauterized opened buboes. Many cities had civic surgeons as well as physicians, and many also served pest houses, plague hospitals, and shut-ins. "Plague surgeons," being more readily available and cheaper to hire, might outnumber plague physicians four or five to one. Some health boards or magistracies recognized the expertise of surgeons and had them serve alongside other professionals. Women barbers and surgeons were known from the 14th century; the latter were common in Naples and Venice but were driven out in England due to fears of witchcraft.

See also: Anatomy and Dissection; Astrology; Bleeding/Phlebotomy; Chauliac, Guy de (Guido Cauliaco); Consilia and Plague Tracts; Hospitals; Medical Education (1300–1500, Medieval Europe); Medical Education (1500–1700, Early Modern Europe); Physicians; Remedies, External; Vesalius, Andeas; Women Medical Practitioners; Zodiac Man.

References

Brockliss, Laurence and Colin Jones. *The Medical World of Early Modern France*. New York: Oxford University Press, 1997.

Pelling, Margaret. "Appearance and Reality: Barber Surgeons, the Body and Disease," in *London 1500–1700: The Making of the Metropolis*, edited by A. L. Beir and Robert Finlay (New York: Longman, 1986), 82–112.

Rawcliffe, Carole. *Medicine and Society in Later Medieval England*. Stroud, Gloucs, UK: Sutton, 1997.

Wyman, A. L. "The Surgeoness: The Female Practitioner of Surgery, 1400–1800." *Medical History* 28 (1984): 22–41.

Sydenham, Thomas (1625–1689)

Thomas was born into the English gentry and attended Oxford University. During the English Civil War, he served in the Parliamentarian cavalry. In return, he received a fellowship to All Souls College to study medicine, which he gave up before earning his M.D. Marrying and settling in London, he practiced medicine among the poorer folk, often accompanied by Robert Boyle, compiling a large record of various illnesses, their purported causes, symptoms, and courses. Since Sydenham had not studied the era's medical theory systematically, he adopted a loose humoral theory and relied on his own observations and case studies. In this he did what Hippocrates had done two millennia earlier, earning himself the nickname "the English Hippocrates."

Sydenham was in London when plague broke out in 1665. Before escaping with his family, he treated several victims in Westminster and more upon his early return to London. From this and previous experience, he published *Method of Curing Fevers Based on His Own Observations* in 1666. He added a fuller discussion of plague ("On Pestilence or Pestilential Fever") in the 1668 edition, dedicated to Robert Boyle, and expanded much of the work into *Medical Observations* (1676). For this last achievement, Cambridge University granted Sydenham an M.D. degree. He never gained full acceptance, however, by either the Royal Society or London's College of Physicians. Both bodies emphasized theory, whereas Sydenham's work reflected his experience that often contradicted Galenism. Based on his observations of symptoms and their courses—especially fevers—he was able to distinguish among various diseases and teach others to do so. What he could not distinguish were causes of various diseases. This led him to the mistaken conclusion that during an epidemic, all diseases tend to become or develop into the epidemic disease. The implications of this notion for treatment are obvious, and Sydenham's reputation ensured that the notion endured until the development of germ theory in the later 19th century.

Sydenham rejected astrological causation of epidemics in favor of a Hippocratic environmentalism and some of Girolamo Fracastoro's ideas of contagion. That "some obscure atmospheric change" brought on plague he considered "established" (Meynell, 1987, 167); disease was spread through the air by fomites or by "effluvia" of corpses. One's humoral balance determined his susceptibility to the disease. Given his general acceptance of Galen's humoralism, Sydenham's suggested remedies were quite familiar: "cooling" diets and the promotion of purgation, especially sweating and ample bloodletting. Nevertheless, he defends them by relating his own observation of their successes: "I have propounded nothing except what I have properly tried" (216–17).

See also: Bleeding/Phlebotomy; Contagion Theory; Diagnosing Plague; Empirics; Humoral Theory; London, Great Plague of (1665–1666); Scientific Revolution.

References

Dewhurst, Kenneth. *Dr. Thomas Sydenham (1625–1689), His Life and Original Writings.* Berkeley: University of California Press, 1966.

Meynell, G. G. "Sydenham, Locke and Sydenham's *De peste sive febre pestilentiali.*" *Medical History* 37 (1993): 330–332.

Symptoms. See *Diagnosing Plague*

Syrups and Electuaries

Arabs and other Muslims were the first apothecaries known to enhance the flavor of certain drugs with sweeteners. Julep was boiled sugar water; syrup a julep with fruit, flower or herb juice added. A 14th-century Muslim regulatory text lists 70 different syrups, from peach to cocoon. The same regulations required the use of Egyptian sugar and disallowed honey. Sugar was considered to be hot and moist, and thus a medicine itself against cold and dry humoral imbalances. The bad-tasting herb or drug could be added to a watery syrup, or it might be boiled down to create a thicker electuary. These were commonly used for daily digestion, as alcohol-based *digestifs* are today in Italy. Roman apothecary Ippolito Ceccarelli's *Antidotario romano* (editions between 1583 and 1668) defined an electuary as a medicinal "simple" prepared with sugar, honey, or syrup. Typically, 16 ounces of sugar balanced 3 ounces of the drug, he wrote.

See also: Alchemy; Apothecaries; Purgatives; Remedies, Internal.

References

Levey, Martin. *Early Arabic Pharmacology.* Leiden: Brill, 1973.

Rawcliffe, Carole. *Medicine and Society in Later Medieval England.* Stroud, Gloucs, UK: Sutton, 1997.

T

Ta'un

At the time of the Black Death, writers in the Arabic language, from Spain to India, utilized two words when writing of the disease. The broader *waba*, as used for example by the physician and theologian Ibn Qayyim al-Jawziyya in his *Medicine of the Prophet* (c. 1348), was used to designate a pestilential disease or epidemic. *Ta'un* was a specific type of *waba*: all *tawa'in* are waba, but not all *waba* are *tawa'in*. Ibn Qayyim is also clear as to the features of *ta'un*: it is an "evil inflammation" that is fatal and is located in the armpit, behind the ear, on the tip of the nose, and in the "soft flesh" of the groin. He quotes the Prophet Muhammad, comparing the glandular swelling to that of a camel. Around the inflammation, the skin grows black or green and ulcerates. He follows the Galenic theory of miasmatic corruption of the air, which putrefies the body's blood, thereby creating a poison that attacks organs. Evil spirits or *djinn* are responsible for the miasma, and invoking good spirits may help one. Physicians are of no help.

Though Muslim theological writers on plague understood the Prophet to have said there was no contagion or infection, Ibn Qayyim and medical authors are clear that *ta'un* is an infectious disease and that remaining around the sick will cause one to become sick. According to *Hadith*, Muhammad taught that one should neither enter nor leave a plague-stricken place, both of which Ibn Qayyim accepts and explains. Significantly, he does not mention that leaving such a place might spread the disease further.

Ibn Qayyim's discussion has a clarity often lacking in contemporary Muslim accounts. Authors often confuse the Arabic terms or rely on context, and other language—*al-wafidah*, "epidemic" or *al-mawtan*, "death" replace *waba* and *ta'un*. In Mamluk Egypt *waba* and *ta'un* are joined by *fasl* and *ta'n* used interchangeably for plague.

See also: Arabic-Persian Medicine and Practitioners; Contagion Theory; Islam and Medicine; Muhammad the Prophet.

References

Conrad, Laurence I. "*Ta'un* and *waba*: Conceptions of Plague and Pestilence in Early Islam." *Journal of the Economic and Social History of the Orient* 25 (1982): 268–307.

Pormann, Peter E. and Emilie Savage-Smith. *Medieval Islamic Medicine*. Washington, DC: Georgetown University Press, 2007.

Stearns, Justin. *Infectious Ideas: Contagion in Premodern Islamic and Christian Thought in the Western Mediterranean*. Baltimore, MD: Johns Hopkins University Press, 2011.

Taxes and Public Finance

An epidemic created financial problems that ranged from concerns to disaster. As for revenue, governments (usually city councils) lost taxpayers through death and flight, trade and manufacturing was often reduced to a trickle, and national governments were reticent at best to provide needed funds. Expenditures rose, varying with the length of the plague season and antiplague measures decided upon or required.

Late medieval and early modern city governments had few sources of income, and all of these were affected during an epidemic. Excise taxes on trade, often called gate taxes, usually provided the lion's share, but plague restrictions on trade and even entrance to the city could reduce these to a trickle. Head and wealth taxes, as well as emergency forced loans from citizens, dried up as the wealthy died or fled to safer locations. Massive death tolls and trade reductions also diminished municipal rents, tolls, port taxes, and fees for services. Though there was an uptick in fines and confiscations of plague-lawbreakers' property, it was often too little and too difficult to collect, as death and flight reduced some civil governments to skeleton crews.

Extraordinary expenditures could run several times annual income. Much went to personnel salaries and wages for guards and watchmen, house cleaners, searchers, corpse carriers, gravediggers, street cleaners; and for nurses, physicians, barber-surgeons, and apothecaries who served the needy, hospitals, and pest houses. These last and other accommodations—huts and convalescent quarters— usually required rents of buildings or land, as well as bedding, medicines, food, cooks, and launderers. Some governments provided surviving victims with new clothing and restitution for property destroyed for being "infected." With many almsgivers to the poor either dead or having fled and clergy busy providing spiritual services (or dead), civil governments often stepped in to help the needy. The sick were relegated to pest houses or hospitals, and the well were fed with publicly supplied bread. But when normal means of provisioning the citizens broke down, shiploads of grain at public expense were required, as were milling, baking, and distribution.

See also: Apothecaries; Crime and Punishment; Governments, Civil; Health Boards, Magistracies,

and Commissions; Physicians, Town; Public Health; Public Sanitation.

References

Byrne, Joseph P. *Daily Life during the Black Death*. Westport, CT: Greenwood Press, 2006.

Cook, Alexandra Parma and Noble David Cook. *The Plague Files: Crisis Management in Sixteenth-Century Seville*. Baton Rouge: University of Louisiana Press, 2009.

Slack, Paul. *The Impact of Plague in Tudor and Stuart England*. New York: Oxford University Press, 1990.

Tears against the Plague

In 1646, many English royalists had fled the isle in the face of Parliamentarian military victories. One was Anglican chaplain John Featly, who took up residence in Flushing, the Netherlands. While there, we are told, he completed a series of 27 pious moral reflections on death and misfortune he published as *A Fountain of Tears*. His immediate audience was a "pious gentlewoman," and the voice he adopted is feminine; *Tears against the Plague* is one portion of *Fountain*. It was published separately and discovered and reprinted during the plague year 1665 by "S. K.," otherwise unknown, who provided a new introduction.

Featly's meditation takes the form of a series of soliloquies, opening with a biblical defense of public mourning during a disaster. The next two establish that plague is God's punishment for sin, and the following two provide biblical examples of plague and stress God's warnings. Featly next treats for whom one ought to pray and ends with special meditations and prayers for one shut in with plague victims and for one struck by the sores.

See also: London, Great Plague of (1665–1666); Morality Literature, Christian; Prayer and Fasting; Shutting In.

Reference

Fealty, John and Scott Rutherford. *Tears Against the Plague: A 17th-century Woman's Devotional*. Cambridge, Mass.: Rhwymbooks, 2000.

Theriac and Mithridatum

The term theriac (treacle, *tiriaq*, *teriaca*) is derived from the Greek *therion* or wild animal; mithridatum is a reference to King Mithridates IV of Pontum of the first century BCE. They were remedies, drugs, used to treat the plague. Mithridates had a Greek physician named Kratevas who concocted a remedy for poison and its pain. It was a complex recipe of four or five dozen herbal and animal ingredients. The "wild animal" may be a reference to the explosive cleansing nature of the drug (sweat, stool) or to the venomous viper used as the active ingredient. The master of Greek *materia medica*, Dioscorides, supposedly recorded the recipe in the first century CE and Galen adopted it in the second as one of his favorite medicines. These passed it along to Byzantine, Arab, and then Western Christian physicians and apothecaries.

Eleventh-century al-Biruni believed there were different types of theriac. The best used a stone (bezoar) created of snake and grass in the stomach of a mountain goat; second was a stone or amber from the secretion of a stag's eye; and least effective was an artificial compound relying on viper flesh. Twelfth-century Ibn Zoar (Avenzoar) used 70 ingredients and reduced the mass first by 10 times and then by seven more by evaporation, molding the result into tablets. During the Middle Ages, the "theriac of Mithridates" was sometimes split into two recipes, theriac and mithridatum, with the latter having a higher opium content.

By the 14th century, theriac was a standard drug recommended for a range of ailments from healing wounds to curing epilepsy. It could be made of virtually any combination of volatile materials, but Christians tended to accept Venetian theriac as the highest quality. By bringing on sweat and evacuation, for humoralists, it was a "hot and dry" drug that was used to combat either a disease that was its opposite—cool and wet—or that had the same properties. Plague was believed to be hot and moist, and theriac's effectiveness was a matter of "like curing like." It worked against plague's poison by opening up the body for expelling it, and, taken with wine or rosewater, was to be used as a prophylactic as well as remedy.

Venetian apothecaries made batches of theriac once a year in a public ritual observed carefully by officials. Its 64 ingredients took 40 days to prepare properly, and the drug underwent aging for 12 years. In the 16th and 17th centuries, the French adopted a similar procedure to ensure a proper product. The astronomer and alchemist Tycho Brahe created his own theriac, supposedly with a Venetian recipe, which he marketed under his name through German apothecaries. He also prepared a recipe for an antiplague elixir that he presented to Emperor Rudolf II. During the 17th century, the drugs remained popular, insofar as producing a result—sweating—was a sign of effectiveness. During the plague of 1626, a single London apothecary created 160 pounds of mithridatum, enough for 15,360 tablets. About the same time, London's College of Physicians decided that theriac did not have to include viper.

See also: Alchemy; Apothecaries; Galen and Galenism; Humoral Theory; Prophylaxes; Remedies, Internal.

References

Griffin, J. P. "Venetian Treacle and the Foundation of Medicines Regulation." *British Journal of Clinical Pharmacology* 58 (2004): 317–325.

Nockels Fabri, Christiane. "Treating Medieval Plague: The Wonderful Virtues of Theriac." *Early Science and Medicine* 12 (2007): 247–283.

Watson, Gilbert. *Theriac and Mithridatium: A Study in Therapeutics*. London: Wellcome History of Medicine Library, 1966.

Third Plague Pandemic

The Second Plague Pandemic ended in Europe with the Russian epidemic of 1770 to 1772, and it ended in the Ottoman Empire, thanks to isolation and quarantine, during the 1830s. In about 30 years, the Third Plague Pandemic began in China. The first reports came from rural Yunnan Province in 1866, and the disease moved slowly, probably due to low population densities and poor transportation. It appeared in the port city of Canton in 1892, where it killed 30,000 in one year, spreading to other Chinese ports and Hong Kong in 1894. Here, Kitasato and Yersin independently discovered the plague pathogen, *Yersinia pestis*, during the same year. In 1896, ships took the disease to Bombay (Mumbai), and it was in Calcutta two years later. British efforts tended to be relegated to the colonial enclaves, and the disease spread from port cities into the rural areas. Russian microbiologist Waldemar Haffkine followed up on Yersin and Shibasaburo's discovery and developed an antiplague vaccine in India in 1896, though with very limited results. Despite aggressive if limited measures and continuing work by the British colonial Indian Plague Research Commission, by 1930, 12,000,000 Indians had died of plague.

Removing bodies of Chinese plague victims, 1910. (Library of Congress)

Plague traveled across the Pacific to Madagascar, Australia (where aggressive rat control kept deaths to 1,363 in Sydney in 1900), Hawaii (1899), and from Honolulu to San Francisco, California, in 1900. The ship *Australia* docked on January 2, and the first plague case was soon found in Chinatown. Officials initially denied plague, then blamed the Chinese community and demanded to try Haffkine's vaccination, but only on Chinese. The Chinese and federal authorities cried racism and argued against the city until active antirat measures went into effect finally in 1903. A second round began after the earthquake and fire of 1906, but reaction was swift and effective, with the last case reported in March 1908. All told, 280 cases were reported and 172 died. Other American port cities, for example, New Orleans, also found cases of plague, but preventive activity tended to be swift. From that time, there has been a reservoir of plague among rodents in the Southwestern United States.

China and Manchuria were hit hard by plague in 1910 and 1911 (pneumonic plague killing 60,000 Manchurians), 1917, and again in 1920 to 1921. After this, the incidence of plague in China dropped significantly, becoming enzootic rather than spawning epidemics. Vietnam, a French colony, and Burma became plague centers as well, producing many of the cases that kept numbers high into the 1950s. That postwar decade saw annual cases fall from the 5,000s to around 500 as insecticides helped keep the fleas down and antibiotics kept victims alive. World Health authorities proclaimed the Pandemic ended in the 1950s, though the Vietnam War stirred up local epidemics into the 1970s.

See also: Bubonic Plague; Bubonic Plague in North America; China; Cordons Sanitaires; Germ Theory; Kitasato, Shibasaburo; Pneumonic Plague; Public Health; Quarantine; Simond, Paul-Louis; Yersin, Alexandre; *Yersinia pestis*.

References

Chase, Marilyn. *The Barbary Plague: The Black Death in Victorian San Francisco.* New York: Random House, 2003.

Echenberg, Myron. *Plague Ports: The Global Urban Impact of Bubonic Plague, 1894–1901.* New York: New York University Press, 2007.

Marriott, Edward. *Plague: A Story of Science, Rivalry, Scientific Breakthrough and the Scourge that Won't Go away.* New York: Holt, 2002.

Thirty Years' War (1618–1648)

Between 1618 and 1648, the major and many minor powers of Europe fought one another in a series of shifting alliances. Hostilities began over religious differences (Catholic vs. Protestant) and dynastic issues in and immediately around the Holy Roman Empire. Soon armies of Dutch Calvinists, Swedish Lutherans, English Anglicans, and Catholics from Spain, France, and Italy were engaging one another across the German imperial territories from the Baltic to northern Italy. The armies were the largest Europe had ever seen, and their potential for destruction was equally huge. When the armies were on the move or otherwise not fighting, their destructive potential was even greater.

Like other premodern armies, these hosted a wide range of diseases, from minor inconveniences to deadly plague, especially after 1630. Originating from various corners of Europe, these forces mixed and mingled, often covering vast distances on complicated campaigns. Because they had to live off of the land, soldiers regularly and often brutally took what they wanted from peasants and townspeople, few of whom could defend themselves. This exposed each to the others' diseases and ravaged the peasants' already low standard of living through plunder and wanton destruction. Soldiers trudged on, often bringing plague fleas and other vectors of disease to yet new groups. Starving refugees fled, often into already overcrowded cities, taking their diseases with them. Armies laid siege to the cities, whose conditions often grew horrific as food became scarce, hygiene nonexistent, and disease rampant. Major epidemics struck in 1622 to 1623, 1625 to 1627, 1629 to 1637, and 1646 to 1650. Plague took the lives of Elector Frederick V (1632), Weimar Dukes Johann Ernst (1627) and Berhard (1639), Imperial generals Henrik Holk (1633) and Walter Butler (1634), and Milan's Spanish governor Gómez Feria (1633). All told, Germany's population dropped by about 50 percent, in some areas by much more.

See also: Armies; Famine; Flight; Hundred Years War.

References

Concannon, R. J. G. "The Third Enemy: The Role of Epidemics in the Thirty Years War." *Journal of World History* 10 (1967): 500–511.

Outram, Quentin. "The Socio-economic Relations of Warfare and the Military Mortality Crises of the Thirty Years' War." *Medical History* 45 (2001): 151–184.

Wilson, Peter H. *The Thirty Years War: Europe's Tragedy.* Cambridge, MA: Harvard University Press, 2009.

"Three Living Meet Three Dead"

The scene became popular after 1350: three cadavers in various states of decay startle three traveling aristocrats—kings early on. In the simplest version, the corpses warn: "What you are we were; what we are you

A 15th-century rendition of the "Three Living Meet Three Dead." The essential warning is to prepare for death by prayer and doing good works. (Dover Pictorial Archives)

will become." The phrasing originated in theologian Peter Damian's epitaph (1072) and appears on many clerical tombs. The meeting evolved later, the best-known example being a poem by minstrel Baudouin of Condé (c. 1285). A Middle-English poem from the mid-15th century, "Three Dead Kings" survives in an Oxford manuscript. A dialogue fleshes out the essential warning: prepare for death by prayer and doing good works. The dynamic is redemptive: the nobles (or kings) are warned and have a chance at salvation. The reanimated corpses prefigure the dogma of the resurrection of the dead at the final judgment while providing a mirror to the living, who are reminded of their mortality. Though generically

Christian, its increased popularity after 1350 reflects the plague-induced concern with sudden death.

Artists painted the scene in churches and cemeteries and miniaturists in Books of Hours and Psalters. *Vifs nous sommes* lists 20 extant French manuscript poetic versions (nine illustrated). It also catalogues 92 frescoes in French churches, 58 in England, and 16 in Italy from before and after 1350. Post-1350 images also appear in Bregninge and Tuse, Denmark (c. 1400 and c. 1460) and Überlingen, Germany (1424). Fresco versions often appear with scenes of the Last Judgment, the Triumph of Death (Pisa's Campo Santo walled graveyard), or the Seven Deadly Sins (Hurstbourne Tarrant, Hampshire, UK).

See also: *Ars moriendi* (*The Art of Dying*); Art, Effects of Plague on; Corpses; Danse Macabre; Death, Depictions of; Triumph of Death.

References

Groupe de recherches sur les peintures murales. *Vifs nous sommes, morts nous sommes.* Vendôme: Editions du Cherche-Lune, 2001.

Kinch, Ashby. "Image, Ideology and Form: The Middle English 'Three Dead Kings.'" *Chaucer Review* 43 (2008): 48–81.

Medieval Wall Painting in the English Parish Church. http://www.paintedchurch.org/ldintro.htm (accessed 3–11–2011).

Toads

Sympathetic medicine, like sympathetic magic, operated on the principle that similar forces counteracted one another. Paracelsians championed this principle from the 1560s into the 18th century. The toad's bumpy skin and often-poisonous nature recommended it as a counteragent to plague. French Dr. Pierre Fabre (*Panchymicum,*

1646) prescribed consuming "salt" extracted from chemically soaked toad ashes to purify one's blood. More often, toad was used externally. In 1665, Dr. John Worthington wore a dried toad in a sack hung from his neck when visiting plague patients. Others pulverized dried toad, mixing it with various herbs and minerals—including arsenic and mercury. This could be used in plasters or moistened with various fluids, including menstrual blood, and shaped into amulets worn from the neck. Early advocates, for example, Peter Turner (*Concerning Amulets*, 1603), wrote in magical terms of the toads "communicating their spiritual qualities," while later physicians, for example, Thomas Willis (*On Fevers*, 1659), borrowed from emerging mechanical and corpuscular notions, imagining the poisons attracting and drawing out victims' "pestilential particles."

See also: Alchemy; Amulets, Talismans, and Magic; Paracelsus and Paracelsianism; Remedies, External.

Reference

Baldwin, Martha. "Toads and Plague: Amulet Therapy in Seventeenth-century Medicine." *Bulletin of the History of Medicine* 67 (1993): 227–247.

Tobacco

In 1721, as plague wracked Marseille, France, Englishman "Eugenius Philalethes's" *Treatise of the Plague* declared, "Those who can take tobacco, would do well to smoke a pipe in the morning, the first thing they do. Dr. Evans, of St John's College in Oxford, told me not long since, that he deigned tobacco to be his chief medicine whenever it should please God to visit us [with plague], and that he would fume his chambers and clothes with nothing else . . . and I have been told that during the last Sickness in London

[1665], the tobacconists escaped the contagion" (p.9).

Tobacco arrived in Western Europe from America between 1556 and 1565. Like other New World plants, tobacco was believed to have medicinal properties. In 1571, Dr. Monardes of Seville claimed its effectiveness on 36 illnesses, a list translated into English in 1577. Smoking the dried leaf, Native American style, was probably the most common use of tobacco, and angered antismokers. In 1604, England's new king James I increased tobacco's import tax 4,000 percent and authored "A Counterblast to Tobacco." Turkish Sultan Murad IV in 1633 decreed that tobacco users were infidels to be executed, a law rescinded in 1647. Murad may have believed that tobacco smoke created a poisonous miasma that caused plague, since Europeans smoked during outbreaks. Indeed, and physicians led the way: during the 1635 to 1636 outbreak in Nijmegen, the Netherlands, Dr. Ysbrand van Diemerbroek smoked as a prophylactic. He had two or three pipe-bowls after breakfast, another three after lunch, and smoked whenever around infected corpses. People believed smoke fumigated the air around them and kept out the poisonous, plague-inducing miasma. Unlike other fumigants, tobacco could be used directly around the face and carried about in the simple clay pipes often seen in 17th-century printed plague scenes. These were especially handy for corpse carriers. A cache of cheap pipes was found in London near plague-era remains during excavations for Metro's Picadilly Line.

Tobacco was also chewed, and its dust sniffed (snuff) and mixed in potions. On June 7, 1665, Londoner Samuel Pepys was alarmed by signs of plague, "so that I was forced to buy some roll tobacco to smell and to chaw—which took away the apprehension" (*Diary*, VI, pg. 120). Philosopher and scientist René Descartes mixed powdered tobacco in wine to induce vomiting, thought to flush out poisons. But smoking remained the norm. Authorities forced London schoolchildren to smoke in 1665 and, at Eton, flogged boys who refused. Tobacco was often advertised, but few sellers went as far as Virginia tobacco planter William Byrd. He wrote *Discourse Concerning the Plague* (1721) and had it published in London. Its 40 pages provided every prophylactic reason to chew, drink, sniff, and smoke Byrd's cash crop.

In 2006, American scientists announced a breakthrough use of tobacco plants in the preparation of the first prophylactic vaccine against bubonic plague; research and testing continue.

See also: Corpse Carriers; Disinfection and Fumigation; Miasma Theory; Prophylaxes; Purgatives.

References

Gilman, Sander. *Smoke: A Global History of Smoking*. London: Reaktion, 2004.

Goodman, Jordan. *Tobacco in History*. New York: Routledge, 1994.

Tracts (Tractates). *See* Consilia and Plague Tracts

Transi Tombs

In the 1390s, French physician Guillaume de Harcigny of Laon and an unknown sculptor devised a new style of tomb sculpture, called a "transi tomb," that showed the transition of the person to the body's state after death. Traditionally, expensive tombs for wealthy and powerful people featured "portraits" of the deceased in low or high relief. The person would be dressed formally as in life, with identification or an epitaph running around the figure. De Harcigny's tomb featured such a life-sized portrait, but beneath it, as if under a table, lay a sculpture of a cadaver, meant to represent the good doctor as he really was. On the one hand, it probably startled many who wandered past, and it was probably meant to. On the other, Laon had suffered four bouts of plague since 1348, and for many, coming unexpectedly upon a cadaver should not have been novel. At about the same time in La Sarraz, Switzerland, the nobleman François de la Sarra had a similar transi tomb prepared, and in 1402, the Avignonese Cardinal De LaGrange in Avignon.

In Canterbury, England, Archbishop Henry Chichele had that island's first transi tomb built in 1424, two decades before his death. On it he had engraved: "I was a pauper born, then to Primate raised / Now I am cut down and ready to be food for worms / Behold my grave/ Whoever you may be who passes by I ask you to remember / You will be like me after you die / All horrible dust, worms, vile flesh" (Cohen, 16). As his own memento mori, or reminder of death, it could hardly have been more fit. To the passerby, the phrase "You will be like me after you die" must have brought to mind the "Three Living Meet Three Dead" poetic and pictorial motif. This suggests that the well-dressed upper figure represents Henry in life, though some modern scholars claim it was Henry postresurrection, his message ultimately a positive one. Given the medieval mind, it was probably both. Bishop Richard Fleming at Lincoln borrowed the form in 1431, and similar tombs appeared in Germany and Austria somewhat later. Germanic folk tended to like including toads and snakes in and on their cadavers, popularly connected as they were to sin, the devil, death, and corruption.

As with other post-1347 macabre imagery, it is easy to claim that the plagues inspired transi tombs, but the influences are no doubt many and subtly mingled. Given the mass graves and oblivion that awaited so many, monuments like these ensured that people would remember. Perhaps the clerics saw them as their final sermons, warning with words and images. Oddly, they are also memorials to humility: in this world, everyone's physical end is dust, worms, and putrefied flesh.

See also: Death, Depictions of; Individualism and Individual Liberties; Mass Graves and Plague Cemeteries.

References
Aberth, John. *From the Brink of the Apocalypse: Crisis and Recovery in Late Medieval England.* New York: Routledge, 2000.

Cohen, Kathleen. *Metamorphosis of a Death Symbol: The Transi Tomb in the Late Middle Ages and the Renaissance.* Berkeley: University of California Press, 1973.

Triumph of Death

Death always wins. The Christian gloss on this fact has always been "be ready." The pictorial motif known as the Triumph of Death predates the hecatombs of the Black Death, but the suddenness, scale, and real horrors of mass deaths lent the motif a real energy and immediacy. Italian poet Petrarch had written on the Triumph of Fame before the plague; after 1348, he turned to the Triumph of Death theme, promoting it across Europe. It appeared in chapels, books of hours, hospitals, and graveyards. At Subiaco, Italy, a 14th-century skeletal horseman plunges a sword into an oblivious noble youth, while at Palermo, a late 15th-century mounted archer mows down his prey. Skeletal Death wages war on the living in these images, hosts of his bony fellows pressing forward as if to sweep life itself off the Earth. In the 15th-century *Très riches heures* book of hours for Duke Jean du Berry, one finds a skeleton host clad with shrouds confronting a contemporary living army of armed and armored soldiers who are just beginning to break and flee. In 1562, Pieter Breughel the Elder created a killing field both vast and personal.

But death does not necessarily mean damnation or oblivion. Like the *Danse Macabre* and "Three Living Meet Three Dead" themes, the Triumph of Death is a warning, not a threat. Death may triumph, but the devil need not. Obliviousness and resistance are futile; penance and redirection of life are not.

See also: *Ars moriendi* (*The Art of Dying*); Art, Effects of Plague on; Corpse Carriers; Corpses; Danse Macabre; Death, Depictions of; Petrarch, Francesco; "Three Living Meet Three Dead."

References

Boeckl, Christine. *Images of Plague and Pestilence: Iconography and Iconology*. Kirksville, MO: Truman State University Press, 2000.

Patrick Pollefrey's "Death in Art." http://www.lamortdanslart.com/triomphe/triumph.htm (accessed 3–11–2011).

Tumbrels

Tumbrels were large, two-wheeled carts used in European cities for carting all manner of goods and waste. Drawn by a single horse, the two-wheel design made them both maneuverable in narrow streets and alleyways and easily dumped by tipping backward on the single axle. During heavy urban outbreaks of plague, corpse removers piled victims' bodies on these sturdy platforms as they moved through the streets. Tumbrels held between 30 and 50 corpses, depending on their original uses. Though illustrations from the 17th century show some tumbrels with arching cloth covers, it appears that most had no covering, making it easier for those who removed bodies via second-story windows. Witnesses wrote of the horror of these wheeled mounds of corpses as they bumped along the uneven pavements: bodies fell off, limbs sprang akimbo, and occasionally signs of life gave pause to the corpse carriers or onlookers.

At the grave pit, the horse backed the tumbrel up to the edge and was then unhitched. The platform tipped back on the axle and the load slid away. Since this process was often carried out at night, it was not unknown to have the cart, horse, load, and driver tumble over the edge into an especially deep pit. The driver was identifiable as the one with the whip. Less often, tumbrels were used to transport living, nonambulatory plague victims to pest houses.

See also: Broadsheets, Broadsides, and Pamphlets; Corpse Carriers; Corpses; Mass Graves and Plague Cemeteries.

Reference

Byrne, Joseph P. *Daily Life during the Black Death*. Westport, CT: Greenwood Press, 2006.

U

Urine and Uroscopy

Collected in the bladder and eliminated through the urethra, urine was long believed to be the filtered overflow of blood from throughout the body. In the absence of modern chemical analysis, observation of urine, or uroscopy, was supposed to reveal much about one's general health or aid in diagnosing illness. Greek physicians pioneered interpretations of their observations, and Arabs refined these in such manuals as Ishaq ibn Sulayman al-Israili's 10th-century *Book on Urine*. To Galenic physicians, combinations of clarity, color, viscosity, texture, weight, smell, residue—and, for some, even taste—revealed much about a patient's condition. Practitioners used such manuals as Henry Daniel's *Book on Judging Urines* (1379), which included a color chart. Like modern stethoscopes, urine flasks or *jordans* were symbols of medieval European physicians, but faith in urinal diagnosis waned from the 16th century and came to be associated with quackery. Paracelsus trusted urinalysis if the fluid were first distilled. Plague doctors appreciated the fact that, unlike taking a pulse or feeling a patient for fever, uroscopy could be done at a distance, even outside the sickroom.

An illustration from a 16th-century German publication showing a physician holding up a urine flask for analysis. (Courtesy of the National Library of Medicine)

See also: Charlatans and Quacks; Diagnosing Plague; Medical Education (1300–1500, Medieval Europe); Paracelsus and Paracelsianism.

References

Rawcliffe, Carole. *Medicine and Society in Later Medieval England*. Stroud, Gloucs, UK: Sutton, 1997.

Siraisi, Nancy. *Medieval and Early Renaissance Medicine*. Chicago: University of Chicago Press, 1990.

Valesco de Tarenta
(d. after 1426)

The Portuguese-born physician first appears as an arts student in Lisbon, from which he journeyed to Paris, where he received his bachelor's degree. From 1382 to 1387, Velasco studied medicine in Montpellier, receiving his license but not the master's diploma. He traveled widely in Iberia and France, eventually joining the household of Gaston III Fébus, Count of Foix. He settled at court and served three counts.

In addition to a book on surgery (1418), Valesco wrote two books for his patrons, a regimen of health (lost) and *On Epidemic and Plague* in 1401. A doctrinaire student of late medieval Galenism, Valesco was at first baffled by plague and its apparent transmission. As others were beginning to do, however, Valesco transcended Galen by reliance on his own experience. He claimed 36 years of experience and survival through "seven or eight epidemics." He identified plague as a pestilential fever attributed to miasmatic poisoning of the air and emphasized cleanliness, personal diet, and hygiene as prophylactics. It was a contagious disease, transmitted when victims exhaled or exuded "venomous fumes" in the presence of people with weakened constitutions. His experience was most evident in his discussion of how the characteristic swellings, or buboes, were best treated to ensure survival. *On Epidemic and Plague* exists in four manuscript versions and was first printed in Turin in 1473. Its orthodoxy and rather simple Latin may help explain its translation

into Spanish, Catalan, Low German, and Hebrew.

See also: Consilia and Plague Tracts; Galen and Galenism; Miasma Theory; Physicians.

Reference

York, William H. "Experience and Theory in Medical Practice during the Later Middle Ages: Velasco de Tarenta (fl. 1382–1426) at the Court of Foix." Ph.D. dissertation, Johns Hopkins University, 2003.

Van Diemerbroeck, Isbrand
(Ysbrand, IJsbrand; 1609–1674)

The Dutch physician and professor studied philosophy in Leiden, The Netherlands, and moved to Angers, France, for his doctorate in medicine. In 1634, Van Diemerbroeck began medical practice in Nijmegen, The Netherlands, just before the plague epidemic of 1635–1637. In the midst of the outbreak, he was named *stadsgeneesheer*, or city physician, overseeing the city's public health measures. In 1646, Van Diemerbroeck relocated to Utrecht, where he served as *stadsgeneesheer* and as Professor of Medicine and Anatomy at the university. He is well known for his *Anatomy of the Human Body* (1672).

During Nijmegen's plague, Van Diemerbroeck treated many victims and provided 120 case histories in his *Four Books on Plague*, published in Latin in 1646. He blamed man's sinfulness for God's punishment, seeing plague as a "venom" that "propagated like yeast through bread." His descriptions of the illness's course within individuals and across the city and of the suffering it caused made this a classic of plague literature. He noted that many refused professional help, relying instead on arsenic-laced amulets and other alternative remedies or prophylactics. He credited his own survival as he worked with case after case to his chewing of cardamom seeds and smoking of tobacco. Like many 17th-century physicians, Van Diemerbroeck rejected bloodletting, but most of his counsels were in line with mainstream, Galenic thought, including room fumigation with burning brimstone. His work was very influential, undergoing nine editions to 1722, including an English translation. It was a major authority during the 1665 plagues in both Amsterdam and London and a key source of English apothecary William Boghurst's 1666 *Loimographia*.

See also: Consilia and Plague Tracts; Disinfection and Fumigation; Physicians; Tobacco.

Reference

Grell, Ole Peter. "Conflicting Duties: Plague and the Obligations of Early Modern Physicians towards Patients and Commonwealth in England and The Netherlands." *Clio Medica* 24 (1993): 131–52.

Van Helmont, Joan Baptista (Johannes; Jan; 1579–1644)

Born to a noble and well-connected family in Brussels, Van Helmont precociously studied at the University of Louvain and later with the Louvain Jesuits. His formal studies left him unsatisfied until he took up medicine at Louvain, earning the M.D. in 1599. He lectured briefly at Louvain and then traveled through Western Europe between 1601 and 1605. Disgusted with the state of medicine in Europe, he resettled in Brussels in 1616.

Van Helmont was a foe of the Galenic and Aristotelian medical establishment and a sympathizer with the Lutheran medical reformer Paracelsus. Van Helmont dabbled in sympathetic magic and retained elements of the Swiss reformer's early chemical sensibilities. He believed in the power of some amulets, rejecting those that used chemical poisons to counteract poison but accepting those featuring gemstones. For example, sapphires absorbed miasma, and amber, when rubbed on certain body points, had attraction power—similar to magnetism—to draw out the "mumial ferment" in which the vital force of plague is embedded. He also developed "zenexton" as an antiplague amulet: a mixture of toad vomit and ocular worms that sympathetically focused the animal's natural fear of humans on the active force of the plague and destroyed it. Unlike religious talismans, Van Helmont understood plague to be a fully natural phenomenon and gave no credence to religious or astrological causes or remedies, a stance that troubled Catholic Church authorities.

For Van Helmont, everything is alive and has its life force. Disease is caused by living seeds that get into various human organs and contend with the organs' life force, or Archeus, thus creating symptoms and death if the vital force is weak. Different seeds in different organs account for such different diseases as plague. He recognized the novelty of his position, calling it the New Philosophy. He called for expansion of Paracelsus's program of chemical studies and the application of regular quantification, for medical chemistry and not humoral balance lay at the root of good health. His short treatise on plague and other writings were published in 1648 and soon found their way to England, where they reinforced Paracelsian chemical physicians and spawned new ones.

See also: Amulets, Talismans, and Magic; Galen and Galenism; Paracelsus and Paracelsianism; Scientific Revolution.

References

Grell, Ole, and Andrew Cunningham. *Religio medici: Medicine and Religion in Seventeenth-Century England.* Aldershot: Scolar Press, 1996.

Pagel, Walter. *Joan Baptista van Helmont: Reformer of Science and Medicine.* New York: Cambridge University Press, 1982.

Venice, Italy

Founded by early medieval refugees, Venice established a republican type of government, run by a duke (*doge*), that looked seaward for expansion. By the 14th century, she had defeated the Pisans and humbled the Genoese among Mediterranean sea powers, had briefly controlled mighty Constantinople, and continued to benefit from coastal colonies from the Black Sea to Dubrovnik. Goods flowed through her canals and warehouses from markets of Northern Europe through the eastern Alpine passes and south to Alexandria and markets of the Mamluk Empire. Venetian merchant fleets also sailed westward to England. Around 1400, as Milan's expansion halted, Venice turned landward, carving out a *terra firma* that brought her into the mainstream of Italian politics and economics.

Plague reached Venice by ships from Black Sea ports through Aegean and Adriatic colonies in 1347. Recent calculations have plague introduced into Venetian Dubrovnik (Ragusa) about November 10 and in Venice two weeks later. In late spring, it flared north and eastward along land routes to Austria and Slovenia. As the disease struck Venice's islands, cemeteries filled and work stopped on two major churches, Sts. Giovanni e Paolo and the Franciscan Frari, as well as the ducal palace. On March 30, the Grand Council chose three "wise men" as temporary commissioners to "preserve public health" and to combat the supposed miasma. They established a form of quarantine in Venetian Istria and emphasized public sanitation in Venice, from clean streets to removal from the city and deep burial of plague corpses (reportedly 600 daily for a time) on the islands of San Erasmo and S. Marco Boccacalme. In July, the Senate assumed control of visitors and suspected victims.

Around 60 percent—between 72,000 and 90,000—of the population is thought to have died. The city of perhaps 130,000 had 18 civic physicians in addition to private physicians and women and Jewish practitioners; by late summer, one physician remained. Nine percent of new citizens were physicians, and in 1382, physicians were forbidden to flee during an epidemic. In 1347, new citizens required 25 years of residency; soon after, the number was dropped to 1. Seventy-five percent of the nobility succumbed, and some 50 noble families were extinguished.

Plague returned decade after decade. Following an episode that killed 15,300, in 1423, authorities decreed a plague hospital, the Lazaretto Vecchio (Old Pest House), be built near the Lido on the Isle of Santa Maria di Nazareth. This was augmented after 1468 with the Lazaretto Nuovo quarantine hospital on San Erasmo. Both were expanded by anchoring boats along the shoreline or constructing shacks. In 1576, San Erasmo sported 1,200 shacks and 3,000 boats; in 1630, workers at the Arsenal shipyard constructed several thousand beds for victims. In 1486, Venice appointed the permanent Magistrato alla sanità (health magistracy)—no physicians—to enforce existing health laws and promulgate new ones to prevent future outbreaks. After a severe plague in 1527 to 1529, it was extended over the terra firma. By 1540, it controlled poor relief, prostitution, and beggars.

In 1575, Venetian authorities called on University of Padua physicians to determine whether they should declare an epidemic. The physicians' outspoken Girolamo Mercuriale declared the threat minimal, and intervention was mortally postponed, as 46,000 of 180,000 residents died during the epidemic of 1575 to 1577. The following and last major Venetian plague began in 1630. Venetians used shutting in to isolate victims, and bills of mortality (*necrologi*) now included all deceased residents, their residences, and even occupations. Religious processions began in June 1630, and the vow to build Santa Maria della Salute church was made on October 22. On the same day, resident poor began to be shipped to a beggars' hospital at San Lazzaro dei Mendicanti. Nevertheless, almost a third of the population perished over two years.

See also: Bills of Mortality; Health Boards, Magistracies, and Commissions; Lazarettos and Pest Houses; Merchants; Mercuriale, Girolamo; Quarantine; St. Roche; Shutting In.

References

Comune di Venezia, Assessorato alla Culturale Belle Arti. *Venezia e la peste, 1348/1797.* Venice: Marsilio Editori, 1979.

Ell, Stephen R. "Three Days in October of 1630: Detailed Examination of Mortality during an Early Modern Plague Epidemic in Venice." *Review of Infectious Disease* 11 (1989): 128–141.

Fenlon, Iain. *The Ceremonial City: History, Memory, and Myth in Renaissance Venice.* New Haven, CT: Yale University Press, 2007.

Vesalius, Andreas (1514–1564)

André Wesele Crabbe was born in Brussels, son of an imperial apothecary. Andreas

Sixteenth-century anatomist and physician Andreas Vesalius. He is often referred to as the founder of modern human anatomy. (Courtesy of the National Library of Medicine)

studied medicine at Louvain and Paris, earning his doctorate at Padua's medical school. At Paris, he learned the importance of correcting "Arabic errors" in Galenic medical texts through first-hand study of corpses. Anatomy and physiology became his specialty, and Vesalius was famed for his public dissections (autopsies) of executed criminals at Padua and Bologna. He compared human and animal physical structures and disproved Galen's claims about human anatomy time and again. During public dissections, Vesalius the physician did the cutting, pointing, and removing traditionally carried out by a lower-status surgeon. He also replaced reading from a Galenic or other traditional anatomy text with his own running commentary. The educational effect was to penetrate the barrier between the physician with his theory and book and the lowly surgeon who got his hands dirty. This encouraged students to rely less on questionable texts and place greater faith in empirically derived information. Despite Vesalius's new model, however, medical schools continued their traditional anatomical pedagogy.

Vesalius's masterpiece was his massive *Seven Books on the Structure of the Human Body* (*De humani corporis fabrica*, Basel, 1543). He also provided abbreviated versions for educational use in German and Latin, the *Epitomi*. The *Fabrica* was an elaboration of his *Six anatomical tables* (Venice, 1538), short texts illustrated with small anatomical illustrations for student use. Revised in 1555, the *Fabrica* was Vesalius's corrective to all previous anatomy works, beautifully and accurately illustrated by an unknown artist who rivaled Leonardo or Titian in skill.

See also: Anatomy and Dissection; Corpses; Galen and Galenism; Medical Education (1500–1700, Early Modern Europe); Medical Humanism.

References

O'Malley, C. D. *Andreas Vesalius of Brussels 1514–1564.* Berkeley: University of California Press, 1964.

Toledo-Pereyra, L. H. "De humani corporis fabrica Surgical Revolution." *Journal of Investigative Surgery* 21 (2008): 232–236.

Vienna, Austria

Vienna was an ancient Danube River crossing and seat of the Dukes of Austria, key feudatories of the Holy Roman Empire in the 14th century. Placed along important regional and international commercial and travel routes, Vienna duly fell into the path of the plague that moved north from Venice through Trent, the Inn Valley, Bavaria, and down the Danube or due north from Dalmatia. There are several contemporary sources for the Black Death in Vienna, including Konrad von Megenberg's *Book of Nature* and the annals of monasteries at Matsee, Neuberg, and Klosterneuberg.

Plague arrived in the early spring of 1349 and manifested itself in April or May. Duke Albrecht II fled to Pukersdorf as daily tolls reached 500. A monk at Zwetl wrote that all victims received the last rites, though the annalist at Neuberg reported that between May 31 and September 29, five large pits at extramural God's Field contained mass burials. One monk wrote that a biblical third of the population died, the other that the same third alone survived. Among these, apparently, were especially large numbers of Jews, as Konrad reported. As in Prague upriver, a new university was planted in Vienna to provide a new generation of physicians. This drew considerably more than the four known apothecaries of the later 14th century and may have encouraged the establishment of a chief medical officer by 1390. In 1405, apothecaries were regulated by the Pharmacy Order, a precursor to later *Pestordnungen* with their much wider powers to prevent epidemics.

Plague returned in 1359, between 1370 and 1374 when 15,000 died, in 1381 when 40,000 were said to have perished, and less seriously in 1398 to 1399. The 15th century saw 13 epidemics and the 16th fewer and less severe outbreaks. In 1585, on the heels of heavy tolls in the later 1570s, the duke established a Director of Health to coordinate prevention and response. High death rates accompanied the outbreak of 1653 to 1656, but worse still was 1678 to 1680. Twenty percent of the population of 110,000 people died over three years as carriages were filled to overflowing with corpses. Afterward, the emperor rewarded 29 loyal physicians who did not flee, and it took a mere year and a half to replace the 20,000 plus with colonies of Germans from upriver. Vienna's final plague epidemic occurred in 1712 to 1714, and the city was prepared. Even so, 9,565 were infected and 8,644 died, including 10 physicians and 50 surgeons.

See also: Chronicles and Annals; Plague Memorials; Churches, Plague.

References

Benedictow, Ole. *The Black Death 1346–1353: The Complete History.* Rochester, NY: Boydell & Brewer, 2004.

Schmölzer, Hilde. *Die Pest in Wien.* Vienna: Österreichischer Bundesverlag Gesellschaft, 1985.

Velimirovic, Boris and Helga. "Plague in Vienna." *Review of Infectious Diseases* 2 (1989): 808–830.

Vinario, Raimondo Chalmel de (Magister Raimundus; Chalmelli; Chalin; d. after 1382)

Born during the second quarter of the 14th century in Vinas, a village in Languedoc, Raimondo studied medicine at the University of Montpellier. Here he remained to practice until relocating to papal Avignon. He became part of the popes' staff, treating curial and other victims of several epidemics.

In 1382, Raimondo wrote *De epidemia*, an account of the plagues of 1347 to 1348, 1362, 1371, and 1382. He believed in celestial causation of plague and claimed that all epidemics became contagious. Every true case of plague was incurable, he stated, since he could cure none. Experience also taught that those victims he bled died, so he limited bleeding. Here his anticlericalism came out: he made sure to bleed the men of the papal curia. He noted the falling virulence of the disease over time: in 1347 to 1348, it attacked about two-thirds of the populace and killed most; in 1360, it made about half sick and some survived; in 1375, about a 10th contracted it and many lived, while in 1382, only about five percent suffered and most survived. Like others, Raimondo observed that later outbreaks killed a higher proportion of children than early ones. His work was revised and printed at Lyon in 1552.

See also: Astrology; Bishops and Popes; Bleeding/Phlebotomy; Consilia and Plague Tracts; Physicians, Court.

Reference

Cohn, Samuel K. *The Black Death Transformed: Disease and Culture in Early Renaissance Europe.* New York: Oxford University Press, 2002.

Virgin Mary

Although the Bible says that Jesus Christ is the perfect intercessor for people before God the Father, it does not stipulate who is the best intercessor before Christ, who is the final judge and accepted by many Christians as the ultimate cause of plague. By the late Middle Ages, Christianity had long been answering the question with the Virgin Mary, Jesus's mother. The preplague, high medieval "cult of Mary," which manifested itself in countless hymns, prayers, icons, churches, and even cities dedicated to Santa Maria, St. Mary, or Notre Dame (Our Lady), reflects this exalted role.

When plague struck Europe in 1347, people naturally blamed Christ the Judge and turned to his mother once again as advocate. In Avignon, Pope Clement had a silver statue of Mary made and processed through

A 17th-century Italian prayer sheet invoking the Virgin Mary's aid and depicting the major plague saints Sebastian (in Roman armor with bow and arrows, crushing Satan in the center) and Roche (in pilgrim's hat, with staff, dog, and tunic pulled up to show bubo at bottom right), along with local saints Adrian, Bennone, and Antonio. Published by Peter de Jode, undated. (Courtesy of the National Library of Medicine)

the streets in 1348, and he concluded his mass for plague time with the priest praying: "Hear us O God our salvation, and at the intercession of Mary, blessed Mother of God, free your people from the terror of your anger . . ." (Horrox, 124). In a Latin prayer found in later 14th-century Books of Hours, Mary is addressed "O glorious star of the sea, save us from the plague. Hear us: for your son who honors you denies you nothing. Jesus, save us, for whom the Virgin Mother prays to you." English poet John Lydgate reworked the text slightly: Mary, "Of infect airs oppress all their utterance / Us to infect, that they have no puissance; /

From their battle be thou our chief defense / That their malice to us do no grievance / Of infecting stroke of pestilence" (Horrox, 124–25). Since God's people's sins had sparked his anger and brought on plague, the prayers of saints were needed to reinforce individual prayer and penitence. And Mary was the most powerful of saints.

Many cities had dedicated themselves to Mary, which made her both a local patron saint and a plague saint, and local churches and icons of Mary became the focus of plague-time ritual. Confraternities, too, had long been dedicated to Mary, and their members organized liturgies and processions designed to draw down Mary's favor for their members, families, and communities. In towns, confraternities, guilds, wealthy nobles, merchants, and clergy had images of Mary created, both prophylactically and in thanks for her successful intercession. Since Mary's heavenly influence revolved around her role as Jesus's mother, the ritual arts generally depicted Mary with the infant Jesus—the Madonna and Child—where other plague saints tended to be shown actively protecting people or kneeling in prayer before Christ enthroned. Since this iconography is so generally prevalent, distinguishing plague-inspired art is tricky. Subtle signs include dark clouds (of miasma), a dark city in the background, or the presence of arrows or quivers; more obvious is the presence of such plague saints as Sebastian or Roche.

The most interesting development in Mary's iconography is the *Misericordia* (mercy). An oversized, standing Mary holds out her arms, extending her cape over a group of smaller figures who are usually praying. Often her protective cape (German *Schutzmantel*) deflects heaven-sent plague arrows, which strike those outside her shadow. The earliest known Misericordia was painted in Genoa around 1372 and featured the archbishop as sheltered devotee. Later versions included robed and hooded confraternity members, clergy, a merchant's family, or a range of types representing a community. The meaning is clear: her devotees did, or will, have her protection. The image, however, seems to infer that Mary can thwart the will of God. Disturbed by this, the Council of Trent (1546–1563) banned the use of the image. Since Protestants denied any intercessory role to saints, including Mary, they abandoned their cults preferring direct communication with God.

See also: Apocalypse and Apocalypticism; Arrows; Art, Effects of Plague on; Books of Hours; Christ; Clement VI, Pope; Ex voto; Lydgate, John; Pope; Prayer and Fasting; Processions.

References

Bailey, Gauvin Alexander, et al., eds. *Hope and Healing: Painting in Italy in a Time of Plague, 1500–1800*. Chicago: University of Chicago Press, 2005.

Boss, Sarah Jane, ed. *Mary: The Complete Resource*. New York: Oxford University Press, 2007.

Horrox, Rosemary. *The Black Death*. New York: Manchester University Press, 1994.

Marshall, Louise. "Manipulating the Sacred: Image and Plague in Renaissance Italy." *Renaissance Quarterly* 47 (1994): 485–532.

Virgin Soil Disease

"Virgin soil" refers to a human population that has never been exposed to a particular pathogen and its disease or that has not been exposed within a very long time. The result of first contact between such a population and a new pathogen is often devastating, depending on the virulence of the pathogen. When an infectious pathogen has never had

contact with a population, the population has had no chance to develop biological immune responses specific to it. Therefore, if the pathogen has the potential to wreak enough damage within the human body to kill it, then that potential will often have full rein. After the startling spike in cases of illness and death, refugees and other carriers will transmit the disease far from the original points of contact to other "virgin" populations that are equally biologically unprepared for it, and the process is repeated. Perhaps the most famous case of such an epidemiological nightmare is the spread of measles, smallpox, and other diseases by Europeans among late 15th- and early 16th-century Amerindian populations. The well-known result was the virtual depeopling of vast regions of the American continents, often far from original points of European contact.

After the pathogen's virulence and the population's lack of biological preparedness, the third factor is the population's cultural understanding of the disease and developed individual and societal means of dealing with it. Some new diseases may present symptoms that suggest known diseases. Customary treatments, drugs, or other responses may or may not bear fruit. When startlingly new symptoms present—for example, great skin blotches or large lumps—the medical community is likely to react in more or less random ways that have little or no effect on the patients. Even if the means for limiting or curing the disease are within the technical understanding of the society, it may make no efforts in those directions simply out of unfamiliarity.

In the premodern world, without understanding of germs and how to contain and fight them, new pathogens cut greats swaths through populations. With modern knowledge and technology, new outbreaks are far less likely to wreak havoc. But the mutability of certain viruses, the rapidity of transportation, and political and social turmoil in areas of Africa and elsewhere from where new pathogens are likeliest to emerge suggest that humans have not subdued the germ.

Was the Black Death a virgin soil outbreak? For all intents and purposes, it should be thought of as one. Since exposure and even recovery from the plague appears not to confer immunity, there was no initial biological defense. Given the domination of antiquated and false medical theories about human anatomy and physiology (humoralism) and the utter misunderstanding of what caused the plague (God, the stars, putrefied air), there was little more positive to do on a patient's level than sedate with opiates and wait. Since historic "plagues" were not unknown to either Christian or Muslim cultures, both responded collectively following previous patterns, for example, flight and isolation of victims. Refugees, however, could easily carry infected fleas, and isolating victims did little to eliminate the rats or fleas.

See also: Black Death (1347–1352); Epidemic and Pandemic; Morbidity, Mortality, and Virulence.

Reference

Crosby, Alfred W. "Virgin Soil Epidemics as a Factor in the Aboriginal Depopulation in America." *The William and Mary Quarterly* 3rd ser. 33 (1976): 289–299.

Wands

Painted rods or wands long were symbols of the physician, not unlike stethoscopes. In early modern Europe, city authorities mandated the use of wands of varying colors for people connected with plague. In 1518, Cardinal Wolsey, Henry VIII's chancellor, ordered all people who were shut up in their home to carry a white rod when out of the house. Up to 1583, such caregivers as doctors and apothecaries and such functionaries as searchers and gravediggers also carried white wands, but after 1583, they carried red. In that year, London's Cornhill neighborhood bought 50 red wands just for corpse inspectors. In 1557, Amsterdam required anyone who visited plague victims or family members of victims to carry a white rod for six weeks after the patient died or recovered. In the 17th century, officials stipulated that they be a meter and a half long. Penalties for failure to carry a required wand varied; in Leiden in 1515, one either provided 2,000 bricks for the city wall or had his hand cut off and was banished.

See also: Clothing; Crime and Punishment; Shutting In.

Reference

Byrne, Joseph. *Daily Life during the Black Death.* Westport, CT: Greenwood, 2006.

Wills and Testaments

Though created by the living, a last will and testament is a contract between the deceased and his or her survivors. Its general effect is to redistribute familial and personal wealth and property from one generation to the next. Its roots were in ancient Roman law and practice, and it was adopted and adapted by medieval Germanic kingdoms. Fully revived with the restoration of Roman Law and the notariate in the 11th and 12th centuries, by the 14th, will making was considered a civic and virtually religious duty.

Testators employed a notary, a paralegal professional to whom the testator dictated his or her instructions. The resulting document was a legal instrument, and the notary knew what it required to have the force of a contract. In addition to funeral and burial arrangements, a father's will included the return of his wife's dowry to her, provision for dowering daughters, naming of his heir who now controlled the bulk of familial wealth and property, provisions for other sons, gifts to friends and other family, pious legacies to the poor, foundations, churches, monasteries, and convents, and funds for postfunereal masses and prayers. An executor who would oversee the distribution of the estate was also named. Women's wills tend to be simpler since women did not usually control familial wealth. These documents could be drawn up at home or in a church or convent and generally required a notary plus several witnesses and perhaps a clergyman, all of whose names appear in the document. A copy was provided to the testator, one was registered publicly, and another recorded in the notary's copybook. People generally prepared wills before undertaking a journey or when ill—more often, perhaps, when on their deathbed.

During plague time, the number of wills filed soared as the sick, the dying, and the cautious prepared for the worst. Codicils (revisions) had to be added as appointed heirs, beneficiaries, or executors died and new ones had to be named. Overworked notaries exposed themselves to the plague, but studies reveal that large numbers remained in plague-stricken cities, and many died carrying out their civic duties. During subsequent plagues, civil authorities reduced the number of required witnesses and other formalities to limit exposure. In some places, wills were dictated out open windows to notaries in the street; in others, notaries were expected to record wills even in pest houses.

Historians use wills for information on inheritance patterns, family structures, pious gift giving, and choices of burial arrangements. They also use annual numbers of wills filed as a mark of death tolls. In London, the average for 1333 to 1348 was 23 wills, in 1349, 352 were produced; in Besançon, the average of 44 climbed to 312 in 1349; and Lübeck's preplague average of six soared to 127 in 1350.

Islamic societies also utilized will making. In Mamluk Egypt, the goods of one dying intestate reverted to the state. Muslim estates in Christian Aragon could be seized by the crown if there were no clear heirs, but plague deaths so disrupted inheritances that royal taxes could not be paid. Wisely, Muslims were left to redistribute property of the intestate as they saw fit.

See also: *Ars moriendi* (*The Art of Dying*); Art, Effects of Plague on; Children; Funerals, Catholic; Funerals, Protestant; Notaries.

References

Cohn, Samuel K. "Last Wills: Family, Women and the Black Death," in his *Women in the Streets: Essays on Sex and Power in Renaissance Italy* (Baltimore, MD: The Johns Hopkins University Press, 1996), 39–56.

Schen, Claire S. *Charity and Lay Piety in Reformation London, 1500–1620*. Burlington, VT: Ashgate, 2002.

Utterback, Kristine T. "The Date and Composition of Bishops' Registers from the Plague Years in the Diocese of Barcelona." *Journal of Ecclesiastical History* 39 (1988): 412–432.

Wray, Shona Kelly. *Communities and Crisis: Bologna during the Black Death*. Boston: Brill, 2009.

Witches and Witchcraft

According to Christian tradition and authorities, witches were men and women who chose to worship and obey Satan in return for favors, powers, or other benefits. Those struck by such seemingly random misfortunes as unexpected illnesses, odd crop failures, or animal deaths often blamed witchcraft. Dealing with Satan was clearly against Church law and often a violation of civil and customary laws. Accusations, trials, and execution of purported witches occurred throughout the Middle Ages but intensified greatly after 1500 in the midst of the Second Pandemic.

In the 1340s, Jews and lepers had been accused, persecuted, and murdered as poisoners of wells, but witches—and even here the claim of witchcraft is often obscure—appear only sporadically as instigators of plague. At Geneva in 1530, 1545, 1567 to 1569, 1571, and 1615; at Chambery in 1577 and Vevey in 1613; and in Savoy and Milan in 1630, diabolically inspired people were accused and tried for spreading a poisonous ointment that set off plague epidemics. Known by the French *engraisseurs* or "greasers," 40 percent of those accused in Geneva were executed,

65 people in 1545 and 1571 alone. Since plague was rarely attributed to Satan, it is not surprising that his supposed minions generally escaped suspicion.

Historians tend to agree, however, that plague added to the societal tensions that created these scapegoats, perhaps several hundred thousand of whom—85 percent of whom were women—suffered persecution and execution from the 1400s well into the 1700s, from Ireland to the Russian steppes. Much of Western Europe suffered witchmania from about 1550 until the end of the Thirty Years' War (1648), about the time plague began to disappear from the continent.

See also: Demons, Satan, and the Devil; Jews.

References

Klaits, Joseph. *Servants of Satan*. Bloomington: Indiana University Press, 1985.

Levack, Brian P. *The Witch-Hunt in Early Modern Europe*. New York: Longman, 1987.

Wither, George (1588–1667)

The English lawyer, soldier, and poet was born near Alton, Hampshire. Educated at Magdalen College, Oxford, and the Inns of Chancery and of Court, his early poetry focused on love. This changed around 1615, when he attained a Puritanical streak that alienated him from the early Stuart court and led him to write hymns and abandon pastoral poetry. He adopted the persona of an Old Testament prophet and took to signing himself Britain's "loyal but despised Remembrancer."

When plague struck London in 1625, Wither remained as observer and attendant to many of the victims. He even developed what appeared to be plague sores. At year's end, he packaged his observations, experiences, complaints, and moral conclusions in his versified *History of the Pestilence*, which he presented to the new king, Charles I. In eight handwritten cantos, Wither has God inflict the plague on sinful Britain; explains the importance of repentance; recounts his own experiences; warns of the abuses and sins he had witnessed; and instructs the king that reform must come from throne and Parliament, lest God's wrath return. In 1628, he self-published a greatly expanded version (580 pages in the 1880 edition) with the title *Britain's Remembrancer*. This was more in line with moralistic tracts and poems by such contemporaries as Thomas Dekker and John Taylor and included theories of natural causation (astrological and miasmatic) and recommendations for a prophylactic regimen. It retains Wither's tortured verses and prophetic voice, however, as he condemns profiteers, charlatans, those who fled, and the very city itself that spawned such wretched creatures.

See also: London, England; Morality Literature, Christian.

Reference

French, J. Milton. *The History of the Pestilence (1625) by George Wither*. Cambridge, MA: Harvard University Press, 1932.

Women Medical Practitioners

Medical care giving and healing in late medieval and early modern Europe were by no means male monopolies. One may imagine that the vast majority of conditions, diseases, and injuries were handled at home and by a woman. Only when the patient worsened might a specialist be called, and this, too, might well have been a woman healer. Women practitioners outnumbered medical school-educated physicians and guild-licensed

A 16th-century woodcut of two midwives comforting a woman sitting in a birthing chair while a third midwife delivers the baby. (Courtesy of the National Library of Medicine)

surgeons thousands to one. Under most circumstances, women were barred from formal medical education or guild membership and were thus unable to share their experience, knowledge, and skills publicly in urban settings.

The most common exception was midwifery, as midwives assisted in all aspects of the birthing process. A male physician or surgeon would only be called upon if there were a problem for which the midwife was unprepared. The midwife's character counted for as much as her skill—often founded in informal apprenticeship—and she was likely to be of the same class as the people she served. Of course, she commanded a fraction of what a male professional would charge and often received payments in kind. Plagues did not stop the community's reproductive cycle, and obstetric services were still needed. Towns that

hired civil physicians and surgeons often also hired public midwives. They might serve the poor gratis and charge wealthier women; they also served in hospitals and pest houses, where their patients both young and mature generally succumbed. Those pregnant and shut in their houses because they or kin had plague also needed midwives' services. In 16th-century Leyden, Holland, the well-provided-for civic midwife complained that wealthy women avoided her because she handled the poor. The pragmatic Dutch ruled that all and only pregnant plague victims would be served. The midwife was not to leave town and was to share her experiences so others could serve better. Leyden never wanted for applicants. About the same time, the first obstetrics book was published in Germany. Aimed at physicians, it marked the shift toward learned male control of even this naturally feminine field.

Women who served as nurses—both laywomen and Catholic nuns—had no competition among male practitioners and had long played key roles in care giving in both such acute care and long-term facilities as orphanages, leprosaria, and hospitals. During epidemics, they served homebound victims, both free and shut in, and those in plague hospitals and pest houses.

Wives of manorial lords, noblewomen, and wives of Protestant clerics often took it upon themselves to know first aid and even more complicated procedures, as well as herb lore, some dentistry, and rudiments of surgery. They served their own families and servants but also retainers, villagers, laborers, and travelers. It was a matter of noblesse oblige as well as practicality, since physicians or surgeons, if available at all, might be days away and far too costly to hire. Sir Thomas More desired that his daughter know physic, and Lady Grace Mildmay had a collection of 250 books on medicine. Significantly, none was on plague. The later 16th and 17th centuries saw increasing numbers of self-help medical books and pamphlets aimed at a literate and lay readership.

Female surgeons were often widows or daughters of surgeons who continued their husbands' or fathers' practices. Early during the Second Pandemic, they might not be licensed but were allowed to practice. Venice recognized their value, and Naples sometimes did. Barber-surgeons' and surgeons' guilds, however, began seeking equity with physicians' guilds and colleges and began restricting and barring female practice in the 15th century. Plague epidemics weakened these barriers as male practitioners fled or died and authorities were desperate for trained personnel. Barriers returned when plague lifted, and society turned back toward male professionalization and willingness to see women healers as witches.

See also: Empirics; Hospitals Lazarettos and Pest Houses; Nurses; Physicians; Surgeons/Barbers.

References

Broomhall, Susan. *Women's Medical Work in Early Modern France.* Manchester: Manchester University Press, 2004.

Donohue, Patricia. *Nursing; the Finest Art.* New York: Mosby, 2010.

Ehrenreich, Barbara and Deirdre English. *Witches, Midwives and Nurses: A History of Women Healers.* New York: The Feminist Press at CUNY, 2010.

Pelling, Margaret. "Unofficial and Unorthodox Medicine," in *Western Medicine: An Illustrated History*, edited by Irvine Loudon (New York: Oxford University Press, 1997), 264–276.

Pomata, Gianna. "Practicing between Earth and Heaven: Women Healers in Early Modern Bologna." *Dynamis* 19 (1999): 119–144.

Wyman, A. L. "The Surgeoness: The Female Practitioner of Surgery, 1400–1800." *Medical History* 28 (1984): 22–41.

Yeoman Farmers and Gentry

In England, the Black Death swept through the countryside and transformed the interstitial classes between the serf and peasant laborers and the landed aristocracy, from bishops and monasteries to the lower nobility. At the lower end were the increasingly independent yeoman farmers and above them the class including Chaucer's *parfit, gentil* knight, the gentry.

As valuable to the landholders of the later Middle Ages as the land were those who made the land produce. The Black Death and recurrent plagues killed and displaced a very large percentage of agricultural labor, which left many landowners to sell off tracts or sit by and watch them revert to their natural state. At the same time, peasants who remained on the land accumulated land, tools, and cash from the deaths of and abandonment of villages by their peers and family, allowing them to take advantage of further available land. As serfdom and forced labor requirements accelerated their disappearance in the 14th century, large landholders spent cash purchasing the labor of day laborers as well as independent farmers. The fall in supply of rural labor due to plague meant that the wages paid rose; however, the Statute of Labourers tried to keep them down. As plague followed plague, the overall population dropped and laborers continued to leave the land for the badly hit cities, availing the yeoman class of still more land. Villages disappeared and enclosure of small plots into large tracts for sheep raising occurred largely in the 15th century

as England's postplague population hit its nadir.

The class of the noble knights, by the Second Pandemic, had several sources of status—birth, marriage, service, or gift—and only incidentally did they ride horses into battle. As landholders, they formed a class beneath the aristocrats and, importantly, above the rising yeoman class. While some were in position to accumulate more land when it became available, others sold off portions to other gentry or to upstart yeomen. Manorial relationships, as between the old landlords and peasants, gave way to negotiated, wage-based arrangements between employers and paid laborers. Gentility was a matter of class, and Chaucer's description of the yeoman forester with this many weapons and crisp green vestments invests him with the desire to rise from commoner to gentleman. But the English crown recognized that too much mobility among classes was destabilizing. The gentry as a class consisted of three levels, with the knights at the top, the esquires in the middle, and gentlemen at the lower end. Income distinguished the classes, and after the plague, as government reached down with its laws to control the increasingly independent commoners many gentry filled law enforcement and judicial offices, for example, coroners, justices of the peace, and even became members of Parliament. In 1413, the Statute of Additions insisted that people appearing before a court of law attest to their social rank. As yeomen reached out toward the gentry and the lower gentry strove to join the upper, England grew into Europe's most dynamic society, with freedom of action and entrepreneurship.

See also: Chaucer, Geoffrey; Demographic Effects of Plague: Europe 1347–1400; Demographic Effects of Plague: Europe 1400–1500; Economic Effects of Plague in Europe; Labourers, Ordinance and Statute of; Nobility; Peasants.

References

Aberth, John. *From the Brink of the Apocalypse: Crisis and Recovery in Late Medieval England.* New York: Routledge, 2000.

Palmer, Robert C. *English Law in the Age of the Black Death, 1348–1381: A Transformation of Governance and Law.* Chapel Hill: University of North Carolina Press, 1993.

Platt, Colin. *King Death: The Black Death and its Aftermath in Late-medieval England.* Toronto: University of Toronto Press, 1996.

Yersin, Alexandre (1863–1943)

Among the first to identify the First and Second Pandemics' plague pathogen with his *Pasteurella pestis*, Alexandre Yersin was raised by his widowed mother in Lavaux, Switzerland. Young Alexandre took an early interest in nature and science. At Lausanne, he prepared for medical school, but in 1884 he traveled to Marburg, Germany, to study botany. While there, he shifted to anatomy and pathology, and after a year, he moved to Paris. He worked briefly in the Hôtel Dieu hospital, then in André Cornil's private bacteriological laboratory. Microbiology was in its early stages, and Yersin had an open field. At Cornil's, he met Louis Pasteur, to whose laboratory he relocated. He studied rabies, diphtheria, and tuberculosis, completing his dissertation on the last in 1889. In the same year, Yersin went to Berlin to study under Robert Koch, the preeminent German microbiologist. His

education now second to none, he returned to Paris, was naturalized a French citizen, and lectured on diphtheria. A vacation as ship's surgeon in Southeast Asia generated a fascination with the region and its people. During a second Asian stay in 1893, Yersin joined the French Colonial Health Service, learned of the plague epidemic in China, and, in June 1894, was admitted to British Hong Kong to study it.

The Third Pandemic had begun in China and came to the West's attention through Hong Kong. While Yersin, working alone and with minimal resources, used his skills in pathology and microbiology to identify the causative agent in plague and prepare a vaccine, a well-supplied Japanese student of Koch's, Shibasaburo Kitasato, was doing the same. The British authorities supplied Kitasato's needs, especially victim corpses, while Yersin lived in a hut and relied on an Italian missionary for subjects. Yersin hypothesized that the distinctive buboes—swollen lymph glands—would be reservoirs of the pathogen, and he was correct. He quickly identified and isolated the plague-causing bacteria and tested their effect on animals, which was lethal. In about a week, Yersin had solved the riddle of the Black Death. Indeed, he was among the first to identify the First and Second Pandemics' plague pathogen with his *Pasteurella pestis*, though this was not based on scientific evidence. In 1971, the pathogen's name was changed to *Yersinia pestis* in Yersin's honor. Kitasato, meanwhile, had serially misidentified a virus and a bacillus as the responsible pathogens, eventually identifying *Y. pestis*.

Yersin determined that the *Y. pestis* could live in soil and that rats played some role in the epidemiology of plague, but Paul-Louis Simond later completed the circle by identifying fleas as transmitters of the bacteria. Yersin also failed to create a stable, effective vaccine for humans, despite some early successes. He established a research station of the Pasteur Institute at Nha Trang, Vietnam, where he continued work on a vaccine. Eventually, he gave up medicine for cattle breeding and rubber tree development.

See also: Bubonic Plague; Germ Theory; Kitasato, Shibasaburo; Koch, Robert; Pasteur, Louis; Simond, Paul-Louis; Third Plague Pandemic; *Yersinia pestis*.

References

Bendiner, Elmer. "Alexander Yersin: Pursuer of Plague." *Hospital Practice* (March 30, 1989): 121–148.

Marriott, Edward. *Plague: A Story of Science, Rivalry, Scientific Breakthrough and the Scourge that Won't Go away.* New York: Holt, 2002.

Yersinia pestis

Yersinia pestis was discovered independently by the student of Louis Pasteur, Alexandre Yersin, and the Japanese student of Robert Koch, Shibasaburo Kitasato, in Hong Kong near the beginning of the Third Plague Pandemic in 1894. They both identified it as the pathogen causing the bubonic plague, which was then raging around them. Originally named *Pasteurella pestis* in honor of Pasteur, the name was changed in 1971. This was in part to differentiate it from other *Pasteurella*-type bacteria, in part to honor Yersin.

Yersinia pestis is a bacterium of the *Enterobacteriaceae* family, and in the same genus are *Y. pseudotuberculosis* and *Y. enterocolitica*. It evolved from *Y. pseudotuberculosis* quite recently, between 1,500 and 20,000 years ago. The mutations provided additional genetic material, allowing it to adapt to a wide range of hosts—including some 80 types of fleas and 200 mammals. Certain of these factors made *Y. pestis* more virulent, or lethal, to its hosts by enabling it to overcome their defenses more easily. The term *enteric* implies the ability to live and be transmitted through water or food, but *pestis* lost this and came to rely upon an insect vector, the flea, for movement between hosts.

It lives quietly in the gut of a cold-blooded flea at about 25°C, but its virulence rises when it enters a host mammal, for example, the rat, whose body temperature is a much warmer 37°C. Unlike other *Yersiniae*, *Y. pestis* does not do well in open environments. It can survive in corpses or in undisturbed, warm soil, like that of a burrowing rodent colony, for up to a year. It is a rod-shaped bacillus between one and one and a half microns long that looks rather like a safety pin and cannot move on its own. It is gram negative but can be stained with Wayson or Giemsa, resulting in bipolarity. It can penetrate into a body through mucous membranes, but not through unbroken skin.

Yersinia pestis has three types or biovariations (biovars) designated *antiqua*, *medievalis*, and *orientalis*, related to different apparent geographical points of origin—Kenya, Kurdistan, and Madagascar, respectively—and bearing responsibility for the three plague pandemics. Genome sequencing beginning in the mid-2000s has uncovered differences between two of the three biovars, including that probably responsible for the Black Death, but research is still in its early stages at this writing. One area of interest is the comparative virulence of the biovars and the genes that are responsible for variations. Knowledge of this can work to manipulate their virulence in both directions: higher for bioweaponry purposes and lower to prevent lethal infection. It is known that a certain genetic factor (the glycoptotein in the shell or capsule that surrounds

Y. pestis) goes into effect at 37°C. This prevents the organism from being enveloped and "eaten" (phagocytosed), inhibiting the action of the human immune system's macrophages. Others locally shut down the immune system's ability to "call for help." This means a rapid effect on the human hosts/victims and very rapid reproduction.

See also: Animals; Black Death: Debate over the Medical Nature of; Bubonic Plague; Bubonic Plague in North America; Diagnosing Plague; End of Second Plague Pandemic: Theories; Fleas; Germ Theory; Pneumonic Plague; Rats and Other Plague Carriers; Septicemic Plague.

References

Achtman, Mark, et al. "Microevolution and History of the Plague Bacillus, *Yersinia pestis*." *Proceedings of the National Academy of Sciences of the USA* 101 (2004): 17, 837–17,842.

Drancourt, Michel, et al. "*Yersinia pestis* as a Telluric, Human Ectoparasite-borne Organism." *Lancet: Infectious Diseases* 6 (2006): 234–241.

Eisen, R. J., et al. "Early-Phase Transmission of *Yersinia pestis* by Unblocked Fleas as a Mechanism Explaining Rapidly Spreading Plague Epizootics." *Proceedings of the National Academy of Sciences of the USA* 103 (2006): 15380–15385.

Haensch, Stephanie, Rafaella Bianucci, et al. "Distinct Clones of *Yersinia pestis* Caused the Black Death." *Public Library of Science Pathogens* 6 (10, 2010): e1001134 doi:10.1371/journal.ppat.101134.

Prentice, M. B., T. Gilbert and A. Cooper. "Was the Black Death caused by *Yersinia pestis*?" *Lancet: Infectious Diseases* Feb. 4, 2004: 72.

Prentice, Michael B. and Lila Rahalison. "Plague." *The Lancet* 369:9568 (2007): 1196–1207.

Skurnik, Mikael, et al., editors. *The Genus Yersinia.* New York: Kluwer, 2003.

Z

Zodiac Man

By 1347, Western physicians had long believed that celestial bodies—including planets, stars, and constellations—played important roles in affecting people's health. According to medical astrology, each of the 12 zodiacal constellations had a direct relationship with one area of the human body. Knowledge of these relationships allowed the physician, surgeon, or patient to schedule or avoid dates for medical procedures to achieve the best result. One's horoscope could also suggest anatomical areas of weakness or strength.

This system, known as *melothesia*, took the visual form of the "Zodiac Man," a nude figure on which was superimposed appropriately the 12 zodiacal signs. This appeared on cards carried by physicians, in medical texts, Books of Hours (e.g., *Les tres riches heures*), almanacs, leechbooks, and astrological tracts. Aries influenced the head and face; Taurus the neck; Gemini shoulders, arms and hands; Cancer chest and stomach; Leo heart and back; Virgo bowels and belly; Libra kidney and buttocks; Scorpio the genitalia; Sagittarius thighs; Capricorn knees; Aquarius shins; and Pisces the feet.

See also: Almanacs; Astrology; Books of Hours; Leechbooks.

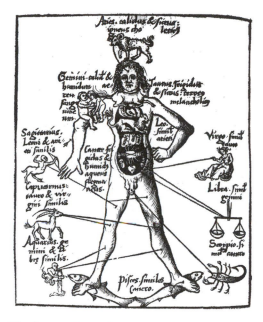

The figure of a zodiac man with the appropriate signs of the zodiac associated with their corresponding body parts. (Courtesy of the National Library of Medicine)

References

Capp, Bernard. *Astrology and the Popular Press: English Almanacs, 1500–1800.* London: Faber and Faber, 1979.

North, J. D. "Medieval Concepts of Celestial Influence," in *Astrology, Science and Society: Historical Essays*, edited by Patrick Curry (Wolfboro, NH: Boydell Press, 1987), 5–18.

Glossary

apprentice In the guild system, a young man engaged by contract with a master in learning the art, craft, or business before working on his own as a journeyman.

bacillus A genus or type of rod-shaped, Gram-stain-positive bacterium.

bacteriology A branch of microbiology that studies bacteria and their effects on other organisms.

bacterium (plural bacteria) A single-celled, free-living, or parasitic organism lacking organized internal structures.

beatify In the Catholic Church, to declare a person "blessed," a step toward being canonized a saint.

bequest A gift (money, land, goods) bequeathed in a will.

biovar Regional variants of a species that have adapted to particular environmental conditions.

bubo (plural buboes) A swollen lymph gland caused by the collection of a large number of dead plague and white blood cells; provides the label "bubonic" to the most common type of *Y. pestis*-caused plague.

Canon Law The official legal code of the Roman Catholic Church.

cauterization Sealing a wound with intense heat.

charnel house Usually part of a cemetery: a facility in which corpses were left until all of the flesh (*carnus*) fell off the bones; bones (*ossa*) would then be taken to an ossuary for permanent storage.

commenda A later medieval partnership arrangement whereby one or more merchant-partners remain at home and one or more accompany their cargo to its destination.

commensal To share a table with; usually a reference to rats that live in proximity to humans.

confession The Catholic sacrament in which the sinner orally lists all sins to a priest, seeking forgiveness and promising to amend his/her moral life. Believed to instill grace and remove spiritual penalties for sin if done sincerely.

corrupt To change the form or substance of something in a manner deemed negative.

cult Within a religion, a set of beliefs and rituals that are apart from but complementary to the main body of belief and ordinary rituals, for example, the Cult of Mary in Catholicism.

cupping A method of drawing out excess "humors" by placing a glass cup on the skin, heating it and thereby creating suction.

dowry A young woman's share of her family's property that was placed in the hands of her new husband upon marriage. In most cultures, it was necessary for a young woman seeking a husband and was returned to her control upon her husband's death.

ecclesiastical Pertaining or belonging to the Church.

egalitarianism Elimination of all social classes and distinctions so that all people are equal.

emetic Substance that promotes or causes vomiting; a form of purgative.

endemic In disease, refers to one that persists indefinitely within a human population, for example, the common cold.

enzootic Endemic, but within an animal population.

episcopal Referring to a Christian bishop, the office, or duties.

epistolary Relating to a letter or correspondence.

epizootic Widespread outbreak of disease within a population of animals.

eschatological Referring to the events or other aspects of the prophesied end of time, especially as described in the biblical Apocalypse/Book of Revelation.

extramural Outside city walls.

focus In an epidemiological context, an area or region in which plague is concentrated and from which it spreads outward.

fomite An inorganic particle thought by some premodern scientists to cause plague in a human body.

fresco A painting or painting technique that uses a fresh or dry (secco) plaster (gesso) base to which mineral pigments are applied; usually indoor walls or ceilings.

funerary Having to do with funerals.

galleys Long, shallow-draft ships propelled by banks of oars usually rowed by prisoners and slaves.

Hadith Muslim writings recounting the life and sayings of the Prophet Muhammad; considered second only to the Koran in religious importance.

hajj In Islam, the pilgrimage to Mecca each Muslim is expected to make at least once; traffic is especially high during the holy month of Ramadan.

iatrochemical Referring to the use of nonorganic substances (e.g., metals, salts) in the treatment of disease.

icon In Orthodox Christian traditions, a stylized painting of a religious figure or scene.

iconography The interpretation of the meaning(s) of imagery in a work of art.

immunity The state of being able to protect the health of a body by containing or destroying intruding pathogens.

intestate Without having made a will.

lay and laity Ordinary Christians who are neither clergy nor members of a monastic order.

legate (papal) A personal representative of the Roman Catholic pope, usually sent to a head of state.

liturgy A Christian church service, especially a Eucharistic service or Mass.

materia medica Plants (sometimes other materials) used in healing.

memento mori Literally, a "reminder of death."

mendicant Literally, a "beggar"; a member of one of the five orders of Catholic friars: Augustinians, Carmelites, Dominicans, Franciscans, or Servites.

microbiology The study of living organisms and life processes too small to be seen with the naked eye.

monotheist A person who believes there is only one god; includes Jews, Christians, and Muslims.

Parlement The judicial branch of the French royal government; organized by region with that of Paris the supreme court.

pathogen A biological agent that has an actual or potential harmful or deadly effect on a host organism.

poison libel The false charge or accusation against a person or group that he or they purposely spread poison in order to kill people.

pomander A ball of aromatic gum and other fragrant materials worn or carried to "purify" pestilential air around a person.

prophylactic A substance, object, or procedure that is thought to protect one from a disease or other harm.

protomedico A physician who served as a town's or region's chief medical official, usually appointed by and answering to a noble or royal authority.

psychosomatic disease One in which a mental state or condition causes a physical illness.

putrefy For an organic substance to decompose in a particularly noxious manner.

putting out system Owners of tools and raw materials would put them into the hands of semiskilled laborers at their home; these people would process the raw materials or create the finished goods in return for pay.

reservoir A geographical area in which a disease pathogen is commonly found, often within animals.

resistance The ability of a person's immune system to limit the impact of a pathogen that has entered his/her body.

sepsis A state of being poisoned by the presence of pathogens in the bloodstream.

sharecropping A contractual arrangement whereby farmers provide labor in return for use of land, equipment, and seed, with the produce shared between farmers and landowner.

sinecure A church position that did not entail serving a congregation but did provide an income.

stele An upright stone slab bearing an inscription or image, usually a memorial.

sterile Free from contaminating microorganisms or other toxins.

subcutaneous Beneath the outmost layers of skin.

suppurate To ooze or discharge pus.

sympathetic action A prescientific notion that similar things can cancel each other out, for example, one poison counteracting another poison.

topos (plural topoi) A common literary topic or theme.

triage The practice in emergency admissions of dividing the sick or wounded into three groups: the dying, the relatively well, and those who would benefit from immediate treatment.

Tridentine Related to the Catholic Church's Council of Trent (1545–1563), from the original Latin name of the town.

votive Related to the making of a vow, usually to God or an intercessory saint during plague time: For example, "If you protect/heal me/my child/the town, I/we will do [X] in thanks."

zoonosis A disease that can, like plague, be transmitted from animals to humans through direct contact or a vector.

Bibliography

The bibliography is organized as follows:
I. Printed and Internet Published Historical Sources
   A) Editions of Plague Consilia, Tracts and Other Medical Sources
   B) Editions of Literary and Other Non-medical Sources
 II. Selected Reference Works
III. Selected Recent Doctoral Dissertations
IV. Secondary Sources: Books and Articles in English (usually)

I. Printed and Internet Published Historical Sources

[Digital Book Index is at http://www.digital bookindex.org/about.htm]

A. Editions of Plague Consilia and Tracts

Aberth, John. *The Black Death: The Great Mortality of 1348–1350*. New York: Bedford, 2005.

Alexandro, Francesco. *Pestis et pestilentium febrium tractatus*. Vercelli: Gulielmus Molinum, 1578. http://whqlibdoc.who.int/rare-books/a56911.pdf.

Bartsocas, Christos. "Two Fourteenth Century Greek Descriptions of the 'Black Death.'" *Journal of the History of Medicine* 21 (1966): 394–400.

Benedetti, Alessandro. *De obseruatione in pestilentia*. Venice: Digital Book Index, 1493.

Bianchelli, Mengo. *Contro alla peste*. Florence: Digital Book Index, 1523.

Blackmore, Richard. *A Discourse upon the Plague*. London: John Clark, 1722. http://whqlibdoc.who.int/rare-books/a57046.pdf.

Browne, Joseph. *A Practical Treatise of the Plague and All Pestilential Infections That Have Happened in This Island for the Last Century*. London: J. Wilcox, 1720. http://whqlibdoc.who.int/rare-books/a56989.pdf.

Canutus text. See Jacobi; Pickett; Vine.

Cermisone, Antonio. *Queste sono recepte facte quasi tute da Magistro Antonio cermisono contra la pestilential*. Milan, 1483.

Chauliac, Guy de. *Inventarium sive Chirurgia Magna*. 2 vols. Edited and translated by Michael McVaugh and Margaret Ogden. Boston: Brill, 1997.

Chiconyeau, François. *A Succinct Account of the Plague at Marseilles: Its Symptoms and the Methods and Medicines Used for Curing It*. LaVergne, TN: Kessinger Publishing, 2010. [Reprint of 1721 translation by "A Physician"]

Colbatch, John. *A Scheme for Proper Methods to Be Taken Should it Please God to Visit Us with the Plague*. London: J. Darby, 1721. http://whqlibdoc.who.int/rare-books/a57045.pdf.

Collectanea medica: medical treatises & prescriptions written by an English scribe. 1450. Digital Book Index.

Commissioners of Health for the Town of Lyon. *L'Ordre publique pour la ville de Lyon pendant la maladie contagious . . . et d'un Traite de la Peste*. Lyon: Antoine Valançol, 1670. http://whqlibdoc.who.int/rare-books/a56931.pdf.

Déchaussé, Leon Augustin. *Parfums et remedes contre la peste*. Paris: Louis-Denis Delatour & Pierre Simon, 1720. http://whqlibdoc.who.int/rare-books/a56920.pdf.

De Mertens, Charles. *Account of the Plague Which Raged at Moscow 1771*. London: 1799. Newtonville, MA: Oriental Research Partners, 1977. Facsimile.

Dinānah, Taha. "Die Schrift von Abī Ǧaʿfar Ahmed ibn ʿAlī ibn Mohammed ibn ʿAlī Hātimah aus Almeriah über die Pest." [Ibn al-Khatimah] *Archiv für Geschichte der Medizin* 19 (1927): 27–81.

Fernel, Jean. *Physiologia* (1567). Translated by John M. Forrester. Philadelphia: American Philosophical Society, 2003.

Ficino, Marsiglio. *Consiglio contra la pestilenzia*. Edited by Enrico Musacchio. Bologna: Cappelli, 1983. Also Digital Book Index.

Forrester, John M., translator, and John Henry, editor. *On the Hidden Causes of Things* [Jean Fernel]*: Forms, Souls and Occult Diseases in Renaissance Medicine*. Boston: Brill, 2005.

Fournier, M. *Observations sur la Nature et le Traitement de la Fievre Pestilentielle, ou la Peste, avec les moyens d'en pre 1777*. Digital Book Index.

Fracastoro, Girolamo. *De contagione*. Translated by C. W. Wright. New York: G.P. Putnam's Sons, 1930.

Gentile da Foligno. *Medici illustris contra pestilentiam consilium feliciter incipit*. 1479. Digital Book Index.

Granjel, Luis S. *Tres escritos sobre pestilencia del Renacimiento español*. Salamanca: Real Academia de Medicina de Salamanca, 1979.

Hancock, Thomas (MD). *Researches into the laws and phenomena of pestilence . . . the plague of London, in 1665*. London, 1821. Digital Book Index.

Harvey, Gideon (MD). *A discourse of the plague, containing the nature, causes, signs, & presages of the pestilence in general*. London, 1665.

Herring, Francis. *Certaine rvles, directions, or advertisments for this time of pestilentiall contagion: with a caueat to those that weare about their neckes impoisoned amulets as a preseruatiue from the plague*. London: William Jones, 1625; reprint New York: Da Capo, 1973.

Hippocrates, Junior (pseud.) *The predicted plague: . . . the prediction, planetary & atmospheric influences considered as cause of Black Plague*. London, 1900. Digital Book Index.

Horrox, Rosemary. *The Black Death*. New York: Manchester University Press, 1994.

Ibn Qayyim al-Jawziyya. *Medicine of the Prophet*. Translated by Penelope Johnstone. Cambridge: Islamic Texts Society, 1998.

Ingrassia, Giovanni Filippo. *Informatione del pestifero et contagioso morbo*. Books I–IV. Edited and introduction by Luigi Ingaliso. Milan: FrancoAngeli, 2005.

"Jacme d'Agramont: regiment de preservacio a epidemia o pestilencia e mortaldats." Edited and translated by M. L. Duran-Reynals and C. E. A. Winslow. *Bulletin of the History of Medicine* 23 (1949): 57–89.

Jacobi, Johannes. *A litil boke the whiche traytied & reherced many gode thinges necessaries for the . . . pestilence (1485?)*. 1910. Digital Book Library.

John de Burdeus (Burgundia). *John de Burdeus or John de Burgundia, Otherwise Sir John de Mandeville, and the Pestilence*. LaVergne, TN: Nabu Reprints, 2010. [Reprint of 1891 edition with original introduction by David Murray]

Joubert, Laurent. *Traitte de la peste.* Montpellier: Jacob Stoer, 1581. http://whqlibdoc.who.int/rare-books/a57044.pdf.

Jung, Ambrosius. *Tractatulus perutilis de pestilentia ex diuersis auctoribus aggregatus / ab eximio arcium et medicinarum.* Augsburg, 1494. Digital Book Index.

Kemp, William. *A brief treatise of the nature, causes, signes, preservation from, and cure of the pestilence.* London, 1665. Digital Book Index.

Kephale, Richard. *Medela pestilentiae: wherein is contained several theological queries concerning the plague.* London, 1665. Digital Book Index.

Kircher, Athanasius. *Athanasii Kircheri e Soc. Iesu scrutinium physico-medicum contagiosae luis, quae pestis dicitur: quo origo.* Rome, 1658. Digital Book Index.

Klebs, Arnold C. "A Catalan Plague-tract of April 24, 1348, by Jacme d'Agramont," in *Report du 6e Congrès international d'histoire de la médecine* (Anvers, France, 1927), 229–232.

Klebs, Arnold C. and E. Droz. *Remedies against the Plague: The Earliest French Tracts.* Paris: E. Droz, 1925.

Knutson, Bengt. 1 *A litil boke the whiche traytied & reherced many gode thinges necessaries for the pestilence.* See Jacobi; Pickett; also Digital Book Index.

Koch, Robert. *Reise-Berichte uber Rinderpest, Bubonenpest in Indien und Afrika, Tsetse- oder Surrakrankheit, Texasfieber.* Berlin, 1898. Digital Book Index.

Lydgate, John. "A diet and doctrine for pestilence," in *The Minor Poems of John Lydgate*, II, edited by Henry Noble McCracken (London: Early English Text Society, 1934), 702–707. [Translated in Byrne, *The Black Death*; pp. 162–167]

Manfredi, Girolamo. *Tractatus de peste.* Bologna: Henricus de Colonia, 1479. Digital Book Index.

Manget, Dr. *Traité de la peste recueilli des meilleurs auteurs anciens & modernes et enrichi de remarques et observations theoriques et pratiques.* Geneva: Philippe Planchet, 1721. http://whqlibdoc.who.int/rare-books/a56993.pdf; also Digital Book Index.

Mead, Richard. *A short discourse concerning pestilential contagion and the methods to be used to prevent it.* London, 1720. Digital Book Index.

Paracelsus. *Fur Pestilentz: ain seer nutzlicher unnd bewerter Tractat, der Christlichen gemayn zu Nutz und Wolfart.* Salzburg, 1554. Digital Book Index.

Pickett, Joseph P. "A Translation of the *Canutus* Plague Treatise," in *Popular and Practical Science of Medieval England*, edited by Lister M. Matheson (East Lansing, MI: Colleagues Press, 1994), 263–282.

Ripamonti, Giuseppe. *La peste di Milano del 1630, Libri cinque, volgarizzati da F. Cusani.* LaVergne, TN: Nabu, 2010. [Facsimile of 1841 imprint.]

Royal College of Physicians of London. *Certain necessary directions as well for the cure of the plague, as for preventing the infection.* London, 1665. Digital Book Index.

Sánchez, María Nieves. *Tratados de la Peste.* Madrid: Arco Libros, 1993.

Savonarola, Michele. *Il trattato in volgare della peste.* Edited by L. Belloni. Rome: For the Società Italiana di medicina interna, 1953.

Sherwood, Thomas. *Practitioner in physic The charitable pestmaster, or, The cure of the plague: a few short & necessary instructions.* London, 1641. Digital Book Index

Sydenham, Thomas. *Methodus curandi febres propriis observationibus superstructura [Method of Treating Fevers].* Edited and translated by G. G. Meynell. Folkstone, UK: Winterdown Books, 1987.

Vine, Guthrie. *A Litil Boke The Which Traytied And Reherced Many Gode Thinges Necessaries For The Pestilence Made By The Bishop Of Arusiens, 1485*. La Vergne, TN: Kessinger Publishing, 2010. [Facsimile of 1910 edition of Canutus Tract translation]

B. Other Primary Sources Related to the Plague

Aberth, John. *The Black Death: The Great Mortality of 1348–1350*. New York: Bedford, 2005.

Anon. (Broadside) "An unparalel'd antidote against the plague, or, A special remedy for a sick soul, whereby a sinner may recover." London, 1665. Digital Book Index.

Anon. (Broadside) "For all persons so soon as they find themselves ill or infected." London, 1665. Digital Book Index.

Bartsocas, Christos. "Two Fourteenth-Century Greek Descriptions of the 'Black Death.'" *Journal of the History of Medicine* 21 (1966): 394–400.

Bellarmine, St. Robert. *The Art of Dying Well*. Manchester, NH: Sophia Institute Press, 1998.

Berengier, Theophile. *Mgr. de Belsunce et la peste de Marseilles*. Paris, 1879. Digital Book Index.

Bertrand, Jean Baptiste. *A Historical Relation of the Plague at Marseilles in the Year 1720*. New York: McGraw-Hill, 1973.

"Bill of Mortality" (London, c. 1583). See Totaro.

Black Death, Sources Concerning the European Plague. Marlborough Wilts., UK: Adam Matthews Publications, 1994. (34 reels of sources)

Boccaccio, Giovanni. *Decameron*. Translated by Mark Musa and Peter Bondanella. New York: Mentor, 1982.

Boghurst, William. *Loimographia: An Account of the Great Plague of London in the Year 1665*. New York: AMS Press, 1976. Also Digital Book Index.

Borromeo, Federico. *La peste di Milano*. Milan: Rusconi, 1987.

Boyle, Robert. *The Works of the Honorable Robert Boyle*. Edited by Thomas Birch. 6 volumes. Hildesheim: Georg Olms, 1966. [Reprint of 1722 edition.]

Broadside. "The general bill of mortallity with a continuation of this present year, 1666." London, 1666. Digital Book Index.

Brooks, Thomas. *A heavenly cordial for all those servants of the Lord that have had the plague (and are recovered)*. London, 1666. Digital Book Index.

Browne, Joseph. *Practical Treatise of the Plague, & all Pestilential Infections that have happened in this island*. London, 1720. Digital Book Index.

Bullein, William. *A Dialogue both pleasant and pietyful* (1564). See Totaro.

Bullein, William. *A dialogue against the fever pestilence*. London: Oxford University Press, 1888; Millwood, NY: Kraus Reprint, 1987.

Byrne, Joseph P. *The Black Death*. Westport, CT: Greenwood, 2004.

Canobbio, Alessandro. *Il successo della peste occorsa in Padova l'anno 1576*. Venice: Gratioso Perchacino, 1577. http://whqlibdoc.who.int/rare-books/a56968.pdf. Also Digital Book Index.

Carvalho, João Manuel Saraiva de. *Diário da peste de Coimbra (1599)*. Lisbon: Fundação Calouste Gulbenkian: Junta Nacional de Investigação Científica e Tecnológica, 1994.

Chiapelli, Alberto. "Gli ordinamenti sanitari del commune di Pistoia contra la pestilenza del 1348." *Archivio Storico Italiano* 4th ser. 63 (1887): 3–24.

Chicoyneau, Francois. *A Succinct Account of the Plague at Marseilles: Its symptoms, & the methods & medicines used for curing it*. London, 1721. Digital Book Index.

Cock, Thomas. *Advice for the poor by vvay of cure and caution*. London, 1665. Digital Book Index.

Cohn, Samuel K. *Popular Protest in Late Medieval Europe*. New York: University of Manchester Press, 2004.

Colbatch, John. *Scheme for proper methods to be taken, should it please God to visit us with the Plague*. 1721. Digital Book Index.

A collection of very valuable and scarce pieces relating to the last plague in the year 1665. http://books.google.com/books?id=RuJbAA AAQAAJ&printsec=frontcover&source=gbs _navlinks_s#v=onepage&q=&f=false.

Dawson, W. R. *A Leechbook or collection of Medical Recipes of the Fifteenth Century*. London: Macmillan, 1934.

Defoe, Daniel. *Due Preparations for the Plague, As Well for Soul as Body*. New York: AMS Press, 1974. Also http://books .google.com/books?id=9wI_AAAAYAAJ &printsec=frontcover&dq=plague&lr=&cd= 88#v=onepage&q&f=false.

Defoe, Daniel. *A Journal of the Plague Year*. Edited by Paula Backscheider (Norton Critical Edition). New York: Norton, 1992. Also Digital Book Index.

Dekker, Thomas. *The Plague Pamphlets of Thomas Dekker*. Washington DC: Scholarly Press, 1994.

Dekker, Thomas. *The Wonderful Year 1603*. London: Folio Press, 1989. See also Totaro.

De Mertens, Charles. *Account of the Plague Which Raged at Moscow 1771*. Newton-ville, MA: Oriental Research Partners, 1977. [Reprint of 1799 translation]

Diedo, Francesco. *Petrus Iudouicus Maldura in vitam Sancti Rochi contra pestem epidimie apud dominum dignissimi intercessori*. Mainz: 1494. Digital Book Index.

Elizabeth I, Queen of England. *Plague Orders*. See Totaro; also for articles and facsimile with transcription, see Historical Collections at the Claude Moore Health Sciences Library at the University of Virginia, http://historical.hsl.virginia.edu/plague/.

Elmer, Peter, and Ole Peter Grell, eds. *Health, Disease and Society in Europe, 1500–1800*. New York: Manchester University Press, 2004.

England & Wales. "By the King, A proclamation, concerning the adjournment of Michaelmas term." [broadside] Oxford, 1665. Digital Book Index.

England & Wales. "By the King. A proclamation concerning the prorogation of the Parliament." [broadside] London, 1665. Digital Book Index.

Evelyn, John. *Diary of John Evelyn*. 6 vols. Edited by E. S. de Beer. Oxford: Clarendon Press, 1955. Vol. 3 (1650–1672).

Fealty, John and Scott Rutherford. *Tears Against the Plague: A 17th-century Woman's Devotional*. Cambridge, MA: Rhwymbooks, 2000.

Giussano, Giovani Pietro. *The Life of St. Charles Borromeo, Cardinal Archbishop of Milan*. 2 vols. New York: Burns and Oates, 1884; facsimile edition of Vol. 1 by Bibliolife, 2010.

Gohlman, William. *The Life of Ibn Sina: A Critical Edition and Annotated Translation*. Albany: State University of New York, 1974.

Goldstein, B. *Levi ben Gerson's Prognostication for the Conjunction of 1345*. Philadelphia: American Philosophical Association, 1990.

Gyug, Richard F. *The Diocese of Barcelona during the Black Death: The Register Notule communium 15 (1348–1349)*. Toronto: Pontifical Institute of Medieval Studies, 1994.

Hammond, E. A. and C. C. Sturgill. "A French Plague Recipe of 1720." *Bulletin of the History of Medicine* 46 (1972): 591–597.

Harrington, Sir John, ed. *The School of Salernum: Regimen sanitatis salerni*. Rome: Edizioni Saturni, 1959. 1607 translation.

Haye, Olivier de la. *Poeme sur la grande peste de 1348.* Ed. by George Guigue. Lyon, 1888.

Hodges, Nathaniel. *Loimologia: Or, an Historical Account of the Plague in London in 1665.* New York: AMS Press, 1994. Also Digital Book Index.

Holbein, Hans. *The Dance of Death. 41 Woodcuts by Hans Holbein the Younger. Complete Facsimile of the 1538 Edition.* New York: Dover, 1972.

Holtzendorff, Franz von. *John Howard und die Pestsperre gegen Ende des achtzehnten Jahrhunderts.* Berlin, 1879. Digital Book Index.

Horrox, Rosemary. *The Black Death.* New York: Manchester University Press, 1994.

Howard, John. *An account of the principal lazarettos in Europe, with various papers [re] the plague, w/observations on some.* London, 1791. Digital Book Index.

"Ibn al-Wardī's *Risālah al-naba' 'an al-waba,'* A Translation of a Major Source for the History for the Black Death in the Middle East." Translated by Michael W. Dols. In *Near Eastern Numismatics, Iconography, Epigraphy and History: Studies in Honor of George C. Miles,* edited by Dickran Kouymjian (Beirut: American University of Beirut Press, 1974), 443–455.

Ibn Battuta. *Voyages of Ibn Battuta.* Volume 4. Hakluyt Society #178. Cambridge: for the Hakluyt Society, 1994.

Ibn Sasra. *A Chronicle of Damascus, 1389–1397.* 2 vols. Trans. by William M. Brinner. Berkeley: University of California Press, 1963.

Jacobus da Voragine. *The Golden Legend.* 2 volumes. Translated by William Ryan. Princeton, NJ: Princeton University Press, 1993.

Jarcho, Saul. *Italian Broadsides Concerning Public Health: Documents from Bologna and Brescia in the Mortimer and Anna Neinken Collection.* Mount Kisko: Futura, 1986.

Jean Fernel's On the Hidden Causes of Things: *Forms, Souls, and Occult Diseases in Renaissance Medicine.* Edited by John M. Forrester. Leiden: Brill, 2005.

Jonson, Ben. *Ben Jonson.* Edited by C. H. Herford, Percy Simpson, and Evelyn Simpson. 11 vols. Oxford: Clarendon Press, 1947.

Langland, William. *Piers Plowman.* Edited by Elizabeth Robertson and Stephen H. A. Shepherd. (Norton Critical Edition). New York: Norton, 2006.

Le Bédoyère, Guy de, ed. *Particular Friends: The Correspondence of Samuel Pepys and John Evelyn.* Woodbridge: Boydell Press, 1997.

Legani, E. S. "Cinque lettere inedited sulla peste di Milano del 1630." *La Rassegna della literatura italiana* 2–3 (1964): 399–409.

Le Muisit, Gilles. *Chronique et annales de Gilles Le Muisit.* Edited by Henri Lemaître. Paris: Libraire Renouard, 1905.

Littré, E. "Opuscule relatif a la peste de 1348." *Bibliotheque de l'Ecole des Chartes* 2 (1840–41): 201–243.

Luther, Martin. "Whether One May Flee from a Deadly Plague," in *Luther's Works*, Vol. 43, edited and translated by G. K. Wienke (Philadelphia: Fortress Press, 1968), 115–138.

Manzoni, Alessandro. *The Betrothed.* Translated by Bruce Penman. New York: Penguin, 1972.

Marcus, Jacob R. *The Jew in the Medieval World: A Source Book: 315–1791.* New York: Atheneum, 1979.

Mead, Matthew. *Solomon's prescription for the removal of the pestilence, or, The discovery of the plague of our hearts.* London, 1666. Digital Book Index.

Mead, Richard. See Digital Book Library

Milbourn, Thomas. *The mourning-cross, or, England's Lord have mercy upon us: containing the certain causes of pestilential disease.* London, 1665. Digital Book Index.

Mondino dei Luzzi. *Anathomia (1316)*. Trans by Charles Singer. In Johannes Ketham, *Fasciculo di Medicina*, Monumenta Medica, II. Florence: R. Lier & Co., 1925.

Moulton, Thomas. "Plague Remedy" (1531). See Totaro.

M. R. *The meanes of preventing, and preserving from, and curing of that most contagious disease called the plague*. London, 1665. Digital Book Index.

Mylius, Andreas. *De testamento tempore pestis condito =: von dem Testament, so zur Zeit der Pest auffgerichtet wird . . .* Leipzig, 1680. Digital Book Index.

Nati, Pietro. *Modo facile et ispedito da conservarsi sano ne tempi pericolo si della pestilenza: con altri trattati*. Florence, 1576. Digital Book Index.

Nicholson, Watson. *Historical Sources of De Foe's Journal of the Plague Year*. Boston: The Stratford Co., 1919.

O'Hara-May, Jane. *Elizabethan Dyetary of Health*. Lawrence, KS: Coronado Press, 1977.

L'Ordre Pvblic povr La Ville de Lyon, pendant la Maladie Contagieufe . . . Augmente . . . d'un Traitte de la Peste. 1670. Digital Book Index.

Parets, Miquel. *A Journal of the Plague Year: The Diary of the Barcelona Tanner Miquel Parets, 1651*. Translated by James S. Amelang. New York: Oxford University Press, 1995.

Pepys, Samuel. *The Diary of Samuel Pepys*. Edited by Robert Latham and William Matthews. 11 vols. Berkeley: University of California Press, 2000. Also Digital Book Index.

Pestblatt. Augsburg 1473. Digital Book Index.

Pistoia City Council (*Aziani*), 1348. "Ordinances for Sanitation in a Time of Mortality (selections)." Internet Medieval Sourcebook: http://www.fordham.edu/halsall/med/pistoia.html.

Robertson, Elizabeth and Stephen H. A. Shepherd, eds. *William Langland: Piers Plowman*. New York: Norton, 2006.

Rosewell, Thomas. *The causes & cure of the pestilence, or, A brief collection of those provoking sins recorded in the Holy Scriptures*. London 1665. Digital Book Index.

Scott, John. *Narratives of two families exposed to the great plague of London, 1665, w/conversations on religious preparations*. 1832. Also http://books.google.com/books?id=yllhAAAAIAAJ&printsec=frontcover&dq=plague&lr=&cd=168#v=onepage&q&f=false.

Shirley, Janet, translator. *A Parisian Journal, 1405–1449*. Oxford: Clarendon Press, 1968; (Beaune, C. ed. *Journal d'un bourgeois de Paris, de 1405 à 1449*. Paris: Livres de Poche, 1990.)

Steinhowel, Heinrich. *Buchlein der Ordnung (Pest Regiment)*. Ulm, 1482. Digital Book Index.

Totaro, Rebecca. *The Plague in Print: Essential Elizabethan Sources, 1558–1603*. Pittsburgh: Duquesne University Press, 2010.

Vesalius, Andreas. *On the Fabric of the Human Body*. 5 volumes. Translated by William Frank Richardson. Novato, CA: Norman Publishing, 2003–2009.

Voigts, Linda E. and Michael R. McVaugh. *A Latin Technical Phlebotomy and Its Middle English Translation*. Philadelphia: American Philosophical Society, 1984.

Wallis, Faith, editor. *Medieval Medicine: A Reader*. Toronto: University of Toronto Press, 2010.

Wither, George. *Britain's Remembrancer*. Breinigsville, PA: Duey Press, 2007.

Wither. *The History of the Pestilence (1625)*. Edited by J. Milton French. Cambridge, MA: Harvard University Press, 1932. Also Digital Book Index, in 2 vols.

Witherley, Thomas (Sir). We who are appointed the physicians for the prevention and cure of the plague, as we implore divine assistance 1665 London: W. J. *A collection of seven and fifty approved receipts good against the plague: taken out of the five books* ... London, 1665. Digital Book Index.

Wu, Lien Te, *et al. Plague: A Manual for Medical and Public Health Workers.* Shanghai: National Quarantine Service, 1936.

Wujastyk, Dominik. *The Roots of Ayurveda.* New York: Penguin Books, 2003.

II. Selected Reference Works

Alexander, Martin, et al., editors. *Encyclopedia of Microbiology.* New York: Academic Press, 2000.

Boslaugh, S., editor. *The Encyclopedia of Epidemiology.* London: SAGE Publications, 2007.

Bynum, W. F. and Helen Bynum, editors. *Dictionary of Medical Biography.* 5 vols. Westport, CT: Greenwood, 2006.

Bynum, W. F. and Roy Porter, editors. *Companion Encyclopedia of the History of Medicine.* 2 vols. New York: Routledge, 1993.

Byrne, Joseph P., editor. *Encyclopedia of Pestilence, Pandemics and Plagues.* 2 vols. Westport, CT: Greenwood Press, 2008.

Glick, Thomas, et al., editors. *Medieval Science, Technology, and Medicine: An Encyclopedia.* New York: Routledge, 2005.

Gorbach, Sherwood L., et al. *Infectious Diseases.* Philadelphia: Lippincott, 2003.

Hatfield, Gabrielle. *Encyclopedia of Folk Medicine: Old World and New World Traditions.* Santa Barbara, CA: ABC-CLIO, 2003.

Heggenhougen, Kris, editor-in-chief. *International Encyclopedia of Public Health.* New York: Elsevier, 2008.

Kiple, Kenneth F., editor. *The Cambridge Historical Dictionary of Disease.* New York: Cambridge University Press, 2003.

Kiple, Kenneth F., editor. *The Cambridge World History of Human Disease.* New York: Cambridge University Press, 2001.

Kohn, George C., editor. *Encyclopedia of Plague and Pestilence.* Revised edition. New York: Facts on File, 2001.

Longe, Jacqueline L. *The Gale Encyclopedia of Medicine,* 5 vols. Stamford, CT: Gale, 2006.

Rashid, Roshdi, editor. *Encyclopedia of the History of Arabic Science.* 3 vols. New York: Routledge, 1996.

Snodgrass, Mary Ellen. *World Epidemics.* Jefferson, NC: McFarlane, 2003.

Vauchez, Andre. *Encyclopedia of the Middle Ages.* New York: Routledge, 2001.

III. Selected Recent Doctoral Dissertations

Bamji, Alexandra. "Religion and Disease in Venice, c. 1620–1700." Ph.D. dissertation, Cambridge University, 2007.

Birkelbach, Karl. "Plague Debate: An Historiographical Analysis of the Retrospective Diagnosis of the Black Death." Ph.D. dissertation, University of Western Australia, 2010.

Boeckl, Christine Maria. "Baroque Plague Imagery and Tridentine Church Reforms." Ph.D. dissertation, University of Maryland, 1990.

Bowers, Kirsty Wilson. "Plague, Politics and Municipal Relations in Sixteenth-Century Seville." Ph.D. dissertation, Indiana University, 2001.

Caudill, Helen Sue. "Plague as a Force in Jacobean Tragedy." Ph.D. dissertation, University of Pittsburgh, 1988.

Clifton, James. "Images of the Plague and Other Contemporary Events of Seventeenth-Century Naples." Ph.D. dissertation, Princeton University, 1987.

Conrad, Lawrence I. "The Plague in the Early Medieval Near East." Ph.D. dissertation, Princeton University, 1981.

Fabbri, Christiane. "Continuity and Change in Late Medieval Plague Medicine: A Survey of 152 Plague Tracts from 1348 to 1599." Ph.D. dissertation, Yale University, 2006.

Goodman, Ailene Sybil. "Explorations of a Baroque Motif: The Plague in Selected Seventeenth-century English and German Literature." Ph.D. dissertation, University of Maryland, 1981.

Heidkamp, Erin E. "A Local Community of 'Locals:' Cistercians of Altenberg Abbey, 1133–1539." Ph.D. dissertation, University of Connecticut, 2009.

Jenks, Stuart. "The Black Death and Würzburg: Michael de Leone's Reaction in Context." Ph.D. dissertation, Yale University, 1977.

Jordan, Louis Edward. "The Iconography of Death in Western Medieval Art to 1350." Ph.D. dissertation, Notre Dame, 1980.

Kawash, Sabri K. "Ibn Hajar al-Asqalani (1372–1449): A Study of the Background, Education and Career of a 'Alim in Egypt." Ph.D. dissertation, Princeton University, 1969.

Laughran, Michelle Anne. "The Body, Public Health, and Social Control in Sixteenth-Century Venice." Ph.D. dissertation, University of Connecticut, 1998.

Marshall, Louise J. "Waiting on the Will of the Lord: The Images of the Plague." Ph.D. dissertation, University of Pennsylvania, 1989.

Palazzotto, Dominick. "The Black Death and Medicine: A Report and Analysis of the Tractates Written between 1348 and 1350." Ph.D. dissertation, University of Kansas, 1974.

Palmer, Richard J. "The Control of Plague in Venice and Northern Italy, 1348–1600." Ph.D. dissertation, University of Kent at Canterbury (UK), 1978.

Phillips, Patrick. "'Fleshes Rage': Ben Jonson and the Plague." Ph.D. dissertation, New York University, 2006.

Stevens, Jane. "The Lazaretti of Venice, Verona and Padua (1520–1580)." Ph.D. dissertation, Cambridge University, 2007.

Stieve, Edwin M. "Medical and Moral Interpretations of Plague in Middle English Literature." Ph.D. dissertation, Michigan State University, 1988.

Varlik, Nükhet. "Disease and Empire: A History of Plague and Epidemics in the Early Ottoman Empire (1453–1600)." Ph.D. dissertation, University of Chicago, 2008.

Vaslef, Irene. "The Role of St. Roch as a Plague Saint: A Late Medieval Hagiographic Tradition." Ph.D. dissertation, Catholic University of America, 1984.

Whitley, A. "Concepts of Ill Health and Pestilence in Fifteenth-century Siena." Ph.D. dissertation, University of London, 2004.

York, William Harry. "Experience and Theory in Medical Practice during the Later Middle Ages: Velasco de Tarenta (fl. 1382–1426) at the Court of Foix." Ph.D. dissertation, Johns Hopkins University, 2003.

IV. Secondary Sources: Books and Articles in English (Primarily)

Aberth, John. "The Black Death in the Diocese of Ely: The Evidence of the Bishop's Register." *Journal of Medieval History* 21 (1995): 275–287.

Aberth, John. *From the Brink of the Apocalypse: Crisis and Recovery in Late Medieval England.* New York: Routledge, 2000.

Aberth, John. *Plagues in World History.* New York: Rowman and Littlefield, 2011.

Abu-Lughod, Janet L. *Cairo: 1001 Years of the "City Victorious."* Princeton, NJ: Princeton University Press, 1971.

Achtman, Mark, et al. "Microevolution and History of the Plague Bacillus, *Yersinia pestis.*" *Proceedings of the National Academy of Sciences of the USA* 101 (2004): 17,837–17,842.

Aers, David. "Justice and Wage-labor after the Black Death: Some Perplexities for

William Langland," in *The Work of Work: Servitude, Slavery, and Labor in Medieval England*, edited by Allen J. Frantzen and Douglas Moffat (Glasgow: Cruithne Press, 1994), 169–190.

Agrimi, Joel and Chiara Cristiani. *Les consilia médicaux*. Turnhout: Brepols, 1994.

Alexander, John T. *Bubonic Plague in Early Modern Russia: Public Health and Urban Disaster*. Baltimore, MD: Johns Hopkins University Press, 1980.

Alexander, John. "Ivan Vien and the First Comprehensive Plague Tractate in Russian." *Medical History* 24 (1980): 419–431.

Alexander, John T. "Catherine II, Bubonic Plague and the Problem of Industry in Moscow." *American Historical Review* 79 (1974): 637–671.

Al-Harithy, Howyda N. "The Complex of Sultan Hasan in Cairo: Reading between the Lines." *Muqarnas* 13 (1996): 68–79.

Allen, Peter Lewis. *The Wages of Sin: Sex and Disease, Past and Present*. Chicago: University of Chicago Press, 2000.

Allmand, C. T. *The Hundred Years War: England and France at War*. New York: Cambridge University Press, 1988.

Amasuno Sárraga, Marcelino V. *La peste en la corona de Castilla durante la segunda mitad del siglo XIV*. Valladolid: Junta de Castilla y León, Consejería de Educación y Cultura, 1996.

Anselment, Raymond, *The Realms of Apollo. Literature and Healing in Seventeenth-Century England*, Newark: University of Delaware Press and Associated University Presses, 1995.

Appleby, A. B. "The Disappearance of the Plague: A Continuing Puzzle." *Economic History Review* 33 (1980): 161–173.

Arikha, Noga. *Passions and Tempers. A History of the Humours*. New York: Ecco, 2007.

Arrizabalaga, Jon. "Facing the Black Death: Perceptions and Reactions of University Medical Practitioners," in *Practical Medicine from Salerno to the Black Death*, edited by Luis Garcia-Ballester, et al. (New York: Cambridge University Press, 1994): 237–288.

Ashtor, Eliyahu. *A Social and Economic History of the Near East in the Middle Ages*. Berkeley: University of California Press, 1976.

Avery, Harold. "Plague Churches, Monuments and Memorials." *Proceedings of the Royal Society of Medicine* 59 (1966): 110–116.

Bailey, Gauvin Alexander, et al., eds. *Hope and Healing: Painting in Italy in a Time of Plague, 1500–1800*. Chicago: University of Chicago Press, 2005.

Baldwin, Martha. "Toads and Plague: Amulet Therapy in Seventeenth-century Medicine." *Bulletin of the History of Medicine* 67 (1993): 227–247.

Banker, James R. *Death and the Community: Memorialization and Confraternities in an Italian Commune in the Late Middle Ages*. Athens: University of Georgia Press, 1988.

Barkai, Ron. "Jewish Treatises on the Black Death (1350–1500): A Preliminary Study," in *Practical Medicine from Salerno to the Black Death*, edited by Luis Garcia-Ballester et al. (New York: Cambridge University Press, 1994), 6–25.

Barroll, John Leeds. *Politics, Plague, and Shakespeare's Theater: The Stuart years*. Ithaca: Cornell University Press, 1991.

Barron, Caroline. *London in the Later Middle Ages: Government and People, 1200–1500*. New York: Oxford University Press, 2004.

Bavel, Bas van. *Manors and Markets: Economy and Society in the Low Countries, 500–1600*. New York: Oxford University Press, 2010.

Bayliss, J. H. "The Extinction of Bubonic Plague in Britain." *Endeavour* 4 (1980): 58–66.

Beaty, Nancy Lee. *The Craft of Dying: A Study in the Literary Tradition of the 'Ars Moriendi' in England*. New Haven, CT: Yale University Press, 1970.

Beidler, Peter G. "The Plague and Chaucer's Pardoner." *Chaucer Review* 16 (1982): 257–269.

Beier, Lucinda McCray. "The Good Death in Seventeenth-century England," in *Death, Ritual, and Bereavement*, edited by Ralph Houlbrooke (London: Routledge, 1989), 43–61.

Bell, Walter George. *The Great Plague in London in 1665*. New York: AMS Press, 1976.

Bendiner, Elmer. "Alexander Yersin: Pursuer of Plague." *Hospital Practice* (March 30, 1989): 121–148.

Benedict, Carol. *Bubonic Plague in Nineteenth-century China*. Stanford: Stanford University Press, 1996.

Benedictow, Ole. *The Black Death 1346–1353: The Complete History*. Rochester, NY: Boydell & Brewer, 2004.

Benedictow, Ole J. *What Disease Was Plague? On the Controversy over the Microbiological Identity of Plague Epidemics of the Past*. Boston: Brill, 2010.

Benedictow, Ole J. *Plague in the Late Medieval Nordic Countries: Epidemiological Studies*. Oslo: Middelalderforlaget, 1992.

Beresford, Maurice and John Hulst. *Deserted Medieval Villages*. London: Lutterworth Press, 1971.

Bergdolt, Klaus. *Der Schwarze Tod in Europa: Die grosse Pest und das Ende des Mittelalters*. Munich: C. H. Beck, 1994.

Berry, H. "A London Plague Bill for 1592, Crich and Goodwyfe Hurde." *English Literary Renaissance* 25 (1995): 3–25.

Biow, Douglas. *Doctors, Ambassadors, Secretaries: Humanism and Professions in Renaissance Italy*. Chicago: University of Chicago Press, 2002.

Biow, Douglas. "The Politics of Cleanliness in Northern Renaissance Italy." *Symposium* 50 (1996): 75–86.

Biraben, Jean-Noel. *Les hommes et la peste en France et dans les pays europeens et mediteraneens*. 2 vols. Paris: Mouton, 1975, 1976.

Bisgaard, Lars and Leif Søndergaard, eds. *Living with the Black Death*. Odense: University of Southern Denmark Press, 2009.

Boeckl, Christine. *Images of Plague and Pestilence: Iconography and Iconology*. Kirksville, MO: Truman State University Press, 2000.

Boring, William C. "William Bullein's *Dialogue against the Fever Pestilence*." *The Nassau Review* 2 (1974): 33–42.

Borodi, N. K. "The Quarantine Service and Anti-epidemic Measures in the Ukraine in the Eighteenth Century." *Soviet Studies in History* 25 (1987): 24–32.

Borsch, Stuart. *The Black Death in Egypt and England*. Austin: University of Texas Press, 2005.

Boss, Sarah Jane, ed. *Mary: The Complete Resource*. New York: Oxford University Press, 2007.

Bower, Rick. "Antidote to the Plague: Dekker's Storytelling in *The Wonderful Year* (1603)." *English Studies* 73 (1992): 229–239.

Bowers, Kristy Wilson. "Balancing Individual and Communal Needs: Plague and Public Health in Early Modern Seville." *Bulletin of the History of Medicine* 81 (2007): 335–358.

Bowsky, William. "The Impact of the Black Death upon Sienese Government and Society." *Speculum* 39 (1964): 368–381.

Bowsky, William. "The Medieval Commune and Internal Violence: Police Power and Public Safety in Siena, 1287–1355." *The American Historical Review* 73 (1967): 1–17.

Boyar, Ebru and Kate Fleet. *A Social History of Ottoman Istanbul*. New York: Cambridge University Press, 2010.

Bray, R. S. *Armies of Pestilence: The Effects of Pandemics on History*. Cambridge: Lutterworth Press, 1998.

Britnell, R. H. "The Black Death in English Towns." *Urban History* 21 (1994): 195–210.

Brock, Thomas D. *Robert Koch: A Life in Medicine and Bacteriology.* Washington, DC: AMS Press, 1999.

Brockliss, Laurence and Colin Jones. *The Medical World of Early Modern France.* New York: Oxford University Press, 1997.

Bühler, C. F. "Lydgate's Rules of Health." *Medium Aevum* 3 (1934): 51–56.

Bühler, C. F. "Prayers and Charms in Certain Middle English Scrolls." *Speculum* 39 (1964): 270–278.

Bullough, Vern L. *Universities, Medicine and Science in the Medieval West.* Burlington, VT: Ashgate, 2004.

Butcher, A. F. "English Urban Society and the Revolt of 1381," in *The English Uprising of 1381*, edited by R. H. Hilton and T. H. Aston (New York: Cambridge University Press, 1984), 84–111.

Butler, Thomas C. *Plague and Other Yersinia Infections.* New York: Plenum Medical Book Co., 1983.

Bylebyl, Jerome L. "Medicine, Philosophy, and Humanism in the Italian Renaissance," in *Science and the Arts in the Renaissance*, edited by John Shirley and F. David Hoeniger (Washington, DC: Folger Shakespeare Library, 1985), 27–49.

Bylebyl, Jerome L. "The School of Padua: Humanistic Medicine in the Sixteenth Century," in *Health, Medicine, and Morality*, edited by Charles Webster (New York: Cambridge University Press, 1979), 335–370.

Byrne, Joseph P. *The Black Death.* Westport, CT.: Greenwood Press, 2004.

Byrne, Joseph P. *Daily Life during the Black Death.* Westport, CT: Greenwood, 2006.

Caldin, W. and H. Raine. "The Plague of 1625 and the Story of John Boston, Parish Clerk of St. Saviours, Southwark." *Transactions of the London and Middlesex Archaeological Society* 23 (1971): 90–99.

Calvi, Giulia. *Histories of a Plague Year: The Social and the Imaginary in Baroque Florence.* Berkeley: University of California Press, 1989.

Camille, Michael. *Master of Death.* New Haven, CT: Yale University Press, 1996.

Campbell, Anna Montgomery. *The Black Death and Men of Learning.* New York: Columbia University Press, 1931.

Camporesi, Piero. *The Fear of Hell.* University Park, PA: Penn State University Press, 1990.

Cantor, Norman. *In the Wake of the Plague.* New York: Free Press, 2000.

Capp, Bernard. *Astrology and the Popular Press: English Almanacs, 1500–1800.* Boston: Faber and Faber, 1979.

Caraman, R. P. *Henry Morse: Priest of the Plague.* London: Longmans, Green and Co., 1957.

Carlin, Claire, ed. *Imagining Contagion in Early Modern Europe.* New York: Palgrave Macmillan, 2005.

Carlino, Andrea. *Books of the Body: Anatomical Ritual and Renaissance Learning.* Trans. by John and Ann C. Tedeschi. Chicago: University of Chicago Press, 1999.

Carmichael, Ann G. "Plague Legislation in the Italian Renaissance." *Bulletin of the History of Medicine* 57 (1983): 508–525.

Carmichael, Ann G. *Plague and the Poor in Renaissance Florence.* New York: Cambridge University Press, 1986.

Carmichael, Ann G. "The Health Status of Florentines in the Fifteenth Century," in *Life and Death in Fifteenth Century Florence*, edited by Marcel Tetel, et al. (Durham, NC: Duke University Press, 1989), 28–45.

Carmichael, Ann G. "Contagion Theory and Contagion Practice in Fifteenth-century Milan." *Renaissance Quarterly* 44 (1991): 213–256.

Carpentier, Elisabeth. *Une ville devant la peste: Orvieto et la Peste Noire de 1348.* Paris: S.E.V.P.E.N., 1962.

Cazes, Hélène. "Apples and Moustaches: Montaigne's Grin in the Face of Infection," in *Imagining Contagion in Early Modern Europe*, edited by Claire L. Carlin (New York: Palgrave Macmillan, 2005), 79–93.

Champion, Justin A. I., ed. *Epidemic Disease in London*. London: Centre for Metropolitan History Working Papers Series 1, 1993.

Champion, Justin A. I. *London's Dreaded Visitation: The Social Geography of the Great Plague in 1665*. London: Historical Geography Research Paper Series 31, 1995.

Chase, Marilyn. *The Barbary Plague: The Black Death in Victorian San Francisco*. New York: Random House, 2003.

Chase, Melissa P. "Fevers, Poisons and Apostemes: Authority and Experience in Montpellier Plague Treatises," in *Science and Technology in Medieval Society*, edited by Pamela Long (New York: New York Academy of Sciences, 1985), 153–169.

Christakos, George, et al. *Interdisciplinary Public Health Reasoning and Epistemic Modeling: The Case of the Black Death*. New York: Springer, 2005.

Christensen, Daniel. *Politics and the Plague in Early Modern Germany: Political Efforts to Combat Epidemics in the Duchy of Braunschweig-Wolffenbüttel during the Seventeenth Century*. Saarbrücken: Verlag Müller, 2008.

Christensen, Peter. ""In these perilous times:" Plague and Plague Policies in Early Modern Denmark." *Medical History* 47 (2003): 413–450.

Cipolla, Carlo. *Cristofano and the Plague: A Study in the History of Public Health in the Age of Galileo*. Berkeley: University of California Press, 1973.

Cipolla, Carlo. "The Plague and Pre-Malthus Malthusians." *Journal of Economic History* 3 (1974): 277–284.

Cipolla, Carlo M. "The 'Bills of Mortality' of Florence." *Population Studies* 32 (1978): 541–548.

Cipolla, Carlo. *Faith, Reason, and the Plague in Seventeenth-Century Tuscany*. New York: W. W. Norton & Company, 1981.

Cipolla, Carlo. *Fighting the Plague in Seventeenth-Century Italy*. Madison: University of Wisconsin Press, 1981.

Cipolla, Carlo. *Miasmas and Disease: Public Health and the Environment in the Pre-industrial Age*. Trans. by Elizabeth Potter. New Haven, CT: Yale University Press, 1992.

Cipolla, Carlo. *Public Health and the Medical Profession in Renaissance Florence*. New York: Cambridge University Press, 1976.

Clifton, James. "Art and Plague in Naples," in *Hope and Healing: Painting in Italy in a Time of Plague, 1500–1800*, edited by Gauvin Alexander Bailey (Chicago: University of Chicago Press, 2005), 97–117.

Closson, Marianne. "The Devil's Curse: The Demonic Origin of Disease in the Sixteenth and Seventeenth Centuries," in *Contagion in Early Modern Europe*, edited by Claire L. Carlin (New York: Palgrave Macmillan, 2005), 63–76.

Cohen, Kathleen. *Metamorphosis of a Death Symbol: The Transi Tomb in the Late Middle Ages and the Renaissance*. Berkeley: University of California Press, 1973.

Cohn, Norman. *The Pursuit of the Millennium*. New York: Oxford University Press, 1990.

Cohn, Samuel K. "The Black Death and the Burning of Jews." *Past & Present* 196 (2007): 3–36.

Cohn, Samuel K. *The Black Death Transformed: Disease and Culture in Early Renaissance Europe*. New York: Oxford University Press, 2002.

Cohn, Samuel K. *The Cult of Remembrance and the Black Death*. Baltimore, MD: Johns Hopkins University Press, 1992.

Cohn, Samuel K. *Cultures of Plague: Medical Thinking at the End of the Renaissance*. New York: Oxford University Press, 2010.

Cohn, Samuel K. "Last Wills: Family, Women and the Black Death," in his *Women in the Streets: Essays on Sex and Power in Renaissance Italy* (Baltimore, MD: Johns Hopkins University Press, 1996), 39–56.

Cohn, Samuel K. *Lust for Liberty: The Politics of Social Revolt in Medieval Europe, 1200–1425.* Cambridge, MA: Harvard University Press, 2006.

Cohn, Samuel K. "Popular Insurrections and the Black Death; a Comparative View." *Past and Present* 195 (2007): 188–204.

Collinson, Patrick. *Archbishop Grindal, 1519–1583. The Struggle for a Reformed Church.* Berkeley: University of California, 1979.

Concannon, R. J. G. "The Third Enemy: The Role of Epidemics in the Thirty Years War." *Journal of World History* 10 (1967): 500–511.

Conrad, Laurence I. "Epidemic Disease in Formal and Popular Thought in Early Islamic Society," in *Epidemics and Ideas*, ed. by Ranger and Slack (Cambridge: Cambridge University Press, 1992), 77–99.

Conrad, Laurence I. "*Ta'un* and *waba*: Conceptions of Plague and Pestilence in Early Islam." *Journal of the Economic and Social History of the Orient* 25 (1982): 268–307.

Conrad, Lawrence I. "Umar at Sargh: The Evolution of an Umayyad Tradition on Flight from the Plague," in *Story-Telling in the Framework of Non-fictional Arabic Literature*, edited by S. Leder (Wiesbaden: Harrassowitz, 1998), 488–528.

Conrad, Laurence I., and Dominik Wujastyk, eds. *Contagion: Perspectives from Pre-Modern Societies.* Aldershot: Ashgate, 2000.

Cook, Alexandra Parma and Noble David Cook. *The Plague Files: Crisis Management in Sixteenth-Century Seville.* Baton Rouge: University of Louisiana Press, 2009.

Coulton, G. G. *The Black Death.* London: Ernest Benn Ltd., 1929.

Crawford, Edward A. "Paul-Louis Simond and His Work on Plague." *Perspectives in Biology and Medicine* 39 (1996): 446–458.

Crawfurd, Raymond. *The Plague and Pestilence in Literature and Art.* Oxford: Clarendon Press, 1914.

Creighton, Charles. *A History of Epidemics in Britain.* 2 vols. 2nd ed. London: Cass, 1965.

Crisciani, Chiara. "Black Death and Golden Remedies: Some Remarks on Alchemy and the Plague," in *The Regulation of Evil*, edited by Agostino Paravicini Bagliani and Francesco Santi (Sismel: Galluzzo, 1998), 7–39.

Cunningham, Andrew and Ole Peter Grell. *The Four Horsemen of the Apocalypse: Religion, War, Famine and Death in Reformation Europe.* New York: Cambridge University Press, 2000.

Curth, Louise Hill. *English Almanacs, Astrology and Popular Medicine, 1500–1700.* New York: Manchester University Press, 2007.

Curth, Louise Hill. "The Medical Content of English Almanacs, 1640–1700." *Journal of the History of Medicine and Allied Sciences* 60 (2005): 255–282.

Cust, R. P. "News and Politics in Seventeenth-Century England." *Past and Present* 112 (1986): 60–90.

Dale, Sharon, et al. *Chronicling History: Chronicles and Historians in Medieval and Renaissance Italy.* State College, PA: Penn State University Press, 2007.

Daniell, Christopher. *Death and Burial in Medieval England.* New York: Routledge, 1997.

Davies, R. H. "The Effect of the Black Death on the Parish Priests of the Medieval Diocese of Coventry and Lichfield." *Bulletin of the Institute of Historical Research* 62 (1989): 85–90.

Davis, David. "The Scarcity of Rats and the Black Death: An Ecological History." *Journal of Interdisciplinary History* 16 (1986): 455–470.

Debré, Patrice. *Louis Pasteur.* Translated by Elborg Forster. Baltimore, MD: Johns Hopkins University Press, 1998.

Delumeau, Jean. *Sin and Fear: The Emergence of a Western Guilt Culture 13th–18th Centuries.* Translated by Eric Nicholson. New York: St. Martin's Press, 1990.

Demaitre, Luke. "Theory and Practice in Medical Education at the University of Montpellier in the Thirteenth and Fourteenth Centuries." *Journal of the History of Medicine and Allied Sciences* 30 (1975): 103–123.

Descatoire, Christine, ed. *Treasures of the Black Death.* London: The Wallace Collection, 2009.

Dewhurst, Kenneth. *Dr. Thomas Sydenham (1625–1689), His Life and Original Writings.* Berkeley: University of California Press, 1966.

Dobson, Mary. *A Chronology of Epidemic Disease and Mortality in Southeast England, 1601–1800.* H.G.R.G. series # 19. London: Historical Geography Research Group, 1990.

Dobson, Mary. *Contours of Death and Disease in Early Modern England.* New York: Cambridge University Press, 1997.

Dodds, Ben and Richard Britnell. *Agriculture and Rural Society after the Black Death: Common Themes and Regional Variations.* Hatfield, Herts, UK: University of Hertfordshire Press, 2008.

Dohar, William J. *The Black Death and Pastoral Leadership: The Diocese of Hereford in the Fourteenth Century.* Philadelphia: University of Pennsylvania Press, 1995.

Dolgova, S. R. "Notes of an Eyewitness of the Plague Riot in Moscow in 1771." *Soviet Studies in History* 25 (1987): 79–90.

Dols, Michael W. *The Black Death in the Middle East.* Princeton, NJ: Princeton University Press, 1977.

Dols, Michael W. "The General Mortality of the Black Death in the Mamluk Empire," in *The Islamic Middle East, 700–1900: Studies in Social and Economic History,* edited by Abraham Udovitch (Princeton, NJ: Princeton University Press, 1981), 404–411.

Donohue, Patricia. *Nursing, The Finest Art.* New York: Mosby, 2010.

Drancourt, Michel and Didier Raoult. "Cause of Black Death." *Lancet: Infectious Diseases* 2 (2002): 459.

Drancourt, Michel and Didier Raoult. "Detection of 400-year-old *Yersinia pestis* DNA in human dental pulp: An approach to the diagnosis of ancient septicemia." *Proceedings of the National Academy of Sciences* 95 (Oct. 27, 1998): 12637.

Drancourt, Michel, et al. "*Yersinia pestis* as a Telluric, Human Ectoparasite-borne Organism." *Lancet: Infectious Diseases* 6 (2006): 234–241.

Dunn, Alastair. *The Great Rising of 1381: The Peasants' Revolt and England's Failed Revolution.* Stroud, Gloucs., UK: Tempus, 2004.

Echenberg, Myron. *Plague Ports: The Global Urban Impact of Bubonic Plague, 1894–1901.* New York: New York University Press, 2007.

Eckert, Edward A. *The Structure of Plagues and Pestilences in Early Modern Europe: Central Europe, 1560–1640.* New York: S. Karger Publishing, 1996.

Eckert, Edward A. "The Retreat of Plague from Central Europe, 1640–1720: A Geomedical Approach." *Bulletin of the History of Medicine* 74 (2000): 1–28.

Editorial. "No Need for Panic about AIDS. Acquired Immune Deficiency Disease, Now Frequent Among Male Homosexuals in the United States, Is Not This Century's Black Death. The Most Urgent Need is to Understand What Is Going On." *Nature* 302 (April 28, 1983): 749.

Ehrenkranz, N. Joel and Deborah Sampson. "Origins of the Old Testament Plagues." *Yale Journal of Biology and Medicine* 81 (2008): 31–42.

Ehrenreich, Barbara and Deirdre English. *Witches, Midwives and Nurses: A History of Women Healers*. New York: The Feminist Press at CUNY, 2010.

Eichenberg, Fritz. *The Dance of Death: A Graphic Commentary on the Danse Macabre through the Centuries*. New York: Abbeville Press, 1983.

Eisen, R. J., et al. "Early-Phase Transmission of *Yersinia pestis* by Unblocked Fleas as a Mechanism Explaining Rapidly Spreading Plague Epizootics." *Proceedings of the National Academy of Sciences of the USA* 103 (2006): 15380–15385.

Eisenstein, Elizabeth L. *The Printing Revolution in Early Modern Europe*. New edition. New York: Cambridge University Press, 2005.

Elmer, Peter and Ole Peter Grell. *Health, Disease and Society in Europe, 1500–1800*. New York: Manchester University Press, 2004.

Esser, Thilo. *Pest, Heilsangst, und Frömmigkeit: Studien zur religiösen Bewältigung der Pest am Ausgang des Mittelalters*. Altenberge: Oros, 1999.

Evans, R. G. *John Wyclif: Myth and Reality*. Downers Grove, IL: IVP, 2006.

Fenlon, Iain. *The Ceremonial City: History, Memory, and Myth in Renaissance Venice*. New Haven, CT: Yale University Press, 2007.

Findlen, Paula, ed. *Athanasius Kircher: The Last Man Who Knew Everything*. New York: Routledge, 2006.

Foa, Anna. *The Jews of Europe after the Black Death*. Berkeley: University of California, 2000.

Forbes, T. R. *Chronicle from Aldgate: Life and Death in Shakespeare's London*. New Haven, CT: Yale University Press, 1971.

Frandsen, Karl-Erik. *The Last Plagues in the Baltic Region, 1709–1713*. Copenhagen: Museum Tusculanum Press, 2010.

French, Katherine L. *The Good Women of the Parish: Gender and Religion after the Black Death*. Philadelphia: University of Pennsylvania Press, 2008.

French, Roger. *Dissection and Vivisection in the European Renaissance*. Burlington, VT: Ashgate, 1999.

French, Roger. *Canonical Medicine: Gentile da Foligno and Scholasticism*. Boston: Brill, 2001.

French, Roger. *Medicine before Science: The Business of Medicine from the Middle Ages to the Enlightenment*. New York: Cambridge University Press, 2003.

French, Roger K. and Andrew Wear, eds. *The Medical Revolution of the Seventeenth Century*. New York: Cambridge University Press, 1989.

Friedman, John B. "'He hath a thousand slayn this pestilence': Iconography of the Plague in the Late Middle Ages," in *Social Unrest in the Late Middle Ages*, edited by Francis X. Newman (Binghamton, NY: Medieval and Renaissance Texts and Studies, 1986), 75–112.

Gage, Kenneth and Michael Kosoy. "Natural History of Plague: Perspectives from More than a Century of Research." *Annual Review of Entomology* 50 (Jan. 2005): 505–528.

Gallagher, Nancy Elizabeth. *Medicine and Power in Tunisia, 1780–1900*. New York: Cambridge University Press, 1983.

Gambaccini, Piero. *Mountebanks and Medicasters: A History of Charlatans from the Middle Ages to the Present*. Jefferson, NC: McFarland and Co., 2004.

Gamsu, Mark. "The Epidemic of Pneumonic Plague in Manchuria 1910–1911." *Past & Present* 190 (2006): 147–183.

Gani, Raymond and Steve Leach. "Epidemiologic Determinants for Modeling Pneumonic Plague Outbreaks." *Emerging Infectious Diseases* 10 (2004): 608–614.

García-Ballester, Luís, and Samuel Kottek. *Medicine and Medical Ethics in Medieval and Early Modern Spain: An Intellectual Approach*. Jerusalem: Magnes Press, 1996.

Geison, Gerald L. *The Private Science of Louis Pasteur*. Princeton, NJ: Princeton University Press, 1995.

Gelpi, A. P. "Saint Sebastian and the Black Death." *Vesalius* 4 (1998): 23–30.

Geltner, Guy. *The Medieval Prison: A Social History*. Princeton, NJ: Princeton University Press, 2008.

Gentilcore, David. *Healers and Healing in Early Modern Europe*. New York: Manchester University Press, 2003.

Gentilcore, David. *Medical Charlatanism in Early Modern Italy*. New York: Oxford University Press, 2006.

Gertsman, Elina. *The Dance of Death in the Middle Ages*. Turnhout: Brepols, 2011.

Getz, Faye Marie. "Black Death and the Silver Lining: Meaning, Continuity, and Revolutionary Change in Histories of Medieval Plague." *Journal of the History of Biology* 24 (1991): 265–289.

Getz, Faye Marie. *Medicine in the English Middle Ages*. Princeton, NJ: Princeton University Press, 1998.

Gilman, Ernest B. *Plague Writing in Early Modern England*. Chicago: University of Chicago Press, 2009.

Gilman, Sander. *Smoke: A Global History of Smoking*. London: Reaktion, 2004.

Ginzburg, Carlo. "Jews, Heretics, Witches," in his *Ecstacies: Deciphering the Witches' Sabbath*, translated by Raymond Rosenthal (New York: Penguin, 1992), 63–86.

Gittings, Clare. *Death, Burial and the Individual in Early Modern England*. London: Croom Helm, 1984.

Godwin, Joscelyn. *Athanasius Kircher: A Renaissance Man and the Search for Lost Knowledge*. New York: Thames and Hudson, 1979.

Goodman, Jordan. *Tobacco in History*. New York: Routledge, 1994.

Gorbach, Sherwood L., et al. *Infectious Diseases*. 3rd edition. New York: Lippincott, Williams & Wilkins, 2004.

Gordon, Bruce and Peter Marshall, eds. *The Place of the Dead: Death and Remembrance in Late Medieval and Early Modern Europe*. New York: Cambridge University Press, 2000.

Gordon, Daniel. "Confrontations with the Plague in Eighteenth-century France," in *Dreadful Visitations*, edited by Alessa Johns (New York: Routledge, 1999), 3–30.

Gottfried, Robert S. *The Black Death: Natural and Human Disaster in Medieval Europe*. New York: The Free Press, 1983.

Gottfried, Robert S. *Epidemic Disease in Fifteenth-Century England: The Medical Response and the Demographic Consequences*. New Brunswick, NJ: Rutgers University Press, 1978.

Gottschall, Dagmar. "Conrad of Megenberg and the Causes of the Plague: A Latin Treatise on the Black Death Composed c. 1350 for the Papal Court in Avignon," in *La vie culturelle et scientifique à la cour des papes d'Avignon*, edited by Jacqueline Hamesse (Turnhout: Brepols, 2006), 319–332.

Gradmann, Christoph and Elborg Forster. *Laboratory Disease: Robert Koch's Medical Bacteriology*. Baltimore, MD: Johns Hopkins University Press, 2009.

Grainger, Ian, et al. *The Black Death Cemetery, East Smithfeld, London*. London: Museum of London, 2008.

Graus, Frantisek. *Pest, Geissler, Judenmorde: Das 14. Jahrhundert als Krisenzeit*. Gottingen: Vandenhoek und Ruprecht, 1987.

Greenberg, S. J. "The "Dreadful Visitation": Public Health and Public Awareness in Seventeenth-century London." *Bulletin of the Medical Library Association* 85 (1997): 391–401.

Gregg, Charles T. *Plague: An Ancient Disease in the Twentieth Century*. Albuquerque: University of New Mexico Press, 1985.

Grell, Ole Peter. "Conflicting Duties: Plague and the Obligations of Early Modern Physicians towards Patients and Commonwealth in England and The Netherlands." *Clio Medica* 24 (1993): 131–152.

Grell, Ole. *Paracelsus: The Man and His Reputation, His Ideas and Their Transformation*. Boston: Brill, 1998.

Grell, Ole Peter and Andrew Cunningham, eds. *Health Care and Poor Relief in Protestant Europe, 1500–1700*. New York: Routledge, 1997.

Grell, Ole Peter, and Andrew Cunningham, eds. *Medicine and the Reformation*. London: Routledge, 1993.

Grell, Ole Peter, Andrew Cunningham and Jon Arrizabalaga. *Centres of Medical Excellence? Medical Travel and Education in Europe, 1500–1789*. Burlington, VT: Ashgate, 2010.

Grell, Ole Peter, Jon Arrizabalaga and Andrew Cunningham, eds. *Health Care and Poor Relief in Counter-Reformation Europe*. New York: Routledge, 1999.

Griffin, J. P. "Venetian Treacle and the Foundation of Medicines Regulation." *British Journal of Clinical Pharmacology* 58 (2004): 317–325.

Grigsby, Bryon Lee. *Pestilence in Medieval and Early Modern English Literature*. New York: Routledge, 2004.

Grmek, Mirko. *Western Medical Thought from Antiquity to the Middle Ages*. Cambridge, MA: Harvard University Press, 1998.

Gross, Ludwik. "How the Plague Bacillus and its Transmission through Fleas Were Discovered: Reminiscences from My Years at the Pasteur Institute in Paris." *Proceedings of the National Academy of Sciences of the United States* 92 (1995): 7609–7611.

Guenée, Bernard. *Between Church and State: The Lives of Four French Prelates in the Late Middle Ages*. Translated by Arthur Goldhammer. Chicago: University of Chicago Press, 1991.

Guerchberg, Sèraphine. "The Controversy over the Alleged Sowers of the Black Death in the Contemporary Treatises on Plague," in *Change in Medieval Society: Europe North of the Alps, 1050–1500*, edited by Sylvia Thrupp (New York: Appleton-Century-Crofts, 1965), 208–224.

Gummer, Benedict. *The Scourging Angel: The Black Death in the British Isles*. New York: Vintage Books, 2010.

Guthke, Karl S. *The Gender of Death: A Cultural History in Art and Literature*. New York: Cambridge University Press, 1999.

Haensch, Stephanie, Rafaella Bianucci, et al. "Distinct Clones of *Yersinia pestis* Caused the Black Death." *Public Library of Science Pathogens* 6 (2010, 10): e1001134 doi:10.1371/journal.ppat.101134.

Hanawalt, Barbara. *Growing Up in Medieval London: The Experience of Childhood in History*. New York: Oxford University Press, 1993.

Harding, Vanessa. "'And one more may be laid there': The Location of Burial in Early Modern London." *London Journal* 14 (1989): 112–129.

Harding, Vanessa. "Burial of the Plague Dead in Early Modern London," in *Epidemic Disease in London*, edited by J. A. I. Champion (London: Centre for Metropolitan History Working Papers Series 1, 1993), 53–64.

Harding, Vanessa. "Whose Body? A Study of Attitudes towards the Dead Body in Early Modern Paris," in *Place of the Dead*, ed. by B. Gordon and P. Marshall (New York: Cambridge University Press, 2000), 170–187.

Harper-Bill, Christopher. "The English Church and English Religion after the Black Death," in *The Black Death in England*, edited by W. M. Ormrod and

P. G. Lindley (Stamford: Paul Watkins, 1996), 79–124.

Harris, Jonathan Gil. *Sick Economies: Drama, Mercantilism and Disease in Shakespeare's England*. Philadelphia: University of Pennsylvania Press, 2004.

Harthan, John P. *Books of Hours*. New York: Random House, 1988.

Harvey, Barbara. *Living and Dying in England, 1100–1540*. Oxford: Oxford University Press, 1993.

Hatcher, John. *The Black Death: A Personal History*. New York: Da Capo, 2008.

Hatcher, John. *Plague, Population, and the English Economy, 1348–1530*. London: Macmillan, 1977.

Hatje, Frank. *Leben und Sterben im Zeitalter der Pest. Basel im 15. bis 17. Jahrhundert*. Basel: Helbing und Lichtenhahn, 1992.

Havercamp, Alfred. "Die Judenverfolgungen zur Zeit des Schwarzen Todes im Gesellschaftsgefüge deutscher Städte," in his *Zur Geschichte der Juden in Deutschland des späten Mittelalters und der frühen Neuzeit* (Stuttgart: Hierseman, 1981), 27–93.

Hawkins, D. "The Black Death and the New London Cemeteries of 1348." *Antiquity* 64 (1990): 637–642.

Hayward, Maria. *Rich Apparel: Clothing and the Law in Henry VIII's England*. Burlington, VT: Ashgate, 2009.

Hays, J. N. *The Burden of Disease*. New Brunswick: Rutgers University Press, 1998.

Healy, Margaret. *Fictions of Disease in Early Modern England: Bodies, Plagues and Politics*. New York: Palgrave, 2002.

Healy, Margaret. "Defoe's Journal and the English Plague Writing Tradition." *Literature and Medicine* 22 (2003): 25–44.

Hecker, Justus F. C. *The Epidemics of the Middle Ages: The Black Death in the Fourteenth Century*. Translated by B. G. Babington. London: Sherwood, Gilbert and Piper, 1835.

Henderson, John. "The Parish and the Poor in Florence at the Time of the Black Death: The Case of San Frediano." *Continuity and Change* 3 (1988): 247–272.

Henderson, John. *Piety and Charity in Late Medieval Florence*. Chicago: University of Chicago Press, 1992.

Henderson, John. *The Renaissance Hospital: Healing the Body and Healing the Soul*. New Haven, CT: Yale University Press, 2006.

Hendrickson, Robert. *More Cunning than Man: A Complete History of the Rat and Its Role in Human Civilization*. New York: Kensington Books, 1983.

Herlihy, David. *The Black Death and the Transformation of the West*. Cambridge, MA: Harvard University Press, 1997.

Hirst, Leonard F. *The Conquest of Plague: A Study of the Evolution of Epidemiology*. Oxford: Oxford University Press, 1953.

Hopkins, Andrew. "Combating the Plague," in *Piety and Plague from Byzantium to the Baroque*, edited by Franco Mormando and Thomas Worcester (Kirksville, MO: Truman State University Press, 2007), 137–151.

Horden, Peregrine. "The Earliest Hospitals in Byzantium, Western Europe and Islam." *Journal of Interdisiplinary History* 35 (2005): 361–389.

Horden, Peregrine. *Hospitals and Healing from Antiquity to the Later Middle Ages*. Burlington, VT: Ashgate, 2008.

Houlbrook, R. A., ed. *Death, Ritual and Bereavement*. New York: Routledge, 1989.

Howard-Jones, N. "Was Shibasaburo Kitasato the Co-discoverer of the Plague Bacillus?" *Perspectives on Biological Medicine* 16 (1973): 292–307.

Houston, R. A. "The Population History of Britain and Ireland 1500–1750," in *British Population History from the Black Death to the Present Day*, ed. by Michael Anderson (New York: Cambridge University Press, 1996), 95–190.

Images of the Plague: The Black Death in Biology, Arts, Literature and Learning. Binghamton, New York: The Gallery, 1977.

Jillings, Karen. *Scotland's Black Death: The Foul Death of the English.* London: Tempus Publishing, 2003.

Jordan, William Chester. *The Great Famine: Northern Europe in the Early Fourteenth Century.* Princeton, NJ: Princeton University Press, 1996.

Kaplan, Barbara Beigun. *"Divulging of Useful Truths in Physick": The Medical Agenda of Robert Boyle.* Baltimore, MD: Johns Hopkins University Press, 1993.

Karlen, Arno. *Man and Microbes: Disease and Plagues in History and Modern Times.* New York: Simon and Schuster, 1995.

Karlen, Arno. *Plague's Progress: A Social History of Man and Disease.* London: V. Gollancz, 1996.

Karlsson, Gunnar. "Plague without Rats: The Case of Fifteenth-century Iceland." *Journal of Medieval History* 22 (1996): 263–284.

Katinis, Teodoro. *Medicina e filosofia in Marsilio Ficino: Il Consilio contro la pestilenza.* Rome: Edizioni di storia e letteratura, 2007.

Kauffman, Christopher. *Tamers of Death.* New York: Seabury, 1976.

Keeling, M. J. and C. A. Gilligan. "Metapopulation Dynamics of Bubonic Plague." *Nature* 19 (October, 2000): 903–906.

Keiser, G. R. "Two Medieval Plague Treatises and Their Afterlife in Early Modern England." *Journal of the History of Medicine and Allied Sciences* 58 (2003): 292–324.

Kelly, John. *The Great Mortality: An Intimate History of the Black Death.* New York: HarperCollins, 2005.

Kelly, Maria. *The Great Dying: The Black Death in Dublin.* Stroud, Gloucs, UK: Tempus, 2003.

Kelly, Maria. *A History of the Black Death in Ireland.* Stroud, Gloucs, UK: Tempus, 2001.

Kharmi, Ghada. "State Control of the Physician in the Middle Ages: An Islamic Model," in *Town and State Physicians in Europe from the Middle Ages to the Enlightenment,* edited by Andrew Russell (Wolfenbüttel Forschungen 17: Herzog August Bibliothek, 1981), 63–84.

Kieckhefer, Richard. "Radical Tendencies in the Flagellant Movement of the Mid-Fourteenth Century." *Journal of Medieval and Renaissance Studies* 4 (1974): 157–176.

Kinch, Ashby. "Image, Ideology and Form: The Middle English 'Three Dead Kings.'" *Chaucer Review* 43 (2008): 48–81.

Kinzelbach, Annemarie. "Infection, Contagion, and Public Health in Late Medieval and Early Modern German Imperial Towns." *Journal of the History of Medicine and Allied Sciences* 61 (2006): 369–389.

Klaits, Joseph. *Servants of Satan.* Bloomington: Indiana University Press, 1985.

Köhler, W. and M. Köhler "Plague as Rats, the Plague of the Philistines." *International Journal of Medical Microbiology* 293 (2003): 333–340.

Konkola, Kari. "More Than a Coincidence? The Arrival of Arsenic and the Disappearance of Plague in Early Modern Europe." *History of Medicine* 47 (1992): 186–209.

Koslofsky, C. M. *The Reformation and the Dead: Death and Ritual in Early Modern Germany, 1450–1700.* Basingstoke: Macmillan, 2000.

Kowal, Areta O. "Danilo Samoilowitz: An Eighteenth-century Ukrainian Epidemiologist and his Role in the Moscow Plague (1770–72)." *Journal of the History of Medicine and Allied Sciences* 27 (1972): 434–446.

Ladurie, Emmanuel LeRoy. *The French Peasantry, 1450–1600.* Translated by Alan Sheridan. Berkeley: University of California Press, 1987.

Lamont-Brown, Raymond. *Royal Poxes and Potions: The Lives of Court Physicians, Surgeons and Apothecaries.* Stroud, Gloucs., UK: Sutton, 2001.

Langer, Lawrence. "Plague and the Russian Countryside: Monastic Estates in the Late Fourteenth and Fifteenth Centuries." *Canadian American Slavic Studies* 10 (1976): 351–368.

Leavy, Barbara Fass. *To Blight with Plague: Studies in a Literary Theme*. New York: New York University Press, 1992.

Lee, Christopher. *1603: The Death of Queen Elizabeth I, the Return of the Black Plague, the Rise of Shakespeare, Piracy, Witchcraft, and the Birth of the Stuart Era*. New York: St. Martin's Press, 2004.

LeGoff, Jacques. *The Birth of Purgatory*. Translated by Arthur Goldhammer. Chicago: University of Chicago Press, 1984.

Lerner, Robert E. "The Black Death and Western Eschatological Mentalities." *American Historical Review* 86 (1981): 533–552; also in *The Black Death: The Impact of the Fourteenth-century Plague*, edited by Daniel Williman (Binghamton, NY: Medieval and Renaissance Texts and Studies, 1982), 77–106.

Lerner, Robert E. "Fleas: Some Scratchy Issues Concerning the Black Death." *The Historian* 8 (2008): 205–229.

Leroux, Neil R. *Martin Luther as Comforter: Writings on Death*. Leiden: Brill, 2007.

Levack, Brian P. *The Witch-Hunt in Early Modern Europe*. New York: Longman, 1987.

Levey, Martin. *Early Arabic Pharmacology*. Leiden: Brill, 1973.

Levine, David. *At the Dawn of Modernity*. Berkeley: University of California Press, 2001.

Lindemann, Mary. *Medicine and Society in Early Modern Europe*. 2nd edition. New York: Cambridge University Press, 2010.

Lindley, Phillip. "The Black Death and English Art: A Debate and Some Assumptions," in *The Black Death in England*, edited by W. M. Ormrod and P. G. Lindley (Stamford: Paul Watkins, 1996), 125–146.

Little, Lester K., ed. *Plague and the End of Antiquity: The Pandemic of 511–750*. New York: Cambridge University Press, 2006.

Llewellyn, Nigel. *The Art of Death: Visual Culture in the English Death Ritual, c. 1500–c. 1800*. London: Reaktion and the Victoria and Albert Museum, 1991.

Local Population Studies. *The Plague Reconsidered: A New Look at its Origins and Effects in Sixteenth and Seventeenth-Century England*. Matlock: Local Populations Studies (Supplement), 1977.

Lucenet, Monique. *Les grandes pestes en France*. Paris: Aubier, 1985.

MacCulloch, Diarmaid. *The Reformation: A History*. New York: Vintage, 2004.

MacCulloch Diarmaid, ed. *The Reign of Henry VIII: Politics, Policy, and Piety*. New York: St. Martin's, 1995.

MacDonald, Michael. "The Career of Astrological Medicine in England," in *Religio Medici*, edited by Peter Grell and Andrew Cunningham (Brookfield, VT: Ashgate: 1996), 62–90.

MacKay, Angus. "Popular Movements and Pogroms in Fifteenth-century Castile." *Past and Present* #55: 33–67, 1972.

MacKay, Ellen. *Persecution, Plague and Fire: Fugitive Histories of the Stage in Early Modern England*. Chicago: University of Chicago Press, 2011.

Markus, R. A. *Gregory the Great and His World*. New York: Cambridge University Press, 1997.

Marriott, Edward. *Plague: A Story of Science, Rivalry, Scientific Breakthrough and the Scourge that Won't Go away*. New York: Holt, 2002.

Marshall, Louise. "Manipulating the Sacred: Image and Plague in Renaissance Italy." *Renaissance Quarterly* 47 (1994): 485–532.

Marshall, Louise. "Confraternity and Community: Mobilizing the Sacred in Times of Plague," *in Confraternities and the Visual Arts in Renaissance Italy: Ritual,*

Spectacle, Image, edited by Barbara Wisch and Diane Cole Ahl (New York: Cambridge University Press, 2000), 20–45.

Martin, A. Lynn. *Plague?: Jesuit Accounts of Epidemic Disease in the 16th Century*. Kirksville, MO: Sixteenth Century Journal Publishers, 1996.

Mate, Mavis E. *Daughters, Wives and Widows after the Black Death: Women in Sussex, 1350–1535*. Rochester, NY: Boydell Press, 1998.

Marmoy, Charles F. A. "The Pesthouse, 1681–1717: Predecessor of the French Hospital." *Huguenot Society of London Proceedings* 25 (1992): 385–399.

Martin, Mathew. "Play and Plague in Ben Jonson's *The Alchemist*." *English Studies in Canada* 26 (2000): 393–408.

Maxwell-Stuart, P. G. *The Chemical Choir: A History of Alchemy*. New York: Continuum, 2008.

McCormick, Michael. "Rats, Communications and Plague: Toward an Ecological History." *Journal of Interdisciplinary History* 34 (2003): 1–25

McCutcheon, Elizabeth. "William Bullein's *Dialogue against the fever pestilence*: A Sixteenth-century Anatomy," in *Miscellanea moreana: Essays for German Marc Hadour*, edited by Clare M. Murphy and Mario di Cesare (Binghamton, NY: Medieval and Renaissance Texts and Studies, 1989), 341–359.

McDaniell, Colleen, and Bernhard Lang. *Heaven: A History*. New York: Vintage, 1990.

McDonald, William C. "Death in the Stars: Heinrich von Mügeln on the Black Plague." *Mediaevalia* 5 (1979): 89–112.

McNeill, William. *Plagues and Peoples*. Garden City, NY: Anchor Press, 1975.

McVaugh, Michael R. *Medicine before the Plague: Practitioners and their Patients in the Crown of Aragon: 1285–1345*. New York: Cambridge University Press, 1993.

McVaugh, Michael. "Surgical Education in the Middle Ages." *Dynamis* 20 (2000): 283–304.

Meiss, Millard. *Painting in Florence and Siena after the Black Death: The Arts, Religion, and Society in the Mid-fourteenth Century*. Princeton, NJ: Princeton University Press, 1951.

Mentgen, Gerd. "Die Pest-Pandemie und die Juden Pogrome der Jahre 1348–1350/1," in *Heiliges Römisches Reich Deutscher Nation 962 bis 1806* (Dresden: Sandstein Verlag, 2006), 298–309.

Meynell, G. G. "Sydenham, Locke and Sydenham's *De peste sive febre pestilentiali*." *Medical History* 37 (1993): 330–332.

Miller, Timothy S. "The Plague in John VI Cantacuzenus and Thucydides." *Greek, Roman and Byzantine Studies* 17 (1976): 385–395.

Mode, Peter. *The Influence of the Black Death on the English Monasteries*. Winasha, WI: George Banta; reprint LaVergne, TN: Kessinger Publishing, 1916/2009.

Mollat, Michel and Philippe Wolff. *The Popular Revolutions of the Late Middle Ages*. Translated by A. L. Lyttonsells. New York: Allen and Unwin, 1973.

Monteano, Peio J. *La ira de Dios: Los navarros en la era de la peste (1348–1723)*. Pamplona: Pamela, 2002.

Monteyne, Joseph. *The Printed Image in Early Modern London: Urban Space, Visual Representation, and Social Exchange*. Burlington, VT: Ashgate, 2007.

Montford, Angela. *Health, Sickness, Medicine, and the Friars in the Thirteenth and Fourteenth Centuries*. Burlington, VT: Ashgate, 2004.

Moote, A. Lloyd and Dorothy C. Moote. *The Great Plague: The Story of London's Most Deadly Year*. Baltimore, MD: Johns Hopkins University Press, 2004.

Moran, JoAnn Hoeppner. "Clerical Recruitment in the Diocese of York, 1340–1530:

Data and Commentary." *Journal of Ecclesiastical History* 34 (1983): 19–54.

Morgenstern S. "Collection of Treatises on Plague Regimen and Remedies published in the German Duchy of Swabia in the XVIIth Century." *Academy Bookman* 26 (1973): 3–20.

Morineau, Michael. "Malthus: There and Back from the Period Preceding the Black Death to the 'Industrial Revolution.' " *Journal of European Economic History* 27 (1998): 137–202.

Mormando, Franco and Thomas Worcester, eds. *Piety and Plague from Byzantium to the Baroque.* Kirksville, MO: Truman State University Press, 2007.

Mullett, Charles F. *The Bubonic Plague and England: An Essay in the History of Preventive Medicine.* Lexington: University of Kentucky Press, 1956.

Nagy, Doreen E. *Popular Medicine in Seventeenth-Century England.* Bowling Green, Ohio: Bowling Green State University Press, 1988.

Naphy, William G. *Plagues, Poisons and Potions: Plague Spreading Conspiracies in the Western Alps c. 1530–1640.* New York: Manchester University Press, 2002.

Naphy, William G. and Andrew Spicer. *The Black Death and the History of Plagues, 1345–1730.* Stroud, Gloucs, UK: Sutton, 2001.

Naphy, William G. and Andrew Spicer. *Plague: Black Death and Pestilence in Europe.* Stroud, Gloucs, UK: Tempus, 2004.

Newman, William and Anthony Grafton, eds. *Secrets of Nature: Astrology and Alchemy in Early Modern Europe.* Cambridge, MA: MIT Press, 2001.

Nicholas, David. *The Domestic Life of a Medieval City: Women, Children and the Family in Fourteenth Century Ghent.* Lincoln: University of Nebraska Press, 1985.

Nicol, Donald. *The Reluctant Emperor: Biography of John Cantacuzenos, Byzantine Emperor and Monk, c. 11295–1383.* New York: Cambridge University Press, 1996.

Nicoud, Marilyn. *Les régimes de santé au moyen Age: Naissance et diffusion d'une écriture médicale (XIIIe–XVe siècle).* 2 volumes. Rome: École française de Rome, 2007.

Niebyl, Peter H. "Galen, Van Helmont and Blood Letting," in *Science, Medicine and Society in the Renaissance*, volume 2, edited by Allen G. Debus (New York: Neale Watkins, 1972), 13–22.

Nightingale, Pamela. *A Medieval Mercantile Community: The Grocers' Company and the Politics and Trade of London, 1000–1485.* New Haven, CT: Yale University Press, 1995.

Nirenberg, David. *Communities of Violence: Persecution of Minorities in the Middle Ages.* Princeton, NJ: Princeton University Press, 1996.

Nockels Fabri, Christiane. "Treating Medieval Plague: The Wonderful Virtues of Theriac." *Early Science and Medicine* 12 (2007): 247–283.

Nohl, Johannes. *The Black Death: A Chronicle of the Plague.* Translated by C. H. Clarke. London: George Allen and Unwin, 1926; reprinted Yardley, PA: Westholme Publishing, 2006.

Norman, Diana. "Change and Continuity: Art and Religion after the Black Death," in her *Siena, Florence and Padua, I: Art, Society and Religion 1280–1400. Interpretative Essays* (New Haven, CT: Yale University Press, 1995), 177–196.

North, J. D. "Medieval Concepts of Celestial Influence," in *Astrology, Science and Society: Historical Essays*, edited by Patrick Curry (Wolfboro, NH: Boydell Press, 1987), 5–18.

North, J. D. "1348 and All That: Oxford Science and the Black Death," in his *Stars,*

Minds and Fate (London: The Hambledon Press, 1989), 361–372.

Nummedal. Tara. *Alchemy and Authority in the Holy Roman Empire*. Chicago: University of Chicago Press, 2007.

Nutton, Vivian. *Ancient Medicine*. New York: Routledge, 2004.

Nutton, Vivian. "Humanist Surgery," in The *Medical Renaissance of the Sixteenth Century*, edited by Andrew Wear et al. (New York: Cambridge University Press, 1985), 75–99.

Nutton, Vivian. *Medicine at the Courts of Europe, 1500–1837*. New York: Routledge, 1990.

Nutton, Vivian, ed. *Pestilential Complexities: Understanding the Medieval Plague*. Supplement #27 to *Medical History*. London: Wellcome Trust for the History of Medicine, 2008.

Nutton, Vivian. "The Reception of Fracastoro's Theory of Contagion: The Seed that Fell among Thorns." *Osiris* 2nd ser. 6 (1990): 196–234.

Nyborg, Ebbe. "The Black Death as Reflected in Scandinavian Art and Architecture," in *Living with the Black Death*, edited by Lars Bisgaard and Leif Søndergaard (Odense: Southern Denmark University Press, 2009), 187–205.

Ober, W. B. and Alloush, N. "The Plague at Granada 1348–1349: Ibn Al-Khatib and ideas of Contagion," in *Bottoms Up!: A Pathologist's Essays on Medicine and the Humanities*, edited by W. B. Ober (Carbondale: Southern Illinois University Press, 1987), 288–293.

O'Boyle, Cornelius. *The Art of Medicine: Medical Teaching at the University of Paris, 1250–1400*. Boston: Brill, 1998.

O'Connor, Mary C. *The Art of Dying Well: The Development of the* Ars moriendi. New York: AMS, 1966.

Ó Gráda, Cormac. *Famine: A Short History*. Princeton, NJ: Princeton University Press, 2009.

O'Malley, C. D. *Andreas Vesalius of Brussels 1514–1564*. Berkeley: University of California Press, 1964.

O'Malley, C. D. *The History of Medical Education*. Berkeley: University of California Press, 1970.

Orent, Wendy. *Plague: The Mysterious Past and Terrifying Future of the World's Most Dangerous Disease*. New York: Free Press, 2004.

Orme, Nicholas. *Medieval Children*. New Haven, CT: Yale University Press, 2003.

Ormrod, W. Mark. "The English Government and the Black Death of 1348–1349," in *England in the Fourteenth Century*, edited by W. M. Ormrod (Woodbridge, Suffolk, UK: Boydell Press, 1986), 175–188.

Outram, Quentin. "The Socio-economic Relations of Warfare and the Military Mortality Crises of the Thirty Years' War." *Medical History* 45 (2001): 151–184.

Pagel, Walter. *Joan Baptista van Helmont: Reformer of Science and Medicine*. New York: Cambridge University Press, 1982.

Palmer, Robert. "The Church, Leprosy and Plague," in *The Church and Healing*, a volume of *Studies in Church History* 19 (1982): 79–99.

Palmer, Robert C. *English Law in the Age of the Black Death, 1348–1381: A Transformation of Governance and Law*. Chapel Hill: University of North Carolina Press, 1993.

Pantin, Sabelle. "Fracastoro's *De contagione* and Medieval Reflection on 'Action at a Distance': Old and New Trends in Renaissance Discourse on Contagion," in *Imagining Contagion in Early Modern Europe*, edited by Claire L. Carlin (New York: Palgrave Macmillan, 2005), 3–15.

Papka, Claudia R. "The Limits of Apocalypse: Eschatology, Epistemology, and Textuality in the *Commedia* and *Piers Plowman*," in *Last Things: Death and the Apocalypse in the Middle Ages*, edited by Carolyn Walker Bynum and Paul Freedman (Philadelphia: University of Pennsylvania Press, 2000), 233–256.

Park, Katherine. *Doctors and Medicine in Early Renaissance Florence*. Princeton, NJ: Princeton University Press, 1985.

Park, Katherine. "Healing the Poor: Hospitals and Medical Assistance in Renaissance Florence," in *Medicine and Charity before the Welfare State*, edited by Jonathan Barry and Colin Jones (New York: Routledge, 1991), 26–45.

Park, Katherine. "The Life of the Corpse: Division and Dissection in Late Medieval Europe." *Journal of the History of Medicine and Allied Sciences* 50 (1995): 111–132.

Parker, Geoffrey. *The Army of Flanders and the Spanish Road, 1567–1659*. New York: Cambridge University Press, 1972.

Pasi Testa, Antonia. "Alle origini dell'Ufficio di Sanità nel ducato di Milano e principato di Pavia." *Archivio storico lombardo* 102 (1976): 376–386.

Pelikan, Jaroslav. *Jesus through the Centuries*. New Haven, CT: Yale University Press, 1999.

Pelling, Margaret. *The Common Lot: Sickness, Medical Occupations and the Urban Poor in Early Modern England*. New York: Longman, 1998.

Pelling, Margaret. *Medical Conflicts in Early Modern London: Patronage, Physicians, and Irregular Practitioners 1550–1640*. New York: Oxford University Press, 2003.

Pelling, Margaret. "Unofficial and Unorthodox Medicine," in *Western Medicine: An Illustrated History*, edited by Irvine Loudon (New York: Oxford University Press, 1997), 264–276.

Perho, I. *The Prophet's Medicine: A Creation of the Muslim Traditionalist Scholars*. Studia Orientalia 74. Helsinki: Finnish Oriental Society, 1995.

Phillips, Patrick. "Fleshes Rage: Ben Jonson and the Plague." Ph.D. dissertation, New York University, 2006.

Pingree, David. "The Diffusion of Arabic Magical Texts in Western Europe," in *La diffusione delle scienze islamiche nel Medio Evo europeo* (Rome: Accademia Nazionale dei Lincei, 1987), 57–102.

Platt, Colin. *King Death: The Black Death and its Aftermath in Late-medieval England*. Toronto: University of Toronto Press, 1996.

Polzer, Joseph. "Aspects of the Fourteenth-Century Iconography of Death and the Plague," in *The Black Death: The Impact of the Fourteenth-century Plague*, edited by Daniel Williman (Binghamton, NY: Medieval and Renaissance Texts and Studies, 1982), 107–130.

Pomata, Gianna. *Contracting a Cure: Patients, Healers, and the Law in Early Modern Bologna*. Baltimore, MD: Johns Hopkins University Press, 1998.

Poos, Larry. *A Rural Society after the Black Death: Essex, 1350–1525*. New York: Cambridge University Press, 1991.

Poos, Larry. "The Social Context of the Statute of Labourers Enforcement." *Law and History* 1 (1983): 27–52.

Pormann, Peter E. and Emilie Savage-Smith. *Medieval Islamic Medicine*. Washington, DC: Georgetown University Press, 2007.

Porter, Stephen. *The Great Plague*. Stroud, Gloucs, UK: Sutton, 1999.

Porter, Stephen. *Lord have Mercy upon Us: London's Plague Years*. Stroud, Gloucs, UK: Tempus, 2005.

Porter, Stephen. *The Popularization of Medicine*. London: Routledge, 1992.

Prentice, M. B., T. Gilbert and A. Cooper. "Was the Black Death caused by *Yersinia pestis*?" *Lancet: Infectious Diseases* (Feb. 4, 2004): 72.

Prentice, Michael B., and Lila Rahalison. "Plague." *The Lancet* 369:9568 (2007): 1196–1207.

Presciutti, Diana Bullen. "David Michael D'Andrea, Civic Christianity in Renaissance Italy: The Hospital of Treviso, 1400–1530." *Medieval Feminist Forum* 44 (2008): 149–152.

Prokhorov, M. F. "The Moscow Uprising of September 1771." *Soviet Studies in History* 25 (1987): 44–78.

Pullan, Brian. "Wage-earners and the Venetian Economy, 1550–1630," in his *Crisis and Change in the Venetian Economy in the Sixteenth and Seventeenth Centuries* (London: Methuen, 1968), 146–174.

Putnam, Bertha Haven. *The Enforcement of the Statute of Labourers during the First Decade after the Black Death*. New York: Columbia University Press, 1908.

Raftis, J. A. "Social Change Versus Revolution: New Interpretations of the Peasants' Revolt of 1381," in *Social Unrest in the Late Middle Ages*, edited by Francis X. Newman (Binghamton: Medieval and Renaissance Texts and Studies, 1986), 3–22.

Ranger, Terence and Paul Slack, editors. *Epidemics and Ideas*. New York: Cambridge University Press, 1992.

Raspe, Lucia. "The Black Death in Jewish Sources: A Second Look at Mayse Nissim." *Jewish Quarterly Review* 94 (2004): 471–489.

Rawcliffe, Carole. *Leprosy in Medieval England*. Rochester, NY: Boydell, 2006.

Rawcliffe, Carole. *Medicine and Society in Later Medieval England*. Stroud, Gloucs, UK: Sutton, 1997.

Raymond, André. *Cairo*. Cambridge, MA: Harvard University Press, 2000.

Reilly, P. Conor. *Athanasius Kircher: Master of a Hundred Arts*. Wiesbaden-Rome: Edizioni del Mondo, 1974.

Reinis, Austra. *Reforming the Art of Dying: The Ars Moriendi in the German Reformation (1519–1528)*. Burlington, VT: Ashgate, 2007.

Reyerson, Kathryn L. "Changes in Testamentary Practice at Montpellier on the Eve of the Black Death." *Church History* 47 (1978): 253–269.

Richards, Jeffrey. *Sex, Dissidence, and Damnation*. New York: Routledge, 1994.

Riley, James C. *The Eighteenth-century Campaign to Avoid Disease*. London: Palgrave MacMillan, 1987.

Robertson, D. W. "Chaucer and the Economic and Social Consequences of the Plague," in *Social Unrest in the Late Middle Ages*, edited by Francis X. Newman (Binghamton: Medieval and Renaissance Texts and Studies, 1986), 49–74.

Robertson, J. C. "Reckoning with London: Interpreting the Bills of Mortality before John Graunt." *Urban History* 23 (1996): 325–350.

Rosen, William. *Justinian's Flea*. New York: Viking, 2007.

Ross, Cheryl L. "The Plague of the Alchemist." *Renaissance Quarterly* 41 (1988): 439–458.

Rothenberg, Gunther. "The Austrian Sanitary Cordon and the Control of Bubonic Plague: 1710–1871." *Journal of the History of Medicine and Allied Sciences* 28 (1973): 15–23.

Rusnock, Andrea A. *Vital Accounts: Quantifying Health and Population in Eighteenth-Century England and France*. New York: Cambridge University Press, 2002.

Russell, Andrew, ed. *The Town and State Physician in Europe from the Middle Ages to the Enlightenment*. Wolfenbüttel Forschungen 17. Wolfenbüttel: Herzog August Bibliothek, 1981.

Russell, Paul A. "Ficino's *Consiglio contro la pestilentia* in the European Tradition." *Verbum, Analecta neolatina*. 1 (1999): 85–96.

Sabine, Ernest. "Butchering in Mediaeval London." *Speculum* 8 (1933): 225–253.

Sabine, Ernest. "City Cleaning in Mediaeval London." *Speculum* 12 (1937): 19–43.

San Juan, Rose Marie. *Rome: A City Out of Print*. Minneapolis: University of Minnesota Press, 2001.

Savage-Smith, Emily. "Attitudes toward Dissection in Medieval Islam." *Journal of the History of Medicine and Allied Sciences* 50 (1995): 67–110.

Schen, Claire S. *Charity and Lay Piety in Reformation London, 1500–1620*. Burlington, VT: Ashgate, 2002.

Schiferl, Ellen. "Iconography of Plague Saints in Fifteenth-century Italian Painting." *Fifteenth Century Studies* 6 (1983): 205–225.

Schirmer, Walter F. *John Lydgate: A Study in the Culture of the Fifteenth Century*. Westport, CT: Greenwood, 1961.

Schmölzer, Hilde. *Die Pest in Wien*. Vienna: Österreichischer Bundesverlag Gesellschaft, 1985.

Schneider, Winfried. *Medical Ethics in the Renaissance*. Washington, DC: Georgetown University Press, 1995.

Scott, John. *Narratives of Two Families*. London: R. B. Seeley and W. Burnside, 1832.

Scott, Susan and Christopher Duncan. *Biology of Plagues: Evidence from Historical Populations*. New York: Cambridge University Press, 2001.

Scott, Susan, and Christopher Duncan. *The Return of the Black Death: The World's Greatest Serial Killer*. Hoboken, NJ: Wiley, 2004.

Seargeant, Philip. "Discursive Diversity in the Textual Articulation of Epidemic Disease in Early Modern England." *Language and Literature* 16 (2007): 323–344.

Sehdev, P. S. "The Origin of Quarantine." *Clinical Infectious Diseases* 35 (2002): 1071–1072.

Shatzmiller, Joseph. *Jews, Medicine, and Medieval Society*. Berkeley: University of California Press, 1994.

Shefer-Mossensohn, Miri. *Ottoman Medicine: Healing and Medical Institutions, 1500–1700*. Albany: SUNY Press, 2009.

Sherman, Irwin W. *The Power of Plague*. Washington, DC: American Society of Microbiologists, 2006.

Shirk, Melanie V. "Violence and the Plague in Aragón, 1348–1351." *Journal of the Rocky Mountain Medieval and Renaissance Association* 5 (1984): 31–39.

Shrewsbury, J. F. *History of Bubonic Plague in the British Isles*. New York: Cambridge University Press, 1970.

Simond, Marc, et al. "Paul-Louis Simond and His Discovery of Plague Transmission by Rat Fleas." *Journal of the Royal Society of Medicine* 91 (1998): 101–104.

Singer, Dorothy W. "The Plague Tractates." *Proceedings of the Royal Society of Medicine* (History of Medicine) 9:2 (1915–16): 159–212.

Singer, Dorothy Waley and Annie Anderson. *Catalogue of Latin and Vernacular Plague Tracts in Great Britain and Eire in Manuscripts Written before the Sixteenth Century*. London: Heinemann Medical Books, 1950.

Siraisi, Nancy. *Avicenna in Renaissance Italy: The Canon and Medical Teaching in Italian Universities after 1500*. Princeton, NJ: Princeton University Press, 1997.

Siraisi, Nancy. "The Faculty of Medicine," in *A History of the University in Europe*, Volume 1, edited by Hilde de Ridder-Symoens (New York: Cambridge University Press, 1992), 360–387.

Siraisi, Nancy. *Medicine at the Italian Universities, 1250–1600*. Leiden: Brill, 2001.

Siraisi, Nancy. *Medieval and Early Renaissance Medicine*. Chicago: University of Chicago Press, 1990.

Skurnik, Mikael, et al., editors. *The Genus Yersinia*. New York: Kluwer, 2003.

Slack, Paul. "Books of Orders: The Making of English Social Policy, 1577–1631." *Transactions of the Royal Historical Society* 5th ser. 30 (1980): 1–22.

Slack, Paul. "The Disappearance of Plague: An Alternative View." *Economic History Review* 2nd ser. 34 (1981): 469–476.

Slack, Paul. *The Impact of Plague in Tudor and Stuart England*. New York: Oxford University Press, 1990.

Slack, Paul. "Metropolitan Government in Crisis: The Response to Plague," in *London: 1500–1700: The Making of the Metropolis*, A. L. Beier and Roger Finlay (New York: Longman, 1986), 60–81.

Slack, Paul. "Responses to Plague in Early Modern England," in *Famine, Disease and the Social Order in Early Modern Society*, edited by Walter R. Schofield (New York: Cambridge University Press, 1989), 167–187.

Slack, Paul. "Responses to Plague in Early Modern Europe: The Implications of Public Health." *Social Research* 55 (1988): 433–453.

Smail, Daniel Lord. "Accommodating Plague in Medieval Marseille." *Continuity and Change* 11 (1996): 11–41.

Smith, Robert S. "Barcelona 'Bills of Mortality' and Population, 1457–1590." *Journal of Political Economy* 44 (1936): 84–93.

Smith, Wesley. *The Hippocratic Tradition*. Ithaca, NY: Cornell University Press, 1973.

Smoller, Laura. "Of Earthquakes, Hail, Frogs, and Geography: Plague and the Investigation of the Apocalypse in the Later Middle Ages," in *Last Things: Death and the Apocalypse in the Middle Ages*, edited by Caroline Walker Bynum and Paul Freedman (Philadelphia: University of Pennsylvania Press, 2000), 156–187.

Snell, William. "Parfit praktisour" or quack? Chaucer's Physician and the Literary Image of Doctors after the Black Death." *Keio Hiyoshi Review of English Studies* 37 (2000): 117–136.

Somerset, Fiona, et al., editors. *Lollards and their Influence on Late Medieval England*. Rochester, NY: Boydell, 2009.

Stathakopoulos, Dionysios. *Famine and Pestilence in the Late Roman and Early Byzantine Empire*. Burlington, VT: Ashgate, 2004.

Stearns, Justin. *Infectious Ideas: Contagion in Premodern Islamic and Christian Thought in the Western Mediterranean*. Baltimore, MD: Johns Hopkins University Press, 2011.

Steinhoff, Judith B. *Sienese Painting after the Black Death: Artistic Pluralism, Politics, and the New Art Market*. New York: Cambridge University Press, 2006.

Strocchia, Sharon T. *Death and Ritual in Renaissance Florence*. Baltimore, MD: Johns Hopkins University Press, 1992.

Stubbs, John. *John Donne: The Reformed Soul: A Biography*. New York: Norton, 2007.

Talvacchia, Bette. "The Double Life of St. Sebastian in Renaissance Art," in *The Body in Early Modern Italy*, edited by Julia Hairston and Walter Stephens (Baltimore, MD: Johns Hopkins University Press, 2010), 226–248.

Taylor, J. "Plague in the Towns of Hampshire: The Epidemic of 1665–1666." *Southern History* 6 (1984): 104–122.

Temkin, Owsei. *Galenism: The Rise and Decline of a Medical Philosophy*. Ithaca: Cornell University Press, 1973.

Theilmann, John and Frances Cate. "A Plague of Plagues: The Problem of Plague Diagnosis in Medieval England." *Journal of Interdisciplinary History* 37 (2007): 371–393.

Thirsk, Joan. *Alternative Agriculture, A History: From the Black Death to the Present Day*. New York: Oxford University Press, 1997.

Thomas, M., et al. "Response to Drancourt and Raoult." *Microbiology* 150 (2004): 264–265.

Toch, Michael. "The Formation of a Diaspora: The Settlement of Jews in the Medieval German *Reich*." *Aschkenas: Zeitschrift für Geschichte und Kultur der Juden* 7 (1997): 55–78.

Toledo-Pereyra, L. H. "*De humani corporis fabrica* Surgical Revolution." *Journal of Investigative Surgery* 21 (2008): 232–236.

Totaro, Rebecca. *Suffering in Paradise: The Bubonic Plague in English Literature from*

More to Milton. Pittsburg: Duquesne University Press, 2005.

Townsend, Eleanor. *Death and Art: Europe, 1200–1530*. London: Victoria and Albert Publishing, 2009.

Tucker, William. "Natural Disasters and the Peasantry in Mamluk Egypt." *Journal of the Economic and Social History of the Orient* 24 (1981): 215–224.

Twigg, Graham. *The Black Death: A Biological Reappraisal*. New York: Schocken Books, 1985.

Ullmann, Manfred. *Islamic Medicine*. Edinburgh: Edinburgh University Press, 1978.

Unschuld, Paul U. *Medicine in China*. Berkeley: University of California Press, 1988.

Ussery, Huling E. *Chaucer's Physician: Medicine and Literature in Fourteenth-century England*. New Orleans: Tulane University Press, 1971.

Utterback, Kristine T. "The Date and Composition of Bishops' Registers from the Plague Years in the Diocese of Barcelona." *Journal of Ecclesiastical History* 39 (1988): 412–432.

Van Os, Henk. "The Black Death and Sienese Painting: A Problem of Interpretation." *Art History* 4 (1981): 237–249.

Velimirovic, Boris and Helga. "Plague in Vienna." *Review of Infectious Diseases* 2 (1989): 808–830.

Walter, J. *Famine, Disease and Social Order in Early Modern Society*. New York: Cambridge University Press, 1989.

Watson, Gilbert. *Theriac and Mithidatium: A Study in Therapeutics*. London: Wellcome History of Medicine Library, 1966.

Watt, Teresa. *Cheap Print and Popular Piety*. New York: Cambridge University Press, 1993.

Watts, Sheldon. *Epidemics and History: Disease, Power and Imperialism*. New Haven, CT: Yale University Press, 1997.

Wear, Andrew. "Fear and Anxiety and the Plague in Early Modern England," in *Religion, Health and Suffering*, edited by J. R. Hinnells and Roy Porter (Oxford, UK: Taylor and Francis, 1999), 339–362.

Wear, Andrew. *Knowledge and Practice in English Medicine, 1550–1680*. New York: Cambridge University Press, 2000.

Webster, Charles. *Paracelsus*. New Haven, CT: Yale University Press, 2008.

Webster, Jill. *Els menorets: The Franciscans in the Realms of Aragon from St. Francis to the Black Death*. Toronto: Pontifical Institute of Mediaeval Studies, 1993.

Weinstein, Donald. "The Art of Dying Well and Popular Piety in the Preaching and Thought of Girolamo Savonarola," in *Life and Death in Fifteenth Century Florence*, edited by Marcel Tetel, et al. (Durham, NC: Duke University Press, 1989), 88–104.

Wheelis, Mark. "Biological Warfare at the 1346 Siege of Caffa." *Emerging Infectious Diseases* 8 (2002): 971–975.

Wieck, Roger S. *Painted Prayers: The Book of Hours in Medieval and Renaissance Art*. New York: Braziller, 1999.

Williams, Gerhild S., et al., eds. *Paracelsian Moments*. Kirksville, MO: Truman State University Press, 2003.

Wilson, F. P. *Plague in Shakespeare's London*. New York: Oxford University Press, 1999.

Wilson, Gilbert. *Theriac and Mithridatum, A Study in Therapeutics*. London: Wellcome Historical Medical Library, 1966.

Wilson, Peter H. *The Thirty Years War: Europe's Tragedy*. Cambridge, MA: Harvard University Press, 2009.

Winslow, Charles-Edward Amory. *The Conquest of Epidemic Disease*. Princeton, NJ: Princeton University Press, 1943.

Wood, Diana. *Pope Clement VI: The Pontificate and Ideas of an Avignon Pope*. New York: Cambridge University Press, 1989.

Wood, J. W., R. J. Ferrell and S. N. Dewitte-Avina. "The Temporal Dynamics of the Fourteenth-century Black Death: New Evidence from English Ecclesiastical Records." *Human Biology* 75 (2003): 427–448.

Wood, James and Sharon DeWitte-Avina "Was the Black Death Yersinial Plague?" *Lancet Infectious Diseases* (June 3, 2003): 327–328.

Wooley, Benjamin. *Heal Thyself: Nicholas Culpeper and the Seventeenth-century Struggle to Bring Medicine to the People.* New York: Harper Collins, 2004.

Wray, Shona Kelly. *Communities and Crisis: Bologna during the Black Death.* Boston: Brill, 2009.

Xing Xiaochen, editor. *History and Development of Traditional Chinese Medicine.* Beijing: Science Press, 1999.

Zeller, Michael. *Rochus: Die Pest und ihr Patron.* Nuremberg: Verlag Hans Böckel, 1989.

Zguta, Russell. "The One-day Votive Church: A Religious Response to the Black Death in Early Russia." *Slavic Review* 3 (1981): 423–432.

Ziegler, Philip. *The Black Death.* New York: Harper and Row, 1969.

Zuckerman, Arnold. *Dr. Richard Mead (1674–1753): A Biographical Study.* Urbana: University of Illinois, 1964.

Zuckerman, Arnold. "Plague and Contagionism in Eighteenth-century England: The Role of Richard Mead." *Bulletin of the History of Medicine* 78 (2004): 273–308.

Index

Note: Bold page numbers refer to main entries.

Peasants, **264–66**, 275; Ciompi revolt, **81**; feudalism and manorialism, 129, **140–42**; Jacquerie, **191**, 275; yeoman farmers and gentry, 141, **365–66**. *See also* Feudalism and manorialism; Yeoman farmers and gentry

Peasants' Revolt, English, **266–67**, 275

Pelagius, 166

Pepys, Samuel, 83, 155, 217, **267–68**, 344

Persecution and execution, 361; anti-Semitism and anti-Jewish violence before the Black Death, **14–16**, 277, 330; Jews as scapegoats, 332, 360; poisoning and plague spreading, 277, **286–87**, 332, 360; witches and witchcraft, 116, **360–61**

Persian Empire, 20. *See also* Arabic-Persian medicine and practitioners

Personal hygiene, 83, 132, 298

Perugia (Italy), 172

Pest houses. *See* Lazarettos and pest houses

Pesthuizen, 280

Pestilence: causes of, 115; use of term, 52. *See also Black Death, Plague,* and *Pestilence* (Terms)

Pestkreuze, 280

Pestsäule, 279–80

Petowe, Henry, 104

Petrarch, Francesco, 102, **268**, 270

Philaretus, 27

Philip II, 185

Philip VI, King, 84, 85

Philistines (Bible), 36–37

"Philosopher's stone," 5

Phlebotomy. *See* Bleeding/phlebotomy

Phlegm (humor), 178

Physicians, 70, 162, **269–71**, 299; Arab-Persian tradition, 20; "bird suit," 269, 270; charlatans and quacks, **70**; chemical physicians, 179, 257; court physicians, **271–72**; empirics, **130**; on health boards, 172; Hippocrates, 27, **174–75**, 178, 231, 235, 327; iatrochemists, 179, 320; Jewish physicians, 193–94; in lazarettos and pest houses, 209; plague doctors, 269–70, 334; *protomedicati*, 18, 270; surgeons/barbers, 52–53, 271, **333–34**; town physicians, **272–73**; wants used by, 359; women medical practitioners,

361–63. *See also* Empirics; Medical education; Medicine; Surgeons/barbers; Women medical practitioners

Physicians, court, **271–72**

Physicians, town, 130, **272–73**

Physick for the Sicknesse (Bradwell), 116

Physiologia (Fernel), 140

Piers Plowman (Landland), 206

Pieta, 25

Pilgrims and pilgrimage, **273–74**

Pistoia (Italy), 94, 210, 301, 326

Plague: AIDS and, **2–3**; anatomy and dissection, 11; Biblical references to, 34–35; bishops and, 292; buboes, 61, 116–17, 196, 202, 211, 311, 366; bubonic plague, **59–61**; causes of: historical theories, 11–12, **67–69**; children and, **72–74**, 147; churches and, **80–81**; clothing and, **82–83**; contagion theory, **88–90**, 310–11; criminal activity and, 96; death toll from, 79; demographic effects of, **106–13**; diagnosis of, **116–17**; dietary regimens for, **118**; earthquakes and, 127, 236, 327; economic effects of, **106–8**, **127–29**; in Europe, **127–29**, **274–78**; exorcism, 196; expulsion of victims, **135–36**; fleas, 12, 59, 60, 67, **145–46**, 328, 366, 367; forewarning of, 327; germ theory, **160–61**, 202; history of in the West (900–1345), **282–83**; humoral theory, 52, 88, 118, 175, **178–79**, 311, 335; in Islamic world, 43–44, 50, 51, 87–88, **106–8**; metaphors for, **234–35**; morbidity, mortality, and virulence, **243–45**; in North America, **61–63**; opportunistic and subsidiary diseases, **118–19**, 277, 283; origins and early spread, **42–46**, 47, **48–51**, 65, 106, **190**; orphans, 73–74; pneumonic plague, 47, 61, **283–84**; poisoning and plague spreading, 277, **286–87**, 332; poverty and, **287–89**; priests and, 291–92; prisoners and, 294; prophylaxes, **296–97**; quarantine, 31, 47, 133, 275, 276, **305–6**; rats and other plague carriers, 12, 59, 67, 131, **307–8**, 328; resistance or immunity to, 134, 307; septicemic plague, **322–23**; shutting in, 184, 277, **325–27**; signs of plague, **327–28**; soldiers and, 21–22;

About the Author

JOSEPH P. BYRNE is a historian and Professor of Honors Humanities at Belmont University in Nashville, Tennessee. Dr. Byrne has written *The Black Death* (Greenwood, 2004) and *Daily Life during the Black Death* (Greenwood, 2006) and edited the *Encyclopedia of Pestilence, Pandemic and Plague* (Greenwood, 2008). He is currently at work on a book about health and wellness in the Renaissance and Enlightenment.

DEMCO